(continued from front flap)

A critique at the end of each chapter assesses the strengths and weaknesses of the person or movement concerned. These conclusions are designed to facilitate comparisons between major factors in the history of Protestant thought.

The bibliography is divided by chapter to indicate additional sources of information for readers who wish to pursue a particular area in greater detail.

As a one volume introduction to the major theological themes of Protestantism; as a source for study groups and individuals who wish to know more about the origins and nature of Protestant theology; and as a welcome addition to the growing body of ecumenical analysis of Christianity, *Historical Protestantism* is a fascinating source of information and insight.

WILLIAM A. SCOTT, S.T.D. Institute Catholique, Paris, France, is Professor of Theology at Le Moyne College, Syracuse, New York.

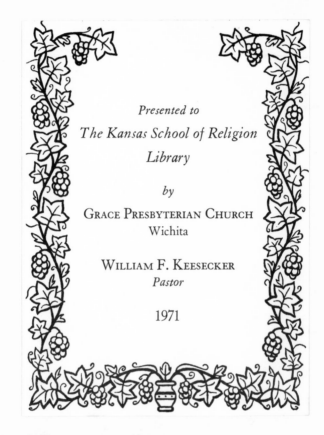

Presented to
The Kansas School of Religion
Library

by

GRACE PRESBYTERIAN CHURCH
Wichita

WILLIAM F. KEESECKER
Pastor

1971

Historical Protestantism

WILLIAM A. SCOTT
Le Moyne College
Syracuse, New York

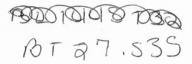

BT 27.S3S

Historical Protestantism: An Historical Introduction to Protestant Theology

Prentice-Hall, Inc., *Englewood Cliffs, New Jersey*

To the memory of
my father and mother

Protestant churches

Prentice-Hall International, Inc., *London*
Prentice-Hall of Australia, Pty. Ltd., *Sydney*
Prentice-Hall of Canada, Ltd., *Toronto*
Prentice-Hall of India Private Limited, *New Delhi*
Prentice-Hall of Japan, Inc., *Tokyo*

© 1971 by Prentice-Hall, Inc.
Englewood Cliffs, N.J.

LIBRARY OF CONGRESS CATALOG CARD NO.: 76–123085
PRINTED IN THE UNITED STATES OF AMERICA

13–389171–2 (p)

13–389205–0 (c)

CURRENT PRINTING (LAST NUMBER):
10 9 8 7 6 5 4 3 2 1

Preface

This book is intended to be an initial introduction to Protestantism and thereby a contribution to the developing dialogue between Protestant and Roman Catholic Christians. It attempts to appraise historical Protestantism from the point of view of a Roman Catholic. To do this, a study is presented of Protestantism in historical perspective. Chapters one through four are a discussion of the initial vision of Protestantism at the time of the Reformation of the sixteenth century as it was expressed by Martin Luther and John Calvin, and by the other two forms that Protestantism took at that time, Anabaptism and Anglicanism.

But it is not enough to study beginnings. One must also see what history has made and is making of those beginnings. What history has made of the Reformation is dealt with in chapters five through seven where Puritanism, Methodism, and nineteenth century liberal Protestantism are studied as representative expressions of Protestant Christianity in the seventeenth, eighteenth, and nineteenth centuries. What history is now making of the Reformation is the subject of chapters eight through twelve where five twentieth century Protestant theologians: Karl Barth, Dietrich Bonhoeffer, Rudolf Bultmann, Reinhold Niebuhr, and Paul Tillich are considered as representative expositors of the meaning of contemporary Protestantism.

Let it be said at the outset that the term Protestantism as used in this book carries a double connotation, one negative, the other positive. The Reformation began as and continues to be a protest *against* certain aspects of late medieval Roman Catholicism. This is the negative implication of the term and until quite recently this has been the sense in which Catholics generally thought of Protestants. In this view, the only acceptable Catholic attitude toward Protestantism was hostility or, at least, wariness, since it was opposed to Catholic beliefs and practices. The chapters which follow will attempt to discuss and evaluate the content of this protest against Roman Catholicism.

But there is another sense in which one can protest. One can protest *for*, speak out in favor of, something. This is by far the more important meaning of the word to Protestants. It is the meaning that needs to assume much more importance in the Catholic view of Protestantism. Sixteenth and twentieth century Protestants alike feel that their primary task has always been to bear witness to a Christianity that is discovered in the Word of God alone. An insistence on the original apostolic faith as that faith is embodied in the Scriptures and an opposition to any form of Christianity which is a deformation of that faith, these, in that order of importance, are the two basic thrusts of Protestantism. These two emphases recur again and again in the pages that follow. To grasp them is to touch the heart of Protestantism.

My grateful thanks are due to Le Moyne college for a faculty research grant and a year's leave of absence which provided me with the assistance and the time needed to complete this book. My gratitude goes out also to my students at Le Moyne over the past five years who have, by their interest and their questions, helped me to work out the ideas which follow. I am grateful, too, to two of my colleagues, Father James Carmody, S. J., and Father Avery Dulles, S. J., for their critical reading of the manuscript. Their suggestions considerably clarified and corrected a number of ideas which might otherwise have remained unclear or incorrect. Last of all, I extend my thanks to Frances E. Morrison, for her careful stylistic reading of the text. What style or clarity is here, owes much to her careful editing.

William A. Scott

Contents

Contents

CHAPTER ONE

Martin Luther

How an insistence on biblical Christianity came to be the hallmark of Protestantism is best understood from a study of the first great Reformer, Martin Luther (1483-1546). It was because Luther set himself against the corruption of Christianity that he found in the church of his time, and because he determined to restore Christianity to the form he found it to have in the New Testament that Protestantism became and remained dominated by two principles of life: (1) *Ecclesia semper reformanda*—the church stands always under the necessity of reform. This is the negative protest; (2) reform must always find its source in a return to God's Word, the Scripture. That is the positive protest.

LUTHER'S PROBLEM

Martin Luther's problem which led him to a radical re-thinking of the Christian message was the problem of salvation: How can I be certain I will be saved? How can I come to the assurance that God looks on me with favor? His questions were theological ones: Who is God? Who am I? How do I relate to Him? His answer was a personal one: I must believe that God is at work in Christ saving me as His Word tells me.

These were the questions and this the answer that dominated and shaped his life. All else is to be read in that light. He could be coarse and vulgar in speech; he could marry a woman who had been a nun; but this and all else in his life, good and bad, can only be seen in perspective if it is seen as flowing from the central core of his life: his strong and sincere quest for a right relation with God. The vehemence and the vulgarity were weapons in defense of what he saw as religious truth. The leaving of the

1

monastery and the subsequent marriage he saw as the logical explication of his deepest religious convictions. He was above all a man of religion. This is the key to understanding him.

Gifted with an intense, scrupulous nature, Luther very early in his life came face to face with his problem: knowing myself for what I am, a sinner, and God for what He is, all just, how can I ever hope to win His favor? His church offered him answers to his problem and he tried them with all the passion of his sincerely religious nature.

Monasticism for the church of that time was the road above all others to God. For the generous soul wanting to give God proof of his love and thereby gain God's approval in return, it was the surest way to salvation. And so in 1505, at the age of 21, he entered the Augustinian Friars at Erfurt. Once in the religious life he gave himself wholeheartedly to it. He was a good monk.

> I was a good monk and I kept the rule of my order so strictly that I may say that if ever a monk got to heaven by his monkery it was I. All my brothers in the monastery who knew me will bear me out. If I had kept on any longer, I should have killed myself with vigils, prayers, reading, and other works.[1]

Austerities became central to his life; nightlong vigils of prayer, corporal punishment, fasting. But none of them gave him the security he sought. Always the question returned: how can I be sure I am doing enough? Is not my sinfulness too great to win His forgiveness? It is impossible for me to become worthy of His love. Thus self-effort, strenuously worked at for a long time (he had already been a monk for twelve years when he posted his ninety-five theses in Wittenberg in 1517) could not give him his assurance. Where else could he turn? There was also the mass and the sacrament of forgiveness for sins. And to these also he gave himself ardently.

Perhaps what one could not earn for oneself could be won through presenting the merits of Christ to the Father. If I offer mass, he thought, that re-presentation of Christ's sacrifice for us to God, He will deign to look on me favorably because of those merits. So, as an ordained priest, he offered the Mass piously and reverently. But the old problem kept returning to torment him. The sacrifice provided only one more occasion for self-doubt. He felt it first on the occasion of his first Mass in 1507. It would return many times thereafter to torment him. It was again the problem of his own unworthiness before God. His own words on that occasion typify the reaction that the Mass tended more and more to arouse in him. As he began the first words of the offertory prayers, the awfulness of what he was about to do burst upon him.

At these words I was utterly stupefied and terror-stricken. I
thought to myself, With what tongue shall I address such Majesty, seeing that all men ought to tremble in the presence of
even an earthly prince? Who am I, that I should lift up mine
eyes or raise my hands to the divine Majesty? The angels surround him. At his nod the earth trembles. And shall I, a miserable little pygmy, say "I want this, I ask for that"? For I am
dust and ashes and full of sin and I am speaking to the living,
eternal and the true God.[2]

His own sinfulness returned to haunt him even at the altar, even while
offering the sacrifice which redeemed him. Here too he was to find no
peace, no assurance of salvation.

What then of Penance, that sacrament for the forgiveness of sins given
by a merciful Father? Here surely God would grant assurance of forgiveness, some sense of hope. But this too was to be no source of solace. He
fell into the pit of scruples and the sacrament only increased his anxiety
and sense of dread. Of the three elements of Penance, confession, contrition and satisfaction, each came to present him with questions he ultimately found unanswerable.[3]

Confession meant to Luther that to be forgiven one must confess one's
sins. But how could he be certain he had done this? It became his constantly recurring experience that he would finish a confession, long and
carefully prepared, only to remember almost immediately some fault or
sin he had forgotten to confess. Little by little the realization dawned on
him that his sinfulness lay a lot deeper than this or that transgression. It
was embedded in his very nature. And that nature enlisted the aid of its
own faculties first to manifest and then to hide its radical corruption.

Will yielded easily, faced by temptation, and then memory conve-
niently forgot the transgression in order that nature might be spared facing
itself. If it were true, Luther reasoned, that the components of his nature
allied themselves together in support of his sinfulness, how could he even
hope to reveal to his confessor the totality of his corruption, no matter
how long and sincerely he searched his conscience? Complete confession
thus became more and more an impossibility for him and so the question:
How can I be sure of forgiveness for sins I do not confess?—became harder
and harder to answer.

Regarding contrition, Luther felt that if God were to forgive, it could
only be because one was sorry for having offended God. Any lesser motive
for sorrow, like fear, could not possibly hope for forgiveness. And having
set the demand thus high, he found he could not scale that height. Was it
possible, he asked himself, for a man, whose supreme object of love was

himself, to place a genuine act of love of God, the only kind of sorrow that deserved God's mercy? He saw it could not be done. The only acceptable form of contrition became an impossibility.

And, as for making satisfaction for sin, here too he saw that sinful man was not capable of doing that. What man could offer adequate satisfaction for offense against an all-holy God?

Thus did Luther learn, in the crucible of his own personal experience over a period of years, that any reliance on sacramental help to win the favor of God that he so desperately sought was illusory. He came finally to the unavoidable conclusion: he could not find within himself—he knew because he had tried long and hard and had failed—the resources needed to win his way to God. At last he saw that his problem lay not with the means available for salvation but with himself. His nature was not capable of using the means. Bouyer sums up his predicament well when he says:

> He had at his disposal any number of means to sanctification. All of these, however—prayer, fasting, monastic discipline, the Sacraments even, still more his own accumulation of petty devotions—he regarded merely as auxiliaries, or rather, stimulants, to his own will. There, precisely, is the point which he saw too vividly ever to forget—namely, that the powerlessness of the human will, in the matter of salvation, is not merely relative, but absolute. It is not that man lacks resources, even powerful ones, to strengthen his will so as to achieve salvation, it is his will which is purely and simply incapable. A feeble workman may achieve great effects with appropriate tools. In the hands of a dead man the most powerful machines are useless.[4]

There was one last means he attempted to use in his struggle for assurance, the merits of the saints. For the church of his time the cult of the saints occupied a prominent place and it was normal for him to turn in this direction in his search for favor with God. If, as daily experience kept bringing home to him ever more acutely, he was unable, because of his own radical sinfulness, to win merit in God's eyes, then, perhaps, an appeal to the merits of the saints would give him some peace. The saints, in the thinking of his age, had, by the exceptional holiness of their lives, won far more merit than was needed for their own salvation. Devotion to them might earn their intercession before God and win from Him the application of their superfluous merits to oneself. Thus, Luther, unable to reach salvation through his own efforts, might still hope for it through the merits of those who, in the eyes of his church, had led lives of extraordinary perfection. For a time he was able to find some assurance in devotion to the saints and in recourse to that treasury of their superabundant merits which, along with the infinite merits won by Christ, were available to the faithful. By prayers and good works he tried to fulfill the conditions requisite to have these merits applied to himself by the church, custodian of that treasury.

But in the end this resource failed him too. He came, finally, to the conclusion that the all-holy God demanded from each human soul all that a man was capable of giving Him by way of a holy life. The very nature of God and man's relation to Him was such as to render the notion of superabundant merit untenable. No man could do less than give God his best and, this being true, no one could be spoken of as giving God more than He had the right to expect. There was no treasury of the saints' merits for Luther to rely upon.

Thus, in the end, Luther found himself in a completely impossible position, bound to earn his own salvation and yet acutely aware of his own inability to do this. The last stage was, predictably, despair: I am lost. This in its turn led to an awful doubt about God Himself. How can I find it in myself, he wondered, to love a God who can put me in such a position? I do not love Him; I hate Him.

> For however irreproachably I lived as a religious, I felt myself in the presence of God to be a sinner with a most unquiet conscience, nor could I trust that I had pleased Him with my satisfaction. I did not love, nay, rather I hated this just God who punished sinners and if not with "open blasphemy" certainly with huge murmurings I was angry with God, saying: "As though it really were not enough that miserable sinners should be eternally damned with original sin, and have all kinds of calamities laid upon them by the law of the ten commandments, God must go and add sorrow upon sorrow and even through the Gospel itself bring His Justice and His Wrath to bear!"[5]

ITS SOLUTION

At this critical juncture Staupitz, his confessor, intervened. What Luther needed, Staupitz saw, was a work that would turn his energies away from introspection. He put his penitent to the task of earning his doctor's degree in theology and subsequently turned over to him his own chair of Scripture at the University of Wittenberg. Luther set himself to study and began lecturing and preaching on the Scriptures. It was here, in the Word of God, that he found his answer.

His study of the Psalms in preparation for a set of lectures on them in 1513-14 was the first step. It helped somewhat to temper his exceedingly harsh picture of God as Demander and Judge. The agony that Christ suffered as depicted in Psalm 22 ("My God, my God, why hast Thou forsaken me?") led him to see how completely Christ had identified Himself with man up to the very point of sharing the sense of utter separation from God because of sin. It was an alienation that Luther himself knew only too well. He saw too that it was the Father who had put Christ to this task in order that Christ might take upon Himself the guilt and penalty of men and satisfy for it. With this realization the light began to break through for Luther. He had been wrong, he realized, in seeing God primarily as Judge. He was that, certainly, but it was the sending of His Son to save that gave the true insight into who God was. He was above all, Love, Mercy, Forgiveness.

Yet one grave problem still remained: the justice of God. All his training in theology, his piety and devotions, the climate of the age in which he lived, had conditioned Luther to see God as just. He would render to each man according to his works. How, if this was true, was it possible, even with his new vision of God as Love, for Luther to escape the just judgment of God? What grounds for hope in God's love did he have with the acute sense of sinfulness that was his? How could God be all just and avoid condemning him?

It was when Luther turned to preparing his lectures on St. Paul's Epistle to the Romans that he found his answer to these questions. He came to see that the justice of God, as Paul used the term, did not mean what he had been taught it meant. Early in the epistle (Rom. 1: 17-18) he met the expression "the justice of God." What did Paul mean by the expression? How was one to understand the phrase: "it is in the Gospel that the justice of God is revealed"? Luther struggled with the passage long and hard and finally he found the key that opened the lock and solved once and for all his search for some assurance of salvation. His own words tell of his momentous discovery.

> I greatly longed to understand Paul's Epistle to the Romans and nothing stood in the way but that one expression, "the justice of God," because I took it to mean that justice whereby God is just and deals justly in punishing the unjust. My situation was that, although an impeccable monk, I stood before God as a sinner troubled in conscience, and I had no

> confidence that my merit would assuage him. Therefore I did
> not love a just and angry God, but rather hated and murmured
> against him. Yet I clung to the dear Paul and had a great
> yearning to know what he meant.
>
> Night and day I pondered until I saw the connection between
> the justice of God and the statement that "the just shall live
> by his faith." Then I grasped that the justice of God is that
> righteousness by which through grace and sheer mercy God
> justifies us through faith. Thereupon I felt myself to be reborn
> and to have gone through open doors into paradise. The whole
> of Scripture took on a new meaning, and whereas before the
> "justice of God" had filled me with hate, now it became to me
> inexpressibly sweet in greater love. This passage of Paul be-
> came to me a gate of heaven. . . .[6]

In these two phrases of St. Paul: "in the Gospel the justice of God is
revealed" and "the just shall live by his faith" and in Luther's understanding of their meaning lies the marrow of his theology, the core of the
Reformation, and the continuing living center of Protestantism. All else in
his thought is an enlargement upon, a deduction from, or implied in, this
fundamental insight.

In the theological tradition wherein Luther had been trained he had
learned to think of the justice of God principally in the punitive sense.
God, in this view, was preeminently the Judge. He knew man's life in all its
detail and demanded strict satisfaction for all his transgressions. His justice
was to be served in its fullness by the imposition of the punishment
warranted. This conception of God had driven Luther to the brink of
despair as he contemplated his own sinfulness and inability to fulfill what
God required of him.

Now he became aware that there was another way of understanding
what was meant by "the justice of God." In the Gospel God's justice is
revealed as something other than Luther had hitherto realized. In simple
language the Good News of the Gospel was that God had expended His
punitive justice on Christ, that by His death Christ, in fulfillment of His
Father's will, took upon Himself the guilt and the debt of man's sins and
paid that debt in full. The demands of the just judge were completely met
on the cross. There the punitive justice of God was satisfied.

But the cross was more than justice satisfied; it was also love revealed.
Precisely because of what Christ did, God treats us differently. In view of
Christ He now declares men just, treats them as saved. He communicates
to men His own justice (i.e., His own holiness). This is the import of Paul's
statement that the justice of God is revealed in the Gospel. His punitive

justice is fulfilled and His justice in the sense of His holiness is communicated to men. Both of these are done because of Christ and that is the
Gospel message. The New Testament revelation is that, in spite of our
sinfulness and inability to merit His forgiveness, God forgives us because of
Christ. No merit of ours has earned this; it is a gratuitous act of divine
love. God loves and saves us in spite of ourselves. Because of Christ's death
God treats us differently than we deserve.

There was one further step in Luther's understanding of Paul. If God
has spoken to man, then man should believe Him when He speaks. It is this
belief which brings that message to the individual personally, effecting in
him that assurance of unmerited salvation of which the Gospel speaks.
"The just man lives by faith," Paul had said. It was as simply stated as
that. A man's faith makes him just, brings him God's holiness and forgiveness, and enables him henceforth to live in the assurance for which Luther
had sought so long. He need not, indeed could not, earn that assurance.
But God, knowing this, gave it to him in Christ. Belief in God acting
through Christ to save him was all he needed to have.

Out of this understanding of Paul came Luther's doctrine of justified
man, as at one and the same time both just and a sinner (*simul justus et
peccator*). On the one hand, man is not different once his faith in God's
love is expressed. He remains of himself still a sinner, incapable of doing
anything which can merit God's favor. But, on the other hand, he is
different because now, in faith, there comes the confidence that God is
giving him salvation, making him just in and through Christ.

As Luther gave himself to the deeper study of the experience he had
gone through, he was able to see that there were three essential elements in
it: the principle of gratuity (*sola gratia*—grace alone), the principle of faith
(*sola fides*—faith alone), and the principle of God's Word (*sola Scriptura*—
scripture alone). For the remainder of his life he was occupied in clarifying, formulating, defending and preaching these three ideas. These are the
foundation on which Protestantism rests.

THE PRINCIPLE OF GRATUITY

God gives salvation gratuitously. Herein lies the answer to Luther's
problem of uncertainty about salvation. He had been seeking to find an
assurance that was based on something he himself did. But the knowledge
that his own painful experience had taught him also brought him to

despair of any assurance from this source. He had learned only too well both the demands that God made of man (man must be holy as God is holy) and his own powerlessness to meet those demands (the constant sense of sinfulness). As a sincere and loyal member of the Church and a good religious he had tried, intensely and perseveringly, to use the means with which the church provided him. Yet one by one they had failed him.

Now he saw that his focus in approaching the problem of salvation had been wrong. He had erroneously assumed that because it was man's problem, the solution too must be worked out by man. God's part was to reward or punish man for his success or failure in solving the problem.

The answer, of course, which he now realized he should have seen, was that salvation is not in man's hands, but in God's and that in a total and absolute sense. Chapters seven and eight of Romans presented a clear picture of the problem and its solution. In Chapter seven, man (every man) finds himself aware of God's law and equally aware of his own desire to follow that law. Yet he soon becomes aware too of another law in his members dragging him in the direction of violating the very law he approves of. "For I know that in me, that is, in my flesh, no good dwells, because to wish is within my power, but I do not find the strength to accomplish what is good" (Rom. 7: 18). The more man struggles to save himself the more certain he becomes of his incapacity. Finally he is, he must be, like Luther, brought to despair. "Unhappy man that I am! Who will deliver me from the body of this death?" (v. 24). It is only to the man who has come to this despairing awareness that the Word of God can say: Who will save you? "The grace of God through Jesus Christ our Lord" (Rom. 7: 25). And Chapter eight goes on to portray the transformation wrought by the Holy Spirit in the soul of the man who has heard and accepted God's promise. Grace is all. Salvation is completely God's work. To it man makes no contribution whatsoever.

THE PRINCIPLE OF FAITH

But this process of God saving man in spite of himself was not something that happened automatically. God does not simply give salvation. He offers it. Man must make his contribution to the process. He must hear the message and then believe in it as personally applicable to himself. Yet in the very act of insisting that man has a contribution to make to his own salvation, Luther, in another of his paradoxes, denies that man himself can make this contribution. If a man comes to believe, it can only be because

God has priorly decided to give him that faith. Even man's faith is a testimony to the absolute gratuity of salvation.

From the side of God, then, grace alone saves; from the side of man, faith alone. In the dialogue of salvation God speaks and man answers; beyond that there is nothing that need or can be added to the process of salvation. Out of the bitterness of his own experience Luther had come to conclude not that man had need of help in achieving salvation but rather that he had an absolute need to be saved by another. There is nothing we can do but believe in our salvation by God.

Here in this dialogue of *sola gratia* and *sola fides* lies the Lutheran rejection of salvation by faith and good works. There is no sense in which man's works can merit his salvation. It is at this point that Luther first comes into sharp conflict with the medieval church. The posting of his ninety-five theses on indulgences on the church door in 1517 is his first overt move against 'merit theology'. It had always been taught in the medieval church, and in recent centuries more one-sidedly than previously, that man was able and indeed required to earn heaven by his own good works. It was true that initial justification was God's gift, earned in no way. But once justified, it was for man to grow in this life of justice by the performance of good works. These did have merit in God's eyes in winning that final state of blessedness which a man would enjoy.

With this position Luther broke. For him faith and faith alone saved. God did all; man did nothing. Even the justified man was unable to place acts that in any sense deserved a reward from God. Even when justified, man remained a sinner (*simul justus et peccator*), and as a sinner he could never win heaven by his own efforts.

What then was the worth of good works in Luther's eyes? Is it to be concluded that he did not urge their performance? Is he saying all that a man need do is believe and beyond that what he does is of no importance? Is he discarding the need for living a good life and opening the door to doing whatever one wishes? This view has been seriously attributed to Luther by some of his critics. His chance remark to Melanchthon, "Sin strongly, but believe even more strongly," has been seized upon as an accurate summary of his position. But to attribute this view to Luther is to calumniate him. He certainly did not hold that faith released one from the performance of good works. J. S. Whale, in *The Protestant Tradition*, has the following to say on this charge.

> Against the reproach constantly repeated by Catholics that he "forbids good works," Luther defends himself frequently, emphatically and effectively. Did his doctrine of Justification

by Faith encourage men to say: "We will take our ease and do
no good works, but be content with faith"? "I answer," said
Luther, "not so, ye wicked men, not so. . . . I have not forbidden good works. I have simply declared that just as a tree must
be good before it can bring forth good fruit, so man must be
made good by God's grace before he can do good." Again:
"The Word is given that thou mayest be cleansed; it quickens
thee to do good works, not to live at ease." Again: "for God
gives no one his grace that he may lie down and do nothing
worth while any more." One of his Latin Propositions of 1520
succinctly states the paradox: "Neither faith nor justification
comes from works; but works come from faith and justification". . . . One glance at his two famous Catechisms shows the
place which he gave to the Commandments of the Law; they
have to be fulfilled.7

It is false, then, to say that Luther's thesis of salvation by faith alone
was understood and taught by him in such a way as to exclude the necessity of good works. But if it be true that he saw the need for works, how
does Luther's view on the process of salvation differ from the position of
the church he left? For that church the classic formulation was that salvation is attained by faith and good works. For Luther the formula was that
man is saved by faith alone, not however, without works. What is the
difference?

The beginning of an answer lies in seeing the diverse answers each
position would give to the question: what is the value of good works? For
the church of the sixteenth century they had value as a means of earning
salvation. For Luther they were the inevitable consequence of having been
saved by God's grace. He himself puts the difference by saying: "Good
works do not make a good man, but a good man does good works."8 In
the one case, works are seen as a cause, along with God's grace, of salvation; in the other, as an effect produced by salvation achieved through
faith.

If faith, then, was so important in the salvific process, what did Luther
understand by the term? For him it was a compound of belief, confidence,
and commitment. Of the three the heart of faith was confidence. In this he
differed from the Roman Church which saw belief, the rational assent to
the truth of revelation, as the essential element. This is not, however, to
say that Luther minimized or dispensed with the need for doctrinal orthodoxy. Quite the contrary, since the whole weight of his writings lay in the
direction of clarifying the content of the Christian faith. It is to say that,
in effect, he demanded two distinct faiths. One was rational assent to the
Christian truth, the other was reliance on God for salvation. The second

tended to be the one on which he put heaviest emphasis. His own torment-
ing experience had taught him that God's message of salvation through
Christ must be heard and answered by faith and so belief is necessary. But
the confidence flowing from this was the most important element. Because
God offers and man accepts, there can be a serene trust that God will be
faithful to what He promises. Man can be confident that God's love once
given will not fail.

Luther saw that this trust was not a once-and-for-all-arrived-at state.
Rather, there always remained the constant need of revitalizing it all
through life, the need too for rejecting any temptation to give it up because of experienced sinfulness. It was to man as sinner that it was first
given; it is to man as sinner that it continues to be given. Man's confidence,
his only hope, is in God's love for him in spite of his sinfulness. This is the
precise Word that God speaks to man in the Gospel.

Arising out of this acceptance of God's love there flows the realization
that one must make every effort to repay that love by loving in return.
One shows one's love by deed, by commitment to God's will, by the
unremitting attempt to live as God wants one to live. It was thus that good
works fitted into Luther's thinking. They are the saved man's spontaneous
response to God's mercy. They do not cause that mercy, nor do they
sustain it. But they are the normal expression of gratitude for the incredi-
ble favor received.

Faith, then, solves the dilemma of the demands of God's law and man's
inability to obey it. It does so by removing not the obligation of the law
but man's lack of capacity to fulfill it. Faith is indeed an emancipation,
not from the law, but from powerlessness in the face of the law and it
effects this release by pointing to where the power to observe the law
comes from, Christ Jesus. In a word, faith, far from releasing man from
obligation, is the only true source of Christian moral conduct. If it does
not imply human activity in response to God's gift of justice, it is not real
faith.

> Faith, however, is something that God effects in us. It changes
> us and we are reborn from God. It puts the old Adam to death
> and makes us quite different men in heart, in mind, and in all
> our powers; and it is accompanied by the Holy Spirit. O, when
> it comes to faith, what a living, creative, active, powerful thing
> it is. It cannot do other than good at all times. It never waits
> to ask whether there is some good work to do. Rather, before
> the question is raised, it has done the deed, and keeps on doing
> it. A man not active in this way is a man without faith.[9]

One last aspect of Luther's understanding of faith calls for attention, its personalism. The religion of his time tended to be a set of social attitudes and practices. It had become too easy to see Christianity as something into which one was born, in which one lived and died without ever having to face the necessity of making a personal commitment to being a Christian. In this world everyone was Christian and the way to live the Christian life was clearly spelled out. One said these prayers, received these sacraments, performed these works of piety. Christianity was all there as a given, a datum of life. But Luther's own purgatory of doubt and uncertainty had cured him of any tendency to accept this externalism.

Faith for Luther was something that occurred only in a very personal context. God's Word of salvation was not spoken to the group. His grace was not offered in general and purely external terms. Rather His Word had a special message for each man and His grace was given only to the individual. The process begins with God taking a prior interest in the individual. He then evidences this interest by offering His message in personal terms through the Holy Spirit who gives the meaning of this invitation for this individual. God's Word is heard by hearing the Spirit say: This is the meaning of God's offer of salvation for you. Thus faith is always a personal encounter. It calls for an entirely personal decision on the part of each man. All of life is lived in this climate of a personal response to a personal invitation in a personal encounter.

Much of Luther's later thinking was but the logical extension of this personalism. He saw that the all-important need was to establish a situation where the individual might come face to face with God without the interference of intermediaries. Thus when he moved toward eliminating external practices of religion, doing away with many of the sacramental means of grace, removing the ordained priesthood, he was simply implementing this basic conviction. Having learned for himself how these practices had kept him from knowing God as He reveals Himself in His Word, he tended to want to remove as many intermediaries as possible between God and the individual soul. He wanted to restore personal commitment to the heart of the religious experience.

THE PRINCIPLE OF GOD'S WORD

Luther's struggle with the problem of salvation found its resolution in his doctrine of salvation gratuitously given by God to the man of faith.

The instrument he had used to reach this conclusion was the Scripture. He concluded that it was there, and only there, in God's Word to man, that the message of salvation was to be found. The Bible alone has authority in communicating God's revelation to man. All that God wants to speak to man is there. But to say this much is not to conclude that the Bible is all-important. It is not. What is all-important is God's Word. The Bible and the Word of God are not exactly the same reality. What is necessary for a man struggling with the problem of salvation is that he become aware of God's activity in solving that problem. The Bible is the story of God's saving activity. It is not that activity; rather it tells man of that activity. It calls attention, points in the direction of the living, active God.

Thus for Luther and for subsequent Protestantism the importance of the Bible is not such that one believes in it but rather that one believes in what it bears witness to, God's Word, God at work in Christ saving us. Hence, the act of faith that Luther makes is not in the Book but in the Word it testifies to. Someone has used the image of a window to portray the Bible's function. One does not look at a window; one looks through it. So it is with the Bible; one looks through its words to see God offering salvation and to respond. The constant concern of Protestantism with vernacular renditions of the Bible and with biblical scholarship takes its origin in Luther's concern with rendering the window as transparent as possible.

How, in Luther's view, is one to understand and interpret the message of the Scriptures? Here care must be taken not to mistake for his view either of the two extremes to which certain later forms of Protestantism carried the principle of the supreme authority of Scripture. Some would come to see the actual words of the Bible as inspired and hence to be interpreted in their strict literal meaning. At the other extreme would be those who would see the meaning of Scripture as completely individual. The only norm for determining its meaning would be what each person, under the Spirit, came to decide was its meaning for him. But both of these positions represent deviations from Luther's own view. He clearly saw the Bible and its understanding as set within the context of the Church.

> ... God's word cannot be without God's people, and conversely, God's people cannot be without God's word. Otherwise, who would preach or hear it preached if there were no people of God? And what could or would God's people believe, if there were no word of God?[10]

The Bible belongs to the Church. To her it was given by God; she alone is responsible for preaching it. Hence, its meaning can only be learned within the community of faith. It is not the individual believer who holds final responsibility for its meaning but the community to which it has been entrusted.

In the practical order what does this principle of the supreme authority of Scripture mean? Or, put another way, how does one come to know what he is to believe? Luther's own experience pointed to three elements as constituting the application of the principle: the Bible itself, tradition, and personal experience.

The Bible

In the words of Scripture which have God for their author the Holy Spirit finds the words He needs to speak to the individual. Thus when one reads or hears the Scripture, the Spirit is at work in the individual soul saying, "This message is true for you." For Luther himself it was particularly the study of the Psalms and Paul's Epistles which led him, under the direction of the Holy Spirit, to the understanding of God's Word as applied to him and to his problem. We will see that for Calvin the influential idea in the Scriptures is the notion of the absolute sovereignty of God. This will lead him to a definite way of writing and a definite course of action in Geneva. In different people the Spirit will use different inspirations to personalize for them the meaning of the Word.

The individual then responds and begins to act in accord with the message. He follows the lead of the Spirit. The activity he then produces gives clear testimony to the unique power of the Word from which it flows. His activity is a convincing proof that this is indeed the Word of God.

Tradition

The voice of the church has been speaking the meaning of the Word of God since that Word was first entrusted to her. Luther, Calvin and the other Reformers were well aware that to know only the Scriptures was not sufficient. One had also to know what the great voices in the church's history, men like Augustine, have said is the Bible's meaning. The preacher and the teacher must be aware of this centuries-old voice of tradition in the church as he approaches his own attempt to understand and communicate its meaning. Luther came to his insight into its essential meaning only after having seriously applied himself to discovering how God's Word had been understood by the early Fathers of the church. Awareness of being part of both a community and a continuity played an important role in the shaping of his final interpretations.

Personal Experience

Lastly, there is the strictly personal task of shaping the message to one's own situation and needs. Luther found his own inner experience—the inability to work out his salvation by his own efforts—at variance with the teaching of the contemporary church that it was by using the external means of grace that a man worked out his own salvation. To that variance he felt compelled to testify. Yet even in protest he did not conceive of himself as breaking with tradition. His conviction was rather that, led by the Spirit and his own arduous study of the voices of tradition, he was returning to the authentic interpretation of God's Word. He thought of himself not as innovator but as conservative and traditionalist in the deepest sense of those terms. He felt that protest was in his case called for as a necessary element in his reverence for the Word of God.

R. M. Brown describes the same personal understanding of the Word of God that each man must come to and puts it in contemporary garb when he writes,

> We must obey God rather than men—even the "men" of the Church, if and when obedience to God and men come into conflict, as they may. They came into conflict in Germany in the '30s. They come into conflict in many parts of the South and the North in the '60s. Martin Luther King's "Letter from a Birmingham Jail," written to eight clergymen who disapproved of his action, is a good example of the spirit of authority in Protestantism. Dr. King does not say that he is acting on his own personal whim. He claims to "be standing in the heritage of all those who, in the name of God, protest injustice"; and so he cites Amos and Paul, Aquinas and Augustine, Martin Luther and John Bunyan, along with many others who make clear to Dr. King that on the issue of racial injustice in Alabama in the 1960's, the burden of proof is not on those who are disobeying unjust laws, but on those who are silently acquiescing to them. And since the latter can be found in great

numbers in the church, the church at this point must be called
to account by those who love the church.[11]

These then are Luther's three fundamental principles. It remains now to
show how his thinking on the church, the sacraments and the Christian
vocation is but the logical working out, in specific areas, of the
implications already present in his three fundamental insights, gratuity,
faith, and God's Word.

THE CHURCH

Luther's thinking on the nature of the church is dominated by two of
his fundamental convictions, the necessarily individual response to the
Spirit's invitation to salvation and the essential sinfulness of human nature.
As we have seen, he felt strongly that there should be no intermediary
between the soul and God. The Spirit of Christ has always been at work in
history inviting individual men to accept God's saving activity on their
behalf and by this acceptance to enter his kingdom. This kingdom of
believers in His Word is the only church Christ intended to found. Thus
the one church which exists by the will of Christ is the community of all
those who have heard and accepted His Word. Luther called this the
church of the creed.

Whatever institutional forms this church takes in the course of time,
and it has taken a variety of them, exist not by His will but by human
decision, by the decision of men to band together in a community of
worship and belief for the advantages that such community affords. But it
must never be forgotten that these particular churches are only human
constructs. Because they are, they will always and inevitably show the
sinfulness and corruption of their creators. Hence too, they will always be
subject to the need for reform. There is no such thing as a finally perfect
structure of the church. Despite man's best efforts to build one, every
visible church, because it is a community of sinful men, will always be
relative, fallible, and imperfect in its attempt to proclaim the Word and
live according to God's will.

In the Roman Church's claim to be the one Church of Christ Luther
saw the attempt of sinful man to absolutize the form of the church; this
can never be done. There can never be one and only one externally
manifest way to worship and serve God. Two aspects of Luther's thought
here make clear the controlling function of his initial insight: (1) the

situation of his time offered him the choice of what he saw as two conflicting authorities, his personal conscience or the teaching authority of the church. It was the first alternative he chose, obedience to the Word of God as he saw it. This became for him the primary authority. What form the church took in his subsequent teaching was determined by the authority of conscience directly subject to the Word of God. Hence it was that, given his choice of authority, he was left with no alternative but to build an explanation of the nature of the church which opposed that of the authority he rejected. In place of a single, divinely-founded, infallible church he substituted his notion of multiple, fallible, humanly-founded churches. It was this church he found in Scripture.

(2) The second aspect to be noted is that for Luther what is initially important is the individual and his relation with God. Once one had established this relation he would be drawn to express it in a community of believers. The Roman vision that saw the individual born of the church yielded to the vision of individuals deciding to structure a church.

In the light of his stress on the church of the creed (an invisible church) which so carefully guards the conscience of the individual, there seemed no need for Luther to give a particular form to the church, to construct a visible church. To begin with, then, he was not concerned with organizing his own church. He felt the Word Itself would lead men to do this spontaneously.

But as the Reformation grew and his thinking developed under the impact of contemporary circumstances, Luther moved more and more definitely towards providing a formal structure for the church. There were two reasons particularly that moved him in this direction. First of all, those who joined with him in furthering the Reformation, men like Zwingli in Zurich and Bucer in Strassburg, began to develop notions of the church which stressed the value of an institutional church for preaching the Word and ordering the religious life of the community. He saw the value of peace, of harmony, of stability, that these structures gave to the life of the church.

Secondly, Luther became increasingly aware that his evangelical vision was not of itself enough to guarantee the success and the continuance of the Reform. Radical groups were springing up which were using his interpretation of the Word of God to serve the cause of rebellion against lawful authority and to introduce chaos into the life of the church. It thus became imperative that he should apply himself to building a concrete form of church life, a form which would provide the locus for proper understanding of God's Word and for the proper living out of the evangelical message.

The value of a definite, organized structure for church life became increasingly obvious. It provided organization, discipline, order and was able to formulate statements of credal belief and forms of worship. It gave organized form to the element of community so essential in the religious experience. Luther came to see that God gathers the church, the community of believers. Men then structure that church in viable and visible form. His own organizational principle was quite simple: the church fulfills its basic function if it is so ordered that it proclaims the pure Gospel and administers Christ's sacraments as He intended. Any church order developed to perform this double task was in his eyes a true form of the church.

For Luther, good pastors carefully chosen and trained were at the heart of this organized church. It was for them to conduct the divine worship at the altar and proclaim the Word in its purity from the pulpit. Careful attention was also given to the religious training of the young and for that purpose he developed his two Catechisms, the *Large Catechism* primarily for use by adults and the *Small Catechism* for children. Both incorporated his view of Christianity that we have already seen. To begin with, a discussion of the ten commandments allowed him to detail man's sinfulness under the Law and his consequent need of God's help. The Apostles' Creed then provided the setting for an exposition of the Gospel message of divine forgiveness. Next the Lord's Prayer was explained as the expression of man's confidence in God's gift of salvation. Finally, the two sacraments of Christ were treated, Baptism and the Lord's Supper. These were seen as the two preeminent means by which God confers His justice on men.

The liturgical worship he set up mirrored his belief that the whole Christian people must understand and be part of the worship of God. Hence all of it was performed in the people's native tongue. He translated the whole of the Scripture into German and appropriate selections from it were woven into the service. At that service the high point was reached when the Word of God was proclaimed and explained by the pastor. A simplified communion service followed. The last element introduced was hymn singing. He himself wrote a number of hymns, both words and music, to express the evangelical faith in song; he also made use of hymns and Psalm versifications borrowed from others.

The whole structure of worship as Luther reconstructed it was different in two dramatic aspects from the worship of the medieval church. First of all, emphasis moved away from the centrality of the priest in the Mass toward focusing on the community joined together in divine worship. Secondly, the center of attention moved away from the altar and the sacrifice to the pulpit and the preaching and teaching of the Word of God.

One might finally summarize Luther's thinking on the church by saying that he never lost his initial conviction that religion is essentially the individual and invisible, interior relation of the soul to God. What concern he manifested for the organizing and structuring of a visible church was wrested from him almost reluctantly by the demands of the concrete historical situation. But once the adjustment was forced on him he gave careful attention to the details of church order. In so doing he developed a liturgy and a church life that was very clearly scriptural and instructional in its orientation.

THE SACRAMENTS

In the area of sacramental theology the determining influence for Luther was the supreme authority of God's Word. Out of that Word he formulated his notion of the meaning of a sacrament as an outward sign of invisible grace, instituted by Christ as evidenced by unmistakably clear words in Scripture, and intended exclusively for Christians. Using this criterion he judged five of the seven sacraments of the medieval church as unscriptural. For him there were only two, Baptism and the Lord's Supper.

Marriage had existed from man's beginnings as a universal practice. It was, therefore, not exclusively Christian nor was its institution to be attributed to Christ, but to God. But though it was not a sacrament it did introduce those who were exchanging vows into a life wherein religion should play a major part. That life together should be blessed by the church.

Confirmation, likewise, found no justification in Christ's words. It was a ceremony added later by the church. "But we read nowhere that Christ ever gave a promise concerning confirmation."[12] "... it is sufficient to regard confirmation as a certain churchly rite, or sacramental ceremony similar to other ceremonies, such as the blessing of water and the like."[13]

His thinking on *Extreme Unction* is interesting as an example of his use of the principle of scriptural authority. Reference to the anointing of the sick is made in the Epistle of St. James (James 5:14 ff.). This might conceivably serve as scriptural warrant for its sacramental nature. But one of the major themes of this epistle was the necessity of good works for salvation, or, put another way, that salvation comes from faith and good works. This, of course, raises the question of whether or not Luther's view of salvation by faith alone takes adequate account of the complete scriptural message regarding the process of salvation.[14] Luther's view was essentially Pauline in its inspiration, as we have seen, and he tended to regard James' point of view with suspicion. He spoke of the letter of James in one place as an "epistle of straw" and again as "not worthy of the spirit of an apostle." Thus, when it was a question of seeing in the epistle's words an indication of the existence of a sacrament of the sick in apostolic times, Luther set this reference aside as having no probative value. "No apostle has the right on his own authority to institute a sacrament."[15] And as far as any indication of institution by Christ is concerned: "And nowhere do we read in the gospel of the sacrament of extreme unction."[16]

Penance was a rite whose value Luther perceived. About its sacramentality he did not seem quite sure. There was no question in his mind that the need for doing penance was a constant theme in Christ's discourses. He saw, therefore, a definite place in the Christian Church for external acts of sorrow for sin. He was also aware of the consolation and peace that confession to a priest could bring to the individual believer. Thus he approved of Penance and of the use of confession by those for whom it was helpful and he recommended confession of one's sins to a brother. What he did object to, however, was that it be institutionalized, made one of those external good works by which a person might be led to believe that he could place a meritorious act and so win God's favor. He saw confession, looked on as a mandatory form of doing penance, as a contradiction of his doctrine of *sola gratia-sola fides*.

Holy Orders was for Luther one of the prime targets of his reform. As he read the signs of his time, clericalism, the domination of the clergy over many areas of life, could be blamed for much of the venality and abuse found in the church. Privilege had been abused and corruption introduced by the excesses of the clergy. In addition, he felt that no significant change could be effected in God's church as long as the clerical order of distinction and authority remained. Introduced by the church, not by Christ, in his view, the rite of ordination did not confer any invisible grace nor indelible mark that was the foundation of a special status in the church. All were of equal membership in the church. Thus, at a stroke, the basis for the clerical theocracy, which he saw as the great evil of the church, was removed.

The church of God would, of course, continue to need its ministers. Let the community of the faithful choose pastors for themselves, men from their own ranks whom they deemed fit to preach the Word, conduct the service and administer Christ's sacraments. Far more scriptural in its roots, and therefore far more characteristic of Christ's church than an ordained and privileged clergy, was the priesthood of all believers. Man had no need for a mediator between himself and God except God's Word. He was to hear the Spirit's voice speaking to him in that Word and to respond to it for himself. But in his response to that Word each believer became a priest for his brethren, in the sense that a man's total response to God's Word included not only his own commitment to God's will but also the responsibility of carrying the Word to his neighbor. Each man brought the divine message to his fellow men, acting as mediator in proclaiming the message of God's mercy by the example of his Christian life.

Thus five sacraments were set aside as lacking an essential element, institution by Christ. There remained for Luther and for Protestantism in general only the two sacraments of *Baptism* and the *Lord's Supper*, or *Eucharist*.

Before proceeding to a discussion of Luther's views on these two sacraments it will be well to stop and consider his general sacramental thinking. For him there was only one real sacrament and that was the Word of God. It was only in this Word that God gave His grace. Here man met God and was saved. Nothing else could add to what was given in this encounter. Hence the other sacraments were only concrete forms, particular actualizations that the Word took because Christ willed it so. In word and act they made God's offer of grace sensibly present; they rendered His Word perceptibly manifest. By so doing they created an opportunity for a fresh response of faith.

The sacramental rites were not of themselves acts that produced grace. Rather, when the Word of God was made present there always had to be a dialogue if that Word was to have its result. The symbolic word and action was God speaking. In addition there always had to be the personal response of individual faith. When both were present, God gave His grace. This was Luther's reaction to the sacramental theology of the medieval church which had come to put so much emphasis on the sacramental action itself. In the Roman view the sacraments produced their effect of grace if the rite was properly performed by the minister and if it was received by the individual without his placing an obstacle in the way of its effectiveness. This approach to the sacrament seemed, in Luther's eyes, to undervalue the person's part in the encounter, to make him only negatively involved in its efficacy. His own stress on the individuality of the religious experience led him to minimize the objective effect produced by the sacrament itself and to emphasize the influence of the individual's reaction on the effect produced. It should be noted, of course, that even the possibility of the individual's contribution took its origin in God's gift, not in his own power. The response of faith was a gift of grace.

The need for personal response in every sacrament caused Luther a serious problem when he came to discussing the sacrament of *Baptism*. This was the occasion, instituted by Christ, for the external profession of one's interior faith. But, if this were true, what justification could be offered for the Baptism of infants? They could not bring personal faith to the sacrament. Luther's answer to this problem seemed to have varied. At one time he saw this sacrament as the prime example of the absolute gratuity of salvation. God simply decided, because He wanted it so, to give the child His grace without any action on the child's part. At another time he saw the community of believers supplying, by their presence in the sponsors, the faith that needed to be present. This was the one occasion where he allowed faith to be vicariously present. The problem, not solved in Luther's time, would return later to introduce into Protestantism a Fundamental division between those who would allow for the Baptism of children and those who, demanding that Luther's own insistence on the presence of personal faith always be verified, practiced only believer's Baptism.

Luther's thinking on the *Eucharist* began with his rejection of the sacrifice of the Mass. For him it was one of the gravest scandals of the medieval church. He took strong exception both to the manner in which it had come to be celebrated and particularly to the thinking offered to justify it. As a young monk he was sent to Rome in 1510 on business for his monastery and while there he was scandalized at the way the Roman clerics offered Mass. Todd paints this picture of his Roman experience:

> It was only later that his experiences at Rome fused into a kind of horror at what came to seem a radical degradation, as he remembered the almost blasphemy with which the priests had seemed to juggle so casually with the sacraments and remembered the worldly lives of themselves and others; the hurried Masses (he tells of the whispers of a priest at an altar next to him as he finished his Mass when Luther was only a third of the way through his own: "Passa, passa . . . , Hurry up, for goodness sake, there are others waiting. . . ."), and the atmosphere of relaxation and self-satisfaction combined with a putrefying legalism, implying an idea of God far distant from anything to be found in the New Testament, a mess from which others had reacted by instituting one reform or another, but which eventually helped to prompt the whole massive Protestant reaction.[17]

But even more serious than his disgust at seeing priests at the altar distractedly mumbling Latin prayers whose meaning in many instances they did not comprehend was his gradually-arrived-at conclusion that the whole thinking which lay behind and was used to justify the offering of the Mass was a blasphemy. Scripture had taught him that Christ's one offering of his life on the cross was all-sufficient. It totally fulfilled the demands of divine justice for sinful man. How then could one speak of re-offering that one all-sufficient sacrifice? Was this not to imply that Christ's work had not fulfilled all justice? The Mass was a calumny on the redemptive sacrifice of the Savior. The presumptuousness of it became even more evident to him when he realized that here was sinful man presuming he could perform an action which would be meritorious in the sight of God. Man's essential evil precluded any such possibility.

Luther, therefore, moved away from the idea of the Mass as a sacrifice in the direction of seeing it as essentially a Eucharistic celebration and thanksgiving service. For him it had two aspects: (1) By its recall of the sacrifice of the cross which effected man's redemption it afforded the believer an opportunity for renewing his gratitude to God for this great gift; (2) the coming together of the faithful for this commemoration of the Lord's Supper provided the occasion for a strong renewal of Christian fellowship and community. The receiving of communion was a perfect expression of that fellowship in the Lord's Body.

Was the Lord Himself really present in the midst of His people at this Eucharist? For Luther the answer was an unequivocal yes. Christ was really and physically present, not however, in terms of the Roman explanation by transubstantiation which smacked too much of scholastic subtlety. Rather, the Lord, who is always and everywhere present, though normally invisibly, chooses this occasion to reveal that presence in visible form. Christ, hiddenly present, removes the veil of that hiddenness at the words of the minister and stands revealed in visible, bodily presence.

In summary then, Luther's sacramental theology was a compound of a variety of elements. It represented his reaction against what he saw as an overstress on the automatically effective operation of the rites themselves. It also represented the application of his scripturally oriented thinking to a specific area of the divine revelation and the implementation of his stress on the individual's part in the salvific process as that was to be applied in the sacraments.

THE CHRISTIAN VOCATION

One last aspect of Luther's thought remains to be touched on: his conception of the nature of the Christian calling. Here too he had a specifically new interpretation of the idea of vocation. When one spoke of vocation at that time, one meant vocation to the priesthood or religious life. Christianity offered the believer two roads to God, one for the ordinary man, led to salvation by way of observance of the commandments while living in the world. This was the less sure way; it was also the more dangerous one because the world was an evil place and offered many obstacles to living a good life.

By far the safer and more perfect road was to enter religious life. Here, withdrawn from the world's temptations, one could more easily please God and by the sacrifice contained in the life of the vows more assuredly win God's favor. It was the religious who more fully lived the Christian calling. The life of the laity was more or less Christian as it approximated this ideal living of Christianity.

Against this concept of the Christian vocation, Luther spoke out strongly. It was misleading and false to the testimony of Scripture to see the more perfect form of Christianity embodied in a withdrawal from the world. God put man in the world that he might work out his salvation there, that he might find his salvation in being merchant, miner, housewife, farmer. It was in these vocations that the Christian fulfilled the will of God for him. Furthermore, the distinction between commandment and counsel certainly found no basis in the Gospels. Christ intended his entire message for all his followers. Each of them was to strive for the fulfillment of the entire Christian Gospel. Last of all, the religious life represented an element in that cast of mind so characteristic of late medievalism which extolled man's efforts as meriting his reward. Religious life, in other words, was built on the false premise that more strenuous efforts win greater reward. This perspective, as we have seen time and time again, represented a distortion in Luther's view. All was God's in salvation and hence no form of the Christian life was any better or any worse in terms of merit than any other form.

Luther is here striking at the roots of medieval monasticism. His thinking will manifest itself in the practical order in his own leaving of religious life and marrying and it will destroy monastic life in the lands where his reform is adopted. The broader implications of this view that Luther takes on the nature of the Christian vocation are well summarized by Brown in the following words:

> What the Reformers did was to cut through that distinction (between religious and lay) and assert that one's calling could be fulfilled in any kind of occupation and not just in a specifically "sacred" one. As Luther put it, the shoemaker can serve God at his bench just as fully as the priest does at the

altar. . . . Thus the "sacredness of the secular" . . . was reaffirmed. One's response to God in love could be carried out wherever one was. All of life was invested with meaning, and all work was invested with dignity.

This view has had a long and complex history. It has raised difficulties; sometimes *all* kinds of work have been too uncritically sanctified, and sometimes Protestantism has become a little too chummy with the worst forms of capitalist expansion. But as a general principle, granted the need for constant redefinition in the light of differing cultural situations, the emphasis on Christian vocation is an important contribution to the ordering of man's total life under God.[18]

CONCLUSION

By way of a final conclusion, how is Luther's position in the history of Christianity to be assessed? There can be no question that he arrived at a view of Christianity sharply differentiated from the Roman Catholicism of his time. It is likewise true that his estimate of the meaning of the Christian religious experience contained authentic and perenially necessary emphases in that experience. His essential contribution seems to have been the rediscovery and reinsertion into the stream of Christian history of certain emphases which had come to be widely undervalued if not totally disregarded in his age. God is all in the salvific process; man must be personally committed by faith to his own salvation; God's Word must be listened to if man is to know what God is offering and asking from man; all these are of the essence of the Christian message.

But to have said this is not to have said all, because the Christian faith in its fullness says there are other equally essential emphases that must be included if one is to talk with completeness of the relation between God and man and of the way by which man comes to God.

(1) It is certainly true that in salvation God is all. But in the Christian revelation it is of equal certainty that God will not save man without his cooperation. In the dialogue of salvation both partners to the dialogue must be active: God and man, To assert the allness of God is not enough. This must be paradoxically countered by asserting also the role of man. Both are involved and hence neither is sufficient alone. It is a distortion of Christianity to overemphasize either term of the dialogue. To overstress God's part tends to reduce man to nothing and thereby robs him of his

necessary contribution to his own salvation. To overstress man's part is to run the risk of granting him an autonomy in his own destiny which Christianity asserts he does not have. Thus at one and the same time God does and does not alone save man and man does and does not contribute to his salvation. In the Christian revelation only the delicate balancing of these opposite and apparently mutually contradictory truths preserves the totality of the truth.

Luther, in reaction against the contemporary church's tendency to exalt the role of man in salvation, laid heavy emphasis on the role of God. In his anxiety to preserve that absoluteness of God he was led to minimize man's role. The consequence of this imbalance is that his thinking is characterized by an excessively pessimistic view of man. Even after God has justified him man is still not able to make any positive contribution to his salvation. He is before and he remains after justification essentially corrupt. But this is, of course, to limit the power of God; it is to say that man is so evil that even God is not able to cure him.

It is sobering to realize that these two positions still seem to characterize the two forms of Christianity. Roman Catholicism, whose overemphasis on man's part in the process of salvation had led to Luther's initial protest, still tends to lay heavy emphasis on man's ability to merit salvation if he performs a set of externally good works. Protestantism, for its part, still looks at man through overly dark glasses. If the ecumenism that characterizes both positions today is to succeed it will be not by resolving the dilemma, God or man, but by preserving the tension, God-man.

(2) For Luther the involvement of the individual in his own salvation by way of faith is all-important. He is right in so insisting. But this insistence on the personal and subjective element in faith needs to be counterbalanced by the equally essential insistence on the objective element in faith. Man must believe, and no proxy can supply this for him. But he does not create that in which he believes; he accepts it. And in the very act of so accepting he is implicitly acknowledging the need for an external authority to determine the content of faith. If there be no such principle of authority then the personalism of faith can degenerate into the sheerest individualism. Each man then supplies not only his personal act of faith but that also in which he believes.

It is certainly true that the person is all-important; yet paradoxically the object to which his faith is directed is equally all-important. And that importance can only be guaranteed if there is an objectively existent authority able to determine the content of man's act of faith. Faith needs to be both subjective and objective.

Again Luther was both right and wrong in his insistence on the need of personal faith. Faced with the excessive objectivity of the Christianity of his time he reacted strongly in the direction of the subjective. It was not enough for a man to be simply and unquestioningly a part of the given Christian structure of society. Creed, sacramental cult, and moral code had no real value unless subjectively assimilated. In this he was right. The individual must make creed, cult, and code his own. The person is all-important in the religious experience. The danger in Luther's stress on the importance of the subjective comes when such emphasis is allowed to exclude or minimize the equally important need in Christianity for an objective content of revelation to which personal faith subscribes. Without such objectively determined content, personal faith becomes pure subjectivism. Man moves to center stage replacing God there. He not only contributes the act of faith but its content as well. If the necessity of individual faith is not countered with the equally definite necessity of objective revelation then faith is relieved of the need for any support outside itself. Thus the door is opened to the elimination of all content (except what is personally decided upon) from belief and the removal of all visible rites, sacraments and other objective means of grace. Man's belief becomes ultimately belief in himself. Luther himself always remained committed to objective revelation as contained in Scripture. But some later forms of Protestantism tended to lose sight of his commitment to objective revelation in their insistence on the all-importance of personal faith.

As noted in the first paradox, God-man, so too here it is tragic to note that the subsequent history of Protestantism and Roman Catholicism tended to become a confrontation between personal faith and objective content. Subjectivity become subjectivism is Protestantism's perennial temptation. Insistence on the need for an authority to determine the objective content of man's belief tends in Roman Catholicism to move constantly towards an excessive authoritarianism. Again the future of contemporary ecumenism depends on its ability to hold in tension without allowing either to dominate, the subjective individual commitment and the objective content of faith determined by a principle of authority.

(3) Lastly, there is truth and error in Luther's insistence that it is only in hearing and responding to God's Word that man can know God's revelation. God's Word must be all in learning the way He has designed for man to come to Him. Yet it is equally true that Christian revelation speaks not only of an event—the life, death and resurrection of Christ, but also of

the meaning of that event—it is in this that God saves man. The same New Testament that speaks of the event speaks also of leaders who speak with authority, giving the authentic interpretation of the event. The community accepts their role and assents to their interpretation.

Thus the Word of God does not stand alone waiting for the private individual to determine its meaning for himself. This could produce as many meanings as there are men and ultimately no objective meaning at all. Rather It stands within a community where there are those whose task it is to explain Its meaning to the fellowship of believers. Or put more succinctly, to deny authentic interpretation is to deny an essential element of God's Word since that Word has built into It indications of Its own authentic interpretation.

God's Word alone is man's sole criterion for salvation; in this Luther saw rightly. Yet again the paradox and the tension appears. God's Word does not stand alone. It has build into It a guaranteed principle of right interpretation. Only with this principle is It understood rightly.

In the Catholicism of his time Luther came to see the primacy of God's Word overshadowed and lost sight of in the Roman tendency not to serve the Word but to subject It to the Church's own purposes. He reacted by cutting the Scriptures free from the church that he saw corrupting it. Correction was needed; the tragedy was that it introduced an unbridgeable chasm between Word and church. Subsequent history has tended to perpetuate that chasm. The Word of God alone as normative continues to be the Protestant emphasis. That the church to whom the Word was entrusted must continue to be its authoritative interpreter, reflects the dominant Catholic emphasis. There is danger in both emphases taken in isolation. One leads toward fragmentation of Christianity and a gradual evacuation of content from the Christian message. The other leads toward subjection of God's Word to human purposes and is liable to end up in a rigid authoritarianism that stifles the Spirit of God as He attempts to speak that Word to the Christian. The final task of contemporary ecumenism is the healing of this rupture of emphases.

We turn now to the other great Reformer, John Calvin, and the elements that he contributed to the formation of the Protestant Tradition.

FOOTNOTES

1Quoted by Roland H. Bainton in *Here I Stand* (New York & Nashville: Abingdon-Cokesbury Press, 1950), p. 45.

2*Ibid.*, p. 41.

3I am here following Bainton's line of thought in *Here I Stand,* pp. 54-56.

4Louis Bouyer, *The Spirit and Forms of Protestantism* (Westminster, Md.: The Newman Press, 1956), p. 9.

5Quoted by Gordon Rupp in *Luther's Progress to the Diet of Worms,* Torchbook edition, (New York: Harper & Row, 1964), p. 33. Reprinted by permission of SCM Press, London.

6Bainton, *Here I Stand,* p. 65.

7J.S. Whale, *The Protestant Tradition,* paperback edition (London and New York: Cambridge University Press, 1959), pp. 93-94.

8Martin Luther, "The Freedom of a Christian" in *Luther's Works,* vol. XXXI, ed. Harold J. Grimm (Philadelphia: Muhlenberg Press, 1957), p. 361.

9——, "Preface to the Epistle of St. Paul to the Romans," *The Reformation Writings of Martin Luther,* vol. II, *The Spirit of the Protestant Reformation,* trans. and ed. Bertram Lee Wolf (New York: Philosophical Library, 1956), p. 288.

10——, "On the Councils and the Church" *Luther's Works,* vol. XLI, ed. Eric W. Gritsch (Philadelphia: Fortress Press, 1966), p. 150.

11Robert M. Brown, "Protestantism and Authority," *Commonweal,* Oct. 9, 1964, p. 71.

12Luther, "The Babylonian Captivity of the Church" in *Luther's Works,* vol. XXXVI, ed. Abdel Ross Wentz (Philadelphia: Fortress Press, 1959) p. 92.

13*Ibid.*

14For a general discussion of Luther's use of Scripture cf. Joseph Lortz, *The Reformation: A Problem for Today* (Westminster, Md.: The Newman Press, 1964), pp. 228-35.

15Luther, *Babylonian Captivity, p. 118,*

16*Ibid.*

17John M. Todd, *Martin Luther* (Westminster, Md.: The Newman Press, 1964, and A. M. Heath, London), pp. 62-63.

18Robert M. Brown, "Classical Protestantism," in *Patterns of Faith in America Today,* ed. F. Ernest Johnson (New York: Harper & Brothers, 1957), pp. 46-47.

CHAPTER TWO

John Calvin

Besides the Lutheranism which developed principally in Germany, by far the largest section of Protestant Christianity derives from another source, the Reformed church tradition with its roots particularly in the Switzerland of Zurich, Basel, and Geneva. And among the men responsible for this vision of Christianity the name of John Calvin (1509-1564) dominates.

Reformed Protestantism finds its origins rather in a movement than in the personal experience of an individual as was true in Luther's case. The movement was biblical humanism championed at the beginning of the sixteenth century by men like Thomas More and Desiderius Erasmus.

The movement was called biblical because it wished to restore the Bible to the center of Christianity. Its central contention was that Scripture is the unique source of knowledge about divine revelation and contains all one must believe to be saved. The leaders of the movement recognized as clearly as Luther the need for the reform of Christianity by a return to the Scriptural teaching; more radically than he, they wanted to restore Christianity, in its beliefs and practices, to the structure patterned in the New Testament.

It was called humanism because it represented a return to humanistic studies, the study of both the ancient classical languages, Greek, Latin, and Hebrew, and of the early Christian Fathers. Tools were developed for the critical study and interpretation of these languages and texts. The results thus obtained were then put at the service of God's Word in new critical texts of the Bible and in the re-opening to scholarship of the works of men like Augustine and Origen. In a word, return was made to the original expression of Christianity as found in the most ancient and critically authenticated texts. It was out of such a background that men like Ulrich Zwingli, Martin Bucer, and John Calvin came.

One further difference between Lutheranism and Reformed Protestant-ism ought to be noted at the beginning and that is the strong activist strain that characterizes the Reformed churches. Luther's church had no mission-ary thrust built into it. It tended to develop under the patronage of the rulers who adopted his views and made his church the church of their realm. The Reformed tradition, on the other hand, emphasized the obliga-tion that lay on its members of securing God's glory by carrying His message to the nations. Hence, unlike Lutheranism, it was missionary oriented. Once begun in the Swiss cantons it spread widely and rapidly. It spread into France and up into the Low Countries. It was carried across the water to Scotland by John Knox where it soon established itself as the state-fostered religion. The Church of England was also strongly influenced in its theology and church structures by the Reformed tradition. The Marian exiles, who spent the years of Mary's reign in the Reformed Swiss communities, carried their Reformed thinking back to England with them and effected its strong presence in the church built by Elizabeth. From England, Reformed Protestantism passed to the New World where, in America, its Presbyterian and Congregational forms were strongly rooted from the beginning. After the Revolutionary War it became and remained the dominant influence in American Protestantism. Hugenot, Covenanter, Dissenter, Puritan, American Protestantism in its principal forms, all trace their beginnings to the Reformed churches that sprang up under Zwingli in Zurich, Bucer in Strassburg, and, above all, John Calvin in Geneva.

CALVIN'S LIFE

Born in 1509 at Noyon in northern France, John Calvin was early destined for the priesthood and was sent when only 14 to prepare for this career in the University of Paris. By 1528 he had switched to law which he studied first at Orleans and then at Bourges. 1531 marked his decision to give himself to the study of Hebrew and the classical languages that he might better penetrate the meaning of the Scripture. It was most probably in these years (1528-31) that his own personal religious crisis developed and his decision was made to give himself henceforth to the service of the sovereign God he found depicted in the Bible. This meant a break with the medieval Catholic church and what he had come to regard as its idolatry and superstition. He himself describes the process of his conversion in the Preface to his *Commentary on the Psalms*.

First, when I was too firmly addicted to the papal superstition to be drawn easily out of such a deep mire, by a sudden conversion, He brought my mind (already more rigid than suited my age) to submission [to Him]. I was so inspired by a taste of true religion and I burned with such a desire to carry my study further, that although I did not drop other subjects I had no zeal for them. In less than one year, all who were looking for a purer doctrine began to come to learn from me, although I was a novice and a beginner.[1]

The most immediate sequel to this decision was a return to Paris for study and writing. By 1534 his new thinking was manifest enough to lead to his involvement in the proceedings for heresy brought against Nicholas Cop, rector of the University of Paris. Calvin was charged with the same tendency to heresy as Cop because of his friendship with Cop. He had to flee Paris and his first stop was Strassburg. McNeill summarizes well Calvin's frame of mind at this juncture. Persecution only hardened him in his resolve.

Behind the harsh reaction of the Sorbonne he saw the whole medieval, papal, hierarchical, and sacramental system sunk through long deterioration into a state of corruption and superstition, inert in the chains of tradition, negligent of the Word of God. Here lay the ultimate hindrance to reform, the stronghold of the persecutors of those who sought it. Cost what it might, Rome itself must be repudiated; others had paid the price. He had known this in an impersonal way for some time; but he had resisted the suggestion, having been "stubbornly addicted" to the Papacy and to the system in which from boyhood he had expected to participate through his later years. Now it was all clear and it was personal. There could be no postponement, no rationalized evasion. The hand of God was laid upon him.[2]

In Strassburg he had the opportunity to see the reformed community, which Martin Bucer had set up, with its own ordered communal life and liturgy. By 1536 he was in Basel where he published his *Institutes of the Christian Religion.* The remainder of his life would be occupied with revising and enlarging this, the greatest of his works. It was and remains one of the monumental statements of Protestant theological thought. With the *Institutes* completed, he set out once again for Strassburg. His journey took him through Geneva where William Farel was at work introducing reform. Farel confronted him and set the course of his future life by convincing him that it was the will of God that he should remain and help build the Reformation in Geneva.

Calvin settled in Geneva, becoming professor of Sacred Letters and assuming the office of pastor in the church of St. Pierre. For two years the work of implementing the reform proceeded slowly because the magistrates and townspeople were not yet ready for the complete submission of the city to God's will that Calvin envisaged. In April of 1538 the contest between Calvin and the General Council for control of the town's spiritual affairs broke out into the open; the issue was the ceremonies of public worship. Calvin and Farel refused to accept the authority of the Council to decide such a directly spiritual matter and they were banished from the city.

Calvin retired to Strassburg and gave himself for three years to working with Bucer for the building up of the Reform there. These years were fruitful ones for him. While there he exercised the pastorate of the congregation of refugees from France. He also took up the task of lecturing and preaching daily. Time was also available for writing and during his stay he published the first of his biblical commentaries, his *Commentary on Romans* (1539). Before the end of his life he would issue commentaries on all of the New Testament and most of the Old. 1540 saw the appearance of his *Little Treatise on the Holy Supper of Our Lord* and his *Reply to Cardinal Sadoleto* (1539) offered his defense for leaving the Roman church.

Last of all, the three years were a valuable experience because they gave Calvin the chance to work with two men from whom he learned much, Sturm and Bucer. John Sturm, the famed humanist, was at the time rector of the school in Strassburg. He would, over the course of the years, make it one of the great humanist schools of Europe. From him Calvin learned much that would be incorporated into his own *collège* in Geneva. From Bucer there was much to learn of church order. He had developed a very close-knit ecclesiastical community where the religious and secular aspects of life flowed together into a harmonious unity wherein the glory of God was sought in all things. Much of the church ordinance Calvin would later set up in Geneva was indebted to Bucer for its inspiration. Thus in many respects the years in Strassburg provided valuable preparation for the life work in Geneva that still lay ahead.

By 1541 the magistrates in Geneva had decided they needed the leadership that only Calvin could supply and a delegation was sent to plead with him to return. With great reluctance, yet under the conviction that God's will called him, Calvin returned to Geneva in September 1541. There he would spend the last twenty-four years of his life building the Holy Commonwealth, God's Kingdom on earth.

HIS THEOLOGY

Much of Calvin's thinking was in accord with Luther's. He too was convinced of the absolute gratuity of salvation, the supreme authority of God's Word, and the need for strong, personal faith. What, however, colored his thinking in all areas and was central to an understanding of his thought was his thinking about God. It was this which distinctly set him apart from Luther. This will be the main focus of our attention.

To begin with, Luther's concentration was on man and the problem of his salvation. For him, religion is essentially man-centered. His thinking about God reflects this anthropocentrism. It is what God does for man that is important to Luther. Calvin's concentration is the exact opposite. For him all is God. His theology is radically theocentric. Man fits into Calvin's concept of religion in terms of his relation to God. What is important is that man learn of God's plan for the world and, having learned it, that he fit himself into the divine scheme of things. It is not for man that God exists; rather the contrary is true and the supreme act of religion for man is to accept this and submit himself humbly to the absolute sovereignty of the all-holy God.[3]

The full implication of this total theocentrism of Calvin will become clear if we analyze three of the basic ideas that dominate his theology: The absolute sovereignty of God, all else exists for God's glory, and the inevitable corollary that flows from both of these principles, his doctrine on predestination.

The Absolute Sovereignty of God

Man's principal purpose in life is, for Calvin, to know God. The God of whom he speaks is God as revealed in Scripture. Much of Calvin's vision of God reflects the Old rather than the New Testament vision of the deity. God, as he knows Him, is utterly transcendent, beyond any thought that we might think of Him. He is totally Other, unknowable (except insofar as He reveals Himself to us and that revelation is more a revelation of His relation to us than it is of His own nature). Put another way, the most basic fact God reveals about Himself is His complete mysteriousness, His absolute hiddenness. To man He is fundamentally incomprehensible. Thus He is the object, not primarily of our knowledge but rather of our adoration. Once this sense of the complete transcendence of God is grasped, one is able to appreciate how completely this understanding of God dominates Calvin.

In His Word God reveals Himself as majestic, awesome, of infinite power, and complete incomprehensibility. Beyond this He shows Himself as the free and sovereign Lord of all that is and all that happens in creation. He is free because He is bound by nothing save His own will. He is, in consequence, subject in no sense to any limit or condition that might be put upon His will by anything that man might do. He is sovereign in the sense that nothing which happens in the created order escapes His will. What happens in his creation happens because He wills it so.

Such, for Calvin, is the only knowledge of God that has any worth for man, a knowledge that leads man to three basic religious attitudes: humble adoration before the mystery and sovereignty of God, acceptance of man's own significance, and total dedication to manifesting the glory of God.

Some very fundamental attitudes within Calvinism flow out of this way of knowing God. Thus, for example, the acceptance of God as essentially mysterious will prevent man's worst sin, idolatry, the tendency to think of God in human terms and to express Him in man-made forms, to make Him what we think Him to be. But God is not a construct of man's mind or imagination. He is a given, completely apart from man's thinking about Him. He is to be accepted as He presents Himself in His Word, not to be speculated about and gradually made over to man's image and likeness. Here lie the roots of Calvinism's perennial suspicion of a natural knowledge of God and its rejection of a natural theology. Man can know nothing of God except what God tells him. What He tells him is contained in His revelation, His Word.

This awe in the presence of the unknown God will find itself also expressed in the attitude adopted by Calvinism with regard to its churches and the form its worship takes. There is an austerity, almost a barrenness, in the lack of any adornment in its churches. This reflects a rejection of visible idolatry. Any statue, painting, stained glass, that man might use to express his idea of God must be rigorously controlled, if not completely excluded, lest man feel he can express the inexpressible. God cannot be expressed in human terms.

The same stark rejection of sensible appeal runs also through their worship. What alone is necessary is that the individual be brought into undistracted contact with God and His Word. Anything that might impede or distract from this personal encounter is to be eliminated. As it is true that man is liable to speak idolatrously in glass, or stone, or wooden image, so too it is far better to use God's Word in speaking of Him than man's own speech for fear of mental and vocal idolatry. Thus, for example, there is much use made in divine worship of the Psalms for both prayers and hymns. These are God's words and the way that God Himself has provided for man to speak about and pray to Him. In using them man is sure that he speaks of and to God rightly.

One is likewise able to understand in this attitude the feeling approaching horror with which Calvin and his followers regard the statues and images, the candles and vestments, the entire sensible appeal of the Roman Catholic liturgy. They are inclined to read here a violation of God's command: "Thou shalt not make unto thyself graven images." In man's attempt to visualize or otherwise make sensible, God and the things of God, there always lurks the temptation to refuse to accept God as He reveals Himself, essentially mysterious and unknowable, and hence to become idolatrous.

All Things Exist for God's Glory (soli Deo gloria)

This unknown and sovereignly free God enters into a freely chosen relation with created reality. All things that exist come from Him; He is their efficient cause. They have also no other end than Him; He is their final cause. Thus, it is for His own purposes that God acts. The redemption wrought by Christ is directed to man and his salvation but that salvation preeminently manifests the glory of God. This being the purpose of the world and of all in it, man's task is to accept and conform himself to this end. He must come to acknowledge that the only reason for which he exists is to give God glory, to reflect the purpose for which God made him. His end is to attain his salvation. But his salvation is part of the over-arching purpose of the world, to give glory to God.

Yet Calvin, in seeing man's end to be the glory of God, does not thereby intend to crush man but rather to raise him to a sure confidence in God. For God's Word makes it clear that He finds His glory in doing good for man. In the final analysis, God's glory is most surely achieved in His saving of men. Herein lies man's surest reason for absolute confidence in God.

In this doctrine of soli Deo gloria two aspects should be particularly noted, (1) Calvin's approach, in his search for assurance of salvation, is different than Luther's, (2) Calvin's view of predestination flows out of this doctrine as a completely logical conclusion.

Luther had rested his confidence that he would be saved on God's promise of gratuitous salvation to sinful man. God will save man despite his unworthiness. Calvin, in his search for the same assurance, came to the conclusion that there is only one absolutely certain, unchanging reality and that is the will of God. Once God decides that His glory is made manifest in the salvation of man then there is nothing that can thwart that will. It is on the will of God that man must come to rely with complete confidence.

Predestination is likewise implicit in this doctrine. God's will is sovereignly free. It is in no way dependent upon or conditioned by any creature. The only condition under which the divine will acts is self-imposed. Its decision is: This creation will give me this particular manifestation of my glory. So it will be. This order of creation will manifest that degree of divine glory that God has predestined it will manifest.

Predestination

It is when this thinking is applied to man that we encounter Calvin's famous doctrine of predestination. As with the rest of created reality, so too with man, all that he does, indeed his final destiny, will be as God has foreordained it would be. God has decided who will be saved and who will be lost in terms of His own will and that decree is irreversible. To suggest that His will is subject to change because of anything man does, whether good or evil, is to blaspheme against His absolute sovereignty.

> We call predestination God's eternal decree by which he determined with himself what he willed to become of each man. For all are not created in equal condition: rather, eternal life is foreordained for some, eternal damnation for others. Therefore, as any man has been created to one or the other of these ends, we speak of him as predestined to life or to death.[4]

One must be careful to qualify Calvin's thinking on this point in two respects. First, he does not claim to do anything in presenting the doctrine of predestination but take into account the clear testimony of God's Word that this is God's plan for men. One need only read, to cite but one of many instances,[5] the ninth chapter of Paul's letter to the Romans to see a description of God choosing whom He will choose and rejecting whom He will reject. "Is not the potter master of his clay, to make from the same mass one vessel for honorable, another for ignoble use?" (Rom. 9:21).

Thus, Calvin is saying, one cannot be selective in reading God's Word. One must read and accept all of that Word and predestination is certainly made explicit in that Word. Secondly, the fact that God predestines is revealed. But beyond that the doctrine is wrapped in mystery. God has not chosen to reveal how the decree is executed, how justice and mercy are served in its execution. Therefore, the only attitude man can adopt that is completely reverent to God's Word is to accept both the fact and the mystery. Any speculation beyond that is idle curiosity about matters that God does not want man to know.

In Calvin's eyes, asking why God acts as He does regarding the salvation of some men and the loss of others is presumptuous. For him it is enough to know that God wills it so.

> For his will is and rightly ought to be the cause of all things that are. For if it has any cause, something must precede it, to which it is, as it were, bound. This is unlawful to imagine. For God's will is so much the highest rule of righteousness that whatever he wills, by the very fact that he wills it, must be considered righteous. When, therefore, one asks why God has so done, we must reply: because he has willed it. But if you proceed further to ask why he so willed, you are seeking something greater and higher than God's will, which cannot be found.[6]

Is it possible for a man to come to know what is God's decision in his own regard? Or, put another way, can a man come to that unshakable assurance that only conviction of predestination to glory can give him? Calvin's answer to this is to describe the process by which a man comes to salvation.

Deep-rooted in every human nature he finds the desire to be master of its own fate, determiner of its own destiny. This is human pride, the conviction each man has that his actions do make a difference in his final destiny. It is the tendency that each one has to play God for himself. It is this universal human urge that is sharply challenged when one comes face to face with the Word of God revealing that He alone determines human destiny.

Once this awareness is reached it demands a response from man. He either accepts the fact that God is all-determining in human destiny or he does not. If he bends in adoring humility before the fact of the divine absoluteness he is at the same time acknowledging his own nothingness and is thus surrendering himself to the will of God. He is equivalently saying: "So be it; for better or worse I submit myself to God's design."

This, for Calvin, is the heart of the act of faith. It is this humble acceptance which gives rise to the absolutely certain conviction that one is destined to glory, is of the number of the elect. God's Spirit rewards man's creaturely surrender with the conviction of salvation. Man comes to believe, to be convinced, that he is saved.

Thus, for the believer the decree of predestination, far from being a source of terror and anxiety, becomes the surest foundation for a serene and unwavering confidence. His conviction of salvation is rooted in the divine will and that is unchangeable. Even though life in its passage may bring frequent doubt, sin, failure, or temptation, these can always be countered and overcome by the recollection of the divine changelessness, God's fidelity to His decree of election. He does not choose on the basis of what a man does; so too He will not change His choice because of what a man does. One may rest secure in the divine fidelity to His own will.

Here in this unshakable confidence lie the deepest roots of that activism so characteristic of Calvinism referred to at the beginning of this chapter. The man of faith is released by that faith from any further self-concern. He is assured of salvation. No further energy need be diverted to worrying about himself. Now the elect is free to direct his energies elsewhere.

At this juncture Calvin makes the point that predestination is not so much to privilege as it is to responsibility. The elect are intended by God to give themselves unceasingly to His service. By election He has forged Himself an instrument for the manifestation of His glory. It becomes the solemn obligation of the elect to work toward the establishment of God's kingdom on earth. For this were they chosen. God has a plan for this world and it is their task to become involved in this world in order to impress God's plan on society.

Of boundless energy in God's cause and supremely fitted to withstand danger, misfortune, opposition, and failure because of his unshakable reliance upon the divine faithfulness, such is Calvin's man of faith. If God is for him, who or what can be against him? The image most readily evoked in the American mind by this description is that of the early American settlers. It was the faith of Calvin that supported them in their harsh environment. Hudson speaks of the role that Calvinism played on the early American scene.

> From a theological point of view, it was the stamp of Geneva which left the deepest mark upon American Protestantism during this early period, when it was being shaped to a common pattern. This is not surprising . . . when one remembers that

Calvinism was well adapted to the needs of men struggling to
tame a wilderness. Sturdy virtues were demanded by the hard
conditions of life in the New World, and these virtues were
supplied by a religious faith which spoke to men in terms of
stern imperatives and high destiny and expressed itself most
characteristically in terms of restless energy, unfaltering confidence, and unblinking acceptance of the harsh facts of life.[7]

The Church

Calvin himself saw that the task imposed upon him by the divine call to
service in Geneva was precisely of this kind, to dedicate himself with every
energy and in spite of whatever opposition to the establishment there of
the Holy Commonwealth. One might summarize his life and work in
Geneva (1541-64) by saying that he spent these years giving form and
structure to Reformed Protestantism. This he did in two ways: By his
writing he gave order and systematic treatment to its theology; by his
activity he developed a thorough, well organized church order.

What Calvin set out to do was build a church patterned on the church
as he found it described in the Word of God. There is, he saw first of all,
an invisible church,

... the society of all the saints, a society which spread over
the whole world, and existing in all ages, yet bound together
by the one doctrine, and the one Spirit of Christ, cultivates
and observes unity of faith and brotherly concord.[8]

For Calvin the members of this church are all those throughout human
history who have been the object of the divine election to glory. At this
point Calvin's thinking on the church should be clarified by Zwingli's
thinking on the notion of covenant. Covenant theology has been central to
Reformed Protestantism's thinking on the church from its very beginnings.

The divine purpose in the creation of the world was that it become the
theatre of His glory. That it might become so, God, at the beginning,
entered into a covenant with man, a covenant of works. Man was in a state
of justice and so he had both the ability and the responsibility for obeying
God in all things. By his complete obedience man was to manifest the
glory of God and by so doing merit his salvation. Thus, before the fall the
divine plan was that salvation would be based on the merit of man's good
works. The fall shattered this covenant once and for all. No longer was
man able to keep the covenant.

God did not, however, abandon man. He decided rather to enter into another covenant, this time a covenant of grace. He chose Israel as His elect that, through her, He might still realize His purpose in creation. With His grace, promised to her if she was faithful to Him, she would be the instrument through which glory would be given to Him. But Israel also failed.

It was then that Christ was sent, He fulfilled the covenant of works perfectly. His life was a total mirroring of the divine glory because it was a complete obedience to the divine will. Thus did He fulfill the covenant of works for men and thereby did He lay the foundation for the covenant of grace of both the Old and the New Testament. Through Him the church comes into being as the new embodiment of the covenant of grace. To her is given the mission and the power to express fully in her life the absolute sovereignty of God. To this church there belong only the elect. She is the society of the faithful whom God has predestined to eternal life. Thus Calvin sees the church as both invisible and visible and he finds that Scripture itself talks of the church in both senses.

> For we have said that Holy Scripture speaks of the church in two ways. Sometimes by the term "church" it means that which is actually in God's presence, into which no persons are received but those who are children of God by grace of adoption and true members of Christ by sanctification of the Holy Spirit. Then, indeed, the church includes not only the saints presently living on earth, but all the elect from the beginning of the world. Often, however, the name "church" designates the whole multitude of men spread over the earth who profess to worship one God and Christ. By baptism we are initiated into faith in him; by partaking in the Lord's Supper we attest our unity in true doctrine and love; in the Word of the Lord we have agreement, and for preaching of the Word the ministry instituted by Christ is preserved. In this church are mingled many hypocrites who have nothing of Christ but the name and outward appearance. There are very many ambitious, greedy, envious persons, evil speakers, and some of quite unclean life. Such are tolerated for a time either because they cannot be convicted by a competent tribunal or because a vigorous discipline does not always flourish as it ought.[9]

Turning attention to the visible church which Calvin saw it to be his task to build in Geneva, the basic premise on which all his thinking regarding the church rests is that Christ Himself indicated what elements He wanted in His church. If, then, the church is to fulfill the glory of God it must structure itself as Christ wills. Put another way, Calvin was convinced that the divine will for all areas of human society was clearly spelled out in God's Word and that it was therefore his obligation to exert every effort to set up a society in Geneva which reflected God's purpose in its least detail.

It was the first function of the church to preach the pure Word of God and to administer Christ's sacraments. But beyond that the church was also responsible for discovering the will of God for human society and for setting up the structures which would ensure that society would manifest the divine glory by obedience to the divine will in all of its activities. His view of the nature and function of the church stands out clearly when compared with the other two views of the church characteristic of early Protestantism.

Luther, as we have seen, was not overly interested in the external and organizational aspects of the church. He felt she fulfilled her purpose if she preached God's Word and administered Christ's sacraments. Beyond that basic function, Scripture itself and the needs of the local community would suggest what church order seemed best. Luther's church was a People's church. To it belonged all the people of a given area. Membership in the church was coterminous with membership in the state. For Luther the church and the state were essentially distinct in their spheres of operation. The first three of the Lord's commandments were the concern of the church. The last seven were the concern of the state. Thus there were two clearly delineated areas of responsibility. Church and state existed side by side, each with its own set of responsibilities.

Anabaptism lay at the other end of the spectrum in its view of the nature of the church. Perfection was attainable in this life and membership in the church was restricted to those who freely chose to give their lives to the pursuit of perfection. The Anabaptist church was, therefore, a separated and a holy church. It was a gathered church of strict believers only and it lived its life in complete separation from the sinful world. The state in the Anabaptist view existed only to control sin and it was meant therefore only for sinners. Believers were to have as little as possible to do with the state. Theirs was a doctrine of absolute separation between church and state. Life for the saints of God was controlled in all its details by the church.

Calvin's view lies midway between the Lutheran and the Anabaptist view. For him all the people of Geneva were to belong to the church. They belonged because they had come to the conviction of election and were eager to live out the full implication of that election. Those not so convinced were not welcome in Geneva. The purpose of the Genevan community was to discover and then live the divine plan. By so doing, it would meet the responsibility implied in election, the manifestation of the divine glory. The function of the state in this view tended to be one of service to the church. The church discovered and promulgated the divine will; it was the task of the state to enforce that will and punish the offender.

Calvin, in a word, took Luther's People's church and transformed it into the Gathered church of Anabaptism without, however, adopting the separatism of Anabaptism. His church included all the community and was, therefore, a People's church; yet all in the church were treated as gathered (willing to live a life directed in all its details by the church).

Calvin's church and each member of it had a triple ideal to strive for, the glorification of God, the service of God and the sanctification of life. The church would embody her quest for that ideal in four characteristic marks: doctrine—the preaching of the pure Word of God; discipline—the subjecting of all of life to the divine will; sacraments—the administering of Christ's sacraments as He instituted them, and ceremonies—the developing of a liturgy and a set of pious exercises for the membership.

When it came to the practical implementation of his ideas on what the church should be, Calvin was precise and specific in his blueprint for church order. His *Ecclesiastical Ordinances of the Church of Geneva* spell out in detail the manner of constructing a society that would be dedicated in all aspects of its life to the service and glory of God. A brief look at its contents will show how specific Calvin was in working out the practical implementation of his theological principles.[10]

Calvin finds that Scripture makes provision for four offices of government in the church: pastors, doctors, elders, and deacons. A pastor is to be chosen with great care. Only after the good habit and conduct of his life has been proven and his good and holy knowledge of the Scripture tested, is he to be admitted to the ministry. In that office it will be his function to proclaim the Word of God, to instruct, admonish, exhort, and censure, to administer the sacraments, and to enjoin brotherly correction.

Doctors will have as their main task the instruction of the faithful in true doctrine. At its highest level this office will call for lectures in biblical theology. But care must also be taken that the young are instructed in languages, humanities, and religion. That this office may be well fulfilled, a school for boys and one for girls is to be established in Geneva.

Elders are to be the overseers of the life of the community. They are to admonish and offer fraternal correction to those whom they find leading a disordered life. Lastly, deacons are to be appointed. They will be of two kinds, those who are to receive and dispense alms for the poor and those charged with caring for the sick. A public hospital is to be maintained as one chief way to care for the poor and the sick.

Following the description of the ministries, careful attention is directed to the sacramental practice. Baptism is to be conferred near the pulpit that all may hear and is to be administered at the time of the sermon, a focal point of the divine service, chosen to underline the sacrament's importance. Calvin's own desire was for the administration of the Lord's Supper at least once a month but the final decision of the Council was four times a year, Easter, Christmas, Pentecost, and the first Sunday of September. The minister is to distribute the bread and the deacons are to assist him in giving the chalice. Specific instructions are then given for Marriage, burial, visitation of the sick and prisoners, and catechetical instruction for the children.

Next there comes a detailed instruction on how to deal with those guilty of infractions of God's law: those holding unorthodox doctrine, those remiss in church-going, those guilty of notorious and public vices. The penalties range in severity from admonition, through exclusion from the Lord's Supper to excommunication.

The records of the Council of the time make evident the great range of human activity that fell under supervision and was punished: dancing, cardplaying, gambling, obscenity, drunkenness, wife-beating, adultery, nonattendance at church. Thus, Calvin's Geneva was an austere theocracy where God's will was spelled out in great detail and strictly enforced. Both the ecclesiastical and secular authorities were called upon to point out and demand observance of what was the will of God for His people. It was felt that by such supervision and vigilance God's glory would be most securely safeguarded.

To those who then or now would find his control of life too detailed and excessively harsh Calvin would reply: For the truly elect the joy they find in the divine election will urge them to search out in all of life the ways and means by which they can give expression to that joy in glad service for the glory of Him who has chosen them.

The Sacraments

One last area of Calvin's thought should be touched on, his sacramental thinking. Here as in all other facets of his thought Calvin turned to the Word of God for his inspiration. There he finds that

> The sacraments themselves were also diverse, in keeping with
> the times, according to the dispensation by which the Lord

was pleased to reveal himself in various ways to men. For
circumcision was enjoined upon Abraham and his descendants
(Gen. 17:10). To it were afterwards added purifications (Lev.
chs. 11 to 15), sacrifices, and other rites (Lev. chs. 1 to 10),
from the law of Moses. These were the sacraments of the Jews
until the coming of Christ.[11]

With the coming of Christ the sacraments of the Old Law were abro-
gated. In their place Christ gave His church two sacraments: Baptism and
the Lord's Supper. Both of these are outward signs,

> . . . by which the Lord seals on our consciences the promises
> of his good will toward us, in order to sustain the weakness of
> our faith. And we in turn attest our piety toward him in the
> presence of the Lord and of his angels and before men.[12]

For Calvin the sacraments fulfill a double function. They serve as sensible signs to constantly reassure men of God's love for them. Christ is the
supreme sign of that love and so the purpose of the sacraments is ". . . the
same office as the Word of God; to offer and set forth Christ to us, and in
him the treasures of heavenly grace."[13]

Their second function is to present men with occasions for the exercise
and increase of their faith. Indeed "they avail and profit nothing unless
received in faith."[14] Each sacramental encounter with Christ offers the
believer an opportunity to reaffirm his acceptance of the salvation God has
given him in Christ.

Baptism is, for Calvin, the "sign of the initiation by which we are
received into the society of the church."[15] It does not deliver a man
". . . from original sin, and from the corruption which has descended from
Adam to all his posterity; . . . ."[16] Rather,

> . . . the Lord promises us by this sign that full and complete
> remission has been made, both of the guilt that should have
> been imputed to us, and of the punishment that we ought to
> have undergone because of the guilt. They also lay hold on
> righteousness, but such righteousness as the people of God can
> obtain in this life, that is, by imputation only, since the Lord
> of his own mercy considers them righteous and innocent.[17]

Calvin is thus at one with Luther in declaring that, when a man is justified,
he remains *simul justus et peccator*, a sinner and yet just because in Christ
God imputes justice to him.

Infants are to receive Baptism because it (like circumcision before it) is the sign and seal of admission into the covenant of grace. The children of believers have by that fact a right to enter the covenant.

> ... the children of believers are baptized not in order that they who were previously strangers to the church may then for the first time become children of God, but rather that, because by the blessing of the promise they already belonged to the body of Christ, they are received into the church with this solemn sign.[18]

Baptism is then the sign of belonging to the covenant. It commits the one baptized to living out the glory of God in all of life and for the child it points forward to God conferring upon him the conviction of his election to glory.

Regarding the *Eucharist,* Calvin concurs with Luther in rejecting its sacrificial character and in his refusal to accept the Roman doctrine of transubstantiation as a satisfactory explanation of the nature of Christ's presence in the sacrament. His own theory of how Christ is present tries to steer a middle course between what he considers to be the extreme of Luther's explanation on the one hand and that of Zwingli on the other.

Luther, as we have seen, held for a real and physical presence of the body and blood of Christ in the sacrament. For him the bread and wine are the body and blood of Christ insofar as they are united with that body and blood. Both substances are really and physically present. Zwingli, on the other hand, bases his interpretation on the doctrine of the Ascension. Christ has ascended into heaven and is with the Father. Hence there can be no question of the real, physical presence of Christ's body in the sacrament. The sacrament is a sign or symbol of the covenant between God and man. The Lord's Supper is a memorial and thanksgiving for this covenant. It is not a means of grace in itself. Thus the words "This is my body" are to be understood as meaning "this signifies or is a sign of my body." There is no physical presence and hence the believer does not receive Christ's body. The Supper is a faith sign. The spiritual gift of Christ's redemption is recalled and received in faith.

Calvin is uneasy with Luther's notion of the local, physical presence of Christ's body. For him this opens the way to adoration of the sacrament and thus a created, material object would come to be adored instead of God. He is in agreement with Zwingli in holding that Christ's body is in heaven.

On the other hand, he is unhappy with the Zwinglian position because it seems to evacuate the sacrament of much of its meaning. Calvin himself felt that the sacrament did have an objective content, that what occurred was not merely a spiritual communion in faith with Christ. The key to his understanding seems to lie in his conception of the nature of a sign.

A sign, first of all, points to something else, draws attention to it. The bread and wine turn us to the contemplation in faith of Christ's humanity and what it does for us.

> ... from the physical things set forth in the Sacrament we are led by a sort of analogy to spiritual things. Thus when bread is given as a symbol of Christ's body we must at once grasp this comparison: as bread nourishes, sustains and keeps the life of our body, so Christ's body is the only food to invigorate and enliven our soul.[19]

But a sign is more than just a pointer in this case; it partakes of the reality toward which it points.

> ... if the Lord truly represents the participation in his body through the breaking of bread, there ought not to be the least doubt that he truly presents and shows his body.
>
> ... when we have received the symbol of the body, let us no less surely trust that the body itself is also given to us.[20]

In the Eucharist Christ really gives the believer what He promised to give, his body and blood.

Care must be taken, however, to clearly differentiate the bread and wine from the body and blood. Both are received; yet sign and reality are distinct. The reality of the body and blood is not identified with the bread and wine yet that reality is really received at the time when the believer eats and drinks the bread and wine.

In summary, Calvin's position would seem to agree with Luther's in stressing the reality of the presence as over against Zwingli's merely symbolic presence. On the other hand, he would seem to approach Zwingli in insisting that the presence is rather spiritual than physical (as Luther would seem to hold).

CONCLUSION

An overall evaluation of Calvin's thinking may follow the same principle that we used in assessing Luther's contribution, namely that Christianity, in its entirety, is the holding in balanced tension of what appear to be mutually exclusive opposites. In reaction against what he saw to be the superstition and idolatry of the Roman church, Calvin, like Luther, returned to the Scriptures to probe again for the authentic voice of Christianity. What he found there was an overpowering sense of the majesty, mystery and transcendence of God. This became the strongly emphasized core of his thinking. That God and His glory be restored to the primacy accorded them in the Scripture is the essential thrust of his thought. Drawn, as he so strongly was, to this idea of God as central, it was inevitable that he should lay almost exclusive stress on this aspect of the Christian message and in the process underplay the also scripturally authenticated role of the human in Christianity.

Rome had moved a good distance toward overasserting that human role and thereby tended to distort the total Christian vision. Devotion to the saints had grown dangerously close to the superstition that by formulas of prayer one could engage their power in controlling the will of God. Indulgences tended to take on the appearance of magic rites whereby one placated an angry tribal God. Thus Calvin was right in putting his finger on the perennial temptation that humans face of wanting to conform God and His will to their own pattern and desire. Man stands always in need of being reminded that the Creator is sovereign and the creature subject. In Calvin's time Christianity, in its strong insistence on the value of external good works and its fostering of devotion to the saints and indulgences, seemed to be giving man a degree of autonomy in working out his salvation that was a distortion of Christianity. Men needed to be reminded strongly that God is the sovereign Lord of all things. This, Calvin did; by so doing he served well the cause of Christianity.

But as with Rome, so with Calvin, stress tended to overstress. Restoring the balance between God and man in the salvific process is not accomplished by overemphasizing the role of either. Calvin's flaw lay precisely here. For one overemphasis, man, he substituted another, God.

Scripture does not see the sovereignty of God as absolutely unconditioned. By his own choice God conditions His will and its execution by the responsible action of man. God does not save or damn a human in spite of what he does. To say that God is all in determining human destiny is a fundamental Christian theme. Equally fundamental is the assertion that man himself is involved in determining his own destiny. One does not portray complete Christianity by excluding or undervaluing either member of the God-man tension.

Robert M. Brown, a contemporary expositor of the Calvinist tradition, points up the values that must be part of a total picture of the sovereignty of God.

> It is important to defend . . . the stress upon the initiatory activity of God, the recognition upon the part of the believer that his salvation is a gift, and not something he has produced through his own resources.

> The integrity of human freedom must not be jeopardized . . . We must retain for the individual his right, if he so chooses, to say "no" to God.

> But we must also allow for a limitless love on God's part which can reach out to those desolate of his love or even of the desire for his love, recognizing the possibility that he may have ways beyond our understanding for bringing men to free acceptance of him.[21]

God's prior activity, freedom, love, these are the components of the balanced Christian view of the sovereignty of God.

One further comment should be made on Calvin's tendency to exclude all that is human from man's worship of God—that all that is human (save sin) is the object of God's love and Christ's redemptive activity and all of it is intended to be directed back to God and His glory. Certainly one of the most constant and noble elements in the Christian tradition has been the enduring quest of the Christian spirit to express in sensible form its adoration of God. One thinks of the stained glass of Chartres, Michelangelo's Sistine Chapel, Handel's Messiah. There is always danger of distortion and many a church in its architecture and interior furnishings bears witness to how far astray man can go in his attempt to give sensible expression to his reverence for God and the things of God. But excess and the recurring tendency to distort are not the norms by which one judges the worth of man's attempts to worship God with all in him that is human. The perennial danger of idolatry and superstition points to the need, not for inhibiting the human spirit's urge to dedicate its creative activity to the worship and glory of God, but for tempering that expression by the constant reminder that God is ultimately inexpressible in human terms.

Calvin, then, reemphasized always valid elements in the Christian revelation. God is the sovereign Lord of all creation and that creation does exist to serve and glorify Him. But he was a child of his age as all men are and so his vision of the nature of the Christian vision was inevitably myopic in some areas. Succeeding ages have tried to balance and thereby complete his thought. Yet even today ecumenical theologians are still engaged in trying to reconcile the apparent opposites that Calvin struggled with. Natural and revealed knowledge of God, the sacraments as signs and symbols and yet as realities of the Lord's presence, the nature of Christ's church and the manner of belonging to it, these and other areas are, as they were in Calvin's time, elements in the Christian revelation which still resist our efforts to penetrate the mystery inherent in them. Yet we have come to recognize, perhaps more sharply today than in many generations, what Calvin always saw quite clearly, that our reflections on these mysteries must always take their origin in God's Word.

Luther is the original, bold and creative thinker. Calvin is more the logician and systematician. Together they are the principal architects of the Protestant Reform. The remainder of Protestant history that we will attempt to trace in its main lines takes on its meaning in terms of a continuation of, or reaction to, the five basic insights of these two men. That history will serve too, to highlight the strength that inheres in these principles when they are sincerely lived. The same history will point up the extreme lengths to which these principles can be pushed, extremes which deserve the name Christian only by stretching that term to its furthest limit of inclusiveness. Finally, by manifesting these extremes, history bears witness to the need for complementing and counterbalancing these essential Christian ideas by other equally authentic Christian values.

FOOTNOTES

[1]From *Calvin: Commentaries,* Library of Christian Classics vol. XXIII, p. 52, translated and edited by Joseph Haroutunian and Louise Pettibone Smith. Published in the U.S.A. by the Westminster Press, 1958. Used by permission.

[2]John T. McNeill, *The History and Character of Calvinism,* 2nd printing with corrections (New York: Oxford University Press, 1957), pp. 114-15.

[3]On this difference between Luther and Calvin cf. Louis Bouyer, *The Spirit and Forms of Protestantism* (Westminster Md.: The Newman Press, 1956.), pp. 59-60.

[4]From *Calvin, Institutes of the Christian Religion,* II. LCC vol. XXI, p. 926, edited by John T. McNeill, and translated by Ford Lewis Battles. The Westminster Press. Copyright   1960, W.L. Jenkins. Used by permission.

[5]J. S. Whale, *The Protestant Tradition,* (London and New York: Cambridge University Press, 1959), p. 142 provides other scriptural evidence of election and reprobation.

6Calvin, *Institutes*, III, 23, 2, LCC, XXI, p. 949.

7Winthrop S. Hudson, *American Protestantism,* paperback edition (Chicago: University of Chicago Press, 1961), pp. 22-23.

8Calvin, *Reply to Sadoleto* in *Tracts and Treatises on the Reformation of the Church,* trans. Henry Beveridge, vol I (Grand Rapids, Mich.: Wm. B. Eerdmans Publishing Co., reprinted in 1958), p. 37. Used by permission of the publisher.

9Calvin, *Institutes,* IV, 1, 7, LCC, XXI, pp. 1021-22.

10The "Draft of the Ecclesiastical Ordinances of the Church of Geneva" may be found in Calvin: *Theological Treatises,* LCC, vol. XXII ed. Rev. J.K.S. Reid (Philadelphia: Westminster Press, 1954), pp. 56-72.

11Calvin, *Institutes,* IV, 14, 20, LCC, XXI, p. 1296.

12*Ibid.*, IV, 14, 1, LCC, XXI, p. 1277.

13*Ibid.*, IV, 14, 17, LCC, XXI, p. 1292.

14*Ibid.*

15*Ibid.,* IV, 15, 1, LCC, XXI, p. 1303.

16*Ibid.,* IV, 15, 10, LCC, XXI, p. 1311.

17*Ibid.*

18Calvin, *Institutes,* IV, 15, 22, LCC, XXI, p. 1323.

19*Ibid.,* IV, 17a, 3, LCC, XXI, p. 1363.

20*Ibid.,* IV, 17, 10, LCC, XXI, p. 1371.

21Robert M. Brown, "Classical Protestantism," in *Patterns of Faith in America Today,* ed. F. Ernest Johnson (New York: Harper & Brothers, 1957), pp. 23-24.

CHAPTER THREE

Anabaptism

Very soon after the Protestant Reform began there started to appear small groups of those who felt that its insistence on the need to return to the Scriptures in order to recover the authentic meaning of Christianity was the all-important key to any real reformation. They accepted Luther's *sola Scriptura* principle but felt that he and the other Reformers had not gone half far enough in their application of this principle to sixteenth century Christian belief and life. They were convinced that so drastic a renewal of Christianity was called for by any serious reading of God's Word that reformation, as Luther and his associates conceived it, was totally inadequate. What was needed, they felt, was a restitution of Christianity without any compromise to the form portrayed in the New Testament. Thus was born the radical Reformation, the reformers of the Reformation, sometimes called the left wing of the Reformation, or more popularly, the Anabaptists (Rebaptizers) so-called because of their practice of rebaptizing all who joined their movement.

The beginnings of Anabaptism (1519-23) were rooted in small groups of earnest, Bible-reading Christians in the Swiss cantons, especially around Zurich. Their reading and discussion of the Bible brought them to see that a return to biblical Christianity in the strictest sense of that word was the only true path to reformation. In accordance with their conviction that the Word of God spoke to them of a church radically different from any Christian church then existing whether Reformed, Lutheran or Roman Catholic, they began to separate themselves from the established churches of the time in order to rebuild the primitive church of which the New Testament spoke.

To begin with, the movement was a quiet and peaceful separation from the world. All that was asked of society and the churches was the right to separate and develop communities modeled on that of the early church. They were sober and pious folk who wanted only to withdraw from the world they saw as sinful and from the churches they viewed as corruptions that they might live together the warm, communal, and totally dedicated kind of life described in the Acts of the Apostles.

Their attempt met unyielding opposition and bitter persecution from society and churches alike. Thousands were exiled or unmercifully destroyed by fire or drowning during the early years and for a time the leadership passed into the hands of revolutionaries who felt sword should be met with sword, persecution by active resistance. There was a brief flurry of revolutionary activity within the movement typified by men like Thomas Muntzer[1] and the infamous Munster incident.[2] But these were temporary aberrations brought on by the fierceness of the persecution. Within a quarter of a century the violence died and the quiet, separated form of Anabaptism reasserted itself as the main line of the movement. In this form the radical Reformation has continued to exist to this day in the rural and out of the way places of the world.

What were the elements of Anabaptism's view of Christianity? Why did that vision set them so radically apart from the rest of Christianity? The answer to these questions lies in understanding the seriousness with which Anabaptism took the principle of Scripture alone and the view of the nature of the church that flowed out of this insistence on Scripture as alone normative in determining what Christianity meant.

ANABAPTIST VISION OF THE CHURCH

The key to grasping Anabaptism is to know their thinking on the nature of the church. And to know that thinking it is necessary to recognize that they took the picture of the church painted in the New Testament as the only licit form of church life. The church must be what she is described as being in the New Testament. That set of documents made it clear to the Anabaptists that the church was meant to be a disciplined community composed only of voluntary believers whose faith determined the pattern of all of life. Only those who saw the total demands that Christianity made on its followers and, seeing, freely accepted these demands in a personally meaningful act of faith, made up the church of apostolic times. In contrast with this kind of church the Anabaptists saw that Christianity, as it existed in the sixteenth century, had come to an almost total identification of church and society. One was born simultaneously into both. Thus, for

Anabaptism, the fundamental reason for the corrupt state of Christianity that he saw all around him was the indiscriminate admission of all into the church.

The same point can be made by contrasting Anabaptism with the position of mainline Protestantism on the nature of salvation. Luther, Calvin and their associates put the essence of the Gospel message in justification by faith. For them confidence that God is at work in Christ saving me is the required Christian response to God's saving offer. Anabaptism would rather see Christianity as rooted fundamentally in the presence and transforming action of the Holy Spirit in the heart of the believer. As they read the Gospel it was not consciousness of justification but commitment to a way of life that was central. For the one tradition, the lives of the early Christians are typical of the way in which a Christian should reply to God's gift of redemption in Christ. For the other, the New Testament pattern of life is not typical of Christian life; it is normative for that life.

These two basic attitudes regarding what it means to be Christian also account for the different approach that the two traditions take in their understanding of the Scripture. Classical Protestantism thought it essential to understand the meaning of justification, of sacrament, of predestination and the like. Theological speculation or intellectual penetration of the Scripture was important if one was to grasp rightly the Christian vision. Faith, in this view, needed to seek understanding of that in which it believed. Anabaptism saw the Gospel rather as a book of life, portraying the life that the saints of God must lead. What was important for them was adhesion to the New Testament form of life, not comprehending what Paul meant by the justice of God. Theologizing on God's Word could produce a sterile formalism in the living of Christianity. One needed rather to read the Book and then live according to the model It proposed.

Once convinced of the corruption of Christianity the Anabaptist moved against the situation first of all by denying the validity of infant baptism and by refusing either to recognize or to practice it. Admission to the church could be only through a process of conversion and infants were not capable of such a process. Only after a man had heard the Word of God, recognized the totality of Its claim on his life, and freely accepted It for himself, could he be baptized. Baptism when conferred was not the cause of one's regeneration. The conversion experience produced that rebirth. Baptism merely confirmed, or better manifested, that state in a public ceremony.

> . . . outward baptism avails nothing so long as we are not inwardly renewed. regenerated, and baptized with the heavenly

> fire and the Holy Ghost of God . . . . In the spiritual strength
> which we have received, we henceforth bind ourselves by the
> outward sign of the covenant in water which is enjoined on all
> believers by Christ. . . .[3]

The New Testament also made it clear that when one entered into the church he entered a separated community. Christ designed His church as a place to which He called His true followers out of the sinful world. In the Anabaptist view the world had always been a place of sin and those who lived in it could not but be sinners. Civil society existed for but one purpose: to control the world's sinfulness by law and power. Because the world was such, the saints of God, dedicated as they were to the total living of Christianity, could not live in it. Theirs must be a separated existence. Total separation was demanded between the church and the world.

As Anabaptism moved to the implementation of this conviction, it demanded of its membership a refusal to participate in any of the world's activities. Thus, for example, a believer could not hold any official position in society. Likewise he was not to have recourse to society's legal system for settlement of disputes. Mutual love among the brethren would provide the norm for settling their own differences. If called into court by a nonbeliever, one went but one refused the swearing of any oaths. Such was forbidden to Christians.

Anabaptism was, of course, realistic enough to recognize the necessity of civil authority if society was to have any order. His normal attitude was, in consequence, to live in peaceful obedience to the civil law as long as it did not command anything which conflicted with what Christianity demanded of him. But at the point where this occurred his only recourse was passive resistance to the law, which implied, on the one hand, a refusal to obey and, on the other, the willing acceptance of whatever penalties such refusal incurred, fine, imprisonment, confiscation of property, exile, even death itself.

The life of the church was not only one of separation from the world; it was also one of opposition to the world. Here again their reading of the New Testament convinced the Anabaptists of the rightness of this view. Early Christianity had known only God's cause. In the spread of His Kingdom its only weapon had been the staff and the Scriptures. The first Christians had traveled everywhere spreading the Word as persuasively as they could but always by peaceful means. Therefore, the sixteenth century believer could live in no other way and call himself Christian. He must be dedicated to peace and to the peaceful spreading of God's Word. In contrast with such a way the state had always used force, war, persecution, violence, and the sword, for the enforcement and spread of its own will. Such a way of life was foreign to Christianity and must be resisted.

> The government magistracy is according to the flesh, but the Christians' is according to the Spirit. Their houses and dwelling remain in this world, but the Christians' are in heaven; their citizenship is in this world, but the Christians' citizenship is in heaven; the weapons of their conflict and war are carnal and against the flesh only, but the Christians' weapons are spiritual, against the fortifications of the devil. The worldlings are armed with steel and iron, but the Christians are armed with the armor of God, with truth, righteousness, peace, faith, salvation and the Word of God. In brief, as is the mind of Christ toward us, so shall the mind of the members of the body of Christ be through Him in all things, that there may be no schism in the body through which it would be destroyed.[4]

The Anabaptist resistance in this matter took a double form. In the first place he was unalterably opposed to war in any form. No true Christian could bear arms in the service of the state. Pacifism was the only possible Christian stance. Only uncompromising resistance, whatever the cost, could be offered to the state's attempt to make one bear arms. In the second place, it was the practice of the state to put its power at the disposal of the church for the enforcement of religious conformity. Protestant and Catholic alike looked on the toleration of religious heterodoxy as a serious social weakness. Error, especially in religion, was a grave danger to the common good and was to be stamped out wherever found. Anabaptism, on the other hand, felt that one had to be free to form and follow his own conscience in the light of God's Word. Force could never be used in support of religious assent. The Anabaptists were convinced they had no choice but to follow the Scriptures as they read them even though the choice brought them into conflict with the established Christian churches and their generally accepted interpretation of the meaning of Christianity. It was inevitable that this insistence on religious liberty would bring down on Anabaptism the wrath of church and state alike. Persecution, suffering, martyrdom for their religious beliefs became their courageously accepted lot. But the persecution served only to strengthen them in their view. For, did not the pages of the New Testament speak of this as the lot of the early Christians? Not only had the primitive church separated from the state, but, in standing apart, she had questioned and opposed the state. This stance had brought persecution, rejection, opposition from the state. The church of the apostles had, in consequence, been a church of martyrs, men willing to bear testimony to the truth with their lives; and that price had been frequently demanded of them. The lesson from this was clear: the church of Christ will always be recognizable by her willingness to suffer. Suffering will always be an essential part of her life. Indeed, it cannot but be that where there is a true church and real Christian witness, opposition will spring up against it. The world is of its nature evil and always will be. The Christian has no choice but to withdraw from it and protest against it. One true mark of Christ's church will always be persecution. If ever the church comes to be accepted and well thought of by the world, it can only mean that the church has abandoned her witness. The community of grace must always stand over against the community of sin. There can be no compromise. So the inevitable lot of the Christian must be exile, persecution and martyrdom. But the testimony of this suffering is one of the surest signs to the believer that he is keeping alive the message and the church of Christ.

INTERNAL STRUCTURE OF THE CHURCH

His separation from the world created for the Anabaptist the need to develop a community of his own to replace that of the world he left and to provide him with the support he needed to live his separated existence. Many of them met the need, as did the Hutterites in Moravia, for example, by setting up completely self-contained and self-supported communities where all was shared in common in accord with what they took to be the mandate of the New Testament. Within this communal structure each plied his own trade for the support of the group. Together in community the brethren lived, worked and worshipped in a life of shared dedication to the living out of God's Will as they found that will expressed in His Word. Whatever form their communal life took, its aim was a life of complete holiness to be achieved through a total commitment to the way of life of the early Christians. To ensure that this end was achieved Anabaptism developed two characteristic instruments, the consensus and the ban.

Consensus

When a man entered Anabaptism it was understood that he did so because, by conscious choice he wanted to seek and follow God's will in living with his brethren. This searching out of the divine will was seen as the constantly recurring responsibility of the entire community. And that will was always to be found in the application of God's Word to whatever the present situation might be. Thus, a major concern for Anabaptism became the creating of circumstances which would allow the entire community, through prayer, reading, and open discussion, to find the meaning of Scripture that applied to this present problem. The meaning of the Word of God was not for them a static, once and for all given; it was rather a living reality and its current application was to be discovered by the group. The Word would find its concrete explication for current circumstances in openness of discussion among the brethren. Because the Spirit of God would be present in these discussions leading each member towards the truth it was to be expected that a consensus would ultimately be reached which would be a commonly agreed upon interpretation. All recognized that each, under the Spirit, bore responsibility for all the others and that only together could they discover what the Spirit wanted them to know and do.

Thus, in its interpretation of the Word of God, Anabaptism tended to take a middle position between those who believed that the authoritative interpretation of the Word of God was the province of the leadership in the church and those who believed that only the individual under the direction of the Spirit could come to the meaning of God's Word for himself. For Anabaptists it was consensus that shaped conscience. The setting was communal prayer and discussion. The end was a commonly achieved interpretation of the Word of God as applied to this situation.

The Ban

Because decisions were communally arrived at, conformity to these decisions was the normal result. But Anabaptism was not unaware of the sinful proclivities of human nature and it developed another instrument to complement the consensus and ensure observance. This was the ban. Should a member of the group manifest a consistent tendency to turn his back on his commitment to holiness, it became the responsibility of the community to banish him from the church. Here again the early church's practice of excommunication was invoked to justify the practice. The well-being of the church demanded that constant vigilance should be exercised over the lives of the members lest sin should find its way into God's church.

For as a city without walls and gates, or a field without
trenches and fences, and a house without walls and doors, so is
also a church which has not the true apostolic exclusion or
ban. For it stands wide open to every seductive spirit, to all
abominations and for proud despisers, to all idolatrous and
wilfully wicked sinners, yes, to all lewd, unchaste wretches,
sodomites, harlots, and knaves, as may be seen in all the large
sects of the world (which, however, pose improperly as the
Church of Christ). Why talk at length? According to my opinion, it is the distinguished usage, honor, and prosperity of a
sincere church if it with Christian discretion teaches the true
apostolic separation, and observes it carefully in solicitous
love, according to the ordinance of the holy, sacred Scriptures.[5]

Two other features were also characteristic of the internal life of the
Anabaptist communities, the priesthood of all believers and the seriousness
with which the Lord's mandate to missionary activity was taken.

Priesthood of all Believers

Whereas Roman Catholicism had a clergy set apart for ministry by the
sacrament of Ordination, Lutheran and Reformed Protestantism, though it
still retained a selected and trained ministry, believed in the priesthood of
all believers in the sense that all believers had the responsibility to minister
the Word to his neighbor. Anabaptism carried the notion of universal
priesthood one further step, again relying on the New Testament testimony to the full participation of all members of the apostolic church both
in the life of the church and in the evangelization of the unbeliever.
Conversion, it was held, conferred full priesthood on all Christians. This
meant that every Christian was empowered to preach, to teach, to conduct
divine worship service, to evangelize. No grade or rank of any kind was
permitted within the Anabaptist church. All were equal and equally capable of ministry. More than any other of the Christian churches, Anabaptism gave the fullness of priesthood to all the brethren.

The Great Commission

Nowhere is the Anabaptist's insistence on the right and responsibility of
every Christian to engage in ministry made clearer than in the seriousness

with which he took the admonition of Christ to preach to all nations. "Go, therefore, make disciples of all nations," was the Great Commission, a command imposed without distinction on every believing Christian. "He sent out His messengers preaching this peace, His apostles who spread this grace abroad through the whole world, who shone as bright, burning torches before all men, so that they might lead me and all erring sinners into the right way, O Lord, not unto me, but unto Thee be praise and honor. Their words I love, their practices I follow."[6]

In the beginning of the movement the execution of this command put wandering preachers and missionaries on all the roads of Europe. But as the movement grew and organized itself, each community came to choose those who would be its representatives in missionary endeavor. The communal living adopted by so many of the congregations provided the possibility of caring for the families of the missionaries while they were away preaching the Word. Yet, though the mission task came to be organized, the Great Commission continued to be seen as binding on all Christians and in the ceremony of admission for new converts each new brother was required to promise to go wherever sent.

Thus did its reading of Scripture bring the radical Reformation to a life of separation and opposition to the world, to communal living, and to voluntary, disciplined fellowship wherein all bore equally the responsibility for holiness and for witness. One last feature of Anabaptism calls for attention, their interpretation of the meaning of History.

MEANING OF HISTORY

Faced as they were with the grim prospect of an unending and almost hopeless struggle against the state and the established churches of Christianity, it became imperative for the Anabaptists, if they were to preserve any sense of their destiny and any assurance of their final victory, to develop a view of history which saw its meaning and purpose as centered not in the great state churches but in their own small conventicles. So they came to their notion of the periodization of history. History was to be read as a series of periods in the execution of the divine plan for mankind. Each period taught its own lesson and made its own contribution to the final meaning of the total process. In each period God was at work in His chosen ones effecting through them His own mysterious purposes. The elect carried the meaning of history; through them He would bring it to its final consummation.

The church of the apostles and early martyrs was the Golden Age of the church's life. It was the age of heroes when believers gladly gave whole-hearted commitment to the living of the Christian life. Using only the weapons of the Lord: meekness, long-suffering, simplicity, single-mindedness, missionary preaching of the Word, charity toward all, the primitive church had grown and conquered the world in spite of almost total opposition by the world and against unceasing persecution and martyrdom. Thus were God's mysterious ways vindicated; His choice of the weak ones of the world to confound the strong validated.

But, in the very hour of victory and again in accord with God's inscrutable purposes, the church fell from righteousness. For most Anabaptists this fall coincided with the reign of Constantine. It was then that Christianity became the official religion of the state. Then was born the Constantinian church, wedded to the power of the state, open to privileged status within the state, subject to all of its corruptive influences. This union of the church and state was and remained the mark of the fallen church. In its wake the union brought infant baptism, mass conversion, and the forced imposition of Christianity on whole peoples. Temporal power became the church's weapon for witness and evangelization of the nonbeliever rather than the sword of the Spirit. Thus did the church lose her initial form as a community of voluntary believers. Membership in her now came to depend not on personal decision but rather on the accident of birth in a Christian land. With that loss, all the corruption and evil that has characterized her life for thirteen hundred years began to be introduced. The church of the Word became the church of the land and in so becoming she ceased to be the true church of Christ.

This state of affairs continued until the sixteenth century with only small, scattered groups of the faithful keeping the church alive during the intervening centuries. Now, in their age, the Anabaptists saw the providence of God beginning again to choose out the small, separated remnant that through them He might start again the restoration of His true church.

It was through Anabaptism, then, and not through Catholicism or Protestantism that the God of history was at work. Their task became what had been the task of His primitive church, to begin again living the life to which Christ called His followers. They were to separate themselves from the state and the corrupt churches, oppose the use of force as a weapon in support of religion, build a strong, communal life with a vigorous, internal discipline. Thereby they would present to the sinful world the true picture of the church of Christ. For this they would be persecuted as His true church had always been.

But all of this was the beginning of the Last Age; they were themselves the instruments chosen by God to inaugurate the end time. He would complete their work by ushering in the final Kingdom of God through a miraculous display of His power. The Day was not far distant when the Lord would appear in might and majesty. Meanwhile His people had their task: the restitution of His church through witness and suffering.

By such a vision of final, triumphant success was Anabaptism able to steel itself against despair. In the sixteenth century the vision and the demanding life it called for captured only a very small percentage of the Reformation movement. The absoluteness of the demands it made on its membership, the life of total separation from the world that was expected and the certainty of relentless persecution, all guaranteed that the movement would remain small. Down through the centuries Anabaptism has continued to remain a minority community within Christianity. Even today the lineal descendants of the radical reformers are relatively few. The most vigorous of those descendants would be the Mennonites and they number only about half a million around the world. There are about one hundred and seventy thousand of them in the United States centered mainly in the Pennsylvania Dutch country and in Virginia, Indians, and Iowa. The remainder are scattered in small groups principally in the Netherlands, Canada, Russia, India, the Congo, and Germany. The other branch that continues the tradition is the Hutterites. They are far smaller than the Mennonites numbering only about eleven thousand in the western provinces of Canada and about forty-five hundred in South Dakota, Montana, and Minnesota. Both these remnants of sixteenth century Anabaptism remain to this day small, highly disciplined, and rigidly separated communities whose life is still very much patterned on the life of the New Testament apostolic church.

CONCLUSION

The decision of Anabaptism that Christianity meant separation from a corrupt world points up the recurrent problem that has faced Christianity all through her history. What does the Gospel say the church should be? Is she to be a hedged vineyard protecting her membership for eternal life or a leaven present in the world and working to bring men to God through the attractiveness of her witness and the completeness of her service?

Anabaptism chose the first as her understanding of what the church

means. The followers of that tradition to this day tend to be found in the
byway places of the world. They have preserved their witness but only at
the price of remaining a small, minority group. In terms of their dedication
to the Great Commission it may be asked: how can a separatist testimony
to the Gospel be taken as a preaching of that Gospel to all creatures? It is
true that the other choice, witness in the world, has often led to overiden-
tification with the world and consequent corruption of the Word of God.
But to say this is only to lead to the further question: need the choice,
indeed should the choice, be only between the two extremes? It would
seem that Anabaptism's strengths, community and discipline learned in
community, are essential. It would seem equally true that such strength is
only really Christian strength when it is seen as preparing for witness to
the world. Separation from the world and witness in it are the two poles
back and forth between which a creative Christian tension must run.

It is interesting to see one of this tradition's most sympathetic contemporary interpreters, Franklin Littell, urging the Mennonite churches to give
serious thought to how their separated witness can best focus its spiritual
power for good in contemporary America. He suggests the inner city as the
best place for their witness. He is, in effect, arguing that the leaven must
be in the mass, not apart; the light must shine in the darkness, not high on
a separated hill, if it is to fulfill its witnessing purpose.

> It seems to me that, as strange as it sounds in an address to a
> people that has been traditionally rural in orientation, the in-
> ner city is precisely the area which calls for the kind of com-
> munity witness for which the sons and daughters of Menno are
> justly noted. In the world which we are moving toward, for
> some time to come the group witness to purity of life, Scrip-
> tural simplicity, non-violence, sharing, spiritual government,
> the "house church" as a community of brethren, etc., will be
> desperately needed. For generations the Mennonites have
> moved into the desert places and through faithfulness, mutual
> aid, and plain hard work turned prairies and jungles into
> garden places. What would be the impact if the Mennonites
> would tackle the most desperate deserts and jungles of
> America, the inner cities from which the prevailing forms of
> culture-religion are fleeing?[7]

From a negative point of view, then, the Anabaptist tradition tends to
blunt the impact of its Christian witness by its insistence on separatism.
From a more positive point of view, the continuing value of Anabaptism's
witness lies, as O'Hanlon notes,[8] in her ability, through the form of life

she leads, to provide the Christian churches with sorely needed freshness of vision. Her accent on the need for a faith that is responsibly arrived at and lived in its fullness suggests that Christianity needs to move away from both a leadership and a membership that is content with formal membership and routine observance. Along the same lines, her strong criticism of a Constantinian church raises the serious question of just how far Christianity can accommodate itself to the culture in which it lives and still retain the freedom it needs to be critical of that culture in the light of the Gospel.

Last of all, Anabaptism evidences a strong emphasis on the local church. For her ". . . the church is not just an automatic ongoing *institution* but an *event* that happens again and again in the worship and life of the local congregation."[9] A renewed Christianity will find her renewal at the local level in churches open to forms of worship that meet the community's felt needs and in churches that make demands on their membership in terms of service to the needs of the surrounding community. Anabaptism can, in a word, offer the Christian churches much light on the meaning of Christian life, worship, and witness.

FOOTNOTES

[1] Muntzer first appeared in history at Zwickau in 1528 where his name was linked with the Zwickau prophets in their opposition to infant baptism and their insistence that the only real method for interpreting the Scriptures was through the work of the Spirit in the heart of the believer. He soon moved to the organization of a secret band of revolutionaries pledged to initiate the kingdom of God on earth by force of arms. In this kingdom all sinners were to be exterminated and the true believers were to live in a community where all possessions were shared in common. It was Muntzer's conviction that the peasants were so misused, their lot so miserable, that little energy or leisure was left to them to attend to the reading of God's Word or developing their faith through prayer. For him, therefore, there could be no real religious reformation without social revolution and so he threw in his lot with the cause of establishing the kingdom by the sword. When the Peasants' war broke out in 1524 he took up the "sword of the saint" to wage war on the godless. By the summer of 1525 he was dead, beheaded by Philip of Hesse after the frightful slaughter of his followers.

[2] In 1534 two Dutch Anabaptists Jan Mathijs and Jan van Leiden came to the north German city of Münster proclaiming that the time of patience with the wickedness of the world was at an end. The saints of God who, until then, had accepted persecution quietly were to rise against the godless and destroy them. A kingdom was proclaimed, the New Jerusalem; herein the millenium would be realized. The town council was ousted and those refusing to accept rebaptism were forced to leave the town. Now began the reign of the saints. All property was made common. Churches and monasteries were plundered. Polygamy was introduced after the example of the

Old Testament patriarchs. At this juncture the local bishop, who was also the lord of the town, laid Münster under siege. The revolutionaries managed to hold out for over a year but finally on June 25, 1535, the episcopal troops took the city. Most of the inhabitants were slaughtered. The bodies of the leaders, after death by torture, were suspended in iron cages from the steeple of a local church.

3*The Complete Works of Menno Simons,* trans. Leonard Verduin, ed. John Christian Wenger, with a biography by Harold S. Bender (Scottdale, Pa.: The Herald Press, 1956), p. 125.

4John C. Wenger, "The Schleitheim Confession of Faith," *The Mennonite Quarterly Review,* XIX, No. 4 (1945), 247-52.

5*The Complete Works of Menno Simons,* p. 962.

6*Ibid.,* p. 71.

7Franklin H. Littell, *A Tribute to Menno Simons* (Scottdale, Pa.: Herald Press, 1961), p. 50.

8Daniel O'Hanlon, S.J., "What Can Catholics Learn from the Free Churches," in *Concilium,* vol. XIV, *Do We Know the Others?* (Glen Rock, N.J.: Paulist Press, 1966) pp. 94-103.

9*Ibid.,* p. 99.

CHAPTER FOUR

Anglicanism

It was only a few years after the Reformation was launched in continental Europe that its influence began to be felt in England. The point in history at which this impact is focused is the reign of Henry VIII (1509-47). Having petitioned the pope for an annulment of his marriage to Catherine of Aragon that he might, by marrying again, provide the throne and England with a male heir, and having been refused his petition, Henry decided to set up in England a national church independent of Rome and subject to himself as its supreme head.

But this single set of events is not of itself the sufficient explanation of how the Reformation came to England. Rather, Henry's petition, the refusal, and the consequent separation from Rome turned out to be the occasion which set free and allowed to begin working far more openly than ever before, forces which had been present in England long before Henry but which had been, until his schism, prevented from producing too drastic a change in the religious and ecclesiastical life of the nation. Henry opened the door to schism and thereby, beyond his own intent, to the Reformation. He introduced change but it was only the prelude to what would follow. Those who counseled him and his successors for the next fifty years would build a reformed church far beyond Henry's own plan.

ANTECEDENTS

Of the forces already at work well before Henry's time the first was a bitter anticlericalism. Ecclesiastical ownership of property was widespread. One estimate would put their holdings at one-third of all the land in

England. Such ownership gave power and real abuse had developed in the
exercise of that power. The clergy monopolized both government and
administration. At one level, many of the common people had come to
hate the clergy for their venality and immorality. At another, the more
educated despised the parish clergy for their ignorance and superstition
and feared and hated the higher clergy for their wealth and power. Thus,
the suppression of the monasteries, the appropriation and redistribution of
their lands, and the break with the Roman church which the clergy served
were, when they came, welcomed or at least accepted without much resistance by most Englishmen.

In process, too, since the late Middle Ages had been the gradual harden-
ing of popular piety into superstition. Christianity's central beliefs, the
Trinity, Incarnation, and Redemption, tended more and more to lose the
attention and devotion of the common people. They were replaced in
popular preaching and piety by an overexaggerated emphasis on hell and
purgatory, their horrors, and how it was possible to escape them. The cult
of Mary and the saints with its long procession of easily abused practices:
relics, pilgrimages, alleged miracles and apparitions, indulgences, became
the core of much of England's Christian belief and practice.

This tendency toward distortion and superstition had gone largely un-
checked because, along with it, there had grown up a serious decline in
clerical learning. The parish clergy tended to be largely uneducated and so
threw up no strong wall against the rising tide of superstition. More serious
in its consequences was the fact that the tradition of learning had dimmed
in the great monasteries of England and very little was the light they shed
on the darkness of the country surrounding them.

By the sixteenth century two further factors had developed: a growing
lay literacy and the advent of books, especially the Bible. It now became
possible for more and more people to see the grotesque deformations in
the understanding of Christianity that had grown up among them. It was
thus not too long a step to move from Henry's break with the Roman
Church, which had permitted such aberrations to exist, to the acceptance
of the doctrinal reforms in that church's teaching which were proposed by
the continental Reformers.

A preview of what was to come had already been given to England two
centuries previously in the person of John Wycliffe (c. 1328-1384).
Wycliffe had seen and opposed the abuses that, even then, were rampant in
the English church. He decried the rich, powerful and worldly clerics,
condemned monasticism, called for a return to the Bible as the sole source
of Christian belief and rejected transubstantiation in favor of a spiritual

presence of Christ in the Eucharist. In a word, he developed many of the positions that would be adopted by the Reformers two hundred years later. But the forces needed to effect the reforms he sought were not yet strong enough in England. What he did accomplish, though, was to bequeath a legacy of dissent to the English church which continued for the next two centuries. When Henry was ready to move against Rome, the tradition of Wycliffe, perpetuated among the Lollards, had produced two effects which would contribute substantially to making Henry's break with Rome far more than a juridical separation. Dickens summarizes these effects.

> By 1530 they had already accomplished their two main services to the Reformation. In the first place fifteenth-century Lollardy helped to exclude the possibility of Catholic reforms by hardening the minds of the English bishops and their officials into a sterile, negative and rigid attitude toward all criticism and toward the English Scriptures. . . . The second and more important function of the Lollards in English history lay in the fact that they provided a springboard of critical dissent from which the Protestant Reformation could overleap the walls of orthodoxy.[1]

IMPLEMENTATION OF THE REFORM

By Henry's reign the time was ripe. His marital problem and the solution he found to it allowed all these factors greater freedom and sharper focus than they had ever had in the past. Now he led England to jurisdictional separation and these forces led her to doctrinal separation from Rome. Henry initiated the revolt from Rome, broke the power of the medieval church in England, and asserted his own supremacy in both church and state. But reformation in the teaching of the church was not in his plans. He remained to his death an orthodox believer in the teachings of Rome and that meant that the English church remained so too.

While Henry lived, the implementation of the Reform in England proceeded very slowly. Henry was more concerned with establishing and extending the royal supremacy than with doctrinal innovation. The latter, on the rare occasions when it occurred, took place because it served the former. But two developments during his reign did lay the groundwork for the future.

First, there was the new availability of the Scriptures in English. Englishmen abroad began producing English translations of the Scriptures. In 1525, for example, William Tyndale brought out an English New Testament in Holland. Copies of it were soon being brought over from Holland in increasing numbers by the English merchants. Along with the other vernacular versions of the Bible now starting to appear, it helped to provide the basis for a growing concern among the English that Christianity be based solely on the Word of God. Thus did Luther's principle of *sola Scriptura* make its way to England.

Secondly, Thomas Cranmer (1489-1556) was created Archbishop of Canterbury by Henry in 1533. By the time of his appointment Cranmer was already a convinced Protestant. He had converted to Lutheranism while on the king's business in Europe. By tradition, doctrine and worship in England were the responsibility of Canterbury's archbishop. Thus, Cranmer found himself in the position of being able to influence strongly what the future course of England's belief and worship would be. In that position, during the reign of Henry and especially of Edward, he was to become the chief architect of liturgical and doctrinal reform in the church in England.

With the accession to the throne of Henry's young son, Edward VI (1547-53), the reform began in earnest. Edward's two Protectors, first Somerset and then Northumberland, were Protestant in their sympathies and thus the power of the state came down on the side of reform. Cranmer, now that he had a freer hand, moved toward reform in liturgy and church life. These were the years during which relics and images were removed from the churches; fasting was abolished; clerical marriage was approved; communion under both kinds was introduced; the practice of private confession was done away with and transubstantiation as an explanation of Christ's presence in the Eucharist was abandoned. A new book for the conduct of liturgical worship was also issued by Cranmer in two versions, the first in 1549 reflecting Luther's views, the second in 1552 rather Zwinglian and Calvinist in its leanings. With this *Book of Common Prayer,* Cranmer was building the future liturgical practice of the English church.

Perhaps the most significant doctrinal reform under Edward was the appearance, under Cranmer's authority, of the *Book of Homilies.* This was a collection of twelve sermons, one of which was to be read each week at Sunday worship service in all the churches of England. Cranmer himself authored three of these sermons, those which dealt with the doctrine of justification. The approach adopted in explaining justification moved toward Luther's position of faith alone as the source of salvation. As Ridley puts it in his life of Cranmer:

> [Cranmer's] doctrine fell a good way short of the new Protestant theology of justification by faith in its Lutheran and Calvinist form. Cranmer went to St. Hilary and St. Ambrose for the plain statements that 'faith alone justifieth' and that 'he which believeth in Christ should be saved without works, by faith alone', and commented: 'What can be spoken more plainly than to say that freely, without works, by faith only, we obtain remission of our sins?' But he immediately qualified this position by explaining that the faith which was necessary for salvation was a true and lively faith, which manifested itself in good living and good works.[2]

The *Book of Homilies* meant that the people of England would hear, at every Sunday worship service, the principal articles of the Christian faith explained in terms that were beginning to reflect the interpretation given those articles by the continental Reformers. These were the years, finally, when the *Forty Two Articles of Belief* were issued. They embodied a definite commitment to the Lutheran *Augsburg Confession* and the writings of Luther and Melanchthon.

Thus, by the end of Edward's short six-year reign, all the changes needed for a Reformed church in England had been promulgated and their enactment begun. But the time was not yet at hand for their final acceptance by the people of England. The Catholic reaction under Queen Mary would go a long way toward assuring that acceptance; and when Elizabeth came to the throne, the Church of England would at last be ready to settle into its definitive form.

Mary, daughter of Catherine of Aragon, was herself a staunch Catholic and her five-year reign (1553-58) was marked by a determined effort to restore Roman Catholicism to England. But five years was too short a time to undo what had been done and achieve her purpose. Indeed, by making almost every mistake she could have made, she deepened England's hostility to Rome and strengthened the English people's receptivity to the Reformation. Her burning and exiling of heretics, her marriage to Philip of Spain, her attempted restoration of church lands and property, her intransigent resistance to all things Protestant, all these alienated her people and doomed her cause. When she was succeeded by Elizabeth (1558-1603) the English were ready for a period of peace and an end to religious division and persecution.

THE ELIZABETHAN SETTLEMENT

What her people wanted, Elizabeth provided, a stable government and a church that was so structured as to serve England's political and social well-being. Together with her bishops, she built a church and a religious life in England that served the cause of peace, order, and stability.

The definitive form of the Church of England, the so-called Elizabethan Settlement, was the produce of a variety of influences and was constructed by men whose Protestantism was representative of most of the major forms of the continental Reform. There were the Marian exiles, many of them clergy and theologians, whose return from five years of banishment in the Rhineland and the cities of Switzerland meant that a strong Reformed influence would be at work in the building of the Church of England. There was also regular correspondence between the English bishops and the German Reformers which guaranteed a Lutheran presence in the English church. Cranmer's liturgy was at hand and it reflected elements of the medieval Catholic liturgy, modified considerably under the influence of the thought of Luther, Calvin and Zwingli. Lastly, the *Forty Two Articles* were in force, providing a statement of belief which was an adaptation to the English scene of German and Swiss doctrinal views.

To these foreign imports, specifically English ingredients were added, the royal supremacy in all matters of religion, and a strong sense of tradition embodied particularly in the preservation of the order of bishops as the cornerstone on which the structure and continuity of the church would rest. Out of all these elements the Church of England was built and built so firmly that four centuries of history have effected only minor modifications in its structure, practice, and belief.

ELEMENTS OF THE ENGLISH REFORM

The continental Reformation, as embodied in the Lutheran and Reformed churches, was fundamentally a theological reform. It inevitably developed and expressed itself in the context of political and social situations. But it was in essence a doctrinal movement. The English Reform, however, did not express itself principally in a doctrinal form. The Church of England as Elizabeth and her bishops built it was a composite of three components: government, belief, and worship. But, as these elements took shape in England they manifested a characteristically English mode of understanding and living Christianity. Thus, the form that government took in the Church of England testified to England's strong reverence for tradition, the belief that what has always been in the church is to be retained because it has proven itself of value. What was enshrined in that Church's book of divine worship, *the Book of Common Prayer,* was not just a set of ceremonies, prayers, and Scripture readings but represented the studied conviction that the worship of God must be as stately, as ordered, as majestic, as human language could make it and biblical to its core. And the English church's expression of doctrinal belief, the *Thirty Nine Articles,* mirrors the English sentiment that articles of faith should be as few and as simple as possible, that how a man lives is of more ultimate consequence than the intellectual expression of his beliefs.

One must understand this blend and interplay of universal Christian themes and English national characteristics if one is to appreciate the spirit of Anglicanism. The Church of England is the paradigm of a *national* church, not so much because the monarch is its supreme head but because Christianity as it is believed and lived in this church is thoroughly English in its expression. In no other church is this blend of universal Christianity and national identity so strikingly present as in the Church of England.

Church Government—Esteem for Tradition

Paramount in the thinking of those who built the Church of England was the belief that they were constructing not a new church but one that preserved strong bonds of unity with the church as it had always been in England. The sign above all others of that continuity was the episcopacy. The episcopal structure of the church stretched back to the beginnings of Christianity and it had its roots in the clear testimony of Scripture. "It is evident unto all men diligently reading Holy Scripture and ancient authors, that from the Apostles' time there have been these orders of Ministers in Christ's Church, Bishops, priests and deacons."[3] Indeed, it was in order that the bishops might be the living embodiment of Christian belief through the ages that Christ had given this form of government to His church. It was the continuous line of bishops from apostolic times that had preserved the faith in unbroken continuity through the centuries, Christian belief owed its preservation and transmission to the episcopacy. That was the bishops' primary task.

Richard Hooker (1553-1600), the greatest of the theologians of Elizabeth's reign, laid out the sense and value of the bishops' role in the church in his *Ecclesiastical Polity.* As he saw it one could formulate several arguments for an episcopal order of church government. The first of these was scriptural. The New Testament bore ample witness to the presence of bishops in the apostolic church. To this one could add the overwhelming testimony of Christian tradition. East and West, for sixteen hundred years, the church had been ruled and taught by bishops. Last of all, it could be argued, and tellingly, that episcopal government had given the church order and stability and continuity. In a word, it worked.

So the Church of England remained what it had always been, an episcopal church. Thus did Elizabeth's advisers stress the continuity of their church with the Catholic church as it had always existed. Their acceptance of the Reformation in doctrinal matters did not, they felt, justify or denote a break in the continuity of the church in England. That church was to be kept in its traditional form while at the same time the effort was to be made to remove the deformations which had crept into that church over the centuries.

On the one hand, then, the Church of England set itself apart from most continental forms of the Reformation which tended to minimize if not abolish the episcopacy because they found little or no justification for it in the Word of God. By so deciding, Anglicanism manifested a much sharper awareness of its identity with the traditional church catholic than the Lutheran and Calvinist Reformers did. These tended rather to look to the apostolic church for their identity, setting aside the church of the intervening centuries.

On the other hand, the English church broke sharply with the Roman Catholic church and its insistence on the centrality and the supremacy of the pope. The order of bishops became, in place of the Supreme Pontiff in the Roman church, the final ruling and teaching body within the church.

This sense of tradition in reformation was in Elizabeth's time and continues to be today, one of the primary elements in Anglicanism's understanding of itself, the conscious attempt to maintain, through its preservation of the episcopacy, continuity with the belief and practice of the church of all the preceding centuries of Christianity. The episcopal order is the embodiment of Anglicanism's accent on the value of tradition in the church.

So strongly does the Church of England feel about the episcopacy as the form of government which Christ Himself gave to His church that she makes it an absolutely necessary element in any proposed reunion of the Christian churches. The Church of England accepts the other Reformation churches as true churches of Christ, authentic preachers of His Word and valid administrators of His sacraments. But a distinction is made in Anglicanism between the being (*esse*) of the church and her well-being (*bene esse*). The first has to do with the essential reality of the church. That reality is had so long as the church is structured to preach Christ's Word of salvation and administer His sacraments. The other Protestant churches are seen as having this essential reality and, therefore, theirs is a saving ministry.

How the church is structured belongs to her well-being, and it is the Anglican position that Christ's will is an episcopally structured church. Grace and salvation do not depend for their presence on the episcopal structure but in terms of any future unity with other Christian churches, Anglicanism insists that only in an episcopally ordered church will the church order be achieved which Christ gave His apostles and intended for His church.

The order of bishops is, in sum, one of the foundation stones on which the Church of England rests her conviction that she has always remained throughout the centuries, in living contact with the church Christ founded.

Doctrine—A Spirit of Comprehensiveness

What the doctrinal commitment of Anglicanism is, how she understands the Christian faith and what is the assent of faith she asks of her membership, are questions that call for varying answers depending upon what expression of Christianity is under consideration.

First of all, to the Christian faith as it is set forth in Scripture the Church of England gives her unqualified assent. Her faith is a biblical faith which she shares with the other Reformation churches. The Bible is the sole rule of faith. Only what is contained in the Scripture must be believed for salvation.

> Holy Scripture containeth all things necessary to salvation; so that whatsoever is not read therein, nor may be proved thereby, is not to be required of any man, that it should be believed as an article of the Faith, or be thought requisite or necessary to salvation.[4]

Secondly, in addition to the authority of Scripture, the Church of England also recognizes what the tradition of the universal church has done, especially in the early centuries, to clarify and develop the understanding of that initial deposit of faith. She, therefore, pays great reverence to the creeds (Apostles', Nicene, and Athanasian) and the teaching of the early Fathers and Councils of the church as embodying the common teaching of Christianity.

The words of James I in his *Premonition to All Most Mighty Monarchs* (1609) epitomize this typical English regard for the doctrinal formulations of the church of the first four centuries.

> I am such a Catholic Christian as believeth the three Creeds, that of the Apostles, that of the Council of Nice, and that of Athanasius, the two latter being paraphrases to the former. And I believe them in that sense as the ancient Fathers and Councils that made them did understand them, to which three Creeds all the ministers of England do subscribe at their Ordination. . . . I admit the Four First General Councils as Catholic and Orthodox. And the said Four General Councils are acknowledged by our Acts of Parliament, and received for orthodox by our Church.[5]

Thirdly, to these expressions of the Christian faith, the sixteenth century church in England felt called upon to add its own set of credal affirmations, the *Thirty Nine Articles.* Yet, in so doing, the bishops did not intend to produce a doctrinal statement demanding the same quality of assent as the Scriptures, Creeds, and early Councils. Their statement was meant, rather, to be a relative statement, relative in the sense that the *Articles* may be characterized as the doctrinal stance adopted by the Church in England at a particular moment in its history in relation to the doctrinal positions being expressed by the other Christian churches at the time. When the *Articles* are read in this light, it is clear that in them Anglicanism is expressing its understanding of the Christian faith in comparison with the understanding of that faith being held and taught by the other three Western Christian churches of the time: the Protestantism of Luther and Calvin, Roman Catholicism, and Anabaptism.

(1) With regard to Lutheranism and the Reformed churches, a series of articles make it evident that the Church of England is in fundamental agreement with their understanding of Christianity. It is, in a word, a Protestant church. Assent is given to Luther's three basic principles: Scripture alone is the source of saving knowledge: faith is central to the attainment of justice; God alone saves, yet in justifying man He produces in him a state from which good works inevitably flow. Calvin's thought is most obviously present in the *Articles'* adoption of his teaching on predestination. The adoption is done, however, in very cautious words that speak only of God's predestination of the elect to glory, saying nothing of those who are lost.

> Predestination to life, is the everlasting purpose of God, whereby (before the foundations of the world were laid) he hath

> constantly decreed by his councel secret to us, to deliver from
> curse and damnation, those whom he hath chosen in Christ
> out of mankind. As the godly consideration of predestination,
> and our election in Christ, is full of sweet, pleasant and
> unspeakable comfort to godly persons, so, for curious and
> carnal persons to have continually before their eyes the sen-
> tence of God's predestination is a most dangerous downfall.[6]

The church, too, is described as the continental Reformation would describe it as "a congregation of faithful men, in the which the Pure Word of God is preached, and the Sacraments be duly administered according to Christ's ordinance."[7] Again, in accord with Reformation thinking, only Baptism and the Lord's Supper are seen as sacraments "ordained of Christ our Lord in the Gospel." The other five Roman sacraments do not have "like nature of sacraments" with them. Thus, it is clear that the positive thrust of the *Articles* is Protestant in its understanding of the Christian faith.

2) The radical Reformation is uncompromisingly rejected by the Church of England in a series of articles which defend the swearing of oaths, assert the right of private property over against the Anabaptist tendency to endorse communal possession of property, and insist that it is lawful for citizens to obey civil authority when it commands what is just. Finally, Anabaptism's insistence on religious liberty, that a man must be free to form and follow his own conscience, is rejected in *Article 18* with its condemnation of the proposition that "every man shall be saved by the Law or Sect which he professeth, so that he be diligent to frame his life according to that law and the light of nature."[8]

(3) The *Articles* are also explicit in their rejection of what the bishops considered to be abuses in belief and practice within late medieval Catholicism. *Article 23* speaks out against belief in Purgatory, the superstitious veneration of images and relics and the invocation of saints. Devotion to the Blessed Sacrament is reprehended in *Article 25*. *Article 28* repudiates transubstantiation as an acceptable explanation of the Real Presence of Christ in the Eucharist. Preferred, rather, is the formula, allowing of either a Zwinglian or Calvinist interpretation, that "the Body of Christ is given, taken and eaten in the Supper, only after an heavenly and spiritual manner. And the means whereby the Body of Christ is received and eaten in the Supper is Faith."[9] Lastly, *Article 31* condemns the Roman emphasis on the sacrificial aspect of the mass, insisting that Christ's sacrifice on the cross was all-sufficient.

The doctrinal position taken in the *Articles* is, then, a mediate one, mediate between the extremism of late medieval Catholicism, on the one hand, and the radical expression of the Reformation embodied in the Anabaptist or Puritan view of Christianity, on the other. It is in this sense that Anglicanism may be called the *via media* (middle way). There is, however, no doubt that this is a Reformation document. It represents a clear commitment to all the basic principles of the Reformation.

This mediate stance in doctrinal matters is, like the episcopal structure, another expression of a typically English characteristic, reasonableness or moderation. Anglicanism has always believed that what constitutes a man a Christian is his acceptance of the Gospel message. The spelling out of that message in precise doctrinal statements and exact rational terms represents man's attempt to put God's revelation into human language. Because such formulations are human language, they ought not to be made into necessary objects of faith. God's revelation, not man's words, are what a Christian should believe and live by. Thus it is that within Anglicanism there has never been a strong insistence that theologically correct, and carefully reasoned expressions of the Christian faith must be assented to by its membership. It prefers, rather, to stress the essentially simple message of the Christian Scriptures, leaving to the individual the task and the right to understand that message in ways that are personally meaningful. Thus, for example, the Church of England recognizes that the New Testament account of the institution of the Eucharist speaks of Christ as really present in that sacrament. The true Christian believes in that presence. Attempts to explain the manner of that real presence are human attempts and the Christian may or may not choose to accept such explanations insofar as they seem helpful to him.

Such an attitude towards doctrine has always meant the presence within Anglicanism of a great flexibility and comprehensiveness in its possession of the Christian faith. The act of faith takes as its object the Scripture message. Beyond that, reasonableness takes over and an extremely broad latitude is granted in interpreting that message. Put another way, what is primarily important in Christianity is not so much what a man gives intellectual assent to as how he lives his life.

Liturgy—Tradition Within Reformation

One central place in Anglicanism is given to episcopal government. The other equally central position is occupied by the liturgical worship of God. Cranmer's *Book of Common Prayer* is the official liturgical book of Anglicanism. For the Church of England, it replaces Rome's four liturgical books: the monk's book of daily prayer, the priest's mass book, the ritual for the conferral of the sacraments, and the bishop's book for ordinations.

Evident in each of the book's four parts is the conviction that controlled its composition, the determination to join together the best of tradition with the best of reformation. This meant that Cranmer was always careful to preserve the ancient liturgical forms, yet always conscious that the liturgy should reflect the Reformation's understanding of the Christian faith.

Thus, he retained the structure of the Roman mass in order to preserve what he felt was tradition's well-proven form of divine worship. But he made it into a communion service, stripping it of its sacrificial emphasis in line with the Reformation conviction that Christ's sacrifice was all-sufficient.

He recognized, too, the soundness of the principle that the church should offer daily prayer of petition, praise and thanks to God and he retained, therefore, the practice of the divine office. But he rewrote the office once prayed by monks, simplifying its format, putting it into the language of the people and moving its recitation to the public churches that the people themselves might understand and participate in it. He saw to it, too, that each of the two daily services of prayer included readings from the Old and New Testaments that the congregation might be fed on the Word of God and, thereby, have the lived experience of the all-sufficiency of God's Word in Christianity.

Yet again, he agreed with the Reformers that the sacraments of Christ were only two in number and he provided the manner of their celebration. But he was traditionalist enough to realize also that the other "commonly called sacraments" had a long and treasured place in the church's life and so the ritual for their conferral was also included.

The Roman tendency in liturgy at the time was to put chief emphasis on the worship of God. The Reformation tendency was to accent the participation and instruction of the congregation. Cranmer's liturgy blends the two, expressing in stately and reverent language, coupled with magnificent orderliness and sober restraint, both the Word and Sacrament aspect of the liturgy. Ample attention was given to both. In no other Christian church is such sustained and serious attention paid to the reading of the Word of God in public worship. Yet, equal place is given to the praising and glorifying of God in sacramental celebration and daily prayer service. Pulpit for preaching and altar for worship, both have their honored place in the *Book of Common Prayer*.

And again, as in episcopal government and in doctrinal commitment, the English character comes through. English piety avoids unseemly display of emotion and shuns sentimentality. It tends rather to be restrained and measured in its expression, quiet rather than ostentatious in its public forms. Cranmer's prayerbook captures that national spirit and expresses it magnificently. The *Book of Common Prayer* stands alongside Luther's *Treatises* and Calvin's *Institutes* as one of the great masterpieces of the Reformation. It makes clear, too, that Anglicanism always has been far more a liturgical than a doctrinal church.

CONCLUSION

The contribution of Anglicanism to the Reformation does not lie primarily in the field of theology as is true in the case of Lutheranism and the Reformed movement, which is not, however, to deny that there has been, since the sixteenth century, a distinguished line of theologians and biblical scholars in the Church of England. It is, rather, to say that she has a particularly strong sense of how man ought to worship God and a unique facility for expressing that worship in appropriate forms and language. The Church of England's other major influence on the history of Protestant Christianity lies in her retention of the episcopal order and through that, her preservation of a much deeper sense of tradition in the church than is true of the other Reformation churches.

As the Christian churches begin working toward reunion more seriously than they have since their separation, there are many who see how well Anglicanism, especially in her worship, her episcopacy, and her reverence for tradition, has kept elements that must be central values to be preserved in any reunited church. Her middle way of moderation between extremes, likewise, offers hope to many as a pattern and a goal for the future of ecumenism. Of the Christian churches she embodies, most obviously, the principle of unity in diversity.

Yet, like most values, her moderation has been bought at a price. That price has meant a growing doctrinal comprehensiveness over the centuries. To preserve Anglicanism's bond of unity has demanded an almost unlimited willingness to tolerate within that unity any and every shade of Christian belief. In consequence, it has grown increasingly difficult to find in Anglicanism any strong sense of a teaching authority to guarantee her continuing possession of the essential elements of Christian fiath.

Mediation and moderation will be key factors for the future of Christianity. Anglicanism, in her history, exemplifies one way in which these values can be embodied in a Christian church. At the same time, her history poses in sharp terms the dilemma that Christianity faces when it tries to house unity and diversity under a single roof.

The problem, faced but not adequately solved by Anglicanism, grows increasingly critical for Christianity in the contemporary pluralistic world. How are the Christian churches to become the one church Christ willed His church to be, while, at the same time, preserving diverse understandings of the Christian faith and varying modes of Christian worship?

FOOTNOTES

[1] A.G. Dickens, *The English Reformation* (London: B.T. Batsford Ltd., and New York: Schocken Books, Inc., 1964), p. 36.

[2] Jasper Ridley, *Thomas Cranmer*, paperback edition (Oxford: University Press, 1966), p. 266. Used by permission of The Clarendon Press, Oxford, England.

[3] From the introduction to the section on the rite of ordination in the *Book of Common Prayer*.

[4] Article 6 of the *Thirty Nine Articles*.

[5] The text is quoted in J. W. C. Wand, *Anglicanism in History and Today* (New York & Toronto: Thomas Nelson and Sons, 1962), p. 52.

[6] Article 17 of the *Thirty Nine Articles*.

[7] Article 19 of the *Thirty Nine Articles*.

[8] Article 18 of the *Thirty Nine Articles*.

[9] Article 28 of the *Thirty Nine Articles*.

CHAPTER FIVE

Puritanism

The England that Elizabeth found upon her accession to the throne had known nothing but religious differences, bloody persecutions, and one government succeeding another for almost twenty years. Sick of religious warfare and confused by the constant shift of governments, the nation wanted nothing so much as peace in religion and stability in the state. Elizabeth read the signs of the times and made it the aim of her reign to provide what was longed for. She would settle the religious situation and give her kingdom a measure of stability in government.

But the problem of religion was not open to easy solution by Elizabeth because her subjects themselves did not agree upon its solution. There was general agreement that there was but one true religion and that the power of the state should lend itself to the support of that religion. But beyond this consensus there was disagreement in answering the question: which is the true religion? The Catholics, by now in the minority, held one view on what was the true religion. The Protestant majority, of course, disagreed. Even among them there was divided opinion on what form religion should take in England.

Elizabeth recognized the difficulty and proposed to solve it by a judicious blend of imposed conformity and broad tolerance. She chose to retain the episcopal form of church as the official framework for the church in England. Bishops were chosen she could depend on and they were given the task of implementing her authority and theirs in terms of a national church with its own system of worship and code of belief. Outward conformity to this church was imposed on the nation. Beyond this each man was free to believe and practice what he wished. It was only when that belief or practice took the form of a disobedience which threatened the peace and stability of the realm that repressive measures were adopted.

THE PURITAN PARTY

For the generality of Englishmen the policy was perfectly acceptable. But one group among her subjects, the Puritans, was unhappy with her policy. It was their conviction, learned during an exile spent in Switzerland imbibing Calvin's view of the church, that Elizabeth's church was an abomination in the sight of the Almighty. This was so because it did not conform to the pure Word of God as the church of Geneva did. For the Puritan, Scripture was the sole authority both for what the church believed and also for what she did. Anything not explicitly authorized in Scripture did not belong in the church. Following this norm they found much in the Elizabethan church clearly at odds with what the Word of God said His Church should be.

For the Anglican theologians, on the other hand, who defended the structure and practice of the Church of England, the answer to the question: what is the authority of Scripture in determining the creed and cult of the church, was different. For them its authority in what was to be believed was absolute. What Scripture taught and only what Scripture taught must be believed. The Word of God was the final word in matters of belief. But in the area of church life and worship, Scripture did not provide complete, specific directions as to what was to be done. The church had always recognized this fact and had, throughout her history, developed forms of worship and norms for living which were best suited to the needs of the age. Thus had Tradition developed, as human reason in the service of the church tried to embody the Scriptural message in appropriate forms. In this field the authority of Scripture was principally negative. Nothing could be instituted in life or worship which was contrary to the teaching of Scripture.

The Puritans, however, would have none of this distinction. Elizabeth's church in terms of what Scripture demanded was a church scarcely reformed at all. It was then their bounden duty, faced with the disparity between the English church and the church that God willed in Scripture, to use all the means at hand to effect the radical purification of their national church. Thus was the party of opposition to Elizabeth's religious policy born, the Puritans, bent on purifying her church of its corruptions. In their view the church had need of a more Scriptural and therefore purer form of government, a purer form of worship, purification of doctrinal beliefs, and a stronger insistence on a holier way of life for the people of England.

For the Puritans, Elizabeth's policy of moderation was at once a frustration and an opportunity. It was a frustration because she would not tolerate their extremism. What were halfway measures for them were peace-keeping policies for her. So long as she lived she would not let them seize power in her church. But it was for the Puritans an opportunity, too, because, provided they did not unduly disturb the peace with their preaching and pamphleteering, she would not crush them completely. So they gained time to unite and to develop their strategy for bringing the church under the control of their vision of what a church should be.

With the passage of time the general lines of their strategy became apparent. Their key idea was organization, the enlistment of the support of those elements of English society which could best ensure the spread and general acceptance of their view of the church. This meant especially the cultivation of the university and the press and the winning to their cause of as many Englishmen as possible, especially the tradesmen, artisans, and merchants of the rising middle class.

The universities, most especially Cambridge, were the cradle of the movement and that in a double sense. From this base the leaders of Puritanism could launch their tracts, pamphlets, and sermons aimed at condemning in the strongest possible language the corruption of the established religion. Along with condemnation, they spoke, too, of the kind of church that God's will, clearly expressed in Scripture, demanded.

In addition to providing the intellectual leadership for the movement, Cambridge also became the source whence flowed a steady stream of preachers prepared to take over, wherever possible, the pulpits of England. Thoroughly committed to the vision of Geneva, these ministers were well equipped with the plain and sober language and the intense earnestness of personal conviction needed to win to their cause the solid middle class merchants and lawyers of the city and the small landholders of the country. It was on this class of society that the full force of their persuasiveness was concentrated.

The press and the rising literacy among the people offered another useful instrument for propaganda; the country began to be filled with Puritan literature. As the years passed, a mounting tide of diaries, autobiographies and biographies, tracts, histories of God's People, programs for the building of the Holy Commonwealth and for living God's will, spread the vision of a church fully reformed and completely purified in accord with the divine will.

THE PURITANS IN POWER

By 1640 the strategy had produced its desired effect. The Long Parliament which began its sessions that year was predominantly Puritan in its outlook which meant that it saw the need for reform of the church as a pressing national problem. During the next ten years it moved to the enactment of that reform. But even as reform began the full effect of Elizabeth's policy, which was continued by her successors, James I (1603-25) and Charles I (1625-49), came to fruition and defeated that reform.

The first effect of that policy was that over the years many of the Puritans gave up hope of ever being able to reform the Church of England. They sought, in voluntary exile, the freedom that God's saints needed to build their purified church. For those who chose America, their holy commonwealth lasted for several generations but faded when the descendants lost the vision of their forebears. The groups that sought refuge in Holland were never large and when they returned to England under the policy of religious toleration in 1688, their impact on the religious life of the nation was minimal. Thus, for a significant segment of Puritanism, Elizabeth's policy produced frustration which led in turn to the choice of exile. Ultimately the exile dissipated the force of their influence.

But by far the most significant effect of Elizabeth's firm restraint was produced among the majority of Puritans who chose to remain in England and suffer through the period of waiting until power fell into their hands. For them her policy provided ample time for differences of opinion to develop regarding the true nature of God's church. These differences produced, in their turn, a splintering of Puritanism into a variety of visions of what the church should be. William Haller puts the matter well.

> Elizabethan policy waiving consistency and ignoring variations of opinion when politically harmless, gave scope for all sorts of men to search the scriptures, to fall in love with their own strange ideas, to espouse fantastic dreams, to collect bands of earnest souls, in short to go and eat forbidden fruit so long as they did not try to upset the apple cart. . . . Thus English Puritanism, denied opportunity to reform the established Church, wreaked its energy during a half century and more upon preaching, and under the impetus of the pulpit, upon unchecked experiment in religious expression and social behavior.[1]

In the Parliament of 1640 which marked the culmination of the Puritan drive to power in the English church two policies came to simultaneous fruition, Elizabeth's religious policy and the Puritan strategy of power. The first, through the fragmentation it produced, guaranteed that the second, once achieved, could not but fail in its attempt to implement its vision of what the church should be. So it turned out. The twenty years until the restoration of the monarchy in 1660 was time enough to prove that the Puritans did not have the unity of vision and power necessary to reform the Church of England according to their own design. Puritanism faded as a significant religious influence in the Church of England.

ELEMENTS OF THE PURITAN VISION

What were the elements of the Puritan vision that produced such passionate, even fanatic dedication among its followers? At the heart of that vision stood Calvin's doctrine of election. The Puritan came through personal conversion to a sense of his own election and a conviction that he was responsible for bringing God's will to his own life, his church and his nation. Three roads, therefore, led out from that center, one to the individual believer and his life, one to the church and its government, belief, and worship, and one to society in general. And all three roads by varying routes reached the same destination, the glory of God. Or put another way, Puritanism could be summarized as Simpson does, in these words:

> The Puritans were elect spirits, segregated from the mass of mankind by an experience of conversion, fired by the sense that God was using them to revolutionize human history and committed to the execution of His will.[2]

The Individual

To enter into the Puritan vision one had first to pass through the door of a personal conversion. In Puritanism one found that door in God's Word and the way above all others for learning God's Word was through the sermons of His godly ministers. The sermon, then, was the key initial experience for the Puritan. The preachers, aware of its crucial importance, directed all the skill of their education to developing a style of preaching which would best effect a personal conversion experience in the members of their congregation. Rhetorical flourish and ornate oratorical devices were shunned in favor of plain, sober language and the use of homely, easily grasped images and parables. Using such means the sermon aimed at producing two succeeding states of soul in the listener: first, a sense of guilt with its accompanying sorrow and yearning for forgiveness, and then the conviction of acceptance by God into the company of His elect with its accompanying dedication to God's will.

To produce this set of effects it was usual for the sermon to begin with a description of the evil of human life. Specifically the intent was to make plainly evident the sinfulness of the life of each one who listened. For this corruption of their lives, men could expect only divine wrath and punishment. The wicked "shall one day be apprehended and arraigned before the bar of God's tribunal seat where the majesty of God shall stand above them with a naked sword of vengeance and a scepter of justice."[3]

From this wickedness there was nothing they could do to escape. Inborn evil was the lot of every son of Adam. Thus were a sense of guilt and sorrow induced. Then into the mood of despair effected by this sobering view of man's condition the preacher injected a note of hope. All was not lost provided a man repented of his sins and abandoned every trace of self-reliance in order to cast all his reliance on Christ, the sole Redeemer. Christ accepted as the only Savior must become the center of one's life. Once this choice was made, consciousness of divine wrath gave way to confidence in God's love. One was thereby introduced into the company of the elect, God's chosen ones. Thus did Puritanism adopt Calvin's conversion experience leading to the assurance of election.

Life now became an unwearying dedication to finding and following the divine will. This quest would, if methodically carried out, preserve, throughout life, a continuing awareness of deserved divine wrath and unmerited divine love. To be sure that the divine will was being totally pursued, all facets of daily life were to be subjected to close scrutiny. Detailed codes of conduct were to be drawn up systematically and followed meticulously. The consciousness of one's own sinfulness was kept constantly alive by a rigorous daily examination of conscience and the noting down in one's diary of the day's failures and successes. The failures testified to one's own corrupt nature; the successes witnessed to God's goodness. The innumerable Puritan diaries, the autobiographies and biographies that survive, witness to the seriousness with which the typical Puritan took this responsibility to serve God in his personal life and thereby manifest the divine glory.

Yet such characterization ought not to become caricature. Sober and serious-minded though the Puritan was, he was not normally an extremist. Life held pleasant implications and enjoyable obligations as well as demanding ones. Family life, conjugal love, friends, the good things of the table, hunting and fishing, all these too were from God and could be used in His service. Single-mindedness regarding life's purpose and moderation in the use of all things were much more typical Puritan attitudes than unrelieved gloom and morbid self-denial.

The Church

In the Puritan eye the church too, perhaps even above all other areas in the life of the nation, stood in need of purification and in implementing that purification a single and simple question was to be asked: what does the Scripture say about the nature of the church? For the Puritan the Bible was the absolute authority in this matter. In it would be found God's own specifications for the organization, the belief and the worship of His church. Hence the rule to be followed in judging all things within the church in England was to ask: does this practice, this belief, this form of government find explicit justification in God's Word? If not, it was to be replaced by the evangelically approved practice, belief and government.

When the Puritans applied their biblical rule to the form and structure of the church, most of them tended not to believe that episcopacy was the scripturally indicated mode of church organization and government. When one examined what form of ministry the Holy Spirit had given to the primitive church it was clear that all ministers of the Word in that church drew their authority as preachers of the Gospel from God's call to ministry and from their selection by the faithful to whom they ministered. The ministers so chosen were referred to as presbyters. Thus New Testament practice indicated that church ministry should be presbyterian in form.

In the early years of Puritanism, while Elizabeth was still queen, most Puritans believed that God's Word called for a church organized along presbyterian lines. The ministers were to be chosen by the people as contrasted with Elizabeth's church where bishops appointed by the crown exercised and regulated ministry.

The Puritans further believed that to this church there should belong all the people of England. It was to be a national church, established and supported by the state. But, though all belonged, yet, within that church there was to be an aristocracy of grace, the elect of God. These saints would exercise the power and provide the ministry. In their hands would lie the authority for formulating the doctrine and determining the life and worship of the church. The church was to be organized into local parishes and each parish was to choose for itself those who would teach (pastors) and those who would lead (elders). Beyond the local level, church polity would be determined by an ascending series of elected assemblies: consistory, classis, provincial and national synods. Within this structure the presbyters (ministers) held final responsibility for the interpretation of Scripture. They would, in consequence, also control the form of life and worship adopted by the church since these could only be derived from the Word of God.

By 1640 the Puritan demands for reform in the church could no longer be denied. Parliament, and therefore power, fell into their hands. The majority of that Long Parliament in 1640 were Puritans who subscribed to Presbyterianism as God's will for His church. In 1643, therefore, that assembly swore a solemn covenant to

> ... endeavor the extirpation of popery, prelacy (that is, Church government by archbishops, bishops, their chancellors and commissaries, deans and chapters, archdeacons and all other ecclesiastical officers depending on that hierarchy). . . .[4]

In fulfillment of that covenant they moved to replace Episcopalianism by Presbyterianism and so long as Parliament held power this remained the form of church life in England.

Not only was there need for reorganizing church order, there was need too for reform in doctrine and practice. In fulfillment of that responsibility an assembly of Puritan divines was convoked by Parliament and that group proceeded to doctrinal and liturgical reformation. After issuing their *Form of Presbyterial Church Government,* they moved to replace the *Book of Common Prayer* with their own liturgical book, the *Directory of Public Worship.* Its chief purpose was to purge Cranmer's liturgy of all its Roman Catholic remnants and to remove all biblically unwarranted practices from divine worship. The application of the biblical criterion to the liturgical and sacramental life of the church uncovered much to be expunged because unauthorized by Scripture. The churches were stripped of all unwarranted liturgical accretions. Mass vestments, copes, gowns, surplices, all were removed and replaced by the simple Geneva gown. Altars were replaced by pulpits; marriage rings, signs of the cross in conferring Baptism, permanent baptismal fonts in the churches were eliminated. In a word, all ritual actions in the divine worship which were corrupt additions to the pure Gospel liturgy were suppressed. Only biblically justified elements were retained. Church service was transformed into a service of the Word, the austere form of worship that Calvinism saw as the only truly scriptural form.

Next the Assembly moved to doctrinal matters. The *Thirty Nine Articles* were set aside and replaced by the *Westminster Confession* and its two companion documents, *The Larger Catechism,* and *The Shorter Catechism.* These were thoroughly Calvinized statements of Christian belief emphasizing, characteristically, the doctrine of the two covenants of works and grace, the divine majesty and sovereignty, and the doctrine of double predestination.

As long as Parliament remained in power the English church was Calvinist in doctrine and practice and presbyterian in church polity. But when Cromwell and his army came to power, Presbyterianism in its turn was set aside as contrary to what God willed for His church. Rather there could be no true Christian church that was not a gathered church.

> . . . For God doth not now make any people, or kindred, or nation his Church; but gathers his Church out of every people and kindred, and nation: and none can be stones of this building, but those that are first elect, and after made precious, through a new birth, and the gift of the Spirit.[5]

The church was not, therefore, to be coextensive with the state nor should there by one established church. It was wrong to impose one form of church on all. Religious liberty ought to be extended to all. It was the conviction of Cromwell and his followers that freedom to form churches as they wished would lead men to set up local congregations of believers. This congregational form was the only form of church polity needed. In this view of the church, membership was to be limited to those only who could produce convincing testimony of a conversion and hence election by God. Only these elect could be of God's church. Structurally the church was to be simply the congregation of the elect in any locale. Beyond this local church, no further organization was needed. Each local community was sufficient unto itself, for were not God's chosen ones able to search the Scripture and discern in it the elements that the church should contain? Were they not also able to find there all the guidelines needed for their life in the world?

But though the local congregation was autonomous and the polity was therefore congregational, it was reasonable to expect, since all members of the church shared election, that God would bring each congregation to the possession of the same Scriptural truth and that therefore the local congregations would enter into voluntary alliance with each other and through that alliance would exercise their combined influence on civil authority and on society at large.

As it turned out Congregationalism, like Presbyterianism, was able to preserve itself as the form of the Church in England only as long as it retained political power. When that was lost, as it had been by 1660, the monarchy was restored and along with it Anglicanism returned and has since remained the established church of England.

Society

The regenerated Puritan for all his concentration on self-scrutiny and self-improvement was not a recluse. He understood that his life of service to God's will was to be lived out in the world. He had no illusions about the world's condition. An evil and sinful place it was and would always be; yet no matter how much he might condemn the world he could not, indeed should not, avoid it. He must live in it, but he was not to reconcile himself to letting the world remain as he found it. Thus the Puritan grasped firmly Calvin's insistence that election was not to privilege but to responsibility. He knew that the truly elect manifests the divine glory by striving to excel in every area of life. For him God's choice implied the fullest possible development of all his talents. As Perry puts it, "The man of God should be a braver warrior, a more enlightened ruler, a more skillful and industrious artisan, and a more successful tradesman because of the divine favor and appointment."[6]

The Puritan recognized that his responsibility for a life in the service of the divine glory was not met solely by the attempt to live God's will as perfectly as possible in his own public life. Society itself needed purification also. His responsibility meant using all the means in his power to set up a state of affairs in the nation in which only the elect would govern or at least the elect would so influence government that a situation would be created which would repress all wickedness in living and thereby create a situation in which as many as possible would have the experience of conversion.

For one short period in English history Puritanism had its chance to implement its dream of an England ruled by the saints. A society dominated in all its details by religious conviction became the policy of the Puritan government during the few brief years of its power. But man being what he is, such a society could enjoy only a fleeting period of existence. Even the Puritan found that he could not for long force his vision on other men and coerce the unregenerate and unconcerned sinner into sanctity. Most Englishment were not prepared to take religion with the deadly seriousness with which the Puritan viewed it. So finally the Puritan vision of a nation dedicated in all aspects of its life to furthering the glory of God failed to capture England.

CONCLUSION

The rise and fall of Puritanism in England offers an intriguing case study in how one is to understand the nature of the Christian church and the Christian life and how one then proceeds to implement that understanding. Put another way, Puritanism is a classic example of the way in which religious extremism works and likewise of the way in which society copes with such extremism. The history of the interplay between those two ways in the case of Puritanism and England is instructive because it depicts one way to answer the question: How are the radical demands of Christianity best implemented in any society?

The Puritan's pathway to making England Christian was a clear-cut one. It began with his conviction of election. From there it was but a short step, one not easily avoided, for the Puritan to come to an awareness of set-apartness which almost imperceptibly led one to a sense of superiority over the generality of men not so chosen. Since this was true, it seemed logical to conclude that the saints had the right to determine, by their searching of the Scriptures, what was right and what was wrong; they had too the corresponding duty to impose this vision on other men. The Puritan did not feel he had fulfilled the purpose of his election until he had demanded of other men the same wholeness of dedication to God's glory that he asked of himself.

Their cause then seemed to them a righteous one. They moved to the adoption of all the means available to share their view with as many as possible. They were above all concerned for acquisition of the power which would enable them to insist that others accept their interpretation of what it meant to be Christian.

Government and society for their part followed the course of toleration and yet control in dealing with Puritanism. That course produced a double effect. It permitted much that was of value in Puritanism to work its way into the fabric of society. Industry, thrift, a god-fearing life, Christianity seen as central to all of life, these were part of the Puritan legacy to future Christian history. On the other hand, the extremism was rendered impotent. Fanaticism, intolerance, compelled religious observance, these were ultimately rejected by the society they attempted to dominate.

To the question: How many men in any society can be brought to conversion and Christian living, the Puritan answer was: most can if church and society are properly ordered. Christian witness became for them the insistence that all be Christian. Society recognized the wrongness of their answer and rejected it.

Puritanism is then ambivalent in its Christian witness. Its vision embodied much that is central to Christianity. Schneider captures the paradoxical nature of the Puritan witness in these words:

> Whenever self-reliance fails, as it sooner or later must, and sinners see themselves as God sees them, piety becomes reincarnate, though the language in which it finds expression may bear little resemblance to that of the Puritans. But whenever sinners become convinced that they are instruments in the hand of God, elected to carry out his holy will, they lose their piety and begin doing good to others. This is an ancient story, and as long as there are sinners, the story of the Puritans will be but one illustration of a universal theme.[7]

In the centuries since Puritanism was dominant in England and America the Christian churches have learned the lesson of religious liberty and that the Christian church exists for service not domination in society. Christians are hopeful today that a witness lived in the context of these values will succeed where the Puritan witness failed. But the question remains the same as that the Puritan faced. What is the nature of Christian witness?

FOOTNOTES

[1] William Haller, *The Rise of Puritanism* (New York: Columbia University Press, 1938), pp. 14-15. Copyright © 1938, Columbia University Press.

[2] Alan Simpson, *Puritanism in Old and New England,* Phoenix edition (Chicago: University of Chicago Press, 1961), p. 39.

[3] Arthur Dent, *A Sermon of Repentaunce,* quoted in M.M. Knappen, *Tudor Puritanism* (Chicago: University of Chicago Press, 1939), p. 343.

[4] From "The Solemn League and Covenant" (1643), quoted in Clyde L. Manschreck, *A History of Christianity* (Englewood Cliffs, N.J.: Prentice-Hall, 1964), II, p. 199.

5William Dell, *The Building and Glory* (1646), quoted in William Haller, *Liberty and Reformation in the Puritan Revolution*, paperback edition (New York: Columbia University Press, 1963), p. 202.

6Ralph Barton Perry, *Puritanism and Democracy*, Torchbook edition (New York: Harper & Row, 1964), p. 92.

7Herbert W. Schneider, *The Puritan Mind* (New York: Holt, Rinehart and Winston, 1958) copyright 1930, © 1958. p. 264.

CHAPTER SIX

Methodism

The final decades of the seventeenth century, which had known so much of religious war and persecution and intolerance, brought a measure of religious peace and stability to England. But at the same time that religion was finding the peace it had not known for many years the climate in which religion lived its life was undergoing drastic alterations which would present Christianity with a whole new set of problems. It is the purpose of this chapter to examine the elements that went to make up this altered religious climate and then to explore the form of Protestant Christianity which emerged as the eighteenth century's most creative Christian response to the crisis of that age.

THE CLIMATE OF THE AGE

Rationalism

During the period running from the latter half of the seventeenth and well into the eighteenth century several movements were at work shaping a quite new philosophical and religious atmosphere. The first of these was the emergence of the Age of Reason. Wearied by the religious wars that had been for so long generated by theological differences, the intellectuals began to move toward seeing religion as something which presented itself as a thoroughly reasonable human attitude.

In its initial stage this movement toward reasonableness saw individual conscience as the ultimate norm in deciding religious truth. In coming to its decision, conscience was enlightened by revelation and formed by reason. But if human intelligence was to reach religious truth this could only be done in a climate that fostered tolerance and freedom of investigation. Thus religious freedom became a basic value in the movement.

When the reasonable man read his Scriptures he recognized them as eminently in accord with reason. Read with an open mind Christ's fulfillment of the Old Testament prophecies and his working of miracles and prophecies lent strong credibility to his claim to divinity. Here was strong proof for the reasonableness of Christianity and therefore for its truth.

From here the movement passed to its second phase, one characterized by a deepening of reliance on reason. A study of the world's religions made it clear that all through history man had expressed his religious instinct in a variety of religions each one of which had its set of beliefs based on reason. From this perspective Christianity was one among the world's religions and like them to be accepted on the basis of its reasonableness. What set it apart from the others was simply that it had its own forms of worship and belief.

It now became evident that if Christianity was a reasonable religion its elements should be subjected to the judgment of reason. Since certain of those elements, like miracles and prophecies, did not admit of reasonable explanation, such elements did not deserve the credence of a reasonable man. Likewise it was seen that there was no place for emotionalism in religion. All it did was to hamper the mind in its search for truth. The final fruit of the movement would not fully ripen until the nineteenth century but the roots are here. Since the Scriptures are human products they too must be tested by human reason and in the end of the movement toward rationalism man came finally to put more confidence in human reason than in the Word of God.

By the beginning of the eighteenth century rationalism had ripened to the point where a growing religious indifferentism was the order of the day. Since all religions were reasonable there was little cause for choosing Christianity rather than one of the others. In fact, if a man lived a reasonable life doing what his reason told him was right then he was essentially a religious man. This being true, there was no great need for belonging to an organized church. And so there was a great falling off in church membership and attendance.

State of the Church in England

For over one hundred and fifty years the church in England had known only strife, dissension, division, and persecution. Most of its energies during that period were devoted to the task of adjusting to each succeeding political crisis. In consequence, when the religious settlement came in 1689 and the church regained some measure of stability and peace, she tended to settle into a period of peaceful return to things as they once had been. But England was no longer what it once had been. Industrialization was on the rise. New towns were springing up; the gap between the classes widened and more and more of the ordinary people found themselves reduced to a life of grinding poverty and hopelessness.

In this new age the church committed two blunders. She retained the old medieval parish structures, now no longer able to meet the needs of the men of this new time, and she tended to identify herself with the gentry rather than the common people. To men who hungered for the consolation that a felt religious experience could bring to hopeless lives she offered preaching that reflected the new trend toward rationalism. The service remained rigidly structured and came to be in many instances more and more perfunctorily performed. The clergy too identified themselves with the squire and the merchant, spending much time with them and increasingly less time attending the parish and the needs of the ordinary parishioners. And thus what the church had to offer spoke less and less convincingly to the majority of men in England. In a word, the church, almost unknowingly, allied herself with the forces of the Age of Reason. Reason increasingly questioned any real need for organized religion. And the conduct of organized religion itself added strength to that questioning.

Deism

To these factors yet another current of the times is to be added, deism. A scientific cosmology was developing. Newton's discoveries brought with them a significant change in man's view of his world. They pointed in the direction of a universe governed in all its parts by law. Like a giant machine of many interlocking parts each of which functioned according to precise and unvarying laws, the universe was both self-operating and self-explanatory in terms of these laws. Whereas formerly God was seen as exercising provident care in the world and the affairs of men, men now began to see Him as the celestial clockmaker. He had created the world as the clockmaker fashions his clock. Once set in motion the universe ran by its own laws with no further need for divine intervention.

For the man of this new scientific world view God was a distant God, unconcerned with the world, otherwise engaged. It was no longer necessary or proper for man to turn to God for explanation of the world and its happenings. It was rather by learning nature's laws that man would come to the solution of his problems. A self-explanatory world contained all that man needed to live his life. Thus for the deist God became impersonal or at least very distant from any concern with man and his world. Divine providence in terms of God's involvement in man's affairs became more and more superfluous.

Together these three currents conspired to create the spirit of the age, a growing reliance on the power of human reason with a concomitant scepticism about the supernatural, a this-world centered view of reality along with the tendency to dismiss belief in the transcendent as pertaining to a more unenlightened, prescientific view of the world and finally a falling off in church attendance in evidence of the widening rift between religion and daily life.

WESLEY'S LIFE

Into such a world John Wesley was born in 1703. By the time he died eighty-eight years later he had fashioned a religious movement which for great numbers of his fellow Englishmen, especially among the lower classes, carried the power to make religious belief and practice central in their lives. Though he did not of design set out to counter the rationalistic and deistic spirit of the age his successfully executed design "to spread Scriptural holiness over the land" provided the century's most effective answer to the spirit of religious indifference which these philosophies fostered.

Wesley's life ran through three phases. The first two of these are of interest principally because they provided the ingredients that fashioned the man of the third period. The first phase, his years at Oxford, was characterized by a strong desire to reach personal perfection. His quest was shared by the other members of the Holy Club at Oxford, a group which included his younger brother Charles and a dozen or more other young men most of whom were preparing for the ministry. All of them were committed to finding the best way to serve God. All were convinced that this search for perfection should be methodically executed. Thus they adopted a life of method for the pursuit of perfection, a set daily order with specific exercises: prayer, reading, fasting several times a week, meetings together each evening to encourage each other and discuss their reading. To this they added corporal works of mercy: almsgiving, visiting the imprisoned, teaching poor children. When, in later years, Wesley began his preaching all over England it was natural to name those who heard his message and followed his detailed program for Christian living, Methodists.

The pivotal experience in the second phase of his life is the period of two years (1535-38) of missionary work in Georgia. At this stage two forces seem to have been at work shaping him. Contact with Moravians during the dangerous voyage to America left him with a lifelong admiration for the depth and unshakable quality of their faith. He found his own faith by contrast with the warmth of theirs more a thing of the mind, an intellectual conviction quite devoid of the warmth so apparent in the Moravians' faith. The second force working on him was a growing sense of failure. His work in America was singularly unsuccessful and the experience induced a period of discouragement and perplexity. He wasnot yet sure of himself nor of what God intended his life work to be. His shipboard diary on his voyage home records his sense of uneasiness.

> On Monday 9 [Jan. 1738] and the following days, I reflected much on that vain desire, which had pursued me for so many years of being in solitude, in order to be a Christian. I have now, thought I, solitude enough. But am I, therefore, the nearer being a Christian? Not if Jesus Christ be the model of Christianity.
> Tues. 24. . . . I went to America to convert the Indians; but oh! who shall convert me? Who, what is he that will deliver me from this evil heart of unbelief?[1]

The third phase began with his experience at the meeting in Aldersgate Street and the effect produced that evening lasted for the remainder of his long life. On May 24, 1738, he went, almost reluctantly, to a church service. There he had his own great personal experience of being saved. Suddenly and more sharply than had ever been true for him before, as he listened to the reading of Luther's *Preface to the Epistle to the Romans,* there came to him a strangely warming conviction that God had, because of Christ, forgiven him his sins.

> In the evening I went very unwillingly to a society in Aldersgate Street, where one was reading Luther's preface to the Epistle to the Romans. About a quarter before nine, while he was describing the change which God works in the heart through faith in Christ, I felt my heart strangely warmed. I felt I did trust in Christ, Christ alone for salvation; and an

assurance was given me that He had taken away my sins, even
mine, and saved me from the law of sin and death.[2]

Now he began to know the mission to which God called him, to bring
the same conviction of salvation to as many of his countrymen as he could
reach. The next fifty-three years were spent in itinerant preaching all over
England. He traveled by horse, by carriage, by foot, up to five thousand
miles a year, preaching to crowds wherever he could gather them, in the
fields, in the slums, on street corners, in meeting houses, spreading Scriptural holiness throughout the land. Always he aimed at arousing in his
hearers a felt experience of salvation.

Wesley was well equipped for the work of his life. He never lost his
consciousness of God and his ability to communicate that experience
through his preaching. But perhaps even more important than this in
guaranteeing the success of his work was his talent for administration, his
genius for reducing to method the ways to insure that the conviction of
salvation once achieved would develop into a lifelong living of Christianity.

HIS METHOD

To bring others to a desire for holiness and to the use of the means for
achieving it became the primary aim of his work. The means he developed
to implement his purpose expanded in variety and effectiveness over the
years. Very soon after his own experience of conversion he began preaching in the fields. The choice of locale was as much determined by finding a
place to accommodate the crowds that flocked to hear him as it was
necessitated by the closing of most of the pulpits of England to him.
Preaching almost anywhere, at almost any time of the day, remained the
heart of his method. He would preach three, four, five times a day, rising
at dawn to catch the laborers before they went to work, talking to them
again in the late afternoon and evening.

To help him he recruited and trained a corps of preachers, clerical and
lay, to cover the face of England with the message of salvation. Always the
preaching had but one aim, to produce and reinforce the felt experience of
being loved and forgiven by God. In the course of time he developed a
college for the training of his preachers, prescribed several hours of reading
for them each day and introduced a system of apprenticeship which would
attach the novice preacher to the veteran for a period of training. As the

movement grew its success and growth depended in large part on the trained lay preachers, a feature of the Christian ministry which was first adopted and most successfully used by the Methodists.

Yet much as Wesley relied on the effectiveness of preaching he always saw it as only a beginning. He would never begin a preaching engagement unless he was sure that he would be able to follow it up by the formation of societies in the places where he preached.

> ... I am more and more convinced that the devil himself desires nothing more than this, that the people of any place should be half-awakened and then left to themselves to fall asleep again. Therefore, I determine, by the grace of God, not to strike one stroke in any place where I cannot follow the blow.[3]

Within these societies the class became the basic group for developing the membership. Normally a group of eleven with a lay leader, they met each week to collect the penny each member gave for the charitable works of the society. This was followed by group prayer, usually extemporaneous and by Bible study together. Members also spent some time talking with each other, giving testimony to the power of God in their lives and confessing their sins. One step up from the class was the band, a smaller group more advanced in their quest for holiness. Love feasts were introduced in imitation of the New Testament Agape. All present took a piece of plain cake and a cup of water together. The communal eating and drinking was followed by the giving of testimony to the Lord's goodness and by hymn singing. Thus was occasion provided for the warm, personal experience of fellowship. Watch night services at the beginning of the year were occasions for a renewal of the covenant with Christ that had been entered into in the initial conversion experience. Beyond these exercises, daily prayer and a weekly day of fasting was recommended to each Methodist. Visitation of all members of the groups was systematically carried out by Wesley and his helpers and unworthy members were constantly being stricken from the lists of membership.

Finally through all the meetings of Wesley's followers there ran the thread of hymn singing. These were written principally by Charles Wesley who produced them in amazing profusion and variety. They early became the hallmark of the Methodist meeting. For the simple and poor people in whom the emotional experience of conversion and the wholehearted living of the Christian life created deep and moving feelings, they provided the perfect outlet for the joy, the peace, the hope that religion had brought into their lives. Hymns became the normal expression of a strongly experienced religious life.

HIS DOCTRINAL EMPHASES

Wesley and his fellow preachers were not innovators in what they preached. Most of them were thoroughly orthodox members of the Church of England, Wesley himself being an ordained minister of that church. In addition it was his continuing insistence that all Methodists should continue to be practicing members of the Church of England. They were to attend divine worship in that church, take communion in it, and never to schedule their own meetings at the time of the Anglican services. Methodism subscribed to the *Thirty Nine Articles* and the *Book of Common Prayer*. They were likewise firmly committed to the basic Reformation positions on the supremacy of Scripture, the need of saving faith and the allness of God in the process of salvation. The distinctiveness of the Methodist preaching and instruction lay rather in its emphases than in the novelty of its doctrines.

For John Wesley, theologizing and the explanation of doctrine was always strictly subordinated to the practical aim of convincing people that they were saved and then providing the means necessary to make this a lifelong commitment to Christian living. His theology was developed in terms of living and thus remained basically simple in its content.

> Our main doctrines which include all the rest, are repentance, faith and holiness. The first of these we account, as it were, the porch of religion; the next the door; the third religion itself.[4]

Methodism did nonetheless have certain characteristic themes. Davies summarizes them under seven headings in his history of Methodism.

> (1) acceptance of the cardinal doctrines of the Christian faith as expressed in the historic creeds combined with the conviction that doctrine not proved in devotion and life and issuing in practical charity is valueless.
>
> (2) the heart of Christianity lies in the personal relation of a man with his Lord, who has saved him, won forgiveness of his sins, and will live in him to transform his character.

(3) the doctrine of the Holy Spirit, the person of the Trinity without whom neither the fulfillment of the Lord's commandments nor the common life of the Christian community is more than a vague aspiration.

(4) an earnest and patient attempt to embody "life in Christ" in personal and social 'holiness' and the formation for this purpose of small groups of committed people who will encourage, correct, instruct, edify and support each other.

(5) the desire to make known the Gospel and above everything else the love and pity of God for each individual sinner, on the widest possible scale and in the most persuasive possible terms.

(6) a generous concern for the material as well as the spiritual welfare of the underprivileged.

(7) the development of a Church Order in which the laity stands alongside the ministry with different but equally essential functions, sharing with the ministry the tasks of preaching the Gospel, caring for the Christian flock and administering the Church's affairs.[5]

Wesley himself likewise had a set of doctrinal emphases which tended to characterize his own understanding of Christianity's meaning. Two of them were positive, his doctrines of Assurance and Perfection; and two were negative, his rejection of Reprobation and of Antinomianism.

The Doctrine of Assurance

The Christian life began, for Wesley, with a definite conversion experience, the felt inner conviction of being forgiven and saved by God through Christ. The fostering of this experience was Wesley's first purpose. Thus the preaching tended to be an attempt to arouse a feeling of being saved. The techniques employed in preaching were chosen to effect this end. It was common for the sermons to dwell on fear and sorrow, themes aimed at as shattering a sense of sinfulness as could be induced. This was then followed by equally strong appeals to confidence in Christ the Savior.

There are those who contend that Wesley considered such a sharply etched experience of sin and salvation as an absolute essential in the process of being saved. Yet his own words on the subject seem to indicate that his own view of the necessity of an experience of assurance was not quite so strongly focused on a single, clearly discernible moment of felt grace. Speaking of the experience of the assurance of salvation Wesley has this to say.

> ... assurance ... Some are fond of the expression; I am not. I hardly ever use it. But I will simply declare ... what are my present sentiments with regard to the thing which is usually meant thereby.
>
> I believe a few, but very few, Christians have an assurance from God of everlasting salvation; and that is the thing which the Apostle terms the plerophory or full assurance of hope. . . .
>
> I believe a consciousness of being in the favour of God (which I do not term plerophory or full assurance, since it is frequently weakened, nay, perhaps interrupted, by returns of doubt or fear) is the common privilege of Christians fearing God and working righteousness.
>
> Yet I do not affirm there are no exceptions to this general rule. Possibly some may be in the favour of God, and yet go mourning all the day long. But I believe this is usually owing either to disorder of body or ignorance of the gospel promises. Therefore I have not for many years thought a consciousness of acceptance to be essential to justifying faith.[6]

Wesley aimed in his preaching at producing in his hearers this awareness of the Divine Presence and he saw it as a state earnestly and constantly to be sought but he was realist enough to know that he could not insist on a sharply defined experience in every case. He was much more concerned with the continuing state of Christian living following on conversion. It was this which ultimately determined the validity of whatever conversion experience one might have. As McConnell puts it:

> The feature of the instantaneous was notable in Wesley's teaching about perfection and this emphasis had pronounced effects upon Methodism's search for religious experience. Anything which resembled or suggested a sharp crisis, anything, in a word, happening suddenly, came to be regarded as especially divine in its origin. . . . [But] Wesley had to admit that there was a gradual work preceding this instantaneous operation of grace, and that there was a growth following it; and he had a hard time giving the pre-eminence to the instantaneous.[7]

The Doctrine of Perfection

Closely allied with his doctrine of Assurance, indeed flowing out of it as its expected consequence, was his doctrine of Perfection. Here Wesley was insisting that once one had experienced the assurance of God's love he could not but give himself to a life of full devotion to Christ. For the assured man life became a never-ending, because never fully achieved, quest for perfection.

Certain of Wesley's comments on perfection might lead one to conclude that he believed one could and should attain a state of complete perfection (sinlessness) in this life. But the insistent evidence of his preaching and ceaseless activity is against this view. This evidence points rather to his understanding that perfection is not so much a state as a direction. It was not just that men might be assured of salvation that he preached and wrote and organized. It was to kindle that assurance first of all but then to provide the continuing thrust towards an ever-growing perfection that he worked.

The converted man was confident of God's love and forgiveness. To this God he then turned over his life that the newly won presence of Christ might go on effecting a more and more profound change in that life. "Faith (which produces assurance) is the door of religion. Holiness (the pursuit consequent on assurance) is religion itself."

Thus Wesley's view of the Christian life and of Christian perfection was a compound of idealism and realism. It was idealistic because it was his belief that inherent in God's Word was the insistence that human nature was capable of great achievement in sanctity. He had, in other words, great confidence in man's ability to grow in holiness through cooperation with the transforming power of Christ working in him. He held that a man whose sins are forgiven does not sin and by that he meant an actual, deliberate violation of the law of God. He believed that one could reach this "Entire Sanctification" in this life. He urged his hearers to work for and expect to attain it. But he never made the claim for himself and seemed rather reluctant to admit its possession by anyone.

His view was realistic too. He did not believe that man should be left to his own devices once assurance was won. He provided him rather with a wide variety of specific activities designed to offer full opportunity for growth. Perfection was for Wesley the putting on of "all the mind of Christ." This was the task of a lifetime for the pursuit of which he offered the method.

Rejection of the Doctrine of Reprobation

The negative emphases in Wesley's teaching tended to take on their meaning in terms of the support they lent to his positive teaching on Perfection. First of all, he was concerned with preserving the full possibility that man could in fact become what God wanted him to be. It was for this reason that he was strong in his rejection of Calvin's theory of Reprobation. This theory saw men lost through the prior decision of God; and therefore in no sense did their free choices affect this decision. Only thus for Calvin was God's absolute sovereignty preserved. Nothing could escape the divine will.

For Wesley the doctrine was open to a number of serious objections. To begin with it rendered the preaching of God's Word worthless. And for him this was unthinkable. To the man convinced of either election or reprobation the preaching of the message of Scripture or the development of its motivation to action was equally fruitless. Again, the view that such a doctrine gave of God seemed seriously to distort the Christian vision of God. "How is this consistent," Wesley asked, "with the Divine Justice or Mercy?" From yet another point of view he saw "that God should be the author of sin and injustice (which must, I think, be the consequence of maintaining this opinion) is a contradiction to the clearest idea we have of the divine nature and perfection."

But his most strenuous objection to Reprobation is its explicit rejection of human freedom. For Wesley the issue of man's final end is certainly open to the influence of man's activity. It is, in some sense at least, what he does that ultimately decides the issue. It is at this point, the point of human freedom that he develops his own view of the process of salvation and man's influence on that process. It is his answer to Reprobation.

There is a universal salvific will on God's part. He wills that all men be saved. In execution of that will full salvific grace is given to each man as he enters the world. That grace will save a man unless and until he deliberately rejects it.

The presence of this prevenient (i.e., preceding any act on man's part) grace is the first sign of the fruits of redemption in every man. This is the first stage in God's applying the redemption to the individual. To be noted is that Wesley is not saying man is born naturally good. He is in accord with the central Protestant affirmation that man as man is "wholly void of the grace of God." Human nature is intrinsically evil as the result of original sin. But

> . . . There is no man that is in a state of mere nature; there is
> no man . . . that is wholly void of the grace of God. No man

living is entirely destitute of what is vulgarly called natural
conscience. But this is not natural: it is more properly termed,
preventing grace. Every man has a greater or less measure of
this, which waiteth not for the call of man . . . which sooner or
later, more or less, enlightens every man that cometh into the
world.8

The man who is born is not, therefore, the natural man. He is redeemed
man and as such he possesses God's prevenient grace which manifests its
presence in two ways. Man has, first of all, a genuinely free will. "A
measure of free will [is] supernaturally restored to every man." Thus
every man is able, not of himself but of God, to choose God and thereby
reply to His prior love. He has, secondly, a preventive conscience. God
gives man, in addition to free will, the ability to recognize that he has this
freedom to choose. That a man is conscious of freedom and convinced
that the use of that freedom affects his destiny is the second of God's
redemptive gifts.

Armed with these two capabilities man is able to work out his salvation.
But awareness of that ability is, for Wesley, to be combined with the
corresponding awareness that working out one's salvation means opening
oneself up to the work of Christ in one's life. For it is ultimately Christ
who saves. Once the Christian becomes aware of this salvific will of God at
work in him the inevitable response will be gratitude which will express
itself not merely in a quest for personal holiness but also in the ministry of
serving love of God and of neighbor. Thus does man cooperate with God
in the working out of his salvation.

Rejection of Antinomianism

Side by side with Wesley's rejection of Reprobation runs his equally
strong rejection of Antinomianism, the tendency which would see in the
assurance of salvation warrant for any type of life one might choose. Such
an attitude would reason: since I am saved why should I worry further
about good activity; the issue of my salvation is already settled. Against
this tendency which cropped up from time to time among his followers
Wesley developed his doctrine of the two justifications, first and final.

On the day of a man's conversion his faith that he is saved initiates his
first justification. His awareness that the righteousness of Christ has been
applied to him marks the beginning of his justified life. But salvation is not
a single experience; it is a process beginning with first justification and
running on through life to final justification at the end. Justification

begins with the salvation experience but it is continued in sanctification, which means that man is certainly accountable for his life. All through the passage from first to final justification the principle that is operative in forming the finally justified man is the faith in Christ which shows itself through love of God and neighbor. It is thus far from sufficient to have undergone the initial experience of conversion. What activity lies between that event and death will finally decide the issue of whether first justification becomes final justification. Only the latter is ultimately determinative of man's eternal destiny.

CONCLUSION

There can be no question that Wesley brought the warmth, the joy, and the peace of religion to thousands who would, without him, have lived lives of poverty and almost complete hopelessness. It was to the common man, largely unnoticed and unserved by the Church of England, that he brought the experience of God. The religious life of England was immeasurably stronger because of his work.

Another way of saying the same thing would be to point out that the religious climate he left behind him was quite different than the one he entered. To the threat placed by rationalism and deism he offered the effective antidote of a religion deeply and personally felt, not reasoned to. The rationalist contended that man should rely only on his reason. Wesley and the Methodists replied that man's reason could be as sure of God as of anything else in life but it was the experience of God not the reasonableness of believing in Him that was decisive for life. To the deist who banished God from the world and human affairs the reply was that God's presence in the human situation could be experienced and a life built on that experience could be a fulfilling one.

There are those who would see Wesley's work as ultimately ineffective since he certainly knew first hand the horrible social conditions of his time and yet there is little indication of his having attempted to effect social change. But such a charge is to accuse him of not having a mid-twentieth century social consciousness. It took a long time to develop the awareness of man's dignity and inherent worth that is the foundation of present social movements. That foundation was only beginning to be laid in his time. A child of his age, he accepted the situation in which he found himself and worked to transform the lives that had to be lived in that situation.

It is also true that for his time he had an acutely developed social sense. He had, for example, a strong sense of the value of education. It was for the education of his people that he founded schools and wrote prodigiously throughout his life. Concern for health led him to found dispensaries for the sick poor and to produce his treatise on *Primitive Physick.* In terms of larger social issues he urged the improvement of prison conditions, opposed traffic in smuggling, evidenced his concern for the condition of French prisoners of war, and was active in support of the movement against slavery. But his major social concern always remained the spiritual care of the people of England.

If a single element in Wesley's approach to Christianity had to be questioned it would be the tendency to rely overly much on the emotional in man's approach to God. Such an approach lays itself open to excess and consequent deception. The Methodist meeting in his day and in the early days of Methodist revivalism in this country had its full quota of mass hysteria, trance, convulsion, all sorts of excessive emotionalism. It was the excess that was fastened on by critics. Yet Wesley himself was aware of the danger, controlled it when he could, and did all that was possible to channel the emotionalism into constructive Christian living. In by far the majority of cases he succeeded. His ultimate testimonial is the transformed lives of those he reached.

Perhaps the best final way to evaluate him is to quote and subscribe to Todd's comparison of Wesley with the first two great Reformers, Luther and Calvin.

> Luther and Calvin began with the great truths. Luther began with the realization that God does all; it is only by faith in him that we can reach eternal life. Calvin began with the sovereignty of God, his immensity and transcendence; until we realize that truth, our religion is as water. Wesley not only began with a great theme; the ideal of holiness; he went on with it, never lapsing into heresy, old or new—in the sense that he never abandoned or opposed the Christian tradition of the Church of England in which he was educated—but developing his understanding of traditional Christianity in an ever maturing expression of the charity of Christ.[9]

FOOTNOTES

[1] *The Journal of John Wesley* as abridged by Nehemiah Curnock, Capricorn Books edition (New York: G. P. Putnam's Sons, 1963), pp. 34-35.

2*Ibid.*, p. 51.

3*Ibid.*, p. 141.

4Quoted by E.H. Sugden in *Standard Sermons of John Wesley* (London: The Epworth Press, 1921), I, 20.

5Rupert E. Davies, *Methodism* (Baltimore: Penguin Books, 1963), pp. 1-2.

6*The Letters of the Rev. John Wesley, A.M.,* ed. John Telford (London: The Epworth Press, 1931), V, 358-59.

7Francis J. McConnell, *John Wesley* (Nashville: Abingdon Press, 1939), p. 201.

8*The History of American Methodism,* 3 vols. vol I, Chap. 1, David C. Shipley, "The European Heritage" (New York & Nashville: Abingdon Press, 1964), I, 35. The quotation is from Wesley's sermon, "On Working Out Our Own Salvation."

9John M. Todd, *John Wesley and the Catholic Church* (London: Hodder & Stoughton, 1958), p. 135. Used by permission of Hodder and Stoughton, Limited.

CHAPTER SEVEN

Nineteenth Century Liberal Protestantism

As Protestantism moved into the nineteenth century it entered an age when its fundamental convictions about the nature of Christianity would be called into radical question by the spirit of the age. Protestant thought in the nineteenth century is the story of Protestantism's attempt to respond to the questions about its faith put to it by a century which, not only in religion, but in every other area of human life was undergoing greater change than man had ever known.

Our attempt here will not be to examine the entire dialogue between religion and culture in the nineteenth century but to try to deal with only three phases of that dialogue in the hope of thereby considering at least three of the main problems with which theology wrestled in that century. The choice of these three is made both because they seem to be the significant areas in the development of nineteenth century Protestant thought and also because they pinpoint the three major areas of concern for that same thought during the present century.

Schleiermacher opened up the question of religion as having other dimensions than the sheerly rational and by so doing pointed up the responsibility Christianity has to couch its message in terms understandable to the men of each succeeding age of history. The question is still with us, for example, in the contemporary death-of-God controversy and its attempt to discover what experience of religion, if any, contemporary man can have. Biblical criticism subjected Christianity's source document, the Bible, to the most searching critical examination and the problem of the meaning of the Word of God is still with us in the program for understanding the meaning of the Scriptures developed by Rudolf Bultmann and his followers and critics. Last of all, Albert Ritschl in his attempt to strip away from Christianity all metaphysical doctrines and make it essentially a moral and ethical code of conduct foreshadowed the twentieth century's continuing concern with the ethical implications of the Christian vision.

FRIEDRICH SCHLEIERMACHER

The first problem to which Protestantism addressed itself in this century was the question posed by the intellectuals of the age: could an intelligent man accept the truth of Christianity and live by it? These were the heirs of the seventeenth and eighteenth century rationalism examined in the last chapter. As the field of human knowledge expanded ever more widely the intellectual found it increasingly difficult to accept the Christian message; it seemed the product of a prior and considerably less enlightened past. It was, in a word, no longer intellectually respectable to be a Christian.

There was another current at work in the beginning of the nineteenth century, countering what was conceived of as the arid and lifeless intellectualism of rationalism. This was the movement of romanticism, the mood of those who preferred other areas of human life than the sheerly intellectual. For them the richness of life lay rather in imagination, in emotion, in the freedom and the individuality of the human person. Their preference lay with the arts, with poetry and drama; emphasis was rather on life's mystery and unexpectedness and unpredictability. For the romanticists, too, religion seemed unacceptable as part of real life since it seemed to concentrate on an appeal to men's minds. It had in it little of the emotional and experiential side of life.

It was to the problem posed by both these movements, perhaps more especially the latter, the problem of making Christianity acceptable to the men of his age, that Friedrich Schleiermacher (1768-1834) dedicated his two great works, *On Religion, Speeches to Its Cultured Despisers* (1799) and *The Christian Faith* (1821-22). His first book was an inquiry into the nature of religion. As the title indicates it was addressed to the cultured of his day for whom belief in Christian dogmas seemed no longer possible. His book is an attempt to render religion acceptable to them.

The basic proposition of the book is that religion is not a set of dogmas, or fixed doctrines to which the intellectual assent of faith is given. Religion is not a manner of thinking and it is not to be identified with creeds or dogmas or theological systems. Rather religion is in its essence an experience, a sense of awareness, a feeling. It arises in each man naturally from his being in the world. It is his reaction to that world. Because man is in the world he has to come to terms with it, to understand it and his place in it. In this coming to terms he is immediately conscious of being dependent, absolutely dependent. In this direct awareness of his situation he is at the same time aware of the Whence of all things, of Him on whom all

things depend, of the Absolute, of God. The same experience, upon
further reflection, brings him to see that dependence is a state he shares
with all other men; they are bound to him and he to them in a shared
condition of absolute dependence.

> The contemplation of the pious is the immediate conscious-
> ness of the universal existence of all finite things, in and
> through the Infinite, and of all temporal things in and through
> the Eternal. Religion is to seek this and find it in all that lives
> and moves, in all growth and change, in all doing and suffering.
> It is to have life and to know life in immediate feeling, only as
> such an existence in the Infinite and Eternal. Where this is
> found religion is satisfied, where it hides itself there is for her
> unrest and anguish, extremity and death. Wherefore it is a life
> in the infinite nature of the Whole, in the One and in the All,
> in God, having and possessing all things in God, and God in
> all.[1]

Put another way, this initial experience could be analyzed as an intuitive realization of all things as united in dependence on God, an immediate
awareness of the finitude of all things and simultaneously of the existence
of the Infinite in which all that is finite exists. A note of caution should be
inserted here. By feeling, Schleiermacher does not refer primarily to an
emotional experience. He means rather an intuitive awareness of reality.
Thus there is a rational (but not only a rational) dimension to feeling.
Novak puts it well in his review of Richard R. Niebuhr's book
Schleiermacher on Christ and Religion: A New Introduction:

> Prof. Niebuhr makes clear that the famous Gefühl or "feeling"
> on which the epistemology of Schleiermacher is based is not
> what would today be called emotive, but rather an abiding
> sense of personal identity, a radical sort of awareness of being
> oneself which is presupposed by all thinking and doing.[2]

The men to whom Schleiermacher writes his *Speeches,* because they
had always thought of religion as a creed to be believed and because they
could no longer give intellectual assent to the Christian or any other creed,
thought of themselves as men without religion, indeed incapable of it. But
they were in error. Like all men they were still able to have the essential
religious experience, the feeling of absolute dependence.

If one studied the world's religions one could see how universally true
was this analysis of the nature of religion. Though all of them have had
their own set of beliefs, it was evident that these beliefs were attempts to

put into specific, rationally apprehended, and intellectually expressed statements the fundamental awareness of the dependence of the finite on the infinite which all of them shared. Nor should it be wondered at that credal formulations have been characteristic of all religions. When the initial religious experience is subjected to reflection, doctrinal expression will inevitably occur. But the result is not to be confused with the cause. Feeling is primary; reason follows with its explanations. Experienced awareness of one's condition is religion; rational expression of belief is its consequence.

In this respect Christianity was like all other religions. It, too, was at base a feeling of dependence. But, and this was what differentiated it from the others, it had an awareness of dependence which was particularly its own. In addition to the universal experience of dependence on God it believed that two additional dimensions of that experience were also part of the religious feeling, a sense of sin and a sense of grace.

> Thus the Christian faith can be simply defined as that feeling or consciousness whose entire content refers to Jesus Christ as its mediator . . . . All that really marks it off from other religions is to be found in the specific structure and quality of its consciousness, as it appears in the person of Jesus Christ, in his individuality and life and in the communication of the same to others.[3]

Schleiermacher's second major work, *The Christian Faith,* spelled out the details of this double sense which differentiated Christianity from other religions. First, with regard to the sense of sin, Schleiermacher argued that though man was capable of experiencing and acknowledging his "fellowship with God," he was also capable of failing to come to or of losing his "God-consciousness." This is what sin is, man's failure to recognize and live by his sense of absolute dependence.

Sin, for Schleiermacher, was isolation, the decision to live by one self and for one self. It was the denial of one's condition; and hence it belonged to an imperfect state of consciousness. Not only did it cut one off from God but it also separated one from that unity with other men which was the consequence of the shared dependence. This state of isolation produced loneliness and misery in a man's life and by so doing confirmed that happiness was only to be found in the acknowledgement of unity with God and with other men. It was only when a man accepted the religious experience that he found peace because he found his true self.

Turning to Christianity's notion of redemption, Schleiermacher argued again that the sense of grace is part of the Christian's experience of religion. At that point in history where the majority of men had lost their God-consciousness, the awareness of their true state, Jesus was sent by God as the Mediator. The significant fact in his life was his mediation. He was the one man who has had complete God-consciousness. He was supremely aware of his relation to God and to other men. For that reason his life exhibited a supreme level of unity with God. Indeed, so perfectly conscious was he of God that this constituted a "veritable existence of God in him." Thus he was at one and the same time the perfect revelation of God to men and the perfect exemplar of what was man's true relation to God.

His mission of mediation is to communicate to men his own perfect intuition of reality, his own consciousness of God. Seen in this light, Christian redemption is, on the one hand, the Christian's coming to consciousness of self as alienated from its true nature because of refusal to accept the feeling of absolute dependence and, on the other, his coming to the experience of being redeemed, of being freed from his isolation, by having communicated to him Christ's own sense of God and sense of unity with God. Redemption is, therefore, not a doctrine; it is an experience. It is not something that is reasoned to; it happens to a man. It is recognized and incorporated into one's life. In the same way, grace is not a belief; it is an experience of the renewal of one's consciousness of God in and through Christ. Reason may and does proceed to formulate this sense of grace for purposes of credal affirmation but grace is the experience not the concept.

From Christ Schleiermacher turned to a consideration of the Christian Church. Here again the role assigned to the Church in a man's life was not what he understood her nature to be so much as what experience his membership in her brought him. Through her membership the Church has been, throughout history, a continual witness to the fact that men have, since her beginning, come to a meaningful God-consciousness through their contact with the life of Jesus as that life is preserved, lived and preached in the Church. She is, in a word, mankind's continuing experience of Christ. In the Church and through the experience of union with God through Jesus that she provides, man is given the place of his union with other men in a shared experience of dependence on God.

One final aspect of Schleiermacher's thinking should be noted. Religion for him had a strongly social and ethical character. Arising out of the awareness of dependence on God and the concomitant awareness of being bound to other men by the bond of shared dependence comes the conviction that these relationships must come to expression in life itself. Isolation, the choice of self, because it is an unnatural existence, a denial of man's basic nature, can bring with it only disaster. Life to be what it is meant to be must be lived in an expressed communion with God and community with other men. The social dimension is a fundamental aspect of religion.

CONCLUSION

In calculating Schleiermacher's legacy to Christian thought it may be noted first of all that in his approach to an understanding of Christianity he developed a way to deal satisfactorily with the serious problems that biblical criticism (our next subject) was causing for the traditional Christian view. The question implicit in the biblical critics' position was: what precisely is the authority of Scripture as the source of Christian belief in the light of the substantially altered view of its message that our historico-critical studies demand? Schleiermacher's view shifted the ground on which religion rested and it thereby removed the necessity of finding answers to the questions posed by biblical criticism. Or perhaps put better, it was for the biblical critic to determine in what sense the Scriptures were to be understood as expressing the primitive church's experience of Christ. Once this was established then that experience could be of value to the present day Christian in understanding his own experience of Christ.

Religion is the personal experience of each man and therefore it carries its own validation. A man surely knows his own experience. Seen from this perspective, it is evident that what a man's reason explicates as its belief is not what comprises religion for him. Rather it is his experience, his awareness of reality which does that for him. Religion understood in this fashion does not require the authority of Scripture, nor the reasoning of philosophy, nor the support of science for its validity. Man experiences religion as true. He intuits its value for himself.

Biblical criticism then is not destructive of religion. Rather it can be helpful. The role of the Bible is to speak to the feeling and experience of man. Scripture's message is for the heart, not the mind. It serves the function of helping man to clarify the experience of dependence on God which arises in him naturally. It adds detail and confirmation to that experience. Biblical criticism, in rendering the message of the Bible clearer and more understandable, allows it to speak more persuasively to man of the meaning of his personal religious experience. In general, then, there is no growth in human knowledge, nor alteration in human understanding that can harm religion because reason in the narrowly intellectual sense does not occupy the central position in religion; experience does.

Again, on the positive side of the ledger, Schleiermacher was very much aware that religion will have little to say to any age unless it understands that age, its problems, its cultural modes of expression, its intellectual preoccupations. Without such understanding it cannot hope to speak its message in accents to which that age will listen. He is among the first in a long line of modern practitioners of Tillich's principle of correlation.

> The method of correlation explains the contents of the Christian faith through existential questions and theological answers in mutual interdependence.[4]

This concern for speaking relevantly as opposed to stressing the timelessness of the Christian message remains the paramount concern of most significant present-day theologians.

Not only did Schleiermacher recognize the need for dialogue with the spirit of his age, he saw too what was the focal point of that dialogue, the individual human person, the self. Man will find Christianity of meaning only if it speaks to him. The locus of religious meaningfulness is, therefore, subjective experience. So his theology takes as its starting point man's understanding of himself and his world. The remainder of his theologizing builds block by block on that experience. The Christian faith is seen as answering to, resonating with, throwing light on, the human situation.

To quote but one among the host of contemporary theologians who see the starting point of theology in very much the same terms, Bernard Lonergan proposes a study of the conversion *experience* as the best starting point for a truly contemporary theology.

> Fundamental to religious living is conversion. . . . For conversion occurs in the lives of individuals . . . When conversion is viewed as an ongoing process, at once personal, communal, and historical, it coincides with living religion. For religion is conversion in its preparation, in its occurrence, in its development, in its consequents, and also alas in its incompleteness, its failures, its breakdowns, its disintegration.

> Now theology and especially the empirical theology of today, is reflection on religion. It follows that theology will be reflection on conversion. But conversion is fundamental to religion. It follows that reflection on conversion can supply theology with its foundation and, indeed, with a foundation that is concrete, dynamic, personal, communal, and historical.[5]

Yet another facet of Schleiermacher's thinking is his return to the great Reformation themes which he pitches in a quite different key. In his insistence on the Infinite as present in and supporting all that is finite he is at one with Calvin's insistence on the absolute sovereignty of God. In grounding all authentic religion in personal experience he is returning to Luther's intense concern for personal involvement as an absolute condition for any true faith. Finally his restoration of Christ to the heart of Christian revelation both re-echoes the Reformation's stress on Christ as the one Lord and Savior and foreshadows what has been increasingly true since his time, a concentration by Christian theologians on Christology as the focal point for understanding Christianity.

From the negative point of view Schleiermacher has not lacked for critics. Their principal uneasiness with his thought has been his strong stress on the subjective element in religion. Unless extreme care is exercised, they argue, the subjective can become sheer subjectivism. The Christian message comes to mean what the individual experiences it to mean for himself. Necessary and valuable as the subjective is, they warn, it needs always to realize that the Word of God is just that, God's Word spoken to man, to be accepted by him in faith and confidence.

Karl Barth, the first great contemporary to react to Schleiermacher's approach, summarizes what continues to be contemporary theology's chief reservation with Schleiermacher: it is ultimately the Bible, not human experience which lies at the foundation of Christianity.

> It is not the right human thoughts about God which form the content of the Bible, but the right divine thoughts about men. The Bible tells us not how we should talk with God but what He says to us; not how we find the way to him, but how he has sought and found the way to us; not the right relation in which we must place ourselves to him, but the covenant which he has made with all who are Abraham's spiritual children and which he has sealed once and for all in Jesus Christ.[6]

BIBLICAL CRITICISM

The second important expression of nineteenth century Protestant thought was the development of a totally new method of studying the meaning of the Scripture. So radically different was the method and so startling its findings that by the end of the century a completely new view of the meaning and authority of the Bible had developed. No longer was it seen as an inerrant set of documents recording God's revelation to men. It remained generally accepted that God spoke through them and in that sense they were inspired books but they were also a set of humanly written documents and as such contained error and contradiction, legend and myth, along with historical facts. Perhaps the most radical result of the movement was the dramatic change effected by the critics in the traditional view of Jesus Christ. The Jesus discovered by the biblical critics was quite different from the Jesus that tradition had known until then.

Biblical criticism applied to the Bible the type of literary analysis to which the other literary productions of the past were being subjected. The critics were convinced that a thorough application of the methods of historical and literary criticism to the Scripture would yield a much more accurate understanding of the Bible than had thus far been achieved. The task of biblical study was conceived to be not so much a study of the text itself as an attempt to get behind the text, to discover what the text was really saying, to separate the text into its various components: fact and fiction, history and legend, ideas intended as distinct from literary forms used to express them.

To achieve this end of a deeper understanding of the text's meaning, the scholars began to ask critical questions regarding the Bible: When were these books written, were the authors really those traditionally accepted to be such, what did the authors really intend to say, what was the effect of history on the thought of the books of the Bible, what relation can be determined between the various books, can a common stock of religious ideas account for the likenesses between the Scripture and the other documents of the ancient Near East?

When applied to the Old Testament this historico-critical method yielded a number of new and startling conclusions. The first five books of the Old Testament were not, as had previously been believed, written by Moses. Different styles, vocabularies, literary forms pointed to a number of authors. Isaiah too was not singly authored but manifested at least two, possibly three or four, different hands in its composition. The creation story in Genesis was not a single unified account, but two distinct traditions had been woven together to give the impression of one account. Many passages previously understood as foretelling the future were now seen to have been written after the event foretold. As the evidence mounted for such views, the traditional position that Scripture was literally true in all that it recorded was gradually undermined.

The major focus of attention of the biblical critics, however, was the New Testament. Specifically their studies concentrated on the person of Jesus or, as Schweitzer later characterized the movement, the work of the scholars became a "guest of the historical Jesus." The task of New Testament study was conceived as involving an attempt to distinguish the words and deeds of the historical Jesus of Nazareth from the interpretations which the Church, in writing the New Testament, added to this basically simple historical portrait. Careful study was needed to separate fact from interpretation of fact or myth in the case of Jesus so that the historical Jesus might be disengaged from the nonhistorical elements that the Church added at a later date. David Strauss' *Life of Jesus* published in 1835-36 will serve as a typical example of the way in which the problem was handled.

David Strauss

To begin with, Strauss (1808-1874), acknowledged that there had been before him two different kinds of attempts to interpret the meaning of Jesus. The orthodox or supernatural approach started with the premise that all the Scripture contained was true, its supernatural (e.g., miracles and prophecies) as well as its natural elements. From this starting point it explained the meaning of the various books, coping as best it could with whatever apparent contradictions it met. The natural or rational approach began with the opposite premise: Only what was historical or rationally explicable could possibly be true. Hence only those passages allowing of rational explanation were to be considered as true. All else was to be eliminated. Strauss found both approaches unsatisfactory and he proposed, in typically Hegelian style, a third method of interpretation, the mythological one, which would achieve a synthesis of the acceptable elements of the two prior types of explanation. The supernatural interpretation was seen as the thesis; the rational as the antithesis and the mythological as the synthesis.

Myth for Strauss means ". . . the clothing in historic form of religious ideas, shaped by the unconsciously inventive power of legend, and embodied in a historic personality."[7] Jesus of Nazareth was a historical person who, in the course of his life and under the influence of the spirit of the age, especially the strong strain of Messianic expectation that characterized the Jewish religious thought of the time, came to believe that he was the Messiah whom the Jews expected. The admiration and reverence he evoked in his followers was so strong that after his death they proceeded, unconsciously, to invest him with legendary and mythical attributes. Their myth-making tendencies were encouraged by the strong Messianic expectations of the contemporary Jews.

All the Messianic allusions of the Old Testament, its references to traits that the future Messiah would have, could quite naturally be absorbed into their increasingly idealized picture of Jesus. The final stage of their mythologizing was the attribution to him of divine qualities. He became for them the Son of God. The Jesus of Scripture is then a combination of historical fact and Christian imagination fashioning a historical figure into a divine person through the process of mythologizing that figure.

A look at the way in which Strauss works out some of the elements of this thesis will clarify his thinking and at the same time provide a typical example of a biblical critic at work.

Jesus of Nazareth

For Strauss, Jesus at some time before his death had come to the conviction that he was the Messiah. The probability was that this was a gradually dawning consciousness. We need not, however, believe that Jesus was a fanatic because he came to this conclusion. He too was, like most of his contemporaries, subject to the suggestive power that myth-making exercised on the men of his time.

Once convinced of his Messiahship, it is easy to conceive how that conviction could have led Jesus to see his own suffering and death as an inevitable consequence of his acceptance of that role. The Old Testament had spoken much of a suffering Messiah, especially Isaiah. The further conclusion that death willingly accepted would possess an atoning power and would exert a powerful spiritual influence on the lives of his followers was also quite understandable. Following this line of thought Strauss could conclude that the death of Jesus was indeed a historical fact but the implications that Christians have found in that death were in large part put there by Jesus, himself a human person, who was formed in his thought patterns by the religious climate of his times.

His Followers

Another strong influence at work in the shaping of the final form of the New Testament was the impact that Jesus' powerful personality had on his apostles and disciples. Much of the detail about him, his healing power, his resurrection, his divinity, is due to their reaction to the strength and attractiveness of his personality. Intimations of his messianic consciousness, for example, would be given to his followers and once the seed was planted their reverence for him would quite naturally lead them to link his deeds and words with the Old Testament descriptions of the future Messiah.

Such a tendency would, for example, explain how the stories of his healings, his prophecies, and his miraculous raisings from the dead made their way into the story of his life. They would be the product of his followers' conviction that the Messiah must surely equal and even surpass the deeds done by the prophets of the Old Testament. Thus the prophet Eliseus had cured Naaman the Syrian of his leprosy; and the same prophet had restored to life the son of the Sunamite woman (*IV Kings:* Chaps. 4-5). Or, again, the transfiguration of the face of Moses after his conversation with God on Sinai would offer obvious background material for the story of the Transfiguration. Such thinking introduced the miraculous stories into the New Testament and led finally to the conclusion that, since he was greater than the prophets of the Old Law, not only did he raise others to life but his own superior power effected his own resurrection.

St. John's Gospel provided Strauss with the last link in his chain of mythological interpretation of the Scripture. Here the person of Jesus moved from the possession of extraordinary power to the status of divinity. By the time John came to write his Gospel he had acquired a familiarity with Greek philosophical thought. That thinking provided him with a series of thought categories: divine sonship, the Logos concept, the notion of preexistence. He came to see all of these as ideal concepts for expressing his own and his fellow Christians' ever deepening reverence for the person of Jesus. When he came to write his life of Jesus these ideas were worked into the fabric of the narrative in such a way that later readers would see them as integral parts of the story of Jesus' life rather than as products of a long period of reflection which had resulted in the weaving together into a single account both historical fact and John's introduction of mythical and philosophical elements into the narrating of these facts.

CONCLUSION

In consequence of Strauss' work and that of the other nineteenth century Protestant biblical scholars a dramatic revolution in the interpretation of Scripture entered the mainstream of Protestant thought. Later scholars would tend to be much less drastic in their application of the new method and Schweitzer's observation at the end of the century that

Strauss' search for myth had led him to underestimate the amount of history in the Gospels was an estimate shared by most scholars.

> ... he overestimates the importance of the Old Testament motives in reference to the creative activity of the legend. He does not see that while in many cases he has shown clearly enough the source of the *form* of the narrative in question, this does not suffice to explain its *origin*. Doubtless, there is mythical material in the story of the feeding of the multitude. But the existence of the story is not explained by reference to the manna in the desert, or the miraculous feeding of a multitude by Elisha. The story in the Gospel has far too much individuality for that, and stands, moreover, in much too closely articulated an historical connexion. It must have as its basis some historical fact. It is not a myth, though there is myth in it.[8]

Yet allowing for all the moderating influence that such criticism has exercised, the historico-critical method of scriptural interpretation still holds the field as the dominant influence in the contemporary study of the Bible. Indeed, the manner of understanding the Word of God not as text but as event which occurs when God speaks to the individual, the meaning and usage of mythological and symbolic language as a vehicle of religious truth, the recurrence of the birth, life, death and rising theme in the literature of most of the world's religion, the historical dimensions of God's dealing with His people, these are the major themes in today's scriptural studies. All of them trace their lineage back to nineteenth century biblical criticism and beyond that back to Luther's principle of *sola Scriptura.*

ALBERT RITSCHL

The third major influence operative in nineteenth century Protestantism was the work of Albert Ritschl (1822-1889). Schleiermacher was a response to romanticism and rationalism. Biblical criticism was Christianity's attempt to come to terms with the new learning and contemporary methods of scholarship. Ritschl represents Christian theology's confrontation with the philosophy of Immanuel Kant. Ritschl's theology was strongly influenced by Kant's thought particularly at two points: the rejection of metaphysics or theoretical speculation as a source of valid knowledge about God; and a strong insistence on religious thought as essentially practical and moral.

Kant, in dealing with the nature of human thought, concluded that man could not know things as they are in themselves. All that could be known were phenomena, things as they presented themselves to the senses, the appearance of things. This being so, it followed that a knowledge of God as He is in Himself (a metaphysical or philosophical knowledge of God) was not a possibility.

But for Kant there was another type of human knowledge. That was the field of moral consciousness, the sphere of man's practical reason. Man is aware of moral obligations that bind him, a series of thou shalts and thou shalt nots. When analyzed out, this moral sense pointed to the existence of One responsible for the existence of this moral imperative in all men. God exists as the necessary postulate to explain man's moral sense and religion is man's recognition that the laws that bind him are commands given by God.

Ritschl accepted this Kantian analysis of the nature of human knowledge and on its basis worked out his interpretation of the meaning of Christianity. His basic premise is that religion and therefore Christianity must be separated from theoretical knowledge. God is apprehended through the moral sense; He is not known rationally. The Christian faith was not, therefore, metaphysical. It was rather moral and ethical. Its primary concern was concrete and practical rather than intellectual and philosophical. Put another way, the object of the Christian message is not concern about the nature of God or Christ but the answer to the question: How is man saved?

Building on this fundamental notion of the practicality of religion Ritschl viewed Christianity as based on value judgments. Man is initially conscious that, though he is part of nature like the other things that surround him, he is unlike the rest of nature in that he sees himself as having a worth and an independence over against nature. Religion offers man an explanation of this consciousness of himself. It provides him with . . . "a solution of the contradiction in which man finds himself, as both a part of the world of nature and a spiritual personality claiming to dominate nature."9

The solution that it gives man is

> . . . faith in superhuman spiritual powers, by whose help the power which man possesses of himself is in some way supplemented and elevated into a unity of its own kind which is a match for the pressure of the natural world. The idea of gods, or Divine powers, everywhere includes belief in their spiritual personality, for the support to be received from above can

only be reckoned on in virtue of an affinity between God and men.[10]

Ritschl is here saying that man makes a value judgment regarding his own worth. He is conscious of a stature above and beyond that of the rest of nature. Implicit in that judgment is the awareness of a Person who is responsible for man's conviction of his own worth and who collaborates with him in his practical assertion of that worth. God is then part and parcel of man's consciousness of his own worth just as for Schleiermacher He is implicit in man's awareness of his dependent state. Thus knowledge of God arises out of a value judgment.

In relation to the objects around him, man judges them as supporting or detracting from his sense of his own worth. They give rise in man to value judgments, feelings of pleasure or pain, happiness or sorrow, guilt or peace, worthwhileness or worthlessness. They are seen as good or bad in terms of whether they help or hinder a man in realizing his own worth.

It should be noted that in this analysis of the nature of religion the feelings and the will play a far more important role than the intellect. For the religious man what is important is the set of values to which he commits himself, not what he knows about the nature of God.

Human history is the place where man has discovered his values and worked out their implementation. For it is in history that movements have grown up dedicated to the pursuit of those values which make life meaningful. It should be concluded then that it is not in nature but in history that God has revealed Himself to man, giving him a sense of his own worth, creating in him a sense of real values and implanting in him the desire to pursue what is worthwhile for human existence.

Jesus Christ and his life are the supreme historical instance of God at work. In him God is revealing Himself as love and at the same time offering this value to man as his supreme ideal. In the life of Jesus man is presented with the paradigm of a total dedication to the highest ideals and their perfect attainment. In Jesus God reveals that love is the highest value to which man can give himself. Therefore what matters for man in the case of Christ is the impact that his moral personality makes on man. Jesus may be called divine because like God he presents man with the highest values and ideals. His divinity is, in Ritschl's words, "the worth to be put on those human achievements of his which suffice for our salvation."[11] Man's faith in Jesus then is at base a value judgment, the conclusion that there is no higher set of aspirations to which man can dedicate himself than those exemplified in Jesus.

But the presentation of an ideal is not his only nor is it his most important work. That lies rather in the reconciliation and justification that he effects in a man. Left to himself man tends to make self-regard and self-concern his principal value. But confrontation with Jesus presents him with love as the highest of human values, love of God and love of neighbor. Belief in Jesus and dedication to his sense of values carries with it the power to make man free from himself and his selfishness and from the alienation from his true self which proceeds from this self regard. Belief in Jesus makes love man's supreme value and brings with it also the power to insert that value into all of life.

It should be clear from this description of Jesus and his work that redemption is understood by Ritschl not so much in terms of an emphasis on Jesus as atoning for the sins of men. He preferred rather to view it in terms of Christ restoring man to his true self and to a true sense of values wherein love holds the primacy. Thus the prime end of the redemption is to bring man to a life based on love and to be redeemed means to accept the values for which Christ gave his life.

The place wherein the redeemed carry on their common pursuit of love also owes its origin to Jesus. He left behind him the value-creating community which is the Church. She serves as the focal point of human aspiration and human endeavor because in her the value system of Jesus is preserved, nourished and preached. In her men can together find and follow the value that God reveals to man through Christ. She is the community of those who have accepted redemption through Christ.

But redemption of the individual and his incorporation into the Church is not the final purpose of the divine plan for history. That purpose is the establishment of the kingdom of God; redemption and church exist to serve that end. The kingdom is to be "the organization of humanity through action inspired by love." It is the divine intention to bring mankind into a universal moral community whose task will be concern for the moral and social needs of the world. Thus the task of the redeemed and of the church is to give themselves to a life of selfless dedication in serving humanity. This life lived out of the motivation of love will contribute to the gradual acceptance of this way of life by other men and thus bring about the inauguration of the kingdom of God on earth.

It is clear then that Christianity, as Ritschl conceives it, is a commitment to moral and ethical value judgments and their implementation in society. But if these judgments are to escape subjectivism, i.e., the individual judgment determining what is right or wrong, good or bad, they must be based not on what the individual might conceive Christianity to be but on what objective, historical investigation establishes as factual in the life and work of Jesus Christ, the founder of Christianity. Like

Schleiermacher, then, Ritschl welcomed biblical criticism because he saw in it the attempt to discover the facts relating to the life of Jesus. This could only help Christianity because in determining who Christ was, what he said and did, this critical investigation would help to provide ever more perfectly the facts in the life of Jesus on which the Church could continue her existence as a value-generating and preserving community.

Ritschl himself was confident that the Scriptures did provide a trustworthy testimony to the life and deeds of Christ yet he was willing to have the biblical critic evaluate that testimony. Whatever might be the outcome of historical investigation, he himself did not feel that Christian faith was evoked by the facts of Jesus' historical existence. It came rather from Jesus as God made him personally present and meaningful in the life of the believer. From Jesus thus presented to the Christian there comes the power of acceptance and the commitment to the values Jesus stands for; there comes also the capability of being free from self-assertion and of dedication to the pursuit, with other men, of the goals of God's kingdom.

It should also be observed that by his insistence on the need for possessing objective facts before making value judgments Ritschl makes clear the distinction between religion and science and the province and competence of both. He saw that the two are needed for the fully human life. It is for science to search out the facts of reality; it is not, however, competent to pass judgment on the human meaning of these facts. This is the task of religion which is competent to attach value meaning to facts. Confusion and conflict occur whenever either strays into the province of the other. Science, for example, should give itself to careful study of the theory of evolution, to the discovery of the facts relating to man's evolving from lower animals. It exceeds its competence, however, if it forms value judgments on these facts.

Religion, on the other hand, needs to listen to science for its factual data; it cannot, for example, speak of man's span on earth as beginning in a garden four thousand years ago if evidence is available indicating that man's presence on earth is of a considerably longer span. But once the facts of man's existence are determined, it is for religion to determine the values which give that life meaning. Both need to respect the competency of the other and rely on the other to fulfill its function.

CONCLUSION

With Ritschl, accent on the practical, ethical, and social implications of Christianity entered the main stream of modern Protestant thought. It has been a central preoccupation of that thought ever since, in the Social Gospel movement with its concentration on the reformation of the social order, in Reinhold Niebuhr's lifelong analysis of the relation between Christianity and society, especially in its political dimension, and last of all in the present attempts of Christian thinkers to bring the Christian faith to bear on the great social issues of race, poverty, war, and international community.

Along with Schleiermacher, Ritschl is also responsible for a line of Christian thought running from his day to the present which is strongly anthropocentric. The starting point for any thought about religion must be man, his experience, his needs, his problems. Karl Barth's thinking will represent the twentieth century's response to this trend in his emphatically theocentric interpretation of Christianity. But the experiential, man-centered approach to thinking about religion is still a dominant trend within Protestantism.

There are those who would hold Ritschl responsible for robbing Christianity of its sense of mystery and its awe in the presence of the transcendent God. He had little patience with mystical experience, pietism, or any approach to Christian faith which did not address itself to the problem of living in and affecting society. Practicality was for him central to authentic religion. Perhaps the best final estimate would be to say that confronted with the two poles between which any true interpretation of the Christian message must steer a middle path: the biblical message and the human situation, Ritschl's emphasis lay on the latter pole. This gives his interpretation all the strength and all the weakness that such a position entails.

FOOTNOTES

1Friedrich Schleiermacher, *On Religion, Speeches to Its Cultured Despisers,* trans. John Oman, Torchbook edition (New York: Harper & Row, 1958), p. 36.

2Michael Novak in *Commonweal,* April 2, 1965, p. 57.

3Richard R. Niebuhr, "Friedrich Schleiermacher," in *A Handbook of Christian Theologians,* ed. by Martin E. Marty and Dean B. Peerman, Meridian Book edition (Cleveland & New York: The World Publishing Co., 1967), p. 31.

4Paul Tillich, *Systematic Theology,* 3 vols. (Chicago: University of Chicago Press, 1951), I, p. 60.

5Bernard Lonergan, S.J., "Theology in Its New Context," in *Theology of Renewal,* ed. L.K. Shook, C.S.B., 2 vols. (New York: Herder and Herder, 1968), I, 44-45.

[6]Karl Barth, *The Word of God and the Word of Man,* Torchbook edition (New York: Harper & Row, 1957), p. 43.

[7]Albert Schweitzer, *The Quest of the Historical Jesus,* Paperback edition (London: A. & C. Block Ltd.; New York: The Macmillan Co. 1966), p. 79.

[8]*Ibid.,* p. 84.

[9]Albert Ritschl, *The Christian Doctrine of Justification and Reconciliation,* trans. J.S. Black, ed. H.R. Mackintosh and A.B. Macaulay, 2nd. ed. (Edinburgh: T. & T. Clark, 1902), p. 199.

[10]*Ibid.*

[11]*Ibid.,* p. 438.

CHAPTER EIGHT

Karl Barth

To say Karl Barth (1886-1968) is to name the giant of twentieth century Protestant theology. His influence on the thinking of all the Christian churches has been enormous and his productivity is unparalleled in this century. There are those who would say that he has done for this age what Luther and Calvin did for theirs and what Aquinas and Augustine had done before them.

Born in Basel in Switzerland in 1886 he did his early training in the great German centers of liberal theology, Berlin, Tübingen, Marburg. At that point in Christian history theology had turned in the direction of a religious anthropology. Man and his religious experience rather than God and his revelation were the characteristic starting point for Christian thought. To that emphasis, liberalism joined a somewhat uncritical optimism about man's innate goodness and perfectibility as well as a great trust in his capacity to build an ever better future for his world.

It was this vision that Barth learned from his masters, from Harnack an understanding of Christianity wherein Jesus, the supreme teacher and revealer of God, but himself a man, was the central focus, from Herrmann that Christian faith and morality flowed from the individual's personal relationship with the person of Jesus, from Gunkel and Schlatter, the latest methods of historical criticism of the Bible.

Thus when he decided to enter the pastoral ministry first for two years at Geneva (1909-11) and then for ten years at Safenwil (1911-21), he was thoroughly committed to liberalism's view of Christianity. But those twelve years of pastoral experience produced a gradually growing disillusionment with liberalism. His first major work, *The Epistle to the Romans,* a commentary on that Pauline letter, reflected this disenchantment. It was the occasion too for his passing from the parish to the university ministry.

Göttingen invited him in 1921 to accept its chair in systematic theology. A brief stay there was followed by periods of teaching at Münster, Bonn, and finally Basel where he taught until his retirement in 1960. During all those years his thinking moved more and more definitively away from liberalism and toward a theology based exclusively on the Word of God.

Barth's rejection of liberalism stemmed from two main causes, the world events occurring during his twelve years as pastor, and his study of the Scriptures. World War I and its aftermath produced mounting evidence that the optimism which liberal theology had developed regarding man, and its projection of a future that would grow increasingly better, needed serious examination and reevaluation. He found his congregation during those years looking to him for answers to the grave problems that the times were forcing upon them and he came to find that the only answers liberalism could provide were the vague and inadequate generalities of a conventional bourgeois morality and a Christianity that had been emasculated by its conformity to the surrounding culture. It had little to say to the irrationality and meaninglessness of the war; nor did it seem able to deal realistically with what events were making more and more clear, that there was a dark side of man, that sin was very much part of him.

Along with his growing uneasiness with liberalism there went a constant study of the Scripture. As he read and pondered he was led to see how different the message of the Bible was from what liberalism had made of it. Asking himself in later years what it was that altered his view of the meaning of Scripture, he wrote

> Was it . . . the discovery that the theme of the Bible, contrary to the critical and to the orthodox exegesis which we inherited, certainly could not be man's religion and religious morality and certainly not his own secret divinity? The stone wall we first ran up against was that the theme of the Bible is the deity of *God,* more exactly God's *deity*—God's independence and particular character, not only in relation to the natural but also to the spiritual cosmos; God's absolutely unique existence, might, and initiative, above all, in His relation to man. Only in this manner were we able to understand the voice of the Old and New Testaments. Only with this perspective did we feel we could henceforth be theologians and in particular, preachers—ministers of the divine Word.[1]

He came, in other words, to see that the Bible has as its primary focus not man but God. It aimed to speak first of God, His transcendence and His sovereign freedom and only then of His judgment on man and His gracious forgiveness of man in spite of that judgment. It concerned itself with

> not the history of man but the history of God! Not the virtues
> of men but the virtues of him who hath called us out of
> darkness into his marvelous light! Not the human standpoint
> but the standpoint of God![2]

In consequence of this newly discovered view of the meaning of Scripture his thinking turned away from the anthropocentrism of liberal theology towards a strict theocentrism. Two stages mark the development of his thought from this point on.

FIRST STAGE

In the first phase his thinking is characterized as a theology of crisis or again as a dialectical theology. In the second phase it becomes a theology of the Word. The term "theology of crisis" is used to describe his earlier thought because the expression sums up the method he used to describe the central message of Scripture at this period.

His thought begins and continues as a protest against the official Christianity of his day. The protest was made in the name of God's Word. That Word did not picture man as innately good; quite the contrary, it saw him as radically and inescapably a sinner, "a sinner through and through." As such, man was incapable of right thinking about God. He had "no point of contact" for relating to God and in consequence all his thought about who God is and what is His relation to men will be in error.

But this is not the only message that Scripture has for man, that he is a sinner. It also constantly accentuates the absolute difference between man and God. God is the "totally Other," the absolutely Transcendent. Between Him and man there is an "infinite qualitative distinction." Liberal theology was wrong then in thinking that man could reach God through his own experience or his own reasoning. The gulf that separated him from God was unbridgeable from man's side. Therefore no attempt on man's part to find God can succeed. The only God that man can possibly know of himself will always be an idol of his own construction. Because God is completely transcendent He is beyond the possibility of man conceiving a correct notion of Him. Such does Scripture say is man's position *vis-à-vis* God.

But the chasm, uncrossable from man's side, can be and has been crossed from God's side. That is the message of Christian revelation, that God has spoken to man. He has revealed Himself to man in Jesus Christ, His Word. Man cannot speak of God; therefore if he is to know God he must listen as God speaks to him.

It is at this point that Barth's thought becomes a crisis theology. God's message to man, when it is spoken to and heard by him, provokes a crisis situation in man's life. He finds himself confronted by a choice, either a refusal to hear the Word which characterizes him a sinner, and the choice to continue on the path of self-reliance, or an openness to that Word, an acceptance of one's state as sinner and the choice of reliance on God as the sole source of salvation. This is the crisis with which God's Word confronts man.

> [Barth] . . . laid great emphasis upon the fact that men could not hear the Word of God without being thrust into a situation where the whole basis of their existence was imperiled—where their lives were at a crisis and where they were judged by God—and where their only hope was in the leap of faith.[3]

From another point of view this stage of Barth's thought is also called a dialectical theology. Such an approach sees the Word of God as God speaking a divine No and a divine Yes to man. It interprets revelation as a series of contrasts set off against each other, each accenting the other: God's holiness and man's sinfulness, God's judgment of man and yet his forgiveness of man, God as creator, man as creature. God is forever saying 'no' to man's sinfulness and to his pretensions to be what he is not. Yet in spite of this he is also forever saying 'yes' to man, lifting him out of his sin and accepting him in spite of his unworthiness. Or, put another way, God deals with man not in terms of a natural 'therefore' but in terms of a divine 'nevertheless'. The message of revelation is not that man is unworthy and therefore God rejects him but rather that man is unworthy and nevertheless God saves him.[4]

All these themes of Barth are summed up in his discussion of the meaning of the cross. Here are all the contrasts between Holy God and sinful man; here meet the divine Yes and the divine No; here finally faith encounters religion. In Christ on the cross God has spoken His Word in condemnation of human sinfulness and in forgiveness of human sin. Here God offers friendship and thereby reveals the meaning of human life. Here finally He asks man to accept Him as He reveals Himself to be. On the cross that Word meets human rejection; Jesus the Word is killed by sinful man. Yet the final message of the cross is not human rejection. That message is rather the divine love and forgiveness which is offered and which persists as God's attitude toward man.

It is here at the cross that faith and religion confront each other. Those responsible for the death of Jesus were the religious men of that time. They are representative of all those who know who God is and how He is to be worshipped, who have built a religion with its holy places, its theological systems, its liturgy and its detailed law of conduct. They are the ones who have domesticated God, made Him over into a god, or more correctly an idol, of their own creation. It is their religion that has made it impossible for them to recognize God when he presents Himself to them in a form or under circumstances other than what they will allow. Religion is the very thing that keeps them from God and makes them sinners. In Barth's words, "religion is the enemy of faith."

Faith, on the other hand, is the opposite of religion. Where religion is man's attempt to relate to God on man's terms, faith is open to accepting God's Word on Who He is and who man is. The man of faith sees the crucifixion as God's Word on human sinfulness and on divine forgiveness. And he sees Jesus Christ as the embodiment of who God is, as His revelation of Himself. He recognizes religion for what it is, man-made forms and structures, human beliefs and attitudes, all that complex of human pride and pretension that leads man to believe he can know God of himself.

From this brief summary of Barth's early method of theologizing, it is evident that two notions stand out strongly in his thinking at this state, the divine transcendence and its corollary, the necessity of revelation.

The Divine Transcendence

Nineteenth century liberalism had, in Barth's mind, reversed the real meaning of revelation. Revelation, as he understood it, was not man's knowledge or experience of God nor was Scripture given to man that he might find in it confirmation of his own idea and his own experience of God. In their eagerness to render Christianity acceptable to their contemporaries, the liberals had moved towards destroying God's transcendence, had brought Him so close that men felt more and more free to make Him over into what their philosophy, their science, and their historical method told them He ought to be. Barth moved to release God from man's notion of who He is by pointing to Scripture's recurring insistence that God is completely other than man and thus can be known only as He reveals Himself.

Because the notion of divine transcendence is at the heart of Barth's thought it is important to be quite clear what he means by it. Transcendence for him is not to be conceived in spatial terms as if by saying God is wholly Other one means He is other-worldly, that He exists somewhere outside this world and its history. Rather transcendence for Barth means God's complete freedom from human attempts to express who He is, where He is to be found, how man relates to Him. He is free of man's holy places and holy times; He is not capturable in metaphysical speculations. He escapes our attempts at a natural theology, a knowledge of Him arrived at by unaided human thought. All we can know of Him, Barth might say, is that we cannot know Him. He comes to man in His own time and place and way. He reveals Himself to man when and how He wishes. As Colin Williams sums up the notion,

> God's transcendence, in the theology of Barth, is the transcendence of our 'other' who meets us in the midst of life as our Lord; it is the transcendence of a Lord who resists all our attempts to control him; but it is not the transcendence of one whose home is in a separate sphere outside our world.[5]

God, in sum, is beyond man's capacity to grasp and know Him. Yet in another sense He is not beyond him but very much present to man by His own choice, in His own way, at His own time and place as revelation makes clear.

Revelation

Transcendence and revelation are correlative ideas. Transcendence makes clear that man's way of knowing God and his expression of that understanding in his religion, his morality, his piety and his culture is all idolatry. Not only is all of this idolatry but also, since man bases his idea and his pursuit of salvation on this erroneous concept of God, he mistakenly believes that he is the fashioner of his own destiny. Thus he is wrong both in his notion of God and in his idea of salvation. From this error he can be rescued only by revelation, by God telling man who He is and what is the road that leads to Him. So we come to revelation.

If God transcends man's power of knowing Him this can only mean man cannot know Him unless He reveals Himself. Transcendence requires revelation if any relationship is to exist between God and man. God has made such a revelation of Himself in Jesus Christ. The whole process of man's relating with God begins when man believes that Jesus Christ is the revelation of God, His Word to men. That revelation, when it is heard, strips man of all his self-reliance, his belief in self-redemption and lays open to him the miracle of God's grace, that he does not save himself; he cannot. God saves him in Christ.

> For the Word of God is not an abstract general idea conceived by the human mind but a particular fact, namely the particular fact of God's actual revelation of Himself and of His will for man in and through the concrete person and work of Jesus Christ, who is Himself the incarnate Word of God, the Lord (Son of God) who became a servant and the servant (the royal man) who became Lord. Hence, the Word of God is a particular event, or rather a series of particular events constituting the *Heilsgeschichte*, particular events which not only happened in the past but continue to happen in this world, in the course of the history of mankind.[6]

SECOND STAGE

By the end of the twenties Barth realized that he was not yet making the Word of God the sole source and criterion of his thinking. Rather he was still strongly wedded to certain philosophical thought forms, especially existentialism as employed by Kierkegaard, as instruments for the presentation and interpretation of the Word of God.

The publication of the first volume of his *Church Dogmatics* in 1932 represents his definitive break with all such reliance on human instruments to explain the Word of God. From now on his thinking attempts to be solely concerned with the exposition of God's revelation of Himself as that revelation is contained in His own Word. He wants to remove any reliance on philosophical, cultural, or anthropological elements as the basis for his exposition of God's Word. Existentialism in particular was to be set aside because it was only another form of liberalism's anthropocentric approach to Christianity.

Now it became his intention to work only with faith-knowledge. He begins with the premise that he has accepted in faith, that God has spoken to man in Christ and it becomes his task to "explicate this self-revelation of God in faithful obedience to His Word." Faith, once it is possessed of God's truth, naturally seeks understanding of that truth.

To one who would ask him: why should I have such faith, what reason is there for accepting as God's Word what you simply assert as such, Barth offers no apologetic, no defense of Christian revelation as truly from God. He replies simply that if Christian theology is rightly grasped, it will prove itself to be true. Revelation is self-authenticating.

His work since then, especially his multi-volumed *Church Dogmatics* is done in careful reliance on that premise of faithful exposition of the Word of God. A thorough treatment of that work is beyond our present purpose. Our discussion will be limited to a treatment of some of the key notions that form the fundamental structure of his thought. We will deal in turn with his notion of revelation, then his thinking on Jesus Christ, the Word of God, and finally say something about the ethical dimension of his thought.

Revelation

Barth's understanding of the meaning of revelation does not begin with a definition of what he means by the term. He begins rather with the concrete reality of revelation. That reality is the event of God's intervention in human history. God reveals by acting. Thus revelation begins not with man and his seeking God. The initiative lies with God. He decides the time and the place and the circumstances of the encounter between Himself and man. Thus the first note Barth strikes is the divine sovereignty and freedom. Were He not to take the initiative, there would be no human knowledge of God. Revelation depends totally on God's decision to reveal. But, having strongly accented the absoluteness of the divine role in revelation, Barth is equally careful to insist on the activity of the human role in responding to revelation. Man's part is not that of passive acceptance. Confronted with God speaking, it is for him to respond in responsible human freedom. There are two partners to the dialogue: He who speaks and he who hears. Man bears the responsibility of a free human act of acceptance. That act is man's faith, his decision to hear and respond in obedience to God's Word.

Next Barth explores the nature of God's revelation, again as that nature manifests itself in human history. God's Word is not a set of propositions to be accepted as true. He does not reveal ideas to be believed. It is not a question of data about God to which one assents intellectually. It is in act that God reveals Himself. His revelation is a series not of words, but of events. He is concerned with showing men who He is, not in communicating truths about Himself. He does not reveal His nature. He reveals Himself in acts done for man.

The same notion may be approached from another perspective by saying that God's revelation is forever active. He did not once and for all
speak what He wished man to know about Him. Rather it is true that
throughout history He is continually in the process of revealing Himself to
men and when that self-disclosure is responded to by faith and obedience
His act has become His Word, His revelation of Himself to this man.

There is a sense in which revelation may be viewed as an objective fact.
In that sense there is only one revelation that God has made of Himself and
that is the event of the life of Jesus Christ. Christ is God's revelation of
who He is and his life and work is a set of objective happenings in history.
Much of Barth's attention is given to exploring the implications of those
events since they are God speaking of Himself in His relations to men. In
them man can read the story of God's judgment on man and yet His final
graciousness in dealing with man. The life, death, and resurrection of Jesus
must always remain the primary, indeed the only, revelation that God
makes of Himself.

Yet, this said, revelation is always in the final sense, subjective. The
subject, man, to whom it is addressed must accept it before it becomes
revelation for him, since the Word has not really been spoken until it has
been heard. God has not, therefore, really revealed Himself until He has,
through the action of the Spirit, brought a man to the free decision of
faith.

> ... the content of the Christian message is neither a subjective
> nor an objective element in isolation, neither man in isolation,
> nor God in isolation, but God and man in their encounter and
> communion, God's dealings with the Christian and the Chris-
> tian's dealings with God.[7]

Finally in his treatment of revelation Barth turns back to where he
started, to God. His last word on the subject is precisely that, an insistence
on the subject of revelation. All through the events by which God speaks
to man, it is He who speaks that is all-important. It is not as an object that
God reveals Himself. He reveals Himself as Subject, as Person. He wants to
give Himself, not knowledge about Himself. What is important in revelation then is not that which is revealed but He who in all His dealings with
men is present revealing Himself. God does not, through revelation, indicate that He judges, teaches, forgives, or loves man. He is rather present in
revelation revealing Himself as He who judges, He who forgives and He
who loves man. In paradoxical terms, there is no object of divine revelation; there is only the Subject who reveals Himself.

Jesus Christ, the Word of God

When Barth turns to a discussion of Jesus as the Word of God he has not really left his central notion of revelation. He is merely approaching it from yet another point of view. The essential affirmation of Christian revelation is that Jesus Christ is the Word of God. That means that in Him is contained God's sole revelation of Himself. He who would know God must know Jesus. It is to be expected then that all of Barth's thought has a "Christological concentration" about it. He sees nothing except in terms of Christ. What Christ is and does is revelation. Or put perhaps more accurately, there is nothing man can know of God except in and through Christ.

One of the sharpest criticisms of Barth's earlier thought was that his insistence on the otherness and transcendence of God was so strong that he seemed to allow little place for any real relationship between God and man. His stress seemed to underline the distance separating them, whereas the Christian faith emphasized, rather, God's closeness to man. Barth's answer to the criticism was that his initial accent on the divine transcendence was a reaction evoked by liberal theology's tendency to rob God of any otherness, to make Him almost wholly immanent in man's experience and his culture.

> Evangelical theology almost all along the line, certainly in all its representative forms and tendencies, had become *religionistic, anthropocentric,* and in this sense, *humanistic. . . .* There is no question about it: here man was made great at the cost of God. . . .[8]

When he felt the point had been made strongly enough that God was completely other than man, he then turned his attention to the "humanity of God," to God turning toward man, to His being with man in the person of Jesus Christ. He himself acknowledged the one-sidedness of his prior view, pointing out that the full Christian vision gives its attention to God being with men and for them. In doing this, however, Christian revelation also brings out clearly that, though God is with man, He is there in sovereign freedom and so He remains even in that being-with, quite other than man.

> But did it not appear to escape us by quite a distance that the *deity* of the *living* God—and we certainly wanted to deal with Him—found its meaning and its power only in the context of

His history and of His dialogue with *man,* and thus in His *togetherness* with man? Indeed—and this is the point back of which we cannot go—it is a matter of *God's* sovereign togetherness with man, a togetherness grounded in Him and determined, delimited, and ordered through Him alone. Only in this way and in this context can it take place and be recognized. It is a matter, however, of God's *togetherness* with man. Who God is and what He is in His deity He proves and reveals not in a vacuum as a divine being-for-Himself, but precisely and authentically in the fact that He exists, speaks and acts as the *partner* of man, though of course as the absolutely superior partner. He who does *that* is the living God. And the freedom in which He does *that* is His deity. It is the deity which as such also has the character of humanity. . . . It is precisely God's *deity* which, rightly understood, includes His *humanity.*[9]

Thus in his later teaching Barth restores balance to his thought. God is the totally Other; yet He chooses to be with man. It is true that He is different from man and the world. But in Christ He affirms man and his world. Though transcendent, He is by His own choice radically present in the world of men.

For Barth the Word of God like revelation does not allow of an *a priori* definition. One comes to understand it by exposure to the person who is the Word of God, Jesus Christ. What is involved is an encounter between two persons in which the one reveals himself and by so doing reveals who God is and what is the nature of the relation He has freely chosen to enter into with man. The Word is a person (Jesus) who acts. In that act God speaks not to men in general but to this particular man. As this man listens God tells him what He has done for him.

Like revelation, the Word of God has also its objective and subjective aspect. Barth's study of the Scripture provides him with the objective content or meaning of that Word. Its subjective aspect is the individual Christian's appropriation of that meaning, an appropriation which is accomplished by the Holy Spirit bringing the individual to faith in, and obedience to, the Word of God. Barth uses the term in a triple sense: The Word is primarily the person of Jesus, but it is also, in a subordinate sense, the witness of Scripture and the preaching of the Church. All three are the Word only when they are heard and responded to.

To be noted also is that the human appropriation of the Word of God is not a once-and-for-all occurrence. God's Word is not a datum or a set of propositions given once and to be assented to at that time. It is that series of acts by which God through Jesus Christ enters into relation with man. Thus it is not a question of having received the Word of God; it is rather a question of being continually in the process of hearing God as He speaks His Word and responding to It.

In Jesus then God speaks, and there are three elements in that speaking, who God is, who man is, and Jesus as the only one in whom God reaches man and man reaches God. The story of Jesus, His life, death and resurrection, speaks of God as one who knows man for what he is, a sinner, but one who, in Christ, judges him, punishes him, and then forgives and saves him. Thus God, as Jesus' life speaks of Him is ultimately the God who loves.

Regarding who man is, Jesus reveals him to himself as at once sinner and forgiven, prideful and yet called to obedience, condemned and yet in Christ elected by God, fallen and yet meant for eternal life with God. He is, in sum, created and sinful, yet saved by grace.

Finally, Jesus Christ speaks of both authoritatively precisely because He is both, God and man. Sharing the nature of both He mirrors, in what He says and is and does, the nature of both. He is the Lord God become Servant, lowering Himself to man's lowliness; He is at the same time Servant as Lord, man raised to God's level. He is the true man; all others are by contrast false to what it means to be a man. He is also 'very' God; in Him the divine plan expresses itself; the divine attributes manifest themselves and God is known for what He truly is, God for man, God with man. In sum, Jesus Christ, at one and the same time, reveals who God is and determines what man ought to be.

THE ETHICAL DIMENSION OF HIS THOUGHT

We have spoken of the first reason that turned Barth away from liberalism, that it was false to the biblical witness. There was another reason closely related to this one, though it lay at a more practical level. Liberalism had also proved itself valueless in providing norms for human action in times of crisis. The first world war and its sequel made all too clear to Barth the inadequacy of human answers to the problems of the world. He realized that, in making revelation man-centered rather than God-centered, liberalism had robbed man of the norms he needed to judge the world and its contemporary situation. No ability to criticize or power to resist inadequate human solutions was left to man if the otherness of God's way of thinking, acting, and judging human events was taken from him. It was only if the man of faith could rely on God's Word to supply him with the answers for human problems that he could exercise his prophetic function of criticizing society. If man's answers alone are available and they do not work, what then is to be done?

Out of this impasse Barth believed man could be led only by the Word of God. That Word spoke of God's way with men. It spoke too of what God expected would be man's way with God and with other men. Revelation speaks not only of what God wants man to know about Him; it speaks too of how man is to act in consequence of that knowledge. He is to act as God Himself has acted, in the humble giving of Himself for the sake of man.

Thus for Barth in his rejection of liberalism two principles became of primary importance, first the acceptance of the Word of God as the only reliable source of human knowledge about the divine, and second, the adoption of the divine solution to the problems that plague man.

The second of these principles led Barth to a deep involvement in many of the great social issues of his lifetime. The resistance of the Confessing Church in Germany to Nazism had him as one of its most outspoken leaders. He was spokesman too for defeated Germany, urging the Allies, soon after the war, to restore to the Germans their political freedom that they might once again begin to develop a sense of responsible political action. Communism knew him as a continuous critic, yet he felt that a good deal of the appeal of Communism was due to the Christian churches and their failure to become involved in the solution to pressing social problems. It was this inertia that made Communism much more attractive as a world-view than Christianity. He was likewise adamant in his opposition to the proliferation of atomic weapons or their use no matter what the provocation.

In summary Barth saw the Christian's task not as withdrawal or noninvolvement in political life but rather as an insistently urgent responsibility to be concerned with the application of God's Word to all areas of life. The responsibility is rooted in man's nature which is a nature shared by all men.

> The minimal definition of our humanity, of humanity generally, must be that it is the being of man in encounter and in this sense the determination of man as being with the other man. [We cannot accept that] man can be a man without the fellow man, an I without the Thou.[10]

CONCLUSION

Barth dominated the theological scene for almost thirty years. But the signs are now multiplying that his influence is on the wane. True to his own deepest convictions he would want it so. He would not want his own theological thinking to become a new system, a new "religion" to be studied and followed slavishly. This could only lead men to yet another idolatry, the belief that they had found a way to speak truly and well of God. Barth himself would want that the only legacy of his thought should be his insistence on the Word of God as the sole source of man's knowledge of God.

But in the eyes of many contemporary theologians Barth's insistence on the transcendence of God is the reason they ultimately find his thought unacceptable. They would agree that at the time when Barth began to write, his insistence on the radical transcendence of God was a needed antidote to the man-centered Christianity that liberalism had developed. Needed too, they would admit, was his striking out at the false optimism that liberal theology had developed in respect to man's own ability to lead a good life, solve his own problems, and build his own future. But yesterday's problems are not today's. For the contemporary theologian the central problem is that of faith, the possibility of belief in God. Allied with that is the other concern for building the best possible world for all men out of the technology that is developing so rapidly. Faith and the construction of a human society are today's concerns and latter-day thinkers tend to fault Barth's way of thinking on both counts.

First of all, his wholly other God does not speak to today's man. So wide and deep is the gulf he has opened between God and man that it does not seem possible or indeed worthwhile to try spanning it. Today's man is a this-worldly man and to speak to him of a God who transcends this world is to speak of what he neither comprehends nor is interested in. Eugene Borowitz summarizes this reason for the present feeling that we have gone beyond Barth.

> Barth's explanation of modern man's failings and hope in what Christ has done for him rests on a radically transcendent sense of God. But contemporary man lives and thinks only in terms of this world, so the vision of a wholly other God who sends salvation like a stone thrown from heaven does not move him.[11]

It is evident from our treatment of what Barth means by transcendence that this objection to Barth is based, at least partially, on a misconception of what transcendence means to him. Yet his language does, in much of his earlier writing, lend itself to such an interpretation. In any case it is clear that, in making God transcendent, Barth has made Him contemporaneously unacceptable. Thus he does not have a contribution to make to the present problem of faith.

A further indictment of Barth's position flows out of the first one. His relegation of God to another world and man's inability to speak of God in any meaningful sense provides one of the foundation stones on which the present death-of-God movement is built. It is but a short step from a wholly other God of whom human language can say nothing intelligible to the conclusion that the reason why man cannot speak of God is because He is not there to be spoken of. At best He may represent man's projections of his hopes and fears, his ideals and his values. Objectively He does not exist; He is only a subjective creation of man. Thus present thinkers would say, not only does Barth not have anything to say to the problem of belief as it is currently experienced; but he also contributes to man's disbelief.

With regard to the other contemporary concern, the building of a better world for all men, and hence total involvement in the city of man and its needs, Barth is also criticized by those who come after him. For Barth the meaning of every event, every movement, every society is always ambiguous. It may speak of God and His will; it may speak only of man and his sinfulness. God is always hidden in His manifestations of Himself in human history. Hence to see any society as reflecting God's presence in the world is to run the risk of idolatry. It is, therefore, extremely difficult to find God present, to say that what one is presently doing to serve the needs of men is clearly God's will. Barth's God, in other words, is so hidden in events that it is well-nigh impossible to discover what is His will in that event. The consequence is that Barth's God provides little by way of specific direction in the building of the better world. As Colin Williams puts it,

> By warning so strongly against the danger of domesticating God in particular religious structures and by insisting so strongly on God's judgment against all our idolatrous attempts to say 'Lo here,' 'Lo there,' Barth fails to give us the help we need in making the dangerous but necessary decisions as to how Christ is calling us to be his servants in the secular events of our time.[12]

To offer this kind of criticism is to say no more than that Barth, like all theologians, theologizes in history. What he or any thinker says is the produce of his time and its needs.

Finally, in this matter of speaking to one's time, it is instructive to note that the history of the past one hundred years has been an example of the very process of dialectic that was so much part of Barth's own method of thought. One could write a history of that period of Christian thought in terms of three stages of development. Liberalism highlighted man's part in the God-man dialogue. The accent was on the immanent, this-worldly character of Christianity. Barth was the worthy champion of the transcendent dimension of Christianity, emphasizing God's primary role in the God-man relation. We are at present in the process of swinging back again to a concentration on the here-and-nowness of religion. If it has meaning then that meaning must be immanent in this world. No other world exists in any significant sense for the men of the sixties.

Once this process is understood, Barth's place in the history of Christian thought is seen as a secure one. He saw and spoke to the needs of his time and in the speaking he towered over most of his contemporaries.

FOOTNOTES

[1] Karl Barth, *The Humanity of God* (Richmond, Va.: John Knox Press, 1966), p. 41.

[2] ——*The Word of God and the Word of Man*, Torchbook ed. (New York: Harper & Row, 1957), p. 45.

[3] Daniel Jenkins, "Karl Barth," in *A Handbook of Christian Theologians*, ed. Martin E. Marty and Dean G. Peerman, Meridian Book ed. (Cleveland & New York: The World Publishing Co., 1967), p. 403.

[4] Georges Casalis, *Portrait of Karl Barth*, trans. and with an introduction by Robert M. Brown, Anchor Book (Garden City, N.Y.: Doubleday & Co., Inc., 1964). The reference is to Brown's paraphrase of Barth's words in the Introduction, p. xxviii.

[5] Colin Williams, *Faith in A Secular Age*, Chapelbook ed. (New York: Harper & Row, 1966), p. 50.

[6] Herbert Hartwell, *The Theology of Karl Barth* (Philadelphia: The Westminster Press, 1964), pp. 22-23. Used by permission.

[7] Barth, *Church Dogmatics*, IV/3, ed. G.W. Bromiley and T. F. Torrance, (Edinburgh: T. & T. Clark, 1960), p. 498.

[8] Barth, *The Humanity of God*, p. 39.

[9] *Ibid.*, pp. 45-46.

[10] Barth, *Church Dogmatics*, III/2, p. 247.

[11] Eugene Borowitz, "God-is-Dead Theology," in *Judaism*, XV, No. 2 (1966), 86.

[12] Williams, *Faith in a Secular Age*, p. 54.

CHAPTER NINE

Dietrich Bonhoeffer

When the name of Dietrich Bonhoeffer (1906-1945) is mentioned, one instinctively asks Godsey's question: "Why is it that his name is being mentioned in the same breath with such theological giants as Barth and Bultmann and Tillich?"[1] There appear to be two elements in an adequate answer to the question. First of all, Bonhoeffer died a martyr. He fulfilled in his own life what he saw the Christian life to mean: 'When Christ calls a man, he bids him come and die."[2] That sacrifice in witness to his belief lends a compelling urgency to what he writes. Men always listen more attentively to one who lives what he believes and dies willingly for it.

The initial attraction to Bonhoeffer then is the arresting testimony of his martyrdom. Once so drawn one finds, as he begins to read the man, the second reason for his present popularity. What he writes speaks to contemporary man of things that concern him in language he understands. What is the meaning of life is the question Bonhoeffer asks, and more specifically, what contribution has Christianity to make to life's meaning? As he formulates his answers to these questions over the years he speaks to two quite different audiences, the men of the church and the men of the world. To the first, his message is always the challenge to make the church what she is meant to be, "Christ-existing-as-community." To the second, his call is to maturity, to a life lived to its fullest in the development of all human potentialities, especially that of human freedom. The world is now, for the first time in its history, making such maturity a realistic possibility.

His ultimate object in that challenge to truthful living and that call to maturity is to bring both church and world to realize that if each is to fulfill its contemporary task each will find it has need of the other. To become what she ought to be the church needs to learn what contemporary man and his world are that she may serve them. Man needs to see that only the church can give him freedom from himself.

The central focus of Bonhoeffer's thought seems best caught in the view of his friend and editor, Eberhard Bethge, who sees that focus as a continually growing awareness of the concreteness of revelation.

> Bethge has shown how Bonhoeffer's passion for the concreteness of revelation provides an explanation for his distinctive attitudes and actions. It led to his interest in the *sociological* form of the church in *Sanctorum Communio,* his questioning in *Act and Being* of the dialectical theologians about how the revelation that is free and not at man's disposal ever becomes concrete revelation, his criticism that in his ethics Emil Brunner neglected to investigate whether the church must risk the proclamation of quite concrete commandments. It explains his continual plea at ecumenical conferences for the risking of a concrete commandment, his concern about the Sermon on the Mount and discipleship, his intransigent position in regard to the ecclesio-political decisions of the Confessing Church. Further, the question drove him to work on his *Ethics,* which asks how the reality of God becomes real on earth and answers that it is only in the context of real life that revelation becomes attached to the penultimate things, that there can be no static separation of the sphere of the world from the sphere of the church. Finally, it brought him to a denial that Christianity was a religion of salvation emphasizing release from this world, and to an affirmation of the "this-worldly" character of the Christian faith.[3]

The journey of his thought parallels the journey of his life. His earlier works, *Sanctorum Communio* (1928) and *Act and Being* (1930), as befits a professor and theologian, tend to concentrate on a theological analysis of the nature of revelation. He passes to a career as pastor, ecumenist, political activist, and finally prisoner and his thought moves ever more steadily in the direction of how revelation is to be related in concrete terms to life itself.

THE NATURE OF REVELATION

The very fact that God has chosen to reveal Himself to man speaks an important initial truth to Bonhoeffer. It says that "God is not free *of* man but *for* man." It says that God has "freely bound Himself to historical man," that He has "placed Himself at man's disposal." It means that "God is there, which is to say: not in eternal non-objectivity but . . . 'haveable,' graspable in His Word within the Church."[4]

Bonhoeffer's first book, his doctoral dissertation, *Sanctorum Communio* (*The Communion of Saints*), addresses itself to an analysis of what God's revelation of His availability means. His question is: what is the church? His answer is that God reveals Himself and thereby makes Himself available to men through Christ in the church.

God's availability, His being *for* man is aimed at meeting man's need. An analysis of what man is, leads Bonhoeffer to conclude that man is by nature essentially social. It is of his very being to be related. It is the divine plan, mirrored in man's nature, that man should live not in aloneness, but in community, *communio* with God and man. But the fall introduced sin into the human situation and sin for Bonhoeffer is separation, alienation, loneliness. From one made for union man became one who lives for self. "The reality of sin . . . places the individual in the utmost loneliness, in a state of radical separation from God and man."[5]

It is at this point that God's availability meets man's need. He reveals Himself as being *for* man; He speaks His Word, expressing Himself as one who loves man; He sends Christ as the expression of who He is and as the solution of mankind's need. The need is communal. There is a solidarity of all men in the fall and its consequent selfishness and separation. The redemption from this state is equally communal because the saving act of Christ is the creation of the community of the redeemed, a *communio sanctorum*, freed from the bondage of selfish existence because it lives by the same principle of life as he lives, love of the other, of God and of man. Thus Christ's task is to restore community to man. This he does by restoring at one and the same time the individual's unity with God and his community with other men.

> But as, when the primal communion with God was rent asunder, human community was rent too, so likewise when God restores the communion of mankind with himself, the community of men with each other is also re-established.[6]

Christ effects this double restoration of communion to man in the church which is most accurately described as "Christ-existing-as-community." It is thus the function of the church to be a communion and that in several senses. It is, first, the locus of humanity's restored community and in that sense the locus of the redemption. It stands, secondly, as the living expression of that which is the ultimate destiny of all humanity, communion with God and man restored in Christ. It is lastly the source from which the fruits of Christ's work are to flow to other men. By what it is and what is says, it speaks the Word, brings "Christ-existing-as-community" to other men.

Described in these terms the church is, of course, an object of faith. The Christian accepts the church thus portrayed as God's revelation of Himself in Christ. But the church may also be viewed from the sociological point of view because it takes shape in history. Viewed thus the ways in which the church has embodied herself in form and structure throughout history may be sociologically analyzed and light shed on what the church is existentially. There is value here but need for caution too for, after sociology has said all it has to say, it has not finally described the nature of the church. For the church is the Word of God active in history. There is that in it which transcends sociological categories.

Bonhoeffer sees also that overstress on the other view of the church, the theological view, is also open to danger. To see the church as only an object of faith runs the risk of seeing her as set apart from the world. Yet her whole function is to be in the world or more accurately to be Christ in the world. To forget that is to forget that the Word is meant to be fully incarnate, to be "Christ revealed as community."[7] Theology and sociology need each other's insights; they also need to be aware of each other's limitations.

Even as he wrote his thesis Bonhoeffer was undergoing a growing disenchantment with the church as he knew it to exist in his own experience. The thesis painted the church as it ought to be; meanwhile life was showing him the church in its real existence. Growing recognition of the gap between the ideal as he described it and its real embodiment led him over the years to a more and more radical criticism of the existing church. But for the present, his hope was that his analysis of the nature of the church would help to provide a vision of what the church ought to be working to become.

Bonhoeffer's next book, *Act and Being,* addressed itself specifically to the subject of revelation. The question he asked was: How is revelation to be conceived? He posits the problem this way:

> There has to be a theological interpretation of what the "being of God in revelation" means and how it is known, of what may be the interrelation of belief as act and revelation as being, and correspondingly of where man stands when seen from the standpoint of revelation. Is revelation merely what is "given" to man in the performance of a certain act, or is there such a thing for him in revelation as a "being"? What form is taken by the concept of revelation if we explain it in terms of the act, and what other form if in terms of a "being?"[8]

Godsey, in his study of Bonhoeffer's theology, summarizes the problem to which Bonhoeffer is addressing himself in these words:

It should be theologically interpreted what "God's being in the revelation" means and how it is known, how faith as act and revelation as being are related and whether revelation is given to man only in the execution of an act or if there is a "being" in the revelation for him.[9]

By way of response to the question Bonhoeffer finds that certain types of theologizing about the nature of revelation describe it in terms of act; others prefer to see it in terms of being.

In the first view God is seen as having revealed himself to man in a series of distinct historical events. He made Himself present to man in a sequence of acts whereby He revealed Himself in history. Revelation is a set of divine acts in relation to man. God reveals Himself in acting. Barth would be a good example of this 'act theology.'

In the second view stress is laid on the continuity of revelation. Here man is seen not so much as the recipient of a set of revelatory acts from God; rather their existence itself (both God's and man's) is a 'being' in revelation. Accent is put on realizing the continuity both of revelation and of man, the continuity of man's possession of and being possessed by revelation. Tillich exemplified this approach to God and to revelation. His is a 'being theology.'

Bonhoeffer sees a certain value in the first kind of thinking. It preserves God's freedom. Whether there will be revelation in His choice. He is not "at man's disposal." If there is a revelation it is because He alone initiates it. But, as we have already seen, God's freedom as He Himself has revealed it is not a freedom *from* man; rather He has elected to exercise His freedom *for* man. He has chosen to enter into relationship with man. His choice is to be in a state of being revealed. Thus Bonhoeffer's own preference is for the second type of approach since he sees it as more accurately reflecting not who God is in Himself but who He is in relation to man.

When these two ways of conceiving revelation are applied to the church the question becomes: how is the church to be thought of? as a series of acts or events in history wherein again and again man responds to revelation? or is it more correct to think of the church as existing in continuity throughout history?

Bonhoeffer's answer is that in the church the value of both 'act' and 'being' thinking on revelation is bound together in a living unity. The church depends for her existence on the act of faith in her and her possession of revelation on the part of the believer. Thus her existence is in one sense contingent on a series of acts. Yet from another point of view it is clear from her history that the church has a continuity of existence. She has a being as the continuing revelation of God. Yet if one had to choose which of the two approaches to the nature of the church is to be preferred, it is clear that Bonhoeffer's choice is for the church as being.

> The Christian communion is God's final revelation: God as "Christ existing as community"; ordained for the rest of time until the end of the world and the return of Christ. It is here that Christ has come the very nearest to humanity, here given himself to his new humanity, so that his person enfolds in itself all whom he has won, binding itself in duty to them, and them reciprocally in duty to him. The "Church" therefore has not the meaning of a human community to which Christ is or is not self-superadded, nor of a union among such as individually seek or think to have Christ and wish to cultivate this common "possession"; no it is a communion created by Christ and founded upon him, one in which Christ reveals himself as ". . . the new man—or rather, the new humanity itself."[10]

The church is then a fellowship of persons. And within that fellowship the saving act of Christ, his death/resurrection is proclaimed over and over again in the act of preaching. The community bears the revelation, indeed *is* the revelation (Christ existing as community) and thus the continuing 'being' of revelation is preserved. The community also speaks and hears the revelation in each act of preaching and each conferral of the sacraments and so the 'act' of revelation is continually reenacted. The church is revelation both in being and in act.

An analysis of faith leads to the same conclusion, that it too has the characteristics of both act and being. Faith continues to be that which sustains the community in existence. And within the community faith finds, in the preaching and sacramental action, the acts which express its own being. Thus Bonhoeffer finds that the church is at one and the same time the continuous being of Christ's revelation and the place where that revelation is made manifest in acts. In her, revelation reveals itself to be both being and act.

As events in Germany became more and more critical, moving ever more ominously towards war, they produced, in Bonhoeffer, a growing disillusionment with the way in which the German Church was meeting the crisis. It was all well and good to theorize about the nature of revelation and of the church. What was now ever more desperately needed was thought and writing on the harsh demands that reality made on the church to implement her thinking in practical action. His question therefore now becomes: What are the practical implications of his thinking on revelation and on the church? How do these realities affect life as it is to be lived in the insistently critical present?

THE CONCRETENESS OF REVELATION

His next book, *The Cost of Discipleship* (1937), is a bridge book in his thinking. It moves away from the dense, abstract thinking of his earlier works and becomes more insistent on the need for an existential embodiment of thought in action. Yet for all of this it has not yet reached the radical religionlessness of his last writings.

The book addresses itself to the problem of grace, to the question: what difference ought its possession to make in a Christian's life? For too long the church has been emasculating grace of its meaning by the way she has preached it. It has become the badge of the comfortable and the self-satisfied. Once a man has accepted Christ as his Lord and Savior he has met the only demand that Christianity makes of him. He may then continue life untroubled by uncertainty about his final salvation. His confidence in Christ has solved that problem for him. So long as his faith remains strong he will be saved. Thus has Luther's principle of *sola fides* been corrupted to justify a life of self-satisfied mediocrity.

The church has corrupted the meaning of grace by converting it from a dearly bought and constantly demanding pearl of great price into a comforting guarantee of salvation without cost. She has transformed grace, which in its authentic form can only be costly, into a caricature of itself which Bonhoeffer labels "cheap grace."

> Cheap grace means grace as a doctrine, a principle, a system. It means forgiveness of sins proclaimed as a general truth, the love of God taught as the Christian "conception" of God. An intellectual assent to that idea is held to be of itself sufficient to secure remission of sins. The Church which holds the correct doctrine of grace has, it is supposed, *ipso facto,* a part in that grace. In such a Church the world finds a cheap covering for its sins; no contrition is required, still less any real desire to be delivered from sin . . . . Cheap grace means the justification of sin without the justification of the sinner. Grace alone does everything, they say, and so everything can remain as it was before.[11]

Over against this parody of grace stands the true grace, the grace that is costly.

> Costly grace is the gospel which must be *sought* again and again, the gift which must be *asked* for, the door at which a man must *knock.* Such grace is *costly* because it calls us to follow, and it is *grace* because it calls us to follow *Jesus Christ.*

It is costly because it costs a man his life, and it is grace
because it gives a man the only true life. It is costly because it
condemns sin, and grace because it justifies the sinner.[12]

Faced with this situation of a grace cheapened by the church and
inconsequential in the life of the individual Christian, Bonhoeffer calls
both back to Christian discipleship. First he paints a picture of the
demands that costly grace make on a man and then deals with how the
church must again become the place of discipleship.

GRACE AND DISCIPLESHIP

In her beginnings the church understood and paid gladly the price that
grace demanded. She gave herself to the total following of Jesus, the
discipleship that required of man his whole life in return for grace. Grace
and discipleship were seen and lived as inseparable. But as "the world was
Christianized and grace became its common property" men lost "the
realization of the costliness of grace" and only within monasticism did the
full price continue to be paid for grace. In his own good time God raised
up Martin Luther to recall once more to men's attention the two parallel
truths: (1) "The only way to follow Jesus was by living in the world,"[13]
and (2) grace costs a man his life. There is no grace without discipleship.
The church has allowed that vision to slip from her gaze. She needs now to
recover it.

The Church needs to relearn that the call to discipleship demands the
response of immediate obedience. Jesus simply says, Follow me. If
accepted, this willingness to follow produces the situation within which
faith can be given. It is at this juncture that the paradoxical quality of
faith becomes apparent. On the one hand, "only those who believe obey"
and on the other hand, "only those who obey believe."[14] It is when the
two come together and are lived that the obedient man of faith is produced.

As the Christian takes up the way of obedience he comes to learn that
discipleship means inescapably the cross. It calls for one "to be aware only
of Christ and no more of self, to see only him who goes before and no
more the road which is too hard for us."[15] The cross of discipleship, if it
is accepted, leads a man into loneliness and Christ demands this of his
followers in order that in their isolation they will come to fix their eyes
only on Him who leads. He cuts a man off from his world, from his father

and mother, wife, children and country, only that he may bring him back
to them through himself. This is true because the same Jesus who separates
us unites us in himself.

> ... The same Mediator who makes us individuals is also the
> founder of a new fellowship. He stands in the center between
> my neighbor and myself. He divides but he also unites.[16]

The long middle section of the book is devoted to developing three
characteristics of Christian ·discipleship: its extraordinariness, its hiddenness, and its distinctiveness. Extraordinariness means "living at the world's
level" but living as Jesus did and this means adopting his love as one's own.
"The cross is the differential" of that love. He loved through suffering up
to death itself. For the Christian disciple this can only mean a life of
suffering love.

Yet the exercise of love by the Christian must always be a hidden thing.
It must above all be hidden from one's self for as soon as "we want to
know our own goodness or love, it has already ceased to be love."[17]
Rather the Christian gives himself in faith to the life of the cross accepting
the paradox that such a way, the way of the cross, "is at once ... the
hidden and the visible ...." way.[18]

Lastly the disciple by the life he leads will be different, yet again he
must not avert to the difference. He simply gives himself to following
Christ, clinging to his word and letting everything else go.[19] Thus he is
distinguished from, yet not set apart from, his fellows. Rather he comes
"to them with an unconditional offer of fellowship, with the single-
mindedness of the love of Jesus."[20]

THE CHURCH, THE PLACE OF DISCIPLESHIP

The demand that grace and discipleship makes on a man is death, death
to self and life, life in Jesus and for others. But if this is the essence of
Christianity why is a church needed? Cannot a man give himself to this life
as an individual? What is there about Christian discipleship that demands a
community, a church? It is to this question that the last section of the
book addresses itself.

The key to the answer to this question lies in a proper understanding of
the Incarnation. Christ did not become *this* man only, but man. He identified Himself with mankind, or as Godsey puts it, "Thus the incarnate Son

of God existed simultaneously as himself and as humanity."[21] Bonhoeffer himself explains in these words:

> As they contemplated the miracle of the Incarnation, the early Fathers passionately contended that while it was true to say that God took human nature upon him, it was wrong to say that he chose a perfect individual man and united himself to him. God was made man, and while that means that he took upon him our entire human nature with all its infirmity, sinfulness and corruption, the whole of apostate humanity, it does not mean that he took upon him the man Jesus. Unless we draw this distinction we shall misunderstand the whole message of the gospel. The Body of Jesus Christ, in which we are taken up with the whole human race, has now become the ground of our salvation.[22]

It is because Jesus Christ bears the new humanity in his body that we cannot find communion with him except in his body. Our fellowship with him is ". . . cleaving to him bodily."[23] This solidarity of ours with Christ in his Body, which is the church (Christ-existing-as-community) is the divine answer to the basic human problem which is also a problem which exists only in solidarity. Adam, created in order that he might be in the image of God, chose his own way to become like God. And this was not *a* man, but man himself who chose. In consequence,

> . . . with the loss of the God-like nature God had given him, man had forfeited the destiny of his being, which was to be like God. In short man had ceased to be man. He must live without the ability to live.[24]

God's answer to this was to come to man in a different image. He decided "to re-create his image in man."[25] This he does by assuming the image of fallen man. Christ in his image newly revealed. The image that Christ bears, however, is not the image of God which Adam first had.

> Rather, it is the image of one who enters a world of sin and death, who takes upon himself all the sorrows of humanity, who meekly bears God's wrath and judgment against sinners, and obeys his will with unswerving devotion in suffering and death, the Man born to poverty, the friend of publicans and sinners, the Man of sorrows, rejected of man and forsaken of God. Here is God made man, here is man in the new image of God.[26]

It is to this image, the "image of his shame," that we must be conformed before we can come to the possession of "the image of his glory." Our union with Christ in his Body allows us to enter this conformity with him. At the same time our communion with him delivers us "from that individualism which is the consequence of sin," and restores us to "solidarity with the whole human race" because "by being partakers of Christ incarnate, we are partakers in the whole humanity which he bore."[27]

Thus does Bonhoeffer see that the cost of discipleship which is union with Christ in his suffering love is the only price that can buy for men the restoration of their solidarity one with another. It is to the paying of this price that the church must once again learn to give herself.

With Bonhoeffer's last two books, *Ethics* and *Letters and Papers From Prison* (both published posthumously), we come to the final period of his life. These are the years of prison and death and the urgency of these experiences is mirrored in the subject matter of these books. Gone are the lofty theological discussions of his former writings. He has come, under the harsh realities of his life, to see that the church, if it is to survive, must come to grips with the agonizing day-by-day problems with which life presents every man. Urgency then is the first note of this period of his life and writing. The second note is harder to see but it is there under the surface. There is an optimism, a conviction always sustaining him, that his beloved church will finally learn her role in the new world coming to birth. Those who see Bonhoeffer writing off the church misread him. He is hard on her, brutally harsh in his criticism, but it is a cruelty which is always aware that the church's pathway must always be, as her Lord's is, through suffering and death. He wants her to suffer and die to all her old forms and ways of living but he wants this precisely that thereby she may be born again to serve the newborn world.

ETHICS

The *Ethics* is unfinished and fragmentary, sometimes difficult in its abstractness, yet like the grinder's sharpening wheel it throws off a series of brilliant sparks which light up his thought and illumine the direction in which it is moving. Rather than a book of a single, coherent argument it is a series of essays all bearing on the problem of what responsible and free Christian life means.

Bonhoeffer believes that we are beyond the day when men are liable to accept a theoretical ethical system. "Ethical fanaticism" too has collapsed, the view of the man who thinks he ". . . can oppose the power of evil with the purity of his will and of his principle."[28]

Today the man who wants to form and follow his conscience finds that he ". . . fights a lonely battle against the overwhelming forces of inescapable situations which demand decisions."[29] Two kinds of response tend to characterize modern man's answer to this situation. There is the man of duty. He does what he is commanded to do. But such a choice means a man loses the ability to place ". . . the deed which is done on one's own free responsibility, the only kind of deed which can strike at the heart of evil and overcome it."[30] Eichmann's plea at his trial that he did only his duty is the extreme example of where this choice can lead one. There are others whose choice is "private virtuousness." This one settles for an individual moral life. Beyond that he will not become involved. Such a one comes sooner or later to realize that this course does not free him from the disquiet he feels for failing to act responsibly in the world. He ends up in either self-destruction or phariseeism.

Faced with the multiplicity and complexity of today's ethical problems "reason, moral fanaticism, conscience, duty, free responsibility and silent virtue . . . ."[31] are reduced to the level of Don Quixote's weapons. They are powerless faced with today's world. Our rusty swords need replacement; we need a new ethical stance.

Bonhoeffer's suggestion is the man armed with wisdom and simplicity. The simple man fixed his gaze solely on God, hearing each day His commandments, His judgments and His mercies. He knows himself "not fettered by principles but bound by love for God . . . ."[32] And it is this simple man who is also wise. He ". . . sees reality in God."[33] He acquires the ". . . best possible knowledge about events . . . "[34] while at the same time realizes that "reality is not built upon principles but that it rests upon the living and creating God."[35] It is God he finds in all reality; it is on Him he relies and His will he follows.

This wise and simple man knows there is one place where God and His world are brought together in harmonious unity, one place where the world is used as God would have it used and that place is the person of Jesus Christ. To this person he gives himself in faith; in Christ he seeks the formation of his moral self. Bonhoeffer finds this moral formation to have three components. It is a conformation to Christ incarnate, crucified and risen.

Christ's incarnation he sees as an affirmation by God of the worthwhileness of the real world. He comes to realize that it must be as true of himself as it was of Christ that

God secures His love against any suggestion that it is not
genuine or that it is doubtful or uncertain, for He himself
enters into the life of man as man and takes upon Himself and
carries in the flesh the nature, the character, and the guilt and
suffering of man.[36]

The Christian is formed also in the likeness of the Crucified and so he
learns to die each day the death of the sinner, bearing the marks of the
wounds which sin inflicts on him. What suffering comes he bears willingly
knowing that thereby he is enabled to die to his own will that he may live
as Christ lives. Finally, he is conformed, too, to the Risen One and so "in
the midst of death he is in life."[37] He knows and lives in the knowledge
that in putting on the form of Christ he both confronts the world and
defeats it.

The church plays an indispensable part in this formation of man into
Christ because the church is not merely ". . . a religious community of
worshippers of Christ but is Christ Himself who has taken form among
men."[38] Thus it is much too narrow a view of the church to see her as
concerned only ". . . with the so-called religious functions of man . . ."[39]
Her concern is rather ". . . with the whole man in his existence in the
world with all its implications."[40] "What matters in the church is not
religion but the form of Christ, and its taking form amidst a band of
men."[41]

In the church, conformed to Christ, this form of Christ is the Christian's fundamental moral stance. How does the Christian proceed to
implement this posture, to reduce it to a concrete principle of life? As
Bonhoeffer sees it he begins by recognizing that Christ was not a theoreti-
cian of what is good; He was a practitioner of love. He affirmed reality,
things as they are, and it was with these that he dealt. The Christian should
then not speak about an ethical system, an ". . . attempt to define that
which is good once and for all. . ."[42] He needs rather to give himself as
Christ did to "the 'among us,' the 'now,' and 'here.' . . ."[43] He needs to
recognize that the form of Christ will take shape in him and must shape his
life ". . . in a manner which is neither abstract nor casuistic, neither pro-
grammatic nor purely speculative."[44] Life for him will mean "concrete
judgments and decisions . . . to be ventured here."[45]

Bonhoeffer is, however, quite aware of the danger of complete subjectivism in moral conduct which is attached to the view just presented. He
goes on to make it clear that morality always has an objective dimension.
One always lives his life in a context and that context determines in large
part the ways in which he will act and react.

... By our history we are set objectively in a definite nexus of experiences, responsibilities and decisions from which we cannot free ourselves again except by an abstraction.[46]

For the true Christian the only truly ethical question is: what is the will of God? Unfortunately the development of Western thought has brought man to a situation where he finds it difficult to find that will. The development has left him with the problem of "thinking in terms of two spheres." It has taught him to distinguish supernatural from natural, sacred from profane. In consequence when he sets out to discover the will of God he is unsure in which of these domains he is to find it and if he looks for it in both he often encounters a conflict between them. Thus

... he abandons reality as a whole and places himself in one or other of the two spheres. He seeks Christ without the world, or he seeks the world without Christ. In either case he is deceiving himself. Or else he tries to stand in both spaces at once and thereby becomes the man of eternal conflict. ...[47]

Bonhoeffer points out that such a view contradicts the view of Scripture which has always known only one reality "... and that is the reality of God, which has become manifest in Christ in the reality of the world."[48] The reality of Christ comprises the reality of the world within itself. In Christ the world is found to have its beginning, its end and its meaning. He created it; it becomes what it is meant to be; it will find its final fulfillment in Him. And thus it is that by "sharing in Christ we stand at once in both the reality of God and the reality of the world."[49] It will be in seeking what Christ would seek that one finds the unity of natural and supernatural.

Returning once again to the sole ethical norm: what is the will of God, Bonhoeffer concludes that it is "nothing other than the becoming real of the reality of Christ with us and in our world."[50]

To clarify further the way in which the Christian life is to be lived, Bonhoeffer introduces the distinction between the last things and the penultimate (things before last) things. The ultimate thing is justification, God's saving of us in Christ. Yet before a man reaches that stage there is much that must first be gone through. These are the penultimate things. The penultimate, which is everything that precedes the justification of the sinner by grace alone, must be taken seriously simply on account of its relation to the ultimate.

In an attempt to grapple with the problem of salvation, Bonhoeffer finds, men tend to choose one of two solutions. There is the radical solution which sees only the ultimate, justification in Christ by grace and faith, as worthwhile. To the attainment of that end all else is sacrificed. In the light of the justice to be attained "everything penultimate in human behaviour is sin and denial."[51] This solution is in effect a total rejection of all things human. It is God alone and reaching Him that matters.

Equally extreme is the position of compromise. In this view the penultimate (perhaps one might say "the things of this world") retains its own right.

> . . . there are still penultimate things which must be done, in fulfillment of the responsibility for this world which God has created. Account must still be taken of men as they are. The ultimate remains totally on the far side of the everyday . . . .[52]

In rejecting both efforts to solve the problem of salvation and of the nature of Christian life, Bonhoeffer reverts yet again to his basic position on the nature of morality. The Christian life means to be conformed to Christ, to the whole Christ. One cannot, therefore, construct a Christian ethic solely on the basis of the Incarnation; nor solely on the basis of the cross or the resurrection. Christ is not any one of these. He is all three: incarnate, dead, and risen. And it is only in the unity of this total view of him that conflict is resolved.

A certain measure of our faith and of our conformity to Christ is in the Incarnation. In that event we learn, and we learn to share, the love of God for His creation. We also believe in and are conformed to the crucified Christ and there ". . . we learn of the judgement of God upon all flesh . . ." We believe finally in the resurrection and in our conformity to Christ risen ". . . we learn of God's will for a new world."[53]

For the Christian then, neither radicalism nor compromise are the solution to life. The Christian life means rather

> . . . being a man through the efficacy of the incarnation; it means being sentenced and pardoned through the efficacy of the cross; and it means living a new life through the efficacy of the resurrection. There cannot be one of these without the rest.[54]

Taking the penultimate seriously means, for Bonhoeffer, two things, being man and being good. In his perspective these things do not of themselves have ultimate value; a man gives himself to them in order that thereby he may prepare the way for the Word. For all of their lack of ultimate significance, however, being a man and being good must always be seen as having an intrinsic value in themselves and a man must always give himself to them with utmost seriousness.

Being a man and being good is not merely an inward process, a turning in on oneself to be sure that one has done all necessary to prepare oneself for the coming of the Lord. "It is [also] a formative activity on the very greatest visible scale."[55] This means a man must be dedicated also to producing the conditions which will allow other men to be men and to be good. One needs to see that taking the "next to last things" earnestly is a "charge of immense responsibility."

> The hungry man needs bread and the homeless man needs a roof; the dispossessed need justice and the lonely need fellowship; the undisciplined need order and the slave needs freedom.[56]

And if the hungry, homeless, dispossessed, lonely, undisciplined, and enslaved do not come to faith then the guilt falls on those who have not met their needs.

The one who takes the penultimate seriously comes to understand that "to provide the hungry man with bread is to prepare the way for the coming of grace."[57] But once again Bonhoeffer sounds the warning that the penultimate always looks to the ultimate. A man is helped to become a man so that having achieved this he may be laid open to the coming of God's grace. ". . . Ultimately it is not indeed a question of the reform of earthly conditions, but it is a question of the coming of Christ."[58]

The responsible Christian, aware of the importance of the penultimate and its relation to the ultimate, will come to conceive of his life in two basic categories: deputyship and responsibility. Deputyship will mean that one sees his life as necessarily modelled on Christ's life; hence it will involve the ". . . complete surrender of one's own life to the other man."[59] In the exercise of that selflessness the Christian relates to ". . . the man who is concretely his neighbor in his concrete possibility."[60]

In every concrete situation of relationship with his neighbor he does as Christ did, he sees ". . . what is necessary and what is 'right' for him to grasp and to do."[61] In so acting one observes, weighs up, assesses, and decides what the situation calls for. The future consequences of one's action, the motivation in one's heart, are also considered. And thus one is prepared ". . . to do what is necessary at the given place and with a due consideration of reality."[62] Having done all of this, having made one's choice and having acted, one is prepared to remain ultimately ignorant of one's own good and evil; to remain completely reliant upon grace. This is "responsible historical action."

Bonhoeffer calls responsibility the way in which we live our life of 'yes' and 'no.' Creation, atonement and redemption are the 'yes' of life. Condemnation and death are its 'no.' Or to put it another way, we are to say 'yes' to creation and redemption in life and 'no' to sin and death. It is in Christ that we learn the 'yes' and 'no' saying of life. For in him

> ... is the 'yes' to what is created, to becoming and to growth, to the flower and to the fruit, to health, happiness, ability, achievement, worth, success, greatness and honour. . . .[63]

In Him we recognize too that "... 'no' means dying, suffering, poverty, renunciation, resignation, humility, degradation, self-denial. . . ."[64]

Saying 'yes' and 'no' to life as Christ did means that, for the Christian, life must be lived in responsible freedom. This will imply that

> the responsible man acts in the freedom of his own self without the support of men, circumstances or principles, but with a due consideration for the given human and general conditions, and for the relevant questions of principle. The proof of his freedom is the fact that nothing can answer for him, nothing can exonerate him, except his own deed and his own self. It is he himself who must observe, judge, weigh up, decide and act. It is man himself who must examine the motives, the prospects, the value and the purpose of his action. But neither the purity of the motivation, nor the opportune circumstances, nor the value, nor the significant purpose of an intended undertaking can become the governing law of his action, a law to which he can withdraw, to which he can appeal as an authority, and by which he can be exculpated and acquitted. For in that case he would indeed no longer be truly free. The action of the responsible man is performed in the obligation which alone gives freedom and which gives entire freedom, the obligation to God and to our neighbor as they confront us in Jesus Christ.[65]

And finally the Christian man is able to recognize that in every choice he makes there is a compound of freedom and of obedience as was true in Christ's life. He perceives that his selfless service to others is at once "... a blind compliance with the law which is commanded by him [by God]. . . ."[66] and an acquiescence "... in God's will out of his own most personal knowledge, with open eyes and a joyous heart . . . ."[67] He accepts gladly the paradox that "obedience without freedom is slavery; freedom without obedience is arbitrary self-will."[68]

Thus does Bonhoeffer conclude his portrait of the Christian moral life. The key to this life is Jesus and the Christian's conformity to Him. The heart of it is the taking seriously of the penultimate while never losing sight of its essential relation to the ultimate. One lives that life in responsible deputyship, with eyes always fixed on Christ, incarnate, dead and risen, the source and goal of all Christian life.

LETTERS AND PAPERS FROM PRISON

In his last book, *Letters and Papers from Prison,* Bonhoeffer takes up again his perennial themes, who is Christ and what is the church. This time, however, his treatment of them is far more radical than heretofore. The problem he is wrestling with first occurs in his letter of April 30, 1944. It becomes immediately clear that he is questioning the very possibility of the continuing existence of Christianity.

> The thing that keeps coming back to me is, what is Christianity, and indeed what is Christ, for us today? The time when men could be told everything by means of words, whether theological or simply pious, is over, and so is the time of inwardness and conscience, which is to say the time of religion as such. We are proceeding towards a time of no religion at all; men as they are now simply cannot be religious any more . . . . What does that mean for "Christianity"?[69]

Subsequent letters explore the reasons why he is so pessimistic about the future of Christianity. Basically his reasons are three: The traditional view of God is no longer an acceptable one; men are no longer interested in an other-worldly salvation; the church misconceives her role in the contemporary world. To meet the crisis he attempts to work out a view of God meaningful to men today, a this-world centered view of salvation and a church willing to adjust to a "religionless Christianity."

The Problem of God

Since the thirteenth century the men of the West have been gradually losing their belief in the traditional God of Christianity, learning how to get along without him. They have been "coming of age," reaching maturity. By now that process is virtually complete. Meanwhile the church in her attempts to deal with the problem has made two fundamental mistakes. She has first of all provided much too abstract a notion of God, stressing that He is the totally Other, the absolutely Transcendent, to be reached mainly by metaphysical speculation. Man's relation to God has been thought of as ". . . a religious relationship to a Supreme Being, absolute in power and goodness. . . ."[70] The church's other mistake has been to encourage men to think of God as a problem solver. He is the solution to death, suffering, pain, evil, sin, those areas of human life for whose meaning man does not have an explanation of his own.

It is now becoming apparent how serious these mistakes have been. Men now realize that if God is to make a difference in life He must be more than a concept, or a Supreme Being. He must somehow be a real experience in the midst of life. If He exists in a world apart, He is no longer of any significance. This world is all-absorbing.

The view of God as problem solver is equally doomed to extinction and that for a quite simple reason. Man is gradually learning to solve more and more of his problems for himself. Fewer and fewer questions remain to be answered by God; less and less is He needed. He will finally be edged out of the world.

> Religious people speak of God when human perception is [often just from laziness] at an end, or human resources fail: it is really always the *Deus ex machina* they call to their aid, either for the so-called solving of insoluble problems or as support in human failure—always, that is to say, helping out human weakness or on the borders of human existence. Of necessity, that can only go on until men can, by their own strength, push those borders a little further, so that God becomes superfluous as a *Deus ex machina*. I have come to be doubtful even about talking of "borders of human existence." Is even death today, since men are scarcely afraid of it any more, and sin, which they scarcely understand any more, still a genuine borderline? It always seems to me that in talking thus we are only seeking frantically to make room for God.[71]

To repair these past mistakes we need to refashion our thinking about God and the manner of our relating to him. The first step is to acknowledge that man has "come of age" and needs to be treated as such. The church must learn to accept the adulthood of man, to see him as capable of living his own life and solving his own problems. It is wrong to go on trying to keep man in tutelage to God; it is a mistake to try to save a place for God in the boundary situations of life.

The attack by Christian apologetic upon the adulthood of the world I consider to be in the first place pointless, in the second ignoble, and in the third un-Christian. Pointless, because it looks to me like an attempt to put a grown-up man back into adolescence, i.e. to make him dependent on things on which he is not in fact dependent any more, thrusting him back into the midst of problems which are in fact not problems for him any more. Ignoble, because this amounts to an effort to exploit the weakness of man for purposes alien to him and not freely subscribed to by him. Un-Christian, because for Christ himself is being substituted one particular stage in the religiousness of man, i.e. a human law.[72]

The next step is to ask and answer the question: Where then does God fit into human life? There are several elements in Bonhoeffer's answer. The first element is his conviction that God ought to be put at the center of life not at its borders.

I should like to speak of God not on the borders of life, but at its centre, not in weakness but in strength, not therefore, in man's suffering and death but in his life and prosperity. On the borders it seems to me better to hold our peace and leave the problem unsolved.[73]

. . . He must be found at the centre of life: in life and not only in death; in health and vigour, and not only in suffering; in activity, and not only in sin. The ground for this lies in the revelation of God in Christ. Christ is the centre of life, and in no sense did he come to answer our unsolved problems. From the centre of life certain questions are seen to be wholly irrelevant, and so are the answers commonly given to them. . . .[74]

The Problem of Salvation

The second element in Bonhoeffer's vision of a contemporary Christianity is to recognize that if God is to be put at the center of life we need also to review our understanding of what salvation means. For too long Christianity has defined salvation in other-worldly terms. Our ultimate fulfillment lies beyond this world; salvation is a process which will finally save us from this world and bring us to God. Such a view sees God as beyond the here and now, as an end to be achieved elsewhere. But it is precisely this God that contemporary man cannot accept. He is totally committed to this world, to living in it, to building it, to enjoying its happiness. The transcendent is neither thinkable nor desirable; thus neither is God.

But there is a view of salvation which speaks to man in a this-worldly framework. It is the Old Testament view which sees redemption and salvation as to be attained in this world and God as a God who leads man through the events in his history to a "... redemption on this side of death. ... Israel is redeemed out of Egypt in order to live before God on earth."[75]

It is this view that the church needs to recover. She must learn that the real focus of Christian hope is not on the life that lies "... upon the far side of the boundary drawn by death."[76] Christians ought to be weaned from looking for "... a last refuge in the eternal from earthly tasks and difficulties."[77] Christian hope from this perspective is the realization that when one comes to faith in Jesus Christ he is then given the life of otherness that is the life of Jesus. In the power of that life he returns to earthly tasks and worldly goals, to community with other men in the building of their world. Thus "Christ takes hold of a man in the centre of his life."[78] Thus does He give him hope for the future of man in this life.

If salvation is so conceived it makes a radical difference in our view of God. No longer is He the totally Other, the absolutely Transcendent. Now in Christ and in the Christian's life of otherness in Christ, He becomes the "beyond in our midst." God in Christ is present in human relations and worldly tasks, in achievement and failure, in joy, happiness and suffering. Thus does it become true that "the transcendent is not infinitely remote, but close at hand,"[79] findable and haveable in the midst of human life.

The love of God that such a relation with Him produces also takes on a new dimension. Like the central theme or melody of a symphony God remains the *cantus firmus* in our life. "... God requires that we should love him eternally with our whole hearts ...."[80] Nevertheless, when the Christian puts on Christ's life of otherness he enters into a life where other loves and other melodies share place with his love of God. Indeed, "earthly affections" developed to the utmost of their limits provide the counterpoint for the love of God.

One last element enters into the vision of God and salvation that Bonhoeffer is building for his contemporaries. It strikes a paradoxical note in comparison with what he has said thus far. The God who can mean most to us is a suffering God. Faced with the enormities of life's demands and his own inadequacies to meet those demands a man may well lose heart. It is in this situation that he needs to make his own the final Christian paradox: God is strongest where He is most weak.

God allows himself to be edged out of the world and on to the cross. God is weak and powerless in the world, and that is exactly the way, the only way, in which he can be with us and help us. Matthew 8:17 makes it crystal-clear that it is not by his omnipotence that Christ helps us, but by his weakness and suffering . . . . The Bible, however, directs him to the powerlessness and suffering of God; only a suffering God can help. To this extent we may say that the process we have described by which the world came of age was an abandonment of a false conception of God, and a clearing of the decks for the God of the Bible, who conquers power and space in the world by his weakness. This must be the starting point for our "worldly" interpretation.[81]

The Problem of the Church

What is the church's role in the face of man's new vision of himself? She needs to recognize how badly she has corrupted the idea of religion. Then she needs to accept with equanimity (indeed Bonhoeffer seems to suggest that she should contribute enthusiastically to it) the advent of "religionless Christianity." Religion as the church has spoken of it and as traditionally practiced has been directed to the individual and he has been in consequence almost exclusively concerned with his own salvation and the development of his own personal prayer life. As a result the needs of the neighbor are forgotten, the problems of the world avoided. Religion in its traditional garb has also tended to be other-worldly, focusing the religious man's attention far more on the attainment of salvation in another world than on involvement in and concern for this world.

The church as the locus of religion has fought too for her position in the world, a segment of life reserved for her, a place to call her own. She has fought for self-preservation and forgotten that she is ". . . her true self only when she exists for humanity."[82] Last of all religion has preyed on man in his weakness. She has tried to keep a place for herself in men's lives where they feel most need. She has fought man's maturity.

Efforts are made to prove to a world thus come of age that it cannot live without the tutelage of 'God.' Even though there has been surrender on all secular problems, there still remains the so-called ultimate questions—death, guilt—on which only 'God' can furnish an answer, and which are the reason why God and the Church and the pastor are needed. Thus we live, to some extent, by these ultimate questions of humanity. But what if one day they no longer exist as such, if they too can be answered without 'God'?[83]

This is religion as Bonhoeffer sees it presently lived in the church and it is this he sees must be replaced by a "religionless Christianity." What he sees coming will be Christianity because Jesus as the man for others will be its focal point—and God as the beyond in our midst will be at its heart. But it will be religionless. This Christianity will replace religion's individualism with community and concern for others. For the metaphysical God in the heavens it will substitute God for the center of life. An otherworldly salvation will yield to redemption sought for, worked toward in this world. And it will be for the man of strength, not of weakness, of achievement not of failure. Yet this same man will find identity in his own experience with the God of weakness and suffering.

Thus in the end it turns out that the vision of "religionless Christianity," which is the heart of Bonhoeffer's thought in his *Letters and Papers,* is a challenge to the church to be what Christ is, one who lives for the selfless service of others. No more fitting conclusion to a study of Bonhoeffer can be found than a citation from the book he was planning to write on the future of Christianity. It is a passage that may well be the last words he had to say to his beloved church. In it he summarizes the work of his lifetime, his final answer to his two questions: What is the church and who is Christ?

> The church is her true self only when she exists for humanity. As a fresh start she should give away all her endowments to the poor and needy. The clergy should live solely on the freewill offerings of their congregations, or possibly engage in some secular calling. She must take her part in the social life of the world, not lording it over men, but helping and serving them. She must tell men, whatever their calling, what it means to live in Christ, to exist for others. And in particular, our own church will have to take a strong line with the blasphemies of *hybris,* power-worship, envy and humbug, for these are the roots of evil. She will have to speak of moderation, purity, confidence, loyalty, steadfastness, patience, discipline, humility, content and modesty. She must not underestimate the importance of human example, which has its origin in the humanity of Jesus, and which is so important in the teaching of St. Paul. It is not abstract argument, but concrete example which gives her word emphasis and power.[84]

CONCLUSION

Any definitive evaluation of Bonhoeffer attempted at present would be premature for two reasons. First of all, his work is only just beginning to be known and studied by Christian theologians. Sufficient time has not yet elapsed for them to assess adequately the impact which his work will ultimately have on the future of Christian thought. Secondly, the most influential portion of his thinking has been his last writings, the *Ethics* and the *Letters and Papers from Prison.* Both of these are only fragmentary and tantalizingly general statements of his thought. His "religionless Christianity," "man come of age," "Jesus as the man for others," will need a good deal more study and development by those who come after him before their real significance and impact can be judged.

Certainly, one thing is clear, Bonhoeffer was perhaps the first to see with complete clarity the almost total separation of religion from life in contemporary society. Joined to that insight was his other radical conviction that Christianity could not heal that separation in any of its traditional forms or any of its traditional ways of speaking about God or Christ or church.

Out of that double insight was born his major contribution and his chief appeal to present Christian thinkers. Any attempt to speak of what religion or Christianity means must begin with the world as it presently exists in all its concreteness and all its immediacy. An affirmation, hopeful yet clear-sighted, of man in his strength, his freedom, his technological mastery of nature and his own life, is the only possible base for the present and future survival of Christianity. It will survive, he was convinced, only if it accepts the death of the civilization and culture which has supported it for many centuries. Acceptance of the secular as the only viable form of human society is the only alternative to death for the Christian churches.

It is this fundamental conviction of Bonhoeffer's that would seem to guarantee the continuing impact of his thought. He accepted the radical transformation of society over the past few centuries as the fact that it is, and saw that Christianity must learn to live in, endorse, and serve this culture or die. In this sense his thought will be seminal for many years to come.

FOOTNOTES

1 From *The Theology of Dietrich Bonhoeffer,* by John D. Godsey. The Westminster Press. W.L. Jenkins, 1960, p. 279. Used by permission.

2 Dietrich Bonhoeffer, *The Cost of Discipleship,* paperback ed. (New York: The Macmillan Company, 1963), p. 99. Reprinted with permission of The Macmillan Company. Copyright 1955 by The MacMillan Company.

3Godsey, *The Theology of Dietrich Bonhoeffer,* pp. 264-5.

4Bonhoeffer, *Act and Being,* trans. Bernard Noble (New York & Evanston: Harper & Row, 1961), pp. 90-91.

5——*The Communion of Saints,* trans. H. Gregor Smith (New York & Evanston: Harper & Row, 1963), p. 106.

6*Ibid.*

7The phrase is used by William Kuhns, *In Pursuit of Dietrich Bonhoeffer* (Dayton, Ohio: Pflaum, 1967), p. 20.

8Bonhoeffer, *Act and Being,* p. 12.

9Godsey, *The Theology of Dietrich Bonhoeffer,* p. 55.

10Bonhoeffer, *Act and Being,* p. 121.

11——*The Cost of Discipleship,* pp. 45-46.

12*Ibid.,* pp. 47-48.

13*Ibid.,* p. 51.

14*Ibid.,* p. 74.

15*Ibid.,* p. 97.

16*Ibid.,* p. 112.

17*Ibid.,* p. 177.

18*Ibid.,* p. 176.

19*Ibid.,* p. 217.

20*Ibid.,* p. 204.

21*Godsey, The Theology of Dietrich Bonhoeffer,* p. 167.

22Bonhoeffer, *The Cost of Discipleship,* pp. 264-5.

23*Ibid.,* p. 266.

24*Ibid.,* p. 338.

25*Ibid.,* p. 339.

26*Ibid.,* p. 340.

27*Ibid.,* p. 341.

28Bonhoeffer, *Ethics,* trans. N. H. Smith, ed. Bethge, Paperback ed. (New York: The MacMillan Co., 1965), p. 66. Reprinted with permission of The Macmillan Company. Copyright 1955 by The Macmillan Company.

29*Ibid.,* p. 66.

30*Ibid.,* p. 66-67.

31*Ibid.,* p. 67.

32*Ibid.,* p. 68.

33*Ibid.*

34*Ibid.,* p. 69.

35*Ibid.*

36*Ibid.,* p. 72.

[37]*Ibid.*, p. 82.

[38]*Ibid.*, p. 83.

[39]*Ibid.*

[40]*Ibid.*, p. 84.

[41]*Ibid.*

[42]*Ibid.*, p. 85.

[43]*Ibid.*, pp. 86-7.

[44]*Ibid.*, p. 88.

[45]*Ibid.*

[46]*Ibid.*, p. 87.

[47]*Ibid.*, p. 197.

[48]*Ibid.*

[49]*Ibid.*

[50]*Ibid.*, p. 212.

[51]*Ibid.*, p. 127.

[52]*Ibid.*

[53]*Ibid.*, pp. 130-31.

[54]*Ibid.*, p. 133.

[55]*Ibid.*, p. 135.

[56]*Ibid.*, p. 137.

[57]*Ibid.*

[58]*Ibid.*, p. 138.

[59]*Ibid.*, p. 225.

[60]*Ibid.*, p. 227.

[61]*Ibid.*

[62]*Ibid.*, p. 233.

[63]*Ibid.*, p. 219.

[64]*Ibid.*

[65]*Ibid.*, pp. 248-49.

[66]*Ibid.*, p. 252.

[67]*Ibid.*

[68]*Ibid.*

[69]Bonhoeffer, *Letters and Papers from Prison,* trans. Reginald H. Fuller, ed. Eberhard Bethge, paperback ed. (New York: The Macmillan Co., 1965), pp. 162-63. Reprinted with permission of The Macmillan Company. Copyright 1953 by The Macmillan Company. ©1967 by SCM Press, Ltd.

[70]*Ibid.*, pp. 237-38.

[71]*Ibid.*, p. 165.

[72]*Ibid.*, pp. 196-97.

73*Ibid.*, pp. 165-66.

74*Ibid.*, p. 191.

75*Ibid.*, p. 205.

76*Ibid.*

77*Ibid.*

78Bonhoeffer, *Letters and Papers*, p. 206.

79*Ibid.*, p. 233.

80*Ibid.*, p. 175.

81*Ibid.*, pp. 219-20.

82*Ibid.*, p. 239.

83*Ibid.*, p. 195-96.

84*Ibid.*, pp. 239-40.

CHAPTER TEN

Rudolf Bultmann

The name of Rudolf Bultmann (*n.* 1884) dominated the theological scene in Europe during the period following Barth's ascendency and prior to the rise of Bonhoeffer's influence. He replaced Barth and was in turn replaced by Bonhoeffer in center stage. Where Barth's attention was fixed on the total otherness of God and the complete impossibility of man's knowing anything about Him unless God decides to reveal Himself, and as Bonhoeffer gave himself to exploring the concrete implications of that revelation for the man of today, Bultmann's focus was on the revelation itself, or more precisely on the vehicle of that revelation, the Scriptures. Bultmann's concern is the development of a manner of interpreting the Scriptures which will make its message comprehensible and meaningful to the modern world. As John Macquarrie puts it in one of his studies of Bultmann,

> ... the main theological interest in Bultmann lies in his attempt to interpret Christianity in such a way that one can be radically skeptical about the factual content of the gospel narrative and yet continue to believe in the essential message of the New Testament. Indeed, Bultmann would go further, maintaining that if the essential Christian message is to gain a hearing in the contemporary world, it must be disengaged from the form in which it is presented in the New Testament.[1]

Bultmann is convinced that the thought patterns which the biblical writers used to convey the message of revelation to their contemporaries are patterns which no longer make sense to Western man. If the Scriptures are to become contemporaneously intelligible then a double task is set for today's biblical scholars. First, the essential message of revelation, what God had to say to man, has to be disengaged from the thought patterns in which that message was first given. Then it needs to be clothed in twentieth century thought patterns and thereby rendered understandable to the men of this time.

The encounter which produces the possibility of Christian belief is always between God speaking and man hearing and answering 'yes'. Therefore the speech of God and the hearing of man must be brought into meaningful contact before faith can occur. Bultmann, in consequence, asks, first of all: Who is man today and how does he conceive of himself? Where does he stand; what situation is he in?

As his tool for answering these questions he chooses existential philosophy and in particular the existential philosophy of Martin Heidegger. He makes this choice because he feels that this is the type of philosophizing which most clearly analyzes the existence of man in his world and most nearly approaches satisfactory answers to the questions that man today asks about himself. It is to man in this situation that the Word of God must now speak.

With this task done Bultmann turns to the other half of his problem, God speaking. When He spoke to the men of the first century He spoke to them as they were situated, within the cultural framework in which they lived. What He wanted to say was embedded in their thought patterns. He accepted their world-view and spoke to them within it. The scholar needs, therefore, to understand the first century situation and its view of reality. Then he must search out and disengage from the Scripture, its vehicle of communication, the Word that God was speaking. What was said needs to be distinguished from how it was said. This process of disentanglement Bultmann calls "demythologizing."

With both these tasks accomplished Bultmann then turns to putting together again the Word of God and the hearing of man. Using existential categories he garbs the essential message of God in contemporary thought patterns. In the light of these remarks about Bultmann's method, what follows will discuss his thought in terms of these three aspects: the contemporary situation of man; the disengagement of the Word of God from its original thought patterns; and; the recasting of that Word in meaningful present day terms.

THE CONTEMPORARY SITUATION OF MAN

As Bultmann, following Heidegger, analyzes present day man, he sees him as both existing, and understanding that he exists, in a world where he is confronted with a variety of possibilities, a choice of ways to live out his life. The two most basic choices for living that face him are authentic or inauthentic existence. In authentic existence man chooses the fullest possible development of himself and all his potentialities whereas inauthentic existence means the choice of turning himself over to the world of things and the collective mass of men to be shaped and fashioned by them.

In Heidegger's view most men in the modern world make the second choice, the surrender of responsibility for one's individuality. It is by far the easier choice and the majority of men settle for it. It is simpler to become one of the collective, depersonalized mass, to consent to its way of life and settle for its values. Far harder is the choice of self-determination. Here a man takes full responsibility for shaping his own life, for choosing his own set of possibilities for living.

These are man's two possible choices for his life and he cannot avoid choosing one of them. Even the decision not to choose between them is a settling for inauthentic existence, a giving of oneself to life as it happens. One must choose either to shape his own life or let himself be shaped by other people and things.

The choice is not a single, once-for-all decision. Life is rather characterized by a constant necessity of choosing between authentic and inauthentic existence. ". . . Each 'now' is the moment of free decision. . . ."[2] And that insistent need for choice is what gives life its chief characteristic—anxiety. Man in his existence is always faced with being and making himself or being made by the world of things.

> For him (Heidegger) the chief characteristic of man's Being in history is anxiety. Man exists in a permanent tension between the past and the future. At every moment he is confronted with an alternative. Either he must immerse himself in the concrete world of nature, and thus inevitably lose his individuality, or he must abandon all security and commit himself unreservedly to the future, and thus alone achieve his authentic Being.[3]

If man makes the choice of inauthentic existence as his way of allaying the anxiety he feels about his existence, then he gives himself to the world, to an exclusive concern with things. His life becomes a quest for security by the acquisition and mastery of things. Yet the harder he struggles the more surely he falls under their domination. Seeking freedom he ends up in slavery. Things become the be-all and the end-all of his life, in a word, his master. In his refusal to see that it is his distinction from things that constitutes his self, he surrenders that distinct selfhood in a continually growing attachment to things. Thus does he become alienated from his true self.

This inauthentic being-in-the-world has its counterpart in an equally inauthentic life of relation with other men (being-with-others). This way of living, like the one just described, is the turning oneself over to the other; in this case to other men, to the collectivity. Here one identifies with our depersonalized society, ceases to accept personal responsibility for one's own existence and submits to being shaped by the group in all matters of decision, of value, of taste. Thus does an individual abdicate himself; thus does he become mediocre, just like everyone else. Thus does he escape the awful sense of insecurity that forever plagues him. He looks to others to give him security, but all they can do is prevent him from becoming himself.

Suppose, on the other hand, that a man, recognizing the two choices open to him, decides for authentic existence. What would this mean and how would he proceed to implement this choice in his life? Here it should be noted that for Heidegger, man is of himself able to implement his choice for authentic existence once he has made it. Bultmann, on the other hand, would hold that man is radically fallen and not able of himself to achieve authentic existence. For this he needs God's help.

The decision for authentic existence is a decision for freedom and that in several senses. It is first a decision for freedom from the world, from the slavery to things and from the tyranny of the collectivity. One decides to take full responsibility for making oneself. He opts for developing his own possibilities for being, rather than letting the other determine what possibilities for living he may actualize. He chooses detachment from the world that he may find his true self for himself.

It is, secondly, a decision for the future and thereby a decision to be free of the past and the slavery to which it has subjected one. The choice is made to give up the past's guilt and failure, and its alienation from the true self in subjection to the other. It means to commit oneself to responsibility for one's future. It is a refusal to accept the determination of the course of one's life by another, no matter what the past might have been. Bultmann is, of course, aware that there is a necessary and inevitable dependence upon the world; yet he believes that there is beyond this an essential self-determination that characterizes authentic existence. He describes the combination this way:

> Although biology and psychology recognize that man is a
> highly dependent being, that does not mean that he has been

handed over to powers outside of and distinct from himself. This dependence is inseparable from human nature, and he needs only to understand it in order to recover his self-mastery and organize his life on a rational basis. If he regards himself as spirit, he knows that he is permanently conditioned by the physical, bodily part of his being, but he distinguishes his true self from it, and knows that he is independent and responsible for his mastery over nature.[4]

In brief, the man who chooses authentic existence decides for true self-realization. He will determine to what things and people his self is given and how this will be done. He will make himself out of the possibilities of existence that are open to him.

THE DISENGAGEMENT OF THE WORD OF GOD

Such is one way of viewing contemporary man and the choices available to him. In addition to his search for authentic existence, this man is also equipped with a definite world view that has been forged for him by the scientific development of the last few centuries. For him ". . . the cause-and-effect nexus is fundamental."[5] Whatever happens in the world has a cause which science has already explained or will some day. Rain gods do not produce rain; atmospheric conditions do. Medicine or surgery cure, not miracles. Everything has its explanation and it is for man to discover that explanation without recourse to mystery or miracle or supernatural explanation of any sort. The natural is naturally explainable. The same is true of modern man's view of history. It is not fate or destiny that determines what will happen. Behind all of history there lies human decision and rational motivation. Thus "modern men take it for granted that the course of nature and of history, like their own inner life and their practical life, is nowhere interrupted by the intervention of supernatural powers."[6]

When this man is confronted with the world as it is described in the Bible he finds himself in a strange and unbelievable place and his tendency is to dismiss it as the dark, superstitious world of prescientific man. It has nothing significant to say to the present scientifically oriented world.

It is, in Bultmann's word, a world of myth." By this he means several different things. He means first of all the description of his world that man gives in order to explain his understanding of himself in that world.

Myth speaks of the power or powers which man supposes he experiences as the ground and limit of his world and of his own activity and suffering. He describes these powers in terms derived from the visible world, with its tangible objects and forces, and from human life, with its feelings, motives and potentialities ... Similarly he may account for the present state and order of the world by speaking of a primeval war between the gods. He speaks of the other world in terms of this world and of the gods in terms derived from human life.[7]

Again, myth is man's way of saying that he believes that ". . . the origin and purpose of the world in which he lives are to be sought not within it but beyond it. . . ."[8] Myth is also the way man speaks to express his sense of dependence, the fact that he is aware of his finiteness and limitation. Lastly, ". . . myth expresses man's belief that in this state of dependence he can be delivered from the forces within the visible world."[9]

All of these meanings of myth and the beliefs they imply are expressed in the world view that is portrayed in the Scriptures.

The cosmology of the New Testament is essentially mythical in character. The world is viewed as a three-storied structure, with the earth in the centre, the heaven above and the underworld beneath. Heaven is the abode of God and of celestial beings—the angels. The underworld is hell, the place of torment. Even the earth is more than the scene of natural, everyday events, of the trivial round and common task. It is the scene of the supernatural activity of God and his angels on the one hand, and of Satan and his daemons on the other. These supernatural forces intervene in the course of nature and in all that men think and will and do. Miracles are by no means rare. Man is not in control of his own life. Evil spirits may take possession of him. Satan may inspire him with evil thoughts. Alternatively, God may inspire his thought and guide his purposes. He may grant him heavenly visions. He may allow him to hear his word of succour or demand. He may give him the supernatural power of his Spirit. History does not follow a smooth unbroken course; it is set in motion and controlled by those supernatural powers. This aeon is held in bondage by Satan, sin and death . . . and hastens towards its end. That end will come very soon, and will take the form of a cosmic catastrophe. It will be inaugurated by the "woes" of the last time. Then the judge will come from heaven, the dead will rise, the last judgment will take place and men will enter into eternal salvation or damnation.[10]

Such a world-view contemporary man finds unacceptable and he dismisses it as ridiculous. He concludes that whatever Scripture has to say belongs to a bygone day. It has nothing to say to today. It is at this point that Bultmann asks his question: Is the message of the New Testament so inextricably bound to the world-view in whose terms it is expressed that one is compelled to reject both the world-view and the message? Or, is it possible to discover an essential message in the Scripture that is valid for all ages of human history and to disengage it from its mythological framework? If this can be done then the possibility of expressing the message in terms of the present world-view arises and with it the hope that the New Testament still has something meaningful to say to our present world.

Bultmann's answer to the question is "yes," the myth and the message are separable. His life's work has been dedicated to "demythologizing" the message of the New Testament, separating myth from message, and then to finding the contemporary philosophical categories in which to express that message. The process of demythologizing is then an attempt to disengage the Word of God from its primitive setting.

As the first step in the process Bultmann makes a distinction between kerygma and myth. Kerygma is God's essential message to man; myth is the framework or world-view within which it is presented. Beginning with the story in which the message is set, i.e., the life of Jesus, Bultmann is quite sceptical about our ability to know anything certain of the life, words and deeds of the historical Jesus. The early Christian community quite soon made him a mythical figure. The facts of his life (whatever they might have been, they are now irrecoverable) underwent a transformation, in the thinking of the primitive Church, and the story of Jesus became the story of ". . . a great, pre-existent, heavenly being who became man for the sake of our redemption. . . ."[11] Conceived by the Holy Spirit and born of a virgin he atoned by his death for men's sins, died, rose, and ascended into heaven. "He will come again on the clouds of heaven to complete the work of redemption and the resurrection and judgment of men will follow. Sin, suffering, and death will then be finally abolished."[12]

Such is the story of Jesus as the New Testament tells it. To men of the present century it contains much of the mythological way of thinking which is simply unacceptable. Their scientific world view makes such thinking an impossibility. Bultmann sums up the contemporary reaction when he says,

> And as for the pre-existence of Christ, with its corollary of
> man's translation into a celestial realm of light, and the cloth-

ing of the human personality in heavenly robes and a spiritual
body—all this is not only irrational but utterly meaningless.
Why should salvation take this particular form? Why should
this be the fulfillment of human life and the realization of
man's true being?[13]

But although the historical facts of the life of Jesus have been irretriev-
ably turned into myth Bultmann believes that it is possible, indeed
absolutely essential, for Christianity to discover in this mythologized story
a message of God to man which is of perennial validity. What is needed is
an attempt to say what the myth says in other terms more acceptable to
modern men. How is this to be done? How is the mythology of the New
Testament to be reinterpreted? What is the message of God for men contained in the New Testament that is still of value to modern man?

THE RECASTING OF THE WORD OF GOD

To uncover what the New Testament has to offer us we must learn to
ask it the proper questions, or put another way, we must know what
questions the Bible is intending to answer before we can ask it the right
questions. For Bultmann the central concern of the New Testament is to
communicate an understanding of human existence. "I think our interest
is really to hear what the Bible has to say for our actual present, to hear
what is the truth about our life and about our soul."[14] The questions to
be asked of it should, therefore, deal with the meaning of human
existence. Man has from his beginning puzzled over and asked himself
questions about the meaning of his existence. There is, therefore, in man a
natural inclination to find the subject matter of the New Testament a
topic of absorbing interest. To profit fully from the treatment of the
subject in Scripture, however, man should take this inbred inclination and
develop it by a personal reflection on his own existence. By so doing he
will bring to sharper focus the questions about himself which cause him
most concern.

Thus armed he will be able to ask the New Testament the proper
existential questions. Bultmann adopts Heidegger's method of inquiry into
the meaning of existence and his questions are derived from reflection
within that philosophical framework. What does the New Testament tell
me about the meaning of my existence? What has it to say about the two

possible ways of existence open to me: authentic and inauthentic? How does it propose that I can achieve authentic existence?

All that can be attempted here is to take a few examples of the way in which he asks questions of the New Testament and how it yields answers to questions asked this way. A further study of his method can best be pursued in his *The Theology of the New Testament,* (Scribners, 1952-55).

Let us limit ourselves to the person of Jesus and the events of his life and ask with Bultmann: What has this to say to me about the meaning of existence? Bultmann begins his answer by asking whether Heidegger's analysis of what authentic existence means is a sufficient answer to the problem of human existence. Is it enough to tell a man what he ought to be? The answer is, of course, no. He must also be told whether or not what he ought to be is an attainable goal. Can a man be what he ought to be, is a question that must be central to any serious discussion of human existence.

The New Testament answer to this question is an unequivocal no. Man is not of himself capable of fighting free of inauthentic existence, slavery to the things of this world. Such deliverance can only be effected by an act of God and this is the kerygma of the New Testament: God has so acted. As Bultmann puts it,

> ... Jesus Christ [is] the eschatological phenomenon... the Saviour through whom God delivers the world by passing judgement on it and granting the future as a gift to those who believe on him . . . .[15]

The New Testament says that man is given the real possibility of authentic existence only through the redemption wrought in Christ.

A man who reflects on his own human situation ought to know from his own experience how inauthentic his existence has been. He should also come, Bultmann would argue, to realize that,

> ... the life he actually lives is not his authentic life, and that he is totally incapable of achieving that life by his own efforts. In short, he is a totally fallen being.[16]

But, unfortunately, this does not happen, for self-reliance carries its own blindness with it. "For self-assertion deludes man into thinking that his existence is a prize within his own grasp."[17] One who has opted for security to be derived from things cannot be convinced of the emptiness of his choice. Thus it becomes apparent that the man who leads the inauthentic life needs to be "delivered from himself" if any possibility of authentic life is to be his. At this point the kerygma of the New Testament again asserts itself: "At the very point where man can do nothing, God steps in and acts—indeed he has acted already—on man's behalf."[18]

Christ is the event in which God acts. Once a man grasps this act as his own in faith he is made free. Freed from himself, he becomes capable of authentic existence. In the moment of this choice of faith this world comes to an end in the sense that man has been freed of it and the inauthenticity it imposes upon him. In this faith man passes over into the possibility of "eschatological existence," a life lived out of this world.

How then is one to view the event of Jesus Christ? In what sense is one to reject it as myth and in what sense is one to retain it as meaningful? In answering the question Bultmann feels ". . . the crux of the matter lies in the cross and resurrection."[19]

The cross is to be accepted as an historical event. Enough evidence exists to be able to fix the date of its occurrence. Its true significance, however, becomes evident when one relates it to the problem of one's existence. Viewed from this perspective one sees that

> to believe in the cross does not mean to concern ourselves with a mythical process wrought outside of us and our world, with an objective event turned by God to our advantage, but rather to make the cross of Christ our own, to undergo crucifixion with him.[20]

Acceptance of the cross means to turn from this world, to accept God's judgment on it and on oneself as belonging to it. It connotes giving up reliance on self which leads only to inauthentic existence in order to place one's reliance on God. In this sense it is a death to self, a crucifixion. It is the radical decision of faith, the commitment of self to God.

Once this choice of identification with the cross has been made one enters into a new life. Dead to sin and to concern with finding security in the things of this world, one has risen to a life of authentic existence. This is the significance of the resurrection, its existential meaning. Is the resurrection as an historical event a myth? Bultmann seems to regard it as such. He seems to understand it as giving final meaning to the cross in the sense that after death there comes life; by losing life new life is found. The New Testament treatment of the resurrection concentrates much more on its significance as the eschatological event than on its historical character.

> If the event of Easter Day is in any sense an historical event additional to the event of the cross, it is nothing else than the

rise of faith in the risen Lord, since it was this faith which led to the apostolic preaching. The resurrection itself is not an event of past history . . . . But the historical problem is not of interest to Christian belief in the resurrection. For the historical event of the rise of the Easter faith means for us what it meant for the first disciples—namely, the self-attestation of the risen Lord, the act of God in which the redemptive event of the cross is completed.[21]

The meaning of the cross/resurrection for the believer is that, through Jesus who was a historical person, God Himself is speaking to man. What He is saying is: Come, through belief in Jesus Christ, to the possession of authentic existence. Bultmann believes that by this radical demythologizing of the story of the New Testament he has put the stumbling block, the *scandalon* of Christianity where it belongs. The point at which man needs to be challenged is not his willingness to accept the mythology of the New Testament. He is to be challenged at the point where the New Testament challenges him, at the point of his self-sufficiency. What modern man is being summoned to accept by the Christian message, is not a three-level universe of heaven, earth, and hell, but the fact that he does not have in himself the power to be his true self. God, through Christ, offers to remedy his radical self-insufficiency. This is what the kerygma of the New Testament calls man to believe in. The response to that call has for Bultmann a triple aspect.

An affirmative response has three aspects: man embraces a new understanding of himself as free from himself and endowed with a new self by divine grace; he accepts the new life which is founded on the grace of God; and he decides on a new understanding of his responsible acting which sees it as born of love.[22]

CONCLUSION

This brief account of how Bultmann proposes to demythologize the New Testament, or perhaps more clearly, how he proposes to ask it to answer questions which are existentially meaningful to modern man, will be sufficient to indicate how controversial an approach to the Scriptures his theological method would be to many Christian theologians.

One thing that surely can be said whether one agrees or disagrees with his method is that he has made the attempt to meet head on *the* religious problem of today, the making of Christianity relevant to today's world. Reginald H. Fuller summarizes Bultmann's positive contribution this way,

> It is generally recognized that Bultmann has rendered a great service by putting his finger on a real problem for the church today, one of which theologians were insufficiently aware during the recovery of biblical theology. That problem is, how to communicate the Christian message to modern man in such a way as to challenge him to a genuine decision.[23]

Granted this contribution, let us look at a few of the problems that his critics have found within his program for demythologizing.

The first set of objections centers around his method. As we have seen, Bultmann tries to translate mythology into existentially meaningful statements. But the problem that immediately arises is: Is the content of the New Testament meant only as an answer to man's existential questions?[24] If so, then much of the New Testament turns out to be meaningless. To take but two examples, St. Paul makes much of the fact that all of creation is fallen and in need of redemption and he looks forward to the time when this will finally be accomplished. But what existential significance can this have for an individual seeking authentic existence for himself?

Again, the New Testament has much to say about eschatology, the end of the world which lies in the future. Yet for Bultmann the most that eschatology seems to yield is the individual's passage from death to life in his choice by faith to enter authentic existence. With that choice he enters the last time. But there is surely a dimension in the eschatology of the New Testament to which such an interpretation does not do full justice. Much is made in St. Paul, for example, of the end of the world and the signs which will accompany it; the Gospels give a good deal of attention to the Last Judgment.

From these and similar objections brought against Bultmann's method it would seem legitimate to conclude that, although his demythologizing does offer a key for a richer understanding of some elements of the New Testament, it cannot by any means be the only method for determining what is of value in the New Testament. Fuller summarizes the force of this set of objections:

> There must then, it is admitted, be interpretation of the Christian myths all the time. But how are they to be interpreted? Bultmann says, existentially. This, as we have seen, is helpful

with those aspects of the New Testament language, of those myths which concern our appropriation of the saving act of God in Christ. But when it comes to speaking of the saving act itself, the use of existentialist interpretation results in the discarding or ignoring of some myths, and in the inadequate interpretation of others. Therefore, despite Bultmann's professed intention, we get elimination of significant areas of the New Testament proclamation. As we have seen, we hear nothing about the church as a corporate fellowship, or of the future, both cosmic and individual. Against this it must be insisted that, true to the professed program of demythologizing, *all* of the New Testament mythology must be retained, and all must be interpreted. And where the existential interpretation is inapplicable, some other kind of interpretation must be discovered. Only so will we avoid taking the witness of the New Testament to the Christ event *à la carte*.[25]

The second major problem that many have with Bultmann is his sense of history. Christianity has been traditionally considered a historical religion, that is, it is a set of beliefs founded finally on a series of historical events, specifically the life of Jesus Christ. Bultmann seems very pessimistic about how much actual historical fact we can know about Jesus. He would admit that there is continuity between history and kerygma, between the life of Jesus and the church's preaching of the meaning of his life. Beyond that, however, he seems unwilling to go. Thus history has been swallowed up in myth and cannot be retrieved. Most of his historical attention is fastened on the present, on what the Christ-event means here and now to the individual. He would characterize the "search for the historical Jesus" as futile. Bishop John Robinson finds that he cannot accept this historical scepticism. It is his feeling that such a stand is too radical a rejection of the tradition of the church. Two thousand years of belief have borne witness to the church's acceptance of the gospel events. The *quod semper et ubique creditur* (what has always and everywhere been believed) of the church cannot be lightly brushed aside. The life of Jesus as historical fact is central to Christianity.[26]

The same objection has been brought by others who have urged that Christianity as a religion needs some base in historical fact; otherwise it would collapse. Macquarrie puts the problem this way,

Does the Christian message summon us to a pure speculative possibility of existence, or to a possibility which has been actualized under the real conditions of historical existence? We could have no confidence about embarking on the first of

these alternatives. So we come back to the question whether
Christianity needs some minimum of factual history, and, if
so, how much?[27]

These are two of the basic problems that are found in Bultmann's work
by his critics. Most of them would agree nonetheless that Bultmann's
contribution to theology has been enormous. For all of the problems
involved in the use of his method, when it is used properly and with due
caution, it can bring the message of the New Testament into much clearer
perspective for the contemporary world. Most would subscribe to Alvin
Porteous' final evaluation of his significance.

> If the church is to be renewed in our day, Christian beliefs
> must somehow "come alive" in some such way as Bultmann
> has tried to make them. The doctrine of sin must be seen as
> the self-made bondage of Everyman to the tyranny of worldly
> securities, rather than the poisonous legacy of a mythical first
> man. The doctrine of salvation must be seen as God's gift to us
> of authentic freedom to be our true selves in service of others,
> rather than the working out of some cosmic plan of redemp-
> tion to which we are called upon to give our intellectual
> acceptance. Similarly, we cannot really claim belief in the
> cross of Christ without taking up our own crosses and follow-
> ing him; nor in his resurrection without exhibiting the power
> of a new life. And finally, we can articulate most convincingly
> our belief in the Kingdom of God, not by our ability to recite
> a timetable of events for the Last Day but by living constantly
> in "the dimension of the eternal," in momentary expectation
> of God's breakthrough into our lives in grace and judgement.
>
> When Christian doctrine has been translated into such exis-
> tential terms as these, the search for the right scandal in the
> Bible has met at least with some degree of positive fulfill-
> ment.[28]

FOOTNOTES

[1] John Macquarrie, "Rudolf Bultmann," in *A Handbook of Christian Theologians*,
Martin E. Marty and Dean G. Peerman, eds. Meridian Book edition (Cleveland & New
York: The World Publishing Co., 1967), p. 460.

[2] Rudolf Bultmann, *Jesus Christ and Mythology* (New York: Charles Scribner's
Sons, 1958), p. 56.

[3]H. W. Bartsch, ed., *Kerygma and Myth*, Torchbook ed. (New York: Harper & Row, 1961), pp. 24-25.

[4]*Ibid.*, p. 6.

[5]Bultmann, *Jesus Christ and Mythology*, p. 15.

[6]*Ibid.*, p. 16.

[7]Bartsch, *Kerygma and Myth*, p. 10.

[8]*Ibid.*

[9]*Ibid.*, p. 11.

[10]*Ibid.*, pp. 1-2.

[11]Bultmann, *Jesus Christ and Mythology*, p. 17.

[12]Bartsch, *Kerygma and Myth*, p. 2.

[13]*Ibid.*, p. 8.

[14]Bultmann, *Jesus Christ and Mythology*, p. 52.

[15]Bartsch, *Kerygma and Myth*, p. 117.

[16]*Ibid.*, p. 30.

[17]*Ibid.*, p. 31.

[18]*Ibid.*

[19]Bartsch, *Kerygma and Myth*, p. 35.

[20]*Ibid.*, p. 36.

[21]*Ibid.*, p. 42.

[22]S. Paul Schilling, *Contemporary Continental Theologians* (Nashville: Abingdon Press, 1966), p. 85.

[23]Reginald H. Fuller, *The New Testament in Current Study* (New York: Charles Scribner's Sons, 1967), p. 13.

[24]*Ibid.*, p. 21.

[25]*Ibid.*, pp. 23-24.

[26]John A. T. Robinson, *Honest to God* (Philadelphia: The Westminster Press, 1965), p. 35.

[27]Macquarrie, *Handbook of Christian Theologians*, p. 460.

[28]Alvin C. Porteous, *Prophetic Voices in Contemporary Theology* (Nashville: Abingdon Press, 1966), p. 95.

CHAPTER ELEVEN

Reinhold Niebuhr

Up until the beginning of the first World War the dominant note in theology both in Europe and America, as we have seen, was nineteenth century liberalism. There was a naive optimism about the inherent goodness of man and his possibilities for indefinite growth in goodness. Barring certain deplorable features like the poverty of the masses which human goodness and scientific know-how would soon erase, the culture and civilization which he had built were good and getting better. All that men needed to do to become what they ought to be was to give themselves unreservedly to the advancement of their world. Thus would they work out their own destiny. There seemed little place or need for the help of God's grace and the doctrine of man's sinfulness attracted scant attention.

World War I destroyed that world and its optimism about man. It laid bare the potential for evil that is always present in man. It exposed man's need for God. European theology was the first to react to the new situation. It did so in the work of Karl Barth with its insistence on the gulf that separated man from God and its stress on man's absolute need for God if he were to overcome his inherent tendency to evil. It was almost fifteen years before the first significant American contribution to the new mood of somberness and realism appeared. The contribution was Reinhold Niebuhr's *Moral Man and Immoral Society,* published in 1932. With its appearance Niebuhr (*n.* 1892) took and held for twenty years and more his position as America's foremost twentieth century theologian.

Yet, Niebuhr did not think of himself as a theologian. His field was rather ethics, or what is sometimes called apologetics, the application of the principles of Christian faith to the complex problems of present-day society. His thought as it developed came to be called Christian Realism. It was Christian because it was his conviction that only in the resources of Christianity could there be found the insights needed to explore and explain the full dimensions of man in both his individual and social nature. If such assistance to understanding man and his world could not be found in the biblical faith then that faith did not deserve to continue in existence.

His thought was at the same time a realism, a willingness to explore in painstaking detail all the complexities of today's human and social problems. Never was the light of faith applied to a situation until he had done all he could to uncover and analyze all its components. The penetration of reality to its depths was the object of his thinking. That thinking was realistic also in its acknowledgment that often the given problem did not allow for a simple, unqualified solution. He knew that man lives with ambiguities, that black and white are rare colors in human situations. His tool for handling this problem of ambiguity was dialectical thinking, the ability to see that every 'yes' calls for a responding 'no.' He became expert in the use of paradoxical statement, balancing one truth against another. He knew how to live with provisional answers, with for-now decisions. He was always aware

> ... that the Christian is "*justus et peccator*," "both sinner and righteous"; that history fulfills and negates the Kingdom of God; that grace is continuous with, and in contradiction to, nature; that Christ is what we ought to be and also what we cannot be; that the power of God is in us and that the power of God is against us in judgment and mercy; that all these affirmations which are but varied forms of the one central paradox of the relation of the Gospel to history must be applied to the experiences of life from top to bottom.[1]

His life's work was to know man in all his dimensions, individual and social, then search the Christian faith for the light it had to shed on man's life in his world.

This chapter will explore the nature of Niebuhr's Christian Realism, first searching out its origins in his own life experience, then uncovering its roots in his understanding of the nature of man as individual and in society, and finally exploring his Christology, especially his thought on the cross of Christ as that which gives meaning to man and history.

ORIGINS OF HIS CHRISTIAN REALISM

Niebuhr's early theological training, done at Yale Divinity School when liberalism was at its height, produced a minister who took seriously the providence of God, affirmed the natural goodness and perfectibility of man, believed that Christian love of neighbor offered the practical solution to all problems of human relationships, and who looked forward optimistically to the Kingdom of God that man would soon definitively establish on earth.

His first assignment was to a parish in Detroit where he had thirteen years to observe at its heart the sprawling growth of American industrialism. It was those years which tempered his optimism and his idealism. He came to learn a number of things. First, he discovered how futile was the preaching of moral idealism. Preaching would never change social inequities. These could only be fought after one had learned first-hand the hurt, the exploitation, the tragedy that industrial society inflicted on so many of its members. Only then would Christian love see the need for getting down to practical involvement in the harsh realities of modern life. It was only through first-hand experience, also, that preaching could learn to sharpen its weapons for a realistic criticism of contemporary society.

First-hand knowledge of what human nature is really like also came to him in those years. Industrialists and auto workers alike made it clear to him that self-interest is a basic motivation in human life. Moreover, for the protection of that self-interest, men will develop a variety of self-deceptions and of social hypocrisies.

Finally he was brought to recognize that self-interest's main instrument in protecting and advancing itself is what he calls "the will to power." The more wealth and power one can amass the greater is one's security against the other. Nothing preserves the self so surely as the possession of power over other men. And since power is so important, the development of whatever means will procure it becomes life's driving force.

The process of disillusionment with liberalism was a gradual one but by the time Niebuhr left Detroit to teach at Union Theological Seminary in 1928 the process was complete. He had become a realist in his view of society and of the way man, on the one hand, was crushed by it and, on the other, manipulated it for his own self-aggrandizement.. He himself had become more truly Christian, too, in his discontent with the churches and their failure to make any impact on the society they supposedly served, and in his recognition that many of them had bowed to the hard facts of the need for survival by blessing the *status quo*. His own course would run in the opposite direction, in the direction of an almost cynical exposure of the ills of man and his society. He had become a Christian realist and was ready to begin work on what would remain the major preoccupation of his life, the study of man in himself and in his relation to society.

THE NATURE OF MAN

Niebuhr's mature analysis of the nature of man is contained in his two-volume work, *The Nature and Destiny of Man*. This is his presentation of the Christian view of man. He finds that this view has three major emphases which he summarizes as follows,

> ... (1) It emphasizes the height of self-transcendence in man's spiritual stature in its doctrine of 'image of God.' (2) It insists on man's weakness, dependence, and finiteness, on his involvement in the necessities and contingencies of the natural world, without, however, regarding this finiteness as, of itself, a source of evil in man. In its purest form the Christian view of man regards man as a unity of God-likeness and creatureliness in which he remains a creature even in the highest spiritual dimensions of his existence and may reveal elements of the image of God even in the lowliest aspects of his natural life. (3) It affirms that the evil in man is a consequence of his inevitable though not necessary unwillingness to acknowledge his dependence, to accept his finiteness and to admit his insecurity, an unwillingness which involves him in the vicious circle of accentuating the insecurity from which he seeks escape.[2]

Thus Niebuhr finds man is created and therefore finite and dependent. He stands over against God the infinite and the transcendent who has nonetheless entered into an intimate relation with man. This creature, man, is a compound of nature and spirit.

> ... Man is a child of nature, subject to its vicissitudes, compelled by its necessities, driven by its impulses, and confined within the brevity of the years which nature permits its varied organic form. ... The other less obvious fact is that man is a spirit who stands outside of nature, life, himself, his reason and the world.[3]

Within the Christian perspective "... man's insignificance as a creature, involved in the process of nature and time, is lifted into significance by the mercy and power of God in which his life is sustained."[4] This dependent yet significant, limited but loved, creature is endowed with the priceless gift of freedom. It is this freedom that chooses the course of his life; it decides what view of reality and what exercise of his being, man will make his own. Freedom elects the relationship between nature and spirit which will characterize man's life.

It is when man comes to exercise that freedom that Niebuhr finds Scripture once more asserting a truth about man. He is a sinner. He will "inevitably but not necessarily" choose to use his freedom wrongly. Because man is nature and spirit there is an ambiguity in his existence. He is at once bound and free, limited in his nature and unlimited in his ability to transcend nature. He stands in and yet above nature.

This ambiguity gives rise to a tension, an anxiety in man, a desire for security in place of the uncertainty of the ambiguity. It is for freedom to resolve the ambiguity, allay the anxiety, provide the security man seeks. Man's freedom may choose to dispel the anxiety in either of two ways. Both the right and the wrong choice are within its power and so man does not choose the wrong necessarily.

The right choice, as Niebuhr sees it, would be for man to accept his creatureliness and his dependence on God. In this choice he elects the transcendent God as the ultimate center of reality. His decision is to accept himself for what he is, weak, finite, ignorant and to trust in God who, revelation tells him, is good, to give him the security he seeks. This is the way of faith, the finding of meaning and security outside the self in God. And it is a real option; the choice is available. "The ideal possibility is that faith in the ultimate security of God's love would overcome all immediate insecurities of nature and history."[5]

But though the ideal possibility is at hand to be chosen it is the message of the Bible that freedom inevitably chooses the other alternative. Man elects to seek security in himself. He denies his creatureliness and becomes his own god. He overestimates his freedom, pretending it is unlimited. He exaggerates his wisdom, stripping it of its relativity. This choice is sin, the refusal to accept finiteness.

Scripture is constant in its description of what constitutes the state of sin. In the myth of the Fall it tells the story of Everyman. Adam is the symbol of each man who chooses his unfettered freedom over his dependence upon the Creator. The prophets of the Old Testament also saw what the essence of sin was.

> The real evil in the human situation, according to the prophetic interpretation, lies in man's unwillingness to recognize and acknowledge the weakness, finiteness and dependence of his position, in his inclination to grasp after a power and security which transcend the possibilities of human existence, and in his effort to pretend a virtue and knowledge which are beyond the limits of mere creatures.[6]

And for Saint Paul in the New Testament, "the sin of man is that he seeks to make himself God. . . ."[7]

This seeking to transcend his finiteness which is man's basic sin is essentially the sin of pride which, Niebuhr finds, takes several forms. In its first form man, anxious about his insecurity, tries to overcome it by seeking power over other people and over things. This is pride of power. It is the sin of the man who, being already in possession of some degree of social power, has come to believe himself secure. He does not find it necessary, therefore, to acknowledge the contingency and dependence of his life. He has deluded himself into believing he is molder of his own destiny, judge of his own values, author of his own existence.[8] But this form of pride is also the sin of the man who has little or no power. The absence of power is the source of his insecurity and he lusts for it and drives toward having it. His pursuit of it will inevitably be at the expense of others. Thus both power and its absence corrupts.

Pride occurs also in the form of intellectual pride.[9] Here man whose knowledge is always finite, makes pretensions to total or final knowledge. It is the sin of the thinker who imagines his own explanation of the meaning of reality to be the final one. It often happens too that this form of pride is used to bolster pride of power. Thus, to use Niebuhr's example of the relations between majority and minority racial groups,

> . . . The majority group justifies the disabilities which it imposes upon the minority group on the ground that the subject group is not capable of enjoying or profiting from the privileges of culture or civilization.[10]

In this kind of wisdom, power and privilege should be reserved to the group wise enough to use it well.

Finally, pride can take a moral form, the form of self-righteousness.[11] Here what seems good to me is by that fact objective moral value. Those who disagree are wrong since their view does not conform to what is objectively right. The pride involved here is the pretentiousness of the finite creature who finds the absolute in his own relative judgments of right and wrong. The classic example is the Pharisee, or perhaps in today's terms, the racist.

Pride is man's primary sin and most men are guilty of it in one or another of its forms. But Niebuhr finds that, in addition to those who allay their insecurity by abusing their freedom, turning a relative into an absolute freedom, there are also those who solve the problem of insecurity by refusing to accept the burden of freedom. Such a one tries to escape from the ". . . responsibilities of self-determination. . . ."[12] by abandoning himself to impulse or desire. Life's problems are not faced; they are evaded in ". . . sexual license, gluttony, extravagance, drunkenness and abandonment to various forms of physical desire . . . ."[13] Niebuhr finds combined in this type of sin both an excessive self-love and at the same time an attempt to escape from the self. He finds too that society visits much sterner penalties on this form of human sin than it does on sins of pride. Yet, in his view, pride is the far more dangerous and destructive form of selfishness.

MAN IN SOCIETY

Sin is not only an individual phenomenon; it has its social dimension too. The components of that social dimension are explored by Niebuhr in his *Moral Man and Immoral Society*. The thesis of this book is that it is possible for the individual to come through faith to a realization that, as a Christian, love should be the dominant factor in his life. Furthermore, the individual is able to express love in his own personal relations with other men. Thus individual man can be moral. The further question is whether society can be moral, whether the love that governs interpersonal relationships can be made an operative principle in inter-societal relationships. The second half of the title indicates Niebuhr's response to the question. The bulk of the book is devoted to explaining why he feels society must be immoral in the sense that the highest moral value, love, cannot be made its basic law of operation.

It is obvious from his doctrine of sin and from his conviction that sin is a universal human phenomenon that Niebuhr, in saying individuals can be moral, is not equating morality with sinlessness. What he does mean is that

> Individual men may be moral in the sense that they are able to consider interests other than their own in determining problems of conduct, and are capable, on occasion, of preferring the advantages of others to their own. They are endowed by nature with a measure of sympathy and consideration for their kind, the breadth of which may be extended by an astute social pedagogy. Their rational faculty prompts them to a sense of justice, which educational discipline may refine and purge of egoistic elements until they are able to view a social situation, in which their own interests are involved, with a fair measure of objectivity.[14]

The same claim, however, cannot be made for groups.

> In every human group there is less reason to guide and to
> check impulse, less capacity for self-transcendence, less ability
> to comprehend the needs of others and therefore more unre-
> strained egoism than the individuals, who compose the group,
> reveal in their personal relationships.[15]

The basic reason for the difference he finds is in the strength of the
"collective egoism" of the group. Pride and the will-to-power over others
may be mastered by the single person. There is a cumulative pride in a
society which is far more resistant to control, far less capable of being
brought under ". . .the dominion of reason or conscience."[16]

It is for this reason that appeals to love of neighbor will never effect
social reform nor will the love ethic suffice to settle disputes between
nations. This being so, differences between groups and the social injustices
which feed on these differences will not yield to ". . . moral and rational
suasion. . . ."[17] In a conflict of interests ". . . power must be challenged
by power."[18] The norm of a society made up of diverse groups, each with
its own will-to-power, cannot be love. It must be justice. And justice is
effected by coming to a reasonably acceptable harmony between the conflicting parties. What man must make his goal for the foreseeable future is

> . . . not the creation of an ideal society in which there will be
> uncoerced and perfect peace and justice, but a society in
> which there will be enough justice, and in which coercion will
> be sufficiently non-violent to prevent his common enterprise
> from issuing into complete disaster.[19]

There will be those who believe injustice can be eliminated by an increase of reason and intelligence and they have some measure of truth on
their side. But ultimately reason cannot overcome the selfishness of an
entire class or nation and those who enjoy privilege will cling to it with or
without the support of reason. Religion, too, must be aware of its limitations when it attempts to provide resources for mediating inter-group
conflict. It can motivate the individual but its effect is considerably less on
the group either that has or that wants privilege.

Nation, class, privileged group, unprivileged proletariat, all are scruti-
nized and the same judgment is passed on all of them. Self-interest is their
breath of life and it is the wise man who recognizes this and who, while
striving to live the ethic of love in his own life and to infuse its spirit into
the groups to which he belongs, is also prepared to work toward the

reasonable compromise which will give to the parties in conflict as close an approximation to justice as the concrete situation allows.

The Christian who is aware of the nature of society and conscious too of the demands of unselfishness which his faith makes on him will view the situations with which life in society will confront him as a series of "impossible possibilities." In each of them he is challenged to live an absolute, the law of love. Because he is a sinner and because society's problems do not yield easily to a solution dictated by love, he is called to an impossibility. Yet, at the same time, if the faith he professes gives him anything it gives him the trust that the possibility somehow exists of implementing love in his society. As William Hordern puts it:

> While there is no situation in which the love-ethic can be applied perfectly, there is no situation in which we cannot come closer to fulfillment of the ideal than we have yet done.[20]

Man is at once and paradoxically the servant and the master of the society he lives in.

CHRIST THE MEANING OF MAN AND HISTORY

Niebuhr's view of man the individual and man in society is a somewhat pessimistic view as we have thus far seen it. The emphasis lies more on man's potentiality for sin than on his possibility for good. For the dimension in his thought that restores the balance and gives the optimism of Christian hope to his thinking one needs to turn to his treatment of Christ. Christ is for Niebuhr both the answer to human sinfulness and key to the meaning of human history.

As we have seen, freedom is an essential component of man's nature. Equally characteristic is the universal misuse he has made of that freedom. Man's action in time, his choices and their effects, are the stuff of which human history is made. Because Niebuhr views man's use of his freedom as both corrupted and corruptive he sees his history as filled with ambiguities and inequities. It is written in a series of crooked lines. Yet Christian faith sees God as writing straight with these crooked lines. It is the divine love for man and God's decision that human history will come out right at its end that casts light on that sinfulness and that history and enables man to find meaning and hope amid all the contradictions, not by the light of his reason but under the illumination of his faith.

The fact of history which faith sees as central and which it uses to shed light on man's sinfulness and history's ambiguities is the fact of Christ and especially the fact of his cross. The cross of Christ has in Niebuhr's thought what Paul Lehmann calls a "... pivotal significance ... both for the human situation and as the clue to the person and work of Christ. ..."21

The cross stands as proof of the presence and power of evil in the world. God is overcome and killed by that evil. Yet it stands, too, for the even stronger presence and power of redeeming grace in the world. In dying God overcomes evil and offers man the same power to overcome. ".... It is God's nature to swallow up evil in himself and destroy it."22 He takes upon Himself the full force of human evil, suffers to death under its impact and thereby conquers its power over man.

This is one meaning and perhaps the deepest and ultimately the most hopeful of its meanings. Yet there are other meanings also. The cross contains a lesson of despair because it points to the sinfulness of man and his hopelessness when left to himself. It is the world that kills God and the world is all of us and so we are all implicated in this rejection of God. As a lesson of optimism the cross reminds that the one who dies is a man, or mroe correctly, *the* man, the second Adam from whom we all descend and with whom we are all identified. And the fact that he is man "... proves that sin is not a necessary and inherent characteristic of life. Evil is not ... a part of essential man."23

To clarify further these various meanings of the cross of Christ, Niebuhr makes use of the concepts of the cross as the wisdom of God and the cross as the power of God. The essential message of the Christian Gospel is that in the cross of Christ both the wisdom of God and His power are made available to man; "... which is to say that not only has the true meaning of life been disclosed (wisdom) but also that resources have been made available to fulfill that meaning (power). In Him the faithful find not only 'truth' but 'grace'."24

First of all, how does the cross reveal the wisdom of God? It is in the cross that man can come to understand the full meaning of the power of God and how its two components, justice and mercy, wrath and forgiveness are reconciled. God cannot love without justice; nor can He be just without mercy. Both these demands of his power are fulfilled in Christ. His justice demands that the evil inherent in man and his history be punished. God's relation with man is not a matter of merely forgiving the sins of man. The divine justice must be fulfilled. "There can be no simple abrogation of the wrath of God by the mercy of God."25 That justice is fully fulfilled in the death of Christ.

But that death of Jesus Christ who is the Son of God also reveals that
God ". . . has a resource of mercy beyond His law and judgment . . . ."[26]
The complete fulfillment of the law of divine justice is at the same time an
act of surpassing mercy because, once the penalty is paid, man is free of
punishment. It is in taking upon Himself the full rigor of the law that God
annuls the necessity of man bearing that rigor. "He has a resource of
mercy beyond His law and judgment but He can make it effective only as
He takes the consequences of His wrath and judgment, upon and into
Himself."[27] Thus is the wisdom of God made manifest, His ability to
reconcile the apparently irreconcilable divine justice and mercy.

The cross manifests another revelation of the wisdom of God and this
one relates to human experience. The human is able to abuse its freedom
and thereby produce evil. It is not, however, able to right the situation it
thus creates. The problem of sin and its effects in human history, though
humanly produced, is not humanly solvable. Man can cause the damage; he
cannot repair it. Nor can God simply repair evil by forgiving it. The situation can be righted only if the demand of evil that it be fully punished be
first met. In this line of thought Niebuhr finds the lesson of the cross for
men. "The fact that God cannot overcome evil without displaying in history His purpose to take the effects of evil upon and into Himself, means
that the divine mercy cannot be effective until the seriousness of sin is
fully known."[28] That is to say, the cross is meant to induce first despair
and only then, hope. Man must first recognize the radical seriousness of his
plight. He must see he has created a situation which he cannot solve and
thus be brought to despair.

It is at this point that Niebuhr introduces the notion of the cross as the
power of God. It is only when a man has come to despair of discovering in
himself the resources to solve his situation that he can produce the sorrow
and the turning to God for help which is the condition for the gift of
divine forgiveness and divine assistance.

> It is in this contrition and in this appropriation of divine
> mercy and forgiveness that the human situation is fully under-
> stood and overcome. In this experience man understands
> himself in his finiteness, realizes the guilt of his efforts to
> escape his insufficiency and dependence and lays hold upon a
> power beyond himself which both completes his incomplete-
> ness and purges him of his false and vain efforts at self-
> completion.[29]

Thus does man come to appropriate both the wisdom and the power of

God that is present in the cross. His recognition of his need for the power of God is at the same time his realization of the wisdom of God. And his appropriation of the power of God is simultaneously the acceptance of His wisdom.

The appropriation of God's power by man has a double meaning. It means, first of all, the presence of God's power in him. In accepting Christ he acknowledges his own inability to save himself, or put another way, he accepts his own sinfulness. It is only on this condition that the empowering presence of Christ becomes his. But when Christ is present the power of new life is also present.

Over against this power of God in us must be set the power of God over us. So long as a man lives and history lasts human pride will continue to set itself against the will of God. Pride will go on introducing corruption into the world. And the power of God will go on condemning human sinfulness, standing in judgment over it.

These two aspects of the power of God need to be kept in continuous tension in a man's life, that God forgives and yet man sins, that grace can lead man to new life and yet at every stage in that life there are present new possibilities for human evil. Every new level of virtue achieved is a new level of possibility for sin.

Life remains, then, forever ambiguous, and the same is true of history. It does not yield itself to an easy understanding of its meaning. Indeed as long as it lasts it will not have its final meaning. What the cross makes clear is that human life and human history do not contain within themselves their own ultimate significance. That is only to be found in Christ and so in God. And God will be found only at life's end and history's completion. Meanwhile the human situation remains always ambiguous.

In his understanding of the meaning of history Niebuhr rejects both the liberal view and the tragic view. Liberal Christianity reads the meaning of the cross in essentially optimistic terms. It sees in what happened there the introduction of vicarious love as ". . . a force in history which gradually gains the triumph over evil. . . ."[30] In this view ". . . the power of love in history, as symbolized by the cross, begins tragically but ends triumphantly. It overcomes evil."[31]

But Niebuhr has learned from his own experience to beware of the optimism of liberalism. He knows that the facts of history give the lie to the thesis of a gradual growth in human goodness. Evil is still very much with us. Along with goodness it too grows as man advances. History has a much more tragic dimension to it than liberalism would allow.

There is another view of the cross which does fuller justice to its meaning. Here the tragedy of history is more heavily accented. For this view the vicarious love that Christ introduced into history does not triumph. It goes unto the end being defeated by human sinfulness. Yet, for all that, it continues to be and to offer to man the true meaning of life. The triumph of Christ's love is not in its victory but in its truth.

> But the idea of the suffering servant in history may also mean that vicarious love remains defeated and tragic in history; but has its triumph in the knowledge that it is ultimately right and true.[32]

Niebuhr finds this explanation of the meaning of history equally unsatisfactory. There is abundant evidence of human goodness. The effect of what Christ did is manifestly present in the world. Both explanations are rejected because neither seems to do full justice to the fact that Jesus is both God and man. He is God and it is as God that he suffers for man's evil. This means that ". . . the contradictions of history are not resolved in history; but they are only ultimately resolved on the level of the eternal and the divine."[33] Yet it is equally true that what Christ did was done as a man in history and for man in history. ". . . God is engaged and involved in history, and is not some unmoved mover, dwelling in eternal equanimity."[34]

For the man of faith there is goodness in history and the power of God is able to effect change for the better in his own life and in society. He is called to responsible action in the world and he is meant to be confident that such action can be effective of good. Yet always he has need of caution. The judgment of God lies on all human action. That action will remain, until the end, a compound of good and evil. No final stage of human goodness is possible in history. Man's task is to strive for the possible and the better but never to settle for what he has achieved as the final coming of the Kingdom of God. That final coming as the title and thesis of one of Niebuhr's books suggests is *Beyond Tragedy*, beyond the ambiguities and contradictions of man's life in this world.

CONCLUSION

Niebuhr's thinking has been an unremitting attempt to apply the insights of the Christian faith to the complexities of contemporary society. The style he has chosen to embody this attempt has been, rather consistently, a devastating analysis of human pretensions and human inadequacies. What he does most expertly is to uncover the danger of a naive optimism regarding man's possibilities and his future. And he does this for the most part without falling into the opposite danger of an unrelieved pessimism about man. From this point of view his realism is just that; it is real. He perceives and describes the good and the bad, the hopeful and the to-be-regretted in man. And one somehow senses that he is right, that the real man is this compound of opposites.

He has had his share of critics, however, and we will close by looking at two major points of criticism brought against him. There are, first of all, among his critics those who would criticize his view of the church and the function it is to play in human life. They would agree that he "... is rightly critical of the sentimentalities, the tyrannies, the obscurantism, and the self-righteousness of the 'churches' in history."[35] But they would question whether for all of its deficiencies, he has given sufficient emphasis to the fact that it is in the church that God's revelation of his relationship with men has been preserved. And by the fact that it does preserve this revelation, it stands in continuing witness against the evil in man and in his society. It stands too as witness that God relates to man in community, not in individuality. It is a people he saves, not individuals. The church for all its failings is the embodiment of divine revelation and relation to man.

By way of answer to one expression of this criticism Niebuhr makes this response,

> I think I have increasingly recognized the value of the Church as a community of grace which, despite historic corruptions, has the "oracles of God," as St. Paul said about Israel. The Church is the one place in history where life is kept open for the final word of God's judgment to break the pride of men and for the word of God's mercy to life up the broken-hearted.[36]

He is quick, however, to add as a qualifying caution the reason which originally led him to criticize the Church.

> But when I see how much new evil comes into life through the pretension of the religious community, through its conventional and graceless legalism and through religious fanaticism, I am concerned that my growing appreciation of the Church should not betray me into this complacency.[37]

His critical spirit will not allow him to exempt from warranted criticism any aspect of life, including the religious aspect, in which humanity is involved. Institutions, especially, must be open to continuing critical appraisal lest the prideful humanity in them should corrupt them.

Another area of his thought which has also drawn sharp negative reaction has been his analysis of human sinfulness. There are those who see in this analysis so pessimistic a view of human nature that it is hard to conceive how a human nature so constituted could even aspire to goodness. Such a view, they contend, tends to paralyze human effort. Others, approaching it from another perspective, see his sketch of human nature's sinfulness as being done in such dark colors that it is hard to imagine how even God could extricate man from the position into which he has put himself.

Others, less extreme in their criticism, find fault with the categories to which he reduces all sin, either pride or sensuality. They would contend that for many men neither category is suitable, or perhaps better, both categories tend to be far too dramatic to describe the state in which they live. Such, for example, are the ones who live quiet, placid lives, undisturbed by the problems around them, unwilling or unable to see any reason why they should show concern or accept responsibility for other men and their needs. Life, except in its individual dimension, is almost a moral vacuum. Yet they are neither proud nor sensual. This segment of humanity is surely as guilty before God as the proud man is. And certainly they are just as dangerous as the man of pride, for they are the ones who create or permit the conditions in society which invite the proud to move in and take over.

To all of these criticisms of his doctrine on sin Niebuhr's response would be, I think, that for him the basic human sin is self-regard. Call it what you will, it is concentration on the self which characterizes all human sinfulness and, unless man has the help of God to overcome this, his situation is helpless. Finally it is in his ruthless dissecting of human self-concern and it corruptive influence on society and on history coupled with his insistence that only divine wisdom and divine power can solve this most fundamental of man's problems, that he has made his lasting contribution.

FOOTNOTES

1Reinhold Niebuhr, *The Nature and Destiny of Man*, vol. II, *Human Destiny*, Paperback edition (New York: Charles Scribner's Sons, 1964), p. 204. Copyright 1941, 1943 Charles Scribner's Sons. Reprinted by permission of the publisher.

2Niebuhr, *Nature and Destiny of Man*, vol. I, *Human Nature*, p. 150.

3*Ibid.*, p. 3.

[4]*Ibid.*, p. 92.

[5]*Ibid.*, p. 183.

[6]*Ibid.*, p. 137.

[7]*Ibid.*, p. 140.

[8]*Ibid.*, pp. 188-89.

[9]*Ibid.*, pp. 194-98.

[10]*Ibid.*, p. 198.

[11]*Ibid.*, pp. 199-203.

[12]*Ibid.*, p. 186.

[13]*Ibid.*, p. 228.

[14]Reinhold Niebuhr, *Moral Man and Immoral Society*, Paperback edition (New York: Charles Scribner's Sons, 1960), p. xi.

[15]*Ibid.*, pp. xi-xii.

[16]*Ibid.*, p. xii.

[17]*Ibid.*, p. xv.

[18]*Ibid.*

[19]Niebuhr, *Moral Man and Immoral Society*, p. 22.

[20]William Hordern, *A Layman's Guide to Protestant Theology*, Paperback ed. (New York: The Macmillan Co., 1962), p. 160.

[21]Paul Lehmann, "The Christology of Reinhold Niebuhr," in *Reinhold Niebuhr: His Religious, Social and Political Thought*, eds. Charles W. Kegley and Robert W. Bretall, paperback ed. (New York: Macmillan Co., 1961), p. 255.

[22]Reinhold Niebuhr, *Beyond Tragedy*, paperback edition (London: James Nisbet & Co., 1937; New York: Charles Scribner's Sons, 1937), p. 168.

[23]*Ibid.*, pp. 167-68.

[24]Niebuhr, *Human Destiny*, p. 98.

[25]*Ibid.*, p. 56.

[26]*Ibid.*, p. 55.

[27]*Ibid.*

[28]*Ibid.*, p. 56.

[29]*Ibid.*, p. 57.

[30]*Ibid.*, p. 45.

[31]*Ibid.*

[32]*Ibid.*

[33]*Ibid.*, p. 46.

[34]*Ibid.*

[35]William J. Wolf, "Reinhold Niebuhr's Doctrine of Man," in *Niebuhr:His Thought*, p. 248.

[36]Niebuhr, "Reply to Interpretation and Criticism," in *Niebuhr: His Thought*, p. 436.

[37]*Ibid.*

CHAPTER TWELVE

Paul Tillich

Twentieth century Protestant theological thought has, in the main, run along three lines. The first of these, begun by Karl Barth, has concentrated on explaining divine revelation as that revelation is found in the Word of God. Emphasis is placed in this approach on the need for man to hear God as He speaks and to respond in faith and obedience. The second line of development, typified by Rudolf Bultmann, has been essentially biblical in its orientation. The attempt is made to find in Scripture what it is that God wants to say to man. To achieve this purpose Scripture is interpreted in terms of what it has to say to man's existential questions: Who am I, what can and should I be?

In Paul Tillich (1886-1965) we come to the main representative of the third line of development, the philosophical understanding of Christian revelation. It will be noted immediately that Tillich's option for a philosophical approach to Christianity is the exact opposite of Barth's. He himself notes the basic difference. Theology, he believes, can be approached in two ways. If the theologian opts to stress the unchangeableness, the perennial truth, of the Christian kerygma rather than the importance of making that message meaningful to man in his situation, then he produces a kerygmatic theology, one which is principally interested in the preservation of the Christian faith in its purity. He believes that Barth's choice is for a theology of this kind and he acknowledges that it keeps Christian truth from the dangers of relativization which are always present when attempts are made to adapt that truth to the contemporary situation. Tillich's choice, on the other hand, is for an "answering theology." In this approach one listens first to the questions that man is asking then frames the Christian message in terms that answer man's questions.

Tillich is well aware that the danger of the first kind of theology is irrelevance and of the second an adaptation which results in distortion and dilution. But it is his own conviction that religion must speak to culture as it is if religion is to make itself present to man. He chooses to run the risk of distortion rather than that of irrelevance.

Tillich is then a philosopher-theologian, that is to say, he believes that philosophy is the instrument to be used in probing the most fundamental of human questions. Once those questions have been uncovered and the human situation implicit in them has been laid bare, then, but only then, does it become possible for the theologian to speak of what Christianity has to say to those questions and that situation.

THE METHOD OF CORRELATION

Tillich speaks of his method of theologizing as the method of correlation. He explains, "the method of correlation explains the contents of the Christian faith through existential questions and theological answers in mutual interdependence. . . ."[1] Unlike Barth who begins with the divine answer, Tillich's point of departure is the human question. His probing for what is the human question carries him over a broad range of human culture because he believes that man best reveals himself in the cultural forms with which he surrounds himself and through which he expresses himself, his interests, his concerns, and his anxieties. For Tillich, painting, theatre, politics, history, sociology, science, depth psychology, literature, philosophy, patterns of life, all of these are grist for the mill of his analysis of the human situation. At the end of that investigation of culture he is in a position to know what questions man asks. Only then does he proceed to theologize, to match divine answer to human question, to show how religion, and specifically Christianity, can help man answer his questions.

Put another way, Tillich views his life work as living in a "boundary situation," on the boundary between philosophy and theology, religion and culture. His task is to understand both and to work for their correlation or better their mutual interpenetration. Underlying this view of the theologian's task is Tillich's conviction that "as the substance of culture is religion, so the form of religion is culture."[2] By this he means that a study of any civilization's cultural forms will uncover either its religious concerns or its lack of such. Or, put the other way around, if religion is present in a culture, it will manifest its presence in all the forms of that culture; if it is not present, the culture will be void of any religious implications.

THE HUMAN SITUATION

Faithful to his method of correlation Tillich's theology is first of all an analysis of man's contemporary situation. He asks: Who is present-day man? How does he conceive of himself? How does he view the meaning of his existence? He answers: For man today as for man in the past the basic question to be asked is, What is the meaning of life?

As man ponders the answer to this question he becomes aware of the basic human condition of finitude. His possession of existence is a very limited one and even that possession is continually threatened by nonexistence. His being is precarious. He could at any moment just as well not be as be. Man knows that he is from moment to moment confronted by the threat of nonbeing. Faced by this threat, how does man give meaning to his life? He needs to find somewhere "the courage to be," to assert that life is worth living in spite of its precariousness.

Put another way, man's awareness of the insecurity of his existence gives rise to anxiety, "the existential awareness of non-being," a concern that perhaps existence does not have a meaning but is rather an absurdity. As Tillich reads the various forms of contemporary cultural expression in psychology, in existentialism, in art and poetry, and in the facts of history and politics he finds ample evidence to support his belief that this anxiety has led modern man to view his human situation as meaningless. His reaction to this meaninglessness has been in terms of despair, apathy, a tendency to self-destruction and a general sense of lack of worthwhileness in life. Out of this anxiety as well as out of this realization of life's limitedness if not pointlessness the same problem arises: where does man find the courage to be, how does he allay his anxiety about life's meaning?

It is Tillich's contention that man chooses to express his courage to be through his freedom. He elects to give life meaning by using his freedom to make the choices that make life meaningful. The basic choice that is made is of self and the freedom inherent therein as the sole source of meaning in life. Implicit in such a decision is a rejection of the essential human condition of finitude. Man decides that he gives rather than finds meaning. Put another way, the choice of self as the source of meaning in life means acting in terms of a denial of what man is, finite, dependent, limited. Thus does man, in his choice of that which will give him the courage to be, deny what he is and separate himself from his true situation. He elects a state of alienation. This state is, for Tillich, the state of sin. In this choice, man at one and the same time makes himself his god and denies who he is, a finite, limited being.

The consequence of this freely chosen state is a sense of separation from one's true being and an ensuing loneliness. Man is estranged from himself and from the One who is really the Ground and Source of his being. It is to this fundamental misuse of freedom in the search for the courage to be that Tillich traces much of the sickness of the men of his time, their sense of despair, emptiness and cynicism, their acceptance of life as meaningless.

> Thus, the state of our whole life is estrangement from others and ourselves, because we are estranged from the Ground of our being, because we are estranged from the origin and aim of our life. And we do not know where we have come from or where we are going. We are separated from the mystery, the depth, and the greatness of our existence. We hear the voice of that depth; but our ears are closed. We feel that something radical, total, and unconditioned is demanded of us; but we rebel against it, try to escape its urgency, and will not accept its promise. We cannot escape, however. If that something is the Ground of our being, we are bound to it for all eternity, just as we are bound to ourselves and to all other life. We always remain in the power of that from which we are estranged. That fact brings us to the ultimate depth of sin: separated and yet bound, estranged and yet belonging, destroyed and yet preserved, the state which is called despair. Despair means that there is no escape. Despair is "the sickness unto death." But the terrible thing about the sickness of despair is that we cannot be released, not even through open or hidden suicide. For we all know that we are bound eternally and inescapably to the Ground of our being. The abyss of separation is not always visible. But it has become more visible to our generation than to preceding generations, because of our feeling of meaninglessness, emptiness, doubt and cynicism—all expressions of despair, of our separation from the roots and the meaning of our life. Sin in its most profound sense, sin as despair, abounds amongst us.[3]

From this state of primal separation from the Ground of his being man is unable to extricate himself. Every effort he makes in that direction is rooted in his chosen condition of estrangement and thereby doomed to failure. Thus all of man's social and political strivings for betterment, his own personal reaching for moral growth, even his practice of religion are of no avail so long as they come from his alienated self.

This is Tillich's analysis of the human situation. As he reads the cultural expressions of that situation he sees these also reflecting the human state of separation from its authentic being. Behind it all he glimpses man asking what has always been his fundamental question: who am I, what is the meaning of my life? At this juncture he is ready to turn from the human question to the divine answer.

THE DIVINE ANSWER

The beginning of an answer lies in man's coming to know himself for what he is, finite and therefore dependent in his being. This admission leads in its turn to an acknowledgment of the One upon Whom man depends and from Whom he has separated himself. This One is not a being among other beings; he is rather the Ground of all being, Being-Itself, the ultimate reality. Thus Tillich names God: "The name of this infinite and inexhaustible depth and ground of all being is *God.* That depth is what the word *God* means."[4]

Tillich believes that an acknowledgment of God as the Ground of being is within the grasp of every man because every man is capable of, indeed has, an ultimate concern. God and ultimate concern are synonyms. Tillich explains,

> ... If that word (God) has not much meaning for you, translate it, and speak of the depths of your life, of the source of your being, of your ultimate concern, of what you take seriously without any reservation. Perhaps, in order to do so, you must forget everything traditional that you have learned about God, perhaps even that word itself. For if you know that God means depth, you know much about Him. You cannot then call yourself an atheist or unbeliever. For you cannot think or say: Life has no depth! Life itself is shallow. Being itself is surface only. If you could say this in complete seriousness you would be an atheist; but otherwise you are not. He who knows about depth knows about God.[5]

A further clarification of what Tillich means by ultimate concern is found in his sermon on the Gospel story of Martha and Mary. The two sisters are used as symbols of the two possible views that a man can take of the meaning of life.

> Martha is concerned about many things, but all of them are finite, preliminary, transitory. Mary is concerned about one thing, which is infinite, ultimate, lasting.[6]

As it is with Martha and Mary so it is with every man.

> Man is concerned about many things: food, shelter, knowl-
> edge, art, social problems, politics—with varying degrees of
> urgency. But a concern becomes ultimate only when it
> demands total surrender and promises total fulfillment. Ulti-
> mate concern is unconditional, total, and infinite. Any
> concern less than this is a preliminary concern, for it is condi-
> tional, partial, and finite.[7]

All men, then, in Tillich's analysis of the human situation have something about which they are ultimately concerned, something that is all-
important to them, something for which they are willing to give their lives.
Ultimate concern is a universal human phenomenon. It follows then that
all men are believers because the name God is the symbol for what concerns a man ultimately.

It would appear that Tillich, in speaking of God as both Ground of
being and ultimate concern, is attempting to throw light on the notion of
God from two different but allied points of view. God is, to begin with,
seen as the depth dimension in life. One meets Him as one plunges below
the surface of reality, where all is superficial and transitory, to the level of
things that really count in one's life. The deeper one drives into the heart
of reality, the closer one comes to what is of final and decisive concern in
one's life. When that point is reached, one has come to that which gives
both being and final meaning to all reality; one has attained to the Ground
of being; one has encountered God.

Tillich now moves to his next point, his contention that, in the Christian message, this God speaks to man as he is in his existential situation of
separation, alienation, and despair. That man yearns for something which
will give him meaning and hope in his life. To that man God speaks in His
Word, Jesus Christ. To that man He holds out in Christ the promise of
"New Being."

THE NEW BEING

In the person of Jesus as portrayed in the New Testament one sees a
man not subject to the separation from the Ground of being that plagues
one's own life. As a man Jesus lived as other men do, in all the circumstances of the human situation. Like other men he too exercised his
freedom, but always within the clear context of who he was, a dependent,

finite and therefore limited being. As such he lived in an uninterrupted acknowledgment of the Ground of his being. In him there was that which Tillich calls perfect "God-manhood." This is man as God intended him to be, man transparent to the depths of being itself. Fully human though he was, he lived not separated from but continuously united with God. He embodied the complete overcoming of all separation from ultimate reality. In a word, he lived what he was, accepting reality for what it was.

Here, in Jesus Christ, lies the power of man's renewal, his reconciliation with himself and with God. Here is the New Being, the principle of human salvation. ". . . reuniting that which is estranged, giving a centre to what is split, overcoming the split between God and man, and man and his world, man and himself."[8] United with him man comes to share the power of that New Being. In the strength of that power he can be liberated from his misuse of freedom; he can be freed from the separation that curses his human existence; he can participate in God-manhood.

But how does man come to participate in this New Being? Christianity says, in a puzzling paradox, man needs only accept the fact that he is accepted. He need only believe and trust that in Christ God gives him the New Being.

> . . .it is as though a voice were saying: "You are accepted. . . .
> Do not try to do anything now; perhaps later you will do
> much. Do not seek for anything;. . .*Simply accept the fact
> that you are accepted*![9]

J. Heywood Thomas neatly paraphrases this Tillichian notion of faith when he says,

> . . . faith is paradoxical in character. It is accepting and being
> accepted, accepting acceptance. Faith accepts the fact that he
> who is separated is accepted.[10]

Once a man has come to this belief and trust he is able to accept himself for what he is: sinner but saved, separated but united to the divine ground. Out of this being accepted he comes to self-acceptance. Thus is he healed. Thus in the power of the New Being does the divine answer reply to the human question: What is the meaning of life.

RELIGION AND CULTURE

A further aspect of Tillich's thought calls for comment, his lifelong interest in the relationship between religion and culture.

A man is religious if he is ultimately concerned, or, put another way, if he affirms that all being has its source and ground in God, Being-Itself. A culture is that complex web of structures, relationships, forms and expressions with which man surrounds himself and through which he expresses who he is and what meaning he gives to life.

The relation between religion and culture, as Tillich reads history, is a dialectical one in which at one point in history each interpenetrates the other and at another time one rejects or stands over against the other. The process by which this relationship expresses itself in history moves through three stages, one replacing and negating the other, only, in its turn, to be negated and replaced. The process is at once cyclic and forward moving like a wheel in motion.

The first type of relation between religion and culture, Tillich calls "theonomy" or a "theonomous culture." In such a period of history man is at peace with himself and at one with the "unconditional." It is a culture which ". . . expresses in its creations an ultimate concern and a transcending meaning not as something strange but as its own spiritual ground."[11] Man reads reality and he accepts his place in it as one who is free, yet finite, capable of unlimited growth yet within a context of limitation. God's law as it manifests itself in the order of things is seen to be in harmony with man's own nature. The culture that such a man creates manifests this acceptance of reality in all of its cultural expressions. All these expressions speak of ultimate concern and of a relationship between man and God and man and man which is integral and authentic. Man is at home in the world because he has found his real place in it. He is very much involved in penetrating and understanding reality yet his expression of that understanding is always in terms of things as they really are. Tillich would cite the early Middle Ages and the beginning period of the Reformation as times in history when such a theonomous culture existed, when God was present in all of society.

But the same history that displays theonomous cultures evidences also a type of culture to which theonomy seems inevitably to yield. This is "heteronomy," the "heteronomous culture." Thus, for example, the high

Middle Ages yielded to the barren externalism and the deadening weight of legalism of the late Middle Ages; the Protestant Reformation gave way to Protestant orthodoxy when the dynamic, living insights of the Reformers were replaced by the systems and codes and laws of their seventeenth century successors.

Heteronomy is a period when a shift occurs in the source from which man draws his awareness of the Ground of being and his relationship to that Ground. In theonomy the source of the awareness is man's own self, particularly his reason assenting to reality as it presents itself to him. Reason and things as they are coincide. But in heteronomy the understanding of reality is imposed upon man from outside himself. "Heteronomy asserts that man, being unable to act according to universal reason, must be subjected to a law, strange and superior to him."[12]

The momentum of a theonomous society continues its existence beyond the time when its cultural forms were the natural expression of how man saw reality. But in heteronomy inner vision, as the source of culture and the root of an authentic view of reality and man's place in it, is replaced by external authority.

Either church or state sets itself up as the arbiter of what a man is to believe and how he is to act. Religion or state validates its authority by claiming to speak for God. Human freedom and cultural creativity are stifled. The external cultural trappings of a theonomous culture continue but the authenticity has gone out of them. They no longer spring from man's own inner vision but are derived from and imposed by law and authority. Sooner or later man rebels against such an externally determined culture. He will not for long accept a meaning of life and an explanation of who he is that is imposed from outside himself.

When the limit of man's tolerance of heteronomy is reached, the stage is set for the movement of history to a third cultural form, "autonomy" or the "autonomous culture." Such a culture is always reactionary, a reaction against the external forces that have imposed a world-view and a culture. It is a movement in the direction of human self-assertion, the insistence that man himself must control the building of his cultural environment. Man becomes the center of all things, the determiner of meaning and its manifold expressions in his society. He lives by his own rationality, making his own laws. It is an autonomy because there is no openness to reality as it is in itself, as is the case in theonomy. Rather the rupture of harmonious correlation between man's vision of meaning and the meaning inherent in reality of itself, which was introduced by heteronomy, is continued. Man does not accept the meaning present in reality. He rather decides what meaning he will allow reality to have and what cultural expression he will give to that meaning. Autonomy, then, is a culture dominated by man's reason. In it man is ultimately concerned about himself. Cultural forms are void of any reference to the ultimate. There is only the here and now, the "conditioned." Tillich sees the Renaissance as an example of autonomous man's rejection of the heteronomy of the late Middle Ages; in eighteenth-century rationalism he reads reason's rejection of Protestant orthodoxy; finally he regards contemporary society as the latest example of an autonomous culture.

KAIROS

At this point Tillich introduces another of his characteristic ideas to describe how one culture comes to pass over into another. This is his notion of *kairos*, a Greek word which, in literal translation means: 'the right or acceptable time.' The term in its general sense refers to the passage from one form of culture to another. In a very particular sense it is used to refer to the coming of Jesus Christ, the New Being. This is the unique *Kairos*, in human history, unique because it has universal significance for all mankind. Apart from this meaning, there is one final use that Tillich makes of the idea. There is only one *Kairos*, but throughout history there have been other *kairoi*, other acceptable times. These are the points in history at which autonomy is ripe for a movement into theonomy.

Tillich believes our own age to be on the verge of such a *kairos*. As he reads the cultural signs of our time, autonomy has just about exhausted itself. Man appears to have come to the point of no return in his attempt to impose his own meaning on the world. The legacy of that attempt has been meaninglessness, absurdity, despair. Life seems to have no depth or meaning. All indications seem to point to the return of religion to culture. As Tillich would put it, autonomy is entering a *kairos* for its return to theonomy. The "acceptable time" appears to be once again present for man to realize the sterility and lack of fulfillment inherent in his self-centered view of reality. Tillich looks forward to a proximate return of man and his culture to a world where the ultimate meaning of things is rooted and grounded in God.

Toward the beginning of our treatment of Tillich, reference was made to his conviction that "as the substance of culture is religion, so the form of religion is culture." The statement offers a convenient vehicle for a final summary of his ideas on religion and culture. In a theonomous culture, religion and culture are closely interrelated. Culture expresses religion's concern with the ultimate and religion gives meaning to all cultural forms. But when theonomy yields to heteronomy, the relation of religion to culture is distorted. Religion dominates in this culture. In such a culture it is not ultimate concern rising up out of man's own inner being that forms and fashions culture. Rather the finite replaces the infinite as the source and ground of culture. A finite authority imposes its own conception of the meaning of reality. Thus the culture becomes an expression of the 'demonic,' a substitution of the conditioned for the unconditional. A distorted religion falsifies the cultural forms.

The passage from heteronomy to autonomy represents another kind of distortion, another dislocation of the right relationship between religion and culture. Culture now rises out of man's self-sufficiency and cannot therefore be a reflection of reality as it truly is. Culture is false in that it is wrongly grounded. Balance and cohesion is only restored when by a return to theonomy, religion is rightly restored to its role as the substance of, as that which gives unconditional meaning to, culture. Culture reassumes its authentic function as the expression in conditioned forms of the true understanding of reality which is based on man's acknowledgment of his relation to God, the Ground of all being.

CONCLUSION

When one comes to an appraisal of Tillich's thought, one is brought face to face with the quandary in which today's Christian thinkers find themselves. Two alternatives seem to be open to them in their attempt to present Christianity to contemporary man. The choice of either alternative appears to involve almost insoluble problems. On the one hand, Barth's choice, a presentation of the Christian faith with accent on God as wholly Other and as standing in judgment on all human achievement, strikes no responsive chord in the heart of modern man. His view that God reveals Himself to man in the Scriptures and that man's only way to God lies in the obedience of faith to this revelation is unacceptable to a generation that has grown up in a world where evidences of man's self-sufficiency grow ever more impressive. Christianity, as Barth presents it, seems to them quite unnecessary.

Tillich opts for the other alternative, to start with man where he is, to analyze the existential situation of man and then show how Christian faith can help man to cope with problems arising out of that situation. By so choosing, Tillich opens himself up to charges from both Christian theologian and secular man.

For the theologian, Tillich's interpretation of the Christian message is open to serious question. To begin with, they say, God, as Tillich describes Him, bears little likeness to the God of traditional Christianity. Tillich's God is not personal since person is a category that can only be used of a being and God is beyond being. He is its Ground. What then, they ask, becomes of the God of Abraham, the Father of our Lord Jesus Christ and the personal God Christian faith has believed in for two millenia?

The theologians also find serious difficulty with Tillich's understanding of Jesus. For Tillich, Jesus was human, not divine. He was the man in whom man's primal separation from the divine ground of being was completely healed. In this sense he was a unique man, but a man, nonetheless. What does this portrait do to the biblical affirmations of his divinity?

Thus the two linchpins of the whole Christian faith, the traditional Christian personalist theism and the divinity of Christ, seem to be unfastened by Tillich. If this is true, what then remains of Christianity? The charge of the theologian, then, is that Tillich has sacrificed the integrity of the Christian message for the sake of contemporary relevance.

On the other hand, Tillich is likewise rejected by contemporary man. Harvey Cox voices that rejection in these terms.

> Tillich's approach has no place for pragmatic man. It is built on the assumption that man by his very nature *must* ask these "ultimate" or existential questions. . . . The difficulty, however, is that they are obviously *not* questions which occur to everyone, or indeed to the vast majority of people. They especially do not occur to the newly emergent urban-secular man.[13]

For all of his attempts to speak contemporaneously, the charge is, Tillich uses the language of nineteenth century idealism. He speaks of a world where the structures of being correspond to the laws of man's reason. His universe of thought is heavy with philosophical terminology, with the tension between being and nonbeing, with the challenge to man to pass from existential separation to union with the Ground of being. But,

> The appeals of Tillich and others of his generation to the "depths of life" invoked by the "meaning" of the old myths are expressions of beliefs and sensibilities that we no longer share.[14]

Man today does not ask the questions that Tillich says it is natural for
him to ask. If this charge be true then Tillich's answers fall on unhearing
ears. Tillich's method of correlation, it would seem, fails of its purpose.
The men of the two worlds he would bring together for mutual enlighten-
ment both find serious fault with his attempt to correlate them.

Protestant Christian thought has traveled a long road from Luther and
Calvin to Barth and Tillich. In some eras the road has passed mostly
through the land of Christian revelation. At other times the road's environ
has been the landscape of human experience with Christian revelation as
the sun illuminating the highway. And sometimes the road has run along
the boundary between the sacred and the secular. The present question, on
which the future depends, is: how is to possible to build that road into the
future in such a way that it runs between irrelevance and adaptation? We
are only at the beginning of tentative probings toward an answer to that
question.

FOOTNOTES

1 Paul Tillich, *Systematic Theology* 3 vols. (Chicago: University of Chicago Press, 1951) I, 60.

2——, *The Interpretation of History* (New York: Charles Scribner's Sons, 1936), p. 50.

3——, *The Shaking of the Foundations,* paperback edition (New York: Charles Scribner's Sons, 1948), pp. 159-60.

4*Ibid.,* p. 57.

5*Ibid.*

6Tillich, *The New Being,* paperback edition *(New York: Charles Scribner's Sons, 1955), p. 152.*

7Carl J. Armbruster, S. J., *The Vision of Paul Tillich* (New York: Sheed and Ward Inc., 1967), p. 25.

8Tillich, *Systematic Theology,* II, 192.

9——, *The Shaking of the Foundations,* p. 162.

10J. Heywood Thomas, *Paul Tillich* (Richmond: John Knox Press, 1966), p. 14.

11Tillich, *The Protestant Era,* paperback abridged edition (Chicago: University of Chicago Press, 1957), p. 57.

12*Ibid.,* p. 56.

13Harvey Cox, *The Secular City* (New York: Macmillan Co., 1965), p. 79.

14John Charles Cooper, *The Roots of the Radical Theology* (Philadelphia: The Westminster Press, 1967), copyright ©1967, The Westminster Press. Used by permission. p. 135.

Bibliography

Reformation

Bainton, Roland, *The Reformation of the Sixteenth Century.* Boston: The Beacon Press, 1952.

Bouyer, Louis, *The Spirit and Forms of Protestantism.* Westminster, Md.: The Newman Press, 1956.

Chadwick, Owen, *The Reformation.* Baltimore: Penguin Books, 1964.

Dillenberger, John and Claude Welch, *Protestant Christianity.* New York: Charles Scribner's Sons, 1954.

Dolan, John, *History of the Reformation.* New York: Desclee Co., 1965.

Lortz, Joseph, *The Reformation: A Problem for Today.* Westminster, Md.: The Newman Press, 1964.

Pauck, Wilhelm, *The Heritage of the Reformation.* New York: Oxford University Press, 1968.

Van de Pol, Willem , *World Protestantism.* New York: Herder and Herder, 1964.

Whale, J.S., *The Protestant Tradition.* Cambridge: Cambridge University Press, 1959.

Martin Luther

Bainton, Roland, *Here I Stand: A Life of Martin Luther.* New York: The New American Library, 1955.

Boehmer, Heinrich, *Martin Luther: Road to Reformation*. New York: Meridian Books, 1957.

Bornkamm, Heinrich, *Luther's World of Thought*. St. Louis: Concordia Publishing House, 1965.

Dillenberger, John, *Martin Luther: Selections From His Writings*. Garden City: Doubleday and Co., Inc., 1961.

Green, V.H.H., *Luther and the Reformation*. New York: Capricorn Books, 1964.

Kerr, Hugh T. (ed.), *A Compend of Luther's Theology*. Philadelphia: The Westminster Press, 1943.

Rupp, E.G., *Luther's Progress to the Diet of Worms*. New York: Harper & Row, 1964.

Rupp, E.G., *The Righteousness of God*. London: Hodder and Stoughton, 1953.

Todd, John, *Martin Luther*. Westminster, Md.: The Newman Press, 1965.

John Calvin

Harkness, Georgia, *John Calvin: The Man and His Ethic*. New York & Nashville: Abingdon Press, 1958.

Kerr, Hugh T. (ed.), *A Compend of the Institutes of the Christian Religion by John Calvin*. Philadelphia: The Westminster Press, 1964.

McNeill, John, *The History and Character of Calvinism*. New York: Oxford University Press, 1954.

Olin, John (ed.), *A Reformation Debate: John Calvin and Jacopo Sadoleto*. New York: Harper & Row, 1966.

Wendel, Francois, *Calvin*. London: William Collins, Sons & Co. Ltd., 1965.

Anabaptism

Bainton, Roland, *The Travail of Religious Liberty.* New York: Harper & Row, 1957.

Estep, William., *The Anabaptist Story.* Nashville, Tenn.: Broadman Press, 1963.

Hershberger, Guy F. (ed.), *The Recovery of the Anabaptist Vision.* Scottdale, Pa.: Herald Press, 1957.

Lecler, Joseph, *Toleration and the Reformation.* New York: Association Press, 1960.

Littell, Franklin, *A Tribute to Menno Simons.* Scottdale, Pa.: Herald Press, 1961.

————, *The Origins of Sectarian Protestantism.* New York: The Macmillan Co., 1964.

Williams, George, *The Radical Reformation.* Philadelphia: The Westminster Press, 1962.

Williams, George and Angel Mergal, (eds.), *Spiritual and Anabaptist Writers,* vol. XXV. *Library of Christian Classics.* Philadelphia: The Westminster Press, 1957.

Anglicanism

Dickens, A.G., *The English Reformation.* New York: Schocken Books, Inc., 1964.

Hughes, Philip, *The Reformation in England* (3 vols.). London: Hollis and Carter, and New York: The Macmillan Co., 1950-54.

Neill, Stephen, *Anglicanism.* Baltimore: Penguin Books, 1958.

Parker, T.M. *The English Reformation to 1558.* London: Oxford University Press, 1950.

Ridley, Jasper, *Thomas Cranmer.* Oxford: The Clarendon Press, 1962.

Rupp, E.G., *Studies in the Making of the English Protestant Tradition.* Cambridge: Cambridge University Press, 1966.

Wand, J. W. C., *Anglicanism in History and Today.* New York and Toronto: Thomas Nelson and Sons, 1962.

Puritanism

Haller, William, *The Rise of Puritanism.* New York: Harper & Row, 1957.

————, *Liberty and Reformation in the Puritan Revolution.* New York: Columbia University Press, 1955.

Knappen, M. M., *Tudor Puritanism.* Chicago: University of Chicago Press, 1939.

Morgan, Edmund, *The Puritan Dilemma.* Boston: Little, Brown and Co., 1958.

Perry, Ralph, *Puritanism and Democracy.* New York: Harper & Row, 1964.

Schneider, Herbert, *The Puritan Mind.* Ann Arbor, Mich.: University of Michigan Press, 1958.

Simpson, Alan, *Puritanism in Old and New England.* Chicago: University of Chicago Press, 1955.

Methodism

Burtner, Robert and Robert Chiles, (eds.), *A Compend of Wesley's Theology.* Nashville, Tenn.: Abingdon Press, 1954.

Cragg, G.R., *The Church and the Age of Reason 1648-1789.* Baltimore: Penguin Books, 1960.

Curnock, Nehemiah (ed.), *The Journal of John Wesley.* New York: Capricorn Books, 1963; G.P. Putnam's Sons.

Davies, Rupert, *Methodism*. Baltimore: Penguin Books, 1963.

McConnell, Francis, *John Wesley*. New York and Nashville: Abingdon Press, 1939.

Rack, Henry, *The Future of John Wesley's Methodism*. Richmond, Va.: John Knox Press, 1965.

Todd, John, *John Wesley and the Catholic Church*. London: Hodder and Stoughton, 1958.

Williams, Colin, *John Wesley's Theology Today*. London: Epworth Press, 1960.

Nineteenth Century Liberal Protestantism

Barth, Karl, *Protestant Thought: From Rousseau to Ritschl*. New York: Harper and Brothers, 1959.

Niebuhr, Richard, *Schleiermacher on Christ and Religion: A New Introduction*. New York: Charles Scribner's Sons, 1964.

Reardon, B.M.G. (ed.), *Religious Thought in the Nineteenth Century*. Cambridge: Cambridge University Press, 1966.

Schleiermacher, Friedrich, *On Religion: Speeches to Its Cultured Despisers*. New York: Harper and Brothers, 1958.

Schweitzer, Albert, *The Quest of the Historical Jesus*. New York: The Macmillan Co., 1961.

Vidler, Alec, *The Church in An Age of Revolution 1789 to the Present Day*. Baltimore: Penguin Books, 1961.

Karl Barth

Barth, Karl, *The Humanity of God*. Richmond, Va.: John Knox Press, 1966.

———, *The Word of God and the Word of Man*. New York: Harper & Row, 1957.

Casalis, Georges, *Portrait of Karl Barth*. Garden City: Doubleday and Co., Inc., 1964.

Hamer, Jerome, *Karl Barth.* Westminster, Md.: The Newman Press, 1962.

Hartwell, Herbert, *The Theology of Karl Barth: An Introduction.* Philadelphia: The Westminster Press, 1964.

Willems, Boniface, *Karl Barth: An Ecumenical Approach to His Theology.* Glen Rock, N.J.: Paulist Press, 1965.

Dietrich Bonhoeffer

Bonhoeffer, Dietrich, *Ethics.* New York: The Macmillan Co., 1965.

————, *Letters and Papers From Prison.* New York: The Macmillan Co., 1962.

————, *Cost of Discipleship.* New York: The Macmillan Co., 1963.

————, *No Rusty Swords.* New York: Harper & Row, 1965.

Godsey, John, *The Theology of Dietrich Bonhoeffer.* Philadelphia: The Westminster Press, 1960.

Kuhns, William, *In Pursuit of Dietrich Bonhoeffer.* Dayton, Ohio: Pflaum Press, 1967.

Marty, Martin (ed.), *The Place of Bonhoeffer.* New York: Association Press, 1962.

Moltmann, Jürgen and Jürgen Weissbach, *Two Studies in the Theology of Dietrich Bonhoeffer.* New York: Charles Scribner's Sons, 1967.

Robertson, E.H., *Dietrich Bonhoeffer.* Richmond, Va.: John Knox Press, 1966.

Vorkink, Peter (ed.), *Bonhoeffer in a World Come of Age.* Philadelphia: Fortress Press, 1968.

Rudolf Bultmann

Bartsch, Hans (ed.), *Kerygma and Myth.* New York: Harper & Row, 1961.

Bultmann, Rudolf, *Jesus and the Word*. New York: Charles Scribner's Sons, 1934.

———, *History and Eschatology*. New York: Harper & Row, 1962.

———, *Jesus Christ and Mythology*. New York: Charles Scribner's Sons, 1958.

Fries, Heinrich, *Bultmann-Barth and Catholic Theology*. Pittsburgh, Pa.: Duquesne University Press, 1967.

Macquarrie, John, *An Existentialist Theology*. New York: Harper & Row, 1965.

———, *The Scope of Demythologizing*. New York: Harper & Row, 1966.

O'Meara, Thomas and Donald Weisser, (eds.), *Rudolf Bultmann in Catholic Thought*. New York: Herder and Herder, 1968.

Reinhold Niebuhr

Carnell, Edward, *The Theology of Reinhold Niebuhr*. Grand Rapids, Mich.: W.B. Eerdmans Publishing Co., 1951.

Harland, Gordon, *The Thought of Reinhold Niebuhr*. New York: Oxford University Press, 1960.

Kegley, Charles and Robert Bretall, (eds.), *Reinhold Niebuhr: His Religious, Social and Political Thought*. New York: The Macmillan Co., 1961.

Niebuhr, Reinhold, *The Nature and Destiny of Man*. 2 vols., New York: Charles Scribner's Sons, 1941-43.

———, *Moral Man and Immoral Society*. New York, Charles Scribner's Sons, 1932.

———, *Beyond Tragedy*. New York: Charles Scribner's Sons, 1937.

———, *The Children of Light and the Children of Darkness*. New York: Charles Scribner's Sons, 1944.

Bibliography

Paul Tillich

Adams, James, *Paul Tillich's Philosophy of Culture, Science and Religion.* New York: Harper & Row, 1965.

Armbruster, Carl, *The Vision of Paul Tillich.* New York: Sheed and Ward, 1967.

Brown, D. M., *Ultimate Concern: Tillich in Dialogue.* New York: Harper & Row, 1965.

Kegley, Charles and Robert Bretall, (eds.), *The Theology of Paul Tillich.* New York: The Macmillan Co., 1962.

Martin, Bernard, *The Existentialist Theology of Paul Tillich.* New Haven: College and University Press, 1964.

McKelway, Alexander, *The Systematic Theology of Paul Tillich.* Richmond, Va.: John Knox Press, 1964.

Tavard, George, *Paul Tillich and the Christian Message.* New York: Charles Scribner's Sons, 1962.

Tillich, Paul, *The New Being.* New York: Charles Scribner's Sons, 1955.

———, *The Shaking of the Foundations.* New York: Charles Scribner's Sons, 1948.

———, *The Religious Situation.* New York: Meridian Books, 1956.

———, *The Theology of Culture.* New York: Oxford University Press, 1964.

———, *The Protestant Era.* Chicago: University of Chicago Press, 1948.

Index

Bonhoeffer, Dietrich (continued)
    Letters and Papers from Prison, 156,
        163-68
    salvation, problem of, 165-67
    Sanctorum Communio, 147, 148-49
Book of Common Prayer (Anglican) 70, 73
        78-79, 80, 89, 102
Book of Homilies (Anglican), 70-71
Borowitz, Eugene, 143
Bouyer, Louis, 4
Brown, R. M., 16-17, 25-26, 50
Bucer, Martin, 31, 32, 33, 34
Bultmann, Rudolf, 111, 146, **173-86,**
        204
    assessment of, 183-86
    "demythologizing" Scripture, 174,
        179-83, 184
    existentialism in, 174-77
    God's Word, disengagement of, 177-
        80
    myth, view of, 177-80
    Scripture, reinterpretation of, 180-83
    Theology of the New Testament, The,
        181-83

Calvin, John, **31-51,** 55, 72, 76, 80, 83,
        86, 91, 106, 109, 118, 130, 216
    assessment of, 48-51
    baptism, place of, 45, 46-47
    church, views on, 41-45
    Commentary on the Psalms, 32-33
    Commentary on the Romans, 34
    covenant with God, 41-42
    *Ecclesiastical Ordinances of the
        Church of Geneva,* 44-45
    Eucharist, place of, 45, 46-47
    God, sovereignty of, 35-37
    Institutes of the Christian Religion,
        33
    life of, 32-34
    *Little Treatise on the Holy Supper of
        Our Lord,* 34
    Predestination, Doctrine of, 38-41
    Reply to Cardinal Sadoleto, 34
    sacraments, place of, 45-48
    Soli Deo Gloria, Doctrine of, 37-38
    theology of, 35-48
Calvinism (*see* Calvin, John)
Cambridge University, 84
Catharine of Aragon, 67, 71
Charles I, 85
Christian Faith, The (Schleiermacher),
        112, 114-16

Christian realism, in Neibuhr, 188, 189-
        202
Christian vocation, 24-26
Church Dogmatics (Barth), 136, 137
Church of England (*see also* Anglicanism),
        32, 72, 82, 83, 96-97, 102, 108
Church of the Creed, 17-18
Commentary on the Psalms (Calvin), 32-33
Commentary on the Romans (Calvin), 34
Communism, 142
Confessing Church, 142
Confirmation, 20
Congregationalism (*see* Puritanism)
Consensus, in Anabaptism, 58-59
Constantine, 62
Cop, Nicholas, 33
Cost of Discipleship, The (Bonhoeffer),
        152-56
Covenant, in Calvin, 41-42
Covenanters, 32
Cox, Harvey, 215
Cranmer, Thomas, 70-71, 78-80, 89
Cromwell, Oliver, 90
Cult of Mary, 68

Davies, Rupert E., 102-103
Deism, 97-98
"Demythologizing" Scripture, 174, 179-
        83, 184
Dickens, A. G., 69
Directory of Public Worship (Puritan),
        89
Dissenters, 32

*Ecclesiastical Ordinances of the Church
        of Geneva,* 44-45
Ecclesiastical Polity (Hooker), 73-74
Edward VI, 70
Eliseus, 122
Elizabeth I, 32, 71, 82, 84, 85, 88
Epistle of St. James, 20
Epistle to the Romans, The (Barth), 130
Epistle to the Romans (St. Paul), 6-9, 38
Erasmus, Desiderius, 31
Ethics (Bonhoeffer), 147, 156-63
Eucharist, 19, 22-24, 45, 46-47
Evangelism, in Anabaptism, 60
Existentialism, in Bultmann, 174-77
Extreme Unction, 20-21

Faith, Principle of, 8, 9-13

Date Due

FEB 1-			
APR 1 8 2017			

Demco 38-297

An Index to Mexican Literary Periodicals

by

Merlin H. Forster

The Scarecrow Press, Inc.
New York and London   1966

TABLE OF CONTENTS

Introduction

1. General

The recent work of Boyd G. Carter,[1] Sturgis E. Leavitt,[2] and John E. Englekirk,[3] as well as publication of an extensive periodical index by G. K. Hall and Company,[4] gives strong indication of an increasing interest in cataloging and indexing the rich and extensive periodical materials of Spanish America which have been virtually without such guides for critical use.[5] The present volume is much more specialized and modest in scope than either the Leavitt index, which includes slightly over 30,000 entries from 56 Spanish American literary periodicals from the 19th and 20th centuries, or the G K. Hall publication, which includes some 250,000 entries selected from an estimated 3,000 Latin American periodicals representing widely diverse fields. The periodicals indexed in this volume come from one country only and from a less extensive chronological period than that covered by the Leavitt index. Much has been gained, however, from such a reduction. This grouping of significant twentieth-century Mexican periodicals, often "little magazines" not included in the larger index publications, has made possible detailed and classified coverage of an important part of Mexican literary expression during a period of some forty years.

2. Selection

The selection of periodicals to be indexed involved several considerations. First, only those literary and cultural journals which began and completed publication during the general period from 1920 to 1960 were considered. Then, because of unavailability of complete collections, such important publications as El Libro y El Pueblo (1922-1935), Letras de México (1937-1947), and Rueca (1944-1948) were regretfully excluded. Also, some effort was made to include publications which were associated with important literary groups in Mexico (such as Contemporáneos, Taller, and Tierra

<u>Nueva</u>). Finally, three journals for which indices already exist in widely scattered places[6] have been reindexed here in order to facilitate their consultation.

The sixteen periodicals finally chosen, though from the same country and general period, are certainly not alike in quality or intent. <u>México Moderno,</u> <u>Contemporáneos,</u> <u>El Hijo</u> <u>Prodigo,</u> and <u>Estaciones,</u> all primarily literary, are certainly more influential publications than the equally literary but much more restricted <u>Poesía,</u> or even <u>Prometeus</u> or <u>Ruta</u>. <u>Romance</u>, with its wide range of articles and sections and its popular style and <u>Forma</u>, a journal of the plastic arts, are probably the least literary of the journals included, although contributions on literature or by important literary figures appeared often in both.[7] The periodicals chosen for indexing, then, represent a varied selection from among recent journals of Mexican literature and culture.

3. Format

The index is divided into two sections: 1) Author List, and 2) Index to Author List. Section I is an alphabetical listing of all materials by author, in which each item is assigned a serial number. Collaborations, translations, and other items of multiple authorship take the serial number of their first occurrence, regardless of whether they first appear under primary author, translator, or first listed collaborator. All subsequent occurrences of such items show the already established serial number in parentheses. Each item also has an abbreviated designation as to literary genre, which appears in parentheses at the end of the entry (see full listing of abbreviations on page facing Section I).

In cases where a particular author has more than one entry, the order of entries is as follows: 1) all items except reviews and translations (listed alphabetically by title); 2) reviews (listed alphabetically under title of the book reviewed); 3) translations (listed alphabetically under translated title). The designation "Anónimo" has been used for all unsigned contributions, and the entries under this designation have been presented first by journal and then alphabetically by title.

Section II is a detailed cross-listing index to Section I,

6

including authors, important secondary references, authors of books reviewed, and subject matter classifications (i. e. , Art, Prose Fiction, History, Philosophy, etc.) In this section reference is made to entries in Section I by using serial numbers assigned there.

4. Acknowledgements

Support for this work has been granted unstintingly over a period of two years by the Graduate College Research Board of the University of Illinois, and also by the Department of Spanish, Italian, and Portuguese, which has given generous supplementary support for acquisition of materials and for manuscript reproduction. I owe special thanks to Professor H. H. Thornberry for his helpful suggestions on classification systems and materials, and to Mr. William H. Huff of the University of Illinois Library for his invaluable help in acquiring and completing collections of periodicals. Finally, I am deeply indebted to Richard M. Reeve and Jane Killam, and also to Gerald W. Petersen, R. R. Hinojosa-Smith, and Jean B. Cortina, without whose combined and conscientious assistance this work would have been virtually impossible.

M. H. F.

Urbana, Illinois
August, 1965

1. Las revistas literarias de Hispanoamérica: Breve historia y contenido. México: Ed. de Andrea (Col. Stadium, No. 24), 1959. 282 pp.

2. Revistas hispanoamericanas: Indice bibliográficio. Santiago de Chile, 1960. 589 pp.

3. "La literatura y la revista literaria en Hispanoamérica." Revista Iberoamericana, XXVII (1961), 9-79, 219-279; XXVIII (1962), 9-73; XXIX (1963), 9-66.

4. Index to Latin-American Periodical Literature, 1929-1960. Boston, 1962. 8 vols. , with Supplement (1963).

5. See Carter, pp. 266-268, for listing of indices and guides to certain periodicals, complete to 1959. Other important publications since then are: Ana Elena Díaz y Alejo et al., Indices de El Domingo (Mexico, 1959), and Indices de El Nacional (Mexico, 1961); Eduardo González Lanuza, Los martinfierristas (Buenos Aires, 1961); Nélida Salvador, Revistas argentinas de vanguardia (Buenos Aires, 1962);

7

Huberto Batis, Indices de El Renacimiento (Mexico, 1963), and Las revistas literarias de México, Vol. I (México, 1963), Vol. II (México, 1964).

6. Leavitt includes México Moderno and Contemporáneos (see also the unpublished M.A. thesis of Alberto M. MacLean, "Indice analítico de la revista Contemporáneos," Texas, 1964), and James K. MacDonald has published an index to Taller in Revista Iberoamericana, XXIX (1963), 325-340. The unpublished Ph.D dissertation of Manuel de Ezcurdia, "La aparición del grupo 'Contemporáneos' en la poesía y en la crítica mexicanas: 1920-1931" (California, Berkeley, 1964), also includes indices of Contemporáneos and Ulises.

7. It should be noted that non-literary articles as well as literary have been indexed in both Romance and Forma, as is the case in the other journals as well.

Summaries of Periodicals

ANTENA. Revista mensual. México, D. F. 5 Numbers, July-
November, 1924. Monthly. Recopilador: Francisco Monterde
García Icazbalceta.

Purpose:

"Esta revista no es portavoz de un grupo--ni literario
ni político . . . [Ella] se halla dispuesta a reconocer todos
los valores intelectuales, sin aceptar o rechazar ciegamente
los consagrados o los desconocidos . . Con un nacionalismo
consciente, no apasionado, dará cohabida a todas las manifes-
taciones de nuestra cultura . . . viendo primero en torno y
después hacia lo lejos" ("Advertencias," I, 2).

Sections:

Anecdotario (commentary); Arte; Ciencia; Letras (book
reviews); Notas (commentary); Radio (Radio Tópicos).

Other Comments:

Very few illustrations. Issues 16-20 pp.

CONTEMPORANEOS. Revista de cultura mexicana. México, D.
F. 11 volumes, 43 Numbers, June, 1928-December, 1931.
Monthly. Editores: Bernardo J. Gastélum, Jaime Torres
Bodet, Bernardo Ortiz de Montellano, and Enrique González
Rojo (1-8). Director: Bernardo Ortiz de Montellano (9-43).

Purpose:

"Nuestra Revista Contemporáneos cumple, con este
número, dos años de vida sin otro programa que ser nueva--
no de novedad pasajera--dentro del marco de su cultura y
su país" (VII, 99).

"En este año 3 la palabra que con más frecuencia se
advierte en las páginas de Contemporáneos es M _ _ _ _ O,
con x o con j, escrita siempre con plumafuente de marca
universal" (X, 97-98).

Sections:

Motivos (book reviews, commentaries on literature and culture, translations, etc.); Bibliografía; Libros de México y sobre México.

Other Comments:

Paper of excellent quality, careful printing, illustrated with numerous reproductions of paintings, engravings, and photographs. Accurate indices at end of each volume. Issues 90-100 pp.

ESTACIONES. Revista literaria de México. México, D. F. 5 Volumes, 20 Numbers, Primavera de 1956-Invierno de 1960. Quarterly. Editores: Elías Nandino (1-12), Alfredo Hurtado (1-10), and Andrés Henestrosa (11-12). Director: Elías Nandino (13-20). Jefe de Redacción: José de la Colina (11-12), and Alí Chumacero (13-20).

Purpose:

"Estaciones aparece animada del propósito de juntar en sus páginas, sin distinción de tendencias o de grupos, a todos los escritores mexicanos . . . . Otro propósito es el de incorporar a nuestra revista colaboraciones del extranjero y estudios acerca de la situación literaria, artística o filosófica de algunos países, a fin de informar de manera amplia a los lectores. Queremos ser mexicanos en nuestro impulso inicial, escribir desde el cielo que nos ampara; pero eso no nos hará sordos para atender a lo que, llegado desde fuera de nuestras fronteras geográficas, signifique una aportación a nuestra cultura" ("Palabras preliminares," I, 1).

Sections:

Libros Recibidos y Comentarios (book reviews); Notas Bibliográficas (book reviews); Ramas Nuevas (supplement); Revistas Recibidas (periodical reviews).

Other Comments:

Each issue has a different cover illustration, and most have other illustrative materials. Issues rather large (100-150 pp.).

FABULA. Hojas de México. México, D. F. 9 Numbers, January-September, 1934. Monthly. Las imprimen Alejandro Gómez Arias y Miguel N. Lira.

Sections:

Libros de México (reviews of books by Mexican authors); Libros para México (reviews of books published abroad about Mexico or at times by Mexican authors).

Other Comments:

Issues fairly small (app. 20 pp.) compared with Contemporáneos or Estaciones. Few illustrations.

LA FALANGE. Revista de cultura latina. México, D. F. 7 Numbers, December, 1922-October, 1923. Monthly. Directores: Jaime Torres Bodet and Bernardo Ortiz de Montellano.

Purpose:

"Cansados de vivir una vida estrecha y de clamar en el fondo de un pozo sin resonancia en donde la voz se ahoga y el ideal se pierde, varios literatos de México se reunen hoy en una falange de poetas y de artistas y editan hoy el primer número de una revista sin odios, sin prejuicios, sin dogmas, sin compromisos . . . [que] se propone:

expresar, sin límites, el alma latina de
América,

reunir a todos los literatos de México que hacen
literatura sana y sincera en un núcleo que
sea exponente de los valores humanos de
nuestra tierra,

servir de índice de la cultura artística nacional a
los demás pueblos del Nuevo Mundo"
("Propósitos," No. 1, 2-3).

Sections:

A. B. C. (commentary); Glosario (commentary); Kodak (humorous sketches); Letras Francesas; Libros (book reviews); Motivos; Poetas Nuevos; Poesía de América.

Other Comments:

Issues 40-60 pp., and each is illustrated by a young

11

painter (Rivera, Lozano, Mérida, and others). Editors claim that all material is strictly unpublished previously.

FORMA. Revista de artes plásticas. México, D. F. 7 Numbers, October, 1926- ?, 1928. Irregular. Director: Gabriel Fernández Ledesma. Representante de la Secretaría de Educación: Salvador Novo (2-7).

Purpose:

"La Secretaría de Educación ha acogido con beneplácito la idea del joven pintor Ledesma de publicar una revista mensual dedicada a las Artes Plásticas de México y patrocina su publicación. En ella se expondrán sucesivamente los múltiples aspectos de la producción nacional, y yo invito a todos los aristas de México a llenar sus páginas" (J M. Puig Casauranc, "Forma").

Sections:

Encuesta (on art and architecture, in 3 issues only), Jaguetes Mexicanos (in color).

Other Comments:

Excellent quality paper, and many plates and illustrations in both color and black and white. Issues 40-50 pp.

EL HIJO PRODIGO. Revista literaria. México, D. F. 13 Volumes, 42 Numbers, April 1943-September, 1946. Monthly. Fundador y editor (1-29): Octavio G. Barreda. Administrador (1-29) y editor (30-42): Isaac Rojas Rosillo. Director (30-42): Xavier Villaurrutia. Redactores: Alí Chumacero, Celestino Gorostiza (1-29), José Luis Martínez (30-40), Octavio Paz, Antonio Sánchez Barbudo, Rafael Solana (30-41), Xavier Villaurrutia (1-29), Leopoldo Zea (42).

Purpose:

"Y esta paradoja debe ser nuestro secreto, nuestro inalienable patronimio que nunca nos podrán arrancar; regreso sin regreso; realidad e imaginación.

Una intensa vida en el mundo imaginativo y un ojo y oído más finos para lo real de la vida cotidiana. Este acoplamiento, pensamos, es lo único que puede librarnos y

12

proporcionarnos una literatura integrada, una literatura humana"
("Imaginación, " I, 8).

Sections:

Correspondencia; Imaginación y Realidad (editorials);
Libros (book reviews); Notas (excerpts from authors of note);
Se Recomienda (in 5 issues only); Teatro (in 2 issues only).

Other Comments:

Series of paintings depicting the Biblical prodigal son
by various artists. Other illustrations. Issues 60-65 pp.,
with indices inside front cover (also complete index of each
volume). Number 39 for June of 1946 special number in
memory of Ramón López Velarde.

MEXICO MODERNO. Revista de letras y arte. México, D. F. 2
Volumes, 16 Numbers, August, 1920-June, 1923. Irregular.
Directores: Enrique González Martínez (I, 1-12), Manuel
Toussaint and Agustín Loera y Chávez (II, 4) Redactores
(II, 1 to II, 3): Vicente Lombardo Toledano, Pedro Henríquez
Ureña, Manuel Gómez Morín, Manuel Toussaint, Daniel Cosío
Villegas, and José Gorostiza.

Sections:

Antología (directed by Salomón de la Selva); El Arte
Musical en el Mundo y Crónica Musical Mexicana (Manuel M.
Ponce); Artes Plásticos de México (Manuel Toussaint); La
Joven Literatura Mexicana (Agustín Loera y Chávez); Letras
Francesas (Jaime Torres Bodet); Libros y Revistas (José
Gorostiza); Repertorio (Salvador Novo); Revista de Libros
(Genaro Estrada); Revistas de Revistas (Jaime Torres Bodet).

Other Comments:

Issues 60-70 pp. with almost no illustrations. No stated editorial purpose, although inside the front cover of the
first issue the following policy is announced: "El material de
esta revista es rigurosamente inédito. Por ningúm motivo se
acepta colaboración que no haya sido solicitada." Numbers
11-12 of Volume I (November, 1921) special issue in honor of
Ramón López Velarde.

POESIA. 3 Numbers, February, 1941-April, 1941. Monthly.
Edita Canek.
Comments:
　　No editorials or sections. Issues 12-34 pp., with works
of only 6 poets included. Photographs of poets are pasted
into individual issues.

PROMETEUS. Revista mexicana de literatura. México, D.F. 3
Numbers, February, 1949-April, 1949. Segunda época: 1
Number, December 1951. Monthly. Director: Francisco M.
Zendejas.
Purpose:
　　"No pretendemos ser anuncio da nada ni encabezar
movimientos estéticos, y con todas las reservas que la
declaración reclama, queremos dejar escrito que hoy, más
que nunca, el hombre está de cara hacia el pasado, no asido
por éste sino ansioso de entregarse y rendirse a todas las
reacciones políticas y morales de la Historia. Porque con-
sidera irreparable una existencia sin símbolos" ("Prometeus, "
1, 12).
Sections:
　　Bibliografía (book reviews).
Other Comments:
　　Issues 60-85 pp., with some sketches, drawings, and
other illustrations. Large amount of translated material with
no source indicated.

ROMANCE. Revista popular hispanoamericana. México, D.F. 2
Volumes, 24 Numbers, February 1, 1940-May 31, 1941. Bi-
weekly. Director: Juan Rejano (1-16). Gerente: Martín Luis
Guzmán (8-16). Director-Gerente: Martín Luis Guzmán (17-24).
Purpose:
　　"Sin carácter de grupo ni de tendencia, pero claramente
partidaria de un aspecto esencial de la cultura: su populariza-
ción, ROMANCE aspira a recoger en sus páginas las
expresiones más significativas--por la calidad de su pensamiento y sensibilidad--del movimiento cultural hispanoamericano
. . . .

14

Naturalmente, este sentimiento hispanoamericano de la cultura, nos obliga, por verdadero, a no encerrarnos, a no renunciar a la cultura de los demás pueblos, sino al contrario, a recogerla para enriquecer la nuestra y hacerla, a la vez, universal . . . ." ("Propósito," 1, 2).

Sections:

Arte; A la Deriva (cultural commentary); Bibliografía (short commentaries on books); Ciencia, Historia, Sociología; En Acecho (short unsigned essays on cultural topics); Espejo de las Horas (political commentary); Los Libros por Dentro (book reviews); Locuras de Cada Día (commentary on a variety of cultural and political topics); La Música; Página de Cine; Revista de Revistas; El Teatro; Ultimas Ediciones y Noticias; Encuesta (on contemporary art and culture).

Other Comments:

Large newspaper format, with issues of consistent size (24 pp.), and with profuse illustrations and photographs.

RUTA. Revista mensual de literatura. México, D. F. 4 Volumes, 12 Numbers, June, 1938-May, 1939. Monthly.

Director: José Mancisidor.

Purpose:

"Ruta . . . es una revista de literatura que dará a conocer al mundo a los escritores mexicanos formados en esta hora en que México crea su destino histórico. A todos los que en ella colaboramos, sólo una idea nos une: la de la defensa de la cultura y el de nuestra lucha firme en contra de su más enconado enemigo: el facismo internacional" ("Trayectoria de Ruta," 1, 63).

Sections:

Asteriscos (cultural commentary); Correo de Ruta (reviews of journals); Libros.

Other Comments:

Issues consistent in size (64 pp.), with very few illustrations. General indices at the end of each volume.

SAGITARIO. Revista del siglo XX. México, D. F. 14 Numbers,

July 15, 1926-May 31, 1927. Irregular. Director: Humberto Rivas.

Purpose:

"Revista del Siglo XX llamamos a nuestra revista y al llamarla así hemos querido dar a entender que en ella tendrán cabida todos los problemas y todas las inquietudes de la época en que vivimos. Hombres de nuestro tiempo, modernos ante todo--respetaremos lo que la tradición tenga de fundamental y de permanente, pero sin caer en las aberraciones clasicistas y casticistas que suelen ser la peor forma de la impotencia. La cultura y su difusión serán nuestro único fin . . ." ("Propósito, " 1, 1).

Sections:

La Instrucción y la Cultura en México (3 issues only); Lecturas y Apostillas (also as Libros Mexicanos and Libros y Revistas); Las Obras y los Días (commentaries by Eugenio d'Ors).

Other Comments:

Issues 15-20 pp., with a variety of illustrative materials. No pagination of any kind.

TALLER. Poesía y crítica. Revista mensual. México, D. F. 12 Numbers, December, 1938-February, 1941. Irregular. Responsables (1-4): Octavio Paz, Rafael Solana, Efraín Huerta, and Alberto Quintero Alvarez. Director: Octavio Paz (5-12). Secretario: Juan Gil-Albert (5-12).

Sections:

La Forma de las Horas (cultural commentary); Notas (book reviews); Tarjetas (commentary).

Other Comments:

Issues 40-100 pp., with scattered sketches and illustrations. Special section at end of each issue on world literary figures of note: Baudelaire, T. S. Eliot, Leopardi, etc.

TIERRA NUEVA. Revista de letras universitarias. México, D. F. 3 Volumes, 15 Numbers, January, 1940-December, 1942. Bimonthly. Responsables: Jorge González Durán, José Luis

Martínez, Alí Chumacero, Leopoldo Zea.

Sections:

Notas (book reviews); Páginas de Hoy (book reviews, combined with Notas after No. 3); Revistas.

Other Comments:

Issues 60-95 pp., with few illustrations. Poetry supplement without pagination included with each issue. Works of Jorge Cuesta, José Luis Martínez, Jorge González Durán, and others appeared here.

ULISES. Revista de curiosidad y crítica. México, D. F. 6 Numbers, May, 1927-February, 1928. Irregular. Editores: Salvador Novo and Xavier Villaurrutia.

Purpose:

"Pero es honrado declarar que Ulises no representa de ninguna manera el 'sentir nacional' . . . . Ulises no implica sino dos criterios, más o menos de acuerdo el uno con el otro. Villaurrutia y yo" (S. N., 6, 37).

Sections:

El Curioso Impertinente (book reviews and commentary, directed by Salvador Novo).

Other Comments:

Issues 30-40 pp., with numerous illustrations.

ABBREVIATIONS

a-e	=	Article and essay
dr	=	Drama
ed	=	Edition
f	=	Prose fiction
il	=	Illustrative material
p	=	Poetry
r	=	Review
tr	=	Translation

SECTION I

Author List

Abra. Pater, Walter Horacio.
"Ascesis" (Trad. Abra) México
Moderno, II (Núm. 3, oc-
tubre de 1922), 183-185. (tr)
1

Abreu Gómez, Ermilo. "Adver-
tencia y notas a la Carta
atenagórica de Sor Juana."
Contemporáneos, VI (Núm. 22,
marzo de 1930), 215-217.
(a-e)   2

----. "Alfonso Reyes." Fábula, Núm. 9 (septiembre de
1934), 171. (a-e)   3

----. "Alfredo Gómez de la
Vega." Sagitario, Núm. 6 (1
de noviembre de 1926), 15.
(a-e)   4

----. "Un aspecto del teatro
romántico: Peón y Contreras."
Contemporáneos, VIII (Núm.
30-31, noviembre-diciembre
de 1930), 222-248. (a-e)   5

----. "Breve historia de mis
libros." El Hijo Pródigo, XI
(Núm. 34, enero de 1946), 9-
16. (a-e)   6

----. "Burla burlando..."
Sagitario, Núm. 14 (31 de
mayo de 1927), 12-15 (dr) 7

----. "La carta atenagórica
de Sor Juana y los jesuitas."
Contemporáneos, IV (Núm. 12,
mayo de 1929), 137-143. (a-e)
8
----. "La commedia del arte."
México Moderno, II (Núm. 9,
mayo de 1921), 162-179 (a-e)
9

----. "Concepto del teatro."
Sagitario, Núm. 11 (15 de
marzo de 1927), 14. (a-e) 10

----. "Del estilo de Martín
Luis Guzmán." Ruta, 10 (marzo
de 1939), 41-42. (a-e)   11

----. "Del parecer la vía de
Góngora, sigo." Ulises, Núm.
3 (agosto de 1927), 39-40.
(a-e)   12

----. "Diálogo del buen decir."
Estaciones, V (Núm. 20, invierno de 1960), 6-22. (a-e) 13

----. "Dos cartas a propósito
de Sigüenza y Góngora." Contemporáneos, III (Núm. 8, enero de 1929), 91-95. (a-e) 14

----. "Ediciones del Primero
sueño de Sor Juana Inés de la
Cruz." Contemporáneos, I (Núm.
3, agosto de 1928), 312-313.
(ed)   15

----. "Ensayo sobre la época de
Sor Juana." Ruta, Núm. 2 (julio
de 1938), 5-22. (a-e)   16

----. "Escrutinio del Popol
Vuh." El Hijo Pródigo, VIII
(Núm. 27, junio de 1945), 163-
164. (a-e)   17

----. "Guía de amantes." Contemporáneos, III (Núm. 9, febrero de 1929), 97-103. (a-e)
18
----. "Historia literaria."
Fábula, Núm. 1 (enero de
1934), 3-5. (a-e)   19

----. "Jesús Guerrero Galván." El Hijo Pródigo, VI (Núm. 20, noviembre de 1944), 88. (a-e) 20

----. "Del Julianillo Valcárcel de los hermanos Machado." Sagitario, Núm. 9 (15 de febrero de 1927), 14. (a-e) 21

----. "La jura de Felipe III en la Nueva España, 1599." La Falange, Núm. 7 (1 de octubre de 1923), 370-374. (a-e) 22

----. "Literatura virreinal mexicana." El Hijo Pródigo, X (Núm. 32, noviembre de 1945), 71-77. (a-e) 23

----. "López Velarde." El Hijo Pródigo, XII (Núm. 39, junio de 1946), 149-150. (a-e) 24

----. "Un loro y tres golondrinas." El Hijo Pródigo, IX (Núm. 28, julio de 1945), 34-55 (dr) 25

----. "Manuel Puga y Acal.-- Manuel de la Parra." Contemporáneos, VIII (Núm. 26-27, julio-agosto de 1930), 95-96. (a-e) 26

----. "La mariposa que voló sobre el mar." Sagitario, Núm. 10 (1 de marzo de 1927), 13. (a-e) 27

----. "Notaciones." Sagitario, Núm. 5 (1 de octubre de 1926), 16. (a-e) 28

----. "Notaciones del arte moderno." Sagitario, Núm. 4 (1 de septiembre de 1926), 6. (a-e) 29

----. "Notas sobre la poesía norteamericana." Estaciones, I (Núm. 3, otoño de 1956), 371-374. (a-e) 30

----. "La obra de Sor Juana." Ruta, Núm. 12 (mayo de 1939), 5-25. (a-e) 31

----. "Panchita." Romance, I (Núm. 20, 15 de enero de 1941), 8 (f) 32

----. "Pelico." El Hijo Pródigo, I (Núm. 2, mayo de 1943). 92-93. (f) 33

----. "El pintor Roberto Montenegro." Forma, II (Núm. 7, 1928), 28-30. (a-e) 34

----. "La poesía de Sigüenza y Góngora." Contemporáneos, VIII (Núm. 26-27, julio-agosto de 1930), 61-90. (a-e) 35

----. "La' Primavera indiana' y el gongorismo" Contemporáneos, III (Núm. 10, marzo de 1929), 265-269. (a-e) 36

----. "El Primero sueño de Sor Juana." Contemporáneos, II (Núm. 4, septiembre de 1928), 46-54. (a-e) 37

----. "Sierra O'Reilly y la novela." Contemporáneos, X (Núm. 35, abril de 1931), 39-73. (a-e) 38

----. "Vida y obra de Sor Juana." Contemporáneos, XI (Núm. 40-41, septiembre-octubre de 1931), 200-206. (a-e) 39

----. "Vida de Sor Juana." Ruta, Núm. 7 (diciembre de 1938), 5-28 (a-e) 40

----. "De las trece obras de Emilio Pettoruti." Sagitario, Núm. 8 (1 de febrero de 1927), 6. (a-e) 41

----. "Trece obras de Emilio Pettoruti." Sagitario, Núm. 7 (1 de enero de 1927), 9-11. (a-e) 42

----. Aclaraciones a la vida de Ruiz Alarcón de Dorothy Schons. Contemporáneos, VI (Núm. 20, enero de 1930), 88-92. (r)   43

----. Antología poética de Salvador Rueda. El Hijo Pródigo, VI (Núm. 19, octubre de 1944), 61. (r)   44

----. "Villa en la historia y en la leyenda" (Reseña de Apuntes sobre la vida militar de Francisco Villa de Nellie Campobello). Romance, I (Núm. 18, 15 de noviembre de 1940), 18. (r)   45

----. Artigas y la revolución americana de Hugo D. Barbagelata. Contemporáneos, VIII (Núm. 30-31, noviembre-diciembre de 1930), 277-278 (r)   46

----. Bibliografía de la independencia de México de Jesús Guzmán y Raz Guzmán. Ruta, Núm. 1 (junio de 1938), 58. (r)   47

----. "Bibliografía de Ruiz de Alarcón," de Pedro Henríquez Ureña aparecida en Boletín del Instituto de Cultura Latino-americana (Núms. 6, 7, 8 y 10). Ruta, Núm. 5 (octubre de 1938), 59-60. (r)   48

----. Capítulos de literatura española de Alfonso Reyes. El Hijo Pródigo, X (Núm. 32, noviembre de 1945, 120. (r)   49

----. Carlos VII, Duque de Madrid del Conde de Rodezno. Contemporáneos, VI (Núm. 21, febrero de 1930), 188-190. (r)   50

----. La casa de doña María de Carlos Luquín. El Hijo Pródigo, III (Núm. 10, enero de 1944), 55. (r)   51

----. Las cien mejores poesías (líricas) mexicanas de Antonio Castro Leal. El Hijo Pródigo, IX (Núm. 29, agosto de 1945), 120. (r)   52

----. Los clásicos revividos. Los clásicos futuros de Azorín. El Hijo Pródigo, XIII (Núm. 40, julio de 1946), 60. (r)   53

----. Crónica de la Merced de P. M. Fray Cristóbal de Aldana. Contemporáneos, V (Núm. 15, agosto de 1929), 72-75. (r)   54

----. Reseña del códice de Chumayel en traducción de Antonio Médiz Bolio. Contemporáneos, VII (Núm. 25, junio de 1930), 248-252. (r)   55

----. Discurso de la novela española contemporánea de Max Aub. El Hijo Pródigo, X (Núm. 31, octubre de 1945), 57-58. (r)   56

----. "Un nuevo libro sobre Siguenza y Góngora" (Reseña de Don Carlos de Siguenza y Góngora, a Mexican Savant of the Seventeenth Century de Irving A. Leonard). Contemporáneos, VII (Núm. 23, abril de 1930), 86-90. (r)   57

----. Los enemigos del teatro de Enrique Díez-Canedo. Taller, I (Núm. 4, julio de 1939), 55-56. (r)   58

----. Ensayos sobre educación de Francisco Giner de los Ríos. El Hijo Prodigo, IX (Núm. 28, julio de 1945), 59-60. (r)   59

----. Entre la piedra y la flor de Octavio Paz. Tierra Nueva, II (Núm. 9-10, mayo-agosto de 1941), 173-174. (r)   60

----. Episodios nacionales de Victoriano Salado Alvarez. El Hijo Pródigo, VIII (Núm. 26, mayo de 1945), 118-119. (r)   61

----. La España del Cid de Ramón Menéndez Pidal. Contemporáneos, IV (Núm. 14, julio de 1929), 345-350. (r)   62

----. El español en Méjico, los Estados Unidos y la América Central (Vol. IV de Biblioteca de dialectología hispano-americana). Ruta, Núm. 11 (abril de 1939), 62-63. (r)   63

----. Esquilo, el creador de la tragedia de Gilbert Murray. El Hijo Pródigo, I (Núm. 6, septiembre de 1943), 382. (r)   64

----. "Flor de romances" (Reseña de Flor nueva de romances viejos de Ramón Menéndez Pidal. Contemporáneos, II (Núm. 5, octubre de 1928), 205-208. (r)   65

----. Flores de pasión y de melancolía de Carlos González Peña. El Hijo Pródigo, XI (Núm. 34, enero de 1946), 57. (r)   66

----. General estoria de Alfonso el Sabio. Contemporáneos, IX (Núm. 34, marzo de 1931), 275-277. (r)   67

----. Gregorio López, el hombre celestial de Fernando Ocaranza. El Hijo Pródigo, V (Núm. 17, agosto de 1944), 122. (r)   68

----. Historia de la literatura española de Angel Valbuena Prat. Ruta, Núm. 6 (noviembre de 1938), 56-57. (r)   69

----. Historia de la literatura mexicana de Julio Jiménez Rueda. El Hijo Pródigo, XIII (Núm. 41, agosto de 1946), 117. (r)   70

----. Historia de la poesía popular dominicana de Emilio Rodríguez Demorizi. Ruta, Núm. 8 (enero de 1939), 54-55. (r)   71

----. Historia literaria de la américa española de Alfredo Coester. Contemporáneos, IX (Núm. 33, feorero de 1931), 185-192. (r)   72

----. El jardín de los niños de Sir Rabindranath Tagore, con notas por Antonio Castro Leal. Ruta, Núm. 7 (diciembre de 1938), 58. (r)   73

----. Mexicayotl de Ramón J. Sender. Romance, II (Núm. 22, 15 de marzo de 1941). 18. (r)   74

----. Nayar de Miguel Angel Menéndez. Romance, II (Núm. 23, 22 de aoril de 1941). 20. (r)   75

----. Nostalgia de la muerte de Xavier Villaurrutia. Ruta, Núm. 2 (julio de 1938), 61-62. (r)   76

----. "Obras de Sigüenza y Góngora." Contemporáneos, II (Núm. 7, diciembre de 1928), 393-396. (r)   77

25

Alardín, Carmen. "La batalla silvestre." Estaciones, II (Núm. 6, verano de 1957), 222-226. (p)   117

----. "Paisaje de lo diario." Estaciones, III (Núm. 12, invierno de 1958), 430. (p)   118

----. Coloquio de amor de Margarita Paz Paredes. Estaciones, II (Núm. 5, primavera de 1957), 99-100. (r)   119

----. Negro Sam del tío Sam de Manuel González Flores. Estaciones, II (Núm. 6, verano de 1957), 230-231. (r)   120

----. Ninón de Rubén Salazar Mallén. Estaciones, II (Núm. 5, primavera de 1957), 98-99. (r)   121

----. Poesía de Demetrio Quiroz Malca. Estaciones, II (Núm. 6, verano de 1957), 231. (r)   122

----. Preludio inmortal a Federico García Lorca de Volga Marcos. Estaciones, II (Núm. 5, primavera de 1957), 99. (r)   123

Alatorre, Antonio. Caillois, Roger. "El escritor en la sociedad" (Trad. Antonio Alatorre y Juan José Arreola). Prometeus, I (Núm. 2, abril de 1949), 75-78. (tr)   124

Alba, Aurelio de. "Un cuento." La Falange, Núm. 2 (1 de enero de 1923), 78-80. (f)   125

Alba, Pedro de. "Artistas y artesanos." Forma, I (Núm. 6, 1928), 1-6. (a-e)   126

----. "Ramón López Velarde, El poeta del amor y de la muerte." México Moderno, II (Núm. 11-12, noviembre-diciembre de 1921), 278-282. (a-e)   127

Alberti, Rafael. "Del pensamiento en un jardín." Taller, II (Núm. 12, enero-febrero de 1941), 5-10. (p)   128

----. "Guía estival del paraíso." Sagitario, Núm. 5 (1 de octubre de 1926), 11. (p)   129

----. "Toro en el mar." Romance, I (Núm. 10, 15, de junio de 1940), 11. (p)   130

----. "Vida bilingüe de un refugiado español en Francia." Romance, I (Núm. 10, 15 de junio de 1940), 11. (p)   131

----. Supervielle, Jules. "La enferma, "Los ojos de la muerta," "El buey." (Trad. Rafael Alberti). Contemporáneos, XI (Núm. 40-41, septiembre-octubre de 1931), 177-180. (tr)   132

Albertos, Ernesto. "Lluvia." Antena, Núm. 1 (julio de 1924), 8. (p)   133

Alcalá, Manuel. "Virgilio y Garcilaso." Tierra Nueva, I (Núm. 6, noviembre-diciembre de 1940), 334-344. (a-e) 134

----. En la cuarta vigilia de Bernardo Casanueva [Mazo]. Tierra Nueva, III (Núm. 15, diciembre de 1942), 166-168. (r)   135

----. Anónimo. "La flauta de jade: poemas chinos." (Trad. Manuel Alcalá). Tierra Nueva, I (Núm. 3, mayo-junio de 1940), 151-153. (tr)   136

27

Anónimo. "Advertencias."
Antena, Núm. 1 (agosto de
1924), 2. (a-e)   191

----. "Lo que merece aplauso
y lo que no lo merece en los
conciertos de radio." Antena,
Núm. 3 (septiembre de 1924),
13-14. (a-e)   192

----. "Acera: Fundación del
cineclub." Contempóraneos,
X (Núm. 36, mayo de 1931),
187-189. (a-e)   193

----. "Antiguos cantares mexicanos"(Trad. Mariano Rojas).
Contemporáneos, IV (Núm. 12,
mayo de 1929), 105-119. (p)
                             194

----. "Desde el número
nueve de esta publicación..."
Contemporáneos, IV (Núm. 11,
abril de 1929), 95. (a-e)
                             195

----. "Escuelas de acción
artística de Cuba." Contemporáneos, XI (Núm. 42-43,
noviembre-diciembre de 1931),
264-267. (il)   196

----. "La máscara del
sombrerón." Contemporáneos,
IX (Núm. 32, enero de 1931),
79. (il)   197

----. "El mundo en tiempo del
surrealismo." Contempo-
ráneos, IX (Núm. 33, febrero
de 1931), 173. (il)   198

----. "Nuestra revista Contemporáneos..." Contempo-
ráneos, VII (Núm. 24, mayo
de 1930), 97. (a-e)   199

----. "Con la impresión de
este número,..." Estaciones,
III (Núm. 10, verano de 1958),
240. (a-e)   200

----. "El Dr. Faubus y Mr.
Erostrato." Estaciones, IV
(Núm. 13, primavera de 1959),
122. (a-e)   201

----. "Editorial." Estaciones,
V (Núm. 18, verano de 1960),
3-5. (a-e)   202

----. "La generación golpeada."
Estaciones, IV (Núm. 13,
primavera de 1959), 120.
(a-e)   203

----. "Laberinto 14." Estaciones, III (Núm. 10, verano de
1958), 208. (a-e)   204

----. "Mercurio de Belvedere."
Estaciones, I (Núm. 2, verano
de 1956), entre 244-245. (il)
                             205

----. "Mínimo homenaje a
Alfonso Reyes." Estaciones,
V (Núm. 17, primavera de
1960), 3. (a-e)   206

----. "Notas." Estaciones, IV
(Núm. 15, otoño de 1959),
284-286. (a-e)   207

----. "Palabras preliminares."
Estaciones, I (Núm. 1, primavera de 1956), 1-2. (a-e)
                             208

----. "Poetas españoles
actuales." Estaciones, IV
(Núm. 15, otoño de 1959), 259.
(a-e)   209

----. "Ramas Nuevas."
Estaciones, II (Núm. 6, verano
de 1957), 204-205. (a-e) 210

----. "Ramas Nuevas." Es-
taciones, II (Núm. 7, otoño de
1957), 330. (a-e)   211
----. "Raúl Anguiano." Estaciones, III (Núm. 9, primavera
de 1958), entre 64 y 65. (il)
                             212

----. "Ultimo panorama de la poesía mexicana." Estaciones, III (Núm. 12, invierno de 1958), 369-370. (a-e)
213

----. Caractéres de la literatura italiana de Luigi Fiorentini. Estaciones, I (Núm. 4, invierno de 1956), 606. (r)
214

----. Cuentos escogidos de Edgar A. Poe. Estaciones, IV (Núm. 13, primavera de 1959), 120-121. (r)   215

----. Esa sangre de Mariano Azuela. Estaciones, I (Núm. 1, primavera de 1956), 127-128. (r)   216

----. Este canto de Raúl Cervantes Ahumada. Estaciones, I (Núm. 1, primavera de 1956), 129. (r)   217

----. Historia de los mapas de G. R. Crone. Estaciones, II (Núm. 5, primavera de 1957), 95-96. (r)   218

----. Honor y gloria de José Attolini. Estaciones, II (Núm. 5, primavera de 1957), 99. (r)   219

----. Los prodigiosos de Hugo Argüelles. Estaciones, II (Núm. 8, invierno de 1957), 485-486. (r)   220

----. Una voz alada y... de un país inexistente de Margarita Mendoza López. Estaciones, I (Núm. 1, primavera de 1956), 129. (r)
221

----. "XXV aniversario del Fondo de Cultura Económica." Estaciones, IV (Núm. 15, otoño de 1959), 368-369. (r)
222

----. Vinnigulasa, cuentos de juchitán de Gabriel López Chiñas. Estaciones, IV (Núm. 13, primavera de 1959), 115-116. (r)   223

----. "Alfonso Reyes." Fábula, Núm. 9 (septiembre de 1934), 163. (a-e)   224

----. "Señales." Fábula, Núm. 1 (enero de 1934), 18. (a-e)
225

----. "Sor Juana Inés de la Cruz." Fábula, Núm. 2 (febrero de 1934), entre 32 y 33. (il)   226

----. "El clima de la tierra." La Falange, Núm. 6 (1 de septiembre de 1923), 352. (p)   227

----. "Comprobación de una leyenda homérica." La Falange, Núm. 6 (1 de septiembre de 1923), 353-354. (a-e)
228

----. "La cultura pública y el ayuntamiento de México." La Falange, Núm. 7 (1 de octubre de 1923), 408-410. (a-e)   229

----. "Chabarcha y el diablillo" (Trad. Rafael Lozano). La Falange, Núm. 4 (1 de julio de 1923), 228-232. (f)
230

----. "Figuras relevantes de América: María Enriqueta." La Falange, Núm. 4 (1 de julio de 1923), 244-245. (a-e)
231

----. "Legítimos versos de Lino Zamora." La Falange, Núm. 1 (1 de diciembre de 1922), 36-39. (p)   232

32

----. "Retrato de desconocida."
El Hijo Pródigo, I (Núm. 3,
junio de 1943), entre 160 y
161. (il)   276

----. "Retrato de Humboldt. "
El Hijo Pródigo, I (Núm. 3,
junio de 1943), entre 160 y
161. (il)   277

----. "Retrato de Sor María
Manuela Josefa. " El Hijo
Pródigo, II (Núm. 7, octubre
de 1943), entre 32 y 33. (il)
                                   278

----. "San Francisco y la
cortesana, " "San Francisco
predicando a los hermanos, "
"San Francisco dando muerte
al Anticristo," "Fray José de
Arriaga, " "Fray José María
Sáenz, " "Fray Ignacio del
Rio," "Fray José María de
Jesús Puelles. " El Hijo
Pródigo, II (Núm. 8, noviem-
bre de 1943), entre 96 y 97.
(il)   279

----. "San Joaquín y la
Virgen. " El Hijo Pródigo,
II (Núm. 9, diciembre de
1943), entre 180 y 181. (il)
                                   280

----. "Viejos cuentos de la
India" (Trad. Daisy Brody y
Antonio Sánchez Barbudo). El
Hijo Pródigo, VIII (Núm. 27,
junio de 1945), 150-156. (f)
                                   281

----. "Como la Anna Boloña
hacía adulterio, y como se
supo. " México Moderno, II
(Núm. 2, septiembre de 1922),
116-119. (a-e)   282

----. "Renan. " México
Moderno, II (Núm. 4, junio de
1923), 251-252. (a-e)
                                   283

----. Reseña de Andamios
interiores de Manuel Maples
Arce. México Moderno, II
(Núm. 2, septiembre de 1922),
126-127. (r)   284

----. "Los dos romanticismos"
(Trad. Salvador Novo). México
Moderno, II (Núm. 3, octubre
de 1922), 188-190. (a-e)
                                   285

----. "Abril. " Prometeus, I
(Núm. 2, abril de 1949),
65-66. (a-e)   286

----. "Mayo. " Prometeus, I
(Núm. 3, mayo de 1949), 139-
140. (a-e)   287

----. "Nota epígrafe. "
Prometeus, II (Núm. 1, diciembre de 1951), 18. (a-e) 288

----. Cuauhtémoc de Héctor
Pérez Martínez. Prometeus,
I (Núm. 1, febrero de 1949),
57-58. (r)   289

----. Imago de Carlos
Spitteler. Prometeus, I (Núm.
1, febrero de 1949), 58-59.
(r)   290

----. Vida y obra de Guillermo
Harvey de Pedro Laín Entralgo.
Prometeus, I (Núm. 1, febrero
de 1949), 58. (r)   291

----. "Acercamiento al problema indígena. " Romance, I
(Núm. 6, 15 de abril de 1940),
7. (a-e)   292

----. "Algunas ideas des-
glosadas de la obra de Hostos."
Romance, I (Núm. 1, 1 de
febrero de 1940), 9. (a-e)
                                   293

----. "América, depositoria de
la cultura. " Romance, I (Núm.
16, 15 de septiembre de 1940),
7. (a-e)   294

----. "Una cueva frente al mar." Romance, I (Núm. 16, 15 de septiembre de 1940), 6. (a-e) 314

----. "La cultura francesa." Romance, I (Núm. 14, 15 de agosto de 1940), 7. (a-e) 315

----. "De la lucha invisible a la guerra." Romance, I (Núm. 5, 1 de abril de 1940), 7. (a-e) 316

----. "Del realismo al impresionismo." Romance, I (Núm. 7, 1 de mayo de 1940), 13. (a-e) 317

----. "La declaracíon de la Junta de la Cultura Española." Romance, I (Núm. 10, 15 de junio de 1940), 20. (a-e) 318

----. "Los delegados del congreso indigenista en Romance." Romance, I (Núm. 8, 15 de mayo de 1940), 20. (a-e) 319

----. "Democracia efectiva." Romance, I (Núm. 11, 1 de julio de 1940), 7. (a-e) 320

----. "El destino de América" Romance, II (Núm. 24, 31 de mayo de 1941), 7. (a-e) 321

----. "El diablo en París." Romance, I (Núm. 12, 15 de julio de 1940), 10. (a-e) 322

----. "La difusión de la cultura en América: E. D. I. A. P.S.A. a los seis meses de comenzar su labor." Romance, I (Núm. 13, 1 de agosto de 1940), 14-15. (a-e) 323

----. "Los dos aspectos de las bibliotecas parlamentarias." Romance, I (Núm. 17, 22 de octubre de 1940), 19. (a-e) 324

----. "Dos centenarios de la historia portuguesa." Romance, I (Núm. 15, 1 de septiembre de 1940), 19. (a-e) 325

----. "250 años de café." Romance, I (Núm. 3, 1 de marzo de 1940), 6. (a-e) 326

----. "Dos épocas en una sola voz de muerte: Entre la espada y la pared de Europa." Romance, I (Núm. 1, 1 de febrero de 1940), 13. (a-e) 327

----. "El ejemplo de Chile." Romance, I (Núm. 13, 1 de agosto de 1940), 7. (a-e) 328

----. "En defensa de la paz." Romance, I (Núm. 8, 15 de mayo de 1940), 7. (a-e) 329

----. "En favor de los intelectuales europeos." Romance, I (Núm. 14, 15 de agosto de 1940), 7. (a-e) 330

----. "Enemigos de América." Romance, I (Núm. 10, 15 de junio de 1940), 7. (a-e) 331

----. "Es posible la guerra de microbios?" Romance, I (Núm. 9, 1 de junio de 1940), 19. (a-e) 332

----. "España al borde." Romance, I (Núm. 17, 22 de octubre de 1940), 7. (a-e) 333

----. "El espíritu de la moda." Romance, I (Núm. 9, 1 de junio de 1940), 12, 17. (a-e)   334

----. "El estado." Romance, II (Núm. 21, 15 de febrero de 1941), 7. (a-e)   335

----. "Europa en el umbral del año nuevo." Romance, I (Núm. 20, 15 de enero de 1941), 7. (a-e)   336

----. "Exposición de bocetos de José Clemente Orozco." Romance, I (Núm. 4, 15 de marzo de 1940), 7. (a-e)   337

----. "El fracaso de la literatura pacifista." Romance, I (Núm. 9, 1 de junio de 1940), 7. (a-e)   338

----. "Goya o la pasión en carne viva." Romance, I (Núm. 1, 1 de febrero de 1940), 12. (a-e)   339

----. "La guerra en el paisaje." Romance, I (Núm. 1, 1 de febrero de 1940), 7. (a-e)   340

----. "Herencia y cultura." Romance, I (Núm. 2, 15 de febrero de 1940), 7. (a-e)   341

----. "Hispanidad, invención y genio de Pablo Picasso." Romance, I (Núm. 2, 15 de febrero de 1940), 13. (a-e)   342

----. "Hispanoamericanismo actual." Romance, II (Núm. 23, 22 de abril de 1941), 7. (a-e)   343

----. "Un homenaje a la ciencia española en el destierro." Romance, I (Núm. 12, 15 de julio de 1940), 20. (a-e)   344

----. "Homenaje a un poeta." Romance, I (Núm. 7, 1 de mayo de 1940), 7. (a-e) 345

----. "Intelectuales en campos de concentración." Romance, I (Núm. 9, 1 de junio de 1940), 20. (a-e)   346

----. "El Japón dentro." Romance, I (Núm. 17, 22 de octubre de 1940), 7. (a-e)   347

----. "Jesualdo en México." Romance, I (Núm. 10, 15 de junio de 1940), 20. (a-e)   348

----. "José Carlos Mariátegui: Una voz viva de América." Romance, I (Núm. 6, 15 de abril de 1940), 6. (a-e) 349

----. "José Guadalupe Posada." Romance, I (Núm. 1, 1 de febrero de 1940), 10. (a-e)   350

----. "La libertad de pensar." Romance, I (Núm. 2, 15 de febrero de 1940), 7. (a-e)   351

----. "La limpieza de las calles a través de la caricatura." Romance, I (Núm. 4, 15 de marzo de 1940), 8. (a-e)   352

----. "Luis Vives, gran humanista español." Romance, I (Núm. 9, 1 de junio de 1940), 9, 22. (a-e)   353

----. "Un manifiesto de los intelectuales chilenos a favor de los refugiados españoles." Romance, I (Núm. 8, 15 de mayo de 1940), 19. (a-e) 354

----. "Más emigrados españoles a América." Romance, I (Núm. 12, 15 de julio de 1940), 7. (a-e) 355

----. "La medicina en la América precolombiana." Romance, I (Núm. 6, 15 de abril), 19. (a-e) 356

----. "La memoria de Juárez." Romance, I (Núm. 12, 15 de julio de 1940), 7. (a-e) 357

----. "El mercado de la Merced." Romance, I (Núm. 1, 1 de febrero de 1940), 25. (a-e) 358

----. "México y la guerra." Romance, II (Núm. 22, 15 de marzo de 1941), 7-8. (a-e) 359

----. "El movimiento romántico: El sentimiento de la libertad." Romance, I (Núm. 5, 1 de abril de 1940), 6. (a-e) 360

----. "Los 'Negro Spirituals' norteamericanos." Romance, II (Núm. 21, 15 de febrero de 1941), 16. (a-e) 361

----. "Neruda o el brillo de la verdad." Romance, I (Núm. 15, 1 de septiembre de 1940), 7. (a-e) 362

----. "Una obra de liberación." Romance, I (Núm. 9, 1 de junio de 1940), 7. (a-e) 363

----. "El 80 aniversario del nacimiento de Henri Bergson." Romance, I (Núm. 2, 15 de febrero de 1940), 12. (a-e) 364

----. "El odio al pensamiento y al hombre." Romance, I (Núm. 15, 1 de septiembre de 1940), 7. (a-e) 365

----. "Pablo Neruda." Romance, I (Núm. 1, 1 de febrero de 1940), 19. (a-e) 366

----. "Un pacífico lugar de Inglaterra, Stratford, el sitio donde nació y donde está enterrado Shakespeare." Romance, I (Núm. 15, 1 de septiembre de 1940), 9. (a-e) 367

----. "Panorama europeo." Romance, II (Núm. 21, 15 de febrero de 1941), 7. (a-e) 368

----. "Una paz efectiva." Romance, I (Núm. 6, 15 de abril de 1940), 7. (a-e) 369

----. "Paz en la guerra." Romance, I (Núm. 3, 1 de marzo de 1940), 7. (a-e) 370

----. "Pintura en el destierro." Romance, I (Núm. 5, 15 de abril de 1940), 12. (il) 371

----. "El premio Nóbel y Gabriela Mistral." Romance, I (Núm. 4, 15 de marzo de 1940), 7. (a-e) 372

----. "El primer congreso de escritores venezolanos." Romance, I (Núm. 11, 1 de junio de 1940), 20. (a-e) 373

41

----. "La pesadilla de Renan" (Reseña de Leviatán de Thomas Hobbes). Romance, I (Núm. 20, 15 de enero de 1941), 19. (r)   413

----. El negro de Cuba de Alberto Arredondo. Romance, I (Núm. 10, 15 de junio de 1940), 19. (r)   414

----. Poesías completas de Antonio Machado. Romance, I (Núm. 19, 18 de diciembre de 1940), 18. (r)   415

----. Psicoanálisis criminal de Luis Jiménez de Asúa. Romance, I (Núm. 19, 18 de diciembre de 1940), 19. (r)   416

----. "Defensa del hombre" (Reseña de Retorno a la libertad de Walter Lippmann). Romance, I (Núm. 18, 15 de noviembre de 1940), 19. (r)   417

----. "O Atenas, o Esparta" (Reseña de They Wanted War de Otto D. Tolischus). Romance, II (Núm. 23, 22 de abril de 1941), 19. (r) 418

----. Los veneros del diablo de Jorge García Granados. Romance, II (Núm. 23, 22 de abril de 1941), 19. (r) 419

----. "Lenin y la cultura." Ruta, Núm. 10 (marzo de 1939), 38-40. (a-e)   420

----. "Trayectoria de RUTA." Ruta, Núm. 1 (junio de 1938), 63. (a-e)   421

----. "A nuestros amigos y lectores." Sagitario, Núm. 5 (1 de octubre de 1926), entre 3 y 4. (a-e)   422

----. "Alfredo Palacios y el imperialismo yanqui." Sagitario, Núm. 2 (1 de agosto de 1926), 14. (a-e)   423

----. "Aspecto de nuestro periodismo: comercio, polilla y mulatez." Sagitario, Núm. 10 (1 de marzo de 1927), 4. (a-e)   424

----. "Cajal en México." Sagitario, Núm. 2 (1 de agosto de 1926), 16. (a-e)   425

----, "Como juega un genio sobre el papel." Sagitario, Núm. 6 (1 de noviembre de 1926), 7, 10. (a-e)   426

----. "España y la política mexicana en materia religiosa." Sagitario, Núm. 2 (1 de agosto de 1926), 7. (a-e)   427

----. "Etnografía colonial y moderna." Sagitario, Núm. 3 (15 de agosto de 1926), 14. (a-e)   428

----. "Federación Internacional de Uniones Intelectuales." Sagitario, Núm. 2 (1 de agosto de 1926), 16. (a-e)   429

----. "Una iniciativa de la revista Forma." Sagitario, Núm. 8 (1 de febrero de 1927),, 2. (a-e)   430

----. "El juego del señor Ors." Sagitario, Núm. 12-13 (30 de abril de 1927), 29. (a-e)   431

----. "Juicios acerca de Sagitario." Sagitario, Núm. 5 (1 de octubre de 1926), 18. (a-e)   432

----. "Los modernos pintores mexicanos: Gabriel Fernández Ledesma." Sagitario, Núm. 2 (1 de agosto de 1926), 8. (a-e)   433

----. "Nuestra portada." Sagitario, Núm. 5 (1 de octubre de 1926), 14. (a-e)   434

----. "Las nuevas secciones de la Liga Anti-Imperialista." Sagitario, Núm. 2 (1 de agosto de 1926), 16. (a-e)   435

----. "La obra cultural y patriótica de la Secretaría de Educación." Sagitario, Núm. 1 (15 de julio de 1926), 3. (a-e)   436

----. "La presentación de Alfredo Gómez de la Vega y el genio sin genio de Luis Pirandello." Sagitario, Núm. 12-13 (30 de abril de 1927), 29. (a-e)   437

----. "Propósito." Sagitario, Núm. 1 (15 de julio de 1926), 4. (a-e)   438

----. "Sagitario en Europa." Sagitario, Núm. 12-13 (30 de abril de 1927), 29. (a-e)   439

----. "La tribu Yaqui no es enemiga del 'Yori'." Sagitario, Núm. 3 (15 de agosto de 1926), 6. (a-e)   440

----. "Versos de este momento, hechos desde el otro mundo" (en el estilo de Luis de Góngora y Argote). Sagitario, Núm. 10 (1 de marzo de 1927), 3. (p)   441

----. El arte en América de José Francés. Sagitario Núm. 11 (15 de marzo de 1927), 17. (r)   442

----. Catálogo de exposiciones de la joven pintura mexicana. Sagitario, Núm. 11 (15 de marzo de 1927), 17. (r)   443

----. "Las fuentes de Stendhal" (Reseña de De L'Amour de Destrutt de Tracy). Sagitario, Núm. 7 (1 de enero de 1927), 17. (r)   444

----. Discursos parlamentarios y Rosales en flor de Alfonso F. Ramírez. Sagitario, Núm. 3 (15 de agosto de 1926), 16. (r)   445

----. Las escuelas al aire libre en México de la Secretaría de Educación Pública. Sagitario, Núm. 10 (1 de marzo de 1927), 17. (r)   446

----. Grandeza mexicana de Bernardo de Balbuena. Sagitario, Núm. 10 (1 de marzo de 1927), 17. (r)   447

----. Historia de las bellas artes en México de José Juan Tablada. Sagitario, Núm. 10 (1 de marzo de 1927), 17. (r)   448

----. El libro de los juicios de José Martí. Sagitario, Núm. 2 (5 de agosto de 1926), 17. (r)   449

----. Maya and Mexican Art de T. A. Joyce. Sagitario, Núm. 11 (15 de marzo de 1927), 17. (r)   450

----. México y México pintoresco de la serie "Orbus Terrarum," ed. Ernest Wasmuth. Sagitario, Núm. 3 (15 de agosto de 1926), 11. (r)   451

----. Las mil y una siestas de Xavier Enciso ("Zutano"). Sagitario, Núm. 14 (31 de mayo de 1927), 18. (r)   452

----. La nueva pintura mexicana con prólogo de Alfredo Ramos Martínez. Sagitario, Núm. 10 (1 de marzo de 1927), 17. (r)   453

----. Pero Galín de Genaro Estrada. Sagitario, Núm. 10 (1 de marzo de 1927), 17. (r)   454

----. Los precursores de la diplomacia mexicana de Isidro Fabela. Sagitario, Núm. 10 (1 de marzo de 1927), 17. (r)   455

----. Principios de estética de Antonio Caso. Sagitario, Núm. 3 (15 de agosto de 1926), 2. (r)   456

----. Reflejos de Xavier Villaurrutia. Sagitario, Núm. 10 (1 de marzo de 1927), 17. (r)   457

----. Relaciones entre México y Venezuela de Manuel Landaeta Rosales. Sagitario, Núm. 11 (15 de marzo de 1927), 7. (r)   458

----. Revista Mexicana de Estudios Históricos. Sagitario, Núm. 14 (31 de mayo de 1927), 18. (r)   459

----. Todo un hombre, una adaptación de una novela de Miguel de Unamuno de Julio de Hoyos. Sagitario, Núm. 2 (1 de agosto de 1926), 13. (r)   460

----. "A partir de este número, Taller verá enriquecido su consejo de redacción..." Taller, I (Núm. 5, octubre de 1939), 6. (a-e)   461

----. "Antonio Machado." Taller, I (Núm. 2, abril de 1939), 28. (a-e)   462

----. "Rafael Vega Albela." Taller, II (Núm. 10, marzo-abril de 1940), 37-38. (a-e)   463

----. "Tarjetas." Taller, I (Núm. 4, julio de 1939), 56-59. (a-e)   464

----. "La flauta de jade: poemas chinos." (Trad. Manuel Alcalá). Tierra Nueva, I (Núm. 3, mayo-junio de 1940), 151-153. (p)   (136)

----. "Sean nuestras primeras líneas un saludo..." Tierra Nueva, I (Núm. 1, enero-febrero de 1940), 3-4. (a-e)   465

----. "Silvestre Revueltas." Tierra Nueva, I (Núm. 4-5, julio-octubre de 1940), 257. (a-e)   466

----. Una noche de mayo de Vidal Álvarez Everoix. Tierra Nueva, I (Núm, 3 mayo-junio de 1940), 189-190. (r)   467

----. "A batallas de amor campos de pluma." Ulises, Núm. 3 (agosto de 1927), 44. (a-e)   468

----. "Al pie de la letra de Ortega y Gasset." Ulises, Núm. 6 (febrero de 1928), 38-39. (a-e)   469

----. "Gide y Lacretelle." Ulises, Núm. 6 (febrero de 1928), 35-37. (a-e)   470

----. "Madrid, meridiano intelectual de hispano-américa." Ulises, Núm. 4 (octubre de 1927), 38-39. (a-e)   471

44

----. "Notas." Ulises, Núm. 2 (junio de 1927), 26-27. (a-e) 472

----. "Ortega y Gasset, espectador." Ulises, Núm. 3 (agosto de 1927), 38-39. (a-e) 473

----. "Extasis. Novela de aventuras" (Reseña de Extasis de Eduardo Villaseñor). Ulises, Núm. 6 (febrero de 1928), 39-43. (r) 474

Anouilh, Jean. "Entreacto" (Trad. Benito Cereno). Prometeus, I (Núm. 2, abril de 1949), 88-91. (a-e) 475

Antón, David. "Viñeta." Estaciones, III (Núm. 9, primavera de 1958), portada. (il) 476

Apango Molina, Ignacio. Brecha en la roca de Héctor Raúl Almanza. Estaciones, I (Núm. 2, verano de 1956), 260-261. (r) 477

Apollinaire, Guillaume. "Cirugía estética" (Trad. Jaime Torres Bodet). Contemporáneos, I (Núm. 3, agosto de 1928), 331-334. (f) 478

----. "Lazos," "El puente de Mirabeau," "Signo," Sombra," "El tercer poema secreto," "Deseo," "Siempre" (Trad. Agustín Bartra). Estaciones, IV (Núm. 15, otoño de 1959), 304-310. (p) 479

Aragón, Louis. "La nueva epopeya francesa." Ruta, Núm. 3 (agosto de 1938), 27-32. (a-e) 480

Aragón Leiva, Agustín. "Sergio M. Eisenstein." Contemporáneos, X (Núm. 36, mayo de 1931), 181-185. (a-e) 481

----. Eisenstein, Sergio M. "Principios de la forma fílmica" (Trad. Agustín Aragón Leiva). Contemporáneos, X (Núm. 36, mayo de 1931), 116-135. (tr) 482

Arai, Alberto T. "Música y cine." Taller, I (Núm. 3, mayo de 1939), 51-53. (a-e) 483

Aranguren, E. "Versos," "Barrio de luz." Sagitario, Núm. 9 (15 de febrero de 1927), 12. (p) 484

Araquistain, Luis. "La gracia de Chesterton." Sagitario, Núm. 3 (15 de agosto de 1926), 15. (a-e) 485

----. La evolución política de iberoamerica de Raúl Carrancá y Trujillo. Sagitario, Núm. 1 (15 de julio de 1926), 17. (r) 486

Arce, David N. "Nocturna palabra." Estaciones, V (Núm. 18, verano de 1960), 127-128. (a-e) 487

Arconada, M. "Un gran periódico madrileño: La Gaceta Literaria." Sagitario, Núm. 10 (1 de marzo de 1927), 16. (a-e) 488

Arconada, César M. "Galdós y su época." Romance, I (Núm. 10, 15 de junio de 1940), 8, 14. (a-e) 489

Arcos, Juan. "Un ciclo de la pintura cubana." Romance, I (Núm. 6, 15 de abril de 1940), 7. (a-e) 490

Arellano Belloc, Francisco. "Canción hogareña." La Falange, Núm. 1 (1 de diciembre de 1922), 27-29. (p) 491

45

Arenales, Ricardo. "Canción de la noche diamantina." México Moderno, II (Núm. 11-12, noviembre-diciembre de 1921), 273-274. (p) 492

----. "Las cinco antorchas contra el viento" (contiene "La carne ardiente," "Canción del tiempo y el espacio," "Paternidad," "Los desposados de la muerte," "Lamentación de octubre"). México Moderno, I (Núm. 2, septiembre de 1920), 77-84. (p) 493

----. "Rosas de una guirnalda de humildad." México Moderno, II (Núm. 9, mayo de 1921), 135-138. (p) 494

----. "El son del viento." La Falange, Núm. 1 (1 de diciembre de 1922), 7-10. (p) 495

----. Antología de poetas modernos de México, publicada por la casa editorial Cultura. México Moderno, I (Núm. 2, septiembre de 1920), 125-128. (r) 496

Arenas, José. "La noche de la decadencia." Estaciones, I (Núm. 4, invierno de 1956), 580-593. (a-e) 497

Arenas Betancourt, Rodrigo. Puerto Cholo de Mario Puga. Estaciones, I (Núm. 2, verano de 1956), 261-262. (r) 498

Arévalo Martínez, Rafael. "Compensación." La Falange, Núm. 2 (1 de enero de 1923), 92. (p) 499

----. "Oíd lo que el trópico encierra...," "Creaturas gozosas." México Moderno, I (Núm. 3, octubre de 1920), 152-153. (p) 500

Arguedas, José María. "La aurora de la canción popular mestiza en el Perú." Romance, I (Núm. 9, 1 de junio de 1940), 10. (a-e) 501

Argüelles, Hugo. "El camino en la caja." Estaciones, III (Núm. 9, primavera de 1958), 89-96. (dr) 502

----. "La costra." Estaciones, V (Núm. 20, invierno de 1960), 88-102. (dr) 503

----. "En el faro." Estaciones, II (Núm. 7, otoño de 1957), 304-313. (dr) 504

----. La picardía mexicana de A. Jiménez. Estaciones, V (Núm. 19, otoño de 1960), 125-126. (r) 505

Argüelles Bringas, Roberto. "Ventarrón," "Secretos," "Desfile cruento." México Moderno, II (Núm. 8, marzo de 1921), 74-77. (p) 506

Argüello, Santiago. "México ante los Estados Unidos en la cuestión de Nicaragua." Sagitario, Núm. 9 (15 de febrero de 1927), 2. (a-e) 507

Aridjis, Homero. "Poema." Estaciones, V (Núm. 20, invierno de 1960), 86-87. (p) 508

Arp, Jean Hans. "Configuración." Estaciones, I (Núm. 1, primavera de 1956), 135. (p) 509

Arreola, Juan José. Caillois, Roger. "El escritor en la sociedad" (Trad. Antonio Alatorre y Juan José Arreola). Prometeus, I (Núm. 2, abril de 1949), 75-78. (tr) (124)

46

Arrieta, Antonio. "Bodegón."
El Hijo Pródigo, XIII (Núm.
40, julio de 1946), entre
32 y 33. (il)   510

Arruza, J. Amber. "Actualidad
de Montaigne." Romance, I
(Núm. 11, 1 de julio de
1940), 3, 10. (a-e)   511

Asch, Nathan. "El campo"
(Trad. Celestino Gorostiza).
Contemporáneos, II (Núm. 5,
octubre de 1928), 144-159.
(f)   512

Asúnsolo R., Enrique. "Alfonso
Reyes." Fábula, Núm. 9
(septiembre de 1934), 171.
(a-e)   513

----. "Centena del desamor."
Poesía, Núm. 1 (febrero de
1941), 10-19. (p)   514

----. "Dolor de primavera."
Poesía, Núm. 1 (febrero de
1941), 20-21. (p)   515

----. "Dos mujeres y una
actriz." El Hijo Pródigo, IX
(Núm. 30, septiembre de
1945), 158-167. X (Núm. 31,
octubre de 1945), 34-53. (dr)
                        516

----. "Ejercicio de invierno."
Estaciones, I (Núm. 4, invierno de 1956), 515-517. (p)
                        517

----. "Noche del trece."
Poesía, Núm. 1 (febrero de
1941), 8-9. (p)   518

----. "Noche del trece."
Fábula, Núm. 2 (febrero de
1934), 30-31. (p)   519

----. "Partida en veinticuatro
octavas." Contemporáneos,
VIII (Núm. 28-29, septiembre-
octubre de 1930), 136-145.
(p)   520

----. "Soneto de la renuncia-
ción con rima de uno del
Dante." Poesía, Núm. 1
(febrero de 1941), 7. (p)
                        521

----. "El teatro en un acto
de Tennessee Williams."
Prometeus, II (Núm. 1, diciembre de 1951), 46-51. (a-e)
                        522

----. "Venus analgésica."
El Hijo Pródigo, IV (Núm. 15,
junio de 1944), 163-172. (dr)
                        523

----. "Viñeta." Estaciones,
I (Núm. 3, otoño de 1956),
portada. (il)   524

----. "Viñeta." Estaciones,
II (Núm. 5, primavera de
1957), portada. (il)   525

----. "Viñeta." Estaciones,
III (Núm. 10, verano de 1958),
portada. (il)   526

----. "Viñeta." Estaciones,
IV (Núm. 13, primavera de
1959), portada. (il)   527

----. Coloquio de Linda y
de Domingo Arenas de Miguel
N. Lira. Fábula, Núm. 6
(junio de 1934), 120. (r)
                        528

----. Romance de gavilanes
de Anselmo Mena. Fábula,
Núm. 4 (abril de 1934), 79.
(r)   529

Asúnsolo, Ignacio; Fernández
Urbina, J. M.; Ruiz,
Guillermo; Rivera, Diego;
Revueltas, Fermín; Domínguez
Bello, Arnulfo; y Centeno,
Francisco. "Encuesta sobre
escultura." Forma, I (Núm.
2, noviembre de 1926), 7-8.
(a-e)   530

Attolini, José. "Erskine Caldwell." Ruta, Núm. 8 (enero de 1939), 48-49. (a-e) 531

----. "Gold poeta." Ruta, Núm. 12 (mayo de 1939), 58-59. (a-e) 532

----. "Substancia del teatro y teatro indoamericano." Ruta, Núm. 6 (noviembre de 1938), 46-47. (a-e) 533

Aub, Max. "Fábula verde." Estaciones, I (Núm. 2, verano de 1956), 171-187. (f) 534

----. "El rapto de Europa o siempre se puede hacer algo." El Hijo Pródigo, X (Núm. 32, noviembre de 1945), 89-110. (dr) 535

----. "La vida conyugal." El Hijo Pródigo, II (Núm. 9, diciembre de 1943), 194-217. (dr) 536

----. Canciones del suburbio de Pio Baroja. El Hijo Pródigo, VII (Núm. 24, marzo de 1945), 187. (r) 537

----. Epigramas americanos de Enrique Díez-Canedo. El Hijo Pródigo, IX (Núm. 28, julio de 1945), 56. (r) 538

----. El obscuro límite de Juan Rejano. Prometeus, I (Núm. 2, abril de 1949), 134-136. (r) 539

----. Otra primavera de Rodolfo Usigli. El Hijo Pródigo, IX (Núm. 30, septiembre de 1945), 182-183. (r) 540

Auclair, Marcela. "Alfonso Reyes." Sagitario, Núm. 12-13 (30 de abril de 1927), 4. (a-e) 541

Averchenko, Arkady. "Mejicano." La Falange, Núm. 4 (1 de julio de 1923), 233-236. (f) 542

Azaña, Manuel. "Estébanez Calderón y Valera." Contemporáneos, V (Núm. 18, noviembre de 1929), 296-317; (Núm. 19, diciembre de 1929), 339-353. (a-e) 543

Azuela, Mariano. "Un grifo." Ulises, Núm. 2 (junio de 1927), 10-13. (f) 544

----. "La lección que no aprendí en las aulas." Fábula, Núm. 7 (julio de 1934), 123-125. (a-e) 545

----. "La luciérnaga." Contemporáneos, I (Núm. 3, agosto de 1928), 235-252. (f) 546

----. "La luciérnaga" Contemporáneos, VII (Núm. 23, abril de 1930), 20-33. (f) 547

----. "La malhora." Contemporáneos, VIII (Núm. 30-31, noviembre-diciembre de 1930), 193-216; IX (Núm. 32, enero de 1931), 42-70. (f) 548

----. "Por el camino de Proust." Contemporáneos, II (Núm. 6, noviembre de 1928), 291-292. (a-e) 549

----. "...Y ultimadamente." Antena, Núm. 4 (octubre de 1924), 4-5. (f) 550

B. "El salón del teatro." Sagitario, Núm. 8 (1 de febrero de 1927), 12. (a-e) 551

B., B. Antes del alba de Ludwig Renn. Ruta, Núm. 10 (marzo de 1939), 58-59. (r) 552

B. , J. Los cholos de Jorge
Icaza. Ruta, Núm. 6
(noviembre de 1938), 58-59.
(r)   553

B. T. , E. Orígenes económicos
y sociales de la guerra de
castas de Héctor Pérez
Martínez. Ruta, Núm. 4
(septiembre de 1938), 61-62.
(r)   554

Bacon, Peggy. "La modelo. "
Contemporáneos, II (Núm. 7,
diciembre de 1928), 335. (il)
                              555

Báez, Edmundo. "Elogio de la
soledad. " El Hijo Pródigo,
I (Núm. 5, agosto de 1943),
299-300. (p)   556

----. "Recuerdo de María
Teresa. " El Hijo Pródigo,
XII (Núm. 38, mayo de 1946),
89-90. (p)   557

----, y Antonio Díaz Conde.
"La soledad o el eco'. "
Estaciones, II (Núm. 7, otoño
de 1957), 246-255. (dr)
                              558

Baeza Flores, Alberto. "Mural
en el aire de México. "
Estaciones, V (Núm. 20,
invierno de 1960), 3-5. (p)
                              559

Balmont, Constantino. "Cartas
de México" (Trad. Xavier
Villaurrutia). México Moderno, II (Núm. 2, septiembre
de 1922), 120-121. (a-e)
                              560

Ballagas, Emilio. "Cárcel de
sombra, " "Cárcel de luz. "
El Hijo Pródigo, V (Núm. 17,
agosto de 1944), 97-99. (p)
                              561

----. "Los 'santos' afrocu-
banos. " Romance, I (Núm. 8,
15 de mayo de 1940), 1-2.
(a-e)   562

Ballesteros, Antonio. "Panorama
de la educación en américa. "
Romance, I (Núm. 4, 15 de
marzo de 1940), 17. (a-e)
                              563

Bancalari, Ignacio L. "El
palacio de la cultura en
México. " Sagitario, Núm. 6
(1 de noviembre de 1926), 8-
9. (a-e)   564

Bañuelos, Juan. "Esta noche y
sus viejos nómadas de blanco. "
Estaciones, III (Núm. 12,
invierno de 1958), 431-432.
(p)   565

Basqueiro Foster, Gerónimo.
Cancionero de Upsala. El
Hijo Pródigo, VII (Núm. 22,
enero de 1945), 60. (r) 566

----. Música y músicos
contemporáneos de Aaron Copland. El Hijo Pródigo, X
(Núm. 33, diciembre de 1945),
181. (r)   567

----. Síntesis de la historia
de la música de Adolfo
Salazar. El Hijo Pródigo, XI
(Núm. 35, febrero de 1946),
114. (r)   568

Barajas, Manuel. "Los filar-
mónicos y el radio. " Antena,
Núm. 2 (agosto de 1924), 12.
(a-e)   569

Barajas Lozano, Ignacio. "Desde
la colina, " "Nocturno. " Antena,
Núm. 2 (agosto de 1924), 7.
(p)   570

----. "Nocturno. " La Falange,
Núm. 1 (1 de diciembre de
1922), 29-30. (p)   571

49

----. "Trilogía mínima." La Falange, Núm. 6 (1 de septiembre de 1923), 339-340. (p)   572

Barcia, Augusto. "Méjico como esperanza." Sagitario, Núm. 1 (15 de julio de 1926), 5-6. (a-e)   573

Barga, Corpus. "Europa y el toro o la guerra de las sorpresas." Romance, I (Núm. 2, 15 de febrero de 1940), 12. (a-e)   574

----. "La noche de Europa." Romance, I (Núm. 5, 1 de abril de 1940), 3. (a-e)   575

Bargallo, Modesto. "Lavoisier y el enigma de los cuatro elementos." Romance, I (Núm. 7, 1 de mayo de 1940), 4-5. (a-e)   576

Barreda, Ignacio María. "Doña Juana María Romero." El Hijo Pródigo, I (Núm. 3, junio de 1943), entre 160 y 161. (il)   577

----. "Doña María Ysabel Antonia Gálves y Estrada." El Hijo Pródigo, I (Núm. 3, junio de 1943), entre 160 y 161. (il)   578

Barreda, Octavio G. "Carlos Orozco Romero." El Hijo Pródigo, XI (Núm. 34, enero de 1946), 31-32. (a-e) 579

----. "Cuaderno de bitacora (Londres, 1929-1930)." El Hijo Pródigo, V (Núm. 16, julio de 1944), 19-25. (a-e)   580

----. "Dados-tres." Contemporáneos, IV (Núm. 11, abril de 1929), 54-60. (f)   581

----. "Juan Soriano." El Hijo Pródigo, VIII (Núm. 25, abril de 1945), 24. (a-e)   582

----. "1939: México literario." Romance, I (Núm. 1, 1 de febrero de 1940), 19. (a-e)   583

----. "Nueva York 1926-1927: teatros." Sagitario, Núm. 10 (1 de marzo de 1927), 2. (a-e)   584

----. "Una página sobre el film Vía Crucis, Las uvas del rencor" (Opiniones de Xavier Villaurrutia, León Felipe, Ramón Gaya, Alberto Quintero Alvarez, Octavio Barreda y Carlos Velo). Romance, I (Núm. 9, 1 de junio de 1940), 11. (a-e)   585

----. "Rufino Tamayo en 1944." El Hijo Pródigo, V (Núm. 18, septiembre de 1944), 141-145. (a-e)   586

----. "Trompos," "Canícula," "Jim y Jack." Contemporáneos, I (Núm. 3, agosto de 1928), 253-260. (f)   587

----. An Anthology of Contemporary Latin-American Poetry de Dudley Fitts. El Hijo Pródigo, I (Núm. 4, julio de 1943), 259. (r)   588

----. La experiencia literaria de Alfonso Reyes. El Hijo Pródigo, I (Núm. 2, mayo de 1943), 122-123. (r)   589

----. El Genil y los olivos de Juan Rejano. El Hijo Pródigo, VII (Núm. 22, enero de 1945), 58. (r)   590

----. "José Gorostiza, o de la inteligencia" (Reseña de

Muerte sin fin). Romance, I
(Núm. 1, 1 de febrero de
1940), 18. (r)   591

----. 338171 T. E. de
Victoria Ocampo. El Hijo
Pródigo, I (Núm. 3, junio de
1943), 187-188. (r)   592

----. Donne, John. "Devociones" (Trad. Octavio G.
Barreda). El Hijo Pródigo,
I (Núm. 1, abril de 1943),
49-57. (tr)   593

----. Eliot, Thomas Stearns.
"Un canto para Simeón" (Trad.
Octavio G. Barreda). Taller,
II (Núm. 10, marzo-abril de
1940), 90-91. (tr)   594

----. Eliot, T. S. "La
música de la poesía" (Trad.
Octavio G. Barreda). El
Hijo Pródigo, I (Núm. 1,
abril de 1943), 21-30. (tr)
                           595

----. Lawrence, David
Herbert. "Mañanas de
México: Día de mercado"
(Trad. Octavio G. Barreda).
Contemporáneos, IX (Núm. 34,
marzo de 1931), 230-243.
(tr)   596

----. Léger, Aléxis Saint-
Léger. ("St. John Perse").
"Anábasis" (Traducción y
prólogo de Octavio G.
Barreda). Contemporáneos,
IX (Núm. 32, enero de 1931),
1-37. (tr)   597

----. Pach, Walter.
"Fluctuat nec mergitur" (Trad.
Octavio G. Barreda). El
Hijo Pródigo, IX (Núm. 28,
julio de 1945), 19-26. (tr)
                           598

----. Richards, I. A. "La
experiencia poética" (Trad.
Octavio G. Barreda). El

Hijo Pródigo, II (Núm 9,
diciembre de 1943), 155-160.
(tr)   599

----. Saroyan, William.
"Entre los perdidos, " "Esti-
mada Greta Garbo, " "Oración"
(Trad. Octavio G. Barreda).
El Hijo Pródigo, I (Núm. 5,
agosto de 1943), 308-311. (tr)
                           600

No entry   601

----. Van Doren, Carl. "La
Torre de Ironía"   (Trad.
Octavio G. Barreda). Contemporáneos, X (Núm. 36, mayo
de 1931), 165-181. (tr) 602

----. Wilder, Thornton. "La
huída a Egipto" (Trad. Octavio
G. Barreda). Contemporáneos,
VIII (Núm. 30-31, noviembre-
diciembre de 1930), 249-253.
(tr)   603

Barrex, Juan Antonio. "Tánger,
ciudad de contradicciones. "
Romance, I (Núm. 10, 15 de
junio de 1940), 12-13. (a-e)
                           604

Barrios, Eduardo. "La antipa-
tía. " La Falange, Núm. 4
(1 de julio de 1923), 197-207.
(f)   605

----. "También algo de mí. "
México Moderno, II (Núm. 3,
octubre de 1922), 151-157.
(a-e)   606

Barrios, Roberto. "La bailar-
ina vestida de verde. " La
Falange, Núm. 2 (1 de enero
de 1923), 93. (p)   607

----. "La flapper. " Antena,
Núm. 5 (noviembre de 1924),
5. (p)   608

----. "Marina." La Falange, Núm. 5 (1 de agosto de 1923), 286-288. (p) 609

Barros Sierra, José. "El artista en Vida y muerte de Silvestre Revueltas," Romance, I (Núm. 17, 22 de octubre de 1940), 5. (a-e) 610

----. "La autobiografía de un artista moderno: A propósito del libro que está escribiendo el pianista Rubinstein." Romance, II (Núm. 21, 15 de febrero de 1941), 17. (a-e) 611

----. "Hacia un ballet mexicano." Romance, I (Núm. 18, 15 de noviembre de 1940), 17. (a-e) 612

----. "El nacimiento de la ópera en el siglo XVII." Romance, II (Núm. 24, 31 de mayo de 1941), 17. (a-e) 613

----. "Los nuevos directores de orquesta mexicanos." Romance, I (Núm. 7, 1 de mayo de 1940), 13. (a-e) 614

----. "La ópera en México: A propósito de la primera representación de la Flauta mágica." Romance, I (Núm. 20, 15 de enero de 1941), 17. (a-e) 615

----. "Otto Klemperer se rebela contra la dictadura musical femenina en los Estados Unidos." Romance, I (Núm. 19, 18 de diciembre de 1940), 17. (a-e) 616

----. "El problema de los artistas jóvenes a propósito de la aparición de Jorge Sandor." Romance, I (Núm. 5, 1 de abril de 1940), 15. (a-e) 617

----. "Radiodifusión libre y transmisiones 'dirigidas'." Romance, I (Núm. 8, 15 de mayo de 1940), 15. (a-e) 618

----. "'Tata Vasco' y su partitura." Romance, II (Núm. 23, 22 de abril de 1941), 17. (a-e) 619

----. "Vida de los ballets rusos." Romance, II (Núm. 22, 15 de marzo de 1941), 17. (a-e) 620

Bartra, Agustín. "Eolo." Prometeus, II (Núm. 1, diciembre de 1951), 26-28. (f) 621

----. "Notas sobre Guillaume Apollinaire." Estaciones, IV (Núm. 15, otoño de 1959), 301-303. (a-e) 622

----. Apollinaire, Guillaume. "Lazos," "El puente Mirabeau," "Signo," "Sombra," "El tercer poema secreto," "Deseo," "Siempre" (Trad. Agustín Bartra). Estaciones, IV (Núm. 15, otoño de 1959), 304-310. (tr) (479)

Baudelaire, Charles. "La Caballera." (Trad. José Emilio Pacheco y y Berny), Estaciones, V (Núm. 18, verano de 1960), 54-55. (p) 623

----. "Trozos escogidos de los Diarios íntimos y de los Consejos a los literatos jóvenes." Taller, II (Núm. 12, enero-febrero de 1941), 82-94. (a-e) 624

Beaton, Cecil. "Los tres Sitwell," "La madre de los Sitwell," "El duque de Beaufort." Prometeus, I (Núm. 2, abril de 1949), entre 128-129. (il)   625

Beauduin, Nicolás. "Huelga de otoño" (Trad. Enrique Fernández Ledesma). Sagitario, Núm. 2 (1 de agosto de 1926), 12. (p)   626

Beham, Hans Sebald. "El hijo pródigo." El Hijo Pródigo, VI (Núm. 19, octubre de 1944), entre 6 y 7. (il)   627

Bejarano, Julio. "Una maldición divina." Romance, I (Núm. 3, 1 de marzo de 1940), 4. (a-e)   628

Beltrán, Neftalí. "Décimas." El Hijo Pródigo, XIII (Núm. 41 agosto de 1946), 86-87. (p)   629

----. "El mar y la niña." Poesía, Núm. 1 (febrero de 1941), 25. (p)   630

----. "Poema." Poesía, Núm. 1 (febrero de 1941), 30-32. (p)   631

----. "Poema de Concha." Ruta, Núm. 6 (noviembre de 1938), 17. (p)   632

----. "Poema de la incercia." Ruta, Núm. 10 (marzo de 1939), 19. (p)   633

----. "Romance." Poesía, Núm. 1 (febrero de 1941), 26-29. (p)   634

----. "Soledad enigma," "Soneto." Taller, II (Núm. 11 julio-agosto de 1940), 37-40. (p)   635

----. "Soneto." El Hijo Pródigo, V (Núm. 18, septiembre de 1944), 140. (p)   636

----. "Soneto." Tierra Nueva, II (Núm. 11-12, septiembre-diciembre de 1941), 209. (p)   637

----. "Soneto," "Canción." El Hijo Pródigo, XI (Núm. 35, febrero de 1946), 83-84. (p)   638

----. Reseña de una traducción de Adonais de Percy Bysshe Shelly, realizada por Manuel Altolaguirre y Antonio Castro Leal. Ruta, Núm. 7 (diciembre de 1938), 57. (r)   639

----. Atardecer sin lirios de Vicente Magdaleno. Ruta, Núm. 6 (noviembre de 1938), 54-55. (r)   640

----. Avance en la madrugada de Carlos Bustos Cerecedo, Estío sin ella de Rafael del Rio R., Canto Kechwa de José María Arguedas. Ruta, Núm. 8 (enero de 1939), 58-60. (r)   641

----. El hacha de León Felipe. Ruta, Núm. 10 (marzo de 1939), 57-58. (r)   642

----. Presagio a la muerte de María Luisa Hidalgo. Ruta, Núm. 6 (noviembre de 1938), 54. (r)   643

Bell, Olive. "O todas las obras de arte visual..." (Trad. Salvador Novo). México Moderno, II (Núm. 2, septiembre de 1922), 124-125. (a-e)   644

Bendezú, Francisco. "El tiempo vacío," "A través de la cerradura de la tormenta." Prometeus, I (Núm. 3, mayo de 1949), 170-171. (p) 645

Benites, Leopoldo. "Luz de mi lámpara pequeña." Sagitario, Núm. 14 (31 de mayo de 1927), 4. (p) 646

Benítez, Fernando. "Tiripetio: Lugar de oro." Romance, I (Núm. 5, 1 de abril de 1940), 10. (a-e) 647

Benítez, José María. "Alegría." La Falange, Núm. 2 (1 de enero de 1923), 96. (p) 648

----. "Amanecer." Estaciones, IV (Núm. 14, verano de 1959), 172-180. (f) 649

----. "El pueblo." Antena, Núm. 5 (noviembre de 1924), 6-7. (f) 650

Benito, Luis de. "El salón de otoño." Sagitario, Núm. 8 (1 de febrero de 1927), 12. (a-e) 651

Bergamín, José. "Las cenizas de una voz o el profesor inalterable." Romance, I (Núm. 4, 15 de marzo de 1940), 1-2. (a-e) 652

----. "Contra tiempo y mareo." El Hijo Pródigo, V (Núm. 17, agosto de 1944), 102-106. (a-e) 653

----. "Las cosas claras." Taller, II (Núm. 8-9, enero-febrero de 1940), 53-55. (a-e) 654

----. "Idealismo y materialismo." El Hijo Pródigo, X (Núm. 33, diciembre de 1945), 137-142. (a-e) 655

----. "Intervención de José Bergamín." Romance, I (Núm. 3, 1 de marzo de 1940), 19. (a-e) 656

----. "Literatura y filosofía." El Hijo Pródigo, III (Núm. 12, marzo de 1944), 147-148. (a-e) 657

----. "Mundo y trasmundo de Galdós." El Hijo Pródigo, I (Núm. 5, agosto de 1943), 292-295. (a-e) 658

----. "Noches de la lírica castellana: La música extremada del maestro Fray Luis de León." Romance, I (Núm. 1, 1 de febrero de 1940), 11. (a-e) 659

----. "Las pequeñeces del demonio." Taller, I (Núm. 6, noviembre de 1939), 5-18. (a-e) 660

----. Vasconcelos, José; González Martínez, Enrique; Gaos, José; Gallegos, José M.; Paz, Octavio; Martínez, José Luis; García-Bacca, David; Jiménez Rueda, Julio; Nicol, Eduardo. "Poesía, mística y filosofía: Debate en torno a San Juan de la Cruz." El Hijo Pródigo, I (Núm. 3, junio de 1943), 135-144. (a-e) 661

----. "Qué es del cuerpo de tu voz? España, cuestión personal." El Hijo Pródigo, VIII (Núm. 27, junio de 1945), 137-143. (a-e) 662

----. "Siete sonetos impuntuales." Taller, I (Núm. 4, julio de 1939), 17-21. (p) 663

54

----. "Tanto tienes cuanto esperas y el cielo padece fuerza o La muerte burlada." El Hijo Pródigo, III (Núm. 10, enero de 1944), 40-53; (Núm. 11, febrero de 1944), 107-119. (dr)   664

----. "Las telarañas del juicio: Qué es poesía?" El Hijo Pródigo, IV (Núm. 13, abril de 1944), 11-20. (a-e)   665

----. "Tendido en el escape volador." El Hijo Pródigo, I (Núm. 2, mayo de 1943), 71-76. (a-e)   666

----. Las amistades peligrosas de Choderlos de Laclos. El Hijo Pródigo, III (Núm. 10, enero de 1944), 55-56. (r)   667

----. La guerra y la paz de Leo Tolstoi. El Hijo Pródigo, II (Núm. 7, octubre de 1943), 58-59. (r)   668

----. Historia de las ideas estéticas en España de Marcelino Menéndez y Pelayo. El Hijo Pródigo, IV (Núm. 14, mayo de 1944), 121-122. (r)   669

----. El pensamiento de Galdós de Arturo Cpadevila y Unamuno. Bosquejo de una filosofía de José Ferrater Mora. El Hijo Pródigo, V (Núm. 16, julio de 1944), 58-59. (r)   670

Bermúdez, María Elvira. "El mundo privado en los novelistas mexicanos de fin de siglo." Estaciones, II (Núm. 8, invierno de 1957), 398-407. (a-e)   671

----. Nocturno dia de Elías Nandino. Estaciones, IV (Núm. 13, primavera de 1959), 112-114. (r)   672

Best, Adolfo. "La novia." La Falange, Núm. 1 (1 de diciembre de 1922), entre 16 y 17. (il)   673

----. "Portada." La Falange, Núm. 2 (1 de enero de 1923), Núm. 3 (1 de febrero de 1923). (il)   674

----. "Radio conferencia sobre México." La Falange, Núm. 1 (1 de diciembre de 1922), 41-45. (a-e)   675

Betz, Maurice. Rilke, Rainer María. "Carta y fragmentos." (Trad. Maurice Betz). Tierra Nueva, I (Núm. 4-5, julio-octubre de 1940), 224-238. (tr)   676

Bianchi, Alfredo A. Tacna y Arica de Joaquín Edwards Bello. Sagitario, Núm. 8 (1 de febrero de 1927), 15. (r)   677

Biddle, George. "Paisaje," "Paisaje mexicano." Contemporáneos, II (Núm. 7, diciembre de 1928), 328-329. (il)   678

Blake, William. "El matrimonio del cielo y del infierno" (Trad. Xavier Villaurrutia). Contemporáneos, II (Núm. 6, noviembre de 1928), 213-243. (a-e)   679

----. "El niño negro" (Trad. Luis Cernuda). Romance, I (Núm. 10, 15 de junio de 1940), 11. (p)   680

Block, Alejandro. "Los escritas" (Trad. Enrique Díez-

Canedo). México Moderno, II (Núm. 1, agosto de 1922), 9-10. (a-e) 681

Blom, Franz. "K'a vum Carranza, el dios que canta," "Chan bor y Carmita, una de sus mujeres," "K'in Obregón con sus cinco mujeres," "Dos mujeres de pura belleza maya. Su rostro es trasunto de las figuras de los monumentos antiguos." Prometeus, I (Núm. 3, mayo de 1949), entre 202-203. (il) 682

----. "Noches en la selva Lacandona." Prometeus, I (Núm. 3, mayo de 1949), 203-206. (a-e) 683

Blumner, Rudolf. "El arte de la danza." Sagitario, Núm. 5 (1 de octubre de 1926), 8-11. (a-e) 684

Bo, Efraín Tomás. El balcón hacia la muerte de Ulises Petit de Murat y El bruto de Arturo Cerretani. El Hijo Pródigo, V (Núm. 17, agosto de 1944), 124. (r) 685

----. La hoguera bárbara de Alfredo Pareja Díez-Canedo. El Hijo Pródigo, VI (Núm. 21, diciembre de 1944), 187-188. (r) 686

----. Sobre la misma tierra de Rómulo Gallegos. El Hijo Pródigo, V (Núm. 18, septiembre de 1944), 188. (r) 687

Boccioni, Umberto. "Forma única de la continuidad en el espacio." Estaciones, I (Núm. 2, verano de 1956), entre 244-245. (il) 688

Bogrand, Ricardo. "Nocturno menor," "Primera lluvia," "Hay veces que las calles,"

"Recado." Estaciones, V (Núm. 17, primavera de 1960), 102-107. (p) 689

Bohet, Víctor. "El aspecto intelectual del antisemitismo." Ruta, Núm. 2 (julio de 1938), 52-54. (a-e) 690

Bonifaz Nuño, Rubén. "Al comienzo." Estaciones, III (Núm. 12, invierno de 1958), 389-390. (p) 691

Bonmariage, Sylvain. "Henri Matisse y la técnica pura." Sagitario, Núm. 8 (1 de febrero de 1927), 7-8. (a-e) 692

Bontempelli, Massimo. "Para la historia del teatro danés" (Trad. Xavier Villaurrutia). Contemporáneos, X (Núm. 36, mayo de 1931), 102-111. (a-e) 693

----. "Sobre una locomotora." Ulises, Núm. 1 (mayo de 1927), 4-8. (f) 694

Borges, Jorge Luis. "Prismas." Sagitario, Núm. 7 (1 de enero de 1927), 4. (p) 695

----. "La recoleta." Contemporáneos, XI (Núm. 40-41, septiembre-octubre de 1931), 139-141. (p) 696

----. "Tranvías." Sagitario, Núm. 4 (1 de septiembre de 1926), 17. (p) 697

Borges, Norah. "Las dos hermanas," "La colegiala," "Ilustración para un libro." Forma, II (Núm. 7, 1928), 9-10. (il) 698

Borja Bolado, F. "De como Horta pagó por ver el mar." Antena, Núm. 3 (septiembre de

1924), 10. (a-e)   699

Botello Barros, Miguel. "En el
trópico," "Beatas," "Autorretrato." Romance, I (Núm.
18, 15 de noviembre de 1940),
15. (il)   700

Bousoño, Carlos. "Invasión de
la realidad." Estaciones, IV
(Núm. 15, otoño de 1959),
274-277. (p)   701

Bovio, G. "El genio y el
pesimismo." La Falange,
Núm. 6 (1 de septiembre de
1923), 352-353. (p)   702

Bragaglia, Antón Giulio. "Cinema
y teatro." Contemporáneos, IX
(Núm. 34, marzo de 1931),
250-275. (a-e)   703

Braque, Georges. "Interior."
Estaciones, I (Núm. 2, verano
de 1956), entre 244-245. (il)
     704

----. "Naturaleza muerta."
Contemporáneos, V (Núm. 15,
agosto de 1929), 63. (il)
     705

Brehme, Hugo. "Catedral de
Campeche," "San Andrés
Chalchicomula," "Tepozotlán."
Sagitario, Núm. 3 (15 de
agosto de 1926), 8-10. (il)
     706

Bremond, Henri. "La poesía
pura" (Trad. Alí Chumacero).
Tierra Nueva, I (Núm. 6,
noviembre-diciembre de 1940),
320-329. (a-e)   707

Brenner, Anita. "Carlos Orozco
como retratista." Forma, I
(Núm. 3, 1927), 4-5. (a-e)
     708
----. "David Alfaro Siqueiros."
Forma, I (Núm. 3, 1927), 4-5.
(a-e)   709

.Breton, André. "Frida Kahlo."
El Hijo Pródigo, XII (Núm. 38,
mayo de 1946), 96. (a-e)
     710

----. "Poema." Estaciones,
I (Núm. 1, primavera de
1956), 135-136. (p)   711

Bretón de los Herreros, Manuel.
"La castañera" (en "Los
españoles pintados por sí
mismos"). Romance, I (Núm.
10, 15 de junio de 1940), 10.
(a-e)   712

Brion, Marcel. Nuevo amor de
Salvador Novo. Fábula, Núm.
3 (marzo de 1934), 60. (r)
     713

Brody, Daisy. Lao-Tze.
"Fragmentos del Tao-te-king"
(Trad. Daisy Brody y Antonio
Sánchez Barbudo). El Hijo
Pródigo, XI (Núm. 35, febrero
de 1946), 97-100. (tr)   714

----. "Viejos cuentos de la
India" (Trad. Daisy Brody y
Antonio Sánchez Barbudo). El
Hijo Pródigo, VIII (Núm. 27,
otoño de 1957), 354. (p) 715

Broido, Rubén. "Vida."
Estaciones, II (Núm. 7, otoño
de 1927), 354. (p)   715

Brull, Mariano. "Preludio,"
"Rosa," "A la rosa desdono-
cida," "A la rosa rosa,"
"Escalas de ruiseñor," "Rosa
sola," "Madrigal a la rosa,"
"Rosa alta," "El ruiseñor a
la ruiseñor a la rosa," "Rosa
sin nombre," "Silencio ante la
rosa," "Cinco minutos de
silencio," "Rosa - Arminda."
"La rosa de mi guarda."
Romance, II (Núm. 21, 15 de
febrero de 1941), 5. (p)
     716

57

Bud, Carmen. "Filosofía en Madrid. " Ruta, Núm. 1 (junio de 1938), 36-40. (a-e)
717

Bueno, Salvador. "El cuento cubano contemporáneo. " El Hijo Pródigo, XIII (Núm. 42, septiembre de 1946), 141-147. (a-e)
718

Bulgakow, B. "Tolstoi íntimo. " Romance, I (Núm. 1, 1 de febrero de 1940), 6; I (Núm. 2, 15 de febrero de 1940), 6, 19. (a-e)
719

Bustamante, Octavio N. "Alfonso Reyes. " Fábula, Núm. 9 (septiembre de 1934), 171-172. (a-e)
720

----. "Ciudades paralelas. " Fábula, Núm. 6 (junio de 1934), 103-106. (a-e)
721

Bustos Cerecedo, Miguel. "Manuel José Othón, gran poeta de su tiempo. " Ruta, Núm. 9 (febrero de 1939), 5-22. (a-e)
722

----. "El mejor poeta de México. " Ruta, Núm. 4 (septiembre de 1938), 56-60. (a-e)
723

----. "Muerte de Aníbal Ponce. " Ruta, Núm. 2 (julio de 1938), 47-48. (a-e)
724

----. Poemas árboles de Elías Nandino. Ruta, Núm. 7 (diciembre de 1938), 59-60. (r)
725

----. Poemas de la tierra de Carlos Carlino. Ruta, Núm. 9 (febrero de 1939), 60-61. (r)
726

----. Presencia de Otto D'Sola. Ruta, Núm. 6

(noviembre de 1938), 55-56. (r)
727

----. Rumbos y nieblas y Amanecer en cualquier camino de Adolfo Sotomayor. Ruta, 8 (enero de 1939), 55-56. (r)
728

----. Tierra del chicle de Ramón Beteta. Ruta, Núm. 1 (junio de 1938), 56-57. (r)
729

----. Tierra herida de Manuel Navarro Luna. Ruta, Núm. 5 (octubre de 1938), 60-61. (r)
730

C. de la, B. Encyclopédie française de M. Julien Cain. Romance, I (Núm. 13, 1 de agosto de 1940), 19. (r) 731

C., L. La vida de Gracus Babeuf de Elías Erenburg. Ruta, Núm. 2 (julio de 1938), 57-59. (r)
732

Cabada, Juan de la. "El grillo crepuscular. " El Hijo Pródigo, I (Núm. 6, septiembre de 1943), 347-352. (f)
733

----. "La mano de Pancho. " Tierra Nueva, III (Núm. 13-14, enero-abril de 1942), 60-68. (f)
734

----. "María 'La voz'. " Taller, I (Núm. 6, noviembre de 1939), 24-43. (f)
735

----. "El tejón y las gallinas. " Romance, I (Núm. 3, 1 de marzo de 1940), 8. (f) 736

Cabrera, Manuel. "Los supuestos del idealismo fenomenológico. " Tierra Nueva, I (Núm. 4-5, julio-octubre de 1940), 208-216. (a-e)
737

----. Sobre los problemas sociales de Carlos Vaz Ferreira. Tierra Nueva, I (Núm. 6, noviembre-diciembre de 1940), 371-373. (r) 738

----. Vida humana, sociedad y derecho de Luis Recaséns Siches. Tierra Nueva, I (Núm. 4-5, julio-octubre de 1940), 284-285. (r) 739

Cabrera, Miguel. "Retrato de la Madre Rosa María del Espíritu Santo." El Hijo Pródigo, II (Núm. 7, octubre de 1943), entre 32 y 33. (il) 740

----. "Retrato de Sor María Agustina Dolores." El Hijo Pródigo, II (Núm. 7, octubre de 1943), entre 8 y 9. (il) 741

----. "Retrato de una religiosa." El Hijo Pródigo, I (Núm. 3, junio de 1943), entre 160 y 161. (il) 742

Cadenazzi, Edgarda. "El lamparero de los alcoholes astrales." Sagitario, Núm. 8 (1 de febrero de 1927), 11. (p) 743

Caillois, Roger. "Actualidad de las sectas" (Trad. Gilberto Owen). El Hijo Pródigo, IV (Núm. 14, mayo de 1944), 89-92. (a-e) 744

----. "La aridez" (Trad. José Luis Martínez). El Hijo Pródigo, I (Núm. 4, julio de 1943), 205-208. (a-e) 745

----. "El escritor en la sociedad" (Trad. Antonio Alatorre y Juan José Arreola.) Prometeus, I (Núm. 2, abril de 1949), 75-78. (a-e) (124)

----. "Imposturas de la poesía" (Trad. José de la Colina). Estaciones, III (Núm. 12, invierno de 1958), 461-465. (a-e) 746

Caldwell, Erskine. "Fuego de cimas." Ruta, Núm. 8 (enero de 1939), 40-42. (f) 747

Calvillo, Manuel. "De amor hallado," "Elegía de ti." Tierra Nueva, I (Núm. 4-5, julio-octubre de 1940), 239-241. (p) 748

Calvillo Madrigal, Salvador. "Amanecer." El Hijo Pródigo, X (Núm. 33, diciembre de 1945), 171-178. (dr) 749

----. "En familia." Estaciones, II (Núm. 5, primavera de 1957), 19-27. (f) 750

----. "El hombre que robó a la muerte." El Hijo Pródigo, XII (Núm. 38, mayo de 1946), 91-95. (f) 751

----. Una botella al mar de Jorge Cuesta, José Gorostiza, Jaime Torres Bodet, Xavier Villaurrutia, y Bernardo Ortiz de Montellano. El Hijo Pródigo, XII (Núm. 38, mayo de 1946), 112-113. (r) 752

----. El de Héctor Morales Saviñón. El Hijo Pródigo, XIII (Núm. 40, julio de 1946), 58, 59. (r) 753

----. Manual de México de Eduardo de Ontañón. El Hijo Pródigo, XIII (Núm. 41, agosto de 1946), 120. (r) 754

Calle, Chita de la. Malaquais, Jean. "Golpes de caña" (Trad. Chita de la Calle). El Hijo Pródigo, IV (Núm. 13, abril de 1944), 44-57; (Núm. 14,

mayo de 1944), 93-109.
(tr)   755

Calleja, Rafael. "Canicas."
Ulises, Núm. 4 (agosto de
1927), 28-30. (a-e)   756

Camargo, Salvador. "Sí, yo
iría a misa." Fábula, Núm.
2 (febrero de 1934), 23-29.
(a-e)   757

Camarillo de Pereyra, María
Enriqueta. ("María
Enriqueta"). "Claridad,"
"Sombra." Antena, Núm. 5
(noviembre de 1924), 3. (p)
                                        758

----. "Contrastes." México
Moderno, II (Núm. 3, octubre
de 1922), 146-147. (p) 759

----. "Los gorriones." Antena,
Núm. 3 (septiembre de 1924),
3-4. (f)   760

----. "Olga Vanof." México
Moderno, I (Núm. 3, octubre
de 1920), 164-169. (f) 761

----. "Optica." La Falange,
Núm. 4 (1 de julio de 1923),
220. (p)   762

----. "La polilla." La Falange,
Núm. 7 (1 de octubre de 1923),
368-369. (a-e)   763

----. "Símbolo." La Falange,
Núm. 2 (1 de enero de 1923),
94. (p)   764

Camín, Alfonso. "Los tres
perfiles." México Moderno,
II (Núm. 11-12, noviembre-
diciembre de 1921), 289-291.
(p)   765

Camp, Santiago Valenti. "Max
Nordau y su concepción de
la ética." Sagitario, Núm. 4

(1 de septiembre de 1926), 13.
(a-e)   766

----. "La sociología y el
realismo objetivo." Sagitario,
Núm. 3 (15 de agosto de
1926), 4-5. (a-e)   767

Campo, Juan del. "Siete
mares." Tierra Nueva, I
(Núm. 3, mayo-junio de 1940),
161-162. (p)   768

Campobello, Nellie. "Martín
Luis Guzmán, a propósito de
El hombre y sus armas."
Ruta, Núm. 6 (noviembre de
1938), 42-43. (a-e)   769

Campobello, Nellie y Gloria.
"Ritmos de Michoacán."
Romance, I (Núm. 17, 22 de
octubre de 1940), 9. (a-e)
                                        770

Campuzano, Juan R. "Altamirano: Niño indígena."
Romance, I (Núm. 15, 1 de
septiembre de 1940), 17.
(a-e)   771

Canade. "La conversación,"
"Autorretrato." Contemporáneos, II (Núm. 7, diciembre
de 1928), 326-327. (il) 772

Cantón, Wilberto L. La casa
del grillo de Alfonso Reyes.
El Hijo Pródigo, VIII (Núm.
26, mayo de 1945), 118. (r)
                                        773

----. Equinoccio de Francisco
Peláez ("Francisco Tario").
El Hijo Pródigo, XIII (Núm.
40, julio de 1946), 57-58.
(r)   774

Capdevila, Arturo. "En el
mar." México Moderno, II
(Núm. 8, marzo de 1921), 73.
(p)   775

60

----. "Nocturno: a Job."
México Moderno, II (Núm. 4,
junio de 1923), 246-248. (p)
776

Capek, Karel. "La muerte de
Arquímedes" (Trad. Antonín
Polacek). Romance, I (Núm.
9, 1 de junio de 1940), 5. (c)
777

Carballido, Emilio. "Misa
primera." Estaciones, I (Núm.
4, invierno de 1956), 570-577.
(dr) 778

----. "Selaginela." Prometeus,
II (Núm. 1, diciembre de
1951), 61-65. (dr) 779

----. Polvos de arroz de
Sergio Galindo. Estaciones,
III (Núm. 10, verano de
1958), 192. (r) 780

Carballo, Emmanuel. "Dos
poemas." Estaciones, IV
(Núm. 13, primavera de 1959),
41-42. (p) 781

Cardenal, Ernesto. Lax, Robert.
"El circo" (Trad. Ernesto
Cardenal). Estaciones, V
(Núm. 19, otoño de 1950), 31-
40. (tr) 782

Cárdenas, Lázaro. "El congreso
indigenista interamericano."
Romance, I (Núm. 7, 1 de
mayo de 1940), 6. (a-e)
783

Cárdenas, Nancy. "Doña
Uncinaria." Estaciones, IV
(Núm. 14, verano de 1959),
201-206. (dr) 784

----. "Teatro Guiñol en la
Cuenca del Papaloapan."
Estaciones, IV (Núm. 14,
verano de 1959), 199-201.
(a-e) 785

Cardona Peña, Alfredo. "Espejo
de la voz." Tierra Nueva, II
(Núm. 11-12, septiembre-
diciembre de 1941), 253-255.
(p) 786

----. "Introducción a la
poesía." Tierra Nueva, I
(Núm. 6, noviembre-diciembre
de 1940), 297-301. (p) 787

----. "El suicida." El Hijo
Pródigo, XI (Núm. 34, enero
de 1946), 33-35. (f) 788

----. "Valle de México." El
Hijo Pródigo, VIII (Núm. 25,
abril de 1945), 30-31. (p)
789

Cardona Vera, José G. "La
raíz." Contemporáneos, XI
(Núm. 42-43, noviembre-
diciembre de 1931), 254-263.
(f) 790

Cardoza y Aragón, Luis. "A
propósito de una exposición."
Ruta, Núm. 2 (junio de 1938),
48-50. (a-e) 791

----. "El autor empieza a
suprimir personajes inútiles."
Sagitario, Núm. 5 (1 de
octubre de 1926), 17-18. (p)
792

----. "Breve tratado de los
cuernos de Anfitrión."
Taller, II (Núm. 11, julio-
agosto de 1940), 27-36. (a-e)
793

----. "Carlos Mérida."
Sagitario, Núm. 11 (15 de
marzo de 1927), 17. (a-e)
794

----. "Dante en Nueva York."
Ruta, Núm. 10 (marzo de
1939), 20-27. (f) 795

----. "Delirio de lirio."
El Hijo Pródigo, I (Núm. 2,
mayo de 1943), 97-102. (a-e)
796

----. "Demagogos de la
poesía: La exposición
surrealista." Taller, II (Núm.
8-9, enero-febrero de 1940),
47-50. (a-e)   797

----. "Dos soledades"("Canto,"
"Federico García Lorca").
Romance, I (Núm. 16, 15 de
septiembre de 1940), 9. (p)
798

----. "Elogio de la embria-
guez." Ruta, Núm. 4
(septiembre de 1938), 5-20.
(a-e)   799

----. "Exposición de artistas
españoles." Romance, I
(Núm. 5, 1 de abril de
1940), 7. (a-e)   800

----. "Federico en Nueva
York." Romance, I (Núm.
13, 1 de agosto de 1940), 1-
2. (a-e)   801

----. "Fez, ciudad santa de
los árabes." Sagitario,
(Núm. 12-13 (30 de abril de
1927), 15-27. (a-e)   802

----. "Oda a Charlot."
Sagitario, Núm. 6 (1 de
noviembre de 1926), 10. (p)
803

----. "El rapto de la torre
Eiffel." Sagitario, Núm. 10
(1 de marzo de 1927), 12.
(f)   804

----. "Rimbaud." Taller, I
(Núm. 4, julio de 1939), 3-5
(paginación independiente).
(a-e)   805

----. "Soledad de la fisiolo-
gia." Taller, I (Núm. 5,
octubre de 1939), 21-26. (p)
806

----. "Torre de Babel."
Contemporáneos, V (Núm. 17,
octubre de 1929), 222-233.
(f)   807

----. Historia de la literatura francesca de Albert
Thibaudet. Romance, I (Núm.
3, 1 de marzo de 1940), 18.
(r)   808

----. Textos y pretextos de
Xavier Villaurrutia. Taller,
II (Núm. 11, julio-agosto de
1940), 73-77. (r)   809

Carleton de Millán, Verna. "El
ocaso de la música francesa."
Ruta, Núm. 1 (junio de 1938),
48-51. (a-e)   810

Carner, José. "Emporio de
tristeza." Romance, I (Núm.
5, 1 de abril de 1940), 1-2.
(a-e)   811

----. "Prometeo y los
cerillos." Romance, I (Núm.
19, 18 de diciembre de 1940),
1, 2, 14. (a-e)   812

Carnés, Luisa. "Gris y rojo."
Romance, I (Núm. 15, 1 de
septiembre de 1940), 4-5.
(n)   813

----. "Los mellizos." Romance, I (Núm. 5, 1 de abril de
1940), 5. (f)   814

----. El bloqueo
del hombre de Clemente
Cimorra. Romance, I (Núm.
14, 15 de agosto de 1940), 18.
(r)   815

Carniado, Enrique. "China poblana." La Falange, Núm. 7 (1 de octubre de 1923), 390-392. (p)   816

Carvajal, María Isabel. ("Carmen Lira"). "La Cucarachita Mandinga." La Falange, Núm. 3 (1 de febrero de 1923), 166-168. (f)   817

Carvalho, Ronald de. "Rubayat," "Juegos pueriles," "Verdad," "Arte poética" (Trad. Jaime Torres Bodet). La Falange, Núm. 5 (1 de agosto de 1923), 264-265. (p)   818

Carrancá y Trujillo, Raúl. "El viento," "Las flechas del gallo." Sagitario, Núm. 9 (15 de febrero de 1927), 12. (a-e)   819

----. Lecturas populares de Esperanza Veláquez Bringas." Sagitario, Núm. 1 (15 de julio de 1926), 17. (r) 820

----. Pareceres. Sagitario, Núm. 4 (1 de septiembre de 1926), 17. (r)   821

----. Patria Grande. Sagitario, Núm. 4 (1 de septiembre de 1926), 17. (r)   822

----. Política trascendental de Salvador Escalón. Sagitario, Núm. 4 (1 de septiembre de 1926), 17. (r)   823

----. La república del Ecuador. El movimiento intelectual iberoamericano de César A. Naveda. Sagitario, Núm. 3 (15 de agosto de 1926), 16. (r)   824

----. La universidad nueva de Alfredo L. Palacios. Sagitario,

Núm. 2 (1 de agosto de 1926), 17. (r)   825

Carrasco, Pedro. "Las estrellas, el hombre y el perro." Romance, I (Núm. 2, 15 de febrero de 1940), 4. (a-e)   826

----. "Hacia los abismos del átomo: Artillería atómica." Romance, I (Núm. 12, 15 de julio de 1940), 4. (a-e) 827

Carrera Andrade, Jorge. "Prisión humana." El Hijo Pródigo, X (Núm. 33, diciembre de 1945), 145-146. (p)   828

Carrillo de Sotomayor, Luis de. "Al ejemplo de las cosas que fueron y se acabaron," "A la ligereza y pérdida del tiempo," "A la duración de un pensamiento," "A un chopo, semejante en desgracia a su amor," "A su amor, en sus males sin remedio," "En el sepulcro de una dama," "A las penas del amor inmortales," "A las prisiones del amor, imposible de romper," "A la caza de unas galoetas turquescas." Taller, II (Núm. 8-9, enerofebrero de 1940), 79-84. (p)   829

Carrillo y Gariel, A. "El arte mexicano de la colonia." Forma, II (Núm. 7, 1928), 22-24. (a-e)   830

Carrington, Leonora. "Conejos blancos." Prometeus, I (Núm. 1, febrero de 1949), 29-32. (f)   831

----. "Penelope" (Trad. José Ferrel). Prometeus, I (Núm. 3, mayo de 1949), 175-202. (dr)   832

----. "Un retrato de la difunta Mrs. Partridge," "Casa de enfrente," "El viaje a Sirio," "Martes," "El ensayo," Prometeus, I (Núm. 2, abril de 1949), entre 94-95. (il)   833

Carrión, Alejandro. "La poesía en un callejón sin salida." Ruta, Núm. 8 (enero de 1939), 50-53. (a-e)   834

Casal, Alfonso. "Momento de Rusia" Contemporáneos, VII (Núm. 24, mayo de 1930), 169-177. (a-e)   835

----. "Norteamérica, paradigma continental." Contemporáneos, X (Núm. 35, abril de 1931), 84-94. (a-e) 836

Casalduero, Joaquín. "Exaltación del ser en Jorge Guillén." El Hijo Pródigo, XIII (Núm. 41, agosto de 1946), 82-85. (a-e)   837

Casanueva Mazo, Bernardo. "En sombra." Tierra Nueva, I (Núm. 2, marzo-abril de 1940), 93-94. (p)   838

----. "Mar de duelo," "Antigua muerte," "Huída." Tierra Nueva, I (Núm. 6, noviembre-diciembre de 1940), 315-319. (p)   839

----. "Sonetos de alta voz." Tierra Nueva, III (Núm. 15, diciembre de 1942), 109-113. (p)   840

----. Estancia en la voz de Manuel Calvillo. Tierra Nueva, III (Núm. 15, diciembre de 1942), 169-171. (r)   841

Casas, Manuel Gonzalo. "El feminismo en la concepción del mundo." Tierra Nueva, III (Núm. 15, diciembre de 1942), 114-120. (a-e)   842

Caso, Antonio. "Ciencia y libertad." Tierra Nueva, I (Núm. 6, noviembre-diciembre de 1940), 293-296. (a-e)   843

----. "El concepto de la historia universal." México Moderno, I (Núm. 1, agosto de 1920), 5-12. (a-e)   844

----. "De las categorías del pensamiento como fundamento de la creencia." México Moderno, I (Núm. 3, octubre de 1920), 138-146. (a-e)845

----. "Rapsodias bíblicas." México Moderno, II (Núm. 3, octubre de 1922), 139-145. (a-e)   846

----. "La sonata y la sinfonía." México Moderno, II (Núm. 7, febrero de 1921), 8-10. (a-e)   847

Cassou, Jean. "Carta de Francia." Ruta, Núm. 8 (enero de 1939), 43-45. (a-e)   848

----. "Cervantes" (Trad. Pedro Geoffroy Rivas). Ruta, Núm. 5 (octubre de 1938), 27-32. (a-e)   849

----. "José Luis Cuevas." Estaciones, I (Núm. 1, primavera de 1956), 114-115. (a-e)   850

Castellanos, Francisco José. Stevenson, Robert Louis. "Carta a un joven que se propone seguir la carrera artística" (Trad. Francisco José Castellanos). Tierra Nueva, II (Núm. 11-12,

septiembre-diciembre de
1941), 210-217. (tr)   851

Castellanos, Julio. "Dibujos."
Contemporáneos, XI (Núm.
40-41, septiembre-octubre de
1931), 133-138. (il)   852

----. "Escenario." Contemporáneos, IX (Núm. 32,
enero de 1931), 89. (il)
853

----. "Maternidad," "Dibujo
para un libro," "Dibujo para
un libro," "Retrato," "El
baño," "Retrato." Contem-
poráneos, III (Núm. 9,
febrero de 1929), 124-129.
(il)   854

----. "Oleo," "Retrato."
Sagitario, Núm. 11 (15 de
marzo de 1927), 3-4. (il)
855

----. "Oleos." Ulises, Núm.
2 (julio de 1927), 16-17. (il)
856

----. "El sombrerón."
Contemporáneos, IX (Núm. 32,
enero de 1931), 80. (il)
857

Castellanos, Rosario. "Crónica
final." Estaciones, II (Núm.
5, primavera de 1957), 16-
18. (p)   858

----. "Cuento." Estaciones,
IV (Núm. 14, verano de
1959), 164-171. (f)   859

----. "Nostalgia," "Linaje."
Estaciones, III (Núm. 12,
invierno de 1958), 412. (p)
860

Castañeda Batres, Oscar. "Vox
Clamantis." Estaciones, III
(Núm. 11, otoño de 1958),
304-305. (p)   861

Castillo, Guillermo. "La
naturaleza virgen es el niño."
Forma, I (Núm. 6, 1928), 7-
11. (a-e)   862

Castillo, Jesús. "Dos danzas
tinecas," "Proseción
hierática." La Falange, Núm.
3 (1 de febrero de 1923), 194-
196. (a-e)   863

Castillo Ledón, Luis. "Un
capítulo de la vida de Miguel
Hidalgo y Costilla." México
Moderno, I (Núm. 2, septiembre de 1920), 67-71. (a-e)
864

----. "México-Tenoxtitlán."
México Moderno, II (Núm. 9,
mayo de 1921), 148-155. (a-e)
865

----. "Vida de Miguel Hidalgo
y Costilla." México Moderno,
II (Núm. 4, junio de 1923),
224-227. (a-e)   866

Castro Jr., Eduardo. "Impresiones sobre Harvard."
Estaciones, II (Núm. 7, otoño
de 1957), 345-353. (a-e)867

Castrovido, Roberto. "El
Triunfo del Carlismo en
España." Romance, I (Núm.
9, 1 de junio de 1940), 10.
(a-e)   868

Castro Leal, Antonio. "Alfonso
Reyes." México Moderno,
II (Núm. 4, junio de 1923),
195-199. (a-e)   869

----. "Arte y moral de
Alarcón." Taller, I (Núm. 5,
octubre de 1939), 13-20. (a-e)
870

----. "Los autores que no
leemos ya: Chesterton."
México Moderno, I (Núm. 1,
agosto de 1920), 18-20. (a-e)
871

----. "Carta de Inglaterra." Contemporáneos, XI (Núm. 38-39, julio-agosto de 1931), 105-112. (a-e)   872

----. "El cazador del ritmo universal." Taller, II (Núm. 8-9, enero-febrero de 1940), 16-24. (f)   873

----. "Las correcciones de Rafael López." El Hijo Pródigo, III (Núm. 11, febrero de 1944), 71-77. (a-e)   874

----. "Don Juan Ruiz de Alarcón y Mendoza." Taller, I (Núm. 5, octubre de 1939), 69-72. (a-e)   875

----. "La elegía del museo." Romance, I (Núm. 17, 22 de octubre de 1940), 1-2. (a-e)   876

----. "El imperialismo andaluz." El Hijo Pródigo, VII (Núm. 22, enero de 1945), 9-13. (a-e)   877

----. "El lucero de la tarde: Notas sobre el poeta inglés John Keats." Romance, I (Núm. 19, 18 de diciembre de 1940), 3, 14. (a-e) 878

----. "La mitología del Siglo XX," Contemporáneos, XI (Núm. 42-43, noviembre-diciembre de 1931), 283-287. (a-e)   879

----. "Oscar Wilde moralista." Romance, I (Núm. 2, 15 de febrero de 1940), 1-2. (a-e)   880

----. "El Príncipe Czerwinski." El Hijo Pródigo, II (Núm. 7, octubre de 1943), 27-31. (f)   881

----. "Ramón López Velarde. México Moderno, II (Núm. 11-12, noviembre-diciembre de 1921), 275-277. (a-e) 882

----. "Respuesta a la encuesta de Romance." Romance, I (Núm. 8, 15 de mayo de 1940), 2. (a-e)883

----. "Ruiz de Alarcón." Romance, I (Núm. 1, 1 de febrero de 1940), 9. (a-e)   884

----. Odas y épodos de Horacio con una introducción de María Rosa Lida. Taller, II (Núm. 8-9, enero-febrero de 1940), 56-58. (r)   885

----. Persons and Places de George Santayana. El Hijo Pródigo, IV (Núm. 13, abril de 1944), 60. (r)   886

----. Poetas novohispanos, estudio, selección y notas de Alfonso Méndez Plancarte. El Hijo Pródigo, VI (Núm. 20, noviembre de 1944), 122-123. (r)   887

----. Salsette descubre América de Jules Romains. El Hijo Pródigo, V (Núm. 17, agosto de 1944), 123. (r)   888

----. Sor Juana Inés de la Cruz, poetisa de corte y convento de Elizabeth Wallace. El Hijo Pródigo, IV (Núm. 14, mayo de 1944), 120. (r)889

----. Lawrence, David Herbert. "De Las mañanas de México" (Trad. Antonio Castro Leal). Romance, I (Núm. 16, 15 de septiembre de 1940), 3, 15. (tr)   890

----. Santayana, George. "Las mansiones de Elena" (Trad. Antonio Castro Leal). El Hijo Pródigo, V (Núm. 16, julio de 1944), 38-41. (tr) 891

Casuso, Teté. "Las estrellas de Hollywood bajan del cielo." Ruta, Núm. 1 (junio de 1938), 41-46. (a-e) 892

Cataño, Eduardo. "Flor en un libro," "Horal." Estaciones, V (Núm. 18, verano de 1960), 42-44. (p) 893

----. "Huellas," "Herido instante," "Germinal." Estaciones, IV (Núm. 13, primavera de 1959), 95-97. (p) 894

----. "Viñeta." Estaciones, I (Núm. 4, invierno de 1956), portada. (il) 895

Cava, José. "Viñeta." Estaciones, II (Núm. 11, otoño de 1958), portada. (il) 896

----. "Viñeta." Estaciones, III (Núm. 12, invierno de 1958), portada. (il) 897

----. "Viñeta." Estaciones, V (Núm. 18, verano de 1960), portada. (il) 898

Cecchi, Emilio. "El Cristo muerto," "La revuelta de Cedillo." (Trad. Jorge Hernández Campos), Estaciones, V (Núm. 17, primavera de 1960), 10-21. (a-e) 899

----. "Mujeres en la ventana," "Anteojos negros." (Trad. Jorge Hernández Campos) Estaciones, V (Núm. 18, verano de 1960), 56-64. (f) 900

Ceja Reyes, Víctor. "La procesión del silencio." Tierra Nueva, I (Núm. 3, mayo-junio de 1940), 157-160. (f) 901

Celaya, Gabriel. "El martillo." Estaciones, IV (Núm. 15, otoño de 1959), 262-265. (p) 902

Centeno, Augusto. "Primavera." Sagitario, Núm. 9 (15 de febrero de 1927), 4. (p) 903

Centeno, Francisco; Fernández Urbina, J. M.; Asúnsolo, Ignacio; Ruiz, Guillermo; Rivera, Diego; Revueltas, Fermín; Domínguez Bello, Arnulfo. "Encuesta sobre escultura." Forma, I (Núm. 2, noviembre de 1926), 7-8. (a-e) (530)

Cereno, Benito. Canto a la primavera de Xavier Villaurrutia. Prometeus, I (Núm. 2, abril de 1949), 131. (r) 904

----. Cuentos crueles del Conde de Villiers de L'Isle-Adam. Prometeus, I (Núm. 2, abril de 1949), 131. (r) 905

----. Anouilh, Jean. "Entreacto" (Trad. Benito Cereno). Prometeus, I (Núm. 2, abril de 1949), 88-91. (tr) (475)

Cernuda, Luis. "Atardecer en la catedral." Taller, II (Núm. 10, marzo-abril de 1940), 15-17. (p) 906

----. "Juan Ramón Jiménez." El Hijo Pródigo, I (Núm. 3, junio de 1943), 148-156. (a-e) 907

----. "Niño tras un cristal," "El éxtasis." Estaciones, III (Núm. 10, verano de 1958), 119-120. (p)   908

----. "Quetzalcoatl." El Hijo Pródigo, II (Núm. 9, diciembre de 1943), 152-154. (p)   909

----. "Tres poetas clásicos." El Hijo Pródigo, IX (Núm. 28, julio de 1945), 9-16. (a-e)   910

----. "La ventana." El Hijo Pródigo, XII (Núm. 37, abril de 1946), 14-15. (p)   911

----. "Vereda del cuco." El Hijo Pródigo, VI (Núm. 20, noviembre de 1944), 78-80. (p)   912

----. Blake, William. "El niño negro" (Trad. Luis Cernuda). Romance, I (Núm. 10, 15 de junio de 1940), 11. (tr)   (680)

----. Keats, John. "Oda al otoño" (Trad. Luis Cernuda). Romance, I (Núm. 10, 15 de junio de 1940), 11. (tr)   913

----. Yeats, W. B. "Ephermera" (Trad. Luis Cernuda). Romance, I (Núm. 10, 15 de junio de 1940), 11. (tr) 914

Cervantes, Enrique A. "Hermandad o confradía de loceros." Forma, I (Núm. 5, 1927), 16-17. (a-e)   915

----. "Una obra artística de orfebrería hecha en la ciudad de Puebla." Forma, I (Núm. 2, noviembre de 1926), 16-17. (a-e)   916

Cervantes, Francisco. "Ciudades de las ánimas." Estaciones, IV (Núm. 14, verano de 1959), 207-210. (p)   917

----. "Túnel donde encontré tu nombre escrito." Estaciones, IV (Núm. 16, invierno de 1959), 411. (p)   918

Cestero, Manuel Florentino. "El inválido." La Falange, Núm. 5 (1 de agosto de 1923), 252-263. (f)   919

----. "Un patio dominicano." La Falange, Núm. 2 (1 de enero de 1923), 83-85. (f)   920

----. "Los reincidentes." México Moderno, II (Núm. 3, octubre de 1922), 158-161. (dr)   921

Cézanne, Paul. "Bañistas." Contemporáneos, V (Núm. 15, agosto de 1929), 65. (il)922

----. "Naturaleza muerta." Estaciones, I (Núm. 2, verano de 1956), entre 244-245. (il)   923

Cirlot, Juan Eduardo. "Suplemento con estudio y antología del surrealismo." Estaciones, I (Núm. 3, otoño de 1956), 406-454. (a-e)   924

Clausel, Joaquín. "Volcanes." El Hijo Pródigo, I (Núm. 4, julio de 1943), entre 212-213. (il)   925

Clercq, Jacques le. "March Dust." Contemporáneos, IV (Núm. 12, mayo de 1929), 123-125. (p)   926

Climent, Enrique. "Retrato de Rosa Marta Sustaita, " "Paisaje

68

de Cuernavaca, " "Retrato de
León Felipe. " Romance, I
(Núm. 20, 15 de enero de
1941), 12-13. (il) 927

Cocteau, Jean. "La farsa del
castillo" (Trad. Xavier
Villaurrutia). Prometeus, II
(Núm. 1, diciembre de 1951),
42-44. (f) 928

----. "Fragmentos sobre
Chirico." Contemporáneos, I
(Núm. 3, agosto de 1928),
261-264. (a-e) 929

Colín, Eduardo. "Alfonso Reyes."
Fábula, Núm. 9 (septiembre
de 1934), 172. (a-e) 930

Colina, José de la. "A la busca
de un Dios perdido." Es-
taciones, III (Núm. 12,
invierno de 1958), 458-460.
(a-e) 931

----. "Un cuadro de Alberto
Gironella, " "Gusano uno, "
"Gusano dos." Estaciones,
III (Núm. 11, otoño de 1958),
288-290. (p) 932

----. "Sobre el caso Pasternak." Estaciones, III (Núm.
12, invierno de 1958), 477-
479. (a-e) 933

----. Cuando pasan las
cigüeñas de Mijail Kelatozov.
Estaciones, III (Núm. 12,
invierno de 1958), 466. (r)
934

----. El lugar de un hombre
de Ramón J. Sender. Es-
taciones, III (Núm. ʻ12, invierno de 1958), 490. (r)
935

----. Luz de aquí de Tomás
Segovia. Estaciones, III
(Núm. 12, invierno de 1958),
489-490. (r) 936

----. La sangre de Medusa
de José Emilio Pacheco y
Berny. Estaciones, III (Núm.
12, invierno de 1958), 489.
(r) 937

----. La strada de Federico
Fellini. Estaciones, III (Núm.
11, otoño de 1958), 323-326.
(r) 938

----. Caillois, Roger. "Imposturas de la poesía" (Trad.
José de la Colina). Estaciones,
III (Núm. 12, invierno de
1958), 461-465. (tr) (746)

Colson, Jaime. "Chaplin y
Cardoza." Sagitario, Núm.
6 (1 de noviembre de 1926),
10. (il) 939

Comas, Juan. "El poblamiento
de América. " Romance, I
(Núm. 11, 1 de julio de 1940),
4, 17. (a-e) 940

----. El plan de los grupos
de estudio de E. Randall
Maguire. Romance, I (Núm.
16, 15 de septiembre de 1940),
19. (r) 941

Comet, César A. "Balcón."
Sagitario, Núm. 7 (1 de enero
de 1927), 15. (p) 942

----. "Nido." Sagitario,
Núm. 6 (1 de noviembre de
1926), 16. (p) 943

Conde Abellán, Carmen. "Surcos."
Sagitario, Núm. 14 (31 de mayo de 1927), 8. (p) 944

Condroyer, Emile. "Des
enfants mexicains." Sagitario,
Núm. 12-13 (30 de abril de
1927), 13. (a-e) 945

Conkling, Hilda. "Agua, " "En
el lago Chaplain, " "Amanecer"

(Trad. Rafael Heliodoro
Valle). México Moderno, II
(Núm. 8, marzo de 1921),
127. (p)   946

Contreras, Francisco. "La
endemoniada." México
Moderno, II (Núm. 8, marzo
de 1921), 90-107. (f) 947

Copland, Aaron. "Carlos
Chávez, compositor." Contemporáneos, II (Núm. 7,
diciembre de 1928), 407-412.
(a-e)   948

Cordero, J. L. "Una broma de
Manuel Castro Padilla."
Antena, Núm. 5 (noviembre de
1924), 8-9. (a-e)   949

Córdoba, Joaquín Fernández de.
"La litografía moreliana del
siglo diecinueve." El Hijo
Pródigo, X (Núm. 32,
noviembre de 1945), 80-84.
(a-e)   950

Cornyn, John Hubert. "Un
antiguo poema azteca."
Sagitario, Núm. 6 (1 de
noviembre de 1926), 16.
(a-e)   951

Coronel, Rafael. "Figura."
Estaciones, I (Núm. 4,
invierno de 1955), entre 492-
493. (il)   952

Corot, Jean Baptiste Camille.
"La mujer en azul," "Vista
de Nantes," "Puente de
Narni," "La Rochell,"
"Magdelena leyendo," "El
torso," "Melancolía," "La
iglesia de Marisell," "Meditación," "Autorretrato."
Romance, I (Núm. 13, 1 de
agosto de 1940), 1, 13. (il)
                            953

Correa, Nicolás de. "Santa
Rosalía." El Hijo Pródigo,

I (Núm. 4, julio de 1943),
entre 212-213. (il)   954

Cortés, Erasto. "Acueducto,"
"Fábrica," "Baile." Forma,
I (Núm. 4, 1927), 26-27. (il)
                            955

Corvalán, Octavio. "América,
¿Tertisferio?" Estaciones, V
(Núm. 18, verano de 1960),
20-29. (a-e)   956

Cosío Villegas, Daniel. "Morado
y oro," "La teoría de la
eternidad." México Moderno,
II (Núm. 2, septiembre de
1922), 94-96. (a-e)   957

----. Bajo el sol de México
de Leonardo Montalbán.
México Moderno, II (Núm. 3,
octubre de 1922), 193. (r)
                            958

----. Puntos sutiles del
Quixote de Emilia Gaspar
Rodríguez. México Moderno,
II (Núm. 4, junio de 1923),
256-257. (r)   959

Coss, Julio Antonio. "Cosas
de todos los días." Es-
taciones, IV (Núm. 13,
primavera de 1959), 93-94.
(f)   960

----. "En busca de la
renovación de nuestro
lenguaje musical." Estaciones,
III (Núm. 10, verano de 1958),
230-236. (a-e)   961

----. "¿Honegger, confor-
mista, incoherente y con-
vencional?" Estaciones, II
(Núm. 8, invierno de 1957),
463-468. (a-e)   962

Costa, Olga. "El programa,"
"Niña." El Hijo Pródigo, X
(Núm. 31, octubre de 1945),
entre 16 y 17. (il)   963

Coto, Juan E. "Flor silvestre."
México Moderno, II (Núm. 11-
12, noviembre-diciembre de
1921), 303. (p)   964

----. "Himno de primavera."
México Moderno, II (Núm. 4
junio de 1923), 244-245. (p)
                               965

----. "Leocópolis." La
Falange, Núm. 3 (1 de
febrero de 1923), 160-161.
(p)   966

Couffon, Claude. "La muerte
lleva el juego" (Reseña de
Pedro Páramo de Juan Rulfo;
Trad. José Emilio Pacheco y
Berny). Estaciones, IV
(Núm. 16, invierno de 1959),
494-495. (r)   967

Covarrubias, Miguel. "Carlos
E. González." La Falange,
Núm. 7 (1 de octubre de
1923), 395. (il)   968

----. "Carlos Mérida." La
Falange, Núm. 3 (1 de
febrero de 1923), 153. (il)
                               969

----. "Diego Rivera." La
Falange, Núm. 2 (1 de enero
de 1923), 127. (il)   970

----. "Genaro Estrada." La
Falange, Núm. 6 (1 de
septiembre de 1923), 361. (il)
                               971

----. "Rodríguez Lozano."
La Falange, Núm. 4 (1 de
julio de 1923), sigue 250.
(il)   972

Cravioto, Alfonso. "Ofrenda a
Urueta," "Tórtola Valencia,"
"Nueva España." México
Moderno, II (Núm. 7, febrero
de 1921), 31-37. (p)   973

----. "Oración fúnebre."
México Moderno, II (Núm. 11-
12, noviembre-diciembre de
1921), 251-254. (a-e)   974

----. "Ser primitivo..."
México Moderno, I (Núm. 5,
diciembre de 1920), 268-269.
(p)   975

Creel, Enrique. "Hermenegildo
y el ángel." Estaciones, II
(Núm. 6, verano de 1957),
177-182. (f)   976

Crespo, Angel. "El sol," "Con
un clavo de paja." Estaciones,
IV (Núm. 15, otoño de 1959),
278-280. (p)   977

Crespo, Gerardo. "Cedro
rojo." Forma, I (Núm. 4,
1927), 25. (il)   978

----. "Grabado en madera."
Forma, I (Núm. 4, 1927), 28.
(il)   979

Crespo, Jorge Juan. "Yo la
vi." México Moderno, II
(Núm. 4, junio de 1923), 253.
(a-e)   980

Crowninshield, Frank. "Tamayo."
Ulises, Núm. 6 (febrero de
1928), 37. (a-e)   981

Cruz, Juan. "La justicia,"
"Mujer peinándose." Tierra
Nueva, II (Núm. 7-8, enero-
abril de 1941), entre 64 y 65.
(il)   982

Cruz, Sor Juana Inés de la. "Carta
atenagórica" (Ed. de Ermilo
Abreu Gómez). Contemporáneos,
VI (Núm. 22, marzo de 1930),
218-268. (a-e, ed)   983

----. "Endechas" (Ed. de Xavier
Villaurrutia). Taller, I (Núm.
7, diciembre de 1939), 59-89.
(p, ed)   984

----. "Liras" (Ed. de Ermilo Abreu Gómez). Contemporáneos, XI (Núm. 40-41, septiembre-octubre de 1931), 120-132. (p, ed) 985

----. "Primero sueño" (Ed. de Ermilo Abreu Gómez). Contemporáneos, I (Núm. 3, agosto de 1928), 272-312. (p, ed) 986

Cuadra, José de la. "Lo que ha de venir." Sagitario, Núm. 9 (15 de febrero de 1927), 13-14. (a-e) 987

Cuesta, Jorge. "Agustín Lazo." Ulises, Núm. 1 (mayo de 1927), 22-24. (a-e) 988

----. "El arte moderno." El Hijo Pródigo, I (Núm. 5, agosto de 1943), 281-285. (a-e) 989

----. "Arte poético," "Este amor no te mira," "Tu voz es un eco." Estaciones, III (Núm. 10, verano de 1958), 144-146. (p) 990

----. "Crítica del reino de los cielos." El Hijo Pródigo, I (Núm. 5, agosto de 1943), 290-291. (a-e) 991

----. "La cultura francesa en México." El Hijo Pródigo, I (Núm. 5, agosto de 1943), 287-290. (a-e) 992

----. "Dibujo." Ulises, Núm. 3 (agosto de 1927), 33-34. (p) 993

----, y Bernardo Ortiz de Montellano. "Dos cartas a propósito de la nota pre-inserta." (sobre La rebelión de las masas de Ortega y Gasset). Contemporáneos, IX (Núm. 33, febrero de 1931), 162-165. (a-e) 994

----. "Notas." Ulises, Núm. 4 (agosto de 1927), 30-37. (a-e) 995

----. "Paraíso encontrado." Tierra Nueva, II (Núm. 11-12, septiembre-diciembre de 1941), 195. (p) 996

----. "Poemas." Contemporáneos, VIII (Núm. 26-27, julio-agosto de 1930), 33-35. (p) 997

----. "Poesía" (Suplemento poético al núm. 15). Tierra Nueva, III (Núm. 15, diciembre de 1942). (p) 998

----. "La poesía de Paul Eluard." Contemporáenos, IV (Núm. 12, mayo de 1929), 130-133. (a-e) 999

----. "Una poesía mística." Romance, I (Núm. 2, 15 de febrero de 1940), 3. (a-e) 1000

----. "El resentimiento en la moral de Max Scheler." Ulises, Núm. 2 (junio de 1927), 17-20. (a-e) 1001

----. "Respuesta a la encuesta de Romance." Romance, I (Núm. 5, 1 de abril de 1940), 2. (a-e) 1002

----. "La resurrección de Don Francisco." Antena, Núm. 1 (julio de 1924), 6-7. (f) 1003

----. "Robert Desnos y el sobrerrealismo." Contemporáneos, V (Núm. 18, noviembre de 1929), 318-322. (a-e) 1004

----. "Salvador Díaz Mirón." El Hijo Pródigo, I (Núm. 5,

agosto de 1943), 285-287.
(a-e)   1005

----. "Sonetos." Contemporáneos, X (Núm. 37, junio de
1931), 193-194. (p)   1006

----. "Sonetos." Contem-
poráneos, XI (Núm. 40-41,
septiembre-octubre de 1931),
142-143. (p)   1007

----. "Sonetos." Taller, II
(Núm. 10, marzo-abril de
1940), 18-20. (p)   1008

----. "Xavier Villaurrutia."
Romance, I (Núm. 11, 1 de
julio de 1940), 11. (a-e)
                         1009

----. La rebelión de las
masas de José Ortega y
Gasset. Contemporáneos, IX
(Núm. 33, febrero de 1931),
152-162. (r)   1010

----. Reflejos de Xavier
Villaurrutia. Ulises, Núm. 1
(mayo de 1927), 28-29. (r)
                         1011

----. Eluard, Paul. "La
invención" (Trad. Jorge
Cuesta). Contemporáneos, IV
(Núm. 12, mayo de 1929),
134-136. (tr)   1012

----. Spender, Stephen. "Sin
el afán que da" (Trad. Jorge
Cuesta). Estaciones, III
(Núm. 10, verano de 1958),
147. (tr)   1013

----. Spender, Stephen.
"Soneto" (Trad. Jorge Cuesta).
Taller, II (Núm. 10, marzo-
abril de 1940), 21. (tr)
                         1014

Cuesta, Víctor. "El ángulo de
la voz." El Hijo Pródigo, II
(Núm. 8, noviembre de 1943),

97. (a-e)   1015

----. "Lenguajes líquidos."
El Hijo Pródigo, V (Núm. 16,
julio de 1944), 37. (dr) 1016

Cuesta y Cuesta, Alfonso.
"Miedo." Ruta, Núm. 11
(abril de 1939), 43-48. (f)
                         1017

Cuevas, José Luis. "Mujeres,"
"La farsa," "El anónimo,"
"La vieja," "El loco." Estaciones, I (Núm. 1, primavera de 1956), entre 120-121.
(il)   1018

Cumming, A. E.; Obregón
Santacilla, Carlos; Montenegro, Roberto; Ituarte,
Manuel M.; Pallares, Alfonso;
Gil, Alberto. "Encuesta sobre
arquitectura." Forma, I (Núm.
3, 1927), 15-16. (a-e) 1019

Cunard, Nancy. "La comida
de hoy." Ruta, Núm. 9
(febrero de 1939), 23-24. (p)
                         1020

----. Canto de España de
Langston Hughes. Ruta, Núm.
1 (junio de 1938), 57-58. (r)
                         1021

Chacón y Calvo, José María.
"La literatura de José Martí."
Romance, I (Núm. 11, 1 de
julio de 1940), 1-2. (a-e)
                         1022

Chagall, Marc. "Yo y mi
aldea." Estaciones, I (Núm.
3, otoño de 1956), entre 454-
455. (il)   1023

Chagoya, Leopoldo. "La dama
de plata." Estaciones, IV
(Núm. 16, invierno de 1959),
469-475. (f)   1024

Champourcin, Ernestina de.
"Límites," "Sueños," "Sole-
dad," "Alborada," "Otoño,"
"Lo eterno," "Interrogación,"
"La siesta," "Ventana,"
"Recurerdos." Romance, I
(Núm. 19, 18 de diciembre de
1940), 5. (p)   1025

----. Juegos y canciones
infantiles de Puerto Rico de
María Cadilla Martínez.
Romance, II (Núm. 24, 31 de
mayo de 1941), 18.   (r)1026

----. Yo quiero libertad de
Isabel de Palencia. Romance,
II (Núm. 22, 15 de marzo de
1941), 19.   (r)   1027

Charlot, Jean. "Carlos Mérida
y la pintura." Contempo-
ráneos, II (Núm. 6, noviembre
de 1928), 262-266. (a-e)
                          1028

----. "José Clemente
Orozco: Su obra monumen-
tal." Forma, I (Núm. 6,
1928), 32-51. (a-e)   1029

----. "Manuel Manilla:Graba-
dor mexicano." Forma, I
(Núm. 2, noviembre de 1926),
18-21. (il)   1030

----. "Nota sobre la pintura
mural de los Mayas." Forma,
I (Núm. 5, 1927), 24. (a-e)
                          1031

----. "Obras." Contem-
poráneos, X (Núm. 37, junio
de 1931), 211-215. (il) 1032

----. "Para las gentes de
buena voluntad." Forma, I
(Núm. 1, octubre de 1926),
34. (a-e)   1033

----. "Pinturas murales
mexicanas." Forma, I (Núm.
1, octubre de 1926), 10-12.
(a-e)   1034

----. "Poemas." Contem-
poráneos, X (Núm. 37, junio
de 1931), 267-271. (p)   1035

----. "Retrato de M. Mar-
tínez Pintao," "Mujeres
desnudas," "Obreros." Forma,
I (Núm. 5, 1927), 25-28. (il)
                          1036

Charry Lara, Fernando. "Influencia de Juan Ramón
Jiménez." Estaciones, III
(Núm. 11, otoño de 1958),
306-308. (a-e)   1037

----. "Silva en el modernismo." Estaciones, III (Núm. 9
primavera de 1958), 15-17.
(a-e)   1038

Chassex, Jean. "Amérique:
1960." (Trad. Hugo Rod-
ríguez-Alcalá), Estaciones, V
(Núm. 18, verano de 1960),
79-83. (p)   1039

Chauveau, Leopold. "La guerra
con Ventripond" (Trad. Roberto
Lago). Romance, I (Núm. 14,
15 de agosto de 1940), 16, 23.
(f)   1040

Chávez, Carlos; Orozco, José
Clemente; Ortiz Monasterio,
Manuel; Owen, Gilberto.
"Encuesta sobre pintura."
Forma, I (Núm. 1, octubre de
1926), 5-6. (a-e)   1041

----. "Música." Ulises, Núm.
2 (julio de 1927), 30-31. (a-e)
                          1042

Chávez, Ezequiel A. "Estudios
de literatura rusa: Al margen
del Crimen y castigo de
Dostoiévsky." México Mod-
erno, II (Núm. 9, mayo de
1921), 139-144. (a-e)   1043

----. "Estudios rusos." México Moderno, I (Núm. 4,

74

noviembre de 1920), 209-219. (a-e) 1044

Chávez Morado, José. "Nido de pájaros extraños." El Hijo Pródigo, X (Núm. 31, octubre de 1945), entre 16 y 17. (il) 1045

Chávez Morado, Juan. "La fuga," "El sueño," "Fusilamiento," "México sombrío." Tierra Nueva, III (Núm. 15, diciembre de 1942), entre 140-141. (il) 1046

Chávez Orozco, Luis. "El mecanismo de la autocracia de Porfirio Díaz." Contemporáneos, X (Núm. 36, mayo de 1931), 144-164. (a-e) 1047

----. "Orígenes de la autocracia de Porfirio Díaz." Contemporáneos, VI (Núm. 21, febrero de 1930), 153-182. (a-e) 1048

----. "El romance en México." Contemporáneos, VII (Núm. 25, junio de 1930), 253-267. (a-e) 1049

Chejov, Antón. "Una petición de mano" (Trad. Xavier Villaurrutia). El Hijo Pródigo, VIII (Núm. 27, junio de 1945), 177-182. (dr) 1050

Chirico, Giorgio de. "Los maniquíes de la torre rosa." Estaciones, I (Núm. 3, otoño de 1956), entre 454-455. (il) 1051

----. "Una Noche." Estaciones, I (Núm. 1, primavera de 1956), 138. (p) 1052

----. "Pequeña antología (Trad. César Moro y

Agustín Lazo). El Hijo Pródigo, VII (Núm. 22, enero de 1945), 33-41. (p) 1053

----. "Telas." Contemporaneos, I (Núm. 3, agosto de 1928), 265-271. (il) 1054

Chumacero, Alí. "Amor es mar," "A tu voz," "Diálogo con un retrato," "A una estatua," "Retorno." Tierra Nueva, III (Núm. 15, diciembre de 1942), 155-162. (p) 1055

----. "Antonio Machado, poeta de España." Tierra Nueva, II (Núm. 7-8, enero-abril de 1941), 74-79. (a-e) 1056

----. "Elegía del marino." El Hijo Pródigo, VI (Núm. 19, octubre de 1944), 32. (p) 1057

----. "En la orilla del silencio," "A una flor inmersa." Tierra Nueva, I (Núm. 4-5, julio-octubre de 1940), 217-220. (p) 1058

----. "Entre mis manos," "Mujer deshabitada." El Hijo Pródigo, II (Núm. 9, diciembre de 1943), 182-183. (p) 1059

----. "Una exposición." Tierra Nueva, I (Núm. 4-5, julio-octubre de 1940), 256. (a-e) 1060

----. "Jorge Cuesta o la traición de la inteligencia." Estaciones, III (Núm. 10, verano de 1958), 141-143. (a-e) 1061

----. "Luz y sombra." Tierra Nueva, II (Núm. 9-10, mayo-agosto de 1941), 171-172. (p) 1062

----. "Mi amante," "Espejo y agua," "El sueño de Adán." El Hijo Pródigo, I (Núm. 2, mayo de 1943), 77-79. (p) 1063

----. "Muerte del hombre." Tierra Nueva, I (Núm. 3, mayo-junio de 1940), 154-156. (p) 1064

----. "Narciso herido," "La transfiguración," "Laurel caído." El Hijo Pródigo, XIII (Núm. 40, julio de 1946), 21-23. (p) 1065

----. "Paráfrasis de la viuda." Estaciones, III (Núm. 12, invierno de 1958), 406. (p) 1066

----. "Páramo de sueños" (Suplemento poético al núm. 6). Tierra Nueva, I (Núm. 6, noviembre-diciembre de 1940). (p) 1067

----. "Poema de amorosa raíz." Tierra Nueva I (Núm. 1, enero-febrero de 1940), 34. (p) 1068

----. "Poesía y destrucción." Tierra Nueva, I (Núm. 6, noviembre-diciembre de 1940), 350-352. (a-e) 1069

----. "Pureza en el tiempo." El Hijo Pródigo, IX (Núm. 30, septiembre de 1945), 147-148. (p) 1070

----. "Ramón López Velarde, el hombre solo." El Hijo Pródigo, XII (Núm. 39, junio de 1946), 145-148. (a-e) 1071

----. Alfonso Gutiérrez Hermosillo y algunos amigos de Agustín Yáñez. El Hijo Pródigo, XI (Núm. 34, enero de 1946), 57. (r) 1072

----. "Una antología" (Reseña de Antología de la poesía mexicana moderna de Manuel Maples Arce.) Tierra Nueva, I (Núm. 6, noviembre-diciembre de 1940), 353-356. (r) 1073

----. Apolo y Coatlicue de Luis Cardoza y Aragón. El Hijo Pródigo, VII (Núm. 23, febrero de 1945), 122-123. (r) 1074

----. Autobiografía de José Clemente Orozco. El Hijo Pródigo, XIII (Núm. 41, agosto de 1946), 118-119. (r) 1075

----. Baudelaire de Aldous Huxley. El Hijo Pródigo, XII (Núm. 38, mayo de 1946), 113. (r) 1076

----. Cantos de la tierra prometida de Juan Cotto. Tierra Nueva, I (Núm. 2, marzo-abril de 1940), 115-116. (r) 1077

----. Castilla. La tradición, el idioma de Ramón Menéndez Pidal. El Hijo Pródigo, XI (Núm. 34, enero de 1946), 59-60. (r) 1078

----. La columna y el viento de Vicente Barbieri. El Hijo Pródigo, I (Núm. 6, septiembre de 1943), 383. (r) 1079

----. Cornucopia de México de José Moreno Villa. Tierra Nueva, I (Núm. 3, mayo-junio de 1940), 185-186. (r) 1080

----. Cuentos vividos y crónicas soñadas de Luis G. Urbina. El Hijo Pródigo, XIII

(Núm. 42, septiembre de 1946), 177. (r)   1081

----. "Educación" (Reseña de Educación y Ciencia de Juan Roura Parella). Tierra Nueva, I (Núm. 4-5, julio-octubre de 1940), 265-267. (r)   1082

----. El escritor según él y según los críticos de Pío Baroja. El Hijo Pródigo, VIII (Núm. 26, mayo de 1945), 120. (r)   1083

----. Espejo de mi muerte de Elías Nandino. El Hijo Pródigo, X (Núm. 32, noviembre de 1945), 122. (r)   1084

----. Fidelidad del sueño de Juan Rejano. El Hijo Pródigo, I (Núm. 2, mayo de 1943), 123-124. (r)   1085

----. Héroes mayas de Ermilo Abreu Gómez. Tierra Nueva, III (Núm. 15, diciembre de 1942), 186-188. (r)   1086

----. Los hombres del alba de Efraín Huerta. El Hijo Pródigo, VII (Núm. 24, marzo de 1945), 184. (r)   1087

----. Hora ciega de Sara de Ibáñez. El Hijo Pródigo, III (Núm. 10, enero de 1944), 57-58. (r)   1088

----. Las ilusiones, El convaleciente, Los oráculos de Juan Gil-Albert. El Hijo Pródigo, VIII (Núm. 27, junio de 1945), 183. (r)   1089

----. Letras de América de Enrique Diéz-Canedo. El Hijo Pródigo, VI (Núm. 21, diciembre de 1944), 185. (r)   1090

----. La marchanta de Mariano Azuela. El Hijo Pródigo, IV (Núm. 13, abril de 1944), 58. (r)   1091

----. Memoria del olvido de Emilio Prados. Tierra Nueva, I (Núm. 3, mayo-junio de 1940), 183-185. (r)   1092

----. Memorias de Victoriano Salado Alvarez. El Hijo Pródigo, XII (Núm. 30, junio de 1946), 175-176. (r)   1093

----. Mi tío don Jesús y otros relatos de Alfonso Gutiérrez Hermosillo. El Hijo Pródigo, IX (Núm. 39, septiembre de 1945), 178. (r)   1094

----. "Michoacán por dentro" (Reseña de Ancla en el tiempo de Alfredo Maillefert). Tierra Nueva, II (Núm. 9-10, mayo-agosto de 1941), 184-185. (r)   1095

----. Mínima muerte de Emilio Prados. El Hijo Pródigo, VI (Núm. 20, noviembre de 1944), 123. (r)   1096

----. Mis mejores poemas de Vicente Aleixandre. Estaciones, II (Núm. 7, otoño de 1957), 320-323. (r)   1097

----. La mujer domada de Mariano Azuela. El Hijo Pródigo, XIII (Núm. 40, julio de 1946), 56-57. (r)   1098

----. El mundo que tú eres de Alfredo Carona Peña. El Hijo Pródigo, III (Núm. 11, febrero de 1944), 121-122. (r)   1099

----. La música por dentro de Rafael Solana. El Hijo

Pródigo, II (Núm. 11, febrero de 1944), 120. (r) 1100

----. La negra Angustias de Francisco Rojas González. El Hijo Pródigo, VII (Núm. 22, enero de 1945), 57. (r) 1101

----. "Pintura mexicana" (Reseña de La nube y el reloj de Luis Cardoza y Aragón). Tierra Nueva, I (Núm. 6, noviembre-diciembre de 1940), 361-365. (r) 1102

----. Nuevos cantares y otros poemas de Alberto Quintero Alvarez. El Hijo Pródigo, I (Núm. 4, julio de 1943), 255-256. (r) 1103

----. Obras completas de Manuel José Othón. El Hijo Pródigo, X (Núm. 31, octubre de 1945), 54-55. (r) 1104

----. Paseo de las mentiras de Juan de la Cabada. Tierra Nueva, I (Núm. 4-5, julio-octubre de 1940), 273-274. (r) 1105

----. Pensativa de Jesús Goytortúa Santos. El Hijo Pródigo, IX (Núm. 29, agosto de 1945), 121. (r) 1106

----. Poemas elementales de Francisco Luis Bernárdez, Persuación de los días de Oliverio Girondo, y El grillo y Claro desvelo de Conrado Nalé Roxlo. El Hijo Pródigo, I (Núm. 1, abril de 1943), 60-61. (r) 1107

----. Poesía española de Joaquín Díez-Canedo y Francisco Giner de los Ríos. El Hijo Pródigo, XII (Núm. 39, junio de 1946), 177-178. (r) 1108

----. Poesía indígena de Angel María Garibay K. Tierra Nueva, I (Núm. 3, mayo-junio de 1940), 191-192. (r) 1109

----. "Cuatro libros" (Reseña de Poesía indígena en traducción de Ángel M. Garibay K.; Crónicas de Michoacán prologadas por Federico Gómez de Orozco; Relaciones históricas de Carlos de Sigüenza y Góngora prologada y anotada por Manuel Romero de Terreros; y Los empeños de una casa de Sor Juana Inés de la Cruz a cargo de Julio Jiménez Rueda). Tierra Nueva, I (Núm. 4-5, julio-octubre de 1940), 286-288. (r) 1110

----. Poetas de México con selección y prólogo de Manuel González Ramírez y Rebeca Torres Ortega. El Hijo Pródigo, XI (Núm. 36, marzo de 1946), 172. (r) 1111

----. Poetas en el destierro de José Ricardo Morales. El Hijo Pródigo, II (Núm. 8, noviembre de 1943), 125-126. (r) 1112

----. Pueblo y canto de Angel de Campo. Tierra Nueva, I (Núm. 1, enero-febrero de 1940), 57-58. (r) 1113

----. Puerta severa de José Moreno Villa. Tierra Nueva, III (Núm. 13-14, enero-abril de 1942), 78-80. (r) 1114

----. Recinto de Octavio Paz. Tierra Nueva, II (Núm. 9-10, mayo-agosto de 1941), 175-177. (r) 1115

----. Romance de José Conde de Enrique González Rojo. Tierra Nueva, I (Núm. 2, marzo-abril de 1940), 111-113. (r)							1116

----. Rosenda de José Rubén Romero. El Hijo Pródigo, XII (Núm. 39, junio de 1946), 176-177. (r)							1117

----. La séptima cruz de Anna Seghers. El Hijo Pródigo, II (Núm. 9, diciembre de 1943), 219. (r)							1118

----. Soledad enemiga de Neftalí Beltrán. El Hijo Pródigo, V (Núm. 16, julio de 1944), 56. (r)							1119

----. 29 cuentistas mexicanos actuales de Manuel Lerín y Marco Antonio Millán. El Hijo Pródigo, X (Núm. 32, noviembre de 1945), 121-122. (r)							1120

----. El venado de Clemente López Trujillo. Tierra Nueva, II (Núm. 11-12, septiembre-diciembre de 1941), 283-284. (r)							1121

----. La vida literaria de México, y la literatura mexicana durante la guerra de independencia de Luis G. Urbina. El Hijo Pródigo, XIII (Núm. 41, agosto de 1946), 116-117. (r)							1122

----. Bremond, Henri. "La poesía pura" (Trad. Alí Chumacero). Tierra Nueva, I (Núm. 6, noviembre-diciembre de 1940), 320-329. (tr)(707)

----. Leclerc, Jorge Luis. "Discurso sobre el estilo" (Trad. Alí Chumacero). Tierra Nueva, III (Núm. 13-14, enero-abril de 1942), 26-34. (tr)							1123

D, J. Amanecer en las ruinas de Hans Habe. Prometeus, I (Núm. 3, mayo de 1949), 219-220. (r)							1124

----. Gran señor y Rajadiablos de Eduardo Barrios. Prometeus, I (Núm. 3, mayo de 1949), 220. (r)							1125

Dalí, Salvador. "Aparto y mano," "Paisaje." Contemporáneos, VII (Núm. 23, abril de 1930), 17-19. (il)							1126

----. "Construcción blanda con alubias hervidas," "Autorretrato." Estaciones, I (Núm. 3, otoño de 1956), entre 454-455. (il)							1127

----. "Poema." Estaciones, I (Núm. 1, primavera de 1956), 139-142. (p)							1128

----. "Salvador Dalí pretende imitar a Leonardo o a Miguel Angel, pero sólo logra remedar a Gustavo Doré," "Un dibujo," "Retrato del padre y de la hermana," "Retrato de Gala," "El asno podrido." Estaciones, II (Núm. 5, primavera de 1957), entre 84-85. (il) 1129

Darío, Rubén. "En la isla de oro." La Falange, Núm. 3 (1 de febrero de 1923), 170-172. (f)							1130

----. "En la última página del 'Romancero del Cid'," "Abrojo," "En el album de Victoria Mayorga Marín." La Falange, Núm. 6 (1 de septiembre de 1923), 334-335. (p)							1131

79

Dauster, Frank. "Aspectos del paisaje en la poesía de Carlos Pellicer. " Estaciones, IV (Núm. 16, invierno de 1959), 387-395. (a-e)   1132

----. "La poesía de Elías Nandino." Estaciones, V (Núm. 19, otoño de 1960), 41-67. (a-e)   1133

----. "El recinto inviolable. " Estaciones, IV (Núm. 14, nerano de 1959), 131-145. (a-e)   1134

----. "El teatro de Xavier Villaurrutia. " Estaciones, I (Núm. 4, invierno de 1956), 479-487. (a-e)   1135

Delevsky, J. "La materialización de la energía. " Romance, I (Núm. 10, 15 de junio de 1940), 4. (a-e)   1136

Delgado, José Manuel. "Esposa para ceremonias. " Estaciones, V (Núm. 18, verano de 1960), 65-71. (dr) 1137

Delgado, José María. "Padre nuestro. " La Falange, Núm. 4 (1 de julio de 1923), 239-240. (p)   1138

Delgado, Juan B. "Elogio de la esmeralda. " Antena, Núm. 4 (octubre de 1924), 5. (p)   1139

Delmar, Meira. "Raíz antigua. " Prometeus, II (Núm. 1, diciembre de 1951), 23. (p)   1140

Demócrito. "Fragmentos filosóficos" (Trad. David García-Bacca). El Hijo Pródigo, II (Núm. 9, diciembre de 1943), 166-175. (a-e)   1141

Derain, André. "Retrato, " "Estudio. " Contemporáneos, V (Núm. 15, agosto de 1929), 60-61. (il)   1142

Derycke, Gaston. "La experiencia romántica. " El Hijo Pródigo, XII (Núm. 37, abril de 1946), 23-24. (a-e) 1143

Deústua, Raúl. "La muerte de los negros. " Prometeus, I (Núm. 3, mayo de 1949), 168-169. (p)   1144

Dìaz, E. "Para amar sin consuelo. " La Falange, Núm. 2 (1 de enero de 1923), entre 128-129. (a-e)   1145

Díaz Arrieta, Hernán. ("Alone"). "Don Andrés. " Tierra Nueva, II (Núm. 11-12, septiembre-diciembre de 1941), 256-262. (a-e)   1146

Díaz Conde, Antonio y Edmundo Báez. "'La soledad o el eco'." Estaciones, II (Núm. 7, otoño de 1957), 246-255. (dr) (558)

Díaz de León, Francisco. "Grabado en madera." Fábula, Núm. 6 (junio de 1934), entre 116-117. (il)   1147

----. "Grabado en madera. " Sagitario, Núm. 4 (1 de septiembre de 1926), 8. (il)   1148

----. "Grabado en madera. " Sagitario, Núm. 9 (15 de febrero de 1927), 3. (il)   1149

----. "Grabados. " Contemporáneos, IX (Núm. 32, enero de 1931), 38-41. (il)   1150

----. "Grabados en madera. " Sagitario, Núm. 9 (15 de febrero de 1927), 16. (il)1151

80

----. "Un pintor japonés en México." Forma, II (Núm. 7, 1928), 1-5. (il)   1152

Díaz Dufóo Jr., Carlos. "El barco." Contemporáneos, XI (38-39, julio-agosto de 1931), 1-30. (dr)   1153

----. "Diálogo." Contemporáneos, I (Núm. 3 agosto de 1928), 229-234. (a-e)   1154

----. "Diálogo." México Moderno, I (Núm. 4, noviembre de 1920), 201-203. (a-e)   1155

----. "Temis municipal." Contemporáneos, IX (Núm. 34, marzo de 1931), 193-205. (dr)   1156

Díaz Rodríguez, Manuel. "En la cruz de fuego." La Falange, Núm. 3 (1 de febrero de 1923), 132-139. (a-e)   1157

Diego, Gerardo. "Fábula de equis y zeda." Contemporáneos, VI (Núm. 21, febrero de 1930), 97-112. (p)   1158

----. "Triunfo." Sagitario, Núm. 4 (1 de septiembre de 1926), 18. (p)   1159

Díez-Canedo, Enrique. "Antonio Machado: poeta español." Taller, I (Núm. 3, mayo de 1939), 7-18. (a-e)   1160

----. "El arte y el tiempo." Romance, I (Núm. 1, 1 de febrero de 1940), 1-2. (a-e)   1161

----. "Consideraciones acerca de un libro de teatro." Romance, I (Núm. 12, 15 de julio de 1940), 1-2. (a-e)   1162

----. "Moreno Villa." Romance, I (Núm. 12, 15 de julio de 1940), 8. (a-e)   1163

----. "Ocho epigramas de oriente" (incluve "Ocaso tropical," "Banyan," "Singapore," "El carabao en el río," "Gallo de pelea," "Stock exchange, Manila," "Volcán de Taal," "Mar y viento.") Tierra Nueva, I (Núm. 3, mayo-junio de 1940), 131-133. (p)   1164

----. "Problemas del teatro." El Hijo Pródigo, V (Núm. 16, julio de 1944), 11-17. (a-e)   1165

----. "Rubén Darío, Juan Ramón Jiménez y los comienzos del modernismo." El Hijo Pródigo, II (Núm. 9, diciembre de 1943), 145-151. (a-e)   1166

----. El gesticulador de Rudolfo Usigli. El Hijo Pródigo, IV (Núm. 13, abril de 1944), 58-59. (r)   1167

----. Juan Ruiz de Alarcón, su vida y su obra de Antonio Castro Leal. El Hijo Pródigo, I (Núm. 3, junio de 1943), 186-187. (r)   1168

----. Letras colombianas Baldomero Sanín Cano. El Hijo Pródigo, IV (Núm. 15, junio de 1944), 184-185. (r)   1169

----. Misterio de Quanaxhuata de José Carner. El Hijo Pródigo, I (Núm. 5, agosto de 1943), 319-320. (r)   1170

----. Numancia de Miguel de Cervantes en versión modernizada de Rafael Alberti. El Hijo Pródigo, II (Núm. 9, diciembre de 1943), 219-220. (r) 1171

----. La vida conyugal de Max Aub. El Hijo Pródigo, IV (Núm. 13, abril de 1944), 59. (r) 1172

----. Block, Alejandro. "Los escritas" (Trad. Enrique Díez-Canedo). México Moderno, II (Núm. 1, agosto de 1922), 9-10. (tr) (681)

----. Masefield, John._ "Los fieles." (Trad. Enrique Díez-Canedo y Martín Luis Guzmán), Contemporáneos, V (Núm. 18, noviembre de 1929), 245-292; (Núm. 19, diciembre de 1929), 354-421. (tr) 1173

----. Pushkin, Alejandro. "El barón avariento" (Trad. Enrique Díez-Canedo). El Hijo Pródigo, V (Núm. 16, julio de 1944), 42-48. (r) 1174

----. Valéry, Paul. "Esbozo de un serpiente" (Trad. Enrique Díez-Canedo). Tierra Nueva, II (Núm. 7-8, enero-abril de 1941), 3-12. (tr) 1175

Dmitrievsky, I. "En las praderas del Uzbequistán." Romance, I (Núm. 12, 15 de julio de 1940), 5. (a-e) 1176

Dodero, Antonio. Kreymborg, Alfred. "El viejo manuscrito" (Trad. Antonio Dodero). La Falange, Núm. 7 (1 de octubre de 1923), 381. (tr) 1177

Domenchina, Juan José. "A propósito de Enrique González Martínez." Romance, I (Núm. 20, 15 de enero de 1941), 3. (a-e) 1178

----. "Azaña, escritor y político." Romance, I (Núm. 18, 15 de noviembre de 1940), 1, 3, 14. (a-e) 1179

----. "Epílogo de James Joyce." Romance, II (Núm. 21, 15 de febrero de 1941), 4. (a-e) 1180

----. "Grandeza y servidumbr' del oficio literario." Romance, II (Núm. 22, 15 de marzo de 1941), 4, 14. (a-e) 1181

----. "Nuevas notas sobre Paul Valéry." Romance, II (Núm. 23, 22 de abril de 1941), 1-2. (a-e) 1182

----. "La poesía española contemporánea." Romance, II (Núm. 24, 31 de mayo de 1941), 5, 13. (p) 1183

----. "Primera elegía jubilar." Romance, I (Núm. 17, 22 de octubre de 1940), 10-11. (p) 1184

Domingo, Marcelino. "Categoría de pueblos." Sagitario, Núm. 3 (15 de agosto de 1926), 6. (a-e) 1185

Domínguez Assiayn, Salvador. "Filosofía de los antiguos mexicanos." Contemporáneos, XI (Núm. 42-43, noviembre-diciembre de 1931), 209-225. (a-e) 1186

Domínguez Bello, Arnulfo; Fernández Urbina, J. M.; Asúnsolo, Ignacio; Ruiz, Guillermo; Rivera, Diego; Revueltas, Fermín; y Centeno, Francisco. "Encuesta sobre

82

escultura." Forma, I (Núm. 2, noviembre de 1926), 7-8. (a-e) (530)

Doniz, Roberto. "Mineros." Estaciones, I (Núm. 4, invierno de 1956), entre 592-593. (il) 1187

Donne, John. "Devociones" (Trad. Octavio G. Barreda). El Hijo Pródigo, I (Núm. 1, abril de 1943), 49-57. (a-e) (593)

Dotor, Angel. "Los grandes españoles contemporáneos: Bonilla y San Martín." La Falange, Núm. 7 (1 de octubre de 1923), 400-403. (a-e) 1188

Dreyfus, Alberto. "Dos estudios sobre el arte contemporáneo." Sagitario, Núm. 8 (1 de febrero de 1927), 9. (a-e) 1189

Durate Guillé, Manuel. "Apertura en el sueño" (Suplemento poético al núm. 2). Tierra Nueva, I (Núm. 2, marzo-abril de 1940). (a-e) 1190

Ducasse, Isidoro. "Prefacio a un libro futuro" (Trad. José Ferrel). El Hijo Pródigo, I (Núm. 6, septiembre de 1943), 365-379. (a-e) 1191

Duchamp, Marcel. "Entre nuestros artículos." Estaciones, I (Núm. 1, primavera de 1956), 142-143. (p) 1192

Dueñas, Guadalupe. "El moribundo." Estaciones, II (Núm. 6, verano de 1957), 171-174. (f) 1193

Duhamel, Georges. "A la sombra de las estatuas" (Trad. Agustín Lazo y Xavier

Villaurrutia). El Hijo Pródigo, XI (Núm. 36, marzo de 1946), 162-171; XII (Núm. 37, abril de 1946), 34-43; (Núm. 38, mayo de 1946), 97-103. (dr) 1194

Durand, José. "Siempre con Alfonso Reyes." Estaciones, V (Núm. 18, verano de 1960), 12-15. (a-e) 1195

Durand, Mercedes. "Primavera," "Verano." Estaciones, (Núm. 6, verano de 1957), 175-176. (p) 1196

----. Samuel Ramos: su filosofar sobre lo mexicano de Juan Hernández Luna. Estaciones, II (Núm. 6, verano de 1957), 192-194. (r) 1197

Durero, Alberto. "El Hijo Pródigo." El Hijo Pródigo, IV (Núm. 15, junio de 1944), entre 132 y 133. (il) 1198

Durtain, Luc. "La época en que vivimos y el heroísmo." Ruta, Núm. 7 (diciembre de 1938), 47-49. (a-e) 1199

----. "La guerra no existe" (Trad. Pedro Geoffroy Rivas). Ruta, Núm. 10 (marzo de 1939), 34-37. (f) 1200

E.D.I.A.P.S.A. "Romance a sus lectores." Romance, I (Núm. 17, 22 de octubre de 1940), 1. (a-e) 1201

Echavarría, Margarita. "Engaño." Estaciones, V (Núm. 18, verano de 1960), 98-106. (f) 1202

Echavarría, Salvador. "Derroteros de la poesía contemporánea." Estaciones, I (Núm. 1 primavera de 1956), 13-26. (a-e) 1203

----. " Qué es la verdad?" Estaciones, I (Núm. 4, invierno de 1956), 492-514. (a-e) 1204

----. "Surrealismo y babelismo." Estaciones, I (Núm. 3, otoño de 1956), 347-357. (a-e) 1205

Echave Ibia, Baltasar de. "María Magdalena." El Hijo Pródigo, I (Núm. 4, julio de 1943), entre 212 y 213. (il) 1206

Echeverría del Prado, Vicente. "Sonetos de la íntima clausura." Estaciones, III (Núm. 12, invierno de 1958), 385-386. (p) 1207

Echeverría Loría, Arturo. "Dos escultores." Tierra Nueva, II (Núm. 7-8, enero-abril de 1941), 64-65. (a-e) 1208

----. "Este pasar junto a la sombra," "Tres ausencias," Tierra Nueva, I (Núm. 3, mayo-junio de 1940), 172-174. (p) 1209

----. "Silencio," "Doble pulso." Tierra Nueva, I (Núm. 6, noviembre-diciembre de 1940), 345-347. (p) 1210

----. "Soledad." Tierra Nueva, I (Núm. 2, marzo-abril de 1940), 110. (p) 1211

----. Canto de Sara de Ibáñez. Tierra Nueva, II (Núm. 9-10, mayo-agosto de 1941), 180-181. (r) 1212

Echeverría R., Manuel. "Yo, aquí." Estaciones, V (Núm. 19, otoño de 1960), 68-73. (f) 1213

Eckhart, Meister. "Dos textos místicos" (Trad. Daisy Brody y Antonio Sánchez Barbudo). El Hijo Pródigo, II (Núm. 7, octubre de 1943), 51-57. (a-e) 1214

Ehrenbourg, Elie. "Moscú." México Moderno, II (Núm. 1, agosto de 1922), 60-61. (p) 1215

Eielson, Jorge Eduardo. "Príncipe de olvido," "Habitación en llamas." Prometeus, I (Núm. 3, mayo de 1949), 166-167. (p) 1216

Eisenstein, Sergio M. "México en las páginas de Eisenstein." Contemporáneos, X (Núm. 36, mayo de 1931), 136-143. (il) 1217

----. "Principios de la forma fílmica" (Trad. Agustín Aragón Leiva). Contemporáneos, X (Núm. 36, mayo de 1931), 110-135. (a-e) (482)

Eliot, Thomas Stearns. "El canto de amor de J. Alfred Prufrock" (Trad. Rodolfo Usigli). Taller, II (Núm. 10, marzo-abril de 1940), 65-69. (p) 1218

----. "Un canto para Simeón" (Trad. Octavio G. Barreda). Taller, II (Núm. 10, marzo-abril de 1940), 90-91. (p) (594)

----. "La fliglia che piange" "Marina" (Trad. Juan Ramón Jiménez). Taller, II (Núm. 10, marzo-abril de 1940), 70, 89. (p) 1219

----. "Los hombres huecos" (Trad. León Felipe). Contemporáneos, IX (Núm. 33, febrero de 1931), 132-136. (p) 1220

----. "Los hombres huecos" (Trad. León Felipe). Taller, II (Núm. 10, marzo-abril de 1940), 85-88. (p)   1221

----. "Miércoles de ceniza" (Trad. Bernardo Ortiz de Montellano). Taller, II (Núm. 10, marzo-abril de 1940), 92-99. (p)   1222

----. "La música de la poesía" (Trad. Octavio G. Barreda). El Hijo Pródigo, I (Núm. 1, abril de 1943), 21-30. (a-e)   (595)

----. "El páramo" (Traducción y prólogo de Enrique Munguía Jr.). Contemporáneos, VIII (Núm. 26-27, julio-agosto de 1930), 7-32.(p)   1223

----. "Qué es un clásico?" (Trad. Rodolfo Usigli). Prometeus, I (Núm. 2, abril de 1949), 105-126. (a-e)   1224

----. "Tierra baldía" (Trad. Angel Flores). Taller, II (Núm. 10, marzo-abril de 1940), 71-84. (p)   1225

Elizondo, Salvador. "Coito, " "Galope en el puerto, " "Canícula, " "Aspid, " "Galope," "Retablo. " Estaciones, V (Núm. 20, invierno de 1960), 60-64. (p)   1226

----. "En torno al Ulises de Joyce. " Estaciones, IV (Núm. 13, primavera de 1959), 98-111. (a-e)   1227

----. "Il miglior fabbro. " Estaciones, V (Núm. 19, otoño de 1960), 3-16. (a-e)   1228

----. "Requiem de junio. " Estaciones, IV (Núm. 14,

verano de 1959), 232-239. (p)   1229

----. Graves, Robert. "Como nieve, " "La puerta, " "Todo estaba en su sitio, " "El suicida en el seto, " "She tells her love while half-asleep. " (Trad. Salvador Elizondo), Estaciones, V (Núm. 17, primavera de 1960), 22-24. (tr)   1230

Elm E. "Respuesta a la encuesta de Romance. " Romance, I (Núm. 3, 1 de marzo de 1940), 2. (p) 1231

Eluard, Paul. "Algunas de las palabras que, hasta ahora me estaban misteriosamente prohibidas. " Estaciones, I (Núm. 1, primavera de 1956), 136-138. (p)   1232

----. "La invención" (Trad. Jorge Cuesta). Contemporáneos, IV (Núm. 12, mayo de 1929), 134-136. (p)   (1012)

Emmanuel, Pierre. "El hombre y el poeta" (Trad. Antonio Sánchez Barbudo). El Hijo Pródigo, I (Núm. 2, mayo de 1943), 89-91. (a-e)   1233

Encina, Juan de la. "Dos exposiciones, Dos artistas. " Romance, I (Núm. 20, 15 de enero de 1941), 7, 8. (a-e)   1234

----. "Imaginería colonial. " Romance, II (Núm. 22, 15 de marzo de 1941), 12-13, 19. (a-e)   1235

----. "Motivos críticos. " Romance, I (Núm. 17, 22 de octubre de 1940), 12. (a-e)   1236

----. "Motivos críticos: Alí Babá en la ciudad de los aires." Romance, I (Núm. 18, 15 de noviembre de 1940), 10. (a-e) 1237

----. "Motivos críticos: Aurelio Arteta." Romance, I (Núm. 19, 18 de diciembre de 1940), 4. (a-e) 1238

----. "Motivos críticos: Del Cuzco a San Miguel." Romance, II (Núm. 24, 31 de mayo de 1941), 9-10. (a-e) 1239

----. "Motivos críticos: Don Artemio de Valle-Arizpe." Romance, II (Núm. 21, 15 de febrero de 1941), 13. (a-e) 1240

----. "Motivos críticos: Escultura tarasca." Romance, I (Núm. 18, 15 de noviembre de 1940), 10. (a-e) 1241

----. "William Hogarth." Romance, II (Núm. 23, 22 de abril de 1941), 3, 12, 13. (a-e) 1242

Enciso, Jorge. "Los frescos cortesianos del Hospital de Jesús." El Hijo Pródigo, I (Núm. 6, septiembre de 1943), 344-345. (a-e) 1243

Enríquez, Carlos. "Vamos a hablar de la Lola." Romance, II (Núm. 21, 15 de febrero de 1941), 6. (f) 1244

Ernst, Max. "El beso," "Enrique IV, la leona de Belfort y un ex-combatiente." Estaciones, I (Núm. 3, otoño de 1956), entre 454-455. (il) 1245

Erro, Luis Enrique. "Las

cuestiones morales." México Moderno, II (Núm 2, septiembre de 1922), 121-122. (a-e) 1246

Escalante, Francisco J. "La astronomía en tiempo de Tut-Anch-Amen." Antena, Núm. 4 (octubre de 1924), 10-12. (a-e) 1247

Escalante, Roberto. "La infame turba." Estaciones, V (Núm. 18, verano de 1960), 74-78. (f) 1248

Escobar, José U. "La sombra de Karamídes." México Moderno, II (Núm. 10, junio de 1921), 216-219. (a-e) 1249

Espejo, Beatriz. "Florencia: 1566," "La misiva del príncipe." Estaciones, IV (Núm. 15, otoño de 1959), 355-357. (f) 1250

----. "La luna en el charco." Estaciones, V (Núm. 19, otoño de 1960), 79-88. (dr) 1251

Esperón, Manuel. "El carro del pulque." Forma, I (Núm. 1, octubre de 1926), 24. (il) 1252

Espina, Antonio. "Ahora, en abril, aquí." Sagitario, Núm. 2 (1 de agosto de 1926), 7. (p) 1253

Estrada, Genaro. "Chufas y capicúas." Antena, Núm. 4 (octubre de 1924), 3-4. (a-e) 1254

----. "De Italia." La Falange, Núm. 2 (1 de enero de 1923), 74-77. (a-e) 1255

----. "Dilucidaciones," "La ciudad colonial." México Moderno, I (Núm. 4, noviembre de 1920), 224-228. (a-e) 1256

----. "Las fiestas de los colegiales de San Ildefonso." México Moderno, I (Núm. 1, agosto de 1920), 29-32. (a-e) 1257

----. "Infierno y paraíso de letras francesas." Contemporáneos, IX (Núm. 34, marzo de 1931), 244-250. (a-e) 1258

----. "Letras minúsculas." México Moderno, II (Núm. 4, junio de 1923), 206-208. (a-e) 1259

----. "Lir-Ate." Sagitario, Núm. 6 (1 de noviembre de 1926), 11. (p) 1260

----. "Panorama," "Lento," "Salto." Contemporáneos, IV (Núm. 13, junio de 1929), 193-200. (p) 1261

----. "Por el camino de Proust." Contemporáneos, II (Núm. 6, noviembre de 1928), 292-296. (a-e) 1262

----. "Preludio," "Retrato," "Tedio," "Asunto," "Madrugada," "Volver." Contemporáneos, I (Núm. 2, julio de 1928), 112-116. (p) 1263

----. "Silencio." Contemporáneos, II (Núm. 7, diciembre de 1928), 319-320. (p) 1264

----. "Sonrisa." Sagitario, Núm. 9 (15 de febrero de 1927), 4. (p) 1265

---- A orillas del Hudson de Martín Luis Guzmán. México

Moderno, II (Núm. 7, febrero de 1921), 62-63. (r) 1266

----. Las alamedas del silencio de Gilberto Rubalcaba. México Moderno, I (Núm. 4, noviembre de 1920), 260. (r) 1267

----. El alma de la escuela del Padre Meneses y varios. México Moderno, II (Núm. 7, febrero de 1921), 71. (r) 1268

----. La cábala del amor de Aurelio Velázquez. México Moderno, I (Núm. 4, noviembre de 1920), 260-261. (r) 1269

----. Cartas de viaje de Alberto María Carreño ("El Monacillo del Sagrario"). México Moderno, I (Núm. 4, noviembre de 1920), 260-261. (r) 1270

----. Las carreteras nacionales de Adolfo A. López. México Moderno, II (Núm. 7, febrero de 1921), 72. (r) 1271

----. Cesarismo democrático de Laureano Vallenilla Lanz. México Moderno, II (Núm. 7, febrero de 1921), 72. (r) 1272

----. Crítica transcendental de M. Vincenzi. México Moderno, I (Núm. 6, enero de 1921), 390. (r) 1273

----. Crónicas coloniales de Ricardo Fernández Guardia. México Moderno, II (Núm. 11-12, noviembre-diciembre de 1921), 312-313. (r) 1274

----. Cuentos de Leónidis Andreieff. México Moderno, I

(Núm. 6, enero de 1921),
388-389. (r)   1275

----. Datos para la historia
de Toluca. Fray Andrés de
Castro de Miguel Salinas.
México Moderno, I (Núm. 5,
diciembre de 1920), 319-320.
(r)   1276

----. Un decenio de política
mexicana de Manuel Calero.
México Moderno, I (Núm. 4,
noviembre de 1920), 263-264.
(r)   1277

----. Doña Catalina Xuárez
Marcayda, primera esposa de
Hernán Cortés y su familia
de Francisco Fernández del
Castillo. México Moderno,
II (Núm. 7, febrero de 1921),
66-68. (r)   1278

----. Les Ecrivains Con-
temporains de l'Amérique
Espagnole de Francisco
Contreras. México Moderno,
I (Núm. 4, noviembre de
1920), 259-260. (r)   1279

----. Estudio relativo a zonas
federales de José L. Cossío.
México Moderno, I (Núm. 3,
octubre de 1920), 193-194. (r)
                                1280

----. Florilegio de Alberto J.
Ureta. México Moderno, I
(Núm. 5, diciembre de 1920),
320. (r)   1281

----. Homenajes póstumos.
Joaquín D. Casasús de Alberto
María Carreño. México
Moderno, II (Núm. 7, febrero
de 1921), 69. (r)   1282

----. Influencias que se
ejercieron en Bolívar de Diego
Carbonell. México Moderno, I
(Núm. 4, noviembre de 1920),
264. (r)   1283

----. Los límites del arte y
algunas reflexiones de moral
y literatura de Andre Gide.
México Moderno, I (Núm. 5,
diciembre de 1920), 319. (r)
                                1284

----. La literatura durante la
guerra de independencia de
Salvador Cordero. México
Moderno, I (Núm. 3, octubre
de 1920), 195. (r)   1285

----. Melpómene de Arturo
Capdevila. México Moderno,
I (Núm. 6, enero de 1921),
389-390. (r)   1286

----. Memoria de Hacienda y
Crédito Público de José E.
Suay. México Moderno, I (Núm
6, enero de 1921), 390. (r)
                                1287

----. Memoria de la Dirección
de la Casa de Moneda y
Oficinas Federales de Ensaye,
Correspondiente al año fiscal
de 1918. México Moderno, I
(Núm. 3, octubre de 1920),
194. (r)   1288

----. Memorias de un vigilante
de José S. Alvarez ("Fray
Mocho"). México Moderno, I
(Núm. 3, octubre de 1920),
194. (r)   1289

----. Notas de las lecciones
del profesor doctor Nicolás
León en la Escuela Nacional de
Bibliotecarios y Archiveros de
Nicolás León. México Moderno
II (Núm. 7, febrero de 1921),
69-70. (r)   1290

----. Obras completas de Amad
Nervo. México Moderno, I
(Núm. 4, noviembre de 1920),
259; II (Núm. 7, febrero de
1921), 69. (r)   1291

----. La organización del Servicio Civil por medio del mérito de Ezequiel A. Chávez. México Moderno, I (Núm. 3, octubre de 1920), 195. (r)
1292

----. Palabras con Flordelina de Luis Aníbal Sánchez. México Moderno, I (Núm. 4, noviembre de 1920), 261. (r)
1293

----. Poemas de Cristián Roeber. México Moderno, I (Núm. 6, enero de 1921), 389. (r)
1294

----. El problema de la tierra y la repoblación de México de Ignacio E. Lozano. México Moderno, I (Núm. 4, noviembre de 1920), 263. (r)
1295

----. Proyecto de Ley para la Creación de una Secretaría de Educación Pública Federal. México Moderno, I (Núm. 4, noviembre de 1920), 262-263. (r)
1296

----. Rubén Darío en Costa Rica. México Moderno, II (Núm. 7, febrero de 1921), 71-72. (r)
1297

----. Ruiseñores del alma de Miguel Galliano Cancio. México Moderno, I (Núm. 3, octubre de 1920), 194. (r)
1298

----. Tesis presentada en la Academia Nacional de Bellas Artes de Miguel de la Torre. México Moderno, I (Núm. 5, diciembre de 1920), 323. (r)
1299

----. La varillita de virtud de Francisco Contreras. México Moderno, I (Núm. 6,

enero de 1921), 389. (r)
1300

----. Veinte Litografías de Taxco de Roberto Montenegro. Contemporáneos, VII (Núm. 24, mayo de 1930), 165-168. (r)
1301

----. Ventura García Calderón y su obra literaria de E. D. Tovar y R. México Moderno, I (Núm. 3, octubre de 1920), 193. (r)
1302

----. Viejos temas de Agustín Basave. México Moderno, I (Núm. 2, septiembre de 1920), 128. (r)
1303

----. The War with Mexico de Justin H. Smith. México Moderno, II (Núm. 7, febrero de 1921), 63-66. (r)
1304

----. Priestley, Herbert Ingram. "La antigua universidad de México (Trad. Genaro Estrada). México Moderno, I (Núm. 1, agosto de 1920), 37-52. (tr)
1305

Estrada, José María. "La niña Gutiérrez," "Retrato," "Don Filomeno Vázquez," "Retrato de mujer," "La niña Concepción Arce," "El padre Catarino Bañuelos y Delgadillo," "Don Miguel Castellano," "Don Secundino González." El Hijo Pródigo, V (Núm. 17, agosto de 1944), entre 96 y 97. (il)
1306

----. "El niño Pablo José Villaseñor." El Hijo Pródigo, V (Núm. 17, agosto de 1944), entre 70 y 71. (il)
1307

Etiemble, René. "Arte del siglo veinte." El Hijo Pródigo, II (Núm. 9, diciembre de 1943), 191-193. (a-e)
1308

Evaci. "El último de los iliteratos." México Moderno, II (Núm. 3, octubre de 1922), 188. (a-e) 1309

Fabela, Isidro. "La puñalada." México Moderno, II (Núm. 10, junio de 1921), 213-215. (p) 1310

Falcón, César. "Poesía revolucionaria: Situación de Rubén Darío y sus herederos." Estaciones, II (Núm. 6, verano de 1957), 115-137. (a-e) 1311

Falgairolle, Adolfo. "Marcel Proust." Sagitario, Núm. 4 (1 de septiembre de 1926), 16. (a-e) 1312

Fardo, Wilfredo B. La propiedad y la expropiación en el derecho mexicano actual de Germán Fernández. Romance, I (Núm. 8, 15 de mayo de 1940), 19. (r) 1313

Fenosa. "Cabeza," "Cabeza." Sagitario, Núm. 11 (15 de marzo de 1927), 16. (il) 1314

Fernández, Justino. "Alfonso Reyes." Fábula, Núm. 9 (septiembre de 1934), 172. (a-e) 1315

----. "Dibujos neoclásicos." El Hijo Pródigo, II (Núm. 9, diciembre de 1943), 163-165. (a-e) 1316

----. "Emilio." Fábula, Núm. 7 (julio de 1934), 133-134. (a-e) 1317

----. "Emilio." Fábula, Núm. 7 (julio de 1934), entre 134-135. (il) 1318

----. "Los frescos de Orozco." El Hijo Pródigo, III (Núm. 12, marzo de 1944), 143-146. (a-e) 1319

----. "Raúl Anguiano." El Hijo Pródigo, VIII (Núm. 27, junio de 1945), 144. (a-e) 1320

Fernández, Miguel Angel. "Poema." Estaciones, II (Núm. 5, primavera de 1957), 56-57. (p) 1321

Fernández, Ramón. "Nota sobre la estética de Proust." (Reseña de Temps retrouvé de Marcel Proust en traducción de Xavier Villaurrutia). Contemporáneos, VI (Núm. 22, marzo de 1930), 269-279. (r) 1322

Fernández, Sergio. "El amor divino." Estaciones, IV (Núm. 14, verano de 1959), 181-192. (a-e) 1323

Fernández C., Antonio. "Salvador Díaz Mirón." Antena, Núm. 4 (octubre de 1924), 10. (a-e) 1324

Fernández Castillón, Amalia. "Poker." Fábula, Núm. 6, (junio de 1934), 107-113. (f) 1325

Fernández del Castillo, Francisco. "El homenaje a Don Joaquín García Icazbalceta." Antena, Núm. 4 (octubre de 1924), 7-8. (a-e) 1326

Fernández de Castro, José Antonio. "Larra y algunos románticos de América." Romance, I (Núm. 7, 1 de mayo de 1940), 12, 20. (a-e) 1327

----. "Humanidad y comprensión de José Martí" (Reseña
de Martí hombre de Gonzalo
de Quesada y Miranda).
Romance, I (Núm. 14, 15 de
agosto de 1940), 19. (r)
1328

Fernández de Córdoba, Joaquín.
"Máscaras tarascas pre-
hispánicas." El Hijo Pródigo,
VII (Núm. 23, febrero de
1945), 77-80. (a-e)   1329

----. "Los perros precolom-
binos." El Hijo Pródigo, VII
(Núm. 24, marzo de 1945),
143-146. (a-e)   1330

----. "Pipas prehispánicas
de la cultura tarasca." El
Hijo Pródigo, VI (Núm. 21,
diciembre de 1944), 144-146.
(a-e)   1331

Fernández Ledesma, Enrique.
"A la fachendosa bizarría
de Alfonso Camín." La
Falange, Núm. 3 (1 de
febrero de 1923), 158-159. (p)
1332

----. "Elegía de la provincia."
México Moderno, II (Núm. 9,
mayo de 1921), 145-147. (p)
1333

----. "El pensamiento y el
arte de Alfonso Reyes."
Sagitario, Núm. 7 (1 de enero
de 1927), 4. (a-e)   1334

----. "Ramón López Velarde."
México Moderno, II (Núm. 11-
12, noviembre-diciembre de
1921), 262-271. (a-e) 1335

----. "Responso moderado."
Antena, Núm. 4 (octubre de
1924), 5-6. (p)   1336

----. Beauduin, Nicolás.
"Huelga de otoño" (Trad.

Enrique Fernández Ledesma).
Sagitario, Núm. 2 (1 de
agosto de 1926), 12. (tr)
(626)

Fernández Ledesma, Gabriel.
"El arte espontáneo de los
presidios." Forma, I (Núm.
1, octubre de 1926), 14-15.
(a-e)   1337

----. "La belleza deportiva."
Forma, I (Núm. 3, 1927),
12-13. (a-e)   1338

----. "Dos máscaras." Forma,
II (Núm. 7, 1928), 26-27.
(a-e)   1339

----. "La fotografía de la
Villa de Guadalupe." Forma,
I (Núm. 2, noviembre de
1926), 10-11. (a-e)   1340

----. "Guillermo Ruiz."
Forma, I (Núm. 2, noviembre
de 1926), 26. (a-e)   1341
----. "Juguetes mexicanos."
Forma, I (Núm. 1, 32-33; Núm. 2,
2, 30-31; Núm. 3, 38-39; Núm.
4, 34-35; Núm. 5, 18-19; Núm.
6, 30-31). (il)   1342
----. "Móvil." Forma, I
(Núm. 1, octubre de 1926),
13. (a-e)   1343

----. "Una nueva escuela de
arte en Michoacán." Forma,
II (Núm. 7, 1928), 37-39.
(a-e)   1344

----. "Para un cartel"
anunciador, " "Cabeza de Haya
de la Torre, " "Otro grabado
para un cartel, " "Retrato de
un obrero tallista." Forma,
I (Núm. 6, 1928), 23-26.
(il)   1345

----. "Primera comunión."
Forma, I (Núm. 3, 1927), 21.
(il)   1346

----. "Relieves de Juan Hernández." Forma, I (Núm. 1, octubre de 1926), 35. (a-e) 1347

----. "Rufino Tamayo." Forma, I (Núm. 5, 1927), 1-4. (a-e) 1348

No entry 1349

----. "Siluetas zacatecanas." Forma, I (Núm. 6, 1928), 12-14. (a-e) 1350

Fernández Mac Grégor, Genaro. "Alfonso Reyes." Fábula, Núm. 9 (septiembre de 1934), 173. (a-e) 1351

----. "El alma en el trasmundo dantesco." El Hijo Pródigo, IV (Núm. 15, junio de 1944), 135-150. (a-e) 1352

----. "Carátulas: José Vasconcelos." México Moderno, II (Núm. 9, mayo de 1921), 156-161. (a-e) 1353

----. "Carátulas:Luis G. Urbina." México Moderno, I (Núm. 5, diciembre de 1920), 270-274. (a-e) 1354

----. "El orto de los Doria." El Hijo Pródigo, III (Núm. 11, febrero de 1944), 81-85. (f) 1355

----. "Una paradoja mental." Fábula, Núm. 5 (mayo de 1934), 33-35. (a-e) 1356

----. "Ramón López Velarde." México Moderno, II (Núm. 11-12, noviembre-diciembre de 1921), 285-288. (a-e) 1357

----. "El viento de Bagdad." El Hijo Pródigo, VII (Núm. 23, febrero de 1945), 85-86. (a-e) 1358

----. Dos o tres mundos de Alfonso Reyes. El Hijo Pródigo, VI (Núm. 20, noviembre de 1944), 121. (r) 1359

Fernández Urbina, J. M.; Asúnsolo, Ignacio; Ruiz, Guillermo; Rivera, Diego; Revueltas, Fermín; Domínguez Bello, Arnulfo; y Centeno, Francisco. "Encuesta sobre escultura." Forma, I (Núm. 2, noviembre de 1926), 7-8. (a-e) (530)

Fernández Valdemoro, Carlos. "Disposición a la muerte." El Hijo Pródigo, VI (Núm. 20, noviembre de 1944), 81-87. (a-e) 1360

Ferrandiz Alborz, F. "Los caminos de la literatura esuatoriana." Ruta, Núm. 12 (mayo de 1939), 49-56. (a-e) 1361

Ferrater Mora, José. "De la contención literaria." El Hijo Pródigo, VI (Núm. 21, diciembre de 1944), 161-164. (a-e) 1362

Ferrel, José. "Nota epígrafe." Prometeus, I (Núm. 3, mayo de 1949), 172. (a-e) 1363

----. Autobiografía de Gianbatista Vico. Prometeus, I (Núm. 2, abril de 1949), 132. (r) 1364

----. Histoire du surrealisme de Maurice Nadau. Prometeus, I (Núm. 1, abril de 1949), 133-134. (r) 1365

----. Carrington, Leonora.
"Penelope" (Trad. José
Ferrel). Prometeus, I (Núm.
3, mayo de 1949), 175-202.
(tr)   (832)

----. Ducasse, Isidoro.
"Prefacio a un libro futuro"
(Trad. José Ferrel). El Hijo
Pródigo, I (Núm. 6, septiem-
bre de 1943), 365-379. (tr)
                              (1191)

----. Montherlant, Henry de.
"Pasifae" (Trad. José Ferrel).
Prometeus, II (Núm. 1,
diciembre de 1951), 29-41.
(tr)   1366

----. Rimbaud, Jean Arthur.
"Las iluminaciones" (Trad.
José Ferrel). El Hijo
Pródigo, V (Núm. 16, julio
de 1944), 49-55. (tr)   1367

----. Rimbaud, Juan Arturo.
"Temporada de infierno"
(Trad. José Ferrel). Taller,
I (Núm. 4, julio de 1939),
7-37. (tr)   1368

Fiebleman, James. "Death of
the God in Mexico." Con-
temporáneos, II (Núm. 7,
diciembre de 1928), 320-323.
(p)   1369

Fiene, Ernest. "Camino de la
ciudad." Contemporáneos, II
(Núm. 7, diciembre de 1928),
334. (il)   1370

Fletcher, John Gould. "La
poesía de D. H. Lawrence"
(Trad. Enrique Munguía Jr.).
Contemporáneos, V (Núm. 18,
noviembre de 1929), 322-328.
(a-e)   1371

Fletcher, William H. "La
poesía de los negros en los
Estados Unidos." Ruta, Núm.

11 (abril de 1939), 5-17.
(a-e)   1372

Flores, Angel. Eliot, Thomas
Stearns. "Tierra baldía"
(Trad. Angel Flores). Taller,
II (Núm. 10, marzo-abril de
1940), 71-84. (tr)   (1225)

Flores, Estéban. "Campo,"
"Paria," "Afinidades."
México Moderno, I (Núm. 5,
diciembre de 1920), 283-284.
(p)   1373

----. Al margen de la Con-
stitución de 1917 de Jorge
Vera Estañol. México
Moderno, I (Núm. 4, noviembre de 1920), 261-262. (r)
                               1374

----. Canciones de la tarde
de Fabio Fiallo. México
Moderno, I (Núm. 4,
noviembre de 1920), 262. (r)
                               1375

Flores, Samuel. "Los jacales."
Sagitario, Núm. 10 (1 de
marzo de 1927), 3. (il) 1376

Florit, Eugenio. "El nombre."
El Hijo Pródigo, V (Núm. 16,
julio de 1944), 33. (p) 1377

Fontains, Mrs. André y
Vauxcelles, Louis. "La talla
directa." Forma I (Núm. 3,
1927), 23-24; (Núm. 4, 1927),
6-7. (a-e)   1378

Fort, Paul. "Baladas francesas" (Trad. Rafael
Lozano). La Falange, Núm.
1 (1 de diciembre de 1922),
56-58. (p)   1379

Fournier, Raoul. "Mi triste
vida." Prometeus, I (Núm. 1
febrero de 1949), 21-25. (f)
                               1380

93

Fraenkel, Michael. "Una nota sobre Hamlet." El Hijo Pródigo, V (Núm. 16, julio de 1944), 34-36. (a-e) 1381

Francés, José. "El arte en América: El ejemplo de los niños mexicanos." Sagitario, Núm. 12-13 (30 de abril de 1927), 7-8. (a-e) 1382

Frank, Waldo. "Antonio Machado, Primer aniversario de su muerte." Romance, I (Núm. 3, 1 de marzo de 1940), 17. (a-e) 1383

----. "Chuquicamata" (Trad. León Felipe). Contemporáneos, XI (Núm. 38-39, julio-agosto de 1931), 31-51. (f) 1384

----. "Retrato de Charles Chaplin." Contemporáneos, IV (Núm. 14, julio de 1929), 289-308. (a-e) 1385

----. "Ya viene el amado." Romance, I (Núm. 7, 1 de mayo de 1940), 3. (f) 1386

Frazer, James George. "La magia y la religión" (Trad. Bernardo Ortiz de Montellano). El Hijo Pródigo, II (Núm. 8, noviembre de 1943), 112-122. (a-e) 1387

Frenk, Mariana. Westheim, Paul. "El espíritu del arte azteca" (Trad. de Mariana Frenk). El Hijo Pródigo, XI (Núm. 34, enero de 1946), 36-46. (tr) 1388

----. Westheim, Paul. "La estética de la pirámide" (Trad. Mariana Frenk). El Hijo Pródigo, VIII (Núm. 27, junio de 1945), 157-162. (tr) 1389

Frías, José D. "Elegía romana."

Antena, Núm. 3 (septiembre de 1924), 4-5. (p) 1390

----. "Makedonius Garza en París." Antena, Núm. 3 (septiembre de 1924), 10. (a-e) 1391

----. "Miguel Lerdo de Tejada y sus calumniadores." Antena, Núm. 5 (noviembre de 1924), 8. (a-e) 1392

----. "Ramón López Velarde." México Moderno, II (Núm. 11-12, noviembre-diciembre de 1921), 295-296. (p) 1393

----. "Salvador Díaz Mirón." Antena, Núm. 4 (octubre de 1924), 10. (a-e) 1394

Friedeberg, Erwin. Traven, Bruno. "La rosa blanca" (Trad. Pedro Geoffroy Rivas y Erwin Friedeberg). Ruta, Núm. 1 (junio de 1938), 30-35. (tr) 1395

Fuentes Mares, José. "Las ideas estéticas de San Agustín." Tierra Nueva, I (Núm. 3, mayo-junio de 1940), 163-171. (a-e) 1396

----. Filosofía de la historia de Emanuel Kant. Tierra Nueva, II (Núm. 11-12, septiembre-diciembre de 1941), 263-268. (r) 1397

Fujimori Seikichi. "El hombre que no aplaudía" (Trad. La Falange, Núm. 7 (1 de octubre de 1923), 407. (r) 1399

G., F. La sombra del sueño de Ignacio Barajas Lozano (de Madrid). La Falange, Núm. 7 (1 de octubre de 1923), 407. (r) 1399

94

Gaddi, Taddeo. "Un milagro de Santo Domingo," Ejecución de San Pedro Mártir. " El Hijo Pródigo, XII (Núm. 37, abril de 1946), entre 16 y 17. (il) 1400

----. "Las virtudes, las artes y las ciencias." El Hijo Pródigo, XII (Núm. 37, abril de 1946), 6. (il) 1401

Gag, Wanda. "Rueca," "Estación del elevado." Contemporáneos, II (Núm. 7, diciembre de 1928), 330-331. (il) 1402

Galerna, Francisco. "Encrucijada." Estaciones, III (Núm. 12, invierno de 1958), 425-426. (p) 1403

----. "El rencor," "Es triste..." Estaciones, II (Núm. 6, verano de 1957), 219-221. (p) 1404

----. Una nueva poesía española con selección e introducción de Max Aub. Estaciones, II (Núm. 7, otoño de 1957), 361-362. (r) 1405

----. Para gozar tu paz de Efraín Huerta. Estaciones II (Núm. 7, otoño de 1957), 362. (r) 1406

----. El retorno de Miguel Guardia. Estaciones, II (Núm. 7, otoño de 1957), 357-358. (r) 1407

Galetar, Margarita. "Dos sonetos." Estaciones, IV (Núm. 14, verano de 1959), 225-226. (p) 1408

Galíndez, Bartolomé. "Un flirt a bordo." México Moderno, II (Núm. 10, junio de 1921), 187-189. (f) 1409

Galindo, Marco Aurelio. Lyeskov, Nicolai. "El centinela" (Traducido y comentado por Marco Aurelio Galindo). Prometeus, I (Núm. 1, febrero de 1949), 33-51. (tr) 1410

Gálvez. "Bodegón." El Hijo Pródigo, XIII (Núm. 40, julio de 1946), entre 32 y 33. (il) 1411

Gallardo M. Roberto. "La historia de Roberto Gallardo M." Prometeus, I (Núm. 3, mayo de 1949), 172-174. (a-e) 1412

Gallegos Rocafull, José María; Vasconcelos, José; González Martínez, Enrique; Gaos, José; Paz, Octavio; Martínez, José Luis; García-Bacca, David; Jiménez Rueda, Julio; Nicol, Eduardo; Bergamín, José. "Poesía, mística y filosofía: Debate en torno a San Juan de la Cruz." El Hijo Pródigo, I (Núm. 3, junio de 1943), 135-144. (a-e) (661)

----. " Es posible la colaboración entre católicos y marxistas?" El Hijo Pródigo, X (Núm. 31, octubre de 1945), 23-33. (a-e) 1413

----. "Esbozo de una dialéctica." El Hijo Pródigo, XIII (Núm. 41, agosto de 1946), 69-78. (a-e) 1414

----. "El sueño de este mundo según los místicos españoles." El Hijo Pródigo, VIII (Núm. 25, abril de 1945), 35-43. (a-e) 1415

Gallo, Joaquín. "El mundo marciano." Romance, I (Núm. 4, 15 de marzo de

1943), 135-144. (a-e) (661)

Garabito Martínez, Jorge.
"Amanecer." Tierra Nueva,
I (Núm. 1, enero-febrero de
1940), 30. (p) 1419

----. Contra la servidumbre
del espíritu de Ezequiel A.
Chávez y Rafael Preciado
Hernández. Tierra Nueva, I
(Núm. 2, marzo-abril de
1940), 121. (r) 1420

García, Genaro. "Morelos."
México Moderno, Núm. 6
(enero de 1921), 338-346.
(a-e) 1421

Garciasol, Ramón de. "A
Miguel Hernández."
Estaciones, IV (Núm. 15,
otoño de 1959), 266-267. (p)
1422

García Ascot, José Miguel.
"Lluvia de noche." Prometeus,
II (Núm. 1, diciembre de
1951), 24. (p) 1423

----. "El parque." Prometeus,
I (Núm. 1, febrero de 1949),
53-55. (p) 1424

----. Cántico de Jorge
Guillén. Prometeus, II (Núm.
1, diciembre de 1951), 67-68.
(r) 1425

----. Las miradas perdidas de
Fina García Marruz.
Prometeus, II (Núm. 1,
diciembre de 1951), 68. (r)
1426

----. La muerte en el alma
de Jean Paul Sartre.
Prometeus, II (Núm. 1,
diciembre de 1951), 68-69.
(r) 1427

García Bacca, Juan David.
"Hacia el matematicismo."

Tierra Nueva, II (Núm. 7-8,
enero-abril de 1941), 13-29.
(a-e) 1428

----. Vasconcelos, José;
González Martínez, Enrique;
Gaos, José; Gallegos, José
M.; Paz, Octavio; Martínez,
José Luis; Jiménez Rueda,
Julio; Nicol, Eduardo;
Bergamín, José. "Poesía,
mística y filosofía: Debate
en torno a San Juan de la
Cruz." El Hijo Pródigo, I
(Núm. 3, junio de 1943),
135-144. (a-e) (661)

----. "El positivismo en
México." El Hijo Pródigo,
VII (Núm. 22, enero de 1945),
21-23. (a-e) 1429

----. La enormidad de España
de Miguel de Unamuno. El
Hijo Pródigo, VII (Núm. 24,
marzo de 1945), 185-186. (r)
1430

----. Los escépticos griegos
de Victor Brochard. El Hijo
Pródigo, XI (Núm. 34, enero
de 1946), 58-59. (r) 1431

----. La esencia de la
filosofía de Guillermo Dilthey.
El Hijo Pródigo, VI (Núm. 20,
noviembre de 1944), 123-124.
(r) 1432

----. La experiencia de Dios
en los místicos españoles de
José M. Gallegos Rocafull.
El Hijo Pródigo, IX (Núm.
28, julio de 1945), 57-58.
(r) 1433

----. Hegel y el idealismo de
Wilhelm Dilthey. El Hijo
Pródigo, V (Núm. 16, julio de
1944), 57. (r) 1434

96

----. Hombre y mundo de Wilhelm Dilthey. El Hijo Pródigo, IV (Núm. 14, mayo de 1944), 122-123. (r) 1435

----. Introducción a las ciencias del espíritu de Wilhelm Dilthey. El Hijo Pródigo, VI (Núm. 19, octubre de 1944), 59-60. (r) 1436

----. Moral de la ciencia de Albert Bayet. El Hijo Pródigo, XI (Núm. 36, marzo de 1946), 174-175. (r) 1437

----. Demócrito. "Fragmentos filosóficos" (Trad. David García-Bacca). El Hijo Pródigo, II (Núm. 9, diciembre de 1943), 166-175. (tr) (1141)

----. Heráclito. "Fragmentos filosóficos" (Trad. Juan David García Bacca). El Hijo Pródigo, III (Núm. 12, marzo de 1944), 166-170. (tr) 1438

----. Plotino. "Sobre lo bello" (Trad. Juan David García-Bacca). El Hijo Pródigo, I (Núm. 5, agosto de 1943), 312-316. (tr) 1439

García Blanco, M. "La mueca de un arte joven." Sagitario, Núm. 10 (1 de marzo de 1927), 15. (a-e) 1440

García Calderón, Ventura. "Carta de amor." México Moderno, Núm. 2 (septiembre de 1920), 65-66. (a-e) 1441

----. "Rubayat." Antena, Núm. 4 (octubre de 1924), 4. (p) 1442

García Godoy, Federico. La

casa de Jaime Torres Bodet (de La Opinión de Santo Domingo). La Falange, Núm. 7 (1 de octubre de 1923), 406-407. (r) 1443

García Lorca, Federico. "Pequeño vals vienés, " "La suite del agua, " "Cuatro baladas amarillas, " "La selva de los relojes, " "Herbarios." Taller, I (Núm. 1, diciembre de 1938), 33-50. (p) 1444

García Marín, José. "Invernal." Tierra Nueva, I (Núm. 1, enero-febrero de 1940), 51-52. (p) 1445

----. La evolución política del pueblo mexicano de Justo Sierra. Tierra Nueva, I (Núm. 3, mayo-junio de 1940), 186-187. (r) 1446

----. La poesía lírica española de Guillermo Díaz-Plaja. Tierra Nueva, I (Núm. 2, marzo-abril de 1940), 120-121. (r) 1447

García Maroto, Gabriel. "Del niño y su estado de gracia." Contemporáneos, XI (Núm. 42-43, noviembre-diciembre de 1931), 268-282. (a-e) 1448

----. "Familia, " "Quick-lunch, " "Mujeres, " "Omnibus." Contemporáneos, VI (Núm. 22, marzo de 1930), 211-214. (il) 1449

----. "La joven pintura mexicana." Sagitario, Núm. 12-13 (30 de abril de 1927), 9-10. (a-e) 1450

----. "La obra de Diego Rivera." Contemporáneos, I (Núm. 1, junio de 1928), 42-75. (a-e) 1451

----. "Ocho dibujos me-
xicanos." Contemporáneos, II
(Núm. 5, octubre de 1928),
136-143. (il)   1452

----. "La revolución artística
mexicana. --Una lección."
Forma, I (Núm. 4, 1927), 8-
16. (a-e)   1453

----. Goya en Zig-Zag de
Juan de la Encina. Con-
temporáneos, II (Núm. 4,
septiembre de 1928), 101-104.
(r)   1454

----. Pruebas de Nueva York
de José Moreno Villa.
Contemporáneos, II (Núm. 7,
diciembre de 1928), 397-402.
(r)   1455

García Marruz, Fina. "Sobre
la rima." El Hijo Pródigo,
VI (Núm. 20, noviembre de
1944), 98-100. (a-e)   1456

García Terrés, Jaime. "Letanías
profanas." Estaciones, III
(Núm. 12, invierno de 1958),
417-418. (p)   1457

Garfias, Pedro. "El ala del
sur." Sagitario, Núm. 14
(31 de mayo de 1927), 6.
(p)   1458

----. "Angelus." Sagitario,
Núm. 7 (1 de enero de
1927), 15. (p)   1459

----. "Una historia extra-
ordinaria." Romance, I
(Núm. 7, 1 de mayo de 1940),
5, 17. (f)   1460

----. "Motivos de la ciudad."
Sagitario, Núm. 10 (1 de
marzo de 1927), 14. (p)
                                 1461

----. "Primavera en Eaton
Hasting." Romance, I (Núm.

15, 1 de septiembre de 1940),
11. (p)   1462

Garibay, Ricardo. "Los
náufragos." Estaciones, I
(Núm. 2, verano de 1956),
188-194. (f)   1463

Garizurieta, César. "Catarsis
del mexicano." El Hijo
Pródigo, XIII (Núm. 40, julio
de 1946), 9-20. (a-e)   1464

Garrido, Luis. "El primer
amor." Antena, Núm. 5
(noviembre de 1924), 6. (f)
                                 1465

----. "La vendedora de amor."
La Falange, Núm. 2 (1 de
enero de 1923), 81-82. (f)
                                 1466

Garza, Ario. "Poema en
tiempo de amor." Estaciones,
III (Núm. 9, primavera de
1948), 87-88. (p)   1467

Garza, Mercedes de la. "Es
un constante ir y venir."
Estaciones, V (Núm. 20,
invierno de 1960), 103-104.
(p)   1468

Gasch, Sebastián. "Salvador
Dalí" (Trad. Humberto Rivas).
Sagitario, Núm. 14 (31 de
mayo de 1927), 9-11. (a-e)
                                 1469

----. "Salvador Dalí"
Contemporáneos, VII (Núm.
23, abril de 1930), 90-92.
(a-e)   1470

Gastélum, Bernardo J. "El
arco de la democracia."
Contemporáneos, V (Núm. 16,
septiembre de 1929), 137-149.
(a-e)   1471

----. "Ciencia del caballero."

Contemporáneos, IV (Núm. 13, junio de 1929), 201-214. (a-e) 1472

----. "Democracia asimétrica." Contemporáneos, II (Núm. 6, noviembre de 1928), 244-256. (a-e) 1473

----. "Espíritu del héroe." Contemporáneos, I (Núm. 1, junio de 1928), 1-14. (a-e) 1474

----. "Un hombre." Contemporáneos, I (Núm. 3, agosto de 1928), 221-228. (a-e) 1475

----. "Intelectualización de la música." El Hijo Pródigo, V (Núm. 17, agosto de 1944), 86-95. (a-e) 1476

----. "Invierno y verano." Contemporáneos, III (Núm. 9, febrero de 1929), 104-119. (a-e) 1477

----. "Pensar en vez de recordar." Contemporáneos, VI (Núm. 20, enero de 1930), 8-20. (a-e) 1478

----. "La revolución mexicana: canción de la libertad." Contemporáneos, IX (Núm. 33, febrero de 1931), 140-151. (a-e) 1479

----. "La teoría del sufragio." Contemporáneos, VII (Núm. 23, abril de 1930), 34-46. (a-e) 1480

----. Diario de viaje de un filósofo de Hermann Keyserling. Contemporáneos, III (Núm. 8, enero de 1929), 74-78. (r) 1481

Gay, Delfina ("Madame de Giradin"). "El disfraz de las bellas: La mujer hacia 1840." Romance, I (Núm. 2, 15 de febrero de 1940), 10. (tr) 1482

Gaya, Ramón. "El aire," "Figurilla," "Tarde." El Hijo Pródigo, VI (Núm. 19, octubre de 1944), 21-23. (p) 1483

----. "Antonio Rodríguez Luna." Romance, I (Núm. 8, 15 de mayo de 1940), 7. (a-e) 1484

----. "Desmaño y justicia de Mariano Orgaz." Taller, II (Núm. 8-9, enero-febrero de 1940), 51-52. (a-e) 1485

----. "Diario de un pintor." El Hijo Pródigo, XIII (Núm. 41, agosto de 1946), 79-81. (p) 1486

----. "Divagación en torno al surrealismo." Romance, I (Núm. 2, 15 de febrero de 1940), 7. (a-e) 1487

----. "Divagaciones de un pintor: Exposición de grabados clásicos." Romance, I (Núm. 13, 1 de agosto de 1940), 7. (a-e) 1488

----. "El extremoso deber del artista." Romance, I (Núm. 4, 15 de marzo de 1940), 10. (a-e) 1489

----. "El grabador Posada." El Hijo Pródigo, I (Núm. 1, abril de 1943), 32. (a-e) 1490

----. "Homenaje a Velázquez." El Hijo Pródigo, X (Núm. 31, octubre de 1945), 9-13. (a-e) 1491

----. "Introducción a la pintura mexicana." Romance, I (Núm. 3, 1 de marzo de 1940), 7. (a-e) 1492

----. "Nuevas anotaciones." Romance, I (Núm. 15, 1 de septiembre de 1940), 5. (a-e) 1493

----. "Una página sobre el film Vía Crucis, Las uvas del rencor" (Opiniones de Xavier Villaurrutia, León Felipe, Ramón Gaya, Alberto Quintero Alvarez, Octavio G. Barreda y Carlos Velo). Romance, I (Núm. 9, 1 de junio de 1940), 11. (a-e) (585)

----. "Palabras de despedida para mis compañeros de redacción." Taller, II (Núm. 11, julio-agosto de 1940), 81-82. (a-e) 1494

----. "Pequeñas anotaciones sobre pintura, crítica, fotografía y poesía." Romance, I (Núm. 10, 15 de junio de 1940), 6. (a-e) 1495

----. "Pintura francesa contemporánea." Taller, I (Núm. 5, octubre de 1939), 49-52. (a-e) 1496

----. "Respuesta a la encuesta de Romance." Romance, I (Núm. 5, 1 de abril de 1940), 2. (a-e) 1497

----. "El señor Domenchina." Taller, II (Núm. 10, marzo-abril de 1940), 57-59. (a-e) 1498

----. "Sonetos de un diario" (incluye "A una verdad," "Al silencio," "Al sufrimiento," "A Dios," "A la lámpara," "A mis amigos"). Taller, I (Núm. 7, diciembre de 1939), 23-26. (p) 1499

----. Canek de Ermilo Abreu Gómez. Romance, II (Núm. 21, 15 de febrero de 1941), 18. (r) 1500

----. Formación y proceso de la literatura venezolana de Mariano Picón Salas. Romance, II (Núm. 23, 22 de abril de 1941), 18. (r) 1501

----. El ingenioso hidalgo Don Quijote de la Mancha de Cervantes publicado por Espasa-Calpe. Romance, I (Núm. 20, 15 de enero de 1941), 18. (r) 1502

Geoffroy Rivas, Pedro. "Balzac: Secretario de su época." Ruta, Núm. 5 (octubre de 1938), 46-49. (a-e) 1503

----. "Dos poemas de Neftalí Beltrán." Ruta, Núm. 7 (diciembre de 1938), 49-51. (a-e) 1504

----. Bajo el comando del pueblo de Cayetano Córdoba Iturburu. Ruta, Núm. 10 (marzo de 1939), 59. (r) 1505

----. Hombres sin mujer de Carlos Montenegro. Ruta, Núm. 2 (julio de 1938), 55-56. (r) 1506

----. Literatura y materialismo dialéctico de John Strachey. Ruta, Núm. 8 (enero de 1939), 56-57. (r) 1507

----. La rebelión de los colgados de Bruno Traven.

Ruta, Núm. 3 (agosto de
1938), 56-57. (r)   1508

----. S F Z 33 de Enrique
Othón Díaz. Ruta, Núm. 4
(septiembre de 1938), 62-63.
(r)   1509

----. Aldington, R. "El
paraíso mismo" (Trad. Pedro
Geoffroy Rivas). Ruta, Núm.
9 (febrero de 1939), 41-49.
(tr)   (142)

----. Cassou, Jean. "Cer-
vantes" (Trad. Pedro
Geoffroy Rivas). Ruta, Núm.
5 (octubre de 1938), 27-32.
(tr)   (849)

----. Durtain, Luc. "La
guerra no existe" (Trad.
Pedro Geoffroy Rivas). Ruta,
Núm. 10 (marzo de 1939),
34-37. (tr)   (1200)

----. Pavlenko, P. "Mayo"
(Trad. Pedro Geoffroy Rivas).
Ruta, Núm. 4 (septiembre de
1938), 43-45. (tr)   1510

----. Traven, Bruno. "La
rosa blanca" (Trad. Pedro
Geoffroy Rivas y Erwin
Friedeberg). Ruta, Núm. 1
(junio de 1938), 30-35. (tr)
                         (1395)

Giaconi, Claudio. "Síntesis
del pensamiento de Albert
Camus." Estaciones, V (Núm.
17, primavera de 1960), 5-9.
(a-e)   1511

Gide, André. "Dos textos."
El Hijo Pródigo, XII (Núm.
37, abril de 1946), 25-29.
(a-e)   1512

----. "Historia de titiro."
El Hijo Pródigo, XI (Núm. 34
enero de 1946), 27-30. (f)
                         1513

----. "Recuerdos literarios y
problemas actuales" (Trad.
Molíns Fábrega). Prometeus,
II (Núm. 1, diciembre de
1951), 6-17. (a-e)   1514

----. "El regreso del hijo
pródigo" (Trad. Xavier
Villaurrutia). Contemporáneos,
III (Núm. 10, marzo de 1929),
239-264. (f)   1515

Gil, Gerónimo Antonio.
"Dibujo," "Dibujo." El Hijo
Pródigo, II (Núm. 9,
diciembre de 1943), entre
163 y 164. (il)   1516

Gil-Albert, Juan. "A los
sombreros de mi madre y
otras elegías." (incluye
"Elegía a los sombreros de
mi madre," "Elegía a la
revelación de mi génesis,"
"Elegía a Chenonceaux,"
"Elegía a un secreto,"
"Elegía a un efímero abrazo,"
"Elegía a mis manos de
entonces," "Elegía a una
tarde purísima." Taller, I
(Núm. 2, abril de 1939), 41-
62. (p)   1517

----. "A un monasterio
griego." El Hijo Pródigo, IX
(Núm. 28, julio de 1945), 27.
(p)   1518

----. "Aldonza Lorenzo." El
Hijo Pródigo, XII (Núm. 37,
abril de 1946), 20-22. (a-e)
                         1519

----. "Emilio Prados de la
'Constelación Rosicler'."
Taller, II (Núm. 11, julio-
agosto de 1940), 68-71. (a-e)
                         1520

----. "En torno a la vocac-
ión." Taller, (Núm. 3, mayo
de 1939), 54-56. (a-e)   1521

----. "Las granadas," "La
lluvia." El Hijo Pródigo, I
(Núm. 3, junio de 1943), 163-
164. (p)   1522

----. "Los ídolos." Taller, I
(Núm. 7, diciembre de 1939),
37-40. (p)   1523

----. "Imprecación a una
divinidad hostil." Taller, II
(Núm. 10, marzo-abril de
1940), 30-36. (p)   1524

----. "Meditaciones
españolas." Taller, I (Núm.
6, noviembre de 1939), 48-
55. (a-e)   1525

----. "El Punto negro de
Gerard de Nerval." El Hijo
Pródigo, X (Núm. 33,
diciembre de 1945), 152-154.
(a-e)   1526

----. "Respuesta a la
encuesta de Romance." Ro-
mance, I (Núm. 7, 1 de mayo
de 1940), 2. (a-e)   1527

----. Hölderlin, Federico.
"Del 'Hyperion' " (Trad.
Juan Gil-Albert). Taller, II
(Núm. 10, marzo-abril de
1940), 5-9. (tr)   1528

Giner de los Ríos, Francisco.
"Antología de Alfonso Reyes."
El Hijo Pródigo, VII (Núm.
22, enero de 1945), 31-32.
(a-e)   1529

----. "El auto de los reyes
magos." Tierra Nueva, I
(Núm. 4-5, julio-octubre de
1940), 242-251. (a-e) 1530

----. "Destino limpio."
Romance, I (Núm. 6, 15 de
abril de 1940), 3. (a-e)
                            1531

----. "La flor." El Hijo

Pródigo, VII (Núm. 22, enero
de 1945), 20. (p)   1532

----. "Hondo cielo." Tierra
Nueva, II (Núm. 11-12,
septiembre-diciembre de 1941),
218-219. (p)   1533

----. "Hoy, febrero, tarde
de tu carta." Tierra Nueva,
I (Núm. 3, mayo-junio de
1940), 180-181. (p)   1534

----. "Pequeña elegía en voz
baja." Tierra Nueva, I (Núm.
6, noviembre-diciembre de
1940), 308-309. (p)   1535

----. "Presencia tuya."
Tierra Nueva, I (Núm. 1,
enero-febrero de 1940), 12-14.
(p)   1536

----. "Tan cerca de vosotros
que el aire se conmueve,"
"Presencia de España," "A
tu honda memoria." Taller,
I (Núm. 6, noviembre de
1939), 44-47. (p)   1537

----. "Angustia y sueño de
Regino Pedroso" (Reseña de
Antología poética y Más allá
canta el mar... de Regino
Pedroso). Romance, I (Núm.
9, 1 de junio de 1940), 18.
(r)   1538

----. Carta de Cristóbal
Colón en que da cuenta del
descubrimiento de América.
Romance, I (Núm. 2, 15 de
1940), 20. (r)   1539

----. "Un libro sobre España
y los españoles" (Reseña de
España, el país y sus
habitantes de Leonardo Martín
Echeverría). Tierra Nueva, I
(Núm. 4-5, julio-octubre de
1940), 271-272. (r)   1540

----. Historia natural y moral de las Indias de José de Acosta. Romance, I (Núm. 13, 1 de agosto de 1940), 19. (r)　　　　　　　1541

----. No son cuentos de Max Aub. El Hijo Pródigo, VII (Núm. 22, enero de 1945), 58-59. (r)　　　　　1542

----. "Forma y color de Emilio Ballagas" (Reseña de Sabor eterno). Romance, I (Núm. 3, 1 de marzo de 1940), 18. (r)　　　1543

Giraudoux, Jean. "No habrá guerra en Troya" (Trad. Xavier Villaurrutia y Agustín Lazo). El Hijo Pródigo, V (Núm. 17, agosto de 1944), 107-120; (Núm. 18, septiembre de 1944), 166-184. (dr)　　　　　　　1544

Glantz, Jacob. "Literatura yiddish contemporánea." Ruta, Núm. 6 (noviembre de 1938), 51-53. (a-e)　1545

Glover, Edward. "Teoría general de la mente." (Trad. Francisco M. Zendejas). Prometeus, I (Núm. 3, mayo de 1949), 143-155. (a-e)
　　　　　　　1546

Godoy, Jorge de. "La estrella del pastor." La Falange, Núm. 3 (1 de febrero de 1923), 140-145. (a-e)　1547

Godoy, Alcayaga, Lucila ("Gabriela Mistral"). "Al pueblo hebreo." La Falange, Núm. 1 (1 de diciembre de 1922), 3-4. (p)　　　1548

----. "Decálogo del artista." México Moderno, I (Núm. 4, noviembre de 1920), 223. (a-e)　　　　　　1549

----. "La misión de Antonio Caso." México Moderno, II (Núm. 1, agosto de 1922), 3-4. (a-e)　　　　　1550

----. "Motivos de San Francisco." La Falange, Núm. 3 (1 de febrero de 1923), 129-131. (a-e)　1551

----. "Norah Borges." Romance, I (Núm. 12, 15 de julio de 1940), 7, 20. (a-e)
　　　　　　　1552

----. "Poemas de éxtasis" (incluye "Estoi llorando," "Esperándote," "Escóndeme," "Dios," "El mundo," "Hablaban de ti."). México Moderno, II (Núm. 2, septiembre de 1922), 69-71. (p)　　　　　　　1553

Golwarz, Sergio. "La simulación en el arte." Estaciones, II (Núm. 5, primavera de 1957), 71-93. (a-e)　1554

Gómez, José. "Cosas memorables de la ciudad de México." El Hijo Pródigo, X (Núm. 32, noviembre de 1945), 111-119. (a-e)　1555

Gómez Arias, Alejandro? Golfo de México de Alfonso Reyes. Fábula, Núm. 8 (agosto de 1934), 159-160. (r)　1556

Gómez-Correa, Enrique. "El prestigio del cuerpo humano." Prometeus, I (Núm. 2, abril de 1949), 92-93. (p)　1557

Gómez de Barquero, Eduardo. "Una heroína romántica." Sagitario, Núm. 6 (1 de noviembre de 1926), 14. (a-e)
　　　　　　　1558

Gómez de la Serna, Ramón. "Lecturas y apostillas."

González, Cutberto. "Escultura."
Forma, I (Núm. 2, noviembre
de 1926), 27. (il)   1579

González, José Luis. "La
despedida de Laura."
Estaciones, I (Núm. 3, otoño
de 1956), 303-316. (f)   1580

González, Miguel. "Cuadros."
Contemporáneos, IX (Núm.
34, marzo de 1931), 208-229.
(il)   1581

González, Natalicio. "Alarcón
y Corneille." Estaciones, II
(Núm. 7, otoño de 1957),
256-262. (a-e)   1582

González, Raúl Renán. "Lauro."
Estaciones, II (Núm. 8,
invierno de 1957), 476-480.
(f)   1583

----. "Lolita." Estaciones,
IV (Núm. 16, invierno de
1959), 410. (p)   1584

----. "Los zopilotes blancos."
Estaciones, IV (Núm. 15,
otoño de 1959), 330-337. (f)
                         1585

González Avelar, Miguel.
"Tiempo, S.A." Estaciones,
III (Núm. 11, otoño de 1958),
309-311. (f)   1586

González Casanova, Pablo.
"Vocablos truncados en el
español de México"
Contemporáneos, VII (Núm.
24, mayo de 1930), 122-147.
(a-e)   1587

----? El honor del ridículo
de Carlos Noriega Hope.
Antena, Núm. 4 (octubre de
1924), 8-9. (r)   1588

----? Luna park: Poema
instantánea del siglo 2 X de

Luis Cardoza y Aragón.
Antena, Núm. 4 (octubre de
1924), 9. (r)   1589

----. Once cuentos cortos de
Rodolfo Navarrete. El Hijo
Pródigo, XII (Núm. 38, mayo
de 1946), 113. (r)   1590

González de Mendoza, José
María. ("El Abate de
Mendoza"). "Cuentos sin-
téticos." Antena, Núm. 2
(agosto de 1924), 5-6. (a-e)
                         1591

----. "Elán." Antena, Núm.
1 (julio de 1924), 6. (a-e)
                         1592

----. "El filtro de Iseo,"
"La virgen de la Torre
Eiffel." Sagitario, Núm. 14
(31 de mayo de 1927), 16. (f)
                         1593

----. "José D. Frías y el
pintor Fujita." Antena, Núm.
3 (septiembre de 1924), 10.
(a-e)   1594

----. "Salvador Díaz Mirón."
Antena, Núm. 4 (octubre de
1924), 10. (a-e)   1595

----. "Tres sketches: Aquel
muerto, La sonrisa de la
Giocconda, El loco." Antena,
Núm. 5 (noviembre de 1924),
3-4. (a-e)   1596

González Durán, Jorge. "Con
Enrique González Martínez."
Tierra Nueva, I (Núm. 1,
enero-febrero de 1940), 15-
19. (a-e)   1597

----. "Cuatro poemas."
Tierra Nueva, I (Núm. 6,
noviembre-diciembre de 1940),
330-333. (p)   1598

----. "En la viva soledad."
Tierra Nueva, II (Núm. 9-10,
mayo-agosto de 1941), 156-159.
(p)   1599

----. "La rosa del cuerpo,"
"La rosa del polvo," "La
flor del agua." El Hijo
Pródigo, III (Núm. 11,
febrero de 1944), 105-106.
(p)   1600

----. "La rosa del sueño."
Tierra Nueva, II (Núm. 11-12,
septiembre-diciembre de 1941),
235. (r)   1601

----. "Seis asonancias y un
epílogo" (Suplemento poético
al núm. 1). Tierra Nueva, I
(Núm. 1, enero-febrero de
1940). (p)   1602

----. "Tres poemas" (incluye
"Poema de la huída" y dos
sin título). Tierra Nueva,
I (Núm. 3, mayo-junio de
1940), 147-150. (p)   1603

----. "Tú, sin muerte."
Tierra Nueva, I (Núm. 4-5,
julio-octubre de 1940), 252-
255. (p)   1604

----. "El héroe fugaz"
(Reseña de De fusilamientos
de Julio Torri). Tierra
Nueva, II (Núm. 7-8, enero-
abril de 1941), 85-91. (r)
                             1605

----. El proceso de Franz
Kafka. Tierra Nueva, I
(Núm. 2, marzo-abril de
1940), 122-125. (r)   1606

----. La rama viva de
Francisco Giñer de los Ríos.
Tierra Nueva, I (Núm. 3,
mayo-junio de 1940), 175-
179. (r)   1607

González Flores, Manuel. "La

sombra." Estaciones, II
(Núm. 6, verano de 1957),
170. (p)   1608

González, León Francisco.
"Inicial," "Psalmo a la
tarde," "Momento vesperal."
México Moderno, Núm. 6
(enero de 1921), 353-355. (p)
                             1609

----. "'La niña pensaba',"
"Ojos ojerosos." Fábula,
Núm. 5 (mayo de 1934), 94-
97. (p)   1610

----. "Oración a Santa Rosa."
La Falange, Núm. 3 (1 de
febrero de 1923), 157-158.
(p)   1611

----. "La rueca," "Domingos
del 'Buen Pastor'." México
Moderno, II (Núm. 3,
octubre de 1922), 148-150.
(p)   1612

----. "Vaga," "Instante."
Antena, Núm. 1 (julio de
1924), 5. (p)   1613

González Martínez, Enrique.
"Al hijo muerto." Romance,
I (Núm. 4, 15 de marzo de
1940), 9. (p)   1614

----. "Arte de Rubén Darío."
Romance, II (Núm. 22, 15
de marzo de 1941), 1-2.
(a-e)   1615

----. "El buitre." Romance,
I (Núm. 4, 15 de marzo de
1940), 9. (p)   1616

----. "La caída," "Retorno,"
"El martillo." La Falange,
Núm. 4 (1 de julio de 1923),
216-217. (p)   1617

----. "Claridad," "El espía,"
"La hamaca," "Peregrinos,"
"El buitre," "Dualidad,"
"Lumbre de llama." Con
temporáneos, III (Núm. 8,
enero de 1929), 1-7. (p)
1618

----. "Defensa de las
academias." Romance, I
(Núm. 8, 15 de mayo de
1940), 6. (a-e)   1619

----. "Hora fracta,"
"Renuncia," "La pesca,"
"Hilos." Ulises, Núm. 6
(febrero de 1928), 3-4. (p)
1620

----. "Meri de toi," "Alma
naciente," "La enemiga."
El Hijo Pródigo, I (Núm. 4,
julio de 1943), 209-210. (p)
1621

----. "Pececillos rojos."
Ulises, Núm. 3 (agosto de
1927), 3-4. (p)   1622

----. "El poema de los siete
pecados." México Moderno,
I (Núm. 1, agosto de 1920),
13-17. (p)   1623

----. Vasconcelos, José;
Gaos, José; Gallegos, José
M.; Paz, Octavio; Martínez,
José Luis; García-Bacca,
David; Jiménez Rueda, Julio;
Nicol, Eduardo; Bergamín,
José. "Poesía mística y
filosofía: Debate en torno a
San Juan de la Cruz." El
Hijo Pródigo, I (Núm. 3,
junio de 1943), 135-144. (a-e)
(661)

----. "Poesías" ("A Antonio
Machado," "Alma en fuga,"
"Júbilo mortal," "Plegaria
de año nuevo"). Romance, I
(Núm. 20, 15 de enero de
1941), 3. (p)   1624

----. "Poesías" ("Aleluya de
la muerte," "Plegaria a la
vida," "Hoja y canción").
Romance, II (Núm. 24, 31 de
mayo de 1941), 3. (p) 1625

----. "Ramón López Velarde."
México Moderno, II (Núm.
11-12, noviembre-diciembre
de 1921), 255-256. (a-e)
1626

----. "Romance del corazón
errabundo," "Corazón fiel,"
"Placer de incertidumbre."
El Hijo Pródigo, VI (Núm. 21,
diciembre de 1944), 147-149.
(p)   1627

----. "El romero alucinado,"
"La ciudad absorta," "Luna
materna." México Moderno,
II (Núm. 7, febrero de 1921),
5-7. (p)   1628

----. "Sábado." Antena, Núm.
3 (septiembre de 1924), 3.
(p)   1629

----. "Siglo cuarenta." Romance, I (Núm. 4, 15 de
marzo de 1940), 9. (p) 1630

----. "El tumulto," "Non
serviam," "Jordán,"
"Desnudez," "Plegaria del
viajero mudo." Contempo-
ráneos, V (Núm. 17, octubre
de 1929), 210-217. (p) 1631

----. "Ultimo viaje,"
"Cansancio." Tierra Nueva,
I (Núm. 2, marzo-abril de
1940), 67-68. (p)   1632

González Mena, Francisco.
"El último lance." México
Moderno, Núm. 5 (diciembre
de 1920), 298-302. (f) 1633

González Morales, Héctor.
"Momento del suicida."

Estaciones, I (Núm. 4, invierno de 1956), 578-579. (p)   1634

González Obregón, Luis. "D. Quijote y el cura Hidalgo." La Falange, Núm. 5 (1 de agosto de 1923), 266-268. (a-e)   1635

----. "Genaro García, su vida y su obra." México Moderno, Núm. 6 (enero de 1921), 356-364. (a-e) 1636

----. "La historia de una encomienda en el siglo XVI." México Moderno, I (Núm. 3, octubre de 1920), 154-158. (a-e)   1637

----. "El homenaje a Don Joaquín García Icazbalceta." Antena, Núm. 3 (septiembre de 1924), 8. (a-e)   1638

González Peña, Carlos. "El príncipe azul." México Moderno, Núm. 6 (enero de 1921), 365-373. (f)   1639

----. Epistolario de Rubén Darío con un estudio preliminar de Ventura García Calderón publicado por la Biblioteca Latino-Americana dirigida por Hugo D. Barbagelata. México Moderno, I (Núm. 1, agosto de 1920), 64. (r)   1640

González Ramírez, Manuel. "Los ojos." Fábula, Núm. 8 (agosto de 1934), 144-150. (f)   1641

----. Mujeres de Eduardo Colín. Fábula, Núm. 8 (agosto de 1934), 159. (r)   1642

González Roa, Fernando. "La decadencia de la democracia y la crisis de la clase media." México Moderno, Núm. 6 (enero de 1921), 348-352. (a-e)   1643

----. "La inmutabilidad del derecho de Propiedad." México Moderno, II (Núm. 10, junio de 1921), 193-198. (a-e)   1644

González Rojo, Enrique. "Alter ego," "Ocaso," "La estrella de mar." México Moderno, I (Núm. 1, agosto de 1920), 56-57. (p)   1645

----. "Círculo." Contemporáneos, V (Núm. 16, septiembre de 1929), 107-111. (f)   1646

----. "Corto circuito." Ulises, Núm. 6 (febrero de 1928), 14-17. (f)   1647

----. "El día más feliz de Charlot." Contemporáneos, II (Núm. 5, octubre de 1928), 113-130. (f)   1648

----. "Díaz Mirón, muerto y vivo." Contemporáneos, I (Núm. 2, julio de 1928), 204-206. (a-e)   1649

----. "Un discípulo argentino de López Velarde." Contemporáneos, I (Núm. 2, julio de 1928), 215-220. (a-e)   1650

----. "Elegías romanas." Taller, I (Núm. 4, julio de 1939), 30-35. (p)   1651

----. "La inocente aventura del trópico." Contemporáneos, I (Núm. 1, junio de 1928), 20-37. (f)   1652

----. "Lugares" Contemporáneos, VII (Núm. 25, junio de 1930), 185-188. (p)
1653

----. "Mil novecientos once." La Falange, Núm. 6 (1 de septiembre de 1923), 338-339. (p)
1654

----. "Oh bien, supremo bien..." La Falange, Núm. 2 (1 de enero de 1923), 96. (p)
1655

----. "Por el camino de Proust." Contemporáneos, II (Núm. 6, noviembre de 1928), 298. (a-e)
1656

----. "Tiempo fiel." Tierra Nueva, I (Núm. 2, marzo-abril de 1940), 69-70. (p)
1657

----. Ambito de Vicente Aleixandre. Contemporáneos, II (Núm. 4, septiembre de 1928), 97-99. (r)
1658

----. "Dama de corazones" (Reseña de Dama de corazones de Xavier Villaurrutia). Contemporáneos, I (Núm. 3, agosto de 1928), 319-321. (r)
1659

----. "Carta a Fantomas-Bergamín" (Reseña de Enemigo que huye de José Bergamín). Contemporáneos, I (Núm. 1, junio de 1928), 92-95. (r)
1660

----. "Epica y economía" (Reseña de El nuevo poema i su orientación hacia una estética económica de Magda Portal). Contemporáneos, II (Núm. 5, octubre de 1928), 208-210. (r)
1661

----. "Ventura García

Calderón y su obra" (reseña de Páginas escogidas de Ventura García Calderón). Contemporáneos, II (Núm. 7, diciembre de 1928), 381-384. (r)
1662

----. Poemas selectos de Agustín F. Cuenca. México Moderno, I (Núm. 2, septiembre de 1920), 123-124. (r)
1663

González Rojo, Enrique Jr. "Tres notas sobre existencialismo." Estaciones, III (Núm. 11, otoño de 1958), 315-322. (a-e)
1664

----. Seis poemas por el hombre de Pedro Duno. Estaciones, II (Núm. 7, otoño de 1957), 226-227. (r)
1665

González y González, Alicia. "La leyenda del rey don Rodrigo." Tierra Nueva, I (Núm. 1, enero-febrero de 1940), 35-44. (a-e)
1666

Gorlier, Carlos Alberto. "Egloga." Estaciones, II (Núm. 7, 1957), 263-264. (p)
1667

Gorostiza, Celestino. "Aspectos del teatro." Contemporáneos, IV (Núm. 12, mayo de 1929), 146-150. (a-e)
1668

----. "Galería de poetas nuevos de México." Contemporáneos, II (Núm. 5, octubre de 1928), 201-205. (a-e)
1669

----. "El nuevo paraíso." Contemporáneos, V (Núm. 17, octubre de 1929), 176-209. (dr)
1670

----. "Payo." Contemporáneos, II (Núm. 7, diciembre de

1928), 336-345. (f)   1671

----. "Teatro judío. "
Contemporáneos, I (Núm. 2,
julio de 1928), 212-213. (a-e)
1672

----. "El teatro y la actitud
mexicana. " Contemporáneos,
VI (Núm. 20, enero de 1930),
39-52. (a-e)   1673

----. Aquí abajo de Francisco
Tario. El Hijo Pródigo, III
(Núm. 10, enero de 1944),
54-55. (r)   1674

----. Dynamo de Eugene O'
Neill. Contemporáneos, V
(Núm. 18, noviembre de
1929), 329-331. (r)   1675

---- Perfiles de Taxco de
Francisco Monterde y Vida
ejemplar de Don José de la
Borda de Manuel Horta.
Contemporáneos, II (Núm. 4,
septiembre de 1928), 99-101.
(r)   1676

----. Asch, Nathan. "El
campo" (Trad. Celestino
Gorostiza). Contemporáneos,
II (Núm. 5, octubre de 1928),
144-159. (tr)   (512)

Gorostiza Alcalá, José. "A
Ramón López Velarde, Q. E.
P. D. " México Moderno, II
(Núm. 11-12, noviembre-
diciembre de 1921), 297-298.
(p)   1677

----. "Acuario. " Sagitario,
Núm. 6 (1 de noviembre de
1926), 16. (p)   1678

----. "Adán, " "Espejo no. "
Contemporáneos, IV (Núm. 12,
mayo de 1929), 97-99. (p)
1679

----. "Alfonso Reyes. "

Fábula, Núm. 9 (septiembre
de 1934), 173-174. (a-e)
1680

----. "Declaración de
Bogotá. " Estaciones, III
(Núm. 12, invierno de 1958),
379-380. (p)   1681

----. "Dibujos sobre un
puerto. " Antena, Núm. 2
(agosto de 1924), 6-7. (p)
1682

----. "Eco. " Sagitario, Núm.
7 (1 de enero de 1927), 11.
(p)   1683

----. "Morfología de La
rueca de aire. " Contem-
poráneos, VII (Núm. 25,
junio de 1930), 240-248.
(a-e)   1684

----. "Notas sobre poesía. "
Estaciones, III (Núm. 9,
primavera de 1958), 1-11.
(a-e)   1685

----. "Vuelvo a ti, " "Gaviota."
México Moderno, I (Núm. 2,
septiembre de 1920), 115-116.
(p)   1686

----. El corazón juglar de
Luis G. Urbina. México
Moderno, II (Núm. 8, marzo
de 1921), 124-125. (r)   1687

----. Desolación de Gabriela
Mistral. México Moderno,
II (Núm. 4, junio de 1923),
255. (r)   1688

----. Escalera de Genaro
Estrada. Contemporáneos, IV
(Núm. 14, julio de 1929),
341-344. (r)   1689

----. Luna de copas de
Antonio Espina. Contemporáneos, V (Núm. 16, septiembre

110

de 1929), 157-159. (r) 1690

----. Optica cerebral de Nahui-Olín. México Moderno, II (Núm. 2, septiembre de 1922), 126. (r) 1691

----. Ordenanzas de gremios de la Nueva España recopilado por Francisco del Barrio Lorenzot. México Moderno, II (Núm. 8, marzo de 1921), 124. (r) 1692

----. Paula y Paulita de Benjamín Jarnés. Contemporáneos, V (Núm. 15, agosto de 1929), 68-69. (r) 1693

----. Rhytion de Araújo Filho. México Moderno, II (Núm. 4, junio de 1923), 256. (r) 1694

----. La segunda dimensión de Moisés Vincenzi. México Moderno, II (Núm. 4, junio de 1923), 255-256. (r) 1695

----. Maurois, André. "La conversación" (Trad. José Gorostiza). Contemporáneos, IV (Núm. 11, abril de 1929), 70-84. (tr) 1696

----. Maurois, André. "La conversación" (Trad. José Gorostiza). Contemporáneos, VII (Núm. 23, abril de 1930), 47-65. (tr) 1697

Gourmont, Remy de. "Fragmentos sobre el estilo" (Trad. José Luis Martínez). El Hijo Pródigo, XII (Núm. 38, mayo de 1946), 104-111. (a-e) 1698

Grabav, Igor. "Una exposición de Bellas Artes en la U. R. S. S. " Romance, II (Núm. 24, 31 de mayo de 1941), 13. (a-e) 1699

Graça Aranha, José Pereira da. "A Ronald de Carvalho" (Trad. Rafael Heliodoro Valle). La Falange, Núm. 5 (1 de agosto de 1923), 300-303. (a-e) 1700

Graves, Robert. "Como nieve, " "La puerta, " "Todo estaba en su sitio, " "El suicida en el seto, " "She tells her love while half-asleep. " (Trad. Salvador Elizondo), Estaciones, V (Núm. 17, primavera de 1960), 22-24. (p) (1230)

Greenwood, Marion. "Mural. " Fábula, Núm. 3 (marzo de 1934), entre 56-57. (il) 1701

Grijalba, Fraiz. "Artistas españoles en la República Dominicana. " Romance, I (Núm. 14, 15 de agosto de 1940), 7. (a-e) 1702

----. "Esposición de Manolo Pascual. " Romance, II (Núm. 21, 15 de febrero de 1941), 9. (a-e) 1703

Grote, Barón Heriberto B. de. Vossler, Karl. "El Primero sueño de Sor Juana" (Trad. Barón Heriberto B. de Crote). Tierra Nueva, II (Núm. 11-12, septiembre-diciembre de 1941), 243-249. (tr) 1704

Guardia, Miguel. "Elegía. " Estaciones, I (Núm. 3, otoño de 1956), 300-302. (p) 1705

----. "Mi casa. " Estaciones, III (Núm. 12, invierno de 1958), 407-411. (p) 1706

----. Obras premiadas 1954-
1955 del Concurso Nacional
de Teatro. Estaciones, I
(Núm. 4, invierno de 1956),
598-600. (r)   1707

Guereña, Jacinto Luis. "La
novela francesa actual. "
Estaciones, IV (Núm. 13,
primavera de 1959), 64-71.
(a-e)   1708

Guerrero, Enrique Gabriel.
"Condición esforzada, " "Ocios
de estío. " Taller, II (Núm.
12, enero-febrero de 1941),
48-51. (p)   1709

----. "Esquema de una carta
al poeta. " El Hijo Pródigo,
VII (Núm. 24, marzo de
1945), 152. (p)   1710

----. "Preludio breve, "
"Música de cámara, "
"Ejercicio de estío. " Taller,
I (Núm. 3, mayo de 1939),
17-20. (p)   1711

Guerrero Galván, J. "Novia
del pueblo. " Estaciones, I
(Núm. 1, primavera de 1956),
entre 112-113. (il)   1712

Guillén, Alberto. "Ingenuidades. "
Antena, Núm. 2 (agosto de
1924), 3-4. (a-e)   1713

Guillén, Fedro. "Una historia
de perros. " Estaciones, I
(Núm. 4, invierno de 1956),
558-566. (f)   1714

Guillén, Jorge. "A lo largo de
las orillas ilustres, " "Luz
diferida, " "Muchachas, "
"Sierpe, " "Vida urbana, "
"Cuerpo veloz, " "Impaciente
vivir. " El Hijo Pródigo, VIII
(Núm. 27, junio de 1945),
145-149. (p)   1715

----. "Amanece, amanezco, "

"Siempre en la isla, " "El
bienventurado. " El Hijo
Pródigo, X (Núm. 32,
noviembre de 1945), 85-86.
(p)   1716

----. "Más esplendor. " El
Hijo Pródigo, I (Núm. 6,
septiembre de 1943), 341-342.
(p)   1717

----. "Una ventana, " "Vacación, " "Tarde mayor. " El
Hijo Pródigo, IV (Núm. 15,
junio de 1944), 151-153. (p)
                                1718

Guillén Zelaya, Alfonso. "En
el tren. " La Falange, Núm.
5 (1 de agosto de 1923), 291-
292. (p)   1719

Gupta, H. L. "Nota sobre
'Bengala dorada' de
Rabindranath Tagore. " La
Falange, Núm. 3 (1 de febrero
de 1923), 169. (a-e)   1720

Gutiérrez, Pedro. "Campesino, "
"Mujer, " "Paisaje, "
"Boxeadores" Contemporáneos,
III (Núm. 10, marzo de 1929),
215-218. (il)   1721

----. "Oleo. " Sagitario, Núm.
12-13 (30 de abril de 1927),
28. (il)   1722

Gutiérrez, Salvador. "Obrero."
Contemporáneos, III (Núm. 10,
marzo de 1929), 214. (il)
                                1723

Gutiérrez Cruz, Carlos.
"Mañanitas, " "El pajarillo, "
"El carbonero. " México
Moderno, II (Núm. 1, agosto
de 1922), 56-58. (p)   1724

Gutiérrez Gutiérrez, Ernesto.
"Años bajo el sol. "
Estaciones, V (Núm. 18,
verano de 1960), 90-93. (p)
                                1725

Gutiérrez Hermosillo, Alfonso. "Alfonso Reyes." Fábula, Núm. 9 (septiembre de 1934), 174. (a-e)   1726

----. "Alusión," "Ocasión." El Hijo Pródigo, V (Núm. 16, julio de 1944), 18. (p) 1727

----. "Anunciación." Poesía, Núm. 2 (marzo de 1941), 35. (p)   1728

----. "Cardona Vera." Contemporáneos, XI (Núm. 42-43, noviembre-diciembre de 1931), 288-293. (a-e)   1729

----. "Carta a un amigo difunto." Ruta, Núm. 4 (septiembre de 1938), 21-24. (p)   1730

----. "Coro." Poesía, Núm. 2 (marzo de 1941), 40-41. (p)   1731

----, y Villaurrutia, Xavier. "Crítica epistolar." El Hijo Pródigo, V (Núm. 17, agosto de 1944), 73-82. (a-e) 1732

----. "Eres mi corazón." Poesía, Núm. 2 (marzo de 1941), 38-39. (p) 1733

----. "Es azul mi hermanita." Poesía, Núm. 2 (marzo de 1941), 36-37. (p)   1734

----. "Greta Garbo," "Soneto," "A una mujer." Tierra Nueva, I (Núm. 4-5, julio-octubre de 1940), 195-197. (p)   1735

----. "Retrato con paisaje." Contemporáneos, V (Núm. 18, noviembre de 1929), 241-242. (p)   1736

----. "Retrato con paisaje."

Contemporáneos, V (Núm. 18, noviembre de 1929), 241-242. (p)   1736

----. "Retrato con paisaje." Contemporáneos, XI (Núm. 40-41, septiembre-octubre de 1931), 144-151. (p) 1737

----. "Sonetos." Contemporáneos, VIII (Núm. 26-27, julio-agosto de 1930), 39-41. (p)   1738

----. "Tratado de la muerte del cuerpo." Poesía, Núm. 2 (marzo de 1941), 42. (p)   1739

----. "Tratados" (incluye "Tratado de la muerte del cuerpo" y "Tratado de la inseguridad"). Fábula, Núm. 6 (junio de 1934), 116-117. (p)   1740

Guzmán, Martín Luis. "Jesús Urueta." México Moderno, II (Núm. 9, mayo de 1921), 129-134. (a-e)   1741

----. "Luz y tinieblas." México Moderno, I (Núm. 3, octubre de 1920), 159-163. (a-e)   1742

----. "Maestros rurales: Kinchil." Ruta, Núm. 3 (agosto de 1938), 33-43. (f)   1743

----. "Palabras del profesor." Romance, I (Núm. 3, 1 de marzo de 1940), 3. (f) 1744

----. "Respuesta a la encuesta de Romance." Romance, I (Núm. 2, 15 de febrero de 1940), 3. (a-e)   1745

----. "Tres coloquios de Pancho Villa." Romance, I

113

(Núm. 12, 15 de julio de 1940), 11. (f)   1746

----. Masefield, John. "Los fieles." (Trad. Enrique Díez-Canedo y Martín Luis Guzmán), Contemporáneos, V (Núm. 18, noviembre de 1929), 245-292; (Núm. 19, diciembre de 1929), 354-421. (tr)   (1173)

H., H. W. "Una antigua librería de Londres." Romance, I (Núm. 4, 15 de marzo de 1940), 12. (a-e)   1747

Hafiz. "Rubayas" (Trad. Rafael Lozano). La Falange, Núm. 3 (1 de febrero de 1923), 150-151. (r)   1748

Halffter, Rodolfo. La música moderna de Adolfo Salazar. El Hijo Pródigo, VII (Núm. 22, enero de 1945), 59-60. (r)   1749

Harring, María S. "Los ángeles custodios." Estaciones, II (Núm. 6, verano de 1957), 217-218. (p)   1750

Hartzenbusch, Juan Eugenio. "El ama de llaves" (En "Los españoles pintados por si mismos"). Romance, I (Núm. 10, 15 de junio de 1940), 10. (a-e)   1751

Heidegger, Martín. "Hölderlin y la esencia de la poesía" (Trad. E. Prado Vertiz y José Luis Martínez). Tierra Nueva, III (Núm. 15, diciembre de 1942), 143-153. (a-e)   1752

Heine, Maurice. "Nota sobre una clasificación psicobiológica de las parestesias sexuales."

Prometeus, I (Núm. 3, mayo de 1949), 159-160. (a-e) 1753

Henestrosa, Andrés. "Alfonso Reyes." Fábula, Núm. 9 (septiembre de 1934), 174. (a-e)   1754

----. "Españolidad de Sarmiento." Romance, I (Núm. 5, 1 de abril de 1940), 11. (a-e)   1755

----. "Gendastu:bi." Tierra Nueva, II (Núm. 9-10, mayo-agosto de 1941), 118-119. (p)   1756

----. "Jorge Isaacs en Tehuantepec." Fábula, Núm. 2 (febrero de 1934), 35-37. (a-e)   1757

----. "Leyendas zapotecas:La tortuga, La golondrina, La campana." Contemporáneos, IV (Núm. 11, abril de 1929), 15-22. (f)   1758

----. "Los muertos que descubrió la guerra." Ruta, 10 (marzo de 1939), 42-44. (a-e)   1759

----. "Retrato de mi madre." Taller, I (Núm. 1, diciembre de 1938), 23-32. (a-e) 1760

----. Canek de Ermilo Abreu Gómez. Tierra Nueva, II (Núm. 7-8, enero-abril de 1941), 71-73. (r)   1761

----. Facundo en su laberinto de Héctor Pérez Martínez. Fábula, Núm. 5 (mayo de 1934), 100. (r)   1762

Henríquez Ureña, Pedro. "La antología de la ciudad." México Moderno, II (Núm. 1

agosto de 1922), 27-29.
(a-e)   1763

----. "Don Juan Ruiz de
Alarcón." El Hijo Pródigo,
XIII (Núm. 40, julio de
1946), 38-47. (a-e) 1764

----. "En busca del verso
puro." Sagitario, Núm. 7
(1 de enero de 1927), 5. (p)
                         1765

----. "En la orilla." México
Moderno, Núm. 6 (enero de
1921), 331-335. (a-e) 1766

----. "Notas sobre literatura
mexicana." México Moderno,
II (Núm. 3, octubre de
1922), 162-165. (a-e) 1767

Heráclito. "Fragmentos
filosóficos" (Trad. Juan
David García Bacca). El
Hijo Pródigo, III (Núm. 12,
marzo de 1944), 166-170.
(a-e)   (1438)

Heredia, José G. "En busca
de las siete ciudades."
Contemporáneos, II (Núm. 5,
octubre de 1928), 160-193.
(a-e)   1768

----. "En busca de las
siete ciudades." Contem-
poráneos, IV (Núm. 14,
julio de 1929), 314-340. (a-e)
                         1769

Hernández, Efrén. "Alfonso
Reyes." Fábula, Núm. 9
(septiembre de 1934), 174-
175. (a-e)   1770

----. "El ángel del subsuelo."
Taller, II (Núm. 12, enero-
febrero de 1941), 52-58. (p)
                         1771

----. "Unos cuantos tomates
en una repisita." Fábula,

Núm. 1 (enero de 1934), 15-
17. (f)   1772

----. "Una historia sin
brillo." Romance, I (Núm.
13, 1 de agosto de 1940),
4-5. (f)   1773

----. "Sobre causas de
títeres." Taller, I (Núm. 2,
abril de 1939), 5-10. (f)
                         1774

----. Canto a Teresa de
Salvador Novo. Fábula,
Núm. 7 (julio de 1934), 139-
140. (r)   1775

Hernández, Mateo. "La
decadencia de la escultura."
Sagitario, Núm. 7 (1 de
enero de 1927), 12. (a-e)
                         1776

Hernández, Porfirio. ("Don
Porfirio"). "Instantáneas:
'La barberías', 'Los
escaparates', 'Los cuartos
de los hoteles'." La Falange,
Núm. 1 (1 de diciembre de
1922), 59-61. (a-e)   1777

----. "El más grande de
los crímenes." Antena, Núm.
2 (agosto de 1924), 7-8.
(a-e)   1778

----. "La natación." Antena,
Núm. 2 (agosto de 1924), 8.
(a-e)   1779

----. "El poder moralizador
de las armas," "La utilidad
de las moscas," "Las
hebillas." La Falange, 3
(1 de febrero de 1923), 176-
178. (a-e)   1780

----. "Los viejos." Antena,
Núm. 2 (agosto de 1924), 8.
(a-e)   1781

115

Hernández Bordes, Ernesto.
"Playa." Fábula, Núm. 4
(abril de 1934), 76. (p) 1782

Hernández Campos, Jorge. "La
buena guerra." Estaciones,
I (Núm. 4, invierno de 1956),
518-550. (f) 1783

----. Cecchi, Emilio. "El
Cristo muerto," "La revuelta
de Cedillo." (Trad. Jorge
Hernández Campos),
Estaciones, V (Núm. 17,
primavera de 1960), 10-21.
(tr) (899)

----. Cecchi, Emilio.
"Mujeres en la ventana,"
"Anteojos Negros." (Trad.
Jorge Hernández Campos)
Estaciones, V (Núm. 18,
verano de 1960), 56-64. (tr)
(900)

Herrasti, Francisco de P.
"Elegía XXIV." Ulises, Núm.
5 (diciembre de 1927), 27-28.
(p) 1784

Herrera Frimont, Celestino.
"Aguilera Malta, novelista
ecuatoriano." Ruta, Núm. 5
(octubre de 1938), 50-51.
(a-e) 1785

----. "Aquellas ramas de
ceiba." Ruta, Núm. 10
(marzo de 1939), 31-33. (n)
1786

----. "Los clásicos de
nuestra historia." Ruta,
Núm. 6 (noviembre de 1938),
43-46. (a-e) 1787

----. "Literatura biográfica
mexicana." Ruta, Núm. 7
(diciembre de 1938), 54-56.
(a-e) 1788

----. "Literatura guerrera
del Chaco." Ruta, Núm. 4

(septiembre de 1938), 53-55.
(a-e) 1789

Herrera Petere, José. "La
cónicas montañas." Romance,
I (Núm. 6, 15 de abril de
1940), 5. (f) 1790

----. "El gran Jefferson
Hope." El Hijo Pródigo, VI
(Núm. 19, octubre de 1944),
26-31. (f) 1791

----. "Hacia la humanización
de la música." Romance, I
(Núm. 6, 15 de abril de
1940), 15. (a-e) 1792

----. "Juana de Dios." El
Hijo Pródigo, I (Núm. 1,
abril de 1943), 33-44. (f)
1793

----. "Manuscrito encontrado
en una bota militar." El
Hijo Pródigo, II (Núm. 9,
diciembre de 1943), 184-190.
(f) 1794

----. "¡Qué encantadora
fiesta!" Taller, I (Núm. 5,
octubre de 1939), 27-35. (f)
1795

----. "Sobre lo grotesco
español." Romance, I (Núm.
3, 1 de marzo de 1940), 9.
(a-e) 1796

----. "Ternura inhumana."
Romance, I (Núm. 2, 15 de
febrero de 1940), 18. (a-e)
1797

----. "Invitación a la
historia" (Reseña de Baraja
de crónicas castellanas de
Ramón Iglesias). Romance, I
(Núm. 10, 15 de junio de
1940), 19. (r) 1798

----. Un cancionero popular
español reunido por Rodolfo

Hallfter. Romance, I (Núm.
2, 15 defebrero de 1940), 15.
(r)   1799

----. Diario de un aspirante
a santo de Georges Duhamel.
Romance, I (Núm. 4, 15 de
marzo de 1940), 18. (r)
                            1800

----. Las montañas y los
hombres de M. Ilin.
Romance, I (Núm. 1, 1 de
febrero de 1940), 20. (r)
                            1801

----. "Nabí o persistencia
del hombre" (Reseña de
Nabí de José Carner).
Romance, I (Núm. 12, 15 de
julio de 1940), 18. (r) 1802

----. "H. G. Wells y las
diferentes clases de
monstruos" (Reseña de El
nuevo origen del mundo de
H. G. Wells). Romance, I
(Núm. 15, 1 de septiembre
de 1940), 18. (r)   1803

----. Piedras blancas de
Pablo L. Landsberg. Romance,
I (Núm. 8, 15 de mayo de
1940), 18. (r)   1804

----. "Oportunidad de Gil
Vicente" (Reseña de Poesías
de Gil Vicente con notas y
prólogo de Dámaso Alonso).
Taller, II (Núm. 10, marzo-
abril de 1940), 53-54. (r)
                            1805

Herrero Estéban, Jacinto.
"Poemas de Avila y Managua."
Estaciones, V (Núm. 19,
otoño de 1960), 21-22. (p)
                            1806

Hidalgo, María Luisa. "Epica
del gusano." Estaciones, I
(Núm. 3, otoño de 1956),
358-359. (f)   1807

----. "Tacto en la distancia."
Tierra Nueva, II (Núm. 7-8,
enero-abril de 1941), 44-46.
(p)   1808

Hinojosa, José María.
"Nuestros huesos," "Vinieron
aves heridas," "Liberación,"
"Arboles en mi vida."
Contemporáneos, IV (Núm. 14,
julio de 1929), 309-313. (p)
                            1809

Hölderlin, Johann Christian
Friedrick. "Cuatro cartas."
El Hijo Pródigo, I (Núm. 4,
julio de 1943), 252-254. (a-e)
                            1810

----. "Del 'Hyperion'" (Trad.
Juan Gil Albert. Taller, II
(Núm. 10, marzo-abril de
1940), 5-9. (f)   (1528)

Horta, Manuel. "El banquete
a Rafael López." Antena,
Núm. 3 (septiembre de 1924),
7. (a-e)   1811

Housman, Alfred Edward.
"Nombre y naturaleza de la
poesía." El Hijo Pródigo, III
(Núm. 11, febrero de 1944),
87-104. (a-e)   1812

Hueng, Tcheng. "La nueva
cultura china." Ruta, Núm.
11 (abril de 1939), 49-54.
(a-e)   1813

Huerta, Efraín. "Absoluto amor."
Poesía, Núm. 2 (marzo de
1941), 49. (p)   1814

----. "Alba de añil." Poesía,
Núm. 2 (marzo de 1941), 50.
(p)   1815

----. "Amante siempre
requerida." Poesía, Núm. 2
(marzo de 1941), 51. (p)
                            1816

----. "El amor." Poesía, Núm. 2 (marzo de 1941), 55-56. (p) 1817

----. "Andrea y el tiempo." Poesía, Núm. 2 (marzo de 1941), 45-46. (p) 1818

----. "Declaración de amor." Ruta, Núm. 2 (julio de 1938), 23-26. (p) 1819

----. "Elegía." Poesía, Núm. 2 (marzo de 1941), 48. (p) 1820

----. "Envío." Poesía, Núm. 2 (marzo de 1941), 47. (p) 1821

----. "Esta región de ruina." Tierra Nueva, II (Núm. 9-10, mayo-agosto de 1941), 123-125. (p) 1822

----. "La estrella en alto." Poesía, Núm. 2 (marzo de 1941), 52-53. (p) 1823

----. "La mariposa loca." Ruta, Núm. 12 (mayo de 1939), 26. (p) 1824

----. "Ordenes de amor." Estaciones, III (Núm. 12, invierno de 1958), 401-403. (p) 1825

----. "Los perros del alba." Prometeus, I (Núm. 1, febrero de 1949), 19-20. (p) 1826

----. "Precursora del alba." Poesía, Núm. 2 (marzo de 1941), 54. (p) 1827

----. "Presencias." Taller, I (Núm. 4, julio de 1939), 54-55. (a-e) 1828

----. "Problema del alma." Taller, II (Núm. 8-9, enero-febrero de 1940), 12-15. (p) 1829

----. "Problema del alma." Taller, II (Núm. 12, enero-febrero de 1941), 46-47. (p) 1830

----. "Problema del alma." El Hijo Pródigo, IV (Núm. 14, mayo de 1944), 82-86. (p) 1831

----. "Tramontar." Taller, I (Núm. 4, julio de 1939), 43-47. (f) 1832

----. "Vals del clavel," "El retorno." El Hijo Pródigo, XI (Núm. 36, marzo de 1946), 141-142. (p) 1833

----. "Verdaderamente," "La poesía enemiga," "Breve canto," "Cuarto canto de abandono." Taller, I (Núm. 1, diciembre de 1938), 14-22. (p) 1834

----. "Una antología de forcejeos" (Reseña de Antología de la poesía mexicana moderna de Manuel Maples Arce. Taller, II (Núm. 12, enero-febrero de 1941), 68-70. (r) 1835

----. Entre dos fuegos de Antonio Sánchez Barbudo. Taller, I (Núm. 1, diciembre de 1938), 60-62. (r) 1836

----. El hombre y el trabajo de Arturo Serrano Plaja. Taller, I (Núm. 1, diciembre de 1938), 62. (r) 1837

----. "Organización del sarcasmo" (Reseña de Niebla de cuernos de José Herrera Petere). Taller, II (Núm. 11, julio-agosto de 1940), 71-73. (r) 1838

----. "La nube exacta y el reloj nublado" (Reseña de La nube y el reloj de Luis Cardoza y Aragón). Taller, II (Núm. 12, enero-febrero de 1941), 70-71. (r) 1839

----. Son nombres ignorados de Juan Gil-Albert. Taller, I (Núm. 1, diciembre de 1938), 62-63. (r) 1840

----. "Bajo las palmeras de la crítica" (Reseña de Textos y pretextos de Xavier Villaurrutia). Romance, I (Núm. 11, 1 de julio de 1940), 18. (r) 1841

----. Viaje a México de Paul Morand. Romance, I (Núm. 4, 15 de marzo de 1940), 18. (r) 1842

Hughes, Langston. "Yo también," "Poema," "Plegaria," "Nota de un suicida" (Trad. Xavier Villaurrutia). Contemporáneos, XI (Núm. 40-41, septiembre-octubre de 1931), 157-159. (p) 1843

Hugnet, Georges. "La hora del pastor." Estaciones, I (Núm. 1, primavera de 1956), 143-144. (p) 1844

Huidobro, Vicente. "Altazor." Contemporáneos, XI (Núm. 40-41, septiembre-octubre de 1931), 152-156. (p) 1845

----. "Poemas" ("Bellas promesas," "Ilusiones perdidas," "Sea como sea"). Romance, I (Núm. 14, 15 de agosto de 1940), 10. (p) 1846

Hurtado, Alfredo. "Carta a Zuno." Estaciones, II (Núm. 8, invierno de 1957), 446-449.

----. "Carta de Alfredo Hurtado al Lic. Guillermo Tardiff." Estaciones, III (Núm. 9, primavera de 1958), 43-48. (a-e) 1848

----. y Nandino, Elías. "Palabras de los editores." Estaciones, II (Núm. 5, primavera de 1957), 3-4. (a-e) 1849

----. "Poema." Estaciones, III (Núm. 9, primavera de 1958), 34. (p) 1850

----. "La poética de Elías Nandino." Estaciones, I (Núm. 1, primavera de 1956), 67-84. (a-e) 1851

----. El arte ruso de Louis Réau. Estaciones, II (Núm. 8, invierno de 1957), 482. (r) 1852

----. Balúm Canán de Rosario Castellanos. Estaciones, II (Núm. 8, invierno de 1957), 481-482. (r) 1853

----. Calavera y jueves santo de Alberto Monterde. Estaciones, II (Núm. 8, invierno de 1957), 482. (r) 1854

----. Coloquio de Amor, poema de Margarita Paz Paredes. Estaciones, II (Núm. 6, verano de 1957), 197. (r) 1855

----. Cruces en Chamula de Francisco Cabrera Nieto. Estaciones, I (Núm. 4, invierno de 1956), 605-606. (r) 1856

----. Dilucidario de Salvador Calvillo Madrigal. Estaciones,

II (Núm. 6, verano de
1957), 194. (r)   1857

----. Eternidad del ruiseñor
de Germán Pardo García.
Estaciones, I (Núm. 4,
invierno de 1956), 602-605.
(r)   1858

----. El filibusterismo de
Jacques y François Gall.
Estaciones, II (Núm. 8,
invierno de 1957), 483-484.
(r)   1859

----. Hueso y carne de Raúl
Prieto. Estaciones, II (Núm.
5, primavera de 1957), 97-98.
(r)   1860

----. Incitaciones y valora-
ciones de Manuel Maples Arce.
Estaciones, II (Núm. 5,
primavera de 1957), 100. (r)
                                 1861

----. Juan Caballero de
Luisa Carnés. Estaciones, II
(Núm. 5, primavera de 1957),
100-101. (r)   1862

----. Negro Sam del tío Sam,
Poemas de Manuel González
Flores. Estaciones, II (Núm.
6, verano de 1957), 195-196.
(r)   1863

----. El nocturno a Rosario
de Wilberto Cantón.
Estaciones, I (Núm. 4,
invierno de 1956), 605. (r)
                                 1864

----. Las palabras perdidas
de Mauricio Magdaleno.
Estaciones, II (Núm. 5,
primavera de 1957), 97. (r)
                                 1865

----. La colección "Los
presentes". Estaciones, I
(Núm. 3, otoño de 1956),
395-401. (r)   1866

----. La vid y el labrador
de Enoch Cancino Casahonda.
Estaciones, II (Núm. 6,
verano de 1957), 197-198. (r)
                                 1867

----. Prampolini, Enrique.
"Concepción del espacio en
las artes plásticas". (Trad.
Alfredo Hurtado). Estaciones,
I (Núm. 2, verano de 1956),
244-248. (tr)   1868

Huxley, Aldous. "El banquete
a Tillotson" (Trad. Samuel
Ramos). México Moderno, II
(Núm. 4, junio de 1923),
209-223. (f)   1869

----. "Baudelaire" (Trad.
José Luis Martínez). El Hijo
Pródigo, VIII (Núm. 27, junio
de 1945), 165-176. (a-e)
                                 1870

----. "Ciudad de México."
(Trad. Xavier Villaurrutia)
Tierra Nueva, II (Núm 9-10,
mayo-agosto de 1941), 169-
170. (a-e)   1871

----. "Diálogos socráticos del
momento" (Trad. Guillermo
Prieto Yeme). México Moderno,
II (Núm. 1, agosto de 1922),
62-63. (a-e)   1872

----. "La influencia de la
ciencia en la literatura
inmortal" (Trad. Salvador
Novo). México Moderno, II
(Núm. 3, octubre de 1922),
187-188. (a-e)   1873

Huyghe, Rene. "La pintura
italiana desde el siglo XIII al
XVI." Romance, I (Núm. 15,
1 de septiembre de 1940), 12-
13. (a-e)   1874

Ibáñez, Sara de. "Liras."
Taller, II (Núm. 12, enero-
febrero de 1941), 34-38. (p)
                                 1875

----. "Sonetos." Taller, II (Núm. 12, enero-febrero de 1941), 39-42. (p) 1876

Ibarbourou, Juana de. "Rebelde." La Falange, Núm. 2 (1 de enero de 1923), 86. (p) 1877

----. "La tarde." México Moderno, I (Núm. 5, diciembre de 1920), 325. (p) 1878

----. "Timonel de mi sueño," "Corazón dolorido de sueños," "Día amargo," "La noche," "Días sin fe." Contemporáneos, III (Núm. 10, marzo de 1929), 193-198. (p) 1879

Ibarra, Jaime. "Esfinge." Sagitario, Núm. 11 (15 de marzo de 1927), 11-12. (f) 1880

----. "Vía Crucis" Contemporáneos, VII (Núm. 25, junio de 1930), 189-210. (a-e) 1881

----. Arbol de Julio J. Casal. Sagitario, Núm. 7 (1 de enero de 1927), 17. (r) 1882

Icaza, Francisco A. de. "Salvador Díaz Mirón." Antena, Núm. 4 (octubre de 1924), 10. (a-e) 1883

----. "Vida amorosa de Lope de Vega." La Falange, Núm. 6 (1 de septiembre de 1923), 317-319. (a-e) 1884

Icaza, Xavier. "Al margen de la vida." México Moderno, I (Núm. 2, septiembre de 1920), 98-101. (a-e) 1885

----. "S. O. S. - 1940." Romance, I (Núm. 19, 18 de diciembre de 1940), 8. (f) 1886

Iduarte, Andrés. "La cosecha del Conde Russell." Romance, I (Núm. 8, 15 de mayo de 1940), 12. (a-e) 1887

----. "Un pintor mexicano en Nueva York: Rufino Tamayo." Romance, I (Núm. 7, 1 de mayo de 1940), 7. (a-e) 1888

Iglesias, Ramón. "Cuarto congreso mexicano de historia." Romance, I (Núm. 2, 15 de febrero de 1940), 20. (a-e) 1889

----. "El historiador y la historia." Romance, I (Núm. 12, 15 de julio de 1940), 17. (a-e) 1890

Iguíñiz, Juan B. "El bachiller D. Cristóbal Bernardo de la Plaza y Jaén y su crónica de la Universidad de México." México Moderno, I (Núm. 5, diciembre de 1920), 275-282. (a-e) 1891

Ijac, Carlos. "La crisis de la enseñanza de la literatura en las universidades burguesas." Ruta, Núm. 11 (abril de 1939), 24-34. (a-e) 1892

Imaz, Eugenio. "La cólera de Descartes." Romance, I (Núm. 7, 1 de mayo de 1940), 11. (a-e) 1893

----. "Platón, loco de amor." El Hijo Pródigo, VII (Núm. 23, febrero de 1945), 81-84. (a-e) 1894

----. El pensamiento vivo de Espinoza de Benito Espinosa. Romance, I (Núm. 4, 15 de marzo de 1940), 18. (r) 1895

Inclán, Federico S. "Claro de luna." Estaciones, III (Núm. 10, verano de 1958), 156-164. (dr) 1896

Ituarte, Manuel M.; Obregón Santacillas, Carlos; Montenegro, Roberto; Pallares, Alfonso; Cumming, A. E.; Robles Gil, Alberto. "Encuesta sobre arquitectura." Forma, I (Núm. 3, 1927), 15-16. (a-e) (1019)

Iturriaga, José E. "Apología de la megalomanía." Tierra Nueva, II (Núm. 11-12, septiembre-diciembre de 1941), 236-240. (a-e) 1897

----. "El fenómeno del proselitismo." Ruta, Núm. 10 (marzo de 1939), 47-53. (a-e) 1898

----. Esquema del siglo XIX de Alfred Weber. Tierra Nueva, III (Núm. 13-14, enero-abril de 1942), 69-74. (r) 1899

----. "Una antinomia resuelta" (Reseña de Libertad y plantificación social de Karl Mannheim). Tierra Nueva, III (Núm. 15, diciembre de 1942), 163-165. (r) 1900

----. Reflexiones sobre la Historia Universal de Jacobo Burkhardt con prólogo de Alfonso Reyes. El Hijo Pródigo, III (Núm. 11, febrero de 1944), 122. (r) 1901

----. Ubicación del arte en la cultura de Rafael Méndez Dorich. El Hijo Pródigo, III (Núm. 12, marzo de 1944), 186. (r) 1902

Izquierdo, María. "Acuarela y viñetas." Taller, I (Núm. 1, diciembre de 1938), entre 32-33. (il) 1903

----. "Oleos." Contemporáneos, V (Núm. 16, septiembre de 1929), 103-106. (il) 1904

J., R. de. Miradas sobre el mundo indolatino de Augusto P. Vistel. Ruta, Núm. 10 (marzo de 1939), 60. (r) 1905

Jacob, Max. "La statue," "Torticolistalle." Ulises, Núm. 1 (mayo de 1927), 3. (p) 1906

Jahn, Jan. Kafka, Franz. "Reproche a mi educación" (Trad. Jan Jahn). Prometeus, I (Núm. 2, abril de 1949), 79-85. (tr) 1907

Jarnés, Benjamín. "Años de aprendizaje y alegría." Contemporáneos, VII (Núm. 23, abril de 1930), 66-77. (a-e) 1908

----. "Apuntes." Sagitario, Núm. 6 (1 de noviembre de 1926), 6. (a-e) 1909

----. "Bibilis." El Hijo Pródigo, V (Núm. 16, julio de 1944), 26-31. (f) 1910

----. "El burlador de sirenas." Romance, I (Núm. 3, 1 de marzo de 1940), 5, 15. (a-e) 1911

----. "Caín y Epimeteo." Romance, I (Núm. 14, 15 de agosto de 1940), 1-2. (a-e) 1912

----. "De Paula y Paulita." Contemporáneos, V (Núm. 15,

agosto de 1929), 69-72. (n)
1913

----. "Gracián, Primor y
rebeldía." Romance, I
(Núm. 2, 15 de febrero de
1940), 11. (a-e)   1914

----. "Lanza y estilo."
Romance, II (Núm. 24, 31 de
mayo de 1941), 1-2. (a-e)
1915

----. "Lo plástico de López
Velarde." Romance, I
(Núm. 20, 15 de enero de
1941), 18. (a-e)   1916

----. "Mañana de vacación."
Sagitario, Núm. 5 (1 de
octubre de 1926), 15-16. (f)
1917

----. "El número 479."
Ulises, Núm. 5 (diciembre de
1927), 8-11. (f)   1918

----. "Orlando el pacífico."
Romance, II (Núm. 22, 15 de
marzo de 1941), 6, 14. (f)
1919

----. "Respuesta a la
encuesta de Romance."
Romance, I (Núm. 2, 15 de
febrero de 1940), 3. (a-e)
1920

----. "Retrato de Yolanda."
Sagitario, Núm. 11 (15 de
marzo de 1927), 7-8. (f)
1921

----. "Teoría del Zumbel."
Contemporáneos, II (Núm. 7,
diciembre de 1928), 305-310.
(c)   1922

----. "La vuelta al semin-
ario." Sagitario, Núm. 10
(1 de marzo de 1927), 5. (f)
1923

----. "Einstein, el apóstol"
(Reseña de Einstein:Hacedor
de universos de H. Gordon
Garbedian). Romance, I
(Núm. 17, 22 de octubre de
1940), 18. (r)   1924

----. "Novela de un apóstol"
(Reseña de En la noche del
mundo de Ofelia Rodríguez
Acosta). Romance, II (Núm.
23, 22 de abril de 1941), 18.
(r)   1925

----. Hernán Cortés de José
de Benito e Isabel la
Católica de Paulita Brook. El
Hijo Pródigo, V (Núm. 18,
septiembre de 1944), 185-186.
(r)   1926

----. "El indio, tema
poético" (Reseña de El indio
en la poesía de la América
española de Aída Cometta
Manzoni). Romance, I (Núm.
17, 22 de octubre de 1940),
18. (r)   1927

----. "Nueva aparición de
Lazarillo" (Reseña de
Lazarillo de Tormes publicado
por Espasa-Calpe). Romance,
II (Núm. 21, 15 de febrero
de 1941), 18. (r)   1928

----. "Museo de la calle"
(Reseña de Nacimiento de
Venus de Jaime Torres Bodet)
Romance, II (Núm. 24, 31 de
mayo de 1941), 18. (r) 1929

----. "Faulkner y lo irracion-
al" (Reseña de Las palmeras
salvajes de William Faulkner).
Romance, II (Núm. 23, 22 de
abril de 1941), 19. (r) 1930

----. "En el campo argentino"
(Reseña de Poetas gauchescos.
Hidalgo, Ascasubi, Del Campo).
Romance, I (Núm. 19, 18 de

diciembre de 1940), 20. (r)
1931

----. "Parsifal en América"
(Reseña de El santo de la
espada de Ricardo Rojas).
Romance, I (Núm. 17, 22 de
octubre de 1940), 18. (r)
1932

Jiménez, Guillermo. "Alfonso
Reyes." Fábula, Núm. 9
(septiembre de 1934), 175.
1933

----. "La danza de Basilea."
Romance, II (Núm. 23, 22 de
abril de 1941), 16. (a-e)
1934

----. "La ventana abierta."
La Falange, Núm. 4 (1 de
julio de 1923), 210-211. (a-e)
1935

----. "Vidas absurdas."
Romance, I (Núm. 20, 15 de
enero de 1941), 8. (f) 1936

Jiménez, Juan Ramón. "Acción
de gracias." Estaciones,
I (Núm. 2, verano de 1956),
249-250. (p)
1937

----. "Aforismos," "Vino,
primero, pura..."
Sagitario, Núm. 10 (1 de
marzo de 1927), 7. (p)
1938

----. "Los árboles." Taller,
II (Núm. 10, marzo-abril de
1940), 10-11. (p) 1939

----. "Burla májica."
Sagitario, Núm. 1 (15 de
julio de 1926), 13. (p) 1940

----. "Emilio Prados."
Romance, I (Núm. 8, 15 de
mayo de 1940), 11. (a-e)
1941

----. "Francisco Giner."
Sagitario, Núm. 7 (1 de
enero de 1927), 7. (a-e)
1942

----. "Luis Cernuda." El
Hijo Pródigo, I (Núm. 6,
septiembre de 1943), 337-340.
(a-e) 1943

----. "Manuel B. Cossío."
Sagitario, Núm. 7 (1 de
enero de 1927), 7. (a-e)
1944

----. "Mar despierto."
Sagitario, Núm. 1 (15 de julio
de 1926), 13. (p) 1945

----. "El más fiel." Romance,
I (Núm. 12, 15 de julio de
1940), 3. (p) 1946

----. "Navegante." Tierra
Nueva, I (Núm. 1, enero-
febrero de 1940), 5-6. (p)
1947

----. "Por dos hieles."
Tierra Nueva, I (Núm. 6,
noviembre-diciembre de 1940),
291-292. (p) 1948

----. "Ricardo Rubio."
Sagitario, Núm. 7 (1 de enero
de 1927), 7. (a-e) 1949

----. Ausencia y canto de
Enrique González Martínez.
Tierra Nueva, I (Núm. 2
marzo-abril de 1940), 111.
(r) 1950

----. Eliot, Thomas Stearns.
"La fligia che piange,"
"Marina" (Trad. Juan Ramón
Jiménez). Taller, II (Núm.
10, marzo-abril de 1940),
70-89. (tr) (1219)

Jiménez Mabarak, Carlos. "La música zapoteca y huave." Prometeus, I (Núm. 2, abril de 1949), 97-102. (a-e) 1951

Jiménez Rueda, Julio. "Un auto de fe." México Moderno, II (Núm. 2, septiembre de 1922), 80-82. (a-e) 1952

----. "Francisco de Quevedo y lo barroco en España." El Hijo Pródigo, X (Núm. 33, diciembre de 1945), 155-160. (a-e) 1953

----. "El guarda-infante." La Falange, Núm. 1 (1 de diciembre de 1922), 13-18. (f) 1954

----. "Los mendigos." Antena, Núm. 2 (agosto de 1924), 4-5. (dr) 1954A

----. "Música y bailes criollos de la Argentina." México Moderno, II (Núm. 10, junio de 1921), 220-225. (a-e) 1955

----. Vasconcelos, José; González Martínez, Enrique; Gaos, José; Gallegos, José M.; Paz, Octavio; Martínez, José Luis; García-Bacca, David; Nicol, Eduardo; Bergamín, José. "Poesía, mística y filosofía: Debate en torno a San Juan de la Cruz." El Hijo Pródigo, I (Núm. 3, junio de 1943), 135-144. (a-e) (662)

----. "El toque de Diana." Contemporáneos, II (Núm. 4, septiembre de 1928), 55-83. (dr) 1956

----. "La visita de Waldo Frank." Contemporáneos, IV (Núm. 14, julio de 1929), 357-358. (a-e) 1957

----. Chilean Short Stories con introducción y selección de Arturo Torres Rioseco. Contemporáneos, IV (Núm. 12, mayo de 1929), 151-153. (r) 1958

----. Rodó y sus críticos publicado por la Biblioteca Latino-Americana dirigida por Hugo D. Barbagelata. México Moderno, I (Núm. 1, agosto de 1920), 64. (r)1959

----. Romains, Jules. "Amadeo y los caballeros en fila" (Trad. Julio Jiménez Rueda). Contemporáneos, IV (Núm. 13, junio de 1929), 215-239. (tr) 1960

Jiménez y Núñez, Victoriano. "Validez de títulos académicos e incorporación de estudios entre España e Hispanoamérica." Sagitario, Núm. 4 (1 de septiembre de 1926), 18. (a-e) 1961

Jodorowsky, Alejandro. "La ópera del orden." Estaciones, V (Núm. 20, invierno de 1960), 26-56. (dr) 1962

Johnson, Eyvind. "La neutralidad y los escritores." Ruta, Núm. 6 (noviembre de 1938), 37-38. (a-e) 1963

Joublanc Rivas, Luciano. "En vano..." La Falange, Núm. 5 (1 de agosto de 1923), 289-290. (p) 1964

----. "Este día," "Lección." México Moderno, II (Núm. 3, octubre de 1922), 169-171. (p) 1965

----. ";Que culpa tienes tú!"
La Falange, Núm. 2 (1 de
enero de 1923), 95. (p)
1966

----. Y sólo yo sabría..."
"De aquel tiempo," "La
castellana que leía el cantar."
México Moderno, I (Núm. 3,
octubre de 1920), 180-183.
(p)   1967

Jouhandeau, Marcelo. "Man-
hattan." Ulises, Núm. 5
(diciembre de 1927), 12-16;
Núm. 6 (febrero de 1928),
21-30. (f)   1968

Joyce, James. "Flood," "On
the Beach at Fontana,"
"Nightpiece," "Simples,"
"A Prayer." Ulises, Núm.
5 (diciembre de 1927), 28-30.
(p)   1969

----. "Un fragmento de
Ulises" (Trad. A. Zamora).
Ruta, Núm. 2 (julio de 1938),
36-42. (f)   1970

Juárez, Erasmo. "Los
nuestros en Nueva York."
Sagitario, Núm. 9 (15 de
febrero de 1927), 4. (a-e)
1971

Juárez, Nicolás B. "La canoa
más ligera." La Falange,
Núm. 4 (1 de julio de 1923),
sigue 250. (a-e)   1972

Juárez Frausto, Manuel. "Yo
conmigo." Tierra Nueva,
I (Núm. 1, enero-febrero de
1940), 47-50. (c)   1973

Juárez Frausto, Pina. "Imágenes"
(incluye "Faro," "Ráfagas,"
"Riscos," "Margarita,"
"Vitral.") Tierra Nueva I
(Núm. 1, enero-febrero
de 1940), 31-33. (p)   1974

----. "El cuentista de la
divagación" (Reseña de
Cuentos de Efrén Hernández).
Tierra Nueva, II (Núm. 9-10,
mayo-agosto de 1941), 182-
183. (r)   1975

----. Prosas de Justo Sierra.
Tierra Nueva, I (Núm. 2,
marzo-abril de 1940), 121-122.
(r)   1976

Junco, Alfonso. "Lo nuestro."
Antena, Núm. 5 (noviembre
de 1924), 7-8. (a-e)   1977

----. "Locura," "En tus
llagas escóndeme." México
Moderno, I (Núm. 1, agosto
de 1920), 59. (p)   1978

Kafka, Franz. "Reproche a
mi educación" (Trad. Jan
Jahn). Prometeus, I (Núm.
2, abril de 1949), 79-85.
(a-e)   (1907)

Kahlo, Frida. "Luther
Burbank." El Hijo Pródigo,
XII (Núm. 38, mayo de
1946), 70. (il)   1979

----. "New York," "Mis
abuelos, mis padres y yo,"
"Lo que me dio el agua,"
"Habitantes de México,"
"Recuerdo de mi herida
abierta," "Mi nana y yo,"
"Recuerdo," "Diego en mi
pensamiento." El Hijo
Pródigo, XII (Núm. 38, mayo
de 1946), entre 96 y 97. (il)
1980

Kandinsky, Vasili. "Ambigüedad."
Estaciones, I (Núm. 3, otoño
de 1956), entre 454 y 455.
(il)   1981

Keats, John. "La Belle Dame
Sans Merci" (Trad. Manuel
Romero de Terreros).

126

México Moderno, II (Núm. 4, junio de 1923), 248-249. (p)   1982

----. "Oda al otoño" (Trad. Luis Cernuda). Romance, I (Núm. 10, 15 de junio de 1940), 11. (p)   (913)

Kegel, Luis Augusto. "Ramón López Velarde." México Moderno, II (Núm. 11-12, noviembre-diciembre de 1921), 300-302. (p)   1983

Kipling, Rudyard. "Como el rinoceronte consiguió su piel." Romance, I (Núm. 10, 15 de junio de 1940), 17. (f)   1984

----. "Dray wara yow dee" (Trad. Alfonso Ortiz). México Moderno, II (Núm. 1, agosto de 1922), 11-19. (f)   1985

----. "Mandaley" (Trad. Rafael Lozano). La Falange, Núm. 4 (1 de julio de 1923), 208-209. (p)   1986

Kitagawa, Tamiji. Autoretrato," "Dibujo," "Mujeres en el baño," "Paisaje," "Dibujo." Contemporáneos, VI (Núm. 21, febrero de 1930), 144-148. (il)   1987

----. "Obrero leyendo," "Juanita," "Vieja indígena," "Flores," "Capilla de San Pedro, en Tlalpan," "Retrato de un joven," "Muchacha endomingada." Forma, II (Núm. 7, 1928), 1-5. (il)   1988

Kononov, A. "Cuentos sobre Chapaiev." Romance, II (Núm. 23, 22 de abril de 1941), 6, 14. (f)   1989

Krauss, Werner. "Un moderno dramaturgo alemán: Georg Kaiser. México Moderno, II (Núm. 4, junio de 1923), 200-204. (a-e)   1990

Kreymborg, Alfred. "Empire." Sagitario, Núm. 10 (1 de marzo de 1927), 4. (p) 1991

----. "El viejo manuscrito" (Trad. Antonio Dodero). La Falange, Núm. 7 (1 de octubre de 1923), 381. (p)   (1177)

Krimov, Yuri. "El petrolero Derbent." Ruta, Núm. 7 (diciembre de 1938), 39-43. (f)   1992

Kuniyoshi, Y. "Las bailarinas." Contemporáneos, II (Núm. 7, diciembre de 1928), 333. (il)   1993

L. R., R. La ruta de Sor Juana de Ermilo Abreu Gómez. Ruta, Núm. 3 (agosto de 1938), 58. (r)   1994

Laborde, Hernán. "Guijarros." Antena, Núm. 4 (octubre de 1924), 7. (a-e)   1995

Lacomba, Juan. "Ciudad." Ulises, Núm. 5 (diciembre de 1927), 11-12. (p)   1996

Lacretelle, Jacques de. "Algo más sobre la poesía pura." Ulises, Núm. 5 (diciembre de 1927), 17-19. (a-e) 1997

Ladrón de Guevara, José. "El congreso de Tucumán." Sagitario, Núm. 1 (15 de julio de 1926), 16. (a-e)   1998

Lafarga, Gastón. "Gerardo Gallegos:El hombre y su obra." Ruta, Núm. 10 (marzo de 1939), 5-18. (a-e) 1999

----. "Mariano Azuela, entrevisto en una novela." Ruta, Núm. 3 (agosto de 1938), 49-51. (a-e) 2000

Lago, Roberto. Chauveau, Leopold, "La guerra con Ventripond" (Trad. Roberto Lago). Romance, I (Núm. 14, 15 de agosto de 1940), 16, 23. (tr) (1040)

Lal Gupta, Heramba. "Guatama Buddha." La Falange, Núm. 2 (1 de enero de 1923), 71-73. (a-e) 2001

Lamarche, Angel Rafael. "Defendamos la literatura." Estaciones, V (Núm. 17, primavera de 1960), 63-67. (a-e) 2002

Landsberg, Pablo Luis. "Piedras blancas." Taller, II (Núm. 8-9, enero-febrero de 1940), 5-11. (f) 2003

Lao-Tze. "Fragmentos del Tao-te-king" (Trad. Daisy Brody y Antonio Sánchez Barbudo). El Hijo Pródigo, XI (Núm. 35, febrero de 1946), 97-100. (a-e) (714)

Lara Isaacs, Alfredo de. "¿Quién? ¡Usted!." Estaciones, IV (Núm. 16, invierno de 1959), 412-415. (f) 2004

Larbaud, Valéry. "Ese vicio impune, la lectura..." (Trad. José Luis Martínez). El Hijo Pródigo, VI (Núm. 20, noviembre de 1944), 101-109. (a-e) 2005

----. "Prólogo a Los de abajo." (Trad. Bernardo Ortiz de Montellano), Contemporáneos, VI (Núm. 21, febrero de 1930), 127-143. (a-e) 2006

Larrea, Juan? Humanismo burgués y humanismo proletario de Aníbal Ponce. Taller, I (Núm. 1, diciembre de 1938), 63-64. (r) 2007

----. "Poesía a vista de pájaro" (Reseña de Piedra y cielo dirigido por Jorge Rojas y El Ciervo herido de Manuel Altolaguirre). Taller, II (Núm. 10, marzo-abril de 1940), 54-57. (r) 2008

Lasso de la Vega, R. Rimbaud, Jean-Arthur. "Después del diluvio" (Trad. R. Lasso de la Vega). Sagitario, Núm. 4 (1 de septiembre de 1926), 6. (tr) 2009

Lawrence, David Herbert. "De Las mañanas de México" (Trad. Antonio Castro Leal). Romance, I (Núm. 16, 15 de septiembre de 1940), 3, 15. (a-e) (890)

----. "Mañanas de México: Día de mercado" (Trad. Octavio G. Barreda). Contemporáneos, IX (Núm. 34, marzo de 1931), 230-243. (a-e) (596)

Lax, Robert. "El circo" (Trad. Ernesto Cardenal). Estaciones, V (Núm. 19, otoño de 1960), 31-40. (p) (782)

Lazo, Agustín. "Antonio." Sagitario, Núm. 10 (1 de

marzo de 1927), 16. (il)
2010

----. "Arte de nuestro
tiempo." Romance, II
(Núm. 21, 15 de febrero de
1941), 12. (a-e)   2011

----. "La capilla de los
españoles." El Hijo Pródigo,
XII (Núm. 37, abril de 1946),
16-17. (a-e)   2012

----. "Cinco acuarelas y un
óleo." Contemporáneos, I
(Núm. 2, julio de 1928), 123-
128. (il)   2013

----. "Las criadas." Ulises,
Núm. 1 (mayo de 1927), 2.
(il)   2014

----. "4 dibujos" Contem-
poráneos, VII (Núm. 23, abril
de 1930), 4-7. (il)   2015

----. "Dibujos." Ulises,
Núm. 6 (febrero de 1928),
31-34. (il)   2016

----. "El drama." Prometeus,
I (Núm. 1, febrero de 1949),
15-18. (a-e)   2017

----. "Homenaje a López
Velarde." El Hijo Pródigo,
XII (Núm. 39, junio de 1946),
124. (il)   2018

----. "Máximo Pacheco."
Forma, I (Núm. 2, noviembre
de 1926), 3-6. (a-e)   2019

----. "Niños." Ulises, Núm.
1 (mayo de 1927), 21. (il)
2020

----. "Nuevos frescos de
Clemente Orozco." Forma,
I (Núm. 1, octubre de 1926),
20-23. (a-e)   2021

----. "La obra de Mariano

Silva Vandeira." El Hijo
Pródigo, X (Núm. 33,
diciembre de 1945), 144.
(a-e)   2022

----. "El paisaje de Clausell."
El Hijo Pródigo, IX (Núm.
28, julio de 1945), 32-33.
(a-e)   2023

----. "Proyecto de Diego
Rivera para un teatro en un
puerto del golfo de México."
Forma, I (Núm. 1, octubre
de 1926), 36-38. (a-e) 2024

----. "Retrato," "Apam,"
"Los amigos," y "Niño."
Forma, I (Núm. 1, octubre
de 1926), 2-4. (il)   2025

----. "Segundo imperio."
El Hijo Pródigo, VIII (Núm.
25, abril de 1945), 44-59;
(Núm. 26, mayo de 1945),
99-117. (dr)   2026

----. "Voz de la pintura
mexicana." El Hijo Pródigo,
I (Núm. 4, julio de 1943),
211-218. (a-e)   2027

----. Autos profanos de
Xavier Villaurrutia. El Hijo
Pródigo, I (Núm. 1, abril
de 1943), 59-60. (r)   2028

----. Maximiliano y Carlota
de Egon Caesar Conte Corti.
El Hijo Pródigo, IV (Núm.
13, abril de 1944), 61-62.
(r)   2029

----. El pacto de Cristina
de Conrado Nalé Roxlo. El
Hijo Pródigo, XII (Núm. 38,
mayo de 1946), 113-114. (r)
2030

----. Tratado de la pintura
de Leonardo de Vinci. El
Hijo Pródigo, VI (Núm. 19,

octubre de 1944), 60. (r)
2031

----. El yerro candente de
Xavier Villaurrutia. El Hijo
Pródigo, VIII (Núm. 26, mayo
de 1945), 118. (r)   2032

----. Chirico, Giorgio de.
"Pequeña antología (Trad.
César Moro y Agustín Lazo).
El Hijo Pródigo, VII (Núm.
22, enero de 1945), 33-41.
(tr)   (1053)

----. Duhamel, Georges.
"A la sombra de las estatuas"
(Trad. Agustín Lazo y Xavier
Villaurruta), El Hijo Pródigo,
XI (Núm. 36, marzo de 1946),
162-171; XII (Núm. 37, abril
de 1946), 34-43; (Núm. 38,
mayo de 1946), 97-103. (tr)
                        (1194)

----. Giraudoux, Jean.   "No
habrá guerra en Troya"
(Trad. Xavier Villaurrutia
y Agustín Lazo).   El Hijo
Pródigo, V (Núm. 17, agosto
de 1944), 107-120; (Núm. 18,
septiembre de 1944), 166-184.
(tr)   (1544)

----. Pirandello, Luigi.   "La
tinaja" (Trad. de Agustín
Lazo y Xavier Villaurrutia).
El Hijo Pródigo, XIII (Núm.
42, septiembre de 1946),
157-167. (tr)   2033

----. Rosso de San Secondo.
"Lazarina entre cuchillos"
(Trad. Gilberto Owen y
Agustín Lazo).   El Hijo
Pródigo, XIII (Núm. 40, julio
de 1946), 48-55; (Núm. 41,
agosto de 1946), 93-103. (tr)
                        2034

Leal, Fernando.   "El circo. "
Prometeus, I (Núm. 3, mayo
de 1949), 161-164. (a-e) 2035

----. "Danza de 'La media
luna', " "Indios vendedores, "
"Yaqui. -- Danza del
'Venadito', " "Timoteo. "
Forma, I (Núm. 3, 1927),
25-28. (il)   2036

----. "Madera. " Sagitario,
Núm. 14 (31 de mayo de
1927), 17. (il)   2037

----. "Madera, " "El modelo
colectivo. " Sagitario, Núm.
14, (31 de mayo de 1927),
3-4. (il)   2038

Leal, Luis.   "La presencia
del soneto. " Estaciones, III
(Núm. 10, verano de 1958),
120-140. (a-e)   2039

----. "Xavier Villaurrutia,
crítico. " Estaciones, IV
(Núm. 13, primavera de
1959), 3-14. (a-e)   2040

Leal Cortés, Alfredo.   "El
triunfo. " Estaciones, IV
(Núm. 14, verano de 1959),
211-224. (f)   2041

Leclerc, Jorge Luis. "Discurso
sobre el estilo" (Trad. Alí
Chumacero). Tierra Nueva,
III (Núm. 13-14, enero-abril
de 1942), 26-34. (a-e) 2042

Leduc, Renato.   "El corsario
beige. " Fábula, Núm. 4
(abril de 1934), 67-70. (f)
                        2043

----. "Romance del emigrante.
Contemporáneos, XI (Núm.
38-39, julio-agosto de 1931),
59-60. (p)   2044

Léger, Aléxis Saint-Léger.
(St. John Perse). "Anábasis"
(Traducción y prólogo de
Octavio G. Barreda).
Contemporáneos, IX (Núm. 32,

enero de 1931), 1-37. (p)
(597)

----. "Imágenes para Crusoe" (Trad. Jorge Zalamea). El Hijo Pródigo, XI (Núm. 35, febrero de 1946), 90-93. (p)
2045

----. "Nieves" (Trad. J. Enrique Moreno de Tagle). Estaciones, I (Núm. 3, otoño de 1956), 362-370. (p) 2046

Lehmann, Rosamond. "Observación de masa y filántropos en harapos." Ruta, Núm. 5 (octubre de 1938), 40-43. (a-e)   2047

Leiva, Raúl. "Diego." Estaciones, II (Núm. 8, invierno de 1957), 370. (p)
2048

----. "La poesía de Carlos Pellicer." Estaciones, II (Núm. 8, invierno de 1957), 378-395. (a-e)   2049

Lenormand, H. R. "A la sombra del mal" (Trad. de Xavier Villaurrutia). El Hijo Pródigo, XI (Núm. 34, enero de 1946), 47-56; (Núm. 35, febrero de 1946), 101-112. (dr)   2050

----. "Un año de teatro en París." Ruta, Núm. 2 (julio de 1938), 43-46. (a-e)
2051

Leñero, Vicente. "Virginidad." Estaciones, V (Núm. 19, otoño de 1960), 23-30. (f)
2052

Leñero Ruiz, Alfonso. "Décimas a Lucifer." Estaciones, II (Núm. 7, otoño de 1957), 314-316. (p)   2053

León, María Teresa. "Norah Lange: Música de su infancia." Romance, I (Núm. 10, 15 de junio de 1940), 6. (a-e)   2054

León Felipe Camino y Galicia. "España." Contemporáneos, VII (Núm. 26-27, julio-agosto de 1930), 36-38. (p)   2055

----. "El gran responsable." Taller, II (Núm. 11, julio-agosto de 1940), 5-26. (p)
2056

----. "Una página sobre el film Vía Crucis, Las uvas del rencor" (Opiniones de Xavier Villaurrutia, León Felipe, Ramón Gaya, Alberto Quintero Alvarez, Octavio G. Barreda y Carlos Velo). Romance, I (Núm. 9, 1 de junio de 1940), 11. (a-e)
(585)

----. "Poesía y dialéctica." Ruta, Núm. 7 (diciembre de 1938), 29-32. (p)   2057

----. "La prueba," "Comenzaremos con la muerte," "Que venga el poeta." Tierra Nueva, II (Núm. 9-10, mayo-agosto de 1941), 99-107. (p)
2058

----. "Respuesta a la encuesta de Romance." Romance, I (Núm. 4, 15 de marzo de 1940), 2. (a-e)
2059

----. "Sobre la tragedia Niebla (Winterset)." Romance, I (Núm. 10, 15 de junio de 1940), 3, 17. (a-e)   2060

----. "Sotillo." Antena, Núm. 2 (agosto de 1924), 4. (p)   2061

----. "Walt Whitman (Habla el prólogo)." Romance, I (Núm. 15, 1 de septiembre de 1940), 3, 8. (p) 2062

----. Eliot, Thomas Stearns. "Los hombres huecos" (Trad. León Felipe). Contemporáneos, IX (Núm. 33, febrero de 1931), 132-136. (tr) (1220)

----. Eliot, Thomas Stearns. "Los hombres huecos" (Trad. León Felipe). Taller, II (Núm. 10, marzo-abril de 1940), 85-88. (tr) (1221)

----. Frank, Waldo. "Chuquicamata." (Trad. León Felipe). Contemporáneos, XI (Núm. 38-39, julio-agosto de 1931), 31-51. (tr) (1384)

Leopardi, Jacobo. "La retama (La ginestra)" (con traducción de Miguel de Unamuno). Taller, II (Núm. 11, julio-agosto de 1940), 83-103. (p) 2063

Lessing, Gotthold Ephraim. "Cartas de Lessing." (Trad. de Angela Selke y Antonio Sánchez Barbudo). El Hijo Pródigo, X (Núm. 33, diciembre de 1945), 161-170. (a-e) 2064

Leyden, Lucas van. "El hijo pródigo." El Hijo Pródigo, V (Núm. 18, septiembre de 1944), entre 134 y 135. (il) 2065

Li Tai-Po. "La isla de los loros." México Moderno, II (Núm. 4, junio de 1923), 249. (p) 2066

Lichtveld, Lou. "Bilingüismo en la enseñanza de indígenas." Ruta, Núm. 1 (junio de 1938), 53-55. (a-e) 2067

----. "El dictador loco." Ruta, Núm. 3 (agosto de 1938), 44-48. (a-e) 2068

Lindo, Hugo. "La estirpe." Estaciones, III (Núm. 12, invierno de 1958), 480-488. (f) 2069

----. "Eutanasia." Estaciones, V (Núm. 17, primavera de 1960), 68-77. (f) 2070

Lira, Miguel N. "Corrido de la niña sin novio." Fábula, Núm. 1 (enero de 1934), 13-14. (p) 2071

----. "Cuando grababa en los pupitres..." Antena, Núm. 1 (julio de 1924), 8. (p) 2072

----. "El Chipujo." Estaciones, V (Núm. 18, verano de 1960), 84-89. (f) 2073

----. "La navaja y la niebla." Estaciones, I (Núm. 1, primavera de 1956), 27-33. (f) 2074

----. Poema de Eduardo Villaseñor. Fábula, Núm. 8 (agosto de 1934), 159. (r) 2075

----. Seamen rhymes de Salvador Novo. Fábula, Núm. 2 (febrero de 1934), 40. (r) 2076

----. Senderillos a ras de Genaro Estrada. Fábula, Núm. 4 (abril de 1934), 79. (r) 2077

----. Las tablas de la conquista de México en las colecciones de Madrid de Genero Estrada. Fábula,

132

Núm. 1 (enero de 1934),
20. (r)   2078

Lira Espejo, Eduardo. "Clásicos
musicales venezolanos de la
colonia. " Romance, I (Núm.
16, 15 de septiembre de
1940), 10. (a-e)   2079

Lizardi Ramos, César. Códice
de Yanhuitlán publicado por
la Academia de Bellas Artes
de Puebla. Romance, I
(Núm. 19, 18 de diciembre
de 1940), 19. (r)   2080

Loera y Chávez, Agustín. "La
joven literatura mexicana. "
México Moderno, II (Núm. 10,
junio de 1921), 226-227. (a-e)
                           2081

----. "La joven literatura
mexicana: Bernardo Ortiz
de Montellano. " México
Moderno, II (Núm. 8, marzo
de 1921), 113-115. (a-e)
                           2082

----. "La joven literatura
mexicana: Carlos Pellicer. "
México Moderno, I (Núm. 5,
diciembre de 1920), 303-311.
(a-e)   2083

----. "La joven literatura
mexicana: Francisco
Monterde García Icazbalceta. "
México Moderno, I (Núm. 4,
noviembre de 1920), 245-250.
(a-e)   2084

----. "La joven literatura
mexicana: Jaime Torres
Bodet, Enrique González
Rojo, Alfonso Junco. "
México Moderno, I (Núm. 1,
agosto de 1920), 53-60. (a-e)
                           2085

----. "La joven literatura
mexicana: José Gorostiza
Alcalá. " México Moderno,

I (Núm. 2, septiembre de
1920), 114-116. (a-e)   2086

----. "La joven literatura
mexicana: Luciano Joublanc
Rivas. " México Moderno, I
(Núm. 3, octubre de 1920),
179-183. (a-e)   2087

----. "La joven literatura
mexicana: Pedro Requena
Legarreta. " México Moderno,
II (Núm. 7, febrero de 1921),
48-52. (a-e)   2088

----. Itinerario contempla-
tivo de Francisco Monterde
y García Izcabalceta. México
Moderno, II (Núm. 4, junio
de 1923), 258. (r)   2089

----. Rumores de mi huerto
y Rincones Románticos de
María Enriqueta Camarillo
de Pereyra. México Moderno,
II (Núm. 4, junio de 1923),
257. (r)   2090

----. Tacámbaro de José
Rubén Romero. México
Moderno, II (Núm. 4, junio
de 1923), 257-258. (r) 2091

Lombardo Toledano, Vicente.
"Definiciones sobre derecho
público. " México Moderno,
II (Núm. 2, septiembre de
1922), 109-111. (a-e)   2092

----. "El eterno problema
del bien. " México Moderno,
I (Núm. 4, noviembre de
1920), 205-208. (a-e)   2093

López, José Ramón. "El
mérito. " La Falange, Núm.
6 (1 de septiembre de 1923),
351-352. (p)   2094

López, Lázaro. "Talla en
madera. " Forma, I (Núm. 2,
noviembre de 1926), 12. (il)
                           2095

López, Rafael. "Ramón López Velarde." México Moderno, II (Núm. 11-12, noviembre-diciembre de 1921), 292-294. (a-e) 2096

López Malo, Rafael. "Elegía a la muerte de Alicia." Fábula, Núm. 5 (mayo de 1934), 98-99. (p) 2097

López Mateos, Esperanza. "Galanteo constructivo." Ruta, Núm. 7 (diciembre de 1938), 51-54. (a-e) 2098

López Páez, Jorge. "Mar a la vista." Estaciones, II (Núm. 5, primavera de 1957), 58-65. (f) 2099

----. "La Señora Solleiro." Estaciones, III (Núm. 10, verano de 1958), 148-155. (f) 2100

López Portillo y Rojas, José. "El poder de las letras." México Moderno, II (Núm. 10, junio de 1921), 204-207. (a-e) 2101

López Trujillo, Clemente. "Antepenúltimo canto del deseo." Tierra Nueva, II (Núm. 9-10, mayo-agosto de 1941), 138-143. (p) 2102

----. "Este afán," "De pueblo en pueblo." Antena, Núm. 1 (julio de 1924), 7-8. (p) 2103

----. "Nocturnos del deshabitado." El Hijo Pródigo, VII (Núm. 23, febrero de 1945), 75-76. (p) 2104

----. "Soledades, muertes y niños." Ruta, Núm. 11 (abril de 1939), 18-23. (p) 2105

----. Páramo de sueños de Alí Chumacero. El Hijo Pródigo, VII (Núm. 23, febrero de 1945), 121-122. (r) 2106

----. El ventrílocuo de Antonio Magaña Esquivel. El Hijo Pródigo, VI (Núm. 21, diciembre de 1944), 184. (r) 2107

López Velarde, Ramón. "El adiós." El Hijo Pródigo, X (Núm. 31, octubre de 1945), 60. (p) 2108

----. "El ancla." México Moderno, II (Núm. 11-12, noviembre-diciembre de 1921), 320. (p) 2109

----. "La conquista," "Anatole France." México Moderno, I (Núm. 2, septiembre de 1920), 85-87. (a-e) 2110

----. "En las tinieblas húmedas...," "Tus dientes," "El mendigo," "Hormigas," "Idolatría." El Hijo Pródigo, XII (Núm. 39, junio de 1946), 138-142. (p) 2111

----. "Lo soez," "La cigüeña." México Moderno, II (Núm. 10, junio de 1921), 185-186. (p) 2112

----. "Mi pecado." La Falange, Núm. 1 (1 de diciembre de 1922), 5. (a-e) 2113

----. "Obra maestra," "Mi pecado," "Novedad de la patria," "Fresnos y álamos," "La flor punitiva," "Lo soez," "José de Arimatea." El Hijo Pródigo, XIII (Núm. 39, junio de 1946), 156-160. (a-e) 2114

----. "Treinta y tres." México Moderno, II (Núm. 11-12, noviembre-diciembre de 1921), 249-250. (p) 2115

----. "Vacaciones," "Gaviota," México Moderno, I (Núm. 4, noviembre de 1920), 220-222. (p) 2116

----. Campo argentino y Versos de Negrita de Fernández Moreno. México Moderno, II (Núm. 7, febrero de 1921), 71. (r) 2117

----. El libro del trópico de Arturo Ambrogi. México Moderno, II (Núm. 7, febrero de 1921), 72. (r) 2118

----. El plano oblicuo de Alfonso Reyes. México Moderno, I (Núm. 5, diciembre de 1920), 323. (r) 2119

López y Fuentes, Gregorio. "El pozo agotado." Ruta, Núm. 1 (junio de 1938), 28-29. (f) 2120

Loureda, Ignacio. "Una carta." Sagitario, Núm. 2 (1 de agosto de 1926), 17. (a-e) 2121

Lowell, Amy. "Opalo" (Trad. Rafael Lozano). La Falange, Núm. 7 (1 de octubre de 1923), 384. (p) 2122

Lozano, F. "Suez, arteria principal del planeta." Romance, I (Núm. 16, 15 de septiembre de 1940), 6. (a-e) 2123

Lozano, Rafael. "Una canción y una ronda." México Moderno, II (Núm. 2, septiembre de 1922), 75-77. (p) 2124

----. "Dos grandes poetas persas: Hafiz y Omar-Al-Khayyan." La Falange, Núm. 3 (1 de febrero de 1923), 150. (a-e) 2125

----. "La literatura francesa de hoy." La Falange, Núm. 1 (1 de diciembre de 1922), 47-50. (a-e) 2126

----. "Los nuevos poetas de los Estados Unidos." La Falange, Núm. 7 (1 de octubre de 1923), 375-380. (a-e) 2127

----. "Oriental." La Falange, Núm. 5 (1 de agosto de 1923), 293-295. (p) 2128

----. El estúpido siglo XIX de Leon Daudet. La Falange, Núm. 1 (1 de diciembre de 1922), 50-51. (r) 2129

----. Les Infants des Hommes de Nicolas Beauduin. La Falange, Núm. 2 (1 de enero de 1923), 122-123. (r) 2130

----. La Livre des Baisers de Jean Second. La Falange, Núm. 1 (1 de diciembre de 1922), 52-54. (r) 2131

----. Anónimo. "Chabarcha y el diablillo" (Trad. Rafael Lozano). La Falange, Núm. 4 (1 de julio de 1923), 228-232. (tr) (230)

----. Fort, Paul. "Baladas francesas" (Trad. Rafael Lozano). La Falange, Núm. 1 (1 de diciembre de 1922), 56-58. (tr) (1379)

----. Hafiz. "Rubayas" (Trad. Rafael Lozano). La Falange, Núm. 3 (1 de febrero de 1923), 150-151. (tr) (1748)

----. Kipling, Rudyard.
"Mandaley" (Trad. Rafael
Lozano). La Falange, Núm.
4 (1 de julio de 1923), 208-
209. (tr)   (1986)

----. Lowell, Amy. "Opalo"
(Trad. Rafael Lozano). La
Falange, Núm. 7 (1 de
octubre de 1923), 384. (tr)
                         (2122)

----. Moreas, Jean
"Estancias" (Trad. Rafael
Lozano). La Falange, Núm.
2 (1 de enero de 1923), 125-
126. (tr)   2132

----. Omar-Al-Kahayyam.
"Rubayas" (Trad. Rafael
Lozano). La Falange, Núm.
3 (1 de febrero de 1923),
151-152. (tr)   2133

----. Sandburg, Carl. "Las
tumbas frías" (Trad. Rafael
Lozano). La Falange, Núm.
7 (1 de octubre de 1923),
385. (tr)   2134

----. Teasdale, Sara. "La
linterna" (Trad. Rafael
Lozano). La Falange, Núm.
7 (1 de octubre de 1923), 385.
(tr)   2135

----. Verlaine, Paul.
"Evocación. " "Spleen, "
"Mujer y gata, " "Streets, "
"Tedio" (Trad. Rafael
Lozano). La Falange, Núm.
3 (1 de febrero de 1923),
189-190. (tr)   2136

Lucrecio Caro, Tito. "De la
naturaleza" (Trad. Agustín
Millares Carlo). El Hijo
Pródigo, IV (Núm. 15, junio
de 1944), 173-181. (p) 2137

Lugones, Leopoldo. "El oro
del otoño. " México Moderno,

II (Núm. 8, marzo de 1921),
126. (p)   2138

Luis, Leopoldo de. "Carta a
Germán Pardo García. "
Estaciones, IV (Núm. 14,
verano de 1959), 159-161.
(p)   2139

----. "Nosotros. " Estaciones,
IV (Núm. 15, otoño de 1959),
268-270. (p)   2140

----. "La poesía de Vicente
Aleixandre: una ascensión
hacia la luz. " Estaciones,
II (Núm. 6, verano de 1957),
157-162. (a-e)   2141

Luisi, Luisa. "Sor Juana
Inés de la Cruz. " Contemporáneos, III (Núm. 9,
febrero de 1929), 130-160.
(a-e)   2142

Lulio, Raimundo. "Proverbios. "
El Hijo Pródigo, I (Núm. 2,
mayo de 1943), 88. (a-e)
                         2143

Luna, Alberto. "El ajuscó. "
Sagitario, Núm. 10 (1 de
marzo de 1927), 11. (il)
                         2144

Luquín, Carlos. "Un juego
poemático de Alfonso Reyes. "
Estaciones, V (Núm. 18,
verano de 1960), 125-126.
(a-e)   2145

Luquín, Eduardo. 'De la
altiplanicie. " Contemporáneos,
VI (Núm. 20, enero de 1930),
81-87. (a-e)   2146

----. "San Angel, " "Xochimilco. " La Falange, Núm. 4
(1 de julio de 1923), 246-247.
(a-e)   2147

----. "El venado." La Falange, Núm. 2 (1 de enero de 1923), 113-115. (f) 2148

----. Al compás de la vida de Luciano Joublanc Rivas. La Falange, Núm. 4 (1 de julio de 1923), 248. (r) 2149

----. Werfel, Franz. "El alma humana y el realismo" (Trad. Eduardo Luquín). Contemporáneos, XI (Núm. 38-39, julio-agosto de 1931), 87-104. (tr) 2150

Lyeskov, Nicolai. "El centinela" (Trad. Marco Aurelio Galindo). Prometeus, I (Núm. 1, febrero de 1949), 33-51. (f) (1410)

Llates, R. "Algunas reflexiones sobre Beethoven" (Trad. Humberto Rivas). Sagitario, Núm. 11 (15 de marzo de 1927), 15. (a-e) 2151

Lleixá, Vicente. "Su quinta dimensión." Estaciones, III (Núm. 10, verano de 1958), 181-186. (f) 2152

M., H. "El profesor Langevin: Su aportación a la ciencia contemporánea." Romance, I (Núm. 15, 1 de septiembre de 1940), 6. (a-e) 2153

M., L. "El avión sin piloto y el problema del aterrizaje sin visibilidad." Romance, I (Núm. 14, 15 de agosto de 1940), 4. (a-e) 2154

M., R. de. "Mm. de Stael: Su estancia en Viena y Rusia." Romance, I (Núm. 16, 16 de septiembre de 1940), 8. (a-e) 2155

M. S., R. "Las palmas." La Falange, Núm. 5 (1 de agosto de 1923), 296-297. (a-e) 2156

Machado, Antonio. "El camino." Taller, II (Núm. 10, marzo-abril de 1940), 39-40. (p) 2157

Machado, José. "Carta de José Machado en la que habla del poeta." Romance, I (Núm. 3, 1 de marzo de 1940), 17. (a-e) 2158

Machado, Manuel. "A una novicia." México Moderno, II (Núm. 10, junio de 1921), 202-203. (p) 2159

Machado de Assis, Joaquim Maria. "El tiempo," "La ópera" (Trad. Julio Torri). La Falange, Núm. 6 (1 de septiembre de 1923), 321-324. (f) 2160

Madero, Sergio René. "Meditación." Estaciones, II (Núm. 8, invierno de 1957), 472-475. (p) 2161

Magaña, Sergio. "Diálogo de los animales." Estaciones, III (Núm. 12, invierno de 1958), 473-476. (dr) 2162

Magaña Esquivel, Antonio. "Herejía de la novela." Romance, I (Núm. 15, 1 de septiembre de 1940), 8. (a-e) 2163

----. "Manuel Eduardo de Gorostiza y su obra dramática." Estaciones, I (Núm. 1, primavera de 1956), 85-91. (a-e) 2164

----. "La puerta de Atlampa." El Hijo Pródigo, I (Núm. 5,

137

agosto de 1943), 301-304. (f)
2165

----. Cornucopia de México
de José Moreno Villa.
Taller, II (Núm. 11, julio-
agosto de 1940), 80-81. (r)
2166

----. Don Justo de José
Gómez Robleda. El Hijo
Pródigo, XIII (Núm. 41,
agosto de 1946), 118. (r)
2167

----. Los santos inocentes
de Rafael Solana. El Hijo
Pródigo, VII (Núm. 23,
febrero de 1945), 122. (r)
2168

----. Seis novelas iguales
entre sí de Octavio N.
Bustamante. El Hijo Pródigo,
VII (Núm. 22, enero de
1945), 58. (r)   2169

----. La vida que te di de
Luigi Pirandello. Romance,
I (Núm. 9, 1 de junio de
1940), 18. (r)   2170

Magdaleno, Vicente. "Soledad,"
"Elegía breve." Fábula,
Núm. 7 (julio de 1934), 135-
136. (p)   2171

Maiakowski, Vladimiro. "Mi
descubrimiento de América."
Ruta, Núm. 3 (agosto de
1938), 18-21. (a-e)   2172

Maillefert, Alfredo. "Alfonso
Reyes." Fábula, Núm. 9
(septiembre de 1934), 175-
176. (a-e)   2173

----. "Francis Jammes."
Fábula, Núm. 1 (enero de
1934), 6-10. (a-e)   2174

Malaquais, Jean. "De la
palabra y del testimonio."

El Hijo Pródigo, VIII (Núm.
25, abril de 1945), 25-29.
(a-e)   2175

----. "Diálogo al revés." El
Hijo Pródigo, I (Núm. 3,
junio de 1943), 168-170. (a-e)
2176

----. "Día uno." Prometeus,
I (Núm. 2, abril de 1949),
127-128. (a-e)   2177

----. "Golpes de caña" (Trad.
Chita de la Calle). El Hijo
Pródigo, IV (Núm. 13, abril
de 1944), 44-57; (Núm. 14,
mayo de 1944), 93-109. (f)
(755)

Mallea, Eduardo A. "Un
libro de Borges." Sagitario,
Núm. 6 (1 de noviembre de
1926), 12-13. (a-e)   2178

Mallo, Maruja. "La popular y
lo plástico de mi obra."
Romance, I (Núm. 11, 1 de
julio de 1940), 13. (a-e)
2179

Man, Ray. "Rayografías."
Contemporáneos, IV (Núm. 13,
junio de 1929), 257-261. (il)
2180

Mancisidor, José. "Los cuentos
de abuelita." Romance, I
(Núm. 2, 15 de febrero de
1940), 5. (f)   2181

----. "Emil Ludwig no es un
titán." Ruta, 8 (enero de
1939), 46-47. (a-e)   2182

----. "En la rosa de los
vientos." Romance, I (Núm.
18, 15 de noviembre de
1940), 8, 14. (f)   2183

----. "En la rosa de los
vientos." Ruta, Núm. 12

(mayo de 1939), 27-38. (f)
2184

----. "El hombre" en "Vida
y muerte de Silvestre
Revueltas." Romance, I
(Núm. 17, 22 de octubre de
1940), 5. (a-e)   2185

----. "Perfil de Silvestre
Revueltas." Ruta, Núm. 2
(julio de 1938), 27-33. (a-e)
2186

----. "Poesía y desesperación."
Ruta, 5 (octubre de 1938), 44-
46. (a-e)   2187

----. "Zolá el hombre."
Romance, I (Núm. 6, 15 de
abril de 1940), 9. (a-e)
2188

----. Contrabando de Enrique
Serpa. Ruta, Núm. 6
(noviembre de 1938), 59-61.
(r)   2189

----. Cuauntémoc. Vida y
muerte de una cultura de
Héctor Pérez Martínez. El
Hijo Pródigo, VII (Núm. 22,
enero de 1945), 57-58. (r)
2190

----. Morelos de Francisco
L. Urquizo. El Hijo Pródigo,
XI (Núm. 34, enero de 1946),
57-58. (r)   2191

----. El teatro en la U. R. S. S.
de Alfredo Gómez de la Vega.
Ruta, Núm. 2 (julio de 1938),
60-61. (r)   2192

----. La vida inútil de Pito
Pérez de José Rubén Romero.
Ruta, Núm. 3 (agosto de
1938), 58-60. (r)   2193

Mantel. "Tepozotlán,"
"Ixtacíhuatl," "Puebla."
Sagitario, Núm. 4 (1 de

septiembre de 1926), 9-11.
(il)   2194

Mañach, Jorge. "Genoveva in
fraganti." Contemporáneos,
I (Núm. 2, julio de 1928),
129-148. (f)   2195

Mar. María del. "Atmósfera
sellada." Estaciones, III
(Núm. 12, invierno de 1958),
387-388. (p)   2196

----. "Elipsis de angustia."
Estaciones, II (Núm. 7, otoño
de 1957), 287-289. (p) 2197

Marcello-Fabri. Rivas,
Humberto. "Paysages" (Trad.
Marcello-Fabri). Sagitario,
Núm. 11 (15 de marzo de
1927), 16. (tr)   2198

Marcos, Volga. "Fanfán
Trigoverde." Estaciones, II
(Núm. 6, verano de 1957),
186-191. (f)   2199

María y Campos, Armando de.
"Los bailes de carnaval en
México durante el siglo
pasado." Romance, II (Núm.
22, 15 de marzo de 1941), 11.
(a-e)   2200

----. "Capítulos inéditos del
teatro en México." Romance,
I (Núm. 18, 15 de noviembre
de 1940), 11, 15. (a-e) 2201

----. "Cátedra de morir:
Fusilamientos de fines del
siglo XIX según las hojas
volantes de Antonio Vanegas
Arroyo." Romance, I (Núm.
19, 18 de diciembre de 1940),
11. (a-e)   2202

----. "El crímen de la
profesa en el folklore nacional."
Romance, II (Núm. 24, 31 de
mayo de 1941), 11. (a-e)
2203

----. "En el teatro mexicano." El Hijo Pródigo, IV (Núm. 13, abril de 1944), 38-43. (a-e)   2204

----. "Laberinto y fracaso musical de Angela Peralta." Romance, I (Núm. 20, 15 de enero de 1941), 11. (a-e)   2205

----. "Orellana, Vanegas Arroyo, Posada: Creadores del mundo mexicano de los títeres." Romance, II (Núm. 21, 15 de febrero de 1941), 11. (a-e)   2206

----. "El teatro en México." Romance, II (Núm. 23, 22 de abril de 1941), 11, 14. (a-e)   2207

Marinello, Juan. "Un artículo sobre Romance." Romance, I (Núm. 9, 1 de junio de 1940), 2. (a-e)   2208

----. "Del nuevo mar." Contemporáneos, IV (Núm. 14, julio de 1929), 284-288. (p)   2209

----. "Primer año de Antonio Machado." Romance, I (Núm. 7, 1 de mayo de 1940), 1-2. (a-e)   2210

----. "Verbo y alusión." Contemporáneos, X (Núm. 35, abril de 1931), 17-31. (a-e)   2211

Mariscal Federico E. "La belleza de nuestros muros." México Moderno, I (Núm. 3, octubre de 1920), 147-151. (a-e)   2212

Márquez, Manuel. "Como vemos y por qué vemos mal o no vemos." Romance, I (Núm. 6, 15 de abril de 1940), 4, 11. (a-e)   2213

Martí, José. "Heredia." Romance, I (Núm. 1, 1 de febrero de 1940), 9. (a-e)   2214

----. "El ideario americano de Martí." Romance, I (Núm. 8, 15 de mayo de 1940), 9. (a-e)   2215

Martín, Luis. "Oleo." Sagitario, Núm. 14 (31 de mayo de 1927), 15. (il) 2216

Martínez, José Luis. "Aldous Huxley." Tierra Nueva, II (Núm. 9-10, mayo-agosto de 1941), 160-168; (Núm. 11-12, septiembre-diciembre de 1941), 196-208; III (Núm. 13-14, enero-abril de 1942), 51-59. (a-e)   2217

----. "Algunos problemas de la historia literaria." El Hijo Pródigo, XI (Núm. 35, febrero de 1946), 71-82. (a-e)   2218

----. "Con Xavier Villaurrutia." Tierra Nueva, I (Núm. 2, marzo-abril de 1940), 74-81. (a-e)   2219

----. "Cuatro pequeñas ausencias." Tierra Nueva, I (Núm. 1, enero-febrero de 1940), 45-46. (p)   2220

----. "Elegía por Melibea y otros poemas" (Suplemento poético al núm. 3). Tierra Nueva, I (Núm. 3, mayo-junio de 1940). (p)   2221

----. "Examen de López Velarde." El Hijo Pródigo, XII (Núm. 39, junio de 1946), 127-137. (a-e)   2222

----. "Julio Torri." Taller, II (Núm. 12, enero-febrero de 1941), 66-68. (a-e) 2223

----. "Las litografías de Julio Prieto." Tierra Nueva, III (Núm. 13-14, enero-abril de 1942), 24-25. (a-e) 2224

----. "Memoria," "Dos poemas a tu olvido." Tierra Nueva, I (Núm. 4-5, julio-octubre de 1940), 205-207. (p) 2225

----. "La muerte en la poesía española del siglo XV." Tierra Nueva, I (Núm. 2, marzo-abril de 1940), 98-109. (a-e) 2226

----. "Nota preliminar." Tierra Nueva, I (Núm. 4-5, julio-octubre de 1940), 221-223. (a-e) 2227

----. "Paul Valéry." Tierra Nueva, I (Núm. 4-5, julio-octubre de 1940), 262-264. (a-e) 2228

----. "Pedro Henríquez Ureña, maestro de México." El Hijo Pródigo, XIII (Núm. 40, julio de 1946), 24-26. (a-e) 2229

----. "La poesía de Luis Cernuda." Tierra Nueva, II (Núm. 7-8, enero-abril de 1941), 80-84. (a-e) 2230

----. Vasconcelos, José; González Martínez, Enrique; Gaos, José; Gallegos, José M.; Paz, Octavio; García-Bacca, David; Jiménez Rueda, Julio; Nicol, Eduardo; Bergamín, José. "Poesía, mística y filosofía: Debate en torno a San Juan de la Cruz." El Hijo Pródigo, I (Núm. 3, junio de 1943), 135-144. (a-e) (661)

----. "Rosa efímera" (Suplemento poético al núm. 7-8). Tierra Nueva, II (Núm. 7-8, enero-abril de 1941). (p) 2231

----. "El sentido cristiano de la muerte." Tierra Nueva, I (Núm. 6, noviembre-diciembre de 1940), 310-314. (a-e) 2232

----. "La técnica en literatura." El Hijo Pródigo, II (Núm. 8, noviembre de 1943), 71-79. (a-e) 2233

----. "Cuenca, poeta de transición" (Reseña de Agustín F. Cuenca. El prosista. El poeta de transición de Francisco Monterde). Tierra Nueva, III (Núm. 15, diciembre de 1942), 180-182. (r) 2234

----. "Laurel" (Reseña de Antología de la poesía moderna en lengua española con prólogo de Xavier Villaurrutia). Tierra Nueva, II (Núm. 11-12, septiembre-diciembre de 1941), 283-284. (r) 2235

----. Bajo el signo mortal... de Enrique González Martínez. El Hijo Pródigo, I (Núm. 1, abril de 1943), 61-62. (r) 2236

----. Concepto de la poesía de José Antonio Portuondo. El Hijo Pródigo, IX (Núm. 30, septiembre de 1945), 179-180. (r) 2237

----. "Conciencia de lo mexicano" (Reseña de Crónicas de la conquista con prólogo de Agustín Yáñez). Romance, I (Núm. 16, 15 de

septiembre de 1940), 18.
(r)   2238

----. "Gutiérrez Nájera,
casi maestro de la prosa"
(Reseña de Cuentos,
crónicas y ensayos de Manuel
Gutiérrez Nájera a cargo
de Alfredo Maillefert).
Tierra Nueva, I (Núm. 6,
noviembre-diciembre de 1940),
357-360. (r)   2239

----. El desterrado de
Enrique Díez Canedo. Tierra
Nueva, I (Núm. 2, marzo-
abril de 1940), 113-115. (r)
                                 2240

----. En torno a José
Hernández de Azorín. Tierra
Nueva, I (Núm. 1, enero-
febrero de 1940), 55-57. (r)
                                 2241

----. Galería de fantasmas.
Años y sombras del siglo
XIX de Enrique Fernández
Ledesma. Tierra Nueva, I
(Núm. 1, enero-febrero de
1940), 57. (r)   2242

----. Grandeza mexicana de
Bernardo de Balbuena con
prólogo de Francisco
Monterde. Tierra Nueva, II
(Núm. 9-10, mayo-agosto de
1941), 190-192. (r)   2243

----. "El teatro por dentro"
(Reseña de Imagen del teatro
de Antonio Magaña Esquivel).
Tierra Nueva, I (Núm. 4-5,
julio-octubre de 1940), 282-
283. (r)   2244

----. El jaiigey de las
ruinas de Sara García
Iglesias. El Hijo Pródigo, V
(Núm. 17, agosto de 1944),
121. (r)   2245

----. Mélange de Paul

Valéry. El Hijo Pródigo, II
(Núm. 9, diciembre de 1943),
221. (r)   2246

----. Muerte sin fin de José
Gorostiza. Tierra Nueva, I
(Núm. 1, enero-febrero de
1940), 54-55. (r)   2247

----. Nueva grandeza
mexicana de Salvador Novo.
El Hijo Pródigo, XII (Núm.
39, junio de 1946), 176. (r)
                                 2248

----. Paseos coloniales de
Manuel Toussaint. Tierra
Nueva, I (Núm. 2, marzo-
abril de 1940), 117-118. (r)
                                 2249

----. "Consciencia de lo
mexicano" (Reseña de El
pensador mexicano de Agustín
Yáñez). Tierra Nueva, I
(Núm. 4-5, julio-octubre de
1940), 268-270. (r)   2250

----. Le petit prince de
Antoine de Saint-Exupery. El
Hijo Pródigo, I (Núm. 6,
septiembre de 1943), 381-382.
(r)   2251

----. "Crítica literaria"
(Reseña de Plenitud de
España de Pedro Henríquez
Ureña). Tierra Nueva, I
(Núm. 4-5, julio-octubre de
1940), 275-277. (r)   2252

----. Poesías profanas de
Fray Manuel Navarrete.
Tierra Nueva I, (Núm. 1,
enero-febrero de 1940), 58-59.
(r)   2253

----. Por quien doblan las
campanas de Ernest
Hemmingway. Tierra Nueva,
III (Núm. 15, diciembre de
1942), 172-175. (r)   2254

142

----. "La prosa de Alfonso Reyes" (Reseña de Los siete sobre Deva de Alfonso Reyes). Tierra Nueva, III (Núm. 15, diciembre de 1942), 176-177. (r)   2255

----. Sociología de la novela de Roger Caillois. El Hijo Pródigo, I (Núm. 3, junio de 1943), 189-190. (r)   2256

----. "Estampa romántica" (Reseña de Teresa de Rosa Chacel). Tierra Nueva, III (Núm. 15, diciembre de 1942), 178-179. (r)   2257

----. Textos y pretextos de Xavier Villaurrutia. Tierra Nueva, I (Núm. 3, mayo-junio de 1940), 182-183. (r)   2258

----. "Grandeza y servidumbre de Marañón" (Reseña de Tiempo viejo y tiempo nuevo de Gregorio Marañón). Tierra Nueva, I (Núm. 6, noviembre-diciembre de 1940), 366-370. (r)   2259

----. Viaje a México de Paul Morand. Tierra Nueva, I (Núm. 2, marzo-abril de 1940), 116-117. (r)   2260

----. Vida en claro de José Moreno Villa. El Hijo Pródigo, VI (Núm. 21, diciembre de 1944), 184-185. (r)   2261

----. La vida que te di de Luigi Pirandello. Tierra Nueva, I (Núm. 3, mayo-junio de 1940), 187-189. (r)   2262

----. Caillois, Roger. "La aridez" (Trad. José Luis Martínez). El Hijo Pródigo,

I (Núm. 4, julio de 1943), 205-208. (tr)   (745)

----. Gourmont, Remy de. "Fragmentos sobre el estilo" (Trad. José Luis Martínez). El Hijo Pródigo, XII (Núm. 38, mayo de 1946), 104-111. (tr)   (1698)

----. Heidegger, Martín. "Hölderlin y la escencia de la poesía" (Trad. E. Prado Vertiz y José Luis Martínez). Tierra Nueva, III (Núm. 15, diciembre de 1942), 143-153. (tr)   (1752)

----. Huxley, Aldous. "Baudelaire." (Trad. José Luis Martínez). El Hijo Pródigo, VIII (Núm. 27, junio de 1945), 165-176. (tr)   (1871)

----. Larbaud, Valéry. "Ese vicio impune, la lectura..." (Trad. José Luis Martínez). El Hijo Pródigo, VI (Núm. 20, noviembre de 1944), 101-109. (tr)   (2005)

Martínez, Juventino. "Héroes del barrio." La Falange, Núm. 7 (1 de octubre de 1923), 398-399. (f)   2263

Martínez, Ricardo. "El astrónomo." El Hijo Pródigo, X (Núm. 31, octubre de 1945), entre 16 y 17. (il)   2264

Martínez Ortega, Judith. "Cristina." El Hijo Pródigo, VI (Núm. 21, diciembre de 1944), 156-160. (f)   2265

Martínez Peñaloza, Porfirio. El oficleido y otros cuentos de Rafael Solana. Estaciones, V (Núm. 17,

primavera de 1960), 114-115.
(r)   2266

----. El sol de octubre de
Rafael Solana. Estaciones,
IV (Núm. 14, verano de
1959), 250-251. (r)   2267

Martínez Pintao. "El Santo
Niño Jesús" y "La oración en
el huerto." Forma, I (Núm.
1, octubre de 1926), 30-31.
(il)   2268

Martínez Sotomayor, José. "El
mar, páginas de un diario de
viaje." El Hijo Pródigo, X
(Núm. 33, diciembre de
1945), 148-151. (a-e) 2269

----. "El puente." Estaciones, II (Núm. 6, verano de
1957), 143-154. (f)   2270

----. "La rueca de aire."
Contemporáneos, VI (Núm.
20, enero de 1930), 21-38.
(f)   2271

Martínez Ulloa, E. "Cultura y
política." Contemporáneos,
VI (Núm. 20, enero de
1930), 57-80. (a-e)   2272

Martínez Valadez, Manuel. "En
un cielo sin mancha," "Como
el mundo cristiano celebra
la pasión." México Moderno,
II (Núm. 4, junio de 1923),
236-237. (p)   2273

----. "Yo te invité
ceremoniosamente," "María
Teresa." México Moderno, II
(Núm. 1, agosto de 1922),
5-8. (p)   2274

Martini, Simone. "Boccaccio.
el Cav. Rodi y otros
retratos," "Laura y otras
mujeres," "La iglesia
militante," "Cristo en el
limbo." El Hijo Pródigo,

XII (Núm. 37, abril de 1946),
entre 16 y 17. (il)   2275

Marré, Luis. "De la muerte,"
"La muchacha del río,"
"Mientes, amigo," "La joven
mariposa," "Otro día," "Oh
Costa." Estaciones, I (Núm.
1, primavera de 1956), 121-
124. (p)   2276

Masefield, John. "Los fieles."
(Trad. Enrique Díez-Canedo
y Martín Luis Guzmán),
Contemporáneos, V (Núm. 18,
noviembre de 1929), 245-292;
(Núm. 19, diciembre de 1929),
354-421. (dr)   (1173)

Masferrer, Alberto. "Los
peces voladores. -- Conversación con unos obreros." La
Falange, Núm. 4 (1 de julio
de 1923), 240-244. (a-e)
                                 2277

Masip, Paulino. "Bagaría ha
muerto." Romance, I (Núm.
13, 1 de agosto de 1940),
3, 5. (a-e)   2278

----. "De quince llevo una."
El Hijo Pródigo, XIII (Núm.
42, septiembre de 1946),
152-156. (f)   2279

----. "El diario de Hamlet
García." Romance, II (Núm.
24, 31 de mayo de 1941), 6,
14, 16. (f)   2280

----. "Don Antonio Machado."
Romance, II (Núm. 21, 15 de
febrero de 1941), 1, 2, 14.
(a-e)   2281

----. "Luis Companys."
Romance, I (Núm. 18, 15 de
noviembre de 1940), 6, 15.
(a-e)   2282

----. "La muerte en el
paraíso." Prometeus, I

144

(Núm. 3, mayo de 1949), 207-216. (f)   2283

Masters, Edgar Lee. "Silencio" (Trad. Salvador Novo). La Falange, Núm. 7 (1 de octubre de 1923), 382-383. (p)   2284

Mata, Emilio R. "Calor y electricidad en Jorge Simon Ohn." Romance, I (Núm. 5, 1 de abril de 1940), 3-4. (a-e)   2285

Matisse, Henri. "Desnudo." Contemporáneos, V (Núm. 15, agosto de 1929), 62. (il)   2286

----. "La lección de piano." Sagitario, Núm. 8 (1 de febrero de 1927), 8. (il)   2287

Maurer, A. "Muchachas." Contemporáneos, II (Núm. 7, diciembre de 1928), 332. (il)   2288

Maurois, André. "La conversación" (Trad. José Gorostiza). Contemporáneos, IV (Núm. 11, abril de 1929), 70-84. (a-e)   (1696)

----. "La conversación" (Trad. José Gorostiza). Contemporáneos, VII (Núm. 23, abril de 1930), 47-65. (a-e)   (1697)

Mayer-Serra, Otto. "La temporada musical en México." Romance, I (Núm. 1, 1 de febrero de 1940), 15. (a-e)   2289

Mayo, Hugo. "Madrugada de los desconocidos," "Otoño de los misterios." Sagitario, Núm. 14 (31 de mayo de 1927), 8. (p)   2290

----. "Polo sur." Sagitario, Núm. 5 (1 de octubre de 1926), 16. (p)   2291

Maza, Francisco de la. "Las capillas abiertas de México." El Hijo Pródigo, VIII (Núm. 26, mayo de 1945), 80-81. (a-e)   2292

----. "José María Estrada." El Hijo Pródigo, V (Núm. 17, agosto de 1944), 96. (a-e)   2293

----. "Retablos barrocos en México." El Hijo Pródigo, IV (Núm. 14, mayo de 1944), 87-88. (a-e)   2294

----. "Tres obras de arte desconocidas." El Hijo Pródigo, II (Núm. 9, diciembre de 1943), 180-181. (a-e)   2295

----. Una pregunta sobre España de Antonio Sánchez Barbudo. El Hijo Pródigo, IX (Núm. 30, septiembre de 1945), 178-179. (r)   2296

Mazaud, Emile. "Un día estupendo" (Trad. Alfonso Reyes). El Hijo Pródigo, III (Núm. 12, marzo de 1944), 171-183. (dr)   2297

Meana, José. "El vuelo de los buitres." El Hijo Pródigo, X (Núm. 31, octubre de 1945), 20-22. (f)   2298

Medina, Luis. "Viñeta." Estaciones, I (Núm. 1, primavera de 1956), portada. (il)   2299

Mediz Bolio, Antonio. "El Chilam Balam de Chumayel." Contemporáneos, IV (Núm. 13, junio de 1929), 240-256. (a-e, tr)   2300

Mejía Sánchez, Ernesto.
"Elegías." Estaciones, II
(Núm. 8, invierno de 1957),
396-397. (p)   2301

----. "Opera mínima."
Estaciones, V (Núm. 20,
invierno de 1960), 23. (p)
                                2302

----. "Un puñado de poesías
desconocidas de Manuel
Gutiérrez Nájera." Estaciones,
IV (Núm. 16, invierno de
1959), 476-484. (a-e) 2303

Mejía Vides, Luis. "A Morazán."
Estaciones, V (Núm. 18,
verano de 1960), 51-53. (p)
                                2304

Meléndez de Espinosa, Juana.
Definiciones de Felix
Dauajare Torres. Estaciones,
V (Núm. 18, verano de 1960),
107-108. (r)   2305

Melo, Gastón. "Acre sabor."
Estaciones, III (Núm. 10,
verano de 1958), 237-239. (f)
                                2306

----. "Manuel 106."
Estaciones, IV (Núm. 14,
verano de 1959), 227-231. (f)
                                2307

Melo, Juan Vicente. "El hilo
de la estrella." Estaciones,
V (Núm. 17, primavera de
1960), 38-45. (f)   2308

----. Benzulul de Eraclio
Zepeda. Estaciones, V
(Núm. 18, verano de 1960),
118-120. (r)   2309

----. Cañón de Juchipila de
Tomás Mojarro. Estaciones,
V (Núm. 18, verano de 1960),
122-124. (r)   2310

----. Chopin de Jesús Bal
y Gay. Estaciones, IV (Núm.
16, invierno de 1959), 496-
499. (r)   2311

----. Galería de títeres de
Guadalupe Amor. Estaciones,
V (Núm. 17, primavera de
1960), 115-117. (r)   2312

----. El laurel de San
Lorenzo de Antonio Castro
Leal. Estaciones, V (Núm.
17, primavera de 1960), 117-
118. (r)   2313

----. La llorona de Carmen
Toscano. Estaciones, V
(Núm. 17, primavera de
1960), 118-119. (r)   2314

----. La mort de Tristán de
Michel del Castillo.
Estaciones, V (Núm. 17,
primavera de 1960), 119-120.
(r)   2315

----. Teatro y Las estatuas
de marfil de Emilio
Carballido. Estaciones, V
(Núm. 18, verano de 1960),
120-122. (r)   2316

Melville, Herman. "Moby
Dick" (Trad. Julio Prieto).
Tierra Nueva, II (Núm. 11-12,
septiembre-diciembre de
1941), 250-252. (f)   2317

Memling, Hans. "Retrato de
hombre," "Eva y Adán."
"Retrato de mujer," "Retrato
de hombre de La Haya," "La
mujer de Tomaso Portinari,"
"Retrato de Tomaso
Portinari," "Tríptico,"
"Retrato de hombre joven de
Londres," "Degollación de
San Juan Bautista," "La
vanidad," "Retrato de hombre
de Florencia," "Retrato de
Van Martín Nieuweurove."

Romance, I (Núm. 10, 15 de junio de 1940), 1, 9. (il) 2318

Mena, Anselmo. "Alfonso Reyes." Fábula, Núm. 9 (septiembre de 1934), 176. (a-e) 2319

----. "Egloga pura." El Hijo Pródigo, VII (Núm. 22, enero de 1945), 14-15. (p) 2320

----. "Greda." Contemporáneos, XI (Núm. 38-39, julio-agosto de 1931), 58. (p) 2321

----. "Soneto." Fábula, Núm. 2 (febrero de 1934), 32. (p) 2322

Mena, Ramón. "El escudo nacional:un códice de piedra." Sagitario, Núm. 3 (15 de agosto de 1926), 7. (a-e) 2323

----. "Mosaicos mexicanos." Forma, I (Núm 4, 1927), 17-21. (a-e) 2324

Méndez Plancarte, Gabriel. "Hidalgo, reformador intelectual." El Hijo Pródigo, VI (Núm. 19, octubre de 1944), 9-20. (a-e) 2325

----. Italia mia de Giovanni Papini. Romance, I (Núm. 11, 1 de junio de 1940), 18. (r) 2326

Méndez Rivas, Joaquín. "Canto al sol." La Falange, Núm. 7 (1 de octubre de 1923), 392-394. (p) 2327

----. "Invocación a Virgilio." La Falange, Núm. 4 (1 de julio de 1923), 218. (p) 2328

Mendizábal, Miguel O. de. "La conquista y la independencia religiosa de los indígenas." Contemporáneos, I (Núm. 2, julio de 1928), 149-199. (a-e) 2329

----. "Evolución religiosa de los pueblos indígenas de México." Contemporáneos, III (Núm. 8, enero de 1929), 32-73. (a-e) 2330

Menéndez Samará, Adolfo. El curso de la vida humana como problema psicológico de Charlotte Buhler. El Hijo Pródigo, IV (Núm. 15, junio de 1944), 185-186. (r) 2331

----. Historia de la filosofía en México de Samuel Ramos. El Hijo Pródigo, I (Núm. 5, agosto de 1943), 317-318. (r) 2332

Mérida, Carlos. "Europa y la pintura en 1928." Contemporáneos, I (Núm. 3, agosto de 1928), 322-330. (a-e) 2333

----. "Guatemala." Sagitario, Núm. 8 (1 de febrero de 1927), 14. (il) 2334

----. "India de Panajachel." La Falange, Núm. 3 (1 de febrero de 1923), entre 168 y 169. (il) 2335

----. "Jesús Castillo," "Wyld Ospina." La Falange, Núm. 3 (1 de febrero de 1923), entre 156 y 157. (il) 2336

----. "John B. Flannagan." El Hijo Pródigo, I (Núm. 5, agosto de 1943), 305-307. (a-e) 2337

----. "Máscaras," "Grupo," "Los caballos y el maguey,"

"Ronda de niños." Contemporáneos, XI (Núm. 38-39, julio-agosto de 1931), 83-86. 2338

----. "Obras." Contemporáneos, II (Núm. 6, noviembre de 1928), 267-272. (il) 2339

----. "Teotihuacán." Sagitario, Núm. 8 (1 de febrero de 1927), 3. (il) 2340

----. Romantic Painting in America de James Thrall Soby y Dorothy C. Miller. El Hijo Pródigo, III (Núm. 12, marzo de 1944), 185-186. (r) 2341

Merino, A. "Respuesta a la encuesta de Romance." Romance, I (Núm. 6, 15 de abril de 1940), 2. (a-e) 2342

Mesa, Diego de. "Pasifae: El toro." Estaciones, IV (Núm. 15, otoño de 1959), 350-354. (f) 2343

Mesa, Enrique de. "'Estalorio', Rey dramático." Sagitario, Núm. 3 (15 de agosto de 1926), 14. (a-e) 2344

Mesonero Romanos, Ramón. "La patrona de huéspedes" (en "Los españoles pintados por sí mismos"). Romance, I (Núm. 10, 15 de junio de 1940), 10. (a-e) 2345

Meza, Guillermo. "Pintor y modelo." El Hijo Pródigo, X (Núm. 31, octubre de 1945), 6. (il) 2346

Michel, Alfonso. "La jaula amarilla." El Hijo Pródigo, X (Núm. 31, octubre de 1945), entre 16 y 17. (il) 2347

Michelena, Margarita. "Aurelia, la bella durmiente." Estaciones, I (Núm. 1, primavera de 1956), 95-98. (a-e) 2348

----. "Lección de cosas." Estaciones, I (Núm. 1, primavera de 1956), 34-41. (p) 2349

----. "Monólogo del buscador." Estaciones, II (Núm. 5, primavera de 1957), 53-55. (a-e) 2350

----. "Monólogo del despierto." Estaciones, III (Núm. 12, invierno de 1958), 391-396. (p) 2351

----. "Un libro necesario" (Reseña de Una manera de morir de Mario Monteforte Toledo). Estaciones, II (Núm. 8, invierno de 1957), 450-453. (r) 2352

Miguel, Francisco. "Líneas." Contemporáneos, V (Núm. 16, septiembre de 1929), 134-136. (il) 2353

Milbreed, Oliver. "Ciencia y libertad." Prometeus, I (Núm. 1, febrero de 1949), 3-10. (a-e) 2354

Millán, María del Carmen. "Poesía y música" (Reseña de Espejismo de Juchitán de Agustín Yáñez). Tierra Nueva, II (Núm. 9-10, mayo-agosto de 1941), 178-179. (r) 2355

Millán y M., Ignacio. "Madame Curie y la terapéutica del cáncer." Ruta, Núm. 4 (septiembre de 1938), 46-53. (a-e) 2356

Millares Carlo, Agustín.
Lucrecio Caro, Tito. "De la
naturaleza" (Trad. Agustín
Millares Carlo). El Hijo
Pródigo, IV (Núm. 15, junio
de 1944), 173-181. (tr)
(2137)

Miranda, Carlos Arbulu.
"Manifiesto de la 'Liga
Antiimperialista'. "
Sagitario, Núm. 14 (31 de
mayo de 1927), 2. (a-e)
2357

Miró, Joan. "Carnaval de
Arlequín, " "Perro que ladra
a la luna. " Estaciones, I
(Núm. 3, otoño de 1956),
entre 454-455. (il)   2358

----. "Pez, " "Paisaje"
Contemporáneos, VII (Núm.
24, mayo de 1930), 148-149.
(il)   2359

Misbnun, Virginia. "Las danzas
de México. " Romance, I
(Núm. 9, 1 de junio de
1940), 15. (a-e)   2360

Mojarro, Tomás. " 'Letras
Mexicanas': un panorama
representativo de la literatura
nacional. " Estaciones, IV
(Núm. 15, otoño de 1959),
376-379. (a-e)   2361

----. "Sahumerio. "
Estaciones, IV (Núm. 15,
otoño de 1959), 311-329. (f)
2362

Molina Enríquez, Renato. "Arte
para los obreros. " Forma,
I (Núm. 3, 1927), 14. (a-e)
2363

----. "Lacas de México:
Los baúles de Olinalá. "
Forma, I (Núm. 6, 1928), 15-
22. (a-e)   2364

----. "Obras de Tina Modotti."
Forma, I (Núm. 4, 1927),
30-33. (a-e)   2365

----. "La pintura mural:
Fermín Revueltas. " Forma,
I (Núm. 3, 1927), 33-36.
(a-e)   2366

Molins Fábrega. Gide, André.
"Recuerdos literarios y
problemas actuales" (Trad.
Molins Fábrica). Prometeus,
II (Núm. 1, diciembre de
1951), 6-17. (tr)   (1514)

Moncada Ivar, Luis. "Aleluya."
Estaciones, IV (Núm. 16,
invierno de 1959), 444-457.
(f)   2367

Monsiváis, Carlos. "Un
argumento para el ave fénix. "
Estaciones, III (Núm. 11,
otoño de 1958), 294-303.
(a-e)   2368

----. "César Vallejo: verso
del sufrimiento americano. "
Estaciones, II (Núm. 7, otoño
de 1957), 331-337. (a-e)
2369

----. "Fino acero de niebla. "
Estaciones, II (Núm. 8,
invierno de 1957), 458-462.
(f)   2370

----. "El último padre de la
iglesia. " Estaciones, IV
(Núm. 13, primavera de
1959), 117-118. (a-e)   2371

----. La hebra de oro de
Emilio Carballido. Estaciones,
III (Núm. 10, verano de
1958), 196-198. (r)   2372

----. Horizonte de Sueños de
María del Mar. Estaciones,
II (Núm. 7, otoño de 1957),
356-357. (r)   2373

----. Los signos perdidos de Sergio Fernández. Estaciones, IV (Núm. 16, invierno de 1959), 488-491. (r)   2374

----. El teatro contemporáneo de Allan Lewis. Estaciones, II (Núm. 7, otoño de 1957), 360-361. (r) 2375

Montaña, Antonio. "El escritor ante la escena." Estaciones, III (Núm. 12, invierno de 1958), 467-472. (a-e) 2376

Montenegro, Roberto. "Carbón para una de las figuras del signo del zodiaco," "El nuevo día," "Retrato retrospectivo," "Rosa Rollando," "Retrato de un anticuario," "La fiesta de la Cruz," "La historia," "El cuento," "Géminis," "El zodiaco," "Bañistas." Forma, II (Núm. 7, 1928), 28-36. (il)   2377

----. "Cristo." La Falange, Núm. 6 (1 de septiembre de 1923), portada. (il)   2378

----. "Dibujo." La Falange, Núm. 6 (1 de septiembre de 1923), entre 346 y 347. (il)   2379

----. Obregón Santacilla, Carlos; Ituarte, Manuel M.; Pallares, Alfonso; Cumming, A. E.; Robles Gil, Alberto. "Encuesta sobre arquitectura." Forma, I (Núm. 3, 1927), 15-16. (a-e)   (1019)

----. "Frescos." Contemporáneos, XI (Núm. 38-39, julio-agosto de 1931), 52-55. (il)   2380

----. "Illustración (1919)." Forma, II (Núm. 7, 1928), 25. (il)   2381

----. "Litografías de Taxco" Contemporáneos, VII (Núm. 24, mayo de 1930), 119-121. (il)   2382

----. "Rufino Tamayo," "Genaro Estrada," "El Marqués de San Francisco," "El chico de la granda." México Moderno, II (Núm. 10, junio de 1921), entre 232-233. (il)   2383

----. "San Francisco de Asís." La Falange, Núm. 6 (1 de septiembre de 1923), entre 330 y 331. (il)   2384

----. "Silencios." Ulises, Núm. 2 (junio de 1927), 28-29. (p)   2385

----. "Tehuana." Forma, I (Núm. 2, noviembre de 1926), 1. (il)   2386

----. "Tehuanas." Fábula, Núm. 4 (abril de 1934), entre 74 y 75. (il)   2387

----. "Viñetas de Novo y Villaurrutia." Ulises, Núm. 4 (agosto de 1927), entre 22 y 23. (il)   2388

Monter, Guillermo. "El mostrador," y "El huacal." Forma, I (Núm. 1, octubre de 1926), 25. (il)   2389

Monterde García Icazbalceta, Francisco. "Alfonso Reyes." Fábula, Núm. 9 (septiembre de 1934), 176. (a-e)   2390

----. "En autógrafo perdido." El Hijo Pródigo, XII (Núm. 39, junio de 1946), 143-144. (a-e)   2391

----. "De autobiografía." Estaciones, V (Núm. 18, verano de 1960), 16-19. (p)   2392

----. "En el remolino." Antena, Núm. 1 (julio de 1924), 13-16. (dr) 2393

----. "Epigramas de José Juan Tablada." Antena, Núm. 2 (agosto de 1924), 10-11. (a-e) 2394

----. "La expresión de Edward Weston." Antena, Núm. 5 (noviembre de 1924), 10-11. (a-e) 2395

----. "Fotografías de Weston." Forma, II (Núm. 7, 1928), 15-16. (a-e) 2396

----. "Guillaume Apollinaire en México." Sagitario, Núm. 4 (1 de septiembre de 1926), 7. (a-e) 2397

----. "Lo que dice el reloj de sol," "Lo que dice la lámpara de aceite," "Lo que dice la pila de agua bendita," "Las nubes," "El enamorado." México Moderno, I (Núm. 4, noviembre de 1920), 247-250. (p) 2398

----. "El oro del ídolo," "El inquisidor." México Moderno, I (Núm. 2, septiembre de 1922), 83-84. (a-e) 2399

----. "La 'pasión' del pintor Gabriel José de Ovalle." El Hijo Pródigo, III (Núm. 11, febrero de 1944), 79-80. (a-e) 2400

----. "La pieza vacía." Antena, Núm. 3 (septiembre de 1924), 7-8. (p) 2401

----. "Pinturas del convento de Guadalupe." El Hijo Pródigo, II (Núm. 8, noviembre de 1943), 95-97. (a-e) 2402

----. "Proteo." Contemporáneos, X (Núm. 37, junio de 1931), 238-262. (dr) 2403

----. "El sainete de palacio." El Hijo Pródigo, XI (Núm. 35, febrero de 1946), 85-87. (a-e) 2404

----. "Vislumbres." La Falange, Núm. 4 (1 de julio de 1923), 195-196. (a-e) 2405

----. Amado Nervo. Acotaciones a su vida y a su obra de Jorge Celso Tíndero. México Moderno, I (Núm. 10, junio de 1921), 239-240. (r) 2406

----. Antología poética de Fernán Silva Valdés. El Hijo Pródigo, V (Núm. 17, agosto de 1944), 123-124. (r) 2407

----. El árbol que canta de Humberto Tejera. México Moderno, I (Núm. 10, junio de 1921), 241. (r) 2408

----. Arte colonial de Manuel Terreros. México Moderno, I (Núm. 10, junio de 1921), 241-242. (r) 2409

----. Cervantes de Benjamín Jarnés. El Hijo Pródigo, IV (Núm. 15, junio de 1944), 184. (r) 2410

----. Del verjel interior de Luis Augusto Méndez. México Moderno, I (Núm. 11-12, noviembre-diciembre de 1921), 315. (r) 2411

----. Don Carlos de Sigüenza y Góngora, erudito barroco de José Rojas Garcidueñas. El Hijo Pródigo, X

(Núm. 33, diciembre de 1945), 179-180. (r)   2412

----. Lecciones de literatura española de Ermilo Abreu Gómez. El Hijo Pródigo, VI (Núm. 19, octubre de 1944), 58-59. (r)   2413

----. Manual de gramática castellana de Carlos Gonzáles Peña. México Moderno, I (Núm. 10, junio de 1921), 240-241. (r) 2414

----. Poemas de Carlos Obligado. México Moderno, II (Núm. 10, junio de 1921), 239. (r)   2415

----. Poemas de corazón amoroso de Luis Felipe Rodríguez. México Moderno, I (Núm. 10, junio de 1921), 241. (r)   2416

----. Poesías de Carlos Guido y Spano. México Moderno, I (Núm. 11-12, noviembre-diciembre de 1921), 314-315. (r)   2417

----. Rayo en la encina de Enrique Uhthoff. El Hijo Pródigo, X (Núm. 31, octubre de 1945), 56-57. (r)   2418

----. Las sinfonías del Popocatépetl de Gerardo Murillo ("Dr. Atl"). México Moderno, I (Núm. 11-12, noviembre-diciembre de 1921), 314. (r)   2419

----. Ternura de Gabriela Mistral. El Hijo Pródigo, XI (Núm. 35, febrero de 1946), 114-115. (r)   2420

----. Visiones urbanas de Armando de María y Campos. México Moderno, II (Núm. 10, junio de 1921), 242. (r) 2421

Montero, José Antonio. "Amargo entre tus manos." Estaciones, IV (Núm. 16, invierno de 1959), 396-397. (p)   2422

Montes de Oca, Marco Antonio. "Contrapunto de la fe." Estaciones, III (Núm. 12, invierno de 1958), 419-422. (p)   2423

----. "Ensayo final," "El caballero de la fe," "Alas que no llegan." Estaciones, III (Núm. 10, verano de 1958), 178-180. (p)   2424

Montherlant, Henri de. "En qué es bueno 1938." Ruta, Núm. 4 (septiembre de 1938), 34-38. (a-e)   2425

----. "Pasifae" (Trad. José Ferrel). Prometeus, II (Núm. 1, diciembre de 1951), 29-41. (dr)   (1366)

Monvel, María. "La sandía," "El pájarillo," "Tiene sueño mi niña..." La Falange, Núm. 5 (1 de agosto de 1923), 297-299. (p)   2426

----. "Tío Conejo y Tía Boa." La Falange, Núm. 6 (1 de septiembre de 1923), 343-344. (f)   2427

Moore, George Foot. "Los profetas." México Moderno, II (Núm. 4, junio de 1923), 252-253. (a-e)   2428

Morales Garcés, Bernardo. "Pedro Jorge Vera." Estaciones, III (Núm. 12, invierno de 1958), 437-438. (a-e)   2429

Morand, Paul. "De la velocidad" (Trad. Antonieta Rivas).

Contemporáneos, V (Núm. 15, agosto de 1929), 35-59. (p) 2430

----. "Pintura en seda," "Business" (Trad. Guillermo de Torre). Sagitario, Núm. 4 (1 de septiembre de 1926), 15. (p) 2431

----. "Un poema: 35.5" (Trad. Jesús S. Soto). Antena, Núm. 4 (octubre de 1924), 6-7. (p) 2432

Moréas, Jean. "Estancias" (Trad. Rafael Lozano). La Falange, Núm. 2 (1 de enero de 1923), 125-126. (p) (2132)

Moreno, Daniel. "El mundo real de La linterna mágica." Estaciones, III (Núm. 9, primavera de 1958), 22-33. (a-e) 2433

Moreno de Tagle, J. Enrique. "A través de la luz, húmeda seda." Estaciones, II (Núm. 6, verano de 1957), 163-169. (f) 2434

----. "En la orilla letal de la palabra." Estaciones, I (Núm. 2, verano de 1956), 160-170. (a-e) 2435

----. "Esquema de México en la retórica del 57." Estaciones, II (Núm. 5, primavera de 1957), 66-69. (a-e) 2436

----. "Poesía y criaturación." Estaciones, III (Núm. 11, otoño de 1958), 251-261. (a-e) 2437

----. "Pueden sustituirse por ruído y lujuria." Estaciones, II (Núm. 8, invierno de 1957), 371-377. (f) 2438

----. Léger, Aléxis Saint-Léger. ("St. John Perse"). "Nieves." (Trad. J. Enrique Moreno de Tagle). Estaciones, I (Núm. 3, otoño de 1956), 362-370. (tr) (2046)

Moreno Villa, José. "El amor a lo sorprendente." Sagitario, Núm. 5 (1 de octubre de 1926), 5. (a-e) 2439

----. "El Arcipreste de Hita." Romance, I (Núm. 8, 15 de mayo de 1940), 3. (a-e) 2440

----. "Canciones a Xochipili, portentoso dios de las flores." El Hijo Pródigo, XI (Núm. 34, enero de 1946), 17-26. (p) 2441

----. "Claridades sobre Picasso. Su pintura, sus poemas, su política." El Hijo Pródigo, IX (Núm. 30, septiembre de 1945), 149-157. (a-e) 2442

----. "Cuatro dibujos." Taller, I (Núm. 1, diciembre de 1938), 33-50. (il) 2443

----. "De la tierra y de la patria." Romance, I (Núm. 4, 15 de marzo de 1940), 3. (a-e) 2444

----. "Embeleso de la confianza." El Hijo Pródigo, VII (Núm. 24, marzo de 1945), 141-142. (p) 2445

----. "Españoles destacados." Sagitario, Núm. 2 (1 de agosto de 1926), 9-10. (a-e) 2446

----. "La filosofía contra la literatura." Romance, I (Núm. 16, 15 de septiembre de 1940), 1-2. (a-e) 2447

----. "Margarita es un cuento o El cuento de Margarita." Tierra Nueva, II (Núm. 7-8, enero-abril de 1941), 66-68. (f)   2448

----. "El oficio." Sagitario, Núm. 3 (15 de agosto de 1926), 11. (a-e)   2449

----. "Porteros." El Hijo Pródigo, XIII (Núm. 42, septiembre de 1946), 136-140. (p)   2450

----. "Topografía de la casa paterna." Taller, I (Núm. 7, diciembre de 1939), 27-36. (a-e)   2451

----. "Unidad en lo gris." "Dingolondango." "Parque selvático." "Para desviarte." "Sal." Romance, I (Núm. 12, 15 de julio de 1940), 8. (p)   2452

Morgan, Claude. "Los partidarios de la muerte." Ruta, Núm. 9 (febrero de 1939), 55-58. (a-e)   2453

Morley, Sylvanus G. "Un jarro maya pintado." Forma, I (Núm. 5, 1927), 22-24. (a-e)   2454

Moro, César. "Algunas reflexiones a propósito de la pintura de Alice Paalen." El Hijo Pródigo, XIII (Núm. 42, septiembre de 1946), 148-150. (a-e)   2455

----. "El fuego y la poesía." El Hijo Pródigo, IV (Núm. 15, junio de 1944), 161-162. (p)   2456

----. "Homenaje a Bonnard." Estaciones, I (Núm. 1, primavera de 1956), 132-133. (p)   2457

----. "El mundo ilustrado." Prometeus, I (Núm. 1, febrero de 1949), 27. (p)   2458

----. "El surrealismo es el cordón." Estaciones, I (Núm. 1, primavera de 1956), 134. (p)   2459

----. Arcane 17 de André Breton. El Hijo Pródigo, IX (Núm. 30, septiembre de 1945), 181-182. (r)   2460

----. Dieu le Veut de René Ristel-Hueber. El Hijo Pródigo, XI (Núm. 35, febrero de 1946), 115. (r)   2461

----. Escultura azteca de Manuel Alvarez Bravo. El Hijo Pródigo, II (Núm. 7, octubre de 1943), 61. (r)   2462

----. La guerra y los niños de Anna Freud y D. Burlingham. El Hijo Pródigo, XIII (Núm. 40, julio de 1946), 59-60. (r)   2463

----. La hija de Iorio de Gabriel D'Annunzio. El Hijo Pródigo, X (Núm. 33, diciembre de 1945), 181-182. (r)   2464

----. Historia de la conquista de México de Guillermo H. Prescott, Historia de la conquista del Peru de Guillermo H. Prescott, Comentarios reales de los Incas de Inca Garcilaso de la Vega, Historia de los Incas de Pedro Sarmiento de Gamboa, Prosa Menuda de Manuel González Prada, y Propaganda y ataque de

Manuel González Prada. El
Hijo Pródigo, XII (Núm. 38,
mayo de 1946), 115-116.
(r)   2465

----. Judith de Jean
Giraudoux. El Hijo Pródigo,
III (Núm. 12, marzo de
1944), 184. (r)   2466

----. Mon coeur mis á nu,
Fusées, Choix de maximes
consolantes sur l'Amour de
Charles Baudelaire. El Hijo
Pródigo, IX (Núm. 28, julio
de 1945), 58-59. (r)   2467

----. Chirico, Giorgio de.
"Pequeña antología" (Trad.
César Moro y Agustín Lazo).
El Hijo Pródigo, VII (Núm.
22, enero de 1945), 33-41.
(tr)   (1053)

----. Peret, Benjamín. "Los
mitos" (Trad. César Moro).
El Hijo Pródigo, IV (Núm.
14, mayo de 1944), 110-119.
(tr)   2468

----. Peret, Benjamín.
"Para pasar el tiempo,"
"Parpadeo," "Allo" (Trad.
César Moro). El Hijo
Pródigo, XII (Núm. 38, mayo
de 1946), 77-78. (tr) 2469

----. Reneville, Roland de.
"Poetas y místicos" (Trad.
César Moro). El Hijo
Pródigo, VI (Núm. 19,
octubre de 1944), 33-43. (tr)
                       2470

----. Serge, Victor. "El
mensaje del escritor" (Trad.
César Moro). El Hijo
Pródigo, VI (Núm. 21,
diciembre de 1944), 150-152.
(tr)   2471

Mota, Fernando. "La cripta."

Estaciones, II (Núm. 8,
invierno de 1957), 410-429.
(dr)   2472

----. "El último Werther."
Estaciones, V (Núm. 17,
primavera de 1960), 54-62.
(dr)   2473

Moussong, Lazlo Javier. "Una
coreografía." Estaciones,
II (Núm. 8, invierno de 1957),
469-471. (dr)   2474

----. "Dos fantasmas breves."
Estaciones, III (Núm. 10,
verano de 1958), 228-229.
(f)   2475

----. "Sesión de jazz con
Stan Kenton." Estaciones, V
(Núm. 17, primavera de
1960), 112-113. (f)   2476

----. "Terrible sueño de
amor." Estaciones, II (Núm.
7, otoño de 1957), 338-341.
(f)   2477

----. Arte abstracto.
Estaciones, III (Núm. 11,
otoño de 1958), 340-343. (r)
                       2478

----. La filosofía americana,
su razón y su sin razón de
ser de Francisco Larroyo.
Estaciones, III (Núm. 9,
primavera de 1958), 100. (r)
                       2479

----. Muerte amurallada de
Raymundo Ramos Gómez.
Estaciones, III (Núm. 9,
primavera de 1958), 100-102.
(r)   2480

----. El puente de José
Martínez Sotomayor.
Estaciones, III (Núm. 11,
otoño de 1958), 336-338. (r)
                       2481

----. Tiempo cercado de Sergio Pitol. Estaciones, IV (Núm. 14, verano de 1959), 245-248. (r)   2482

Munguía, Enrique Jr. "Apuntes para una dicotomía humana." Contemporáneos, VIII (Núm. 30-31, noviembre-diciembre de 1930), 254-259. (a-e)
                                          2483

----. "D. H. Lawrence" Contemporáneos, VII (Núm. 23, abril de 1930), 81-86. (a-e)   2484

----. "Entierro." Contemporáneos, V (Núm. 18, noviembre de 1929), 243. (p)   2485

----. "Etica y maquinismo." Contemporáneos, VIII (Núm. 28-29, septiembre-octubre de 1930), 175-180. (a-e)
                                          2486

----. "Exposición de fuga," Contemporáneos, VI (Núm. 22, marzo de 1930), 196-200. (a-e)   2487

----. "Marina con retrato de mujer." Contemporáneos, VIII (Núm. 30-31, noviembre-diciembre de 1930), 220-221. (p)   2488

----. Le forcat innocent de Jules Supervielle. Contemporáneos, VIII (Núm. 30-31, noviembre-diciembre de 1930), 275-276. (r) 2489

----. Poesías de Enrique González Martínez. Contemporáneos, VIII (Núm. 30-31, noviembre-diciembre de 1930), 272-275. (r)   2490

----. Eliot, Thomas Stearns. "El páramo" (Traducción y

prólogo de Enrique Munguía Jr.). Contemporáneos, VIII (Núm. 26-27, julio-agosto de 1930), 7-32. (tr)   (1223)

----. Fletcher, John Gould. "La poesía de D. H. Lawrence," (Trad. Enrique Munguía Jr.). Contemporáneos, V (Núm. 18, noviembre de 1929), 322-328. (tr)   (1371)

Muñoz, Rafael F. "Una biografía." Estaciones, IV (Núm. 14, verano de 1959), 147-158. (f)   2491

----. "Mezquites." Ruta, Núm. 2 (julio de 1938), 34-35. (f)   2492

Murillo, Gerardo. ("Dr. Atl"). "A la sombra de un árbol," "El huehuentón," "Los grandes conos." México Moderno, II (Núm. 1, agosto de 1922), 54-55. (p)   2493

----."¡Arribal! Arriba!" Antena, Núm. 5 (noviembre de 1924), 4-5. (a-e)   2494

----. "La estancia en la montaña," "Un luminoso día," "La noche." México Moderno," I (Núm. 10, junio de 1921), 208-212. (p)   2495

----. "Los retablos del señor del hospital." Forma, I (Núm. 3, 1927), 17-20. (a-e)   2496

----. "Los ritmos de la vida." México Moderno, II (Núm. 3, octubre de 1922), 166-168. (p)   2497

----. "Ritmos de la vida," "Arma tu barca y empújala al océano." La Falange,

156

Núm. 1 (1 de diciembre de 1922), 11-12. (p)   2498

Murray, Gilbert. "Roma y Grecia." México Moderno, II (Núm. 2, septiembre de 1922), 123-124. (a-e) 2499

Mutis, Alvaro. "Antes que cante el gallo." Estaciones, V (Núm. 17, primavera de 1960), 80-101. (f)   2500

Nandino, Elías. "Carta a Jaime Torres Bodet." Estaciones, III (Núm. 11, otoño de 1958), 241-247. (a-e)   2501

----. "Con este ejemplar..." Estaciones, V (Núm. 20, invierno de 1960), portada. (a-e)   2502

----. "Contestación a Diego Rivera." Estaciones, II (Núm. 8, invierno de 1957), 368. (p)   2503

----. "Después del surrealismo...¿Qué?" Estaciones, I (Núm. 3, otoño de 1956), 379-386. (a-e)   2504

----. "Estudio y pequeña antología poética de Emilio Ballagas." Estaciones, I (Núm. 2, verano de 1956), 202-237. (a-e)   2505

----. "Nocturno cuerpo." Estaciones, III (Núm. 12, invierno de 1958), 382-384. (p)   2506

----. "Nocturno descenso." Estaciones, III (Núm. 11, otoño de 1958), 262-263. (p)   2507

----. "Nocturno llanto." Estaciones, II (Núm. 7, otoño de 1957), 243-245. (p)   2508

----, y Alfredo Hurtado. "Palabras de los editores." Estaciones, II (Núm. 5, primavera de 1957), 3-4. (a-e)   2509

----. "Poema al corazón." El Hijo Pródigo, II (Núm. 8, noviembre de 1943), 98-99. (p)   2510

----. "Poema de mi fuga." Prometeus, II (Núm. 1, diciembre de 1951), 19-20. (p)   2511

----. "Poesía de Xavier Villaurrutia." Estaciones, I (Núm. 4, invierno de 1956), 460-468. (a-e)   2512

----. "El poeta." Estaciones, V (Núm. 18, verano de 1960), 9-11. (p)   2513

----. "Retrato." Estaciones, I (Núm. 4, invierno de 1956), 457-459. (a-e)   2514

----. "Sonetos en incendio." Estaciones, IV (Núm. 16, invierno de 1959), 398-399. (p)   2515

----. "Suplemento en homenaje a la memoria del poeta y pintor peruano César Moro." Estaciones, I (Núm. 1, primavera de 1956), 130-131. (a-e)   2516

----. Acto propicio de Fernando Sánchez Mayans. Estaciones, III (Núm. 11, otoño de 1958), 334. (r) 2517

----. Al pie de la letra de Rosario Castellanos. Estaciones, IV (Núm. 14, verano de 1959), 242-243. (r)   2518

----. Algo de amor y otros poemas de Sabás Cruz Garcia. Estaciones, I (Núm. 4, invierno de 1956), 606. (p)
2519

----. Amantes, poemas de Jorge Caitán Durán. Estaciones, IV (Núm. 16, invierno de 1959), 487. (r)
2520

----. Anécdotas, cuentos y relatos de José Rojas Garcidueñas. Estaciones, I (Núm. 4, invierno de 1956), 607. (r)
2521

----. Las artes plásticas en Jalisco de José G. Zuno. Estaciones, II (Núm. 7, otoño de 1957), 325. (r)
2522

----. Asonante final y otros poemas de Eugenio Florit. Estaciones, II (Núm. 5, primavera de 1957), 96-97. (r)
2523

----. Los Cantares de Piza de Ezra Pound. Estaciones, II (Núm. 6, verano de 1957), 198. (r)
2524

----. Canto llano de Nuria Parés. Estaciones, V (Núm. 18, verano de 1960), 115-116. (r)
2525

----. El cristianismo medieval y moderno de Charles Guignebert. Estaciones, II (Núm. 7, otoño de 1957), 325-326. (r)
2526

----. Desatadura de Jesús Arellano. Estaciones, III (Núm. 11, otoño de 1958), 333. (r)
2527

----. Dos poemas de Wilberto Cantón. Estaciones, I (Núm.

2, verano de 1956), 262-263. (r)
2528

----. Elegías y otros poemas de Walter González Penelas. Estaciones, I (Núm. 4, invierno de 1956), 607. (r)
2529

----. Ensayos japoneses de Manuel Maples Arce. Estaciones, IV (Núm. 14, verano de 1959), 243. (r)
2530

----. Escuela de cortesanos de Wilberto Cantón. Estaciones, I (Núm. 4, invierno de 1956), 606. (r)
2531

----. La eternidad esquiva de Fernando González Urízar. Estaciones, IV (Núm. 14, verano de 1959), 243. (r)
2532

----. Exilio de Sara García Iglesias. Estaciones, II (Núm. 7, otoño de 1957), 324-325. (r)
2533

----. El extraño, poemas de Leopoldo de Luis. Estaciones, II (Núm. 7, otoño de 1957), 323-324. (r)
2534

----. Gilberto Owen y su obra de José Rojas Garcidueñas. Estaciones, I (Núm. 1, primavera de 1956), 128. (r)
2535

----. Glosas y décimas de México con selección e introducción de Vicente T. Mendoza. Estaciones, II (Núm. 6, verano de 1957), 194-195. (r)
2536

----. Hemerografía potosina de Joaquín Meade. Estaciones,

I (Núm. 4, invierno de 1956), 607. (r) 2537

----. Historia de la medicina de J. A. Hayward. Estaciones, I (Núm. 1, primavera de 1956), 127. (r) 2538

----. El libro vacío de Josefina Vicens. Estaciones, III (Núm. 11, otoño de 1958), 332-333. (r) 2539

----. Palabra de Mauricio de la Selva. Estaciones, I (Núm. 1, primavera de 1956), 128. (r) 2540

----. Palabras en reposo de Alí Chumacero. Estaciones, I (Núm. 1, primavera de 1956), 128. (r) 2541

----. Perfil de la raíz de Ricardo Bogrand. Estaciones, I (Núm. 2, verano de 1956), 257. (r) 2542

----. Plegaria grave de Luisa Pasamanik. Estaciones, III (Núm. 11, otoño de 1958), 333-334. (r) 2543

----. Pliegos de testimonios de Marco Antonio Montes de Oca. Estaciones, II (Núm. 5, primavera de 1957), 94-95. (r) 2544

----. Poemas (1953 a 1955) de Rosario Castellanos. Estaciones, II (Núm. 6, verano de 1957), 196-197. (r) 2545

----. Poemas con bastón de Arnoldo Liberman. Estaciones, IV (Núm. 14, verano de 1959), 243-244. (r) 2546

----. Tiempo de Isidro Conde. Estaciones, II (Núm. 6, verano de 1957), 197. (r) 2547

----. Viaje impreciso, poemas de Alfredo G. Roggiano. Estaciones, IV (Núm. 16, invierno de 1959), 487. (r) 2548

Nava, J. Guadalupe. "Hierros forjados." Forma, I (Núm. 1, octubre de 1926), 29. (il) 2549

Navarrete, José Antonio. "Vuelve la noche." Estaciones, III (Núm. 9, primavera de 1958), 97-98. (p) 2550

Navarro, Gustavo A. ("Tristán Marof"). "Un raro y original escritor." La Falange, Núm. 5 (1 de agosto de 1923), 303-305. (a-e) 2551

Navarro Sánchez, José Adalberto. "Soneto del gozo," "Soneto del gozo quebrantado." Tierra Nueva, II (Núm. 7-8, enero-abril de 1941), 69-70. (p) 2552

Naveda, César A. "Hispanoamérica y sus destinos." Sagitario, Núm. 8 (1 de febrero de 1927), 13. (a-e) 2553

Nelken, Margarita. "Raúl Anguiano." Estaciones, III (Núm. 9, primavera de 1958), 49-75. (a-e) 2554

Nelson, Alma. "Algunas impresiones de México." La Falange, Núm. 5 (1 de agosto de 1923), 309. (a-e) 2555

Nérval, Gerard de. "El desdichado." (Trad. José Emilio Pacheco y Berny). Estaciones, IV (Núm. 13, primavera de 1959), 91. (p) 2556

----. "Verídica historia del canard." Romance, I (Núm. 3, 1 de marzo de 1940), 10. (a-e)   2557

Neuman, Elsa M. "Fragmento de la novela Que...¿Yo preocupada?." Estaciones, III (Núm. 10, verano de 1958), 222-227. (f)   2558

Neuvillatte, Alfonso de. "Los dos compadres." Estaciones, II (Núm. 6, verano de 1957), 206-208. (f)   2559

Nicol, Eduardo. Vasconcelos, José; González Martínez, Enrique; Gaos, José; Gallegos, José M.; Paz, Octavio; Martínez, José Luis; García-Bacca, David; Jiménez, Rueda, Julio; Bergamín, José. "Poesía, mística y filosofía: Debate en torno a San Juan de la Cruz." El Hijo Pródigo, I (Núm. 3, junio de 1943), 135-144. (a-e)   (661)

----. La filosofía de Maimónides de José Gaos. Romance, I (Núm. 16, 15 de septiembre de 1940), 18. (r)
                                   2561

Nielson, B. "Algunas impresiones sobre México." La Falange, Núm. 5 (1 de agosto de 1923), 310. (a-e)
                                   2562

Nieto Caballero, Luis E. "Encuentro de Gabriela Mistral." Estaciones, II (Núm. 5, primavera de 1957), 28-35. (a-e)   2563

Noguera, Eduardo. "La cerámica prehispánica." El Hijo Pródigo, VII (Núm. 22, enero de 1945), 16-19. (a-e)
                                   2564

Noulet, Emilie. "Una carta inédita de Mallarmé." El Hijo Pródigo, III (Núm. 10, enero de 1944), 28-31. (a-e)
                                   2565

----. "Poe en la poesía francesa." El Hijo Pródigo, II (Núm. 7, octubre de 1943), 11-23. (a-e)   2566

----. Syncopes de Alain Bosquet. El Hijo Pródigo, V (Núm. 16, julio de 1944), 59. (r)   2567

Novaro, Octavio. "Pertenezco a una raza condenada." Estaciones, III (Núm. 12, invierno de 1958), 404-405. (p)   2568

----. "Poema en U," "Fórmula del recuerdo." Fábula, Núm. 8 (agosto de 1934), 156-157. (p)   2569

Novás Calvo, Lino. " 'Aliados' y 'alemanes'." Romance, I (Núm. 17, 22 de octubre de 1940), 8, 14. (f)   2570

----. "Apunte sobre mulatería." Romance, I (Núm. 6, 15 de abril de 1940), 3. (a-e)
                                   2571

----. "Dos poetas para alcaldes." Romance, I (Núm. 8, 15 de mayo de 1940), 8. (a-e)   2572

----. "Integración de una nacionalidad." Romance, I (Núm. 20, 15 de enero de 1941), 9. (a-e)   2573

----. "Pablo, soldado conocido" (Reseña de Aventuras del soldado desconocido cubano de Pablo de La Torriente-Brau). Romance, I

(Núm. 18, 15 de noviembre de 1940), 18. (r) 2574

Novo, Salvador. "El arte de la fotografía." Contemporáneos, IX (Núm. 33, febrero de 1931), 165-172. (a-e) 2575

----. "Breve romance de ausencia." Contemporáneos, XI (Núm. 40-41, septiembre-octubre de 1931), 167-168. (p) 2576

----. "Confesiones de pequeños filósofos." La Falange, Núm. 7 (1 de octubre de 1923), 396-397. (a-e) 2577

----. "Confesiones de pequeños filósofos." Antena, Núm. 1 (julio de 1924), 7. (a-e) 2578

----. "El corrector de pruebas: Cuestiones gongorinas de Alfonso Reyes." Ulises, Núm. 4 (octubre de 1927), 39-40. (r) 2579

----. "El curioso impertinente." Ulises, Núm. 1 (mayo de 1927), 29-31. (a-e) 2580

----. "Las escuelas al aire libre." Forma, I (Núm. 1, octubre de 1926), 16-17. (a-e) 2581

----. "El gallo y el arcipreste." Romance, I (Núm. 1, 1 de febrero de 1940), 3, 10. (a-e) 2582

----. "Glosa incompleta en tres tiempos sobre un tema de amor." Contemporáneos, VIII (Núm. 26-27, julio-agosto de 1930), 42-45. (p) 2583

----. "Margarita de niebla y Benjamín Jarnés." Ulises, Núm. 5 (diciembre de 1927), 24-26. (a-e) 2584

----. "México siempre." Fábula, Núm. 3 (marzo de 1934), 43-49. (a-e) 2585

----. "1959." Estaciones, III (Núm. 12, invierno de 1958), 381. (p) 2586

----. "Notas sobre la poesía de los negros en los Estados Unidos." Contemporáneos, XI (Núm. 40-41, septiembre-octubre de 1931), 197-200. (a-e) 2587

----. "Odio, muerte y eruditos." Sagitario, Núm. 9 (15 de febrero de 1927), 5-6. (a-e) 2588

----. "Palabras extrañas," "El amigo ido." Ulises, Núm. 1 (mayo de 1927), 9. (p) 2589

----. "La pesca y la flecha (Adivinanza)." Ulises, Núm. 2 (junio de 1927), 25-26. (a-e) 2590

----. "Poema." Sagitario, Núm. 4 (1 de septiembre de 1926), 14. (p) 2591

----. "Poemas." Ulises, Núm. 5 (diciembre de 1927), 3-4. (p) 2592

----. "Puebla-México." Sagitario, Núm. 11 (1 de marzo de 1927), 9-10. (a-e) 2593

----. "¡Qué México!" La Falange, Núm. 6 (1 de septiembre de 1923), 346-349. (f) 2594

----. "Radio-conferencia sobre el radio." Antena, Núm. 2 (agosto de 1924), 11-12. (a-e)   2595

----. "La renovación imposible," "Charcos," "Viaje." México Moderno, II (Núm. 2, septiembre de 1922), 78-79. (p)   2596

----. "Return ticket." Ulises, Núm. 2 (junio de 1927), 21-24; Núm. 3 (agosto de 1927), 15-28; Núm. 4 (octubre de 1927), 10-28. (a-e)   2597

----. "Viaje." Antena, Núm. 3 (septiembre de 1924), 6. (p)   2598

----. El secreto de los robots de M. Chapek. México Moderno, II (Núm. 4, junio de 1923), 253-254. (r) 2599

----. Anónimo. "Los dos romanticismos" (Trad. Salvador Novo). México Moderno, II (Núm. 3, octubre de 1922), 188-190. (tr)   (285)

----. Bell, Olive. "O todas las obras de arte visual..." (Trad. Salvador Novo). México Moderno, II (Núm. 2, septiembre de 1922), 124-125. (tr)   (644)

----. Huxley, Aldous. "La influencia de la ciencia en la literatura inmortal" (Trad. Salvador Novo). México Moderno, II (Núm. 3, octubre de 1922), 187-188. (tr)   (1873)

----. Masters, Edgar Lee. "Silencio" (Trad. Salvador Novo). La Falange, Núm. 7 (1 de octubre de 1923) 382-383. (tr)   (2284)

----. Pound, Ezra. "N. Y." (Trad. Salvador Novo). La Falange, Núm. 7 (1 de octubre de 1923), 384. (tr)   2600

Núñez y Domínguez, José de J. "Madrigal doméstico." Antena, Núm. 2 (agosto de 1924), 4. (p)   2601

----. "Meditación de primavera." México Moderno, Núm. 6 (enero de 1921), 336-337. (p)   2602

----. "La tísica." La Falange, Núm. 5 (1 de agosto de 1923), 285-286. (p)   2603

O. de Mendizábal, Miguel. "Los animales en los tejidos y bordados indígenas." Forma, I (Núm. 3, 1927), 7-11. (a-e)   2604

Obregón Santacilla, Carlos. "Consideraciones sobre arquitectura moderna; el hastío de la curva." Forma, I (Núm. 3, 1927), 41-44. (a-e)   2605

----. Montenegro, Roberto; Ituarte, Manuel M.; Pallares, Alfonso; Cumming, A. E.; Robles Gil, Alberto. "Encuesta sobre arquitectura." Forma, I (Núm. 3, 1927), 15-16. (a-e)   (1019)

Ocampo, Isidoro. "Pepenador," "Vino la otra." Tierra Nueva, II (Núm. 9-10, mayo-agosto de 1941), entre 144-145. (il)   2606

Ocampo, María Luisa. "El teatro mexicano contemporáneo." Antena, Núm. 1 (julio de 1924), 12-13. (a-e)   2607

Ochoa, Enriqueta. "La sequía." Estaciones, I (Núm. 3, otoño de 1956), 360-361. (p) 2608

O'Gorman, Edmundo. "Alfonso Reyes." Fábula, Núm. 9 (septiembre de 1934), 176. (a-e) 2609

----. "Carta de un autor agradeciendo un plagio." El Hijo Pródigo, VIII (Núm. 25, abril de 1945), 61. (a-e) 2610

----. "Una divagación." Fábula, Núm. 5 (mayo de 1934), 91-93. (a-e) 2611

----. Del ensayo americano de Medardo Vitier. El Hijo Pródigo, X (Núm. 31, octubre de 1945), 59-60. (r) 2612

----. Escritos inéditos de Fray Servando Teresa de Mier con introducción, notas y ordenación de textos por J. M. Miquel i Vergés y Hugo Díaz-Thomé. El Hijo Pródigo, VIII (Núm. 25, abril de 1945), 60-61. (r) 2613

----. El hombre Colón y otros ensayos de Ramón Iglesia. El Hijo Pródigo, VI (Núm. 21, diciembre de 1944), 185-186. (r) 2614

----. Mina, el español frente a España de J. M. Miquel i. Vergés. El Hijo Pródigo, IX (Núm. 28, julio de 1945), 56. (r) 2615

----. Torquemada de Thomas Hope. El Hijo Pródigo, VIII (Núm. 26, mayo de 1945), 121-122. (r) 2616

Ohanian, Armen. "El centinela de Kremenetz." Ruta, Núm. 6 (noviembre de 1938), 33-36. (f) 2617

Omar-Al-Khayyam. "Rubayas" (Trad. Rafael Lozano). La Falange, Núm. 3 (1 de febrero de 1923), 151-152. (p) (2133)

Ordaz Rocha, Luis. "Los siete días." Antena, Núm. 3 (septiembre de 1924), 6. (p) 2618

Orgambide, Pedro G. "El niño alucinado." Estaciones, IV (Núm. 15, otoño de 1959), 344-349. (f) 2619

Oribe, Emilio. "La danza en el mar." México Moderno, I (Núm. 8, marzo de 1921), 89. (p) 2620

Orlando, Felipe. "Las voces." Estaciones, V (Núm. 18, verano de 1960), 94-97. (a-e) 2621

Orozco, Carlos. "Retrato de Izca Farías," "Retrato de la Srta. Victoria Marín." Forma, I (Núm. 3, 1927), 4-5. (il) 2622

Orozco, José Clemente. "Del arte y otras cosas." El Hijo Pródigo, I (Núm. 6, septiembre de 1943), 364. (a-e) 2623

----. "El Demonio," "La humanidad," "Un jinete," "La gran Meretriz," "El dolor humano," "El Angel ata al Demonio." El Hijo Pródigo, III (Núm. 12, marzo de 1944), entre 144 y 145. (il) 2624

----. Ortiz Monasterio, Manuel; Owen, Gilberto; Chávez, Carlos. "Encuesta sobre pintura." Forma, I (Núm. 1, octubre de 1926), 5-6. (a-e)   (1041)

----. "Estudio," "La chole," "Desnudo," "Trabajo," "Paz," "Justicia," "Soldaderas." Forma, I (Núm. 1, octubre de 1926), 20-23. (il)   2625

----. "Frescos." Contemporáneos, III (Núm. 8, enero de 1929), 24-31. (il)   2626

----. "Obras recientes de José Clemente Orozco" (Incluye "Requiem," " 'El plan'," "The Subway," "Street Corner.") Contemporáneos, IV (Núm. 12, mayo de 1929), 126-129. (il) 2627

----. "Retrato de la señora Eva Sikelianos," "Oleo," "Escenas de la Revolución." Contemporáneos, V (Núm. 18, noviembre de 1929), 293-295. (il)   2628

Orozco Muñoz, Francisco. "Alfonso Reyes." Fábula, Núm. 9 (septiembre de 1934), 176. (a-e)   2629

----. "Los animalistas totonacos." El Hijo Pródigo, V (Núm. 16, julio de 1944), 32. (a-e)   2630

----. "El arte totonaca del antiguo México." El Hijo Pródigo, I (Núm. 2, mayo de 1943), 94-96. (a-e)   2631

----. "Como un consejo," "En el muelle de Gante," "Amistad." México Moderno, I (Núm. 6, enero de 1921), 329-330. (p)   2632

----. "Con el corazón angustiado," "Síntesis." México Moderno, I (Núm. 3, octubre de 1920), 133. (p)   2633

----. "El cráneo de cristal." Fábula, Núm. 4 (abril de 1934), 75. (a-e)   2634

----. "Diego Rivera." Fábula, Núm. 4 (abril de 1934), 74. (a-e)   2635

----. "Invitación al dolor," "Noticias del pueblo," "El hombre que se creyó feliz." México Moderno, II (Núm. 2, septiembre de 1922), 90-91. (a-e)   2636

----. "Los que se fueron." La Falange, Núm. 7 (1 de octubre de 1923), 363-365. (p)   2637

----. "Pequeñas esculturas mexicanas." El Hijo Pródigo, IV (Núm. 13, abril de 1944), 24. (a-e)   2638

----. Saadí. "Sentencias" (Trad. Francisco Orozco Muñoz). La Falange, Núm. 2 (1 de enero de 1923), 66-70. (tr)   2639

Orozco Romero, Carlos. "Cabeza," "Mujer sentada," "Cabeza," "Retrato." Contemporáneos, V (Núm. 17, octubre de 1929), 218-221. (il)   2640

----. "La mujer que espera," "La tormenta," "La mujer del guante," "Paisaje," "Autorretrato," "El paricutín," "Mujer," "Retrato." El Hijo Pródigo, XI (Núm. 34, enero de 1946), entre 48 y 49. (il)   2641

----. "Pescador de nubes."
Estaciones, I (Núm. 1,
primavera de 1956), entre
112-113. (il)   2642

Ors, Eugenio d'. "Historia de
una claudicación." Sagitario,
Núm. 3 (15 de agosto de
1926), 12-13. (p)   2643

----. "Los laicos y los
otros." Sagiatrio, Núm. 5
(1 de octubre de 1926), 12-13.
(p)   2644

----. "Mahatma Gandhi."
Sagitario, Núm. 4 (1 de
septiembre de 1926), 5. (a-e)
                                 2645

----. "Paul-Jean Toulet."
Sagitario, Núm. 1 (15 de
julio de 1926), 14. (p) 2646

----. "Sobre el mongolismo."
Sagitario, Núm. 2 (1 de
agosto de 1926), 12. (p)
                                 2647

Ortega, Gregorio. "Godoy,
traductor de France." Antena,
Núm. 3 (septiembre de 1924),
10-11. (a-e)   2648

Ortiz, Alfonso. Kipling,
Rudyard. "Dray wara yow
dee" (Trad. Alfonso Ortiz).
México Moderno, II (Núm. 1,
agosto de 1922), 11-19. (tr)
                                 (1985)

Ortiz, César. "Uvas del
rencor" (Reseña de Grapes of
Wrath de John Steinbeck).
Romance, I (Núm. 6, 15 de
abril de 1940), 18. (r) 2649

Ortiz, Fernando. "El tabaco
y los ritos purificadores de
los pecados." Romance, I
(Núm. 17, 22 de octubre de
1940), 4, 15. (a-e) 2650

Ortiz de Montellano, Bernardo.
"Adición (al cuaderno de
lecturas de Alfonso Reyes)."
Contemporáneos, IX (Núm.
33, febrero de 1931), 184-
185. (a-e)   2651

----. "Alfonso Reyes."
Fábula, Núm. 9 (septiembre
de 1934), 177. (a-e)   2652

----. "Aniversario 3."
Contemporáneos, X (Núm. 30,
mayo de 1931), 97-98. (a-e)
                                 2653

----. "Antiguos cantares
mexicanos." Contemporáneos,
IV (Núm. 12, mayo de 1929),
100-104. (a-e)   2654

----. "Antiguos cantares
mexicanos." Contemporáneos,
XI (Núm. 40-41, septiembre-
octubre de 1931), 115-119.
(p)   2655

----. "Antología de Jean
Charlot." Contemporáneos,
X (Núm. 37, junio de 1931),
263-266. (a-e)   2656

----. "Aventuras de la novela."
Contemporáneos, I (Núm. 2,
julio de 1928), 207-209. (a-e)
                                 2657

----. "La cabeza de Salomé."
El Hijo Pródigo, I (Núm. 3,
junio de 1943), 165-167. (dr)
                                 2658

----. "Cantares," "Amor
como yo lo entiendo..."
Antena, Núm. 3 (septiembre
de 1924), 5. (p)   2659

----. "Los cinco sentidos."
La Falange, Núm. 7 (1 de
octubre de 1923), 394. (p)
                                 2660

----. "Cuadernos del Plata." Contemporáneos, V (Núm. 19, diciembre de 1929), 427-429. (a-e)   2661

----. "Definiciones para la estética de...". Contemporáneos, III (Núm. 10, marzo de 1929), 199-205. (a-e)   2662

----. "Desolación," "Resignación." México Moderno, I (Núm. 8, marzo de 1921), 114-115. (p) 2663

----, y Cuesta, Jorge. "Dos cartas a propósito de la nota preinserta" (sobre La rebelión de las masas de Ortega y Gasset). Contemporáneos, IX (Núm. 33, febrero de 1931), 162-165. (a-e)   (994)

----. "Elegía." El Hijo Pródigo, VIII (Núm. 25, abril de 1945), 21-23. (p) 2664

----. "Epica popular" (Contiene "Corrido de Julián Blanco"). Contemporáneos, III (Núm. 10, marzo de 1929), 271-279. (a-e)   2665

----. "Esquema de la literatura mexicana moderna." Contemporáneos, X (Núm. 37, junio de 1931), 195-210. (a-e)   2666

----. "Este era un rey...," "El loro," "Meditación." La Falange, Núm. 4 (1 de julio de 1923), 226-227. (p)   2667

----. "Feria." Sagitario, Núm. 11 (15 de marzo de 1927), 8. (p) 2668

----. "El fusil del insurgente." La Falange,

Núm. 6 (1 de septiembre de 1923), 344-345. (p) 2669

----. "Hipnoticias de México." El Hijo Pródigo, I (Núm. 6, septiembre de 1943), 353-354. (a-e) 2670

----. "Lección." La Falange, Núm. 3 (1 de febrero de 1923), 164-165. (p) 2671

----. "Letra muerta," "Tercer son de altiplanicie." Contemporáneos, VIII (Núm. 26-27, julio-agosto de 1930), 46-51. (p) 2672

----. "Literatura de la revolución y literatura revolucionaria" Contemporáneos, VIII (Núm. 23, abril de 1930), 77-81. (a-e) 2673

----. "Literatura del pueblo y de los niños." La Falange, Núm. 1 (1 de diciembre de 1922), 31-32. (f) 2674

----. "Marcial Rojas." Contemporáneos, VIII (Núm. 28-29, septiembre-octubre de 1930), 192. (a-e) 2675

----. "Martirio de la guitarra." Contemporáneos, IX (Núm. 34, marzo de 1931), 279. (p) 2676

----. "Mi reino." La Falange, Núm. 5 (1 de agosto de 1923), 288-289. (p) 2677

----. "Navegación del alma." Fábula, Núm. 3 (marzo de 1934), 55-56. (p) 2678

----. "Nota previa." Taller, II (Núm. 10, marzo-abril de 1940), 63-64. (a-e) 2679

----. "Notas de un lector de poesía." Contemporáneos,

VIII (Núm. 26-27, julio-
agosto de 1930), 91-95. (a-e)
2680

----. "La obra de Valéry y
el pensamiento ruso. "
Contemporáneos, XI (Núm.
40-41, septiembre-octubre
de 1931), 187-197. (a-e)
2681

----. "Pesca, " "Historia, "
"Agrarismo, " "Horizonte, "
"Dibujo, " "Encendedor de
estrellas, " "Oración, "
"Ultimo sueño. " Contem-
poráneos, I (Núm. 1, junio
de 1928), 38-42. (p) 2682

----. "El pescadito, " "Yo soy
la viudita, " "La pájara
pinta. " La Falange, Núm. 2
(1 de enero de 1923), 100-101.
(p)   2683

----. "Poesía. " Contem-
poráneos, VI (Núm. 22,
marzo de 1930), 193-195. (p)
2684

----. "Poesías de Robinson"
(incluye "Gravedad, "
"Gaceta, " y "Motivos negros').
Contemporáneos, II (Núm. 5,
octubre de 1928), 109-112.
(p)   2685

----. "Por el camino de
Proust. " Contemporáneos, II
(Núm. 6, noviembre de 1928),
298-300. (a-e)   2686

----. "Primero sueño. "
Contemporáneos, X (Núm. 35,
abril de 1931), 1-12. (p)
2687

----. "Romance de las
hebritas de oro, " "El milano,"
"Canciones de cuna. " La
Falange, Núm. 1 (1 de
diciembre de 1922), 32-35.
(p)   2688

----. "Segundo número de
poesía. " Contemporáneos,
XI (Núm. 38-39, julio-agosto
de 1931), 113. (a-e)   2689

----. "Segundo sueño
(Anestesia). " Romance, I
(Núm. 13, 1 de agosto de
1940), 9. (p)   2690

----. "El soldadito de plomo."
La Falange, Núm. 2 (1 de
enero de 1923), 99. (p) 2691

----. "Son de altiplanicie. "
Contemporáneos, V (Núm. 16,
septiembre de 1929), 81-86.
(p)   2692

----. "Sonetos antiguos. "
El Hijo Pródigo, X (Núm. 33,
diciembre de 1945), 143. (p)
2693

----. "Sueño al mar, " "Quiero decir: el ángel, "
"Materia de la vida. " El
Hijo Pródigo, III (Núm. 12,
marzo de 1944), 141-142.
(p)   2694

----. "Suma de poesía. "
Contemporáneos, IV (Núm. 12,
mayo de 1929), 143-145.
(a-e)   2695

----. "Supervielle, poeta de
alta mar. " Contemporáneos,
X (Núm. 35, abril de 1931),
79-81. (a-e)   2696

----. "Teatro de títeres --
El sombrerón. " Contem-
poráneos, IX (Núm. 32, enero
de 1931), 71-96. (dr) 2697

----. "Visita del maestro
Pedro San Juan. " Contem-
poráneos, V (Núm. 16,
septiembre de 1929), 156-157.
(a-e)   2698

----. Anfora sedienta de Rafael Heliodoro Valle. La Falange, Núm. 2 (1 de enero de 1923), 118. (r) 2699

----. "Una antología nueva" (Reseña de Antología de la poesía mexicana moderna de Jorge Cuesta). Contemporáneos, I (Núm. 1, junio de 1928), 76-81. (r) 2700

----. La aventura y el orden de Guillermo de Torre. El Hijo Pródigo, III (Núm. 11, febrero de 1944), 120-121. (r) 2701

----. Camino de Carlos Pellicer. Contemporáneos, V (Núm. 16, septiembre de 1929), 150-152. (r) 2702

----. Crucero de Genaro Estrada. Contemporáneos, II (Núm. 4, septiembre de 1928), 84-86. (r) 2703

----. De mi block de Pedro Erasmo Callorda (ed.). México Moderno, I (Núm. 8, marzo de 1921), 123. (r) 2704

----. Del carillón íntimo de Emilio Menéndez Barriola. México Moderno, I (Núm. 8, marzo de 1921), 123. (r) 2705

----. Historia de la literatura mexicana de Carlos González Peña. Contemporáneos, III (Núm. 9, febrero de 1929), 177-180. (r) 2706

----. Los hombres que dispersó la danza de Andrés Henestrosa. Contemporáneos, VIII (Núm. 30-31, noviembre-diciembre de 1930), 276-277. (r) 2707

----. Intemperie de Fernán Silva Valdés y Boletines de mar y tierra de Jorge Carrera Andrade. Contemporáneos, VIII (Núm. 30-31, noviembre-diciembre de 1930), 269-271. (r) 2708

----. "Librería de viejo" (Reseña de Memorias del marqués de San Basilio de autor anónimo). Contemporáneos, II (Núm. 7, diciembre de 1928), 412-415. (r) 2709

----. Pensamientos y formas. Notas de viaje de Alberto Masferrer. México Moderno, II (Núm. 8, marzo de 1921), 123-124. (r) 2710

----. Romancero gitano de Federico García Lorca. Contemporáneos, II (Núm. 4, septiembre de 1928), 104-108. (r) 2711

----. "Vida de Cortés" (Reseña de La vie de Fernand Cortés de Jean Babelon). Contemporáneos, II (Núm. 7, diciembre de 1928), 388-393. (r) 2712

----. Eliot, Thomas Stearns. "Miércoles de ceniza" (Trad. Bernardo Ortiz de Montellano). Taller, II (Núm. 10, marzo-abril de 1940), 92-99. (tr) (1222)

----. Frazer, James George. "La magia y la religión" (Trad. Bernardo Ortiz de Montellano). El Hijo Pródigo, II (Núm. 8, noviembre de 1943), 112-122. (tr) (1387)

----. Larbaud, Valéry. "Prólogo a Los de abajo." (Trad. Bernardo Ortiz de Montellano), Contemporáneos, VI (Núm. 21, febrero de 1930), 127-143. (tr) (2006)

----. Tagore, Rabindranath. "Poemas" (Trad. Bernardo Ortiz de Montellano). La Falange, Núm. 1 (1 de diciembre de 1922), 45. (tr) 2713

----. Valéry, Paul. "Conversación sobre la poesía" (Trad. Bernardo Ortiz de Montellano). Contemporáneos, VIII (Núm. 26-27, julio-agosto de 1930), 3-6. (tr) 2714

Ortiz Monasterio, Manuel; Orozco, José Clemente; Owen, Gilberto; Chávez, Carlos. "Encuesta sobre pintura." Forma, I (Núm. 1, octubre de 1926), 5-6. (a-e) (1041)

Ortiz Reyes, José. "Sosa." Romance, I (Núm. 16, 15 de septiembre de 1940), 16-17. (f) 2715

Ortiz Saralegui, Juvenal. "Federico García Lorca y Rafael Barradas." Romance, I (Núm. 19, 18 de diciembre de 1940), 9. (a-e) 2716

Ortiz Vidales, Alfredo. 'Dos poemas." Fábula, Núm. 7 (julio de 1934), 137-138. (p) 2717

Orrego E., Atenor. La muerte en las manos de Julián Gorkin. Estaciones, II (Núm. 6, verano de 1957), 198-201. (r) 2718

Osorio, Adrián. "La catedral de México." Fábula, Núm.

5 (mayo de 1934), entre 96-97. (il) 2719

Osorio, José Salomón. "El puerto." Antena, Núm. 4 (octubre de 1924), 7. (p) 2720

Ostrovsky, Nicolás. "Y el acero fue templado." Ruta, Núm. 12 (mayo de 1939), 39-48. (f) 2721

Otero, Blas de. "Parábolas y dezires." Estaciones, IV (Núm. 15, otoño de 1959), 271-273. (p) 2722

Otero Silva, Miguel. "El libertador." Ruta, Núm. 5 (octubre de 1938), 26. (p) 2723

Ovalle, José de. "La flajelación," "La corona de espinas," "La sentencia," "La crucifixión," "La lanzada," "El descendimiento." El Hijo Pródigo, III (Núm. 11, febrero de 1944), entre 80 y 81. (il) 2724

Owen, Gilberto. "Anti-orfeo." Sagitario, Núm. 14 (31 de mayo de 1927), 5. (p) 2725

----. "Autorretrato o del subway." Contemporáneos, IV (Núm. 12, mayo de 1929), 120-122. (p) 2726

----. "Canción del alfarero." La Falange, Núm. 6 (1 de septiembre de 1923), 340-342. (p) 2727

----. "Carta." Contemporáneos, VIII (Núm. 28-29, septiembre-octubre de 1930), 97-110. (p) 2728

----. "Desvelo." Ulises, Núm. 1 (mayo de 1927),

10-11. (p) 2729

----. "Encuentros con Jorge
Cuesta." El Hijo Pródigo,
III (Núm. 12, marzo de 1944),
137-140. (a-e) 2730

----. Orozco, José Clemente;
Ortiz Monasterio, Manuel;
Chávez, Carlos. "Encuesta
sobre pintura." Forma, I
(Núm. 1, octubre de 1926),
5-6. (a-e) (1041)

----. "Examen de pausas."
Contemporáneos, I (Núm. 2,
julio de 1928), 97-111. (f)
2731

----. "Pachuca." Ulises,
Núm. 2 (junio de 1927), 8-10.
(f) 2732

----. "Playa de veraneo."
Antena, Núm. 4 (octubre de
1924), 7. (p) 2733

----. "Poema en que se usa
mucho la palabra amor."
Contemporáneos, II (Núm. 7,
diciembre de 1928), 323-324.
(p) 2734

----. "Poesía -¿Pura?-Plena."
Sagitario, Núm. 10, (1 de
marzo de 1927), 6. (a-e)
2735

----. "La poesía,
Villaurrutia y la crítica."
Sagitario, Núm. 9 (15 de
febrero de 1927), 8. (a-e)
2736

----. "Pureza." Sagitario,
Núm. 10 (1 de marzo de
1927), 6. (p) 2737

----. "Sinbad el varado."
El Hijo Pródigo, II (Núm. 7,
octubre de 1943), 24-26. (p)
2738

----. "Teologías,"
"Maravillas de la voluntad,"
"Interior," "Novela,"
"Poética." Ulises, Núm. 5
(diciembre de 1927), 5-7.
(p) 2739

----. Los alimentos
terrestres de André Gide.
El Hijo Pródigo, II (Núm. 7,
octubre de 1943), 59. (r)
2740

----. El diablo en el cuerpo
de Raymond Radiguet. El
Hijo Pródigo, IV (Núm. 14,
mayo de 1944), 120-121. (r)
2741

----. Invitación a la muerte
de Xavier Villaurrutia. El
Hijo Pródigo, IV (Núm. 13,
abril de 1944), 59-60. (r)
2742

----. Pájaro pinto de Antonio
Espina. Ulises, Núm. 1
(mayo de 1927), 26-27. (r)
2743

----. Poemas intemporales
de Porfirio Barba Jacob. El
Hijo Pródigo, III (Núm. 10,
enero de 1944), 55. (r) 2744

----. Variaciones sobre la
poesía de Eduardo González
Lanuza. El Hijo Pródigo, III
(Núm. 10, enero de 1944),
59. (r) 2745

----. Caillois, Roger.
"Actualidad de las sectas"
(Trad. Cilberto Owen). El
Hijo Pródigo, IV (Núm. 14,
mayo de 1944), 89-92. (tr)
(744)

----. Rosso de San Secondo.
"Lazarina entre cuchillos"
(Trad. Gilberto Owen y
Agustín Lazo). El Hijo

Pródigo, XIII (Núm. 40, julio de 1946), 48-55; (Núm. 41, agosto de 1946), 93-103. (tr)   (2034)

----. Smedley, Agnes. "El automóvil núm. 1469" (Trad. Gilberto Owen). El Hijo Pródigo, III (Núm. 10, enero de 1944), 35-39. (tr) 2745A

----. Valéry, Paul. "Pequeños textos, comentarios de grabados" (Trad. Gilberto Owen). Contemporáneos, II (Núm. 4, septiembre de 1928), 34-39. (tr)   2746

P., D. de. "Leon Tolstoi y Máximo Gorki: Entrevistas y correspondencia." Romance, II (Núm. 22, 15 de marzo de 1941), 3. (a-e)   2747

P., J. Bases para un Congreso Centroamericano de Obreros de Eduardo Alvarez. México Moderno, II (Núm. 7, febrero de 1921), 70-71. (r) 2748

P. S., N. Historia política de la revolución de Miguel Alessio Robles. Ruta, Núm. 2 (julio de 1938), 56-57. (r)   2749

Paalen, Alice. "Gruta." Estaciones, I (Núm. 1, primavera de 1956), 144. (p)   2750

----. "La nuit hindoe," "La lune et son reflet," "La promenade," "Le cyclope," "La souris," "La fiesta de abril," "Out of Africa," "Twilight." El Hijo Pródigo, XIII (Núm. 42, septiembre de 1946), entre 148 y 150. (il)   2751

----. "La peau de soleil." El Hijo Pródigo, XIII (Núm.

42, septiembre de 1946), 128. (il)   2752

Pach, Walter. "El arte en México." Forma, II (Núm. 7, 1928), 19-21. (a-e)   2753

----. "Aspectos desconocidos de la pintura mexicana." El Hijo Pródigo, I (Núm. 3, junio de 1943), 157-162. (a-e)   2754

----. "Fluctuat nec mergitur" (Trad. Octavio G. Barreda). El Hijo Pródigo, IX (Núm. 28, julio de 1945), 19-26. (a-e)   (598)

----. "Impresiones sobre el arte actual de México." México Moderno, II (Núm. 3, octubre de 1922), 131-138. (a-e)   2755

----. Medieval American Art de Pal Kelemen. El Hijo Pródigo, I (Núm. 6, septiembre de 1943), 382-383. (r) 2756

Pacheco, León. "La pintura de Rodríguez Lozano." Contemporáneos, IV (Núm. 11, abril de 1929), 85-88. (a-e)   2757

----. "El secreto de Manuel Rodríguez Lozano." Sagitario, Núm. 9 (15 de febrero de 1927), 9-10. (a-e)   2758

----. "Secretos, debilidades." Ulises, Núm. 6 (febrero de 1928), 18-20. (a-e)   2759

Pacheco, Máximo. "Columpio," "El grito," "El hogar," "Descanso de los aguadores," "Jacal," "Obrero muerto." Forma, I (Núm. 2, noviembre de 1926), 3-6. (il)   2760

----. "Los dos huérfanos."
Forma, I (Núm. 3, 1927), 29.
(il)   2761

Pacheco y Berny, José Emilio.
"Arbol entre dos muros."
Estaciones, II (Núm. 12,
invierno de 1958), 433-436. (p)
                                  2762

----. "Del frágil laberinto."
Estaciones, IV (Núm. 14,
verano de 1959), 162-163. (p)
                                  2763

----. "Egloga octava."
Estaciones, V (Núm. 18,
verano de 1960), 6-8. (p)
                                  2764

----. "El enemigo muerto."
Estaciones, IV (Núm. 16,
invierno de 1959), 405-409.
(f)   2765

----. "Eva." Estaciones, II
(Núm. 5, primavera de 1957),
70. (p)   2766

----. "Guerra Florida."
Estaciones, III (Núm. 9,
primavera de 1958), 77-81.
(p)   2767

----. "Obituario." Estaciones,
III (Núm. 9, primavera de
1958), 108. (a-e)   2768

----. "Soneto." Estaciones,
III (Núm. 11, otoño de 1958),
314. (p)   2769

----. "Tríptico del gato."
Estaciones, II (Núm. 6, verano
de 1957), 209-216. (f) 2770

----. Adela y yo de Rubén
Salazar Mallén. Estaciones,
III (Núm. 9, primavera de
1958), 106-107. (r)   2771

----. Al pie de la letra de
Rosario Castellanos. Estaciones,

IV (Núm. 14, verano de
1959), 245. (r)   2772

----. Alas de Rafael Solana.
Estaciones, III (Núm. 9,
primavera de 1958), 105-106.
(r)   2773

----. Barrabás de Par
Lagerkvist. Estaciones, II
(Núm. 7, otoño de 1957),
363-364. (r)   2774

----. Bernardo de Balbuena.
La vida y la obra de José
Rojas Garcidueñas. Estaciones,
IV (Núm. 14, verano de
1959), 249-250. (r)   2775

----. Calle mayor de Juan
Antonio Bardem. Estaciones,
IV (Núm. 16, invierno de
1959), 500-501. (r)   2776

----. Caminos del diablo y de
Dios de Ventura Gómez
Dávila. Estaciones, IV (Núm.
16, invierno de 1959), 501.
(r)   2777

----. "La colección 'Lenguas
y estudios literarios'."
Estaciones, IV (Núm. 15,
otoño de 1959), 380-384. (r)
                       2778

----. Coloquio de amor de
Margarita Paz Paredes.
Estaciones, II (Núm. 6,
verano de 1957), 228-229. (r)
                       2779

----. Crónica de la
revolución mexicana de
Roberto Blanco Moheno.
Estaciones, III (Núm. 9,
primavera de 1958), 104-105.
(r)   2780

----. La cruzada de los
niños de Marcel Schwob.
Estaciones, IV (Núm. 15,

172

otoño de 1959), 358-360. (r)
2781

----. Cuentistas mexicanos modernos con selección e introducción de Emmanuel Carballo. Estaciones, II (Núm. 6, verano de 1957), 229. (r) 2782

----. D. F. Colección Teatro Mexicano de Emilio Carballido. Estaciones, II (Núm. 6, verano de 1957), 230. (r)
2783

----. El destino de Lázaro de Manuel Andújar. Estaciones, IV (Núm. 16, invierno de 1959), 496. (r) 2784

----. La dignidad en Don Quixote de Francisco Monterde. Estaciones, IV (Núm. 14, verano de 1959), 249. (r) 2785

----. El ensayo mexicano moderno de José Luis Martínez. Estaciones, III (Núm. 11, otoño de 1958), 327-331. (r) 2786

----. Ensayos escogidos de Miguel de Montaigne. Estaciones, IV (Núm. 16, invierno de 1959), 501-502. (r) 2787

----. La estación violenta de Octavio Paz. Estaciones, III (Núm. 11, otoño de 1958), 334-336. (r) 2788

----. Flor de juegos antiguos de Agustín váñez. Estaciones, IV (Núm. 14, verano de 1959), 248. (r) 2789

----. Historia mundial desde 1914 hasta 1950 de David Thomson. Estaciones, IV

(Núm. 14, verano de 1959), 249. (r) 2790

----. Jorge Cuesta: Poesía de Elías Nandino. Estaciones, III (Núm. 10, verano de 1958), 198-199. (r) 2791

----. Lienzos de sueño de Manuel Mejía Valera. Estaciones, IV (Núm. 14, verano de 1959), 244. (r)
2792

----. El lugar donde crece la hierba de Luisa Josefina Hernández. Estaciones, IV (Núm. 16, invierno de 1959), 499-500. (r) 2793

----. Malditos de Wilberto Cantón. Estaciones, IV (Núm. 14, verano de 1959), 244. (r)
2794

----. Muertes históricas de Martín Luis Guzmán. Estaciones, III (Núm. 11, otoño de 1958), 338-340. (r)
2795

----. La mujer domada de Mariano Azuela. Estaciones, II (Núm. 7, otoño de 1957), 362-363. (r) 2796

----. Obras completas de Mariano Azuela. Estaciones, V (Núm. 17, primavera de 1960), 120-122. (r) 2797

----. Paz o guerra atómica de Albert Schweitzer. Estaciones, III (Núm. 11, otoño de 1958), 343-346. (r)
2798

----. Las peras del olmo de Octavio Paz. Estaciones, II (Núm. 7, otoño de 1957), 358-360. (r) 2799

----. Piedra de sol de Octavio Paz. Estaciones, III (Núm. 9, primavera de 1958), 99. (r) 2800

----. Primeros versos de Gilberto Owen. Estaciones, II (Núm. 7, otoño de 1957), 355-356. (r) 2801

----. Las raíces irritadas de Edmundo Valadés. Estaciones, III (Núm. 9, primavera de 1958), 107-108. (r) 2802

----. La región más transparente de Carlos Fuentes. Estaciones, III (Núm. 10, verano de 1958), 193-196. (r) 2803

----. Robespierre de Mario Mazzuchelli. Estaciones, IV (Núm. 16, invierno de 1959), 502-503. (r) 2804

----. Sin tregua de Jaime Torres Bodet. Estaciones, II (Núm. 8, invierno de 1957), 486-487. (r) 2805

----. El sótano de Lini M. de Vries. Estaciones, IV (Núm. 16, invierno de 1959), 502. (r) 2806

----. Tiempo cercado de Sergio Pitol. Estaciones, IV (Núm. 14, verano de 1959), 244. (r) 2807

----. Todo ángel es terrible de Guillermo Francovich. Estaciones, IV (Núm. 16, invierno de 1959), 502. (r) 2808

----. Ulises Criollo de José Vasconcelos. Estaciones, III (Núm. 9, primavera de 1958), 102-103. (r) 2809

----. Verso y dolor de Miguel Hernández de Jacinto Palacios. Estaciones, III (Núm. 10, verano de 1958), 191. (r) 2810

----. La vid y el labrador de Enoch Cancino Casahonda. Estaciones, II (Núm. 6, verano de 1957), 227-228. (r) 2811

----. Vida de Morelos de Alfonso Teja Zabre. Estaciones, IV (Núm. 16, invierno de 1959), 502. (r) 2812

----. Baudelaire, Charles. "La caballera. " (Trad. José Emilio Pacheco y Berny), Estaciones, V (Núm. 18, veranode 1960), 54-55. (tr) (623)

----. Couffon, Claude. "La muerte lleva el juego" (Reseña de Pedro Páramo de Juan Rulfo; Trad. José Emilio Pacheco y Berny). Estaciones, IV (Núm. 16, invierno de 1959), 494-495. (tr) (967)

----. Nérval, Gerard de. "El desdichado. " (Trad. José Emilio Pacheco y Berny). Estaciones, IV (Núm. 13, primavera de 1959), 91. (tr) (2556)

Padilla, Hugo. "Poema. " Estaciones, III (Núm. 11, otoño de 1958), 248-250. (p) 2813

----. "Poema. " Estaciones, IV (Núm. 15, otoño de 1959), 299-300. (p) 2814

Páez de Ribera, Ruy. "Dezir contra la provesa. " México Moderno, II (Núm. 2,

(1 de agosto de 1922), 14.
(a-e)   2816

----. "Mensaje a la juventud
mexicana." Sagitario, Núm.
11 (15 de marzo de 1927), 4.
(a-e)   2817

----. "Nicaragua:Resolución
de la 'Unión Latino-Americana'." Sagitario, Núm. 11
(15 de marzo de 1927), 10.
(a-e)   2818

Palacios, Emanuel. "Anónimo
del ahorcado." Contempo-
ráneos, VIII (Núm. 26-27,
julio-agosto de 1930), 52-54.
(p)   2819

----. "Fauna de vidrio."
Fábula, Núm. 4 (abril de
1934), 71-73. (a-e)   2820

----. "Muerta." Contempo-
ráneos, V (Núm. 18,
noviembre de 1929), 244. (p)
                         2821

----. "Paisajes y confesiones."
Taller, I (Núm. 4, julio de
1939), 48-50. (a-e)   2822

----. "Río." Contemporáneos,
XI (Núm. 40-41, septiembre-
octubre de 1931), 169-170.
(p)   2823

Palafox y Mendoza, Don Juan de.
"De la naturaleza del indio."
El Hijo Pródigo, VII (Núm. 23,
febrero de 1945), 100-108;
(Núm. 24, marzo de 1945),
153-165. (a-e)   2824

Pallais, A. H. "Los
maitines de la niña más
linda de la ciudad." La
Falange, Núm. 3 (1 de
febrero de 1923), 161-162.
(p)   2825

Pallares, Alfonso; Obregón
Santacilla, Carlos;
Montenegro, Roberto;
Ituarte, Manuel M.; Cumming,
A. E.: Robles Gil, Alberto.
"Encuesta sobre arquitectura."
Forma, I (Núm. 3, 1927),
15-16. (a-e)   (1019)

Parada León, Ricardo. "La
agonía." Antena, Núm. 2
(agosto de 1924), 13-15,
Núm. 3 (septiembre de 1924);
Núm. 11-13; 4 (octubre de 1924);
Núm. 12-14; 5 (octubre de 1924);
11-15. (dr)   2826

----. "Ponce, compositor
eficaz." Antena, Núm. 5
(noviembre de 1924), 8. (a-e)
                         2827

Pardo, Wilfredo B.
Delincuentes políticos y
políticos delincuentes de Noé
de la Flor. Romance, I
(Núm. 3, 1 de marzo de
1940), 19. (r)   2828

----. "Un estudio sobre el
problema filosófico del
derecho" (Reseña de Vida
humana, sociedad y derecho
de Luis Recaséns Siches).
Romance, I (Núm. 10, 15 de
junio de 1940), 19. (r) 2829

Pardo García, Germán.
"América en el cuento."
Estaciones, I (Núm. 1,
primavera de 1956), 99-105.
(a-e)   2830

----. "Centauro en primavera,"
"Frutal amor," "Floral amor,"
"Amor en sus banderas,"
"Centauro vencedor," "Hombre
centauro." Estaciones, II
(Núm. 5, primavera de 1957),
5-8. (p)   2831

----. "Fantasía del pan." Estaciones, III (Núm. 11, otoño de 1958), 353-368. (p) 2832

----. "Testimonios del viento." Estaciones, II (Núm. 8, invierno de 1957), 430-445. (p) 2833

----. Palabra de Mauricio de la Selva. Estaciones, I (Núm. 2, verano de 1956), 254-255. (r) 2834

Partida, Rafael L. Shildt, Runar. "El ahorcado" (Trad. Rafael L. Partida). El Hijo Pródigo, XII (Núm. 39, junio de 1946), 165-174. (tr) 2835

Parra, Felix. "Bodegón." El Hijo Pródigo, XIII (Núm. 40, julio de 1946), 6. (il) 2836

Parra, Manuel de la. "El tintinámbulo, " "Anochecer." México Moderno, I (Núm. 1, agosto de 1920), 23-25. (p) 2837

Pasamanik, Luisa. "Nocturno." Estaciones, IV (Núm. 14, verano de 1959), 193-198. (p) 2838

Paso, Fernando del. "Dos sonetos de lo diario." Estaciones, III (Núm. 12, invierno de 1958), 423-424. (p) 2839

Pater, Walter. "Ascesis" (Trad. Abra) México Moderno, II (Núm. 3, octubre de 1922), 183-185. (a-e) (1)

Pavlenko, P. "Mayo" (Trad. Pedro Geoffroy Rivas). Ruta, Núm. 4 (septiembre de 1938), 43-45. (f) (1510)

Pavón Flores, Mario. "Diario

lírico de un maestro." Ruta, Núm. 9 (febrero de 1939), 35-40. (f) 2840

----. Singladura de César Garizurieta. Ruta, Núm. 1 (junio de 1938), 58-59. (r) 2841

Paz, Octavio. "A tres jóvenes amigos." Ruta, Núm. 5 (octubre de 1938), 52-58. (a-e) 2842

----. "Bajo tu clara sombra" (Suplemento poético al núm. 9-10). Tierra Nueva, II (Núm. 9-10, mayo-ágosto de 1941). (p) 2843

----. "La casa de España." Taller, I (Núm. 1, diciembre de 1938), 57-58. (a-e) 2844

----. "Constante amigo." Taller, I (Núm. 4, julio de 1939), 53. (a-e) 2845

----. "Diario de un soñador." El Hijo Pródigo, VII (Núm. 24, marzo de 1945), 147-151. (a-e) 2846

----. "Juan Soriano." Tierra Nueva, II (Núm. 11-12, septiembre-diciembre de 1941), 241-242. (a-e) 2847

----. "El mar." Taller, I (Núm. 3, mayo de 1939), 41-44. (a-e) 2848

----. "Máscaras del alba." Estaciones, III (Núm. 9, primavera de 1958), 12-14. (p) 2849

----. "Medianoche, " "Primavera a la vista, " "Junio." El Hijo Pródigo, V (Núm. 17, agosto de 1944), 83-85. (p) 2850

----. "El muro, " "Olvido. "
El Hijo Pródigo, II (Núm. 9,
diciembre de 1943), 161-162.
(p)   2851

----. "Noche de resurreccio-
nes." Taller, II (Núm. 10,
marzo-abril de 1940), 25-29.
(p)   2852

----. "Noches" (Contiene
"Nacimiento" y "El
desconocido"). El Hijo
Pródigo, I (Núm. 1, abril de
1943), 18-20. (p)   2853

----. "Oda al sueño. " Taller,
I (Núm. 4, julio de 1939),
36-39. (p)   2854

----. "Una obra sin joroba. "
Taller, I (Núm. 5, octubre
de 1939), 43-45. (a-e) 2855

----. "Pablo Neruda en el
corazón. " Ruta, Núm. 4
(septiembre de 1938), 25-33.
(a-e)   2856

----. "Palabras en la sombra,"
"Adiós a la casa, "
"Epitafio para un poeta. " El
Hijo Pródigo, IX (Núm. 31,
octubre de 1945), 17-19. (p)
                           2857

----. "Poesía de soledad y
poesía de comunión. " El
Hijo Pródigo, I (Núm. 5,
agosto de 1943), 271-278.
(a-e)   2858

----; Vasconcelos, José;
González Martínez, Enrique;
Gaos, José; Gallegos, José
M.; Martínez, José Luis;
García-Bacca, David;
Jiménez Rueda, Julio; Nicol,
Eduardo; Bergamín, José.
"Poesía, mística y filosofía:
Debate en torno a San Juan
de la Cruz. " El Hijo Pródigo,

I (Núm. 3, junio de 1943),
135-144. (a-e)   (661)

----. "Respuesta a la encuesta
de Romance. " Romance, I
(Núm. 7, 1 de mayo de 1940),
2. (a-e)   2859

----. "Semillas para un
himno. " Estaciones, III
(Núm. 12, invierno de 1958),
397-398. (p)   2860

----. "7 P. M. ," "La calle, "
"El regreso. " El Hijo
Pródigo, VIII (Núm. 26, mayo
de 1945), 82-84. (p)   2861

----. "Silvestre Revueltas. "
Taller, II (Núm. 12, enero-
febrero de 1941), 61-63.
(a-e)   2862

----. "El testimonio de los
sentidos. " Romance, I (Núm.
3, 1 de marzo de 1940), 9.
(a-e)   2863

----. "Vigilias. " Taller, I
(Núm. 1, diciembre de 1938),
3-13. (a-e)   2864

----. "Vigilias. " Taller, I
(Núm. 7, diciembre de 1939),
11-12. (a-e)   2865

----. "Vigilias. " Tierra
Nueva, II (Núm. 7-8, enero-
abril de 1941), 32-43. (a-e)
                           2866

----. Archipiélago de mujeres
de Agustín Yáñez. El Hijo
Pródigo, I (Núm. 6,
septiembre de 1943), 380.
(r)   2867

----. Breve antología lírica
de Manuel José Othón con
prólogo y selección de Jesús
Zavala. El Hijo Pródigo, I
(Núm. 4, julio de 1943), 256.
(r)   2868

177

----. "Invitación a la novela" (Reseña de La educación de los sentidos, parte I: el envenado de Rafael Solana). Taller, I (Núm. 6, noviembre de 1939), 66-68. (r) 2869

----. Entre apagados muros de Efrén Hernández. El Hijo Pródigo, I (Núm. 4, julio de 1943), 255. (r) 2870

----. Historias e invenciones de Féliz Muriel de Rafael Dieste. El Hijo Pródigo, II (Núm. 8, noviembre de 1943), 125. (r) 2871

----. "Lawrence en español" (Reseña de La mujer que se fue a caballo de D. H. Lawrence). Romance, I (Núm. 1, 1 de febrero de 1940), 18, 19. (r) 2872

----. Mundo de perdición de José Bergamín. Taller, II (Núm. 11, julio-agosto de 1940), 65-68. (r) 2873

----. Ocnos de Luis Cernuda. El Hijo Pródigo, I (Núm. 3, junio de 1943), 188-189. (r) 2874

----. Páginas escogidas de José Vasconcelos con selección y prólogo de Antonio Castro Leal. Taller, II (Núm. 12, enero-febrero de 1941), 64-66. (r) 2875

----. Los presocráticos: Jenófanes, Parménides y Empédocles con traducción, prólogo y notas de David Garcia-Bacca. El Hijo Pródigo, II (Núm. 7, octubre de 1943), 60-61. (r) 2876

----. Sabor eterno de Emilio Ballagas. Taller, II (Núm.

10, marzo-abril de 1940), 52-53. (r) 2877

----. San Juan de Max Aub. El Hijo Pródigo, I (Núm. 5, agosto de 1943). 318-319. (r) 2878

----. "Razón de ser" (Reseña de El tema de nuestro tiempo de José Ortega y Gasset). Taller, I (Núm. 2, abril de 1939), 30-34. (r) 2879

----. Torres de amor de Lorenzo Varela. El Hijo Pródigo, I (Núm. 2, mayo de 1943), 124. (r) 2880

Pellicer y Cámara, Carlos. "Las canciones de Peñíscola." Ruta, Núm. 1 (junio de 1938), 20-27. (p) 2881

----. "Cuatro sonetos bajo el signo de la cruz." Romance, I (Núm. 4, 15 de marzo de 1940), 9. (p) 2882

----. "Dos sonetos de junio." Estaciones, III (Núm. 12, invierno de 1958), 374-375. (p) 2883

----. "Elegía nocturna." Taller, II (Núm. 10, marzo-abril de 1940), 12-14. (p) 2884

----. "Esquemas para una oda tropical." Estaciones, II (Núm. 6, verano de 1957), 155-156. (p) 2885

----. "Estudios." Contemporáneos, XI (Núm. 40-41, septiembre-octubre de 1931), 171-174. (p) 2886

----. "Exágonos." Ulises, Núm. 2 (junio de 1927), 7. (p) 2887

178

----. "Grupos de figuras." Contemporáneos, VIII (Núm. 26-27, julio-agosto de 1930), 55-60. (p)   2888

----. "Noche en el agua." El Hijo Pródigo, II (Núm. 8, noviembre de 1943), 80-81. (p)   2889

----. "La puerta." Fábula, Núm. 1 (enero de 1934), 11-12. (p)   2890

----. "Son de viento en las palmas...," "Yo no sé qué tiene el mar...," "En negro se desafina...," "Recuerdos de Iza," "Homenaje a Amado Nervo." México Moderno, I (Núm. 5, diciembre de 1920), 305-311. (p)   2891

----. "Sonetos de otoño," "A Eduardo Villaseñor," "Sonetos a los arcángeles." Taller, I (Núm. 7, diciembre de 1939), 5-10. (p)   2892

----. "3 sonetos a Dios," "Amanece en mis ojos." Estaciones, I (Núm. 1, primavera de 1956), 8-12. (p)   2893

----. "Trópico." Antena, Núm. 2 (agosto de 1924), 7. (p)   2894

----. Un libro de poemas de Elim. México Moderno, I (Núm. 8, marzo de 1921), 125. (r)   2895

----. Romanzas interiores de Angel Corao. México Moderno, I (Núm. 8, marzo de 1921), 125. (r)   2896

El Pensador Imberbe. "Respuesta a la encuesta de Romance." Romance, I (Núm. 3, 1 de marzo de 1940), 2. (a-e) 2897

Peña, Margarita. "Los nuevos." Estaciones, V (Núm. 20, invierno de 1960), 65-78. (a-e)   2898

Peret, Benjamín. "Háblame." Estaciones, I (Núm. 1, primavera de 1956), 144-145. (p)   2899

----. "Los mitos" (Trad. César Moro). El Hijo Pródigo, IV (Núm. 14, mayo de 1944), 110-119. (a-e) (2468)

----. "Para pasar el tiempo," "Parpadeo," "Allo" (Trad. César Moro). El Hijo Pródigo, XII (Núm. 38, mayo de 1946), 77-78. (p)   (2469)

Pereyra, Carlos. "Penumbras de museo." México Moderno, I (Núm. 4, noviembre de 1920), 229-234. (a-e)   2900

Pérez de Aguilar, Antonio. "Alacena." El Hijo Pródigo, XIII (Núm. 40, julio de 1946), entre 32 y 33. (il)   2901

----. "Alacena con diversos objetos." El Hijo Pródigo, I (Núm. 4, julio de 1943), entre 212-213. (il)   2902

Pérez de Ayala, Ramón. "De la seriedad." México Moderno, II (Núm. 2, septiembre de 1922), 121. (a-e)   2903

Pérez de Oliva, Fernán. "Diálogo de la dignidad del hombre." El Hijo Pródigo, XI (Núm. 36, marzo de 1946), 143-161. (a-e)   2904

Pérez Ferrero, Miguel. "Andén." Contemporáneos, II (Núm. 6, noviembre de 1928),

257-261. (f) 2905

----. "Angela, Anita, Adriana, etc..." Sagitario, Núm. 8 (1 de febrero de 1927), 10. (f) 2906

----. "El arte nuevo como agresión" Contemporáneos, VII (Núm. 24, mayo de 1930), 150-165. (a-e) 2907

Pérez Martínez, Hector. "Alfonso Reyes." Fábula, Núm. 9 (septiembre de 1934), 177. (a-e) 2908

----. "Canción que dice:amor." Fábula, Núm. 2 (febrero de 1934), 33-34. (p) 2909

----. "Dédalo." Ruta, Núm. 7 (diciembre de 1938), 33-38. (f) 2910

----. Ciudadanos armados de Manuel de la Peña. Fábula, Núm. 1 (enero de 1934), 20. (r) 2911

----. La Conquête Spirituel du Mexique de Robert Ricard. Fábula, Núm. 4 (abril de 1934), 80. (r) 2912

----. Historia de la literatura castellano de Abigail Mejía. Fábula, Núm. 4 (abril de 1934), 80. (r) 2913

Pérez Salazar, Francisco. "Dos cartas a propósito de Sigüenza y Góngora." Contemporáneos, III (Núm. 8, enero de 1929), 86-90. (a-e) 2914

Pérez y Soto, Atenógenes. "Salvador Díaz Mirón." Antena, Núm. 4 (octubre de 1924), 10. (a-e) 2915

Perrín, André. "En Morbacka, casa natal de Selma Lagerlof." Romance, I (Núm. 13, 1 de agosto de 1940), 12. (a-e) 2916

Pettorutti, Emilio. "Fortunato Depero, el artista dinámico por excelencia." Sagitario, Núm. 12-13 (30 de abril de 1927), 2. (a-e) 2917

Phelps, Ruth Shepard. "Dante" (Trad. Guillermo Prieto Yeme). México Moderno, II (Núm. 1, agosto de 1922), 59-60. (a-e) 2918

Picasso, Pablo. "Arlequín sentado," "Retrato de Jaime Sabartes," "Retrato de Conchita," "Mujer sentada." Estaciones, II (Núm. 5, primavera de 1957), entre 84-85. (il) 2919

----. "Guitarra y galleta," "Vaso y compotera," "Mujeres desnudas," "Segadores," "La familia de Arlequín," "Trance de muerte," "La mujer del artista," "Mujeres en la fuente," "Tres músicos," "Oleo." Romance, I (Núm. 2, 15 de febrero de 1940), 13. (il) 2920

----. "Naturaleza muerta." Contemporáneos, V (Núm. 15, agosto de 1929), 66. (il) 2921

----. "28 Noviembre XXXV." Estaciones, I (Núm. 1, primavera de 1956), 145-146. (p) 2922

----. "Vida." Estaciones, I (Núm. 2, verano de 1956), entre 244-245. (il) 2923

Picón-Salas, Mariano. "Un agitador venezolano de 1840." Romance, I (Núm. 20, 15 de

enero de 1941), 10. (a-e)
2924

----. "El mundo: La época
(Pequeña meditación de la
guerra)." Romance, I (Núm.
12, 15 de julio de 1940), 14.
(a-e)   2925

Pierre-Quint, León. "Norteamérica desconocida." Ruta,
Núm. 6 (noviembre de 1938),
48-50. (a-e)   2926

Piñol M., J. "Los glaciares
y las primeras civilizaciones."
Romance, I (Núm. 13, 1 de
agosto de 1940), 6. (a-e)
2927

Pirandello, Luigi. "La tinaja"
(Trad. de Agustín Lazo y
Xavier Villaurrutia). El Hijo
Pródigo, XIII (Núm. 42,
septiembre de 1946), 157-167.
(dr)   (2033)

Pitol, Sergio. "En familia."
Estaciones, III (Núm. 11,
otoño de 1958), 264-272. (f)
2928

----. "Las meninas."
Estaciones, IV (Núm. 16,
invierno de 1959), 418-441.
(dr)   2929

----. "Soñar, acaso!"
Estaciones, IV (Núm. 13,
primavera de 1959), 30-40.
(dr)   2930

----. "Victorio Ferri cuenta
un cuento." Estaciones, III
(Núm. 9, primavera de 1958),
82-86. (f)   2931

Pizarro Suárez, Nicolás.
Fujimori, Seikichi. "El
hombre que no aplaudía"
(Trad. Nicolás Pizarro
Suárez). Ruta, Núm. 5

(octubre de 1938), 38-39.
(tr)   (1398)

Plá y Beltrán. "Soldados de
España." Ruta, Núm. 5
(octubre de 1938), 25. (p)
2932

Plotino. "Sobre lo bello"
(Trad. Juan David García
Bacca). El Hijo Pródigo, I
(Núm. 5, agosto de 1943),
312-316. (a-e)   (1439)

Poe, Edgar Allan. "Presumien-
do." Romance, I (Núm. 4,
15 de marzo de 1940), 5. (f)
2933

Polacek, Antonín. Capek,
Karel. "La muerte de
Arquimedes" (Trad. Antonín
Polacek). Romance, I
(Núm. 9, 1 de junio de 1940),
5. (f)   (777)

Poliansky, D. "El teatro de
los buriato-mongolés."
Romance, II (Núm. 22, 15 de
marzo de 1941), 16, 17. (a-e)
2934

Ponce, Aníbal. Fourier de
Armond y Maubliac. Taller,
II (Núm. 8-9, enero-febrero
de 1940), 68-69. (r)   2935

Ponce, Manuel M. "A propósito
de 'Le Tombeau de Debussy'."
México Moderno, I (Núm. 8,
marzo de 1921), 108-112.
(a-e)   2936

----. "El arte musical en el
mundo," "Crónica musical
mexicana." México Moderno,
I (Núm. 10, junio de 1921),
235-237. (a-e)   2937

----. "Un bello ejemplo."
México Moderno, I (Núm. 2,
septiembre de 1920), 102-107.
(a-e)   2938

----. "Cuatro canciones olvidades en la tierra." El Hijo Pródigo, IX (Núm. 29, agosto de 1945), 89-90. (p) 2939

----. "En defensa propia." México Moderno, I (Núm. 6, enero de 1921), 374-381. (a-e) 2940

----. "La enseñanza musical obligatoria." México Moderno, I (Núm. 5, diciembre de 1920), 294-297. (a-e) 2941

----. "Una iniciativa." México Moderno, I (Núm. 7, febrero de 1921), 45-47. (a-e) 2942

----. "Poema." El Hijo Pródigo, VI (Núm. 21, diciembre de 1944), 153-155. (p) 2943

----. "S. M. El Fox." México Moderno, I (Núm. 9, mayo de 1921), 180-181. (a-e) 2944

----. "Saint-Saens." México Moderno, II (Núm. 4, junio de 1923), 238-243. (a-e) 2945

----. "El suplicio del concertista." México Moderno, I (Núm. 1, agosto de 1920), 33-36. (a-e) 2946

----. "Wagner y la IX Sinfonía." México Moderno, I (Núm. 4, noviembre de 1920), 235-244. (a-e) 2947

Pondal Ríos, Sixto. "Infancia." El Hijo Pródigo, XIII (Núm. 42, septiembre de 1946), 151. (p) 2948

Poniatowska, Elena. "Alvaro Mutis." Estaciones, V (Núm. 17, primavera de 1960),

78-79. (a-e) 2949

----. "Poemas." Estaciones, II (Núm. 6, verano de 1957), 183-185. (p) 2950

----. "El retiro." Estaciones, V (Núm. 17, primavera de 1960), 25-37. (f) 2951

Portal, Magda. "Norah Borges." Forma, II (Núm. 7, 1928), 9-10. (a-e) 2952

Porter, Liliana. "Viñeta." Estaciones, IV (Núm. 14, verano de 1959), portada. (il) 2953

----. "Viñeta." Estaciones, IV (Núm. 15, otoño de 1959), portada. (il) 2954

Portuondo, José Antonio. "E. Díez-Canedo y las letras de América." El Hijo Pródigo, VII (Núm. 22, enero de 1945), 28-30. (a-e) 2955

----. El tonel de Diógenes de Manuel González Prada. El Hijo Pródigo, VIII (Núm. 26, mayo de 1945), 120-121. (r) 2956

Porras Troconis, Gabriel. "La disolución de la Gran Colombia." México Moderno, I (Núm. 3, octubre de 1920), 170-178. (a-e) 2957

Posada, Adolfo. "Acercamiento espiritual hispanoamericano." Sagitario, Núm. 2 (1 de agosto de 1926), 4-6. (a-e) 2958

Posada, José Guadalupe. "Calavera Catrina," "Jarabe de ultratumba," "Suicidio de un hispano en el Teatro Arbeu," "El ahorcado," "La muerte del General Manuel

González, presidente de la República," "Mujer que echa plomo derretido a su marido," "Linchamiento de la Bejarano," "El Chalequero." El Hijo Pródigo, I (Núm. 1, abril de 1943), entre 48 y 49. (il)   2959

----. "Fusilamiento." El Hijo Pródigo, I (Núm. 1, abril de 1943), portada. (il)   2960

Pound, Ezra. "N. Y." (Trad. Salvador Novo). La Falange, Núm. 7 (1 de octubre de 1923), 384. (p)   (2600)

Pradenas Jara, Hernán. "¿Qué es América y qué somos los americanos?" Estaciones, V (Núm. 19, otoño de 1960), 105-116. (a-e)   2961

Prados, Emilio. "Canto a la soledad." Taller, II (Núm. 10, marzo-abril de 1940), 22-24. (p)   2962

----. "Cuerpo perseguido." Taller, I (Núm. 4, julio de 1939), 22-28. (p)   2963

----. "Dos canciones." Romance, I (Núm. 8, 15 de mayo de 1940), 11. (p) 2964

----. "Dos poemas de amor." El Hijo Pródigo, IV (Núm. 13, abril de 1944), 21-23. (p)   2965

----. "Noche humana." Romance, I (Núm. 8, 15 de mayo de 1940), 11. (p) 2966

----. "Nuevo amor." Tierra Nueva, II (Núm. 7-8, enero-abril de 1941), 30-31. (p)   2967

----. Heidegger, Martín.

"Hölderlin y la esencia de la poesía" (Trad. E. Prado Vertiz y José Luis Martínez). Tierra Nueva, III (Núm. 15, diciembre de 1942), 143-153. (tr)   (1752)

Prampolini, Enrique. "Concepción del espacio en las artes plásticas" (Trad. Alfredo Hurtado). Estaciones, I (Núm. 2, verano de 1956), 244-248. (a-e)   (1868)

Prassinos, Gisele. "Anuncio." Estaciones, I (Núm. 1, primavera de 1956), 146-147. (p)   2968

Prebisch, Alberto. "Manuel Rodríguez Lozano." Forma, I (Núm. 4, 1927), 2. (a-e)   2969

Priento, Valerio. "Las capitulares de los libros de coro." Forma, I (Núm. 2, noviembre de 1926), 13-15. (a-e)   2970

Priestley, Herbert Ingram. "La antigua universidad de México" (Trad. Genaro Estrada). México Moderno, I (Núm. 1, agosto de 1920), 37-52. (a-e)   (1305)

Prieto, Julio. "Cuatro cuadros recientes de José Chávez Morado." Tierra Nueva, III (Núm. 15, diciembre de 1942), 139-141. (a-e)   2971

----. "Cuatro maderas." Tierra Nueva, I (Núm. 4-5, julio-octubre de 1940), forma parte del Suplemento poético al núm. 4-5. (il)   2972

----. "Dos litografías de Ocampo." Tierra Nueva, II

(Núm. 9-10, mayo-agosto de 1941), 144-145. (a-e) 2973

----. "Dos litografías de Raúl Anguiano." Tierra Nueva, I (Núm. 6, noviembre-diciembre de 1940), 348-349. (il) 2974

----. "Golfo de México." Fábula, Núm. 9 (septiembre de 1934), entre 168 y 169. (il) 2975

----. "Litografías." Tierra Nueva, III (Núm. 13-14, enero-abril de 1942), entre 24 y 25. (il) 2976

----. "Mascara." Fábula, Núm. 1 (enero de 1934), entre 12-13. (il) 2977

----. Melville, Herman. "Moby Dick" (Trad. Julio Prieto). Tierra Nueva, II (Núm. 11-12, septiembre-diciembre de 1941), 250-252. (tr) (2317)

Prieto Yeme, Guillermo. Huxley, Aldous. "Diálogos socráticos del momento" (Trad. Guillermo Prieto Yeme). México Moderno, II (Núm. 1, agosto de 1922), 62-63. (tr) (1872)

----. Phelps, Ruth Shepard. "Dante" (Trad. Guillermo Prieto Yeme). México Moderno, II (Núm. 1, agosto de 1922), 59-60. (tr) (2918)

----. Romains, Jules. "Opiniones literarias de Victor Hugo," "La moda de psicoanálisis" (Trad. Guillermo Prieto Yeme). México Moderno, II (Núm. 1, agosto de 1922), 61-62. (tr) 2978

Prieto y Romero, Ramón.

"Ruta." Sagitario, Núm. 9 (15 de febrero de 1927), 8. (p) 2979

Prieto y Souza, L. "Concurso para el pabellón de México en Sevilla." Forma, I (Núm. 1, octubre de 1926), 39-42. (a-e) 2980

Puente, J. Jesús. "Respuesta a la encuesta de Romance." Romance, I (Núm. 6, 15 de abril de 1940), 2. (a-e) 2981

Puértolas, Agustín S. "Melodía interior." Prometeus, II (Núm. 1, diciembre de 1951), 53-60. (f) 2982

Puga, Mario. "Antonio Machado: el hombre y la política." Estaciones, I (Núm. 3, otoño de 1956), 331-342. (a-e) 2983

Puig Casauranc, José Manuel. "El abismo entre dos clases proletarias." Sagitario, Núm. 4 (1 de septiembre de 1926), 3. (a-e) 2984

----. "El estado que guarda el ramo de educación pública." Sagitario, Núm. 5 (1 de octubre de 1926), 3. (a-e) 2985

----. "Los intelectuales de Austria y los odios del proletario." Sagitario, Núm. 4 (1 de septiembre de 1926), 3. (a-e) 2986

----. "Introducción." Forma, I (Núm. 1, octubre de 1926), 1. (a-e) 2987

Pujula, Pedro. "Jean Richepin." Sagitario, Núm. 8 (1 de febrero de 1927), 12. (a-e) 2988

Pushkin, Alejandro. "El barón avariento" (Trad. Enrique Díez-Canedo). El Hijo Pródigo, V (Núm. 16, julio de 1944), 42-48. (dr) (1174)

Quevedo, Francisco de. "Canción fúnebre a la muerte de don Luis Carrillo de Sotomayor." Taller, II (Núm. 8-9, enero-febrero de 1940), 75-77. (p) 2989

----. "Una carta de Francisco de Quevedo a Don Manuel Serrano del Castillo." El Hijo Pródigo, I (Núm. 2, mayo de 1943), 117-121. (a-e) 2990

----. "Sobre la necedad y la muerte." El Hijo Pródigo, IX (Núm. 30, septiembre de 1945), 168-177. (a-e) 2991

Quijano, Alejandro. "Alfonso Reyes." Fábula, Núm. 9 (septiembre de 1934), 177-178. (a-e) 2992

----. "Una carta del conquistador D. Gonzalo Jiménez de Quesada." México Moderno, I (Núm. 5, diciembre de 1920), 285-293. (a-e) 2993

----. "Ramón López Velarde." México Moderno, I (Núm. 11-12, noviembre-diciembre de 1921), 297-298. (a-e) 2994

Quintana, Jorge. "Admiración y comprensión de Martí en Cuba." Romance, I (Núm. 8, 15 de mayo de 1940), 9. (a-e) 2995

----. "Un bibliógrafo cubano: Fermín Peraza." Romance, I (Núm. 11, 1 de junio de 1940), 19. (a-e) 2996

----. Santander de Fernando González. Romance, I (Núm. 15, 1 de septiembre de 1940), 19. (r) 2997

Quintero Alvarez, Alberto. "Carta al amigo que vive junto al mar." Taller, II (Núm. 12, enero-febrero de 1941), 42-45. (p) 2998

----. "Cauda de la palabra." Tierra Nueva, III (Núm. 13-14, enero-abril de 1942), 19-23. (p) 2999

----. "En busca de la ignorancia." Romance, I (Núm. 4, 15 de marzo de 1940), 10. (a-e) 3000

----. "Enrique González Rojo." Taller, I (Núm. 4, julio de 1939), 29. (a-e) 3001

----. "Estancias" (incluye "Retorno," "Vida desecha," "La niñez terrenal," "Yo profeso."). Taller, I (Núm. 6, noviembre de 1939), 19-23. (p) 3002

----. "Los inquilinos de la filosofía." Taller, I (Núm. 5, octubre de 1939), 45-49. (a-e) 3003

----. "Una página sobre el film Vía Crucis, Las uvas del rencor" (Opiniones de Xavier Villaurrutia, León Felipe, Ramón Gaya, Alberto Quintero Alvarez, Octavio G. Barreda y Carlos Velo). Romance, I (Núm. 9, 1 de junio de 1940), 11. (a-e) (585)

----. "Poema de los lobos." Ruta, Núm. 8 (enero de 1939), 28-31. (p) 3004

185

----. "Sobre la inteligencia." Taller, I (Núm. 1, diciembre de 1938), 54-56. (a-e) 3005

----. "El tiempo contemplado." Taller, I (Núm. 2, abril de 1939), 11-14. (p) 3006

----. "Tuyo es el reino." Romance, I (Núm. 11, 1 de julio de 1940), 5. (f) 3007

----. Canek de Ermilo Abreu Gómez. Taller, II (Núm. 12, enero-febrero de 1941), 74. (r) 3008

----. Claro abismo de Germán Pardo García. Taller, II (Núm. 12, enero-febrero de 1941), 75. (r) 3009

----. "En el mar de Platón" (Reseña de Filosofía y poesía de María Zambrano). Taller, II (Núm. 8-9, enero-febrero de 1940), 62-64. (r) 3010

----. "La fatalidad en Kafka" (Reseña de La metamorfosis de Franz Kafka, trad. y prólogo de Jorge Luis Borges). Taller, I (Núm. 2, abril de 1939), 37-39. (r) 3011

----. Muerte sin fin de José Gorostiza. Taller, I (Núm. 7, diciembre de 1939), 44-46. (r) 3012

----. "Vida y poesía plenas" (Reseña de Poesía 1898-1939 de Enrique González Martínez). Romance, I (Núm. 1, 1 de febrero de 1940), 18, 19. (r) 3013

----. "El poeta León Chestov" (Reseña de Las revelaciones de la muerte de León Chestov). Taller, I (Núm. 3, mayo de 1939), 39-41. (r) 3014

----. La vida que te di de Luigi Pirandello. Taller, II (Núm. 11, julio-agosto de 1940), 77-79. (r) 3015

Quiñones, Horacio. "Cuarto de enfermo." Fábula, Núm. 8 (agosto de 1934), 158. (a-e) 3016

R., T. El gran dictador de H. G. Wells. Romance, II (Núm. 21, 15 de febrero de 1941), 19. (r) 3017

Radványi, Netty. ("Seghers, Anna"). "Leyendas de Artemisa" (Trad. Angela Selke y Antonio Sánchez Barbudo). El Hijo Pródigo, V (Núm. 18, septiembre de 1944), 154-165. (f) 3018

Ramírez, Alfonso Francisco. "Alonso de Cabrera." Estaciones, II (Núm. 7, otoño de 1957), 290-294. (a-e) 3019

Ramírez, J. Martín. "El centro popular de pintura de San Pablo." Forma, II (Núm. 7, 1928), 6-8. (a-e) 3020

Ramírez Cabañas, Joaquín. "Propósito." La Falange, Núm. 6 (1 de septiembre de 1923), 336-337. (p) 3021

----. "Xochimilco." Contemporáneos, III (Núm. 8, enero de 1929), 13-17. (a-e) 3022

Ramos, José Manuel. "Antenas" Antena, Núm. 2 (agosto de 1924), 12-13. (a-e) 3023

----. "Radio tópicos." Antena, Núm. 1 (julio de 1924), 17-19. (a-e) 3024

Ramos, Leopoldo. "Adve-
nimiento." Poesía, Núm. 3
(abril de 1941), 67-68. (p)
3025

----. "Dicha." Poesía, Núm.
3 (abril de 1941), 59. (p)
3026

----. "Un paso." Poesía,
Núm. 3 (abril de 1941), 64-65.
(p)   3027

----. "Siempreviva." Poesía,
Núm. 3 (abril de 1941), 62-
63. (p)   3028

----. "Tu beso." Poesía,
Núm. 3 (abril de 1941), 60-
61. (p)   3029

----. "Tus pasos." Poesía,
Núm. 3 (abril de 1941), 66.
(p)   3030

Ramos, Samuel. "Antonio Caso:
La campaña anti-positivista."
Ulises, Núm. 1 (mayo de
1927), 12-20, Núm. 2 (junio
de 1927), 5-6. (a-e)   3031

----. "El caso Strawinsky."
Contemporáneos, V (Núm. 15,
agosto de 1929), 1-32; (Núm.
16, septiembre de 1929), 112-
133. (a-e)   3032

----. "La cultura criolla."
Contemporáneos, XI (Núm. 38-
39, julio-agosto de 1931), 61-
82. (a-e)   3033

----. "La danza." Forma, I
(Núm. 3, 1927), 6. (a-e)
3034

----. "Ensayos estéticos: La
caricatura." Forma, I
(Núm. 1, octubre de 1926),
8-9. (a-e)   3035

----. "El genio desconocido."
Sagitario, Núm. 9 (15 de

febrero de 1927), 11. (a-e)
3036

----. "Las ideas filosóficas
en México después de la
Reforma." México Moderno,
II (Núm. 1, agosto de 1922),
35-38. (a-e)   3037

----. "El irracionalismo."
Ulises, Núm. 3 (agosto de
1927), 5-13. (a-e)   3038

----. "Mimesis y creación en
las artes plásticas."
Estaciones, II (Núm. 7, otoño
de 1957), 233-238. (a-e)
3039

----. "El ocaso de Ariel."
La Falange, Núm. 5 (1 de
agosto de 1923), 305-308.
(a-e)   3040

----. "El sueño de México."
Contemporáneos, VI (Núm. 21,
febrero de 1930), 113-126; VII
(Núm. 24, mayo de 1930),
103-118. (a-e)   3041

----. "El teatro en Francia."
La Falange, Núm. 2 (1 de
enero de 1923), 123-124. (a-e)
3042

----. Huxley, Aldous. "El
banquete a Tillotson" (Trad.
Samuel Ramos). México
Moderno, II (Núm. 4, junio
de 1923), 209-223. (tr)(1869)

----. Worringer, Wilhelm.
"Abstracción y proyección
sentimental" (Trad. Samuel
Ramos). El Hijo Pródigo, III
(Núm. 12, marzo de 1944),
155-165. (tr)   3043

Ramos Gómez, Raymundo J.
"Canción inusitada." Estaciones,
II (Núm. 8, invierno de
1957), 455-457 (p)   3044

----. "Cuerpo ritual. "
Estaciones, III (Núm. 10,
verano de 1958), 209-213. (p)
3045

----. "Estancia definitiva. "
Estaciones, IV (Núm. 13,
primavera de 1959), 72-73.
(p)   3046

----. "Poema del amor
libre. " Estaciones, II (Núm.
7, otoño de 1957), 302-303.
(p)   3047

Ramos Martínez, Alfredo.
"Ideas generales sobre la
evolución del arte en México. "
Sagitario, Núm. 12-13 (30
de abril de 1927), 5-6. (a-e)
3048

Rebolledo, Efrén. "Extremado
realismo" (Reseña de Le mur
de Jean Paul Sartre). Ro-
mance, I (Núm. 2, 15 de
febrero de 1940), 18. (r)
3049

Rebolledo, J. Enrique.
"Maiakovski o las formas de
la acción. " Romance, I (Núm.
7, 1 de mayo de 1940), 8.
(a-e)   3050

----. Sobre los problemas
sociales de Vaz Ferreira.
Romance, I (Núm. 4, 15 de
marzo de 1940), 19. (r)
3051

Rejano, Juan. "Angel de las
nieblas: La piedra solitaria
de Bécquer. " Romance, I
(Núm. 14, 15 de agosto de
1940), 11, 17. (a-e) 3052

----. "Entre dos reinos. "
El Hijo Pródigo, V (Núm. 18,
septiembre de 1944), 146-148.
(p)   3053

----. "Escala de la ausencia."

Taller, II (Núm. 8-9, enero-
febrero de 1940), 25-27. (p)
3054

----. "Para un aniversario:
García Lorca y España. "
Romance, I (Núm. 15, 1 de
septiembre de 1940), 20.
(a-e)   3055

----. "Rebelión de sombras. "
El Hijo Pródigo, X (Núm. 31,
octubre de 1945), 14-15. (p)
3056

----. "Sobre la soledad. "
Romance, I (Núm. 7, 1 de
mayo de 1940), 9.   (a-e) 3057

----. "Trébol de octubre. "
Estaciones, II (Núm. 8,
invierno de 1957), 408-409.
(p)   3058

----. "Vallejo entre el clamor
y el silencio" (Reseña de
España, aparta de mí este
cáliz de César Vallejo).
Taller, II (Núm. 10, marzo-
abril de 1940), 47-51. (r)
3059

----. "Las vidas iluminadas. "
Romance, I (Núm. 3, 1 de
marzo de 1940), 9. (a-e)
3060

----. "Vivir en dos dimen-
siones. " Romance, I (Núm.
12, 15 de julio de 1940), 11.
(a-e)   3061

----. Don Lindo de Almería
en el cielo de México de
José Bergamín y Rodolfo
Halffter. Romance, I Núm. 1,
(1 de febrero de 1940), 5. (r)
3062

----. España, El país y los
habitantes de L. Martín
Echeverría. Romance, I

188

(Núm. 13, 1 de agosto de 1940), 19. (r) 3063

----. Historia del nazismo de Konrad Heiden. Romance, I (Núm. 1, 1 de febrero de 1940), 20. (r) 3064

----. La hora de España de Joaquín Navasal y de Mendiri. Romance, I (Núm. 1, 1 de febrero de 1940), 20. (r) 3065

----. "Cuerpo de sombra" (Reseña de Memoria del olvido de Emilio Prados). Romance, I (Núm. 10, 15 de junio de 1940), 18. (r) 3066

----. "Entendimiento y voluntad de Pascal" (Reseña de El pensamiento vivo de Pascal de Francois Mauriac). Romance, I (Núm. 13, 1 de agosto de 1940), 18. (r) 3067

----. "El héroe entre nosotros" (Reseña de Vida privada de Napoleón de Octave Anbry). Romance, I (Núm. 11, 1 de julio de 1940), 18. (r) 3068

Rembrandt van Ryn, Harmensz. "El hijo pródigo." El Hijo Pródigo, I (Núm. 6, septiembre de 1943), entre 334 y 335. (il) 3069

Renán González, Raúl. "El hilo de la tarde." Estaciones, V (Núm. 18, verano de 1960), 30-41. (c) 3070

----. Más humano que divino de William Spratling. Estaciones, V (Núm. 17, primavera de 1960), 128. (r) 3071

René-Jean. "L'etonnante exposition de jeunes peintres et dessinateurs décoles enfantines mexicaines." Sagitario, Núm. 12-13 (30 de abril de 1927), 11. (a-e) 3072

Reneville, Roland de. "Poetas místicos" (Trad. César Moro). El Hijo Pródigo, VI (Núm. 19, octubre de 1944), 33-43. (a-e) (2470)

Renn, Ludwig. "De la estrategía de maniobras a la estrategía de aniquilamiento." Romance, I (Núm. 9, 1 de junio de 1940), 6. (a-e) 3073

Renourad, P. "Alfonso Daudet." Romance, I (Núm. 16, 15 de septiembre de 1940), 13. (a-e) 3074

Requena Legarreta, Pedro. "Entre las sombras," "En esta copa cristal...," "La alegoría del águila." México Moderno, I (Núm. 7, febrero de 1921), 50-52. (p) 3075

Revueltas, Fermín: Fernández Urbina, J. M.; Asúnsolo, Ignacio; Ruiz, Guillermo; Rivera, Diego; Domínguez Bello, Arnulfo; y Centeno, Francisco. "Encuesta sobre escultura." Forma, I (Núm. 2, noviembre de 1926), 7-8. (a-e) (530)

----. "Mujer orante." Forma, I (Núm. 3, 1927), 32. (il) 3076

Revueltas, José. "El abismo." Ruta, Núm. 5 (octubre de 1938), 33-37. (f) 3077

----. "La 'Carta a un amigo difunto'." Taller, I (Núm. 4, julio de 1939), 51-52. (a-e) 3078

----. "El corazón verde."
Tierra Nueva, II (Núm. 11-12,
septiembre-diciembre de 1941),
220-234. (f)   3079

----. "Dios en la tierra."
Tierra Nueva, II (Núm. 7-8,
enero-abril de 1941), 47-52.
(f)   3080

----. "El encuentro."
Romance, I (Núm. 16, 15 de
septiembre de 1940), 5. (f)
                                3081

----. "La Iglesia y el hombre."
Taller, I (Núm. 1, diciembre
de 1938), 51-53. (a-e) 3082

----. "Profecía de España."
Taller, I (Núm. 2, abril de
1939), 28-30. (a-e)   3083

----. "El quebranto."
Taller, I (Núm. 2, abril de
1939), 15-27. (f)   3084

----. "El saurio inmóvil."
El Hijo Pródigo, I (Núm. 1,
abril de 1943), 31. (f) 3085

----. "La soledad." Ruta,
Núm. 11 (abril de 1939), 35-
42. (f)   3086

----. De la nada a millonario
de Egon Jameson. Romance,
I (Núm. 5, 1 de abril de
1940), 18. (r)   3087

Rey, María Ramona. "¿Tú das
el paso?..." Tierra Nueva I,
(Núm. 2, marzo-abril de
1940), 95-97. (f)   3088

----. Aires de México de
Ignacio Manuel Altamirano
prologado y recompilado por
Antonio Acevedo Escobedo.
Tierra Nueva, II (Núm. 7-8,
enero-abril de 1941), 92-93.
(r)   3089

Reyes, Alfonso. "A Margarita
y a Manuel Toussaint en sus
bodas de plata." Estaciones,
I (Núm. 2, verano de 1956),
250-252. (p)   3090

----. "Análisis de una
metáfora." La Falange, Núm.
7 (1 de octubre de 1923),
366-367. (a-e)   3091

----. "Ausencia y presencia
del amigo." El Hijo Pródigo,
V (Núm. 16, julio de 1944),
9-10. (a-e)   3092

----. "Los buitres y los
ojos." Fábula, Núm. 9
(septiembre de 1934), 164-165.
(a-e)   3093

----. "La caída." Contem-
poráneos, III (Núm. 8, enero
de 1929), 8-12. (a-e) 3094

----. "El calendario: Un
propósito, Una lección, El
otro extremo." Antena, Núm.
1 (julio de 1924), 3-5. (a-e)
                                3095

----. "El Cipango y la
Antilia." Tierra Nueva, I
(Núm. 1, enero-febrero de
1940), 7-11. (a-e)   3096

----. "La 'Conquista de
México (1519-1521)', por
Miguel González." Contem-
poráneos, IX (Núm. 34, marzo
de 1931), 206-207. (a-e) 3097

----. "Correr la pólvora."
Tierra Nueva, II (Núm. 9-10,
mayo-agosto de 1941), 108-115.
(a-e)   3098

----. "Crítica epistolar."
El Hijo Pródigo, XII (Núm. 37,
abril de 1946), 60-61. (a-e)
                                3099

----. "Cuaderno de lecturas."
Contemporáneos, VIII (Núm.
28-29, septiembre-octubre
de 1930), 180-191. (a-e)
3100

----. "Cuaderno de lecturas:
De la traducción." Contemporáneos, IX (Núm. 33,
febrero de 1931), 174-184.
(a-e)   3101

----. "Charca de luz."
Sagitario, Núm. 12-13 (30 de
abril de 1927), 4. (p)   3102

----. "De Shakespeare
considerado como fantasma."
Sagitario, Núm. 5 (1 de
octubre de 1926), 7. (a-e)
3103

----. "Discurso por Virgilio."
Contemporáneos, IX (Núm. 33,
febrero de 1931), 97-131.
(a-e)   3104

----. "2 casi sonetos." Contemporáneos, XI (Núm. 40-41,
septiembre-octubre de 1931),
175-176. (p)   3105

----. "En torno a una obra de
Lulio." Tierra Nueva, I
(Núm. 4-5, julio-octubre de
1940), 259-261. (a-e) 3106

----. "Exégesis fácil de
Mallarmé." Estaciones, I
(Núm. 2, verano de 1956),
149-157. (p)   3107

----. "Exposición Enrique
Riverón." Sagitario, Núm. 7
(1 de enero de 1927), 16.
(a-e)   3108

----. "Fantasía del viaje,"
"Amado Nervo," "Filosofía a
Lálage." México Moderno, I
(Núm. 3, octubre de 1920),
134-137. (p)   3109

----. "Los filósofos de las
islas." El Hijo Pródigo, VI
(Núm. 20, noviembre de 1944),
73-77. (p)   3110

----. "Goethe y la filosofía
del dibujo." Romance, I
(Núm. 1, 1 de febrero de
1940), 3. (a-e)   3111

----. "Grecia y su hermosa
falsificación del pasado."
Estaciones, III (Núm. 10,
verano de 1958), 113-118.
(a-e)   3112

----. "Infancia," "Golfo de
México," "Gaviotas."
Fábula, Núm. 9 (septiembre
de 1934), 166-170. (p)   3113

----. "Lo popular en
Góngora." Ruta, Núm. 1
(junio de 1938), 3-19. (a-e)
3114

----. "Mitología de las
cobras." Contemporáneos, VII
(Núm. 23, abril de 1930),
8-16. (a-e)   3115

----. "Motivos de 'Laoconte'."
México Moderno, II (Núm. 2,
septiembre de 1922), 112-114.
(a-e)   3116

----. "La 'Obra soñada' de
Mallarmé." Estaciones, I
(Núm. 1, primavera de 1956),
3-7. (a-e)   3117

----. "Ocio y placeres del
periódico." Contemporáneos,
VII (Núm. 24, mayo de 1930),
178-183; (Núm. 25, junio de
1930), 267-271; VIII (Núm.
30-31, noviembre-diciembre
de 1930), 259-268. (a-e)
3118

----. "Palinodia del polvo."
Romance, I (Núm. 9, 1 de
junio de 1940), 1-2. (a-e) 3119

191

----. "Pasión y muerte de dona Engraçadinha." El Hijo Pródigo, XII (Núm. 37, abril de 1946), 9-13. (f)   3120

----. "El personaje de este drama..." Estaciones, II (Núm. 5, primavera de 1957), 9-15. (a-e)   3121

----. "Ramón Gómez de la Serna." México Moderno, I (Núm. 8, marzo de 1921), 78-85. (a-e)   3122

----. "La reacción contra Goethe." Estaciones, I (Núm. 3, otoño de 1956), 293-299. (a-e)   3123

----. "Retrato," "El llanto." Estaciones, III (Núm. 12, invierno de 1958), 371-373. (p)   3124

----. "Los siete sobre Deva." Romance, I (Núm. 20, 15 de enero de 1941), 1, 2. (a-e)   3125

----. "Los últimos siete sabios." El Hijo Pródigo, I (Núm. 1, abril de 1943), 9-17. (a-e)   3126

----. "Undecimilia." El Hijo Pródigo, IX (Núm. 29, agosto de 1945), 85-86. (p)   3127

----. "Urna de Alarcón." Taller, I (Núm. 5, octubre de 1939), 7-11. (a-e) 3128

----. Mazaud, Emile. "Un día estupendo" (Trad. Alfonso Reyes). El Hijo Pródigo, III (Núm. 12, marzo de 1944), 171-183. (tr)   (2297)

Reyes, Fernando. "Mujer en oración" Contemporáneos, III (Núm. 10, marzo de 1929), 219. (il)   3129

----. "Oleo." Sagitario, Núm. 12-13 (30 de abril de 1927), 3. (il)   3130

Reyes, Neftalí Ricardo. ("Pablo Neruda"). "Arte poética," "Diurno doliente." Contemporáneos, X (Núm. 35, abril de 1931), 32-35. (p)   3131

----. "Colección nocturna." Contemporáneos, XI (Núm. 40-41, septiembre-octubre de 1931), 163-166. (p) 3132

----. "Discurso." Tierra Nueva, II (Núm. 9-10, mayo-agosto de 1941), 120-122. (a-e)   3133

----. "Liras de Luis Martín, Sor Juana Inés de la Cruz, el conde de Rebolledo, doña Cristobalina, y el conde de Villamediana" (Selección y discurso, en verso, de la lira por Pablo Neruda). Taller, I (Núm. 6, noviembre de 1939), 69-91. (p)   3134

----. "Oda de invierno al río Mapocho." Ruta, Núm. 3 (agosto de 1938), 22. (p) 3135

----. "Versos de Sara de Ibáñez." Taller, II (Núm. 12, enero-febrero de 1941), 34. (a-e)   3136

Reyes Nevares, Salvador. "De la novela." Estaciones, II (Núm. 7, otoño de 1957), 272-286. (a-e)   3137

----. "Hacia una literatura nacional." Estaciones, II (Núm. 5, primavera de 1957), 40-50. (a-e)   3138

----. "Notas sobre el surrealismo." Estaciones, I

192

(Núm. 3, otoño de 1956), 317-330. (a-e) 3139

----. "Notas sobre La región más transparente." Estaciones, III (Núm. 10, verano de 1958), 165-177. (a-e) 3140

----. Mis páginas mejores de Vicente Aleixandre. Estaciones, II (Núm. 7, otoño de 1957), 319-320. (r) 3141

Reyes Ruiz, J. Jesús. "Elegía de soledad." Tierra Nueva, I (Núm. 2, marzo-abril de 1940), 82-83. (p) 3142

----. "Poema a la madre ausente," "El torbellino," "Elogio de Aguascalientes," "Poema a la novia provinciana." (Suplemento poético al núm. 4-5) Tierra Nueva, I (Núm. 4-5, julio-octubre de 1940). (p) 3143

Ricard, Robert. "Algunas publicaciones recientes sobre México." Contemporáneos, X (Núm. 37, junio de 1931), 271-281. (r) 3144

Richards, I. A. "La experiencia poética" (Trad. Octavio G. Barreda). El Hijo Pródigo, II (Núm. 9, diciembre de 1943), 155-160. (a-e) (599)

Rigol, Jorge. "Un film ejemplar: Los trece." Ruta, Núm. 9 (febrero de 1939), 53-55. (a-e) 3145

Rilke, Rainer María. "Carta y fragmentos." (Trad. Maurice Betz). Tierra Nueva, I (Núm. 4-5, julio-octubre de 1940), 224-238. (a-e) (676)

Rimbaud, Jean-Arthur. "Después del diluvio" (Trad. R. Lasso de la Vega).

Sagitario, Núm. 4 (1 de septiembre de 1926), 6. (p) (2009)

----. "Las iluminaciones" (Trad. José Ferrel). El Hijo Pródigo, V (Núm. 16, julio de 1944), 49-55. (a-e) (1367)

----. "Temporada de infierno" (Trad. José Ferrel). Taller, I (Núm. 4, julio de 1939), 7-37 (paginación independiente). (p) (1368)

Río R., Rafael del. "A tu muerte." Tierra Nueva, I (Núm. 4-5, julio-octubre de 1940), 258. (p) 3146

Rioja, Enrique. "Los animales descontentos eternos." Romance, II (Núm. 23, 22 de abril de 1941), 4, 14. (a-e) 3147

----. "Farsa y engaño en el mundo viviente." Romance, II (Núm. 21, 15 de febrero de 1941), 10, 16. (a-e) 3148

----. "El mar, residencia de monstruos luminosos." Romance, I (Núm. 1, 1 de febrero de 1940), 4. (a-e) 3149

----. "La naturaleza creadora de locuras, excesos y dislates." Romance, II (Núm. 24, 31 de mayo de 1941), 4, 12. (a-e) 3150

Ríos, Carlos Alfonso. "Dos poemas." Prometeus, I (Núm. 3, mayo de 1949), 165-166. (p) 3151

Ríos, Fernando de los. "Estados Unidos y México." Sagitario, Núm. 6 (1 de

noviembre de 1926), 4-5.
(a-e)   3152

Ríos, Juan. "El asilo de
lunáticos." Prometeus, I
(Núm. 2, abril de 1949),
103-104. (p)   3153

Ríos P. Joaquín. Angel sin
cabeza de Vicki Baum.
Prometeus, I (Núm. 2, abril
de 1949), 136-137. (r) 3154

Rivas, Antonieta. Morand, Paul.
"De la velocidad" (Trad.
Antonieta Rivas). Contem-
poráneos, V (Núm. 15,
agosto de 1929), 35-59. (tr)
                                 (2430)

Rivas, Antonio. En torno a
nosotras de Margarita Nelken.
Ulises, Núm. 5 (diciembre de
1927), 22-23. (r)   3155

Rivas, Humberto. "Una carta."
Sagitario, Núm. 2 (1 de
agosto de 1926), 17. (a-e)
                                 3156

----. "El cuento y la cuenta
de oro de América."
Sagitario, Núm. 14 (31 de
mayo de 1927), 4. (a-e)
                                 3157

----. "La incomprensión y la
intolerancia." Sagitario,
Núm. 3 (15 de agosto de
1926), 3. (a-e)   3158

----. "Mar." Sagitario, Núm.
5 (1 de octubre de 1926), 12.
(p)   3159

----. "Paysages" (Trad.
Marcello-Fabri). Sagitario,
Núm. 11 (15 de marzo de
1927), 16. (p)   (2198)

----. "Poemas de la casa."
Sagitario, Núm. 7 (1 de
enero de 1927), 15. (p) 3160

----. "Prosas viajeras."
Sagitario, Núm. 9 (15 de
febrero de 1927), 15. (a-e)
                                 3161

----. "Proyecciones."
Sagitario, Núm. 4 (1 de
septiembre de 1926), 4. (a-e)
                                 3162

----. "Proyecciones."
Sagitario, Núm. 5 (1 de
octubre de 1926), 4. (a-e)
                                 3163

----. "Tránsito." Sagitario,
Núm. 6 (1 de noviembre de
1926), 16. (p)   3164

----. "El viento." Sagitario,
Núm. 10 (1 de marzo de
1927), 8-11. (dr)   3165

----. "Votiva." "Pianísimo."
"Copas." "Retorno."
Sagitario, Núm. 1 (15 de
julio de 1926), 15. (p) 3166

----. Gasch, Sebastián.
"Salvador Dalí" (Trad.
Humberto Rivas). Sagitario,
Núm. 14 (31 de mayo de
1927), 9-11. (tr)   (1469)

----. Llates, R. "Algunas
reflexiones sobre Beethoven"
(Trad. Humberto Rivas).
Sagitario, Núm. 11 (15 de
marzo de 1927), 15. (tr)
                                 (2151)

Rivas Panedas, José. "Almoha-
da." Sagitario, Núm. 7
(1 de enero de 1927), 12. (p)
                                 3167

----. "Dulzura." Sagitario,
Núm. 11 (15 de marzo de
1927), 12. (p)   3168

----. "Estación." Sagitario,
Núm. 10 (1 de marzo de
1927), 13. (p)   3169

----. "Invenciones del alba," "Notas del alba." Sagitario, Núm. 5 (1 de octubre de 1926), 6. (p) 3170

----. "Jardín." Sagitario, Núm. 8 (1 de febrero de 1927), 5. (p) 3171

----. "Jardín invernal." "Invierno." "Ya están." Sagitario, Núm. 1 (15 de julio de 1926), 6. (p) 3172

----. "Lejos." Sagitario, Núm. 9 (15 de febrero de 1927), 11. (p) 3173

----. "Mis pasos." Sagitario, Núm. 4 (1 de septiembre de 1926), 17. (p) 3174

----. "Sentencias de amanecer," "Plenilunio." Sagitario, Núm. 6 (1 de noviembre de 1926), 15. (p) 3175

Rivas Sáinz, Arturo. "Belleza, arte y poesía en la estética de Santayana." El Hijo Pródigo, III (Núm. 12, marzo de 1944), 153-154. (a-e) 3176

----. "Concepto de la zozobra." El Hijo Pródigo, III (Núm. 10, enero de 1944), 9-25. (a-e) 3177

----. "La grupa de Zoraida." El Hijo Pródigo, XII (Núm. 39, junio de 1946), 161-164. (a-e) 3178

----. "La melodía." Estaciones, I (Núm. 1, primavera de 1956), 42-66. (a-e) 3179

----. "Metáfora e imagen." El Hijo Pródigo, V (Núm. 18, septiembre de 1944), 149-153.

(a-e) 3180

----. "Poesía de filosofar." El Hijo Pródigo, I (Núm. 2, mayo de 1943), 80-84. (a-e) 3181

----. "Poesía de significar." Tierra Nueva, II (Núm. 7-8, enero-abril de 1941), 53-63. (a-e) 3182

----. "Respuesta a la encuesta de Romance." Romance, I (Núm. 6, 15 de abril de 1940), 2. (a-e) 3183

----. Les Abeilles D'Aristée de Wladimir Weidle. El Hijo Pródigo, IV (Núm. 15, junio de 1944), 182-183. (r) 3184

----. El arco y la lira de Octavio Paz. Estaciones, I (Núm. 3, otoño de 1956), 402-404. (r) 3185

----. Batlle, héroe civil de Justino Zavala. El Hijo Pródigo, XIII (Núm. 42, septiembre de 1946), 179. (r) 3186

----. El deslinde. Prolegómenos a la teoría literaria de Alfonso Reyes. El Hijo Pródigo, V (Núm. 17, agosto de 1944), 121. (r) 3187

----. Historia de la literatura rusa de Pablo Schostakovsky. El Hijo Pródigo, XI (Núm. 36, marzo de 1946), 173-174. (r) 3188

----. Investigaciones sobre el Quijote apócrifo de Joaquín Espín Real, Filosofía del Quijote de David Rubio y La invención del Quijote de Arturo Marasso. El Hijo

Pródigo, III (Núm. 10, enero de 1944), 58-59. (r)   3189

----. La literatura española de Nicolás González Ruiz. El Hijo Pródigo, VII (Núm. 23, febrero de 1945), 123-124. (r)   3190

----. Lo eterno y lo temporal en el arte de Octavio N. Derisi y El sentido del cine de Sergio M. Eisenstein. El Hijo Pródigo, VI (Núm. 21, diciembre de 1944), 188. (r)   3191

----. Papel social del intelectual de Florián Znaniecki. El Hijo Pródigo, IV (Núm. 15, junio de 1944), 186. (r)   3192

----. Teseo de Eduardo Dieste. El Hijo Pródigo, IX (Núm. 29, agosto de 1945), 122. (r)   3193

----. Tratado de poética de Alberto Hidalgo. El Hijo Pródigo, V (Núm. 18, septiembre de 1944), 187. (r)   3194

Rivera, Diego M.   "El arte de la revolucion." Sagitario, Núm. 1 (15 de julio de 1926), 7-12. (a-e)   3195

----. "Carta." Estaciones, II (Núm. 8, invierno de 1957), 365-367. (a-e)   3196

----. "De pintura y otras cosas que no lo son." La Falange, Núm. 5 (1 de agosto de 1923), 269-271. (a-e)   3197

----. "Dibujo." La Falange, Núm. 2 (1 de enero de 1923), entre 80 y 81. (il)   3198

----. "Dibujo." La Falange, Núm. 2 (1 de enero de 1923), entre 82 y 83. (il)   3199

----. "Dibujo a lápiz." Forma, I (Núm. 3, 1927), 37. (il)   3200

----. "En Yucatán." La Falange, Núm. 2 (1 de enero de 1923), entre 96 y 97. (il)   3201

----. "Escultura," "Talla directa." Forma, I (Núm. 3, 1927), 2-3. (a-e)   3202

----. Fernández Urbina, J. M.; Asúnsolo, Ignacio; Ruiz, Guillermo; Revueltas, Fermín; Domínguez Bello, Arnulfo; y Centeno, Francisco. "Encuesta sobre escultura." Forma, I (Núm. 2, noviembre de 1926), 7-8. (a-e)   (530)

----. "Los frutos," "La selva," "La hacienda," "La costa." Sagitario, Núm. 1 (15 de julio de 1926), 8-11. (il)   3203

----. "Hombre que fuma," "Naturaleza muerta," "Paisaje tropical," "Paisaje americano," "Anfiteatro," "El Jordán," "Viñaderos," "Mujer etrusca," "Retratos." Forma, I (Núm. 5, 1927), 29-35. (il)   3204

----. "Oleos y fragmentos de murales." Ulises, Núm. 5 (diciembre de 1927), entre 16 y 17. (il)   3205

----. "El reparto de ejidos," Forma, I (Núm. 5, 1927), 20-21. (il)   3206

----. "El trapiche." Sagitario, Núm. 7 (1 de enero de 1927), 8. (il)   3207

Rivera, Gerardo. Las andanzas
de Hernán Cortés y otros
excesos de Artemio de Valle-
Arizpe. Romance, II (Núm.
24, 31 de mayo de 1941), 18.
(r)   3208

Robledo, Antonio. "El hijo
pródigo." El Hijo Pródigo,
I (Núm. 1, abril de 1943),
entre 6 y 7. (il)   3209

Robles Gil, Alberto; Obregón
Santacilla, Carlos;
Montenegro, Roberto;
Ituarte, Manuel M.; Pallares,
Alfonso; Cumming, A. E.
"Encuesta sobre arquitectura."
Forma, I (Núm. 3, 1927),
15-16. (a-e)   (1019)

Roca, Deodoro. "La paz y el
petróleo." México Moderno,
II (Núm. 4, junio de 1923),
250-251. (a-e)   3210

Rodell, John S. "Maxwell
Anderson; Una crítica" (Trad.
Rodolfo Usigli). El Hijo
Pródigo, II (Núm. 9,
diciembre de 1943), 176-179.
(a-e)   3211

Rodin, Auguste. "El hijo
pródigo." El Hijo Pródigo,
I (Núm. 5, agosto de 1943),
entre 268 y 269. (il)   3212

Rodríguez, Claudio. "Llegada a
la estación de Avila."
Estaciones, IV (Núm. 15,
otoño de 1959), 281-283. (p)
                               3213

Rodríguez, Eugenio. "Viñeta."
Estaciones, II (Núm. 8,
invierno de 1957), portada.
(il)   3214

Rodríguez, Luis Angel. "La
inquisición en México."
Romance, I (Núm. 7, 1 de
mayo de 1940), 9. (a-e)3215

----. "Respuesta a la
encuesta de Romance."
Romance, I (Núm. 3, 1 de
marzo de 1940), 2. (a-e)
                               3216

Rodríguez, Luis Felipe.
"Chipojo." Romance, II
(Núm. 23, 22 de abril de
1941), 17. (f)   3217

Rodríguez Alcalá, Hugo.
"Abril cruzando el mundo,"
"Eternidad," "Otoño."
Estaciones, IV (Núm. 16,
invierno de 1959), 442-443.
(p)   3218

----. "Lloro de luna."
Estaciones, IV (Núm. 13,
primavera de 1959), 92. (p)
                               3219

----. Chassex, Jean.
"Amérique:1960." (Trad. Hugo
Rodríguez-Alcalá),
Estaciones, V (Núm. 18,
verano de 1960), 79-83. (tr)
                          (1039)

Rodríguez Chicharro, César.
"Ella, la poesía," "El
columpio." Estaciones, IV
(Núm. 16, invierno de 1959),
416-417. (p)   3220

----. "El loco." Estaciones,
III (Núm. 9, primavera de
1958), 35-37. (f)   3221

Rodríguez Lozano, Manuel.
"Cuernavaca." La Falange,
Núm. 4 (1 de julio de 1923),
entre 232 y 233. (il)   3222

----. "Dibujos." Contem-
poráneos, X (Núm. 35, abril
de 1931), 13-16. (il)   3223

----. "Hondazos." Sagitario,
Núm. 11 (15 de marzo de
1927), 6. (a-e)   3224

----. "Mujer sentada," "Velorio," "El corrido," "Mujer sentada," "La banca." Forma, I (Núm. 4, 1927), 1-5. (il) 3225

----. "El obrero." La Falange, Núm. 4 (1 de julio de 1923), portada. (il) 3226

----. "Oleos." Contemporáneos, IV (Núm. 11, abril de 1929), 61-69. (il) 3227

----. "Tebo." Fábula, Núm. 8 (agosto de 1934), 154. (a-e) 3228

Rodríguez Luna, Antonio. "Naturaleza muerta," "Interior," "Jaula con pájaros," "Naturaleza muerta." Romance, I (Núm. 20, 15 de enero de 1941), 12-13. (il) 3229

Rodríguez Mata, Magdalena. "Más sobre los clásicos." Estaciones, III (Núm. 12, invierno de 1958), 446-457. (a-e) 3230

Rodríguez Orgaz, Mariano. "Vicisitudes arquitectónicas de la Plaza Mayor de México." Romance, I (Núm. 13, 1 de agosto de 1940), 11. (a-e) 3231

Rojas, Fermín. "Los agachados." Estaciones, I (Núm. 4, invierno de 1956), entre 592-593. (il) 3232

Rojas, Marcial. "Un extemporáneo." Contemporáneos, II (Núm. 5, octubre de 1928), 199-200. (a-e) 3233

----. "Moralidades legendarias." Contemporáneos, I (Núm. 2, julio de 1928), 214-215. (a-e) 3234

----. "La muerte de Andrenio." Contemporáneos, V (Núm. 19, diciembre de 1929), 426-427. (a-e) 3235

----. "Notas de conversación." Contemporáneos, V (Núm. 18, noviembre de 1929), 335-336. (a-e) 3236

----. Seguro azar de Pedro Salinas. Contemporáneos, III (Núm. 9, febrero de 1929), 185-186. (r) 3237

Rojas, Mariano. Anónimo. "Antiguos cantares mexicanos" (Trad. Mariano Rojas). Contemporáneos, IV (Núm. 12, mayo de 1929), 105-119. (tr) (194)

Rojas Garcidueñas, José. El Padre Kino, misionero y gobernante de Fortino Ibarra de Anda. El Hijo Pródigo, X (Núm. 33, diciembre de 1945), 180-181. (r) 3238

Rojas Giménez, Alberto. "De El extranjero." Sagitario, Núm. 11 (15 de marzo de 1927), 2. (p) 3239

Rojas González, Francisco. "El carro caja." El Hijo Pródigo, X (Núm. 32, noviembre de 1945), 87-88. (f) 3240

----. "El último tótem." El Hijo Pródigo, IX (Núm. 28, julio de 1945), 28-31. (f) 3241

Rojas Paz, Pablo. "Exposición Palomar." Sagitario, Núm. 7 (1 de enero de 1927), 16. (a-e) 3242

Rojas Rosillo, Isaac. Isabel
Moctezuma de Sara García
Iglesias. El Hijo Pródigo,
XII (Núm. 39, junio de
1946), 177. (r)   3243

Rolland, Romain. "Nicolas
Ostrovsky." Ruta, Núm. 12
(mayo de 1939), 57-58. (a-e)
                         3244

Romains, Jules. "Amadeo y los
caballeros en fila" (Trad.
Julio Jiménez Rueda).
Contemporáneos, IV (Núm. 13,
junio de 1929), 215-239. (dr)
                         (1960)

----. "Opiniones literarias
de Victor Hugo," "La moda
de psicoanálisis" (Trad.
Guillermo Prieto Yeme).
México Moderno, II (Núm. 1,
agosto de 1922), 61-62.
(a-e)   (2978)

Romano Muñoz, José. "La
doble solución al problema
del valor de la vida"
Contemporáneos, III (Núm.
10, marzo de 1929), 206-213.
(a-e)   3245

----. "Ni irracionalismo ni
racionalismo, sino filosofía
crítica." Ulises, Núm. 4
(agosto de 1927), 4-10. (a-e)
                         3246

Romero, Francisco. "Caprichos
y transcripciones." Romance,
I (Núm. 17, 22 de octubre de
1940), 11. (a-e)   3247

----. "Hume y el problema
de la causalidad." Romance,
I (Núm. 12, 15 de julio de
1940), 19. (a-e)   3248

Romero, José Rubén.
"Alfonso Reyes." Fábula,
Núm. 9 (septiembre de
1934), 178. (a-e)   3249

Romero Brest, Jorge. "Exposición de obras de Emilio
Pettoruti." Romance, I
(Núm. 16, 15 de septiembre
de 1940), 7. (a-e)   3250

----. "Vida artística en la
Argentina." Romance, I
(Núm. 9, 1 de junio de
1940), 7. (a-e)   3251

Romero de Terreros, Manuel.
("El Marqués de San
Francisco"). "Acuarelas
mexicanas del siglo XIX."
El Hijo Pródigo, III (Núm. 10,
enero de 1944), 32-33. (a-e)
                         3252

----. "Después de la lluvia..."
México Moderno, II (Núm. 6,
enero de 1921), 347. (p) 3253

----. "Escudos de monja."
El Hijo Pródigo, VI (Núm.
19, octubre de 1944), 24-25.
(a-e)   3254

----. "La escultura de la
Nueva España." México
Moderno, II (Núm. 1,
agosto de 1922), 30-34.
(a-e)   3255

----. "Miguel González."
Contemporáneos, X (Núm. 35,
abril de 1931), 83-84. (il)
                         3256

----. "Obras de hierro."
Forma, I (Núm. 6, 1928), 27-
29. (a-e)   3257

----. "El papagayo de
Huichilobos." México Moderno,
I (Núm. 2, septiembre de
1920), 108-113. (f)   3258

----. Keats, John. "La Belle
Dame Sans Merci" (Trad.
Manuel Romero de Terreros).
México Moderno, II (Núm. 4,

junio de 1923), 248-249. (tr)
(1982)

Romo, Herbert. "Viñeta."
Estaciones, V (Núm. 17,
primavera de 1960), portada.
(il)   3259

----. "Viñeta." Estaciones,
V (Núm. 20, invierno de
1960), portada. (il)   3260

Rooseroeck, Gust. L. van, y
Rafael A. Soto. "Un
olvidado precursor del
modernismo: Della Rocca de
Vergalo." La Falange, Núm.
3 (1 de febrero de 1923),
183-187. (a-e)   3261

Ros, Antonio. "Homero padeció
tracoma." Romance, I
(Núm. 20, 15 de enero de
1941), 19. (a-e)   3262

Rosa, Leopoldo de la. "La
amiga." México Moderno, I
(Núm. 2, septiembre de
1920), 94-97. (p)   3263

----. "Canción de una
estrella y un río." La
Falange, Núm. 5 (1 de agosto
de 1923), 284. (p)   3264

Rosa, Pedro de la. "Paisaje."
Contemporáneos, III (Núm.
10, marzo de 1929), 220. (il)
                        3265

Rosado Vega, Luis. "De paso."
La Falange, Núm. 6 (1 de
septiembre de 1923), 336. (p)
                        3266

Rosales, Salatiel. El ala de la
montaña y Las nuevas
capillas de Flavio Herrera.
La Falange, Núm. 2 (1 de
enero de 1923), 116-118. (r)
                        3267

Rosenzweig, Carmen.
"Descendimiento de Albert
Camus." Estaciones, V
(Núm. 18, verano de 1960),
72-73. (a-e)   3268

----. "Inclinar la cabeza."
Estaciones, IV (Núm. 13,
primavera de 1959), 74-75.
(f)   3269

Rosey, Gui. "He aquí todos
siglos pasados a filo de
espada." Estaciones, I
(Núm. 1, primavera de 1956),
147-148. (p)   3270

Rossi, Attilio. "Las artes
plásticas en la Argentina."
Romance, I (Núm. 11, 1 de
julio de 1940), 12-13. (a-e)
                        3271

Rosso de San Secondo.
"Lazarina entre cuchillos"
(Trad. Gilberto Owen y
Agustín Lazo). El Hijo
Pródigo, XIII (Núm. 40, julio
de 1946), 48-55; (Núm. 41,
agosto de 1946), 93-103.
(dr)   (2034)

Ruiz, Guillermo. Fernández
Urbina, J. M.; Asúnsolo,
Ignacio; Rivera, Diego;
Revueltas, Fermín;
Domínguez Bello, Arnulfo; y
Centeno, Francisco.
"Encuesta sobre escultura."
Forma, I (Núm. 2,
noviembre de 1926), 7-8.
(a-e)   (530)

----. "Raza." Forma, I
(Núm. 3, 1927), 1-3. (il)
                        3272

Ruiz Cabañas, Samuel.
"Blasón." La Falange, Núm.
2 (1 de enero de 1923), 65.
(p)   3273

----. "Cubismo." La Falange, Núm. 2 (1 de enero de 1923), 95. (p)   3274

Ruiz de Alarcón y Mendoza, Juan. "Fragmentos sobre el amor y las mujeres." Taller, I (Núm. 5, octubre de 1939), 75-89. (dr)   3275

Ruiz Esparza, Juan Manuel. "Alfonso Reyes." Fábula, Núm. 9 (septiembre de 1934), 178. (a-e)   3276

----. "Ultima voluntad," "Estival." Fábula, Núm. 8 (agosto de 1934), 151-153. (p)   3277

Ruiz Harrell, Rafael. "Rosa de Camotlán." Estaciones, III (Núm. 10, verano de 1958), 214-221. (f)   3278

Russell, Dora Isella. "La poesía, oficio secular." Estaciones, III (Núm. 9, primavera de 1958), 38-42. (a-e)   3279

S. La caída de Carranza. -- De la dictadura a la libertad de varios autores. México Moderno, I (Núm. 5, diciembre de 1920), 320-321. (r)   3280

Saadí. "Sentencias" (Trad. Francisco Orozco Muñoz). La Falange, Núm. 2 (1 de enero de 1923), 66-70. (a-e)   (2639)

Saavedra, Rafael M. "La 'cruza'." México Moderno, II (Núm. 2, septiembre de 1922), 97-108. (dr)   3281

----. "La noche de los muertos." Antena, Núm. 5 (noviembre de 1924), 9-10. (f)   3282

----. "Pancho Domínguez en la Huasteca." Antena, Núm. 5 (noviembre de 1924), 8. (a-e)   3283

Saavedra Faxardo, Diego. "Idea de un príncipe político christiano." El Hijo Pródigo, XII (Núm. 37, abril de 1946), 44-57. (a-e)   3284

Sabines, Jaime. "Dos poemas breves." Estaciones, III (Núm. 12, invierno de 1958), 413-414. (p)   3285

----. "La enfermedad viene de lejos." Estaciones, I (Núm. 4, invierno de 1956), 567-569. (p)   3286

----. "Tío Chagua." Estaciones, III (Núm. 9, primavera de 1958), 18-21. (p)   3287

Sabisch. "Viñeta." Estaciones, IV (Núm. 16, invierno de 1959), portada. (il)   3288

Sáenz, Marta. "Doña Pastora explica." Estaciones, V (Núm. 18, verano de 1960), 45-50. (f)   3289

----. "Sócrates y Platón." Estaciones, V (Núm. 19, otoño de 1960), 89-94. (f)   3290

Sáinz, Gustavo. "El brillante color de la violencia." Estaciones, V (Núm. 17, primavera de 1960), 46-53. (f)   3291

----. "La deshabitada." Estaciones, V (Núm. 19, otoño de 1960), 17-20. (f)   3292

----. "Introducción a la ópera del orden." Estaciones,

V (Núm. 20, invierno de 1960), 24-25. (a-e) 3293

----. "El sol en los brazos." Estaciones, IV (Núm. 13, primavera de 1959), 78-90. (f) 3294

----. "Viñeta." Estaciones, V (Núm. 19, otoño de 1960), portada. (il) 3295

----. Amor de Henry Green. Estaciones, V (Núm. 19, otoño de 1960), 118-120. (r) 3296

----. La conciencia de Zeno de Italo Svevo (pseud. Ettore Schmitz) Estaciones, V (Núm. 19, otoño de 1960), 120. (r) 3297

----. Dark Bridwell de Esther Chelminsky. Estaciones, V (Núm. 19, otoño de 1960), 120-121. (r) 3298

----. El empleo del tiempo de Michel Butor. Estaciones, V (Núm. 19, otoño de 1960), 117. (r) 3299

----. James Joyce por él mismo de Jean Paris. Estaciones, IV (Núm. 13, primavera de 1959), 118-120. (r) 3300

----. La Jeunesse D'André Gide de Jean Delay. Estaciones, IV (Núm. 14, verano de 1959), 251-254. (r) 3301

----. La justicia de enero de Sergio Galindo. Estaciones, IV (Núm. 13, primavera de 1959), 116-117. (r) 3302

----. Lienzos de sueño de Manuel Mejía Valera. Estaciones, IV (Núm. 16,

invierno de 1959), 487-488. (r) 3303

----. La muchacha debajo del león de André Pieyre de Mandiarques. Estaciones, V (Núm. 19, otoño de 1960), 118. (r) 3304

----. El último justo de André Schwarz-Bart. Estaciones, V (Núm. 19, otoño de 1960), 123-125. (r) 3305

----. La verdadera vida de Sebastián Knight de Vladimir Nabokov. Estaciones, V (Núm. 19, otoño de 1960), 121-123. (r) 3306

Salas Viu, Vicente. "Ramón desarraigado." Romance, I (Núm. 10, 15 de junio de 1940), 6. (a-e) 3307

Salazar, Adolfo. "Cafés con música." El Hijo Pródigo, II (Núm. 8, noviembre de 1943), 82-87. (f) 3308

----. "Figuras con paisaje." El Hijo Pródigo, VII (Núm. 23, febrero de 1945), 91-99. (a-e) 3309

----. "Paisaje con figuras, notas e impresiones de la 'otra' Italia." El Hijo Pródigo, VI (Núm. 20, noviembre de 1944), 89-97. (a-e) 3310

----. "Retrato de la Madre Lugarda María de la Luz." El Hijo Pródigo, II (Núm. 7, octubre de 1943), entre 32 y 33. (il) 3311

----. Las dos Españas de Fidelino de Figueiredo. El Hijo Pródigo, VI (Núm. 21,

diciembre de 1944), 186-187.
(r)   3312

Salazar, Juan B. "Fauna
mexicana:El tlacuache, El
borrego salvaje, El berrendo,
El elefante marino."
Contemporáneos, IV (Núm. 12,
mayo de 1929), 169-192. (a-
e)   3313

Salazar, Toño. "Alfonso Reyes."
Fábula, Núm. 9 (septiembre
de 1934), entre 174 y 175.
(il)   3314

----. "Ricardo Arenales."
La Falange, Núm. 1 (1 de
diciembre de 1922), 6. (il)
                               3315

Salazar Bondy, Sebastián.
"Cuerpo para olvidar," "Amo
a Lot." Prometeus, I (Núm.
3, mayo de 1949), 167-168.
(p)   3316

Salazar Mallén, Rubén.
"Acuario." Contemporáneos,
VI (Núm. 22, marzo de 1930),
201-210. (f)   3317

----. "Cinta." Contempo-
ráneos, III (Núm. 8, enero de
1929), 18-23. (f)   3318

----. "Diagnóstico de una
traición." Estaciones, I
(Núm. 3, otoño de 1956), 387-
394. (a-e)   3319

----. "Espuma." Contempo-
ráneos, IV (Núm. 11, abril
de 1929), 1-14. (f)   3320

----. "Miedo," "San
Ambrosio." Estaciones, III
(Núm. 11, otoño de 1958),
291-293. (f)   3321

----. La educación sentimental de Jaime Torres Bodet.
Contemporáneos, VI (Núm.

21, febrero de 1930), 186-
188. (r)   3322

----. Indagación del Choteo
de Jorge Mañach. Contem-
poráneos, II (Núm. 10, marzo
de 1929), 270-271. (f)   3323

----. Influencia de la sal en
la distribución geográfica
de los grupos indígenas de
México de Miguel O. de
Mendizábal. Contemporáneos,
IV (Núm. 13, junio de 1929),
269-272. (r)   3324

----. El positivismo en
México de Leopoldo Zea. El
Hijo Pródigo, I (Núm. 2,
mayo de 1943), 124-125. (r)
                               3325

----. Sin novedad en el
frente de Enrich María
Remarque. Contemporáneos,
V (Núm. 15, agosto de
1929), 75-78. (r)   3326

Salazar Viniegra, Leopoldo.
"Don Juan y el amor."
Contemporáneos, IV (Núm. 11,
abril de 1929), 23-53. (a-e)
                               3327

----. Ensayo de psicología
de la adolescencia de
Ezequiel A. Chávez.
Contemporáneos, V (Núm. 16,
septiembre de 1929), 153-156.
(r)   3328

Salazar y Chapela, E. "Un
día de guerra." Romance, I
(Núm. 4, 15 de marzo de
1940), 12. (a-e)   3329

----. "La mujer inglesa en
la guerra." Romance, I
(Núm. 6, 15 de abril de
1940), 12. (a-e)   3330

----. "Un libro sobre México"

203

(Reseña de An eye-witness of Mexico de R. H. K. Marett). Romance, I (Núm. 9, 1 de junio de 1940), 18. (r) 3331

----. "García Lorca en Londres" (Reseña de Lament for the death of a bullfighter and other poems, trad. A. L. Lloyd; Poems, trad. Stephen Spender y J. L. Gili). Romance, I (Núm. 7, 1 de mayo de 1940), 18. (r) 3332

Salinas, Pedro. "Nueve o diez poetas." El Hijo Pródigo, VIII (Núm. 26, mayo de 1945), 71-79. (a-e) 3333

----. "Poesías de Luis Carrillo de Sotomayor." Taller, II (Núm. 8-9, enero-febrero de 1940), 73-74. (a-e) 3334

----. "Querencia." El Hijo Pródigo, I (Núm. 4, julio de 1943), 219-220. (p) 3335

Salmón, André. "Manuel Rodríguez Lozano." Forma, I (Núm. 4, 1927), 2. (a-e) 3336

Sánchez, Pedro C. "Astronomía y geodesia." Contemporáneos, II (Núm. 7, diciembre de 1928), 346-380. (a-e) 3337

Sánchez Barbudo, Antonio. "A la orilla del mundo." El Hijo Pródigo, I (Núm. 1, abril de 1943), 44-48. (a-e) 3338

----. "La casa de comidas." El Hijo Pródigo, VII (Núm. 22, enero de 1945), 24-27. (f) 3339

----. "España como esperanza." El Hijo Pródigo, IV (Núm. 13, abril de 1944), 25-37. (a-e) 3340

----. "Lo que hace al verdadero escritor." Romance, I (Núm. 13, 1 de agosto de 1940), 9, 11. (a-e) 3341

----. "Poesías rufianescas." El Hijo Pródigo, XIII (Núm. 40, julio de 1946), 34-37. (a-e) 3342

----. "Primavera-otoño, 1938." Taller, II (Núm. 11, julio-agosto de 1940), 41-61. (f) 3343

----. "Recuerdos de un estilo." El Hijo Pródigo, IX (Núm. 29, agosto de 1945), 96-104. (f) 3344

----. "El sentimiento de la derrota." El Hijo Pródigo, I (Núm. 4, julio de 1943), 221-229. (p) 3345

----. "Sobre un ser alado que se apoyaba en un sillín." Romance, I (Núm. 5, 1 de abril de 1940), 9. (a-e) 3346

----. "Sueños de grandeza." El Hijo Pródigo, II (Núm. 7, octubre de 1943), 33-40. (f) 3347

----. "Valle Inclán y su paisaje." Romance, I (Núm. 2, 15 de febrero de 1940), 9. (a-e) 3348

----. "Viaje a un lago." El Hijo Pródigo, XII (Núm. 38, mayo de 1946), 79-88. (f) 3349

----. "Un violinista."

Romance, I (Núm. 8, 15 de mayo de 1940), 5. (f) 3350

----. Asedio a Dilthey de Eugenio Imaz. El Hijo Pródigo, IX (Núm. 30, septiembre de 1945), 180-181. (r) 3351

----. Un aspecto del orden cristiano y La figura de este mundo de José M. Gallegos Rocafull. El Hijo Pródigo, II (Núm. 8, noviembre de 1943), 123-124. (r) 3352

----. El clarividente de Lion Feutchwanger. El Hijo Pródigo, IV (Núm. 14, mayo de 1944), 122. (r) 3353

----. "La maravilla en la sangre" (Reseña de Crónicas de la conquista). Taller, I (Núm. 5, octubre de 1939), 55-60. (r) 3354

----. Cuenca Ibérica de Miguel de Unamuno. El Hijo Pródigo, I (Núm. 4, julio de 1943), 256-257. (r) 3355

----. China en armas de Agnes Smedley. El Hijo Pródigo, V (Núm. 16, julio de 1944), 57-58. (r) 3356

----. Delicioso el hereje de Adolfo Salazar. El Hijo Pródigo, XII (Núm. 37, abril de 1946), 58-59. (r) 3357

----. Descontento creador de Romualdo Brughetti. El Hijo Pródigo, V (Núm. 18, septiembre de 1944), 186-187. (r) 3358

----. Dios en la tierra de José Revueltas. El Hijo

Pródigo, VI (Núm. 20, noviembre de 1944), 121-122. (r) 3359

----. Don Ramón María del Valle-Inclán de Ramón Gómez de la Serna. El Hijo Pródigo, VII (Núm. 23, febrero de 1945), 123. (r) 3360

----. "K. Mansfield o la vida pequeña" (Reseña de En la bahía de Katherine Mansfield). Romance, I (Núm. 2, 15 de febrero de 1940), 18. (r) 3361

----. El español del éxodo y del llanto de León Felipe. Taller, II (Núm. 8-9, enero-febrero de 1940), 58-61. (r) 3362

----. "Fanatismo y misticismo" (Reseña de Ensayos de Adolfo Menéndez Samará). Romance, I (Núm. 11, 1 de julio de 1940), 18. (r) 3363

----. Fray Diego Valadés. Escritor y grabador franciscano del siglo XVI de Francisco de la Maza. El Hijo Pródigo, X (Núm. 31, octubre de 1945), 55-56. (r) 3364

----. El gran Meaulnes de Alain Fournier. Taller, I (Núm. 7, diciembre de 1939), 46-52. (r) 3365

----. Il est un jardin de Jacqueline Dupuy. El Hijo Pródigo, XI (Núm. 36, marzo de 1946), 175-176. (r) 3366

----. Mal de ciudad de Isidoro Sagües. El Hijo

Pródigo, IX (Núm. 28, julio de 1945), 59. (r) 3367

----. Mañanas en México de D. H. Lawrence. El Hijo Pródigo, I (Núm. 1, abril de 1943), 58-59. (r) 3368

----. Melodía de amor y la muerte del corneta Cristóbal Rilke. Romance, I (Núm. 4, 15 de marzo de 1940), 18. (r) 3369

----. Menéndez Pelayo y las dos Españas de Guillermo de Torre. El Hijo Pródigo, II (Núm. 9, diciembre de 1943), 220-221. (r) 3370

----. "Antonio Machado" (Reseña de Obras completas de Antonio Machado). Taller, II (Núm. 12, enero-febrero de 1941), 11-33. (r) 3371

----. Pages de journal de André Gide. El Hijo Pródigo, XII (Núm. 38, mayo de 1946), 114-115. (r) 3372

----. El pasajero de José Bergamín. El Hijo Pródigo, I (Núm. 6, septiembre de 1943), 380-381. (r) 3373

----. "Aparición de un novelista" (Reseña de Paseo de mentiras de Juan de la Cabada). Romance, I (Núm. 15, 1 de septiembre de 1940), 18. (r) 3374

----. El pensamiento vivo de Séneca de María Zambrano. El Hijo Pródigo, VII (Núm. 24, marzo de 1945), 184-185. (r) 3375

----. Los pintores italianos del Renacimiento de Bernardo Berenson. El Hijo

Pródigo, VI (Núm. 19, octubre de 1944), 60-61. (r) 3376

----. Las ratas de José Bianco. El Hijo Pródigo, III (Núm. 12, marzo de 1944), 185. (r) 3377

----. Realidad del alma de C. G. Jung. Romance, I (Núm. 14, 15 de agosto de 1940), 19. (r) 3378

----. El saber y la cultura de Max Scheler. Romance, I (Núm. 1, 1 de febrero de 1940), 18. (r) 3379

----. El sitio de Sebastopol de Boris Voyetejov y Doce meses que cambiaron el mundo de Larry Lesueur. El Hijo Pródigo, II (Núm. 11, febrero de 1944), 122-123. (r) 3380

----. La última vez que vi París de Elliot Paul. El Hijo Pródigo, I (Núm. 5, agosto de 1943), 320. (r) 3381

----. Viaje sin retorno de Henry Shoskes. El Hijo Pródigo, VIII (Núm. 27, junio de 1945), 183-184. (r) 3382

----. Vida y obra de Galdós de Joaquín Casalduero. El Hijo Pródigo, III (Núm. 10, enero de 1944), 56-57. (r) 3383

----. Eckhart, Meister. "Dos textos místicos" (Trad. Daisy Brody y Antonio Sánchez Barbudo). El Hijo Pródigo, II (Núm. 7, octubre de 1943), 51-57. (tr) (1214)

----. Emmanuel, Pierre. "El hombre y el poeta" (Trad. Antonio Sánchez Barbudo. El Hijo Pródigo, I (Núm. 2, mayo de 1943), 89-99. (tr) (1233)

----. Lao-Tze. "Fragmentos del Tao-te-king" (Trad. Daisy Brody y Antonio Sánchez Barbudo). El Hijo Pródigo, XI (Núm. 35, febrero de 1946), 97-100. (tr) (714)

----. "Viejos cuentos de la India (Trad. Daisy Brody y Antonio Sánchez Barbudo). El Hijo Pródigo, VIII (Núm. 27, junio de 1945), 150-156. (tr) (281)

----. Lessing, Gotthold Ephraim. "Cartas de Lessing" (Trad. de Angela Selke y Antonio Sánchez Barbudo). El Hijo Pródigo, X (Núm. 33, diciembre de 1945), 161-170. (tr) (2064)

----. Radványi, Netty. ("Seghers, Anna"). "Leyendas de Artemisa" (Trad. Angela Selke y Antonio Sánchez Barbudo). El Hijo Pródigo, V (Núm. 18, septiembre de 1944), 154-165. (tr) (3018)

Sánchez de Ocaña, Rafael. "La sombra de Robespierre." Romance, I (Núm. 11, 1 de julio de 1940), 9. (a-e) 3384

----. "Temblor de almas." Romance, I (Núm. 3, 1 de marzo de 1940), 5. (a-e) 3385

Sánchez Mayans, Fernando. "Las cosas eternas." Estaciones, II (Núm. 7, otoño de 1957), 297-301. (f) 3386

----. "Ciudad abandonada." Estaciones, III (Núm. 12, invierno de 1958), 415-416. (p) 3387

----. "Poema a un artista difunto." Estaciones, I (Núm. 3, otoño de 1956), 343-346. (p) 3388

----. "El regreso marino." Prometeus, II (Núm. 1, diciembre de 1951), 21-22. (p) 3389

----. "Sonetos al dolor." Prometeus, I (Núm. 3, mayo de 1949), 156-157. (p) 3390

----. Cementerio de pájaros de Griselda Alvarez. Estaciones, I (Núm. 1, primavera de 1956), 125. (r) 3391

----. Panorámica de las letras I. Ramón López Velarde de Rafael Cuevas. Estaciones, I (Núm. 4, invierno de 1956), 596-597. (r) 3392

----. Tarumba de Jaime Sabines. Estaciones, I (Núm. 2, verano de 1956), 255-257. (r) 3393

----. Teatro: El Malentendido, Calígula, El estado de sitio, y Los justos de Albert Camus. Prometeus, II (Núm. 1, diciembre de 1951), 66-67. (r) 3394

Sánchez Rivero, Angel. "Fragmentos de un diario." Contemporáneos, VIII (Núm. 28-29, septiembre-octubre de 1930), 146-163. (a-e) 3395

Sánchez-Sáez, Braulio.

"Literatura del Brasil: Hombres y libros del pasado año." Romance, II (Núm. 24, 31 de mayo de 1941), 20. (a-e) 3396

Sánchez Vázquez, Adolfo. "La decadencia del héroe." Romance, I (Núm. 4, 15 de marzo de 1940), 10. (a-e) 3397

----. "En torno a la picaresca." Romance, I (Núm. 8, 15 de mayo de 1940), 6. (a-e) 3398

----. "Sonetos." Taller, II (Núm. 12, enero-febrero de 1941), 59-60. (p) 3399

----. "Perfil del cuento" (Reseña de Antología del cuento hispanoamericano de Víctor Domínguez Silva). Romance, I (Núm. 14, 15 de agosto de 1940), 18. (r) 3400

----. "En torno a un libro de José Ma. Arguedas sobre el arte popular indio y mestizo" (Reseña de Canto Kechwa.) Romance, I (Núm. 9, 1 de junio de 1940), 19. (r) 3401

----. Ciclo de vírgenes de Manuel Ponce. Romance, I (Núm. 6, 15 de abril de 1940), 18. (r) 3402

----. Eduardo VII y su época de André Maurois. Romance, I (Núm. 1, 1 de febrero de 1940), 20. (r) 3403

----. Ensayos de Juan Marinello. Romance, I (Núm. 2, 15 de febrero de 1940), 19. (r) 3404

----. Flor cerrada de Juvenal Ortiz Saralegui. Romance, I (Núm. 5, 1 de abril de 1940), 18. (r) 3405

----. "Fourier o el socialismo utópico" (Reseña de Fourier de Armond y Maubliac). Romance, I (Núm. 6, 15 de abril de 1940), 19. (r) 3406

----. "Gil Vicente poeta lírico" (Reseña de una selección de su poesía por Dámaso Alonso). Romance, I (Núm. 8, 15 de mayo de 1940), 18. (r) 3407

----. Reseña de Historia comparada de los pueblos de Europa de Charles Seignotos. Romance, I (Núm. 4, 15 de marzo de 1940), 19. (r) 3408

----. "Pancho Villa el héroe y el hombre" (Reseña de Memorias de Pancho Villa, Tercera parte, de Martín Luis Guzmán). Romance, I (Núm. 7, 1 de mayo de 1940), 18. (r) 3409

----. Nietzche de Henri Lefebvre. Romance, I (Núm. 16, 15 de septiembre de 1940), 18. (r) 3410

----. "La nueva generación poética de Colombia" (Reseña de la colección Piedra y cielo). Romance, I (Núm. 10, 15 de junio de 1940), 18. (r) 3411

----. La rama viva de Francisco Giner de los Ríos. Romance, I (Núm. 13, 1 de agosto de 1940), 18. (r) 3412

----. "El auto sacramental de nuestro tiempo" (Reseña de Tres en uno de Juan Bartolomé Roxas). Romance, I (Núm. 12, 15 de julio de 1940), 18. (r) 3413

Sandburg, Carl. "Memoir of a Proud Boy." Ulises, Núm. 2 (junio de 1927), 3-4. (p) 3414

----. "Las tumbas frías" (Trad. Rafael Lozano). La Falange, Núm. 7 (1 de octubre de 1923), 385. (p) (2134)

Sandóiz, Alba. "La empalada." El Hijo Pródigo, XIII (Núm. 41, agosto de 1946), 88-90. (f) 3415

Sanjuan, Pedro. "Música nueva." Contemporáneos, V (Núm. 17, octubre de 1929), 161-175. (a-e) 3416

Santacruz, Agustín. "El ahorcado." Ruta, Núm. 4 (septiembre de 1938), 39-42. (f) 3417

Santa Cruz, Francisco. "Composición mural," "Dibujo," "Dibujo," "Figura." Contemporáneos, VI (Núm. 20, enero de 1930), 53-56. (il) 3418

Santa Cruz, Mario. "Anatole France, novelista filósofo, y esteta." Antena, Núm. 1 (julio de 1924), 9-11. (a-e) 3419

Santaló Sors, Marcelo. "Mas allá de las estrellas." Romance, I (Núm. 20, 15 de enero de 1941), 4. (a-e) 3420

----. "Mil millones de estrellas." Romance, I (Núm. 9, 1 de junio de 1940), 4. (a-e) 3421

Santayana, George. "Aversión al platonismo." México Moderno, II (Núm. 3, octubre de 1922), 185-186. (a-e) 3422

----. "Las mansiones de Elena" (Trad. Antonio Castro Leal). El Hijo Pródigo, V (Núm. 16, julio de 1944), 38-41. (a-e) (891)

Santos, Ninfa. "Si nada más oyeras." El Hijo Pródigo, XII (Núm. 37, abril de 1946), 18-19. (p) 3423

Santos Chocano, José. "El nocturno del regreso al hogar." La Falange, Núm. 2 (1 de enero de 1923), 87-89. (p) 3424

Santoyo, Matías. "Tehuana." Forma, I (Núm. 2, noviembre de 1926), 2. (il) 3425

Santullano, Luis. "El cínico, el mar y la montaña: Recuerdos y nostalgias." Romance, I (Núm. 11, 1 de julio de 1940), 6. (a-e) 3426

Saroyan, William. "Entre los perdidos," "Estimada Greta Garbo," "Oración" (Trad. Octavio G. Barreda). El Hijo Pródigo, I (Núm. 5, agosto de 1943), 308-311. (a-e) (600)

Sayago, Fernando. "Lo que falta a los conciertos de radio." Antena, Núm. 1 (julio de 1924), 19. (a-e) 3427

Schaeffner, André. "Los grandes maestros de la

música: Igor Strawinsky."
Romance, I (Núm. 14, 15 de
agosto de 1940), 6. (a-e)
3428

Schons, Dorothy. "Nuevos
datos para la biografía de
Sor Juana." Contemporáneos,
III (Núm. 9, febrero de
1929), 161-176. (a-e)   3429

Segovia, Tomás. "Los jardines
allá," "Alegría," "Vivido."
Estaciones, III (Núm. 12,
invierno de 1958), 427-429.
(p)   3430

----. "Lluvia estival."
Estaciones, IV (Núm. 14,
verano de 1959), 146. (p)
3431

Ségur, Condesa de. "Una carta
a su pequeño hijo Jacques
de Pitray" (Trad. Francisco
Zendejas). Prometeus, II
(Núm. 1, diciembre de 1951),
45. (a-e)   3432

Selke, Angela. Lessing, Gotthold
Ephraim. "Cartas de
Lessing" (Trad. de Angela
Selke y Antonio Sánchez
Barbudo). El Hijo Pródigo,
X (Núm. 33, diciembre de
1945), 161-170. (tr) (2064)

----. Radványi, Netty.
("Seghers, Anna"). "Leyendas
de Artemisa" (Trad. Angela
Selke y Antonio Sánchez
Barbudo). El Hijo Pródigo,
V (Núm. 18, septiembre de
1944), 154-165. (tr) (3018)

Selke, Rodolfo. Tolstoi, Alexis.
"San Petersburgo." (Trad.
Rodolfo Selke). El Hijo
Pródigo, V (Núm. 17, agosto
de 1944), 100-101. (tr)
3433

Selva, Mauricio de la. "Antonio

de Undurraga y vanguardia
pan-hispánica." Estaciones,
III (Núm. 10, verano de
1958), 187-190. (a-e)   3434

----. "Carta a mi hijo."
Estaciones, V (Núm. 20,
invierno de 1960), 79-81.
(p)   3435

----. "Cuartro novelistas."
Estaciones, IV (Núm. 16,
invierno de 1959), 458-468.
(a-e)   3436

----. "Un hombre tímido."
Estaciones, II (Núm. 7, otoño
de 1957), 265-271. (f)   3427

----. "Imagen de Diego
Rivera." Estaciones, II
(Núm. 8, invierno de 1957),
369. (p)   3438

----. "Poemas cortos para
la ausencia tuya."
Estaciones, II (Núm. 5,
primavera de 1957), 36-39.
(p)   3439

----. Los aborígenes de las
Antillas de Felipe Pichardo
Moya. Estaciones, I (Núm.
4, invierno de 1956), 595-
596. (r)   3440

----. Antología de Miguel
Hernández. Estaciones, V
(Núm. 20, invierno de 1960),
116-117. (r)   3441

----. Balzac de Jaime Torres
Bodet. Estaciones, IV (Núm.
16, invierno de 1959), 503-
504. (r)   3442

----. Campanas de barro,
Poemas y corridos de
Alfonso Leñero Ruiz.
Estaciones, II (Núm. 6,
verano de 1957), 196. (r)
3443

----. Cantares de Cocibolca de Francisco Hernández Segura. Estaciones, V (Núm. 18, verano de 1960), 113-115. (r)   3444

----. Casi el Paraíso de Luis Spota. Estaciones, II (Núm. 7, otoño de 1957), 317-318. (r)   3445

----. Conflictos y armonías en torno a Cuba de Emeterio S. Santovenia. Estaciones, I (Núm. 4, invierno de 1956), 601-602. (r)   3446

----. Conversaciones con Nehru de Tibor Mende. Estaciones, II (Núm. 7, otoño de 1957), 318. (r)3447

----. La corruptora de Guy des Cars. Estaciones, V (Núm. 20, invierno 1960), 114-116. (r)   3448

----. Daniela de Luisa Rinser. Estaciones, V (Núm. 20, invierno de 1960), 121-123. (r)   3449

----. De Rimbaud a Pasternak y Quasimodo de Max Henríquez Ureña. Estaciones, V (Núm. 20, invierno de 1960), 117-118. (r)   3450

----. Enrique Gómez Carrillo: El cronista errante de Edelberto Torres. Estaciones, I (Núm. 4, invierno de 1956), 600-601. (r)   3451

----. Esa Sangre de Mariano Azuela. Estaciones, I (Núm. 2, verano de 1956), 253-254. (r)   3452

----. Escándalo en Troya de Eva Hemmer Hansen.

Estaciones, V (Núm. 20, invierno de 1960), 106-108. (r)   3453

----. El escritor en la sociedad de masas y breve teoría de la traducción de Francisco Ayala. Estaciones, I (Núm. 2, verano de 1956), 258-259. (r)   3454

----. Fábula del tiburón y las sardinas, América Latina estrangulada de Juan José Arévalo. Estaciones, II (Núm. 5, primavera de 1957), 96. (r)   3455

----. Francisco Gavidia y Rubén Darío, Semilla y floración del modernismo de Cristóbal Humberto Ibarra. Estaciones, V (Núm. 17, primavera de 1960), 125-128. (r)   3456

----. García Moreno El santo del patíbulo de Benjamin Carrión. Estaciones, V (Núm. 18, verano de 1960), 108-109. (r)   3457

----. Los hechos de la vida de George Gamow. Estaciones, V (Núm. 17, primavera de 1960), 122-123. (r)   3458

----. El héroe de las mil capas de Joseph Campbell. Estaciones, V (Núm. 17, primavera de 1960), 123-124. (r)   3459

----. Hijas de las alegría de Guy des Cars. Estaciones, V (Núm. 20, invierno de 1960), 108-110. (r)   3460

----. Historia de las ideas contemporáneas en Centro América de Rafael Heliodoro

Valle. Estaciones, V (Núm. 18, verano de 1960), 116-118. (r)   3461

----. Historia prodigiosa de Adolfo Bioy Casares. Estaciones, I (Núm. 2, verano de 1956), 259-260. (r) 3462

----. Los índios de las américas de John Collier. Estaciones, V (Núm. 20, invierno de 1960), 110-111. (r)   3463

----. Los inocentes de Manuel Lamana. Estaciones, V (Núm. 18, verano de 1960), 112-113. (r)   3464

----. Introducción al estudio de Grecia de A. Petrie. Estaciones, II (Núm. 7, otoño de 1957), 317. (r)   3465

----. Los jilgueros de Joel Marrokín. Estaciones, V (Núm. 17, primavera de 1960), 124-125. (r) 3466

----. "La literatura en los Breviarios." Estaciones, IV (Núm. 15, otoño de 1959), 370-375. (r)   3467

----. Manual de Zoología fantástica de Jorge Luis Borges y Margarita Guerrero. Estaciones, II (Núm. 6, verano de 1957), 195. (r)   3468

----. Morelos y Bolívar de Vicente Sáenz. Estaciones, II (Núm. 7, otoño de 1957), 318-319. (r)   3469

----. Obras completas de Alfonso Reyes. Estaciones, V (Núm. 20, invierno de 1960), 118-120. (r)   3470

----. El papel del economista como asesor oficial de W. A. Johr y H. S. Singer. Estaciones, II (Núm. 7, otoño de 1957), 326. (r)   3471

----. El Perú, retrato de un país adolescente de Luis Alberto Sánchez. Estaciones, IV (Núm. 16, invierno de 1959), 492-493. (r)   3472

----. La pintura prehistórica de Alan Hougton Brodrick. Estaciones, I (Núm. 4, invierno de 1956), 594-595. (r)   3473

----. Poesías completas de Manuel Altolaguirre. Estaciones, V (Núm. 19, otoño de 1960), 126-128. (r)   3474

----. El poeta que se volvió gusano y otras historias verídicas de Fernando Alegría. Estaciones, I (Núm. 1, primavera de 1956), 126-127. (r)   3475

----. Los reinos del ser de George Santayana. Estaciones, V (Núm. 18, verano de 1960), 109-110. (r)   3476

----. El revés y el derecho de Albert Camus. Estaciones, IV (Núm. 16, invierno de 1959), 491-492. (r)   3477

----. Se oyen las musas de Truman Capote. Estaciones, IV (Núm. 16, invierno de 1959), 493-494. (r)   3478

----. Sobre literatura y filosofía de José Mancisidor.

Estaciones, II (Núm. 5, primavera de 1957), 96. (r) 3479

----. Sobre los ángeles de Rafael Alberti. Estaciones, V (Núm. 18, verano de 1960), 110-112. (r) 3480

----. Tendencia a la corrupción de R. E. Barker. Estaciones, V (Núm. 20, invierno de 1960), 105-106. (r) 3481

----. El tiempo de la ira de Luis Spota. Estaciones, V (Núm. 20, invierno de 1960), 111-114. (r) 3482

----. Un verde paraíso de Marcos Victoria. Estaciones, V (Núm. 20, invierno de 1960), 120-121. (r) 3483

Selva, Salomón de la. "Alejandro Hamilton: Sonata." Romance, II (Núm. 22, 15 de marzo de 1941), 5. (p) 3484

----. "Antología" sobre Macías. México Moderno, II (Núm. 3, octubre de 1922), 179-182. (ed) 3485

----. "Rubén Darío." Romance, II (Núm. 21, 15 de febrero de 1941), 3. (a-e) 3486

----. "Tu amor desmesurado, por codicioso pierde..." México Moderno, I (Núm. 8, marzo de 1921), 86-87. (p) 3487

----. "Urgencias centro-americanas: verdad, amor." México Moderno, II (Núm. 3, octubre de 1922), 174-178. (a-e) 3488

----. Divertidas aventuras del nieto de Juan Moreira de Roberto J. Payró. México Moderno, II (Núm. 3, octubre de 1922), 193-194. (r) 3489

----. Problems in Pan Americanism de Samuel Guy Inman. México Moderno, II (Núm. 2, septiembre de 1922), 128-129. (r) 3490

----. The Psychology of Social Life del Dr. Charles Platt. México Moderno, II (Núm. 2, septiembre de 1922), 129. (r) 3491

----. Remanso de silencio de Joaquín Ramírez Cabañas. México Moderno, II (Núm. 3, octubre de 1922), 188-190. (r) 3492

----. Una vida en el cine de Alberto Masferrer. México Moderno, II (Núm. 2, septiembre de 1922), 127. (r) 3493

Serge, Victor. "El mensaje del escritor" (Trad. César Moro). El Hijo Pródigo, VI (Núm. 21, diciembre de 1944), 147-149. (a-e) (2471)

----. Journal de guerre de Jean Malaquais. El Hijo Pródigo, III (Núm. 12, marzo de 1944), 184-185. (r) 3494

Serpa, Enrique. "Eran tres marineros..." Ruta, Núm. 6 (noviembre de 1938), 18-19. (p) 3495

Serrano, Luis G. "Azulejos y paneles policromos de la época de la colonia." Forma, I (Núm. 5, 1927), 10-15. (a-e) 3496

Serrano Plaja, Arturo. "Estos son los oficios," "Aquí no llora nadie," "De un Diario de un viaje de emigrantes". Romance, I (Núm. 14, 15 de agosto de 1940), 10. (p) 3497

Severianin, Igor. "Día de primavera," "Día de verano," "Día de otoño," "Victoria Regia" (Trad. Jorge Villardo). Sagitario, Núm. 12-13 (30 de abril de 1927), 14. (p) 3498

Shildt, Runar. "El ahorcado" (Trad. de Rafael L. Partida). El Hijo Pródigo, XII (Núm. 39, junio de 1946), 165-174. (dr) (2835)

Sierra, José Barros. "La ópera no quiere morir." Romance, I (Núm. 4, 15 de marzo de 1940), 15. (a-e) 3499

Silva, Jonás de. "Coração." México Moderno, I (Núm. 5, diciembre de 1920), 326-327. (p) 3500

Silva Valdés, Fernán. "Canto a las playas del Uruguay." Romance, I (Núm. 20, 15 de enero de 1941), 10. (p) 3501

Silva Vandeira, Mariano. "Salomé." El Hijo Pródigo, I (Núm. 7, julio de 1943), entre 212-213. (il) 3502

Silva y Aceves, Mariano. "Campanitas de plata." México Moderno, I (Núm. 1, agosto de 1920), 26-28. (p) 3503

----. La educación contemporánea de Carlos Octavio Bunge. México Moderno, I (Núm. 3, octubre de 1920), 195-196. (r) 3504

----. Moral ocasional de Manuel Velázque Andrade. México Moderno, I (Núm. 7, febrero de 1921), 68. (r) 3505

Sinclair, Upton. "El arte y lo inmediato." Ruta, Núm. 7 (diciembre de 1938), 44-46. (a-e) 3506

Siqueiros, David Alfaro. "Cabeza," "Obrero." Forma, I (Núm. 2, noviembre de 1926), 22-24. (il) 3507

----. "Un ensayo de pintura colectiva." Romance, I (Núm. 4, 15 de marzo de 1940), 7. (a-e) 3508

----. "La visita a la cárcel," "Zapata," "La madre proletaria," "Blanca Luz Brumen," "Niño," "Paisaje," "La familia." Romance, I (Núm. 17, 22 de octubre de 1940), 1, 13. (il) 3509

Smedley, Agnes. "El automóvil núm. 1469" (Trad. Gilberto Owen). El Hijo Pródigo, III (Núm. 10, enero de 1944), 35-39. (f) (2745a)

Smith, Logan Pearsall. "Merengues" (Trad. Eduardo Villaseñor). México Moderno, II (Núm. 1, agosto de 1922), 60. (a-e) 3510

Sócrates. "Dos cuadritos socráticos" (Trad. Juan David García Bacca). El Hijo Pródigo, VIII (Núm. 26, mayo de 1945), 94-98. (a-e) 3511

Solana, Rafael. "La capilla dorada." El Hijo Pródigo, VIII (Núm. 26, mayo de 1945), 85-89. (p) 3512

----. "El concerto." El Hijo Pródigo, I (Núm. 4, julio de 1943), 230-235. (f)   3513

----. "Diario, epígrafes y apuntes para la novela La educación de los sentidos." Taller, I (Núm. 3, mayo de 1939), 44-50. (a-e)   3514

----. "Diciembre," "Enero," "Febrero." Estaciones, III (Núm. 12, invierno de 1958), 399-400. (p)   3515

----. "Dos poemas." Taller, I (Núm. 4, julio de 1939), 40-42. (p)   3516

----. "En busca de la prosa." Taller, I (Núm. 6, noviembre de 1939), 63-65. (a-e)   3517

----. "Estrella que se apaga." El Hijo Pródigo, XI (Núm. 36, marzo de 1946), 127-133. (f)   3518

----. "Jaime Torres Bodet." Estaciones, II (Núm. 6, verano de 1957), 105-109. (a-e)   3519

----. "José Juan Tablada." El Hijo Pródigo, IX (Núm. 30, septiembre de 1945), 135-137. (a-e)   3520

----. "La mujer de sal." Taller, II (Núm. 8-9, enero-febrero de 1940), 28-41. (f)   3521

----. "Notas sobre la pintura de María Izquierdo." Taller, I (Núm. 1, diciembre de 1938), entre 32-33. (a-e)   3522

----. "La pastoral." Tierra Nueva, III (Núm. 15, diciembre de 1942), 121-130. (f)   3523

----. "La patria chica de López Velarde." El Hijo Pródigo, XII (Núm. 39, junio de 1946), 151-155. (a-e) 3524

----. "La piedra." El Hijo Pródigo, IV (Núm. 15, junio de 1944), 154-158. (f)   3525

----. "Poemas." El Hijo Pródigo, X (Núm. 32, noviembre de 1945), 78-79. (p)   3526

----. "El retorno del adjetivo." Romance, I (Núm. 5, 1 de abril de 1940), 9. (a-e)   3527

----. "Tres ciudades distantes." Estaciones, I (Núm. 2, verano de 1956), 195-197. (p)   3528

----. Una antología de la poesía mexicana de Arturo Torres Rioseco. Taller, I (Núm. 3, mayo de 1939), 57-58. (r)   3529

----. Las cien mejores poesías mexicanas modernas de Antonio Castro Leal. Taller, I (Núm. 2, abril de 1939), 34-37. (r)   3530

----. De la materia suspirable de Vicente Echeverría. El Hijo Pródigo, X (Núm. 32, noviembre de 1945), 122. (r)   3531

----. Ensayo de un crimen de Rodolfo Usigli. El Hijo Pródigo, VIII (Núm. 25, abril de 1945), 60. (r) 3532

----. Libro de las soledades del poniente y La corona de Ricardo E. Molinari. Taller,

II (Núm. 10, marzo-abril de 1940), 46. (r)   3533

----. Moctezuma, el de la silla de oro de Francisco Monterde. El Hijo Pródigo, XI (Núm. 35, febrero de 1946), 113-114. (r)   3534

----. "Nueva cultura." Taller, II (Núm. 8-9, enero-febrero de 1940), 68-69. (r)   3535

----. Palabras en la niebla de Ignacio Barajas Lozano. El Hijo Pródigo, X (Núm. 32, noviembre de 1945), 122. (r)   3536

----. Poemas de las islas invitades de Manuel Altolaguirre y Pleamar de Rafael Alberti. El Hijo Pródigo, V (Núm. 17, agosto de 1944), 122-123. (r)   3537

----. Poesía de Enrique González Martínez. Taller, I (Núm. 3, mayo de 1939), 57. (r)   3538

----. El viajero alucinado de Agustín Loera y Chávez. El Hijo Pródigo, XII (Núm. 37, abril de 1946), 58. (r)   3539

Solar, Hernán del. "Poetas chilenos de hoy y mañana." Ruta, Núm. 10 (marzo de 1939), 54-56. (a-e)   3540

Solís, José M. "Falena." Antena, Núm. 5 (noviembre de 1924), 6. (p)   3541

----. "Hijo vela tu alma." La Falange, Núm. 6 (1 de septiembre de 1923), 337-338. (p)   3542

Sologuren, Javier. "Noción de la mañana," "Elegía." Prometeus, I (Núm. 3, mayo de 1949), 169. (p)   3543

----. "Poetas jóvenes del Perú." Prometeus, I (Núm. 3, mayo de 1949), 165. (p)   3544

----. "Torre de la noche." Prometeus, I (Núm. 2, abril de 1949), 67. (p)   3545

Soriano, Juan. "La bella jardinera." El Hijo Pródigo, X (Núm. 31, octubre de 1945), entre 16 y 17. (il)

----. "Homenaje a Guadalupe Dueñas." Estaciones, III (Núm. 11, otoño de 1958), 312-313. (a-e)   3547

----. "Oleos." Tierra Nueva, II (Núm. 11-12, septiembre-diciembre de 1941), entre 240 y 241. (il)   3548

Soto, Jesús S. "El canto de la lluvia," "Tarde religiosa." México Moderno, I (Núm. 10, junio de 1921), 227-228. (p)   3549

----. Morand, Paul. "Un poema: 35 5" (Trad. Jesús S. Soto). Antena, Núm. 4 (octubre de 1924), 6-7. (tr)   (2432)

Soto, Rafael A. y Gust. L. van Rooseroeck. "Un olvidado precursor del modernismo: Della Rocca de Vergalo." La Falange, Núm. 3 (1 de febrero de 1923), 183-187. (a-e)   3550

Soupault, Philippe. "La personalidad de Cuevas." Estaciones, I (Núm. 1,

primavera de 1956), 115-
120. (a-e)   3551

Spender, Stephen. "Sin el afán
que da" (Trad. Jorge
Cuesta). Estaciones, III
(Núm. 10, verano de 1958),
147. (p)   (1013)

----. "Soneto" (Trad. Jorge
Cuesta). Taller, II (Núm.
10, marzo-abril de 1940),
21. (p)   (1014)

Stevenson, Robert Louis.
"Carta a un joven que se
propone seguir la carrera
artística" (Trad. Francisco
José Castellanos). Tierra
Nueva, II (Núm. 11-12,
septiembre-diciembre de
1941), 210-217. (a-e) (851)

Stoyanov, Ludmia. "La
tendencias ideológicas de la
literatura búlgara contemporánea." Ruta, Núm. 10
(marzo de 1939), 28-30.
(a-e)   3552

Suárez, Dolores. "Canción."
Fábula, Núm. 3 (marzo de
1934), 58-59. (p)   3553

Sucre, José María de. "La
palabra optimista de
América." Sagitario, Núm.
14 (31 de mayo de 1927), 7.
(a-e)   3554

Supervielle, Jules. "La enferma,"
"Los ojos de la muerta,"
"El buey." (Trad. Rafael
Alberti). Contemporáneos,
XI (Núm. 40-41, septiembre-
octubre de 1931), 177-180.
(p)   (132)

----. "Poème." Contem-
poráneos, V (Núm. 19,
diciembre de 1929), 337-338.
(p)   3555

----. "Le sculpteur."
Sagitario, Núm. 11 (15 de
marzo de 1927), 16. (p)
                    3556

T., E. B. El hombre y sus
armas de Martín Luis
Guzmán. Ruta, Núm. 7
(diciembre de 1938), 58-59.
(r)   3557

T., M. Animula de Mariano
Silva. México Moderno, I
(Núm. 5, diciembre de
1920), 321-322. (r)   3558

Tablada, José Juan. "Habla
el marinero," "Nevasca,"
"Cabaret," "El viejo vestido
de azul." El Hijo Pródigo,
IX (Núm. 30, septiembre
de 1945), 138-143. (p) 3559

----. "Já, Já, Já." México
Moderno, I (Núm. 4,
noviembre de 1920), 204.
(p)   3560

----. "Reminescencia." La
Falange, Núm. 2 (1 de
enero de 1923), 89-90. (p)
                    3561

----. "Retablo a la memoria
de Ramón López Velarde."
México Moderno, I (Núm.
11-12, noviembre-diciembre
de 1921), 257-261. (p) 3562

----. "Versos de una reina."
México Moderno, I (Núm.
10, junio de 1921), 190-192.
(p)   3563

----. "Los zopilotes."
México Moderno, II (Núm.
4, junio de 1923), 205. (p)
                    3564

Taborda, Saúl. "Hans Tietze
y el expresionismo."
Sagitario, Núm. 5 (1 de

octubre de 1926), 14. (a-e)
3565

Tagore, Rabindranath. "Bengala dorada." La Falange, Núm. 3 (1 de febrero de 1923), 169. (p)   3566

----. "El jardín de los niños" (Suplemento poético al núm. 11-12). Tierra Nueva, II (Núm. 11-12, septiembre-diciembre de 1941). (p)   3567

----. "Poemas" (Trad. Bernardo Ortiz de Montellano). La Falange, Núm. 1 (1 de diciembre de 1922), 45. (p)   (2713)

Tapia Bolívar, Daniel. "El solitario del Escorial." Romance, II (Núm. 23, 22 de abril de 1941), 5, 14. (a-e)
3568

----. La bahía de silencio de Eduardo Mallea. Romance, II (Núm. 23, 22 de abril de 1941), 18. (r)   3569

----. Fiebre de Miguel Otero Silva. Romance, I (Núm. 20, 15 de enero de 1941), 18. (r)   3570

----. "De Carlos IV a Franco" (Reseña de Orígenes próximos de la España actual de Angel Ossorio y Gallardo). Romance, II (Núm. 24, 31 de mayo de 1941), 19. (r) 3571

----. Vidas de santos españoles publicado por la Biblioteca Nueva. Romance, II (Núm. 22, 15 de marzo de 1941), 19. (r)   3572

Tamayo, Rufino. "Acuarelas y óleos." Contemporáneos,

II (Núm. 4, septiembre de 1928), 40-45. (il)   3573

----. "Cabeza," "Mujeres saltando la cuerda," "Perro y serpiente," "Mujer blanca," "Enamorados," "Luna de miel," "Carnaval," "Mujer con una jaula." El Hijo Pródigo, V (Núm. 18, septiembre de 1944), entre 144 y 145. (il)   3574

----. "Oaxaca," "Mujeres," "Hermanas," "Niños," "India oaxaqueña," "Cabezas," "Tres hombres," e "Indias de Yalalag." Forma, I (Núm. 5, 1927), 1-4. (il)   3575

Tanguy, Ives. "Fin de la rampa." Estaciones, I (Núm. 3, otoño de 1956), entre 454-455. (il)   3576

Tauro, Alberto. "Ciencia y democracia." Ruta, Núm. 9 (febrero de 1939), 50-53. (a-e)   3577

----. "Reflejos de los problemas nacionales en la evolución de la literatura peruana." Romance, I (Núm. 19, 18 de diciembre de 1940), 10. (a-e)   3578

Teasdale, Sara. "La linterna" (Trad. Rafael Lozano). La Falange, Núm. 7 (1 de octubre de 1923), 385. (p)
(2135)

Tebo. "Dibujo." Fábula, Núm. 8 (agosto de 1934), entre 154-155. (il)   3579

Teixidor, Felipe. "Ex libris y bibliotecas de México" Contemporáneos, VII (Núm. 25, junio de 1930), 214-239. (a-e)   3580

Teja Zabre, Alfonso. "Alfonso Reyes." Fábula, Núm. 9 (septiembre de 1934), 178-179. (a-e)   3581

----. "Un ciclo de cultura criolla." Ruta, Núm. 6 (noviembre de 1938), 5-16. (a-e)   3582

----. "El mexicanismo de don Juan Ruiz de Alarcón." Fábula, Núm. 4 (abril de 1934), 63-66. (a-e)   3583

Téllez Toledo, Juan. "Los espiritistas." El Hijo Pródigo, I (Núm. 4, julio de 1943), entre 212-213. (il)   3584

Terán, Juan Manuel. "La definición de la ética y sus problemas fundamentales." Tierra Nueva, II (Núm. 9-10, mayo-agosto de 1941), 146-155. (a-e)   3585

----. "El problema de la justica en Aristóteles." Tierra Nueva, I (Núm. 2, marzo-abril de 1940), 84-92. (a-e)   3586

----. Dos ideas de la filosofía de José Gaos y Francisco Larroyo. Tierra Nueva, I (Núm. 2, marzo-abril de 1940), 118. (r) 3587

----. El logicismo autónomo de Alberto T. Arai. Tierra Nueva, II (Núm. 11-12, septiembre-diciembre de 1941), 267-268. (r)   3588

----. Nueva historia de la filosofía de Wilhelm Windelband. Tierra Nueva, II (Núm. 7-8, enero-abril de 1941), 94-96. (r)   3589

Téry, Simone. "El pensamiento francés amordazado." Romance, I (Núm. 15, 1 de septiembre de 1940), 16. (a-e)   3590

Thomas, Bernhard. "La doble anomalía de la existencia judía y sus consecuencias." Romance, I (Núm. 16, 15 de septiembre de 1940), 4, 11. (a-e)   3591

Tirado Fuentes, René. "Alfonso Reyes." Fábula, Núm. 9 (septiembre de 1934), 179. (a-e)   3592

----. "Canción." Fábula, Núm. 4 (abril de 1934), 77-78. (p)   3593

----. Almas de perfil de Margarita Urueta. Fábula, Núm. 8 (agosto de 1934), 160. (r)   3594

Tizón, Héctor. "Frontera." Estaciones, IV (Núm. 15, otoño de 1959), 338-343. (f)   3595

Tolsa, Manuel. "Dibujo." El Hijo Pródigo, II (Núm. 9, diciembre de 1943), entre 142 y 143. (il)   3596

Tolstoi, Alexis. "San Petersburgo" (Trad. Rodolfo Selke). El Hijo Pródigo, V (Núm. 17, agosto de 1944), 100-101. (f)   (3433)

Tomás Bo, Efraín. Papeles de recienvenido de Macedonio Fernández. El Hijo Pródigo, VII (Núm. 24, marzo de 1945), 186. (r)   3597

Toral Moreno, Alfonso. "El buitre." Estaciones, I (Núm. 1, primavera de 1956), 92-94. (f)   3598

219

Torner, Florentino M. "Flaubert o la pasión literaria." Romance, I (Núm. 18, 15 de noviembre de 1940), 5. (a-e)   3599

----. "Julián Besteiro." Romance, I (Núm. 17, 22 de octubre de 1940), 6. (a-e)   3600

----. "La realidad y el arte." Romance, I (Núm. 11, 1 de julio de 1940), 7. (a-e)   3601

----. "Rousseau:Héroe del sentimiento." Romance, I (Núm. 4, 15 de marzo de 1940), 11. (a-e)   3602

----. "Perspectivas americanas" (Reseña de El destino de la América Latina de Samuel Guy Inman). Romance, II (Núm. 24, 31 de mayo de 1941), 19. (r)   3603

----. "Retablo de experiencias" (Reseña de Grandes católicos compilado por Rev. P. Claude Williamson). Romance, I (Núm. 20, 15 de enero de 1941), 20. (r)   3604

----. "El hombre por dentro" (Reseña de La herencia y otros ensayos de ciencia popular de Julián Huxley). Romance, I (Núm. 19, 18 de diciembre de 1940), 19. (r)   3605

----. "Cristóbal Colón:Vida, misterios y milagros del almirante de la mar océana" (Reseña de Vida del muy magnífico señor don Cristóbal Colón de Salvador de Madariaga). Romance, II (Núm. 21, 15 de febrero de 1941), 18. (r)   3606

Toro, Alfonso. "El carácter del pueblo español." México Moderno, I (Núm. 7, febrero de 1921), 19-30. (a-e)   3607

Toruño, Juan Felipe. "Viaje sin sol." Estaciones, I (Núm. 4, invierno de 1956), 551-554. (p)   3608

Torre, Claudio de la. "Juguete y velero." Sagitario, Núm. 3 (15 de agosto de 1926), 15. (p)   3609

Torre, Guillermo de. Morand, Paul. "Pintura en seda," "Business" (Trad. Guillermo de Torre). Sagitario, Núm. 4 (1 de septiembre de 1926), 15. (tr)   (2431)

Torres, José. "La doctrinas de Freud en la patología mental." México Moderno, II (Núm. 1, agosto de 1922), 39-53. (a-e)   3610

Torres Bodet, Jaime. "Aniversario de Proust." Contemporáneos, II (Núm. 6, noviembre de 1928), 280-291. (a-e)   3611

----. "Aspecto de la biografía." Contemporáneos, III (Núm. 8, enero de 1929), 79-85. (a-e)   3612

----. "Amor." Antena, Núm. 5 (noviembre de 1924), 4. (p)   3613

----. "Calcomanía." Sagitario, Núm. 7 (1 de enero de 1927), 15. (p) 3614

----. "Calle," "Perdón," "Estrella," "Tierra," "La noria." Estaciones, II

(Núm. 6, verano de 1957), 110-114. (p) 3615

----. "Cándido o de la estadística." Contemporáneos, I (Núm. 1, junio de 1928), 82-86. (a-e) 3616

----. "Carta." La Falange, Núm. 2 (1 de enero de 1923), 91-92. (p) 3617

----. "Carta de amor." México Moderno, II (Núm. 2, septiembre de 1922), 85-89. (p) 3618

----. "Cercanía de López Velarde." Contemporáneos, VIII (Núm. 28-29, septiembre-octubre de 1930), 111-135. (a-e) 3619

----. "Cielo," "Epílogos." Antena, Núm. 1 (julio de 1924), 5-6. (p) 3620

----. "Civilización." La Falange, Núm. 7 (1 de octubre de 1923), 386-387. (p) 3621

----. "Una comida a propósito de una encuesta." Sagitario, Núm. 10 (1 de marzo de 1927), 7. (a-e) 3622

----. "Comprobando Toledo." Contemporáneos, IV (Núm. 14, julio de 1929), 273-283. (f) 3623

----. "Continuidad." El Hijo Pródigo, I (Núm. 3, junio de 1943), 145-147. (p) 3624

----. "La danza," "Sueño." Sagitario, Núm. 14 (31 de mayo de 1927), 6. (p) 3625

----. "Desnudo," "Canción de cuna." Contemporáneos, VI (Núm. 20, enero de 1930), 1-7. (p) 3626

----. "Desnudo," "Otoño." Ulises, Núm. 6 (febrero de 1928), 13. (p) 3627

----. "Diario de Poil de Carotte." Contemporáneos, X (Núm. 35, abril de 1931), 74-78. (a-e) 3628

----. "Domingo." Ulises, Núm. 3 (agosto de 1927), 29-33. (f) 3629

----. "Dos poetas de España: Gerardo Diego y Rafael Alberti." Sagitario, Núm. 11 (15 de marzo de 1927), 13-14. (a-e) 3630

----. "La exposición del libro mexicano." La Falange, Núm. 1 (1 de diciembre de 1922), 45-46. (a-e) 3631

----. "Fragmentos de una niñez." Romance, I (Núm. 20, 15 de enero de 1941), 6, 14. (a-e) 3632

----. "¿Homenaje a Benavente?" Contemporáneos, III (Núm. 9, febrero de 1929), 181-185. (a-e) 3633

----. "Invitación al viaje." Contemporáneos, V (Núm. 16, septiembre de 1929), 87-102. (a-e) 3634

----. "Máximas y mínimas de la costumbre." Contemporáneos, II (Núm. 7, diciembre de 1928), 311-318. (a-e) 3635

----. "¿Memorias?

¿Biografías?." Contempo-
ráneos, I (Núm. 2, julio
de 1928), 200-204. (a-e)
3636

----. "El momento literario
en México." La Falange,
Núm. 1 (1 de diciembre de
1922), 40-41. (a-e) 3637

----. "Nocturno mar."
Estaciones, III (Núm. 12,
invierno de 1958), 376-378.
(p) 3638

----. "Una novela de
Huysmans: Al revés."
México Moderno, I (Núm. 7,
febrero de 1921), 38-44.
(a-e) 3639

----. "Ocaso," "El poema de
la razón doliente,"
"Reproche." México Moderno,
I (Núm. 1, agosto de 1920),
54-55. (p) 3640

----. "Palabra," "Lirio,"
"Desnudo," "Uva,"
"Manzana," "Otoño," "Vaso."
Contemporáneos, I (Núm. 1,
junio de 1928), 15-19. (p)
3641

----. "Páramo." Contem-
poráneos, X (Núm. 36,
mayo de 1931), 99-101. (p)
3642

----. "Perspectiva de la
literatura mexicana actual."
Contemporáneos, II (Núm. 4,
septiembre de 1928), 1-33.
(a-e) 3643

----. "Pirandello sin
palabras." Contemporáneos,
I (Núm. 2, julio de 1928),
209-212. (a-e) 3644

----. "Pórtico." Contem-
poráneos, XI (Núm. 40-41,

septiembre-octubre de 1931),
181-183. (p) 3645

----. "Ricardo Gómez
Robelo." Antena, Núm. 3
(septiembre de 1924), 8-9.
(p) 3646

----. "Rosa," "Arte poética,"
"Madrugada," "Flecha,"
"Pureza," "Diamante,"
"Otra rosa," "En vano,"
"Epitafio," "Regreso".
Romance, I (Núm. 18, 15 de
diciembre de 1940), 9. (p)
3647

----. "Ruptura." Sagitario,
Núm. 9 (15 de febrero de
1927), 7. (p) 3648

----. "Serenata de Schubert."
Contemporáneos, I (Núm. 1,
junio de 1928), 91-92. (a-e)
3649

----. "Sueño del hospital"
Contemporáneos, VII (Núm.
24, mayo de 1930), 99-102.
(p) 3650

----. "Tarjetas de visita."
Contemporáneos, II (Núm. 5,
octubre de 1928), 211-212.
(a-e) 3651

----. "Vivir," "Al pasar
por la escuela," "La lluvia,"
"Siempre." La Falange,
Núm. 4 (1 de julio de 1923),
219. (p) 3652

----. Hiver Caraibe de Paul
Morand y Histoire de Paola
Ferrani de Jacques de
Lacretelle. Contemporáneos,
IV (Núm. 13, junio de 1929),
262-268. (r) 3653

----. "Magia negra y magia
blanca" (Reseña de Magic
Noire de Paul Morand.)

222

Contemporáneos, I (Núm. 3, agosto de 1928), 314-319. (r)   3654

----. Meditaciones de un idealista de Luis Garrido. Contemporáneos, II (Núm. 7, diciembre de 1928), 384-387. (r)   3655

----. Nadja de André Breton. Contemporáneos, II (Núm. 5, octubre de 1928), 194-199. (r)   3656

----. "Novela y nube" (Reseña de Novela como nube de Gilberto Owen). Contemporáneos, II (Núm. 4, septiembre de 1928), 87-90. (r)   3657

----. Nuevas canciones de Antonio Machado. Antena, Núm. 2 (agosto de 1924), 8-9. (r)   3658

----. Poèmes de Tendresse de Ernest Prevost. La Falange, Núm. 1 (1 de diciembre de 1922), 54-56. (r)   3659

----. El romero alucinado de Enrique González Martínez. La Falange, Núm. 5 (1 de agosto de 1923), 280-283. (r)   3660

----. Santa Teresa y otros ensayos de Américo Castro. Contemporáneos, V (Núm. 17, octubre de 1929), 234-238. (r)   3661

----. Scènes de la Vie Future de Georges Duhamel. Contemporáneos, VIII (Núm. 28-29, septiembre-octubre de 1930), 164-175. (r)   3662

----. Apollinaire, Guillaume. "Cirugía estética" (Trad.

Jaime Torres Bodet). Contemporáneos, I (Núm. 3, agosto de 1928), 331-334. (tr)   (478)

----. Carvalho, Ronald de. "Rubayat," "Juegos pueriles," "Verdad," "Arte poética" (Trad. Jaime Torres Bodet). La Falange, Núm. 5 (1 de agosto de 1923), 264-265. (tr) (818)

----. Silva, Jonás de. "Coração" (Trad. Jaime Torres Bodet). México Moderno, I (Núm. 5, diciembre de 1920), 327. (tr)   (3500)

Torres Morales, Rubén. "Poema." Estaciones, II (Núm. 7, otoño de 1957), 344. (p)   3663

----. "Los rostros en la roca." Estaciones, IV (Núm. 13, primavera de 1959), 76-77. (p)   3664

----. "Torre final." Estaciones, II (Núm. 7, otoño de 1957), 342-343. (p)   3665

Torres Rioseco, Arturo. "Aire de sentimiento," "Rosa del sueño." Estaciones, IV (Núm. 13, primavera de 1959), 62-63. (p)   3666

----. "Apunte." Contemporáneos, XI (Núm. 38-39, julio-agosto de 1931), 56-57. (p)   3667

----. "Estudios literarios: José Martí." La Falange, Núm. 3 (1 de febrero de 1923), 172-175. (a-e) 3668

----. "Mujer mexicana. "
La Falange, Núm. 4 (1 de
julio de 1923), 222-223. (p)
3669

----. "Ricardo Güiraldes. "
Ruta, Núm. 8 (enero de
1939), 5-27. (a-e)   3670

Torri, Julio. "Alfonso Reyes. "
Fábula, Núm. 9 (septiembre
de 1934), 179. (a-e)   3671

----. "El descubridor, " "La
amada desconocida. " Tierra
Nueva, I (Núm. 2, marzo
abril de 1940), 71-73.
(a-e)   3672

----. "En el valle de
Josafat. " Antena, Núm. 2
(agosto de 1924), 3. (dr)
3673

----. "La feria. " México
Moderno, II (Núm. 2,
septiembre de 1922), 92-93.
(a-e)   3674

----. "La humilidad premia-
da. (Apólogo). " México
Moderno, I (Núm. 1, agosto
de 1920), 21. (a-e)   3675

----. "Machado de Assis. "
La Falange, Núm. 6 (1 de
septiembre de 1923), 320-
321. (a-e)   3676

----. "Para aumentar la
cifra de accidentes. " México
Moderno, I (Núm. 1, agosto
de 1920), 21-22. (a-e)   3677

----. "Plautina. " Fábula,
Núm. 5 (mayo de 1934), 90.
(a-e)   3678

----. "Por el camino de
Proust. " Contemporáneos,
II (Núm. 6, noviembre de
1928), 300-303. (a-e)   3679

----. "Prosas. " Ulises,
Núm. 3 (agosto de 1927),
13-14. (a-e)   3680

----. "Xenias, " "La
procesión, " "El mal actor
de sus propias emociones. "
Contemporáneos, II (Núm. 5,
octubre de 1928), 131-135.
(a-e)   3681

----. El alma nueva de las
cosas viejas de Alfonso
Cravioto. México Moderno,
I (Núm. 11-12, noviembre-
diciembre de 1921), 311-312.
(r)   3682

----. Dramma per musica
de Antonio Caso. México
Moderno, I (Núm. 2,
septiembre de 1920), 124-
125. (r)   3683

----. En la verbena de
Madrid de Ventura García
Calderón. México Moderno,
I (Núm. 6, enero de 1921),
387-388. (r)   3684

----. Machado de Assis,
Joaquim Maria. "El tiempo, "
"La ópera" (Trad. Julio
Torri). La Falange, Núm.
6 (1 de septiembre de 1923),
321-324. (tr)   (2160)

Torriente, Loló de la.
"Dostoiewski: La fascinación
de Dimitri Karamazav. "
Ruta, Núm. 5 (octubre de
1938), 5-24. (a-e)   3685

Toscano, Salvador. "Arte e
historia tarascos. " El Hijo
Pródigo, XI (Núm. 36,
marzo de 1946), 136-140.
(a-e)   3686

----. "La cerámica tarasca."
El Hijo Pródigo, I (Núm. 5,
agosto de 1943), 296-298.
(a-e)   3687

----. "Las ideas
políticas de Ramón López
Velarde." Taller, I (Núm.
3, mayo de 1939), 31-38.
(a-e)   3688

Toscano, Carmen. "Tenías el
mundo en las manos, "
"Déjame pasar de largo, "
"Este era el poema. "
Estaciones, I (Núm. 2,
verano de 1956), 241-243. (p)
                         3689

Toussaint, Manuel. "A colores."
La Falange, Núm. 3 (1 de
febrero de 1923), 181-182.
(p)   3690

----. "Arte americano. "
Romance, I (Núm. 6, 15 de
abril de 1940), 1-2. (a-e)
                         3691

----. "Estudio sobre
Teposcolula." Forma, I
(Núm. 2, noviembre de
1926), 37-41. (a-e)   3692

----. "Paseos coloniales,
(Tepotzotlán). " México
Moderno, I (Núm. 2,
septiembre de 1920), 77-84.
(a-e)   3693

----. "El problema de la
educación artística en
México. " México Moderno,
II (Núm. 4, junio de 1923),
228-235. (a-e)   3694

----. "Retratos de monjas. "
El Hijo Pródigo, II (Núm. 7,
octubre de 1943), 32. (a-e)
                         3695

----. "Tasco." Contemporáneos, II (Núm. 6, noviembre
de 1928), 273-279. (a-e)
                         3696

----. "Viajes alucinados. "
La Falange, Núm. 1 (1 de

diciembre de 1922), 19-23.
(a-e)   3697

----. "Viajes alucinados. "
México Moderno, II (Núm. 1,
agosto de 1922), 23-26.
(a-e)   3698

----. Disertaciones de un
arquitecto de Jesús T.
Acevedo. México Moderno,
I (Núm. 1, agosto de 1920),
64. (r)   3699

----. Juan Gabriel Borkman
de Henrick Ibsen con
traducción y prólogo de
Carlos Barrera. México
Moderno, I (Núm. 1, agosto
de 1920), 64. (r)   3700

----. Prometeo vencedor de
José Vasconcelos. México
Moderno, I (Núm. 1, agosto
de 1920), 64. (r)   3701

----. Versos de José Martí.
México Moderno, I (Núm. 1,
agosto de 1920), 64. (r)
                         3702

Traven, Bruno. "La rosa
blanca" (Trad. Pedro
Geoffroy Rivas y Erwin
Friedeberg). Ruta, Núm. 1
(junio de 1938), 30-35. (f)
                       (1395)

Turrent Rozas, Lorenzo.
"Dice el pueblo." Ruta, Núm.
6 (noviembre de 1938), 39-
42. (a-e)   3703

----. "Jack." Ruta, Núm. 8
(enero de 1939), 32-39. (f)
                         3704

----. "Jorge Amado y la
novela iberoamericana. "
Ruta, Núm. 2 (julio de 1938),
50-52. (a-e)   3705

----. "Manuel José Othón, colono mental?" Ruta, Núm. 3 (agosto de 1938), 51-53. (a-e)　　　3706

----. "Realismo y expresión." Ruta, Núm. 11 (abril de 1939), 55-57. (a-e)　　　3707

----. Reseña de un folleto de la Liga Pro-Cultura Alemana en México. Ruta, Núm. 8 (enero de 1939), 58. (r)　　　3708

----. Peleando con los milicianos de Pablo de la Torriente-Brau. Ruta, Núm. 9 (febrero de 1939), 59. (r)　　　3709

Tzara, Tristán. "El poeta en la sociedad." Ruta, Núm. 11 (abril de 1939), 57-61. (a-e)　　　3710

Unamuno, Miguel de. "Carta inédita." La Falange, Núm. 4 (1 de julio de 1923), 245-246. (a-e)　　　3711

----. "Juan Manso: Cuento de muertos." Romance, I (Núm. 1, 1 de febrero de 1940), 5, 22. (f)　　　3712

----. Leopardi, Jacobo. "La retama (La genestra)" (con traducción de Miguel de Unamuno). Taller, II (Núm. 11, julio-agosto de 1940), 83-103. (tr)　　　(2063)

Undurraga, Antonio de. "Carta atlántica," "Oda a la tierra sin estaciones," "Amor argonauta." Estaciones, V (Núm. 19, otoño de 1960), 74-78. (p)　　　3713

----. "Papiros en los muros de los Mayas." Estaciones,

V (Núm. 20, invierno de 1960), 57-59. (p)　　　3714

----. "Soliloquio inmemorial para Ana." Estaciones, IV (Núm. 13, primavera de 1959), 28-29. (p)　　　3715

Uranga, Emilio. Sociología del Renacimiento de Alfred von Martin. El Hijo Pródigo, XIII (Núm. 42, septiembre de 1946), 178-179. (r) 3716

Urueta, Margarita. "A solas." Fábula, Núm. 8 (agosto de 1934), 143. (a-e)　　　3717

----. "Caparazón." Estaciones, IV (Núm. 16, invierno de 1959), 400-404. (dr)　　　3718

Urzaiz Rodríguez, Eduardo. "El espíritu varonil de Sor Juana." El Hijo Pródigo, VIII (Núm. 25, abril de 1945), 11-20. (a-e)　　　3719

Urrutia y Araña, Don Luis de. El soldado desconocido de Salomón de la Selva. México Moderno, II (Núm. 1, agosto de 1922), 65. (r)　　　3720

Usigli, Rodolfo. "Los cuartetos de T. S. Eliot y la poesía, arte impopular." El Hijo Pródigo, II (Núm. 8, noviembre de 1943), 88-94. (a-e)　　　3721

----. "Estética de la muerte." El Hijo Pródigo, XIII (Núm. 40, julio de 1946), 29-31. (a-e)　　　3722

----. "La familia cena en casa." El Hijo Pródigo, VI (Núm. 21, diciembre de 1944), 165-183; VII (Núm. 22, enero de 1945), 42-56;

(Núm. 23, febrero de 1945),
109-120. (dr)   3723

----. "El gesticulador. "
El Hijo Pródigo, I (Núm. 2,
mayo de 1943), 103-116,
(Núm. 3, junio de 1943),
171-185, (Núm. 4, julio de
1943), 236-251. (dr)   3724

----. "Teatro desnudo. "
Ruta, Núm. 1 (junio de
1938), 51-52. (dr)   3725

----. Eliot, Thomas Stearns.
"El canto de amor de J.
Alfred Prufrock" (Trad.
Rodolfo Usigli). Taller, II
(Núm. 10, marzo-abril de
1940), 65-69. (tr)   (1218)

----. Eliot, Thomas Stearns.
"¿Qué es un clásico?" (Trad.
Rodolfo Usigli). Prometeus,
I (Núm. 2, abril de 1949),
105-126. (tr)   (1224)

----. Rodell, John S.
"Maxwell Anderson:Una
crítica" (Trad. Rodolfo
Usigli). El Hijo Pródigo, II
(Núm. 9, diciembre de 1943),
176-179. (tr)   (3210)

V., C. Nocturnos de Xavier
Villaurrutia. Fábula, Núm.
2 (febrero de 1934), 38-39.
(r)   3726

Valadez, Miguel. "El cuento de
Juan Pablo. " La Falange,
Núm. 6 (1 de septiembre
de 1923), 325-330. (f)   3727

Valcárcel, Luis E. "Significado
del arte inkaico. " Sagitario,
Núm. 7 (1 de enero de
1927), 13-14. (a-e)   3728

Valdelomar, Abraham. "El
toreo. " La Falange, Núm.
3 (1 de febrero de 1923),
154-156. (a-e)   3729

Valéry, Paul. "Conversación
sobre la poesía" (Trad.
Bernardo Ortiz de
Montellano). Contempo-
ráneos, VIII (Núm. 26-27,
julio-agosto de 1930), 3-6.
(a-e)   (2714)

----. "Esbozo de una
serpiente" (Trad. Enrique
Díez-Canedo). Tierra
Nueva, II (Núm. 7-8, enero-
abril de 1941), 3-12. (p)
                            (1175)

----. "Introducción a la
Poética" (Trad. Ricardo de
Alcázar). Estaciones, I
(Núm. 2, verano de 1956),
265-290. (a-e)   (139)

----. "Pequeños textos,
comentarios de grabados"
(Trad. Gilberto Owen).
Contemporáneos, II (Núm. 4,
septiembre de 1928), 34-39.
(a-e)   (2746)

Valldeperes, Manuel. "Angel
Botello Barros." Romance,
I (Núm. 18, 15 de
noviembre de 1940), 7, 15.
(a-e)   3730

----. "Lugones, poeta de la
exaltación partriótica. "
Romance, I (Núm. 11, 1 de
julio de 1940), 6. (a-e)
                             3731

Valle, Rafael Heliodoro. "El
calabazo de Ayacucho. "
Forma, I (Núm. 5, 1927),
5-7. (a-e)   3732

----. "Una cena con Valle-
Inclán." La Falange, Núm.
3 (1 de febrero de 1923),
179-181. (a-e)   3733

----. "El congreso de
escritores y de artistas. "
La Falange, Núm. 4 (1 de

julio de 1923), 237-239.
(a-e)   3734

----. "Elegía juvenil."
México Moderno, I (Núm.
11-12, noviembre-diciembre
de 1921), 283-284. (p)   3735

----. "El loco en la ventana."
La Falange, Núm. 4 (1 de
julio de 1923), 220-222. (p)
                     3736

----. "El perfume en la
Nueva España." La Falange,
Núm. 1 (1 de diciembre de
1922), 24-26. (a-e)   3737

----. "Plata de Guanajuato."
La Falange, Núm. 7 (1 de
octubre de 1923), 387-389.
(p)   3738

----. "Salvador Díaz Mirón."
Antena, Núm. 4 (octubre de
1924), 10. (a-e)   3739

----. "Sarcófago." México
Moderno, I (Núm. 8, marzo
de 1921), 88. (p)   3740

----. "Trilogía y otros
versos." Romance, II
(Núm. 23, 22 de abril de
1941), 9. (p)   3741

----. "Bibliografía Centro-
Americana de 1920." México
Moderno, I (Núm. 10, junio
de 1921), 243-244. (r)   3742

----. Reseña de un libro de
María Monvel. La Falange,
Núm. 2 (1 de enero de
1923), 120-121. (r)   3743

----. Bajo la cruz del sur
de Julio Jiménez Rueda.
La Falange, Núm. 2 (1 de
enero de 1923), 121. (r)
                     3744

----. Estudios indostánicos
de José Vasconcelos.
México Moderno, I (Núm.
10, junio de 1921), 238-239.
(r)   3745

----. La lente opaca de
Flavio Herrera. México
Moderno, I (Núm. 11-12,
noviembre-diciembre de
1921), 313. (r)   3746

----. México hacia el fin
del virreinato español de
Gregorio Torres Quintero.
México Moderno, I (Núm.
11-12, noviembre-diciembre
de 1921), 312. (r)   3747

----. Por la verdad histórica
de Manuel Calderón
Ramírez. México Moderno,
I (Núm. 10, junio de 1921),
242. (r)   3748

----. Raíz Salvaje de Juana
de Ibarbourou. La Falange,
Núm. 5 (1 de agosto de
1923), 312-313. (r)   3749

----. El universal ilustrado
de Carlos Noriega Hope.
La Falange, Núm. 2 (1 de
enero de 1923), 121. (r)
                     3750

----. Conkling, Hilda.
"Agua," "En el lago
Chaplain," "Amanecer"
(Trad. Rafael Heliodoro
Valle). México Moderno, I
(Núm. 8, marzo de 1921),
127. (tr)   (946)

Valle, R. del. "Tríptico:
cubismo, escultura
futurista, y estridentismo."
Antena, Núm. 4 (octubre de
1924), 6. (a-e)   3751

Valle-Arizpe, Artemio de.
"Alfonso Reyes íntimo."
Antena, Núm. 1 (julio de

1924), 11-12. (c) 3752

----. "Las flores del pino."
La Falange, Núm. 5 (1 de
agosto de 1923), 272-279. (f)
3753

Valle Inclán, Ramón María del.
"Nos vemos!" México
Moderno, II (Núm. 2,
septiembre de 1922), 67-68.
(p) 3754

----. "La tienda de
Herbolario." Sagitario,
Núm. 3 (15 de agosto de
1926), 5. (p) 3755

Van Doren, Carl. "La torre
de ironía." (Trad. Octavio
G. Barreda) Contempo-
ráneos, X (Núm. 36, mayo de
1931), 165-181. (a-e) (602)

Varela, Blanca. "Elegía," "El
sueño." Prometeus, I (Núm.
3, mayo de 1949), 170. (p)
3756

Varela, Lorenzo. "Al paso de
una injusticia." Romance, I
(Núm. 16, 15 de septiembre
de 1940), 5. (a-e) 3757

----. "Baudelaire." Taller,
II (Núm. 12, enero-febrero
de 1941), 79-81. (a-e) 3758

----. "Galería de arte de la
Librería de Cristal:
Exposición hispano mexicana."
Romance, I (Núm. 14, 15 de
agosto de 1940), 12-13. (a-e)
3759

----. "El héroe." Taller, I
(Núm. 5, octubre de 1939),
37-41. (a-e) 3760

----. "El ilusionista."
Romance, I (Núm. 14, 15 de
agosto de 1940), 5, 14. (f)
3761

----. "Una literatura de la
derrota." Romance, I
(Núm. 9, 1 de junio de
1940), 5. (a-e) 3762

----. "Noviembre en la
esperanza." Taller, I (Núm.
7, diciembre de 1939), 41-
43. (a-e) 3763

----. "La realidad y el
deseo." Romance, I (Núm.
2, 15 de febrero de 1940),
9. (a-e) 3764

----. "El siglo en el
corazón." Romance, I (Núm.
5, 1 de abril de 1940), 9.
(a-e) 3765

----. Aldeia das aguias de
Guedes de Amorim.
Romance, I (Núm. 10, 15 de
junio de 1940), 18. (r) 3766

----. Capítulos de literatura
española de Alfonso Reyes.
Romance, I (Núm. 3, 1 de
marzo de 1940), 18. (r)
3767

----. Paseo de mentiras de
Juan de la Cabada. Taller,
II (Núm. 12, enero-febrero
de 1941), 71-73. (r) 3768

----. Plenitud de España de
Pedro Henríquez Ureña.
Romance, I (Núm. 13, 1 de
agosto de 1940), 18. (r)
3769

----. "La flauta y el pito;
el tambor y el salmo; y la
poesía." (Reseña de
Poesía de Rafael Alberti).
Taller, II (Núm. 10, marzo-
abril de 1940), 41-45. (r)
3770

----. Poesías completas de
Rafael Alberti. Romance, I
(Núm. 6, 15 de abril de

1940), 18. (r)   3771

----. Poesías escogidas de
Juan José Domenchina.
Romance, I (Núm. 5, 1 de
abril de 1940), 18. (r) 3772

----. "Las astillas olorosas
de Tala" (Reseña de Tala de
Gabriela Mistral). Taller,
I (Núm. 5, octubre de 1939),
60-63. (r)   3773

----. Tilín García de Carlos
Enríquez. Romance, I
(Núm. 7, 1 de mayo de
1940), 18. (r)   3774

----. "El victorial, biografía
caballeresca castellana"
(Reseña de El victorial).
Romance, I (Núm. 8, 15 de
mayo de 1940), 18. (r) 3775

Vargas, Elvira. "Por las rutas
del sureste." Romance, I
(Núm. 6, 15 de abril de
1940), 8. (a-e)   3776

Varonna y Pera, Enrique José.
"Poemas en prosa." México
Moderno, II (Núm. 2,
septiembre de 1922), 72-74.
(p)   3777

Vasconcelos, José. "Arte
indostánico:La arquitectura.
Estilos hindú y dravídico."
México Moderno, I (Núm. 5,
diciembre de 1920), 265-267.
(a-e)   3778

----. "Elogio de Cuauhtémoc."
La Falange, Núm. 2 (1 de
enero de 1923), 103-106.
(a-e)   3779

----. "El fusilado." El Hijo
Pródigo, VII (Núm. 23,
febrero de 1945), 87-90. (f)
        3780

----. "Himnos breves."

México Moderno, I (Núm. 1,
agosto de 1920), 1-4. (p)
        3781

----. González Martínez,
Enrique; Gaos, José;
Gallegos, José M. ; Paz,
Octavio; Martínez, José
Luis; García-Bacca, David;
Jiménez Rueda, Julio;
Nicol, Eduardo; Bergamín,
José. "Poesía, mística y
filosofía; Debate en torno a
San Juan de la Cruz." El
Hijo Pródigo, I (Núm. 3,
junio de 1943), 135-144.
(a-e)   (661)

----. "Ramón López Velarde."
México Moderno, I (Núm.
11-12, noviembre-diciembre
de 1921), 272. (a-e) 3782

----. Trilogía dramática de
A. Granja Irigoyen. La
Falange, Núm. 6 (1 de
septiembre de 1923), 358.
(r)   3783

Vauxcelles, Louis, y Mrs.
André Fontains. "La talla
directa." Forma, I (Núm.
3, 1927), 23-24; (Núm. 4,
1927), 6-7. (a-e)   (1378)

Vázques, José María. "Re-
trato de una dama." El
Hijo Pródigo, I (Núm. 4,
julio de 1943), entre 202 y
203. (il)   3784

Vázques Amaral, José. "Nota
sobre 'Cristóbal Colón' y
otros poemas de Sidney Salt."
Ruta, Núm. 10 (marzo de
1939), 44-47. (a-e) 3785

Veblen, Thorstein. "Teoría
del vestido." El Hijo
Pródigo, VIII (Núm. 25,
abril de 1945), 32-34. (a-e)
        3786

230

Vega, Fausto. "Asunto de novelas." Estaciones, III (Núm. 11, otoño de 1958), 273-287. (a-e)   3787

Vega Albela, Rafael. "Amorosamente," "Solo el hombre." Taller, I (Núm. 3, mayo de 1939), 22. (p)   3788

----. "Canciones," "Sonetos." Taller, II (Núm. 8-9, enero-febrero de 1940), 42-45. (p)   3789

----. "Luz en el destierro." Taller, I (Núm. 7, diciembre de 1939), 55-57. (a-e)   3790

----. "El proceso en el espíritu proteico de Franz Kafka." Romance, I (Núm. 5, 1 de abril de 1940), 18. (a-e)   3791

----. La educación de los sentidos o el envenenado de Rafael Solana. Romance, I (Núm. 2, 15 de febrero de 1940), 18. (r)   3792

----. "Poesía y profecía de Jorge de Lima" (Reseña de un libro de poesía de Jorge de Lima). Taller, II (Núm. 8-9, enero-febrero de 1940), 65-67. (r)   3793

Vela, Arqueles. "André Breton globe-trotter aux pas perdus." Ruta, Núm. 1 (junio de 1938), 47-48. (a-e)   3794

----. "La epopeya y la novela." Ruta, Núm. 3 (agosto de 1938), 23-26. (a-e)   3795

Velasco, Alfredo. "Tres poemas." Fábula, Núm. 6 (junio de 1934), 118-119. (p)   3796

Velasco, José María. "Paisaje." El Hijo Pródigo, I (Núm. 4, julio de 1943), entre 212-213. (il)   3797

Velázque, Alberto. "Canto elegiaco a Julián Besteiro." Romance, I (Núm. 17, 22 de octubre de 1940), 6. (p)   3798

----. "Las siete palabras de la pasión." Romance, II (Núm. 23, 22 de abril de 1941), 9. (p)   3799

Velázquez Bringas, Esperanza. "Informes del Departamento de Bibliotecas del mes de junio." Sagitario, Núm. 3 (15 de agosto de 1926), 2. (a-e)   3800

Velázquez Chávez, Agustín. "La pintura de la historia de los Estados Unidos de Diego Rivera." Romance, I (Núm. 18, 15 de noviembre de 1940), 12, 13, 15. (a-e)   3801

----. "El Prometeo de Orozco." Romance, I (Núm. 19, 18 de diciembre de 1940), 12-13. (a-e)   3802

----. "El Siqueiros de 1923 a 1931." Romance, I (Núm. 17, 22 de octubre de 1940), 13. (a-e)   3803

Velo, Carlos. "Una página sobre el film Vía Crucis, Las uvas del rencor" (Opiniones de Xavier Villaurrutia, León Felipe, Ramón Gaya, Alberto Quintero Alvarez, Octavio G. Barreda y Carlos Velo). Romance, I (Núm. 9, 1 de junio de 1940), 11. (a-e)   (585)

231

----. "Ritmo y cinema."
Romance, I (Núm. 2, 15 de
febrero de 1940), 17. (a-e)
3804

----. "Símbolos en plata."
Romance, I (Núm. 4, 15 de
marzo de 1940), 3. (a-e)
3805

Vera, Pedro Jorge. "Luto
eterno." Estaciones, III
(Núm. 12, invierno de 1958),
439-445. (f)   3806

Vergés, J. M. Miquel i.
"Bolívar e Iturbide."
Romance, I (Núm. 4, 15 de
marzo de 1940), 6. (a-e)
3807

----. "El primer periódico
insurgente: El despertador
americano." Romance, I
(Núm. 12, 15 de julio de
1940), 6, 18. (a-e)   3808

Verhesen, Fernand. Las ostras
o la literatura de Rubén
Salazar Mallén. Estaciones,
IV (Núm. 13, primavera de
1959), 114-115. (r)   3809

Verlaine, Paul. "Apunte de
Rimbaud, de memoria."
Taller, I (Núm. 4, julio de
1939), 6. (il)   3810

----. "Evocación," "Spleen,"
"Mujer y gata," "Streets,"
"Tedio" (Trad. Rafael
Lozano). La Falange, Núm.
3 (1 de febrero de 1923),
189-190. (p)   (2136)

Verona, Enrique José. "Poemas
en prosa." México Moderno,
I (Núm. 7, febrero de
1921), 3-4. (p)   3811

Verzman, I. "Juan Jacobo
Rousseau." Ruta, Núm. 3

(agosto de 1938), 54-55.
(a-e)   3812

Villa, Dr. "Indios" (con
introducción de Bernardo
Ortiz de Montellano).
Contemporáneos, XI (Núm.
42-43, noviembre-diciembre
de 1931), 233-253. (a-e)
3813

Villardo, Jorge. Severianin,
Igor, "Día de primavera,"
"Día de verano," "Día de
otoño," "Victoria Regia"
(Trad. Jorge Villardo).
Sagitario, Núm. 12-13
(30 de abril de 1927), 14.
(tr)   (3498)

Villaseñor, Eduardo.
"Anécdota." Contemporáneos,
VI (Núm. 21, febrero de
1930), 149-152. (p)   3814

----. "Ayer." Sagitario,
Núm. 7 (1 de enero de 1927),
6. (p)   3815

----. "Cantabria." Sagitario,
Núm. 11 (15 de marzo de
1927), 6. (a-e)   3816

----. "Cuando." Prometeus,
I (Núm. 2, abril de 1949),
86-87. (p)   3817

----. "El culto del éxito."
Sagitario, Núm. 8 (1 de
febrero de 1927), 5. (a-e)
3818

----. "De la curiosidad."
El Hijo Pródigo, VII (Núm.
24, marzo de 1945), 135-140.
(a-e)   3819

----. "Las dos culturas."
México Moderno, II (Núm. 1,
agosto de 1922), 20-22.
(a-e)   3820

----. "Extasis, novela de aventuras." Ulises, Núm. 6 (febrero de 1928), 39-43. (n)   3821

----. "Judía," "La fuente." México Moderno, II (Núm. 3, octubre de 1922), 172-173. (p)   3822

----. "Nubes," "Hoy." Sagitario, Núm. 9 (15 de febrero de 1927), 7. (p)   3823

----. "Poemas." El Hijo Pródigo, I (Núm. 6, septiembre de 1943), 346. (p)   3824

----. "Xaimaca, Don Segundo Sombra: ¿De qué se trata?" Sagitario, Núm. 10 (1 de marzo de 1927), 14.   (a-e)
3825

----. Visionario de Nueva España de Genaro Estrada. Sagitario, Núm. 5 (1 de octubre de 1926), 13.   (r)   3826

----. Smith, Logan Pearsall. "Merengues" (Trad. Eduardo Villaseñor). México Moderno, II (Núm. 1, agosto de 1922), 60. (tr)   (3510)

Villaseñor, Jorge A.   "La escena del beso." Estaciones, IV (Núm. 15, otoño de 1959), 287-298. (dr)   3827

Villaurrutia, Xavier. "A la memoria de Rafael López." El Hijo Pródigo, I (Núm. 5, agosto de 1943), 321. (a-e)   3828

----. "Agustín Lazo." Forma, I (Núm. 1, octubre de 1926), 2-4. (a-e)   3829

----. "Agustín Lazo y el teatro." El Hijo Pródigo, XI (Núm. 35, febrero de 1946), 88-89. (a-e)   3830

----. "Alfredo Zalce." Contemporáneos, X (Núm. 36, mayo de 1931), 185-186. (a-e)   3831

----. "Amor condusse noi ad una morte." Taller, I (Núm. 4, julio de 1939), 15-16. (p)   3832

----. "Arabe sin hurí." Fábula, Núm. 3 (marzo de 1934), 50-54. (a-e)   3833

----. "Atmósferas." Antena, Núm. 3 (septiembre de 1924), 5. (p)   3834

----. "El ausente." Tierra Nueva, III (Núm. 13-14, enero-abril de 1942), 35-50. (dr)   3835

----. "Autocrítica." Ulises, Núm. 3 (agosto de 1927), 40-42. (a-e)   3836

----. "Cartas a Olivier." Ulises, Núm. 2 (junio de 1927), 13-17. (a-e)   3837

----. "Cézanne." Sagitario, Núm. 11 (15 de marzo de 1927), 4. (p)   3838

----. "Con la mirada humilde..." Estaciones, II (Núm. 6, verano de 1957), 141-142. (p)   3839

----. "Crepuscular." Estaciones, I (Núm. 2, verano de 1956), 158-159. (p)   3840

----. "Crítica cinematográfica." Estaciones, IV (Núm. 13, primavera de 1959), 15-27. (a-e)   3841

----, y Gutiérrez Hermosillo, Alfonso. "Crítica epistolar."

El Hijo Pródigo, V (Núm. 17, agosto de 1944), 73-82. (a-e)
(1732)

----. "Cuaderno de apuntes." Estaciones, I (Núm. 4, invierno de 1956), 488-491. (a-e)   3842

----. "Cuaderno de apuntes." Estaciones, II (Núm. 6, verano de 1957), 138-140. (a-e)   3843

----. "Un cuadro de la pintura mexicana actual." Ulises, Núm. 6 (febrero de 1928), 5-12. (a-e)   3844

----. "Debate en torno de Walt Whitman." Romance, I (Núm. 10, 15 de junio de 1940), 1-2. (p)   3845

----. "Décima muerte." Romance, I (Núm. 11, 1 de julio de 1940), 11. (p) 3846

----. "Diálogo." La Falange, Núm. 4 (1 de julio de 1923), 212-215. (a-e)
3847

----. "Epigramas de Boston." Prometeus, I (Núm. 1, febrero de 1949), 13-14. (p)
3848

----. "Epílogo." La Falange, Núm. 4 (1 de julio de 1923), 190-191. (a-e)   3849

----. "Estancias nocturnas," "Madrigal sombrío." El Hijo Pródigo, IX (Núm. 28, julio de 1945), 17-18. (p)   3850

----. "El éxodo." El Hijo Pródigo, I (Núm. 2, mayo de 1943), 85-88. (a-e)
3851

----. "Exposición." Forma, I (Núm. 2, noviembre de 1926), 32. (a-e)   3852

----. "Exposición Lazo." Sagitario, Núm. 10 (1 de marzo de 1927), 16. (a-e)   3853

----. "Fichas sin sobre para Lazo." Contemporáneos, I (Núm. 2, julio de 1928), 117-122. (a-e)   3854

----. "Fórmula moral de Octavio de Romeu." Sagitario, Núm. 9 (15 de febrero de 1927), 10. (a-e)   3855

----. "Fragmento de sueño." Ulises, Núm. 3 (agosto de 1927), 34-38. (f)   3856

----. "Gérard de Nerval." Romance, I (Núm. 17, 22 de octubre de 1940), 3. (a-e)   3857

----. "Guía de poetas norteamericanos." Contemporáneos, II (Núm. 4, septiembre de 1928), 91-97. (a-e)   3858

----. "Henríquez Ureña, humanista moderno." Contemporáneos, II (Núm. 7, diciembre de 1928), 402-407. (a-e)   3859

----. "Historia de Diego Rivera." Forma, I (Núm. 5, 1927), 29-31. (a-e)   3860

----. "Invitación a la muerte." El Hijo Pródigo, I (Núm. 6, septiembre de 1943), 355-363; II (Núm. 7, octubre de 1943), 41-50; II (Núm. 8, 1943), 100-111. (dr)   3861

----. "José Clemente Orozco y el horror." Romance, I (Núm. 1, 1 de febrero de 1940), 1, 7. (a-e)   3862

----. "Juan Cordero." El Hijo Pródigo, IX (Núm. 30, septiembre de 1945), 144-146. (a-e)   3863

----. "Julio Castellanos." Ulises, Núm. 2 (junio de 1927), 27-28. (a-e)   3864

----. "Julio Ruelas, dibujante y pintor." El Hijo Pródigo, XIII (Núm. 41, agosto de 1946), 91-92. (a-e)   3865

----. "Luis Cardoza y Aragón." Romance, I (Núm. 16, 15 de septiembre de 1940), 9. (a-e)   3866

----. "Manuel Alvarez Bravo." El Hijo Pródigo, IX (Núm. 29, agosto de 1945), 87-89. (a-e)   3867

----. "Mauricio Leal." La Falange, Núm. 1 (1 de diciembre de 1922), 62-63. (f)   3868

----. "La mulata de Córdoba." El Hijo Pródigo, VII (Núm. 24, marzo de 1945), 166-183. (dr)   3869

----. "Nocturno." Tierra Nueva, I (Núm. 3, mayo-junio de 1940), 134-135. (p)   3870

----. "Nocturno." El Hijo Pródigo, III (Núm. 11, febrero de 1944), 78. (p)   3871

----. "Nocturno amor,"

"Nocturno de los angeles," "Nocturno rosa," "Nocturno mar," "Cementerio en la nieve." Estaciones, I (Núm. 4, invierno de 1956), 469-478. (p) 3872

----. "Nocturno de la estatua." Contemporáneos, II (Núm. 7, diciembre de 1928), 324-325. (p) 3873

----. "Nocturno en que nada se oye." Contemporáneos, V (Núm. 15, agosto de 1929), 33-34. (p) 3874

----. "Nocturno eterno." Contemporáneos, XI (Núm. 40-41, septiembre-octubre de 1931), 184-186. (p) 3875

----. "Novo, corrector." Antena, Núm. 3 (septiembre de 1924), 11. (a-e) 3876

----. "Nuestro amor." El Hijo Pródigo, XI (Núm. 36, marzo de 1946), 134-135. (p) 3877

----. "Otro nocturno." Contemporáneos, VII (Núm. 23, abril de 1930), 1-3. (p) 3878

----. "Una página sobre el film Vía Crucis, Las uvas del rencor" (Opiniones de Xavier Villaurrutia, León Felipe, Ramón Gaya, Alberto Quintero Alvarez, Octavio G. Barreda y Carlos Velo). Romance, I (Núm. 9, 1 de junio de 1940), 11. (a-e) (585)

----. "Pedro Prado." Antena, Núm. 2 (agosto de 1924), 9-11. (a-e) 3879

----. "Poesía." Ulises, Núm. 4 (octubre de 1927),

3. (p) 3880

----. "Pueblo." Sagitario, Núm. 7 (1 de enero de 1927), 15. (p) 3881

----. "Pueblo." La Falange, Núm. 5 (1 de agosto de 1923), 290-291. (p) 3882

----. "Respuesta a la encuesta de Romance." Romance, I (Núm. 4, 15 de marzo de 1940), 2. (a-e) 3883

----. "Revista de exposiciones." Forma, I (Núm. 1, octubre de 1926), 28. (a-e) 3884

----. "El romanticismo y el sueño." Romance, I (Núm. 15, 1 de septiembre de 1940), 1-2. (a-e) 3885

----. "Sáinz de la Maza." Contemporáneos, IX (Núm. 34, marzo de 1931), 278. (a-e) 3886

----. "Soledad." La Falange, Núm. 7 (1 de octubre de 1923), 389-390. (p) 3887

----. "Soneto del temor a Dios." Prometeus, II (Núm. 1, diciembre de 1951), 18. (p) 3888

----. "Títulos." Contemporáneos, I (Núm. 1, junio de 1928), 81-82. (a-e) 3889

----. "La tónica de Efrén Rebolledo." Contemporáneos, V (Núm. 19, diciembre de 1929), 422-426. (a-e) 3890

----. "El yerro candente." El Hijo Pródigo, VI (Núm. 19, octubre de 1944), 44-57; (Núm. 20, noviembre de 1944),

110-120. (dr) 3891

----. Adonais de Percy
Bysshe Shelley (Trad. Manuel
Altolaguirre y Antonio
Castro Leal). Taller, I
(Núm. 1, diciembre de 1938),
59-60. (r) 3892

----. Antología de cuentos
mexicanos e hispano
americanos con selección de
Salvador Novo. La Falange,
Núm. 5 (1 de agosto de
1923), 313. (r) 3893

----. Antología de la
literatura mexicana de Carlos
Castillo. El Hijo Pródigo,
V (Núm. 16, julio de 1944),
56-57. (r) 3894

----. El arte en la Rusia
actual de Esperanza
Velázquez Bringas. La
Falange, Núm. 4 (1 de julio
de 1923), 249-250. (r) 3895

----. Caballito del diablo de
José Bergamín. El Hijo
Pródigo, I (Núm. 2, mayo de
1943), 123. (r) 3896

----. Carmina áurea de
Miguel D. Martínez Rendón.
La Falange, Núm. 6 (1 de
septiembre de 1923), 357.
(r) 3897

----. Las cien mejores
poesías mexicanas modernas
de Antonio Castro Leal. El
Hijo Pródigo, X (Núm. 33,
diciembre de 1945), 179. (r)
3898

----. La communion des
forts de Roger Caillois. El
Hijo Pródigo, I (Núm. 6,
septiembre de 1943), 381.
(r) 3899

----. El crimen de tres

bandas de Rafael Solana. El
Hijo Pródigo, IX (Núm. 29,
agosto de 1945), 120-121. (r)
3900

----. Cuadernos de plata de
Alfonso Reyes. Contem-
poráneos, VI (Núm. 21,
febrero de 1930), 183-186.
(r) 3901

----. Le chateau de grisou
de César Moro. El Hijo
Pródigo, II (Núm. 7,
octubre de 1943), 59. (r)
3902

----. Etudes littéraires de
E. Noulet. El Hijo Pródigo,
VI (Núm. 20, noviembre de
1944), 123. (r) 3903

----. Ficciones de Jorge
Luis Borges. El Hijo
Pródigo, VIII (Núm. 26,
mayo de 1945), 119. (r)
3904

----. Figura, amor y muerte
de Amado Nervo de
Bernardo Ortiz de Montellano.
El Hijo Pródigo, II (Núm. 9,
diciembre de 1943), 218. (r)
3905

----. Fuga de Navidad de
Alfonso Reyes. Contem-
poráneos, V (Núm. 16,
septiembre de 1929), 152-153.
(r) 3906

----. Geórgicas de Joaquín
Méndez Rivas. La Falange,
Núm. 6 (1 de septiembre de
1923), 355-356. (r) 3907

----. El hombre del buho
de Enrique González
Martínez. El Hijo Pródigo,
VI (Núm. 19, octubre de
1944), 58. (r) 3908

237

----. Huellas de Alfonso Reyes. La Falange, Núm. 4 (1 de julio de 1923), 248-249. (r) 3909

----. Introducción a la poesía frances de Thierry Maulnier. Taller, I (Núm. 6, noviembre de 1939), 56-59. (r) 3910

----. Jacinto Benavente de Federico de Onís. La Falange, Núm. 7 (1 de octubre de 1923), 404. (r) 3911

----. Juan Ramón Jiménez en su obra de Enrique Díez-Canedo. El Hijo Pródigo, V (Núm. 18, septiembre de 1944), 185. (r) 3912

----. "Viajes, viajeros" (Reseña de Lettres espagnoles de Jacques de Lacretelle, España virgen de Waldo Frank, y España fiel de Manuel Gómez Morín). Contemporáneos, I (Núm. 1, junio de 1928), 87-91. (r) 3913

----. Littérature de Jean Giraudoux. El Hijo Pródigo, IV (Núm. 15, junio de 1944), 182. (r) 3914

----. México-pregón de Miguel N. Lira. Fábula, Núm. 1 (enero de 1934), 19. (r) 3915

----. Oaxaca de Manuel Toussaint. Ulises, Núm. 1 (mayo de 1927), 24-26. (r) 3916

----. Obras completas de Ramón López Velarde. El Hijo Pródigo, VII (Núm. 23, febrero de 1945), 121. (r) 3917

----. Los ojos extasiados de Miriam Elim. La Falange, Núm. 5 (1 de agosto de 1923), 313-314. (r) 3918

----. El paisajista José María Velasco de Juan de la Encina. El Hijo Pródigo, III (Núm. 10, enero de 1944), 54. (r) 3919

----. La part de Diable de Denis de Rougemont. El Hijo Pródigo, I (Núm. 4, julio de 1943), 257-258. (r) 3920

----. Poemas de Jorge Luis Borges. El Hijo Pródigo, IV (Núm. 13, abril de 1944), 60-61. (r) 3921

----. Poesías completas de Luis G. Urbina. El Hijo Pródigo, XIII (Núm. 40, julio de 1946), 56. (r) 3922

----. La puerta de Rubén Azócar. La Falange, Núm. 7 (1 de octubre de 1923), 405. (r) 3923

----. "Juan Chabás y el pudor" (Reseña de Puerto de Sonilva de Juan Chabás). Contemporáneos, I (Núm. 3, agosto de 1928), 334-336. (r) 3924

----. El puerto y otros poemas de Enrique González Rojo. Antena, Núm. 1 (julio de 1924), 8. (r) 3925

----. Las rosas de Engaddi de Rafael Arévalo Martínez. La Falange, Núm. 5 (1 de agosto de 1923), 314. (r) 3926

----. Rusia. Espejo saludable de Rafael Calleja.

La Falange, Núm. 7 (1 de octubre de 1923), 404-405. (r) 3927

----. Segundo imperio de Agustín Lazo. El Hijo Pródigo, XII (Núm. 38, mayo de 1946), 112. (r) 3928

----. Seis problemas para Don Isidro de H. Bustos Domecq. El Hijo Pródigo, I (Núm. 5, agosto de 1943), 320-321. (r) 3939

----. Sonetos mexicanos de Francisco González Guerrero. El Hijo Pródigo, XI (Núm. 35, febrero de 1946), 113. (r) 3930

----. Sor Adoración del Divino Verbo de Julio Jiménez Rueda. La Falange, Núm. 6 (1 de septiembre de 1923), 356-357. (r) 3931

----. La torre de Joaquín Cifuentes Sepúlveda. La Falange, Núm. 7 (1 de octubre de 1923), 405-406. (r) 3932

----. Transitable cristal de Eduardo González Lanuza y Solo en el tiempo de González Carballho. El Hijo Pródigo, III (Núm. 11, febrero de 1944), 121. (r) 3933

----. Tres poetas filósofos de George Santayana. El Hijo Pródigo, I (Núm. 3, junio de 1943), 187. (r) 3934

----. El último puritano de George Santayana. Romance, I (Núm. 19, 18 de diciembre de 1940), 18. (r) 3935

----. Viajes alucinados: Rincones de España de Manuel Toussaint. Antena, Núm. 1 (julio de 1924), 9. (r) 3936

----. Vuelta de Emilio Prados. Ulises, Núm. 5 (diciembre de 1927), 20-22. (f) 3937

----. The Wind that Swept Mexico de Anita Brenner. El Hijo Pródigo, II (Núm. 8, noviembre de 1943), 123. (r) 3938

----. Balmont, Constantino. "Cartas de México" (Trad. Xavier Villaurrutia). México Moderno, II (Núm. 2, septiembre de 1922), 120-121. (tr) (560)

----. Blake, William. "El matrimonio del cielo y del infierno" (Trad. Xavier Villaurrutia). Contemporáneos, II (Núm. 6, noviembre de 1928), 213-243. (tr) (679)

----. Bontempelli, Massimo. "Para la historia del teatro danés" (Trad. Xavier Villaurrutia). Contemporáneos, X (Núm. 36, mayo de 1931), 102-111. (tr) (693)

----. Cocteau, Jean. "La farsa del castillo" (Trad. Xavier Villaurrutia). Prometeus, II (Núm. 1, diciembre de 1951), 42-44. (tr) (928)

----. Chejov, Antón. "Una petición de mano" (Trad. Xavier Villaurrutia). El Hijo Pródigo, VIII (Núm. 27, junio de 1945), 177-182. (tr) (1050)

----. Duhamel, Georges. "A la sombra de las estatuas" (Trad. Agustín Lazo y Xavier Villaurrutia), El Hijo Pródigo, XI (Núm. marzo de 1946), 162-171; XII (Núm. 37, abril de 1946), 34-43; (Núm. 38, mayo de 1946), 97-103. (tr) (1194)

----. Gide, André. "El regreso del hijo pródigo" (Trad. Xavier Villaurrutia). Contemporáneos, III (Núm. 10, marzo de 1929), 239-264. (tr) (1515)

----. Giraudoux, Jean. "No habrá guerra en Troya" (Trad. Xavier Villaurrutia y Agustín Lazo). El Hijo Pródigo, V (Núm. 17, agosto de 1944), 107-120; (Núm. 18, septiembre de 1944), 166-184. (tr) (1544)

----. Huxley, Aldous. "Ciudad de México." (Trad. Xavier Villaurrutia). Tierra Nueva, II (Núm. 9-10, mayo-agosto de 1941), 169-170. (tr) (1871)

----. Lenormand, H. R. "A la sombra del mal" (Trad. Xavier Villaurrutia). El Hijo Pródigo, XI (Núm. 34, enero de 1946), 47-56; (Núm. 35, febrero de 1946), 101-112. (tr) (2050)

----. Pirandello, Luigi. "La tinaja" (Trad. Agustín Lazo y Xavier Villaurrutia). El Hijo Pródigo, XIII (Núm. 42, septiembre de 1946), 157-167. (tr) (2033)

Villena, Enrique de. "Arte de trovar." El Hijo Pródigo, IX (Núm. 29, agosto de

1945), 105-119. (a-e) 3939

Volkov, V. "La lámpara de aladino." Romance, II (Núm. 23, 22 de abril de 1941), 10. (a-e) 3940

Vossler, Karl. "El Primero sueño de Sor Juana" (Trad. Barón Heriberto B. Grote). Tierra Nueva, II (Núm. 11-12, septiembre-diciembre de 1941), 243-249. (a-e) (1704)

Walden, Hernwarth. "Carta de Alemania." Sagitario, Núm. 4 (1 de septiembre de 1926), 15. (a-e) 3941

----. "Poème." Sagitario, Núm. 11 (15 de marzo de 1927), 16. (p) 3942

Wasilievska, Wanda. "El arco iris. "El Hijo Pródigo, III (Núm. 12, marzo de 1944), 149-152. (f) 3943

Watteau, Jean Antoine. "Los placeres del baile, " "El campamento, " "La amante inquieta, " "El amor en el teatro italiano, " "Autorre-trato, " "El embarque para Citerea, " "El trovador. " Romance, I (Núm. 8, 15 de mayo de 1940), 1. 13. (il) 3944

Weber, Delia. "El había ido de viaje, " "Voy por el camino. " México Moderno, II (Núm. 1, agosto de 1922), 63-64. (a-e) 3945

Welsh, Donald. "La catedral. " La Falange, Núm. 5 (1 de agosto de 1923), 310-311. (a-e) 3946

Werfel, Franz. "El alma humana y el realismo" (Trad. Eduardo Luquín). Contemporáneos, XI (Núm. 38-39, julio-agosto de 1931), 87-104. (a-e)   (2150)

Westheim, Paul. "El espíritu del arte azteca" (Trad. Mariana Frenk). El Hijo Pródigo, XI (Núm. 34, enero de 1946), 36-46. (a-e) (1388)

----. "La estética de la pirámide" (Trad. Mariana Frenk). El Hijo Pródigo, VIII (Núm. 27, junio de 1945), 157-162. (a-e)   (1389)

----. "Pintores veracruzanos." El Hijo Pródigo, IV (Núm. 15, junio de 1944), 159-160. (a-e)   3947

Weston, Edward. "Conceptos del artista." Forma, II (Núm. 7, 1928), 17. (a-e)   3948

----. "Los daguerrotipos." Forma, I (Núm. 1, octubre de 1926), 7. (a-e)   3949

----. "Fábrica," "Juguetes mexicanos," "Juguetes mexicanos," "W. C." Forma, II (Núm. 7, 1928), 16-18. (il)   3950

----. "Fotografías." Contemporáneos, XI (Núm. 40-41, septiembre-octubre de 1931), 160-162. (il) 3951

Westphalen, Emilio Adolfo. "La rama dorada." El Hijo Pródigo, XII (Núm. 37, abril de 1946), 30-33. (a-e)   3952

Wilcock, Juan Rodolfo. "Primer día," "Cuatro años." El Hijo Pródigo, III (Núm. 10, enero de 1944), 34. (p) 3953

Wilder, Thornton. "La huída a Egipto" (Trad. Octavio G. Barreda). Contemporáneos, VIII (Núm. 30-31, noviembre-diciembre de 1930), 249-253. (dr)   (603)

Worringer, Wilhelm. "Abstracción y proyección sentimental" (Trad. Samuel Ramos). El Hijo Pródigo, III (Núm. 12, marzo de 1944), 155-165. (a-e) (3043)

Wyld Ospina, Carlos. "La carreta tropical." La Falange, Núm. 3 (1 de febrero de 1923), 162-163. (p)   3954

Wyzewa, Teodor de. "Correspondencia del crítico de Koenigsberg." Romance, I (Núm. 12, 15 de julio de 1940), 3. (a-e)   3955

Xavier, Héctor. "Viñeta." Estaciones, I (Núm. 2, verano de 1956), portada. (il)   3956

Ximeno y Planes, Rafael. "Dibujo," "Dibujo," "Dibujo." El Hijo Pródigo, II (Núm. 9, diciembre de 1943), entre 163 y 164. (il)   3957

Xirau, Joaquín. "Los dos reinos." Tierra Nueva, I (Núm. 4-5, julio-octubre de 1940), 198-204. (a-e) 3958

----. "La fenomenología." Romance, I (Núm. 10, 15 de junio de 1940), 5. (a-e)   3959

----. "La fenomenología." Romance, I (Núm. 14, 15 de agosto de 1940), 3, 9. (a-e)   3960

----. "La fenomenología: Heidegger." Romance, I (Núm. 20, 15 de enero de enero de 1941), 5, 15. (a-e) 3961

----. "Fidelidad." Romance, I (Núm. 3, 1 de marzo de 1940), 1-2. (a-e) 3962

Yáñez, Agustín. "Alfonso Reyes." Fábula, Núm. 9 (septiembre de 1934), 180. (a-e) 3963

----. "Diez libros mexicanos." Fábula, Núm. 5 (mayo de 1934), 86-89. (a-e) 3964

----. "Pasión y convalecencia." Ruta, Núm. 6 (noviembre de 1938), 26-32. (f) 3965

----. "La patria del Periquillo." Romance, I (Núm. 5, 1 de abril de 1940), 3-4. (a-e) 3966

----. "El sueño del cura." El Hijo Pródigo, XI (Núm. 35, febrero de 1946), 94-96. (f) 3967

----. Antología del pensamiento de lengua española en la edad contemporánea con introducción y selección de José Gaos. El Hijo Pródigo, XI (Núm. 36, marzo de 1946), 172-173. (r) 3968

----. Este pueblo de América de Germán Arciniegas. El Hijo Pródigo, X (Núm. 31, octubre de 1945), 58-59. (r) 3969

Yeats, William Butler. "Ephemera" (Trad. Luis Cernuda). Romance, I (Núm. 10, 15 de junio de 1940), 11. (p) (914)

Ygobone, Aquiles D. "La obra del instituto cultural Argentino-Mexicano en Buenos Aires." Romance, I (Núm. 8, 15 de mayo de 1940), 17. (a-e) 3970

Z. V., J. Medio tono de Rodolfo Usigli. Ruta, Núm. 5 (octubre de 1938), 59. (r) 3971

Zabre, Solón. "Apuntes para un ensayo: Sobre Dante, Cervantes y Goethe." Ruta, Núm. 3 (agosto de 1938), 5-17. (a-e) 3972

----. "Descartes o el método de la duda." Ruta, Núm. 9 (febrero de 1939), 25-34. (a-e) 3973

----. Corrientes culturales que definen al Periquillo de Bernabé Godoy V. Ruta, Núm. 1 (junio de 1938), 59-61. (r) 3974

Zahar, Alfonso. "Areopagítica." Tierra Nueva, III (Núm. 13-14, enero-abril de 1942), 75-77. (a-e) 3975

Zalamea, Jorge. Léger, Aléxis Saint-Léger ("St. John Perse"). "Imágenes para Crusoe" (Trad. Jorge Zalamea). El Hijo Pródigo, XI (Núm. 35, febrero de 1946), 90-93. (tr) (2045)

Zalce, Alfredo. "Litografías." Contemporáneos, X (Núm. 36, mayo de 1931), 112-115. (il) 3976

----. "Paisaje de Yucatán." El Hijo Pródigo, X (Núm. 31, octubre de 1945), entre 16 y 17. (il) 3977

Zaldumbide, Gonzalo. "Un elegíaco ecuatoriano."

México Moderno, I (Núm. 7, febrero de 1921), 11-18. (a-e) 3978

Zambrano, María. "La destrucción de la filosofía en Nietzsche." El Hijo Pródigo, VII (Núm. 23, febrero de 1945), 71-74. (a-e) 3979

----. "La destrucción de las formas." El Hijo Pródigo, IV (Núm. 14, mayo de 1944), 75-81. (a-e) 3980

----. "Poema y sistema." El Hijo Pródigo, V (Núm. 18, septiembre de 1944), 137-139. (a-e) 3981

----. "Poesía y filosofía." Taller, I (Núm. 4, julio de 1939), 5-14. (a-e) 3982

----. "Sobre la vacilación actual." El Hijo Pródigo, IX (Núm. 29, agosto de 1945), 91-95. (a-e) 3983

----. Descartes y Husserl de Francisco Romero. Taller, I (Núm. 6, noviembre de 1939), 59-62. (r) 3984

Zamora, A. Joyce, James. "Un fragmento de Ulises" (Trad. A. Zamora). Ruta, Núm. 2 (julio de 1938), 36-42. (tr) (1970)

Zarraga, Angel. "Oda a la Virgen de Guadalupe." Contemporáneos, XI (Núm. 42-43, noviembre-diciembre de 1931), 226-232. (p) 3985

Zavala, Jesús. "Ambrosio Ramírez, traductor de Horacio." Romance, I (Núm. 18, 15 de noviembre de 1940), 2. (a-e) 3986

----. "El poeta mexicano Manuel José Othón." Romance, I (Núm. 11, 1 de julio de 1940), 16. (a-e) 3987

----. El inútil dolor de José de J. Núñez y Domínguez. Antena, Núm. 3 (septiembre de 1924), 9. (r) 3988

----. La poesía de San Juan de la Cruz de Dámaso Alonso. El Hijo Pródigo, VIII (Núm. 27, junio de 1945), 184-185. (r) 3989

----. Quetzalcoatl de Humberto Tejera. Antena, Núm. 3 (septiembre de 1924), 9-10. (r) 3990

Zea, Leopoldo. "Esquema para una historia de la filosofía." El Hijo Pródigo, VI (Núm. 21, diciembre de 1944), 137-143. (a-e) 3991

----. "Esquema para una historia de la filosofía." El Hijo Pródigo, IX (Núm. 29, agosto de 1945), 73-84. (a-e) 3992

----. "La filosofía en Aristóteles." Tierra Nueva, I (Núm. 6, noviembre-diciembre de 1940), 302-307. (a-e) 3993

----. "Heráclito." Tierra Nueva, I (Núm. 1, enero-febrero de 1940), 20-29. (a-e) 3994

----. "Pensamiento y trayectoria de Ortega y Gasset." El Hijo Pródigo, III (Núm. 11, febrero de 1944), 85-86. (a-e) 3995

----. "El sentido de responsibilidad en la filosofía actual." Tierra Nueva, I (Núm. 3, mayo-junio de 1940), 136-146. (a-e) 3996

----. "El sentido judío de la muerte." Tierra Nueva, III (Núm. 15, diciembre de 1942), 131-137. (a-e) 3997

----. Ensimismamiento y alteración de José Ortega y Gasset. Tierra Nueva, I (Núm. 2, marzo-abril de 1940), 118-120. (r) 3998

----. Esencia y formas de la simpatía de Max Scheler. El Hijo Pródigo, I (Núm. 4, julio de 1943), 258-259. (r) 3999

----. Filosofía de la ilustración de Ernst Cassirer. El Hijo Pródigo, II (Núm. 8, noviembre de 1943), 124-125. (r) 4000

----. Hacia un nuevo humanismo de Samuel Ramos. Tierra Nueva, I (Núm. 6, noviembre-diciembre de 1940), 374-378. (r) 4001

----. "La historia en el siglo XIX" (Reseña de Historia e historiadores en el siglo XIX de G. P. Gooch). Tierra Nueva, III (Núm. 15, diciembre de 1942), 183-185. (r) 4002

----. Ideología y utopía de Karl Mannheim. Tierra Nueva, II (Núm. 11-12, septiembre-diciembre de 1941), 269-272. (r) 4003

----. Meyerson y la física moderna de Antonio Caso.

Tierra Nueva, I (Núm. 1, enero-febrero de 1940), 53-54. (r) 4004

----. El nuevo psicoanálisis de Karen Horney. El Hijo Pródigo, III (Núm. 11, febrero de 1944), 123. (r) 4005

----. Política de Victoria de Antonio Gómez Robledo. Tierra Nueva, II (Núm. 9-10, mayo-agosto de 1941), 186-189. (r) 4006

----. Spinoza de Carl Gebhardt. Tierra Nueva, I (Núm. 4-5, julio-octubre de 1940), 278-281. (r) 4007

Zegri, Armando. "La tragedia del nubio," "Sugerencia," "Tristezas de la senectud," "La simpatía de lo ridículo." La Falange, Núm. 3 (1 de febrero de 1923), 146-149. (a-e) 4008

Zelaya, Antonio. "Elogio de la traición." La Falange, Núm. 6 (1 de septiembre de 1923), 350-351. (p) 4009

----. La casa de Jaime Torres Bodet. La Falange, Núm. 6 (1 de septiembre de 1923), 331-333. (r) 4010

Zendejas, Francisco. "Ave devorada por tiburones." Estaciones, II (Núm. 7, otoño de 1957), 295-296. (p) 4011

----. "Avión que vuela sobre la ciudad olvidada." Estaciones, II (Núm. 5, primavera de 1957), 51-52. (p) 4012

----. "Editorial." Prometeus,

II (Núm. 1, diciembre de 1951), 3-5. (a-e)   4013

----. "Las 'esencias' en la literatura." El Hijo Pródigo, XIII (Núm. 42, septiembre de 1946), 131-135. (a-e)   4014

----. "¿Freud o Jung?" Prometeus, I (Núm. 3, mayo de 1949), 141-143. (a-e) 4015

----. "Leonora Carrington." Prometeus, I (Núm. 2, abril de 1949), 94-95. (a-e)

----. "El mundo reconquistado de James Joyce." El Hijo Pródigo, XII (Núm. 38, mayo de 1946), 73-76. (a-e)   4017

----. "Nota epígrafe." Prometeus, II (Núm. 1, diciembre de 1951), 52. (a-e) 4018

----. "Poesía y libertad." Prometeus, I (Núm. 1, febrero de 1949), 11-12. (a-e)   4019

----. "Positivos y negativos." Estaciones, I (Núm. 4, invierno de 1956), 555-557. (a-e)   4020

----. "Se murió cuando quiso." Prometeus, II (Núm. 1, diciembre de 1951), 25. (p)   4021

----. "¿Traición o protesta? : El caso de Ezra Pound." Prometeus, I (Núm. 2, abril de 1949), 68-74. (a-e)   4022

----. Babel de Enrique González Martínez. Prometeus, I (Núm. 2, abril de 1949), 131-132. (r)

4023

----. Baudelaire, poeta existencial de José Miguel García Ascot. Prometeus, II (Núm. 1, diciembre de 1951), 69-70. (r)   4024

----. La danza y el ballet de Adolfo Salazar. Prometeus, I (Núm. 3, mayo de 1949), 218-219. (r)   4025

----. Decir lo de primavera de Fernando Sánchez Mayans. Prometeus, II (Núm. 1, diciembre de 1951), 70. (r)   4026

----. Historia de la literatura griega de C. M. Bowra. Prometeus, I (Núm. 3, mayo de 1949), 217-218. (r)   4027

----. Left Hand, Right Hand!; The Scarlet Tree; Great Morning!; Laughter in the Next Room de Sir Osbert Sitwell. Prometeus, I (Núm. 2, abril de 1949), 129-130. (r)   4028

----. Glover, Edward. "Teoría general de la mento." (Trad. Francisco M. Zendejas). Prometeus, I (Núm. 3, mayo de 1949), 143-155. (tr)   (1546)

----. Ségur, Condesa de. "Una carta a su pequeño hijo Jacques de Pitray" (Trad. Francisco Zendejas). Prometeus, II (Núm. 1, diciembre de 1951), 45. (tr)   (3432)

Zervos, Christian. "Peintures d'enfants." Sagitario, Núm. 12-13 (30 de abril de 1927), 12. (a-e)   4029

Zorrilla, Oscar. "Acuarela
II." Estaciones, IV (Núm.
16, invierno de 1959), 485-
486. (f)   4030

----. La appassionata y El
alfarero de Héctor Azar.
Estaciones, IV (Núm. 14,
verano de 1959), 240-241.
(r)   4031

----. Cuentos del desierto
de Emma Dolujanoff.
Estaciones, IV (Núm. 14,
verano de 1959), 241-242.
(r)   4032

Zulueta, Luis de. "Ante un
centenario: Juan Enrique
Pestalozzi." Sagitario, Núm.
8 (1 de febrero de 1927),
11. (a-e)   4033

Zull, Ivan. "Cosas de familia."
Estaciones, I (Núm. 2, verano de 1956), 198-201. (f)
                            4034

Zummern, Alfred. "El
problema de las relaciones
económicas internacionales."
Sagitario, Núm. 2 (1 de
agosto de 1926), 15. (a-e)
                            4035

Zúñiga, Francisco. "Desnudo,"
"Cabeza de niña." Tierra
Nueva, II (Núm. 7-8. enero-
abril de 1941), entre 64 y
65. (il)   4036

A

Abra, 1
Abreu Gómez, Ermilo, 2-90,
 983, 985, 986, 1086, 1500,
 1761, 1994, 2413, 3008
Abril, Xavier, 91-93
Acevedo, Jesús, 94, 3699
Acevedo Escobedo, Antonio, 95-
 105, 3089
Aceves Navarro, Gilberto, 106
Acosta, Agustín, 107
Acosta, José de, 1541
Acosta, Julio, 108-112
Acosta, Oscar, 113
Adjucto-Botelho, Pero, 114
Aeschylus, 64
Agosti, Héctor P., 115
Aguilera Malta, Demetrio, 1785
Aguirre, Manuel, 116
Aguirre, Mirta, 82
Alardín, Carmen, 117-123
Alatorre, Antonio, 124
Alba, Aurelio de, 125
Alba, Pedro de, 126, 127
Alberti, Rafael, 128-132, 1171,
 3480, 3537, 3630, 3770, 3771
Albertos, Ernesto, 133
Alcalá, Manuel, 134-136
Alcázar, Ricardo de, 81, 137-139
Alcíbar, José de, 140
Alcover, Juan, 147
Alchvang, A., 141
Aldana, P. M. Fray Cristóbal
 de, 54
Aldington, R., 142
Alegría, Fernando, 3475
Aleixandre, Vicente, 143, 144,
 1097, 1658, 2141, 3141
Alessio Robles, Miguel, 2749
Alfonso el Sabio, 67
Alienes Urosa, Julián, 145
Almanza, Héctor Raúl, 477
Alomar, Gabriel, 146, 147

Alonso, Dámaso, 1805, 3407,
 3989
Altamirano, Ignacio Manuel,
 771, 3089
Altolaguirre, Manuel, 148-152,
 639, 2008, 3474, 3537, 3892
Alvarado, José, 153-163
Alvarez, Eduardo, 2748
Alvarez, Francisco Javier, 164
Alvarez, Griselda, 3391
Alvarez, José S., 1289
Alvarez Bravo, Dolores, 165
Alvarez Bravo, Manuel, 166-
 168, 2462, 3867
Alvarez Everoix, Vidal, 467
Amado, Jorge, 3705
Ambrogi, Arturo, 2118
Amero, Emilio, 169-170
Amezcua, José, 171
Amo, Julián, 172-174
Amor, Guadalupe, 2312
Amorim, Guedes de, 3766
Amparo Dávila, María, 175
Anbry, Octave, 3068
Anderson, Maxwell, 3210, 3211
Andrenio (see Gómez de
 Baquero, Eduardo)
Andreieff, Leónidis, 1275
Andrés de Aguirre, Ginés de,
 177
Andújar, Manuel, 2784
Angel, Abraham, 178-181
Anguiano, Raúl, 182-187, 212,
 1320, 2554, 2974
Angulo, Gaspar de, 188
Anistar, Mauricio, 189, 190
Anónimo, 136, 191-474
Anouilh, Jean, 475
ANTHROPOLOGY, 428, 940,
 3440, 3463
Antón, David, 476
Apango Molina, Ignacio, 477

Apollinaire, Guillaume, 478
479, 622, 2397
Aragon, Louis, 480
Aragón Leiva, Agustín, 481, 482
Arai, Alberto T. , 483, 3588
Aranguren, E. , 484
Araquistain, Luis, 485, 486
Arce, David N. , 487
Arciniegas, Germán, 3969
Arconada, César M. , 489
Arconada, M. , 488
Arcos, Juan, 490
ARCHITECTURE
    European, 1019, 2012, 2605,
        3778
    Mexican, 245, 564, 1236,
        2024, 2212, 2292, 2980,
        3231, 3692, 3699
    Spanish American, 1239, 1389
Arellano, Jesús, 2527
Arellano Belloc, Francisco, 491
Arenales, Ricardo, 492-496, 3315
Arenas, José, 497
Arenas Betancourt, Rodrigo, 498
Arévalo, Juan José, 3455
Arévalo Martínez, Rafael, 499,
    500, 3926
Arguedas, José María, 501, 641,
    3401
Argüelles, Hugo, 220, 502-505
Argüelles Bringas, Roberto, 506
Argüello, Santiago, 507
Aridjis, Homero, 508
Aristotle, 3586, 3993
Armond y Maubliac, ?, 2935,
    3406
Arp, Jean Hans, 509
ART
    Classical
        criticism of, 1488
        reproductions, passim,
            consult under artist
    European
        criticism of, 41, 42, 258,
            311, 312, 339, 342, 380,
            391, 393, 426, 598, 651,
            692, 800, 929, 1238, 1242,
            1284, 1378, 1469, 1470,
            1485, 1491, 1496, 1699, 1702,
            1703, 1852, 1874, 2031,
            2333, 2446, 2656, 2716,
            2917, 3376, 3395, 3565,
            3730, 3895, 4016

    reproductions, passim,
        consult under artist
    General, 29, 256, 384, 388,
        497, 644, 989, 1189, 1241,
        1308, 1316, 1487, 1489, 1493,
        1554, 1576, 1776, 1868, 1902,
        2011, 2363, 2623, 2907, 3043,
        3309, 3473, 3751
    Japanese
        criticism of, 1339
    Mexican, passim, consult
        under artist
    North American
        criticism of, 305, 2337, 2341
    Spanish American
        criticism of, 314, 442, 490,
            794, 1208, 1343, 2756, 2952,
            3108, 3242, 3250, 3251, 3271,
            3401, 3728, 3732
    reproductions, passim,
        consult under artist
Arteta, Aurelio, 1238
Arredondo, Alberto, 414
Arreola, Juan José, 124
Arrieta, Antonio, 510
Arruza, J. Amber, 511
Ascasubi, Hilario, 1931
Asch, Nathan, 512
Asúnsolo, Ignacio, 530
Asúnsolo R. , Enrique, 513-529
Atl, Dr. (see Murillo, Gerardo)
Attolini, José, 219, 531-533
Aub, Max, 56, 534-540, 1172,
    1405, 1542, 2878
Auclair, Marcela, 541
Averchenko, Arkady, 542
Ayala, Francisco, 3454
Azaña, Manuel, 543, 1179, 3568
Azócar, Rubén, 3923
Azorín (see Martínez Ruiz, José)
Azuela, Mariano, 216, 544-550,
    1091, 1098, 2000, 2006, 2651,
    2796, 2797, 3452

B

B. , 551
B. , B. , 552
B. , T. , E. , 554
Babelon, Jean, 2712
Bacon, Peggy, 555
Bach, Johann Sebastian, 2487
Báez, Edmundo, 556-558

Bioy Casares, Adolfo, 3462
Blake, William, 679, 680
Blanco-Fombona, Rufino, 176
Blanco Moheno, Roberto, 2780
Block, Alejandro, 681
Blom, Franz, 682, 683
Blumner, Rudolf, 684
Bó, Efraín Tomás, 685-687, 3597
Boccioni, Umberto, 688
Bogrand, Ricardo, 689, 2542
Bohet, Víctor, 690
Bolívar, Simón, 1283, 2723, 3469, 3807
Bonifaz Nuño, Rubén, 691
Bonilla y San Martín, Adolfo, 1188
Bonmariage, Sylvain, 692
Bonnard, ?, 2457
Bontempelli, Massimo, 693, 694
Borges, Jorge Luis, 695-697, 2178, 2661, 3011, 3468, 3904, 3921
Borges, Norah, 698, 1552, 2952
Borja Bolado, F., 699
Bosquet, Alain, 2567
Botello Barros, Angel, 3730
Botello Barros, Miguel, 700
Bousoño, Carlos, 701
Bovio, G., 702
Bowra, C. M., 4027
Bragaglia, Antón Giulio, 703
Braque, Georges, 704, 705
Brehme, Hugo, 451, 706
Bremond, Henri, 707
Brenner, Anita, 708, 709, 3938
Breton, André, 710, 711, 2460, 3656, 3794
Bretón de los Herreros, Manuel, 712
Brion, Marcel, 713
Brodrick, Alan Hougton, 3473
Brody, Daisy, 281, 714, 1214
Broido, Rubén, 715
Brook, Paulita, 1926
Brughetti, Romualdo, 3358
Brull, Mariano, 716
Bud, Carmen, 717
Buddha, 2001
Bueno, Salvador, 718
Buhler, Charlotte, 2331
Bulgakow, B., 719
Burbank, Luther, 1979

Burkhardt, Jacobo, 1901
Burlingham, D., 2463
Bustamante, Octavio N., 720, 721, 2169
Bustos Cerecedo, Carlos, 641
Bustos Cerecedo, Miguel, 722-730
Butor, Michel, 3299

C

C., L., 732
C. de la B., 731
Cabada, Juan de la, 733-736, 1105, 3374
Cabrera, Alonso de., 3019
Cabrera, Manuel, 737-739
Cabrera, Miguel, 740-742
Cabrera Nieto, Francisco, 1856
Cadenazzi, Edgarda, 743
Cadilla Martínez, María, 1026
Caillois, Roger, 124, 744-746, 2256, 3899
Cain, M. Julien, 731
Calderón de la Barca, 109
Calderón Ramírez, Manuel, 3748
Caldwell, Erskine, 531, 747
Calero, Manuel, 1277
Calvillo, Manuel, 748, 841
Calvillo Madrigal, Salvador, 749-754, 1857
Calle, Chita de la, 755
Calleja, Rafael, 756, 3927
Callorda, Pedro Erasmo, 2704
Camargo, Salvador, 757
Camarillo de Pereyra, María Enriqueta, 231, 758-764, 2090
Camín, Alfonso, 765
Camp, Santiago Valenti, 766, 767
Campbell, Joseph, 3459
Campo, Angel de, 1113
Campo, Estanislao del, 1931
Campo, Juan del, 768
Campobello, Gloria, 770
Campobello, Nellie, 45, 769, 770
Campos Alatorre, Cipriano, 102
Campuzano, Juan R., 771
Camus, Albert, 1511, 3268, 3394, 3477
Canade, ?, 772
Cantón, Wilberto L., 773, 774, 1864, 2528, 2531, 2794

250

Capdevila, Arturo, 670, 775, 776, 1286
Capek, Karel, 777
Capote, Truman, 3478
Carballido, Emilio, 778-780, 2316, 2372, 2783
Carballo, Emmanuel, 781, 2782
Carbonell, Diego, 1283
Cardenal, Ernesto, 782
Cárdenas, Lázaro, 783
Cárdenas, Nancy, 784, 785
Cardona Peña, Alfredo, 786-789
Cardona Vera, José G., 790, 1729
Cardoza y Aragón, Luis, 791-809, 1074, 1102, 1589, 1839, 3866
Carleton de Millán, Verna, 810
Carlino, Carlos, 726
Carner, José, 811, 812, 1170, 1802
Carnés, Luisa, 813-815, 1862
Carniado, Enrique, 816
Carona Peña, Alfredo, 1099
Cars, Guy des, 3448, 3460
Carvajal, María Isabel, 817
Carvalho, Ronald de, 818, 1700
Carr-Saunders, A. M., 174
Carrancá y Trujillo, Raúl, 486, 819-825
Carrasco, Pedro, 826, 827
Carreño, Alberto María, 1270, 1282
Carrera Andrade, Jorge, 828, 2708
Carrillo de Sotomayor, Luis de, 829, 2989, 3334
Carrillo y Gariel, A., 830
Carrington, Leonora, 831-833, 4016
Carrión, Alejandro, 834
Carrión, Benjamín, 3457
Casahonda, Enoch Cancino, 1867
Casal, Alfonso, 835, 836
Casal, Julio J., 1882
Casalduero, Joaquín, 837, 3383
Casanueva Mazo, Bernardo, 135, 838-841
Casas, Manuel Gonzalo, 842
Casasús, Joaquín D., 1282
Caso, Antonio, 456, 843-847, 1550, 3031, 3683, 4004
Cassirer, Ernst, 4000

Cassou, Jean, 848-850
Castellanos, Francisco José, 851
Castellanos, Julio, 852-857, 3864
Castellanos, Rosario, 858-860, 1853, 2518, 2545, 2772
Castañeda Batres, Oscar, 861
Castillo, Carlos, 3894
Castillo, Guillermo, 862
Castillo, Jesús, 863
Castillo, Michel del, 2315
Castillo Ledón, Luis, 864-866
Castro, Américo, 3661
Castro, Eduardo Jr., 867
Castro, Fray Andrés de, 1276
Castro Leal, Antonio, 52, 73, 639, 869-891, 1168, 2313, 2875, 3530, 3892, 3898
Castro Padilla, Manuel, 949
Castrovido, Roberto, 868
Casuso, Teté, 892
Cataño, Eduardo, 893-895
Cava, José, 896-898
Cecchi, Emilio, 899, 900
Ceja Reyes, Víctor, 901
Cejador y Frauca, Julio, 2588
Celaya, Gabriel, 902
Céline, ?, 2453
Centeno, Augosto, 903
Centeno, Francisco, 530
Cereno, Benito, 475, 904, 905
Cernuda, Luis, 680, 906-914, 1943, 2230, 2874
Cervantes, Enrique A., 915, 916
Cervantes, Francisco, 917, 918
Cervantes, Miguel de, 849, 959, 1171, 1502, 2410, 2785, 3189, 3972
Cervantes Ahumada, Raúl, 217
Cerretani, Arturo, 685
Cestero, Manuel Florentino, 919-921
Cézanne, Paul, 992, 923
Cid, El, 163
Cifuentes Sepúlveda, Joaquín, 3932
Cimorra, Clemente, 815
Cirlot, Juan Eduardo, 924
Clausel, Joaquín, 925, 2023
Clerq, Jacques le, 926
Climent, Enrique, 927

Cocteau, Jean, 928, 929
Coester, Alfredo, 172
Colín, Eduardo, 930, 1642
Colina, José de la, 746, 931-938
Colson, Jaime, 939
Collier, John, 3463
Comas, Juan, 404, 940, 941
Comet, César A., 942, 943
Companys, Luis, 2282
Conan Doyle, Sir Arthur, 1664
Conde, Isidro, 2547
Conde Abellán, Carmen, 944
Condroyer, Emile, 945
Conkling, Hilda, 946
Conte Corti, Egon Caesar, 2029
Contreras, Francisco, 947, 1279, 1300
Copland, Aaron, 567, 948
Corao, Angel, 2896
Cordero, J. L., 949
Cordero, Juan, 3863
Cordero Salvador, 1285
Córdoba, Joaquín Fernández de, 950
Corneille, Pierre, 1582
Cornyn, John Hubert, 951
Coronel, Rafael, 952
Corot, Jean Baptiste Camille, 953
Cortés, Erasto, 955
Cortés, Hernán, 87, 1278, 1926, 2712, 3208
Corvalán, Octavio, 956
Correa, Nicolás de, 954
Cosío Villegas, Daniel, 957-959
Coss, Julio Antonio, 960-962
Cossío, José L., 1280
Cossío, Manuel B., 1944
Costa, Olga, 963
Coto, Juan E., 964-966, 1077
Couffon, Claude, 967
Covarrubias, Miguel, 968-972, 3035
Cravioto, Alfonso, 973-975, 3682
Creel, Enrique, 976
Creft, José de, 258
Crespo, Angel, 977
Crespo, Gerardo, 978, 979
Crespo, Jorge Juan, 980
Cristobalina, doña, 3134
Crone, G. R., 218
Crowninshield, Frank, 981
Cruz, Juan, 982, 1208

Cruz, Sor Juana Inés de la, 2, 8, 15, 16, 31, 37, 39, 40, 226, 661, 889, 910, 983-986, 1110, 1704, 2142, 2404, 2519, 3134, 3429, 3719
Cuadra, José de la, 987
Cuéllar, ?, 2433
Cuenca, Agustín F., 1663, 2234
Cuesta, Jorge, 752, 988-1014, 1061, 2700, 2730, 2791
Cuesta, Víctor, 1015, 1016
Cuesta y Cuesta, Alfonso, 1017
Cuevas, José Luis, 850, 1018, 3551
Cuevas, Rafael, 3392
Cumming, A. E., 1019
Cunard, Nancy, 1020, 1021
Curie, Madame, 2356
Chabás, Juan, 3924
Chacel, Rosa, 2257
Chacón y Calvo, José María, 1022
Chagall, Marc, 1023
Chagoya, Leopoldo, 1024
Champourcin, Ernestina de, 1025-1027
Chapek, M., 2599
Chaplin, Charles, 1385
Charlot, Jean, 803, 1028-1036, 2656
Charry Lara, Fernando, 1037, 1038
Chassex, Jean, 1039
Chaveau, Leopold, 1040
Chávez, Carlos, 948, 1041, 1042
Chávez, Ezequiel A., 1043, 1044, 1292, 1420, 3328
Chávez Morado, José, 1045, 2971
Chávez Morado, Juan, 1046
Chávez Orozco, Luis, 1047-1049
Chekhov, Anton, 1050
Chelminsky, Esther, 3298
Chesterton, Gilbert Keith, 485, 871
Chestov, León, 3014
Chirico, Giorgio de, 929, 1051-1054
Chopin, Frédéric Francois, 2311
Chumacero, Alí, 707, 1055-1123, 2106, 2541

D

D., J., 1124, 1125
Dalí, Salvador, 1126-1129, 1469,
1470
DANCE (see MUSIC)
D'Annunzio, Gabriel, 2464
Dante Alighieri, 1352, 2918,
3972
Darío, Rubén, 1130, 1131, 1166,
1297, 1311, 1615, 1640, 3456,
3486
Dauajare Torres, Fleix, 2305
Daudet, Alfonse, 3074
Daudet, Leon, 2129
Dauster, Frank, 1132-1135
de Mille, Cecil B., 2371
Debussy, Claude, 2936
Delay, Jean, 3301
Delevsky, J., 1136
Delgado, José Manuel, 1137
Delgado, José María, 1138
Delgado, Juan B., 1139
Della Rocca de Vergalo, 3261,
3550
Delmar, Meira, 1140
Democritus, 1141
Depero, Fortunato, 2917
Derain, André, 1142
Derisi, Octavio N., 3191
Derycke, Gaston, 1143
Descartes, René du Perron,
1893, 3973, 3984
Desnos, Robert, 1004
Deustua, Raúl, 1144
Díaz, E., 1145
Díaz, Enrique Othón, 1509
Díaz, Porfirio, 1047, 1048
Díaz Arrieta, Hernán, 1146
Díaz Conde, Antonio, 558
Díaz de León, Francisco, 250,
1147-1152
Díaz Dufóo, Carlos Jr., 1153-
1156
Díaz Mirón, Salvador, 1005,
1324, 1394, 1595, 1649, 1883,
2915, 3739
Díaz-Plaja, Guillermo, 1447
Díaz Rodríguez, Manuel, 1157
Díaz-Thomé, Hugo, 2613
Diderot, Denis, 158
Diego, Gerardo, 1158, 1159,
3630

Dieste, Eduardo, 3193
Dieste, Rafael, 2871
Díez-Canedo, Enrique, 58,
538, 681, 1090, 1160-1175,
2240, 2955, 3912
Díez Canedo, Joaquín, 1108
Dilthey, Wilhelm, 1432, 1434-
1436, 3351
Dmitrievsky, I., 1176
Dodero, Antonio, 1177
Dolujanoff, Emma, 4032
Domecq, H. Bustos, 3929
Domenchina, Juan José, 1178-
1184, 1498, 3772
Domingo, Marcelino, 1185
Domínguez, Pancho, 3283
Domínguez Assiayn, Salvador,
1186
Domínguez Bello, Arnulfo, 530
Domínguez Silva, Víctor, 3400
Doniz, Roberto, 1187
Donne, John, 593
Dos Passos, John, 2593
Dostoievsky, Fedor
Michailovitch, 1043, 1044,
3685
Dotor, Angel, 1188
DRAMA
British and North American
criticism of, 411, 522,
584, 880, 1381, 2060, 3103,
3211
in translation, 603, 832,
1173
Danish
criticism of, 693
French
criticism of, 551, 1582,
2051, 2130, 2466, 3042,
3394,
in translation, 1194, 1366,
1482, 1544, 1960, 2297
General, 395, 2017, 3162
German
criticism of, 1990
in translation, 2835
Italian
criticism of, 9, 437, 2170,
2262, 2464, 3015, 3644
in translation, 2033, 2034
Jewish
criticism of, 1672
Mexican, passim, consult

253

under author
Norwegian
  criticism of, 3700
Russian
  criticism of, 304, 1174,
  2192, 2599, 2934, 3940
  in translation, 1050
Spanish
  criticism of, 10, 21, 27,
  109, 137, 460, 870, 875,
  1162, 1165, 1171, 1530,
  1582, 1884, 2164, 2344,
  2418, 2855, 2878, 3128,
  3633, 3911
Spanish American
  criticism of, 533, 1237,
  2030
  original works, passim,
  consult under author
Dreyfus, Alberto, 1189
D'Sola, Otto, 727
Duarte Guillé, Manuel, 1190
Ducasse, Isidoro, 1191
Duchamp, Marcel, 1192
Dueñas, Guadalupe, 1193, 2769,
  3547
Duhamel, Georges, 1194, 1800,
  3662
Duno, Pedro, 1665
Dupuy, Jacqueline, 3366
Durand, José, 1195
Durand, Mercedes, 1196, 1197
Durero, Alberto, 1198
Durtain, Luc, 1199, 1200

E

E.D.I.A.P.S.A., 1201
ECONOMICS; 145, 146, 307,
  326, 2984, 2986, 3471, 4035
Echavarría, Margarita, 1202
Echavarría, Salvador, 1203-1205
Echave Ibia, Baltasar de, 1206
Echeverría, Leonardo Martín,
  1540, 3063
Echeverría, Vicente, 3531
Echeverría del Prado, Vicente,
  1207
Echeverría Loría, Arturo, 1208-
  1212
Echeverría R., Manuel, 1213
Eckhart, Meister, 1214

EDITORIAL COMMENT
Antena, 191
Contemporáneos, 195, 199,
  2651, 2653, 2675, 2689
Estaciones, 200, 202, 204,
  206, 208, 210, 211, 1849,
  2502, 2509, 2516, 2768
Fábula, 224, 225
La Falange, 233, 234
Forma, 244, 254, 430, 2987
El Hijo Pródigo, 259
Prometeus, 286, 287
Romance, 298, 375, 385,
  389, 392, 1201
Ruta, 421
Sagitario, 422, 424, 431, 434,
  438, 439, 2121, 3156
Taller, 461, 464, 1494
Tierra Nueva, 465
EDUCATION
European, 1082, 4033
Latin American, 563, 1268,
  1961, 3970
Mexican, 404, 436, 446,
  1296, 1305, 1619, 2436,
  2985, 3504, 3800
Edwards Bello, Joaquín, 677
Ehrenbourg, Elie, 732, 1215
Eielson, Jorge Eduardo, 1216
Einstein, Albert, 1924
Eisenstein, Sergei M., 481,
  482, 1217, 3191
Elim, Miriam, 2895, 3918
Eliot, Thomas Stearns, 594,
  959, 1218-1225, 2679, 3721
Elizondo, Slavador, 1226-1230
Elm, E., 1231
Eluard, Paul, 999, 1012, 1232
Emmanuel, Pierre, 1233
Empedocles, 2876
Encina, Juan de la, 1234-1242,
  1454, 3913
Enciso, Jorge, 1243
Enciso, Xavier, 452
Enríquez, Carlos, 1244, 3774
Ernst, Max, 1245
Erro, Luis Enrique, 1246
Escalante, Francisco J., 1247
Escalante, Roberto, 1248
Escalón, Salvador, 823
Escardó, Florencio, 103
Escobar, José U., 1249

Figueiredo, Fidelino de, 3312
Fiorentini, Luigi, 214
Fitts, Dudley, 588
Flannagan, John B. , 2337
Flaubert, Gustave, 3599
Fletcher, John Gould, 1371
Fletcher, William H. , 1372
Flor, Noé de la, 2828
Flores, Angel, 1225
Flores, Estéban, 1373-1375
Flores, Samuel, 1376
Florit, Eugenio, 1377, 2523
Fontains, Mrs. André, 1378
Fort, Paul, 1379
Fournier, Alain, 295, 3365
Fournier, Raoul, 1380
Fraenkel, Michael, 1381
France, Anatole, 2110, 3419
Francés, José, 442, 1382
Francovich, Guillermo, 2808
Frank, Waldo, 1383-1386, 1957, 3913
Frazer, James George, 1387, 3952
Frenk, Mariana, 1388, 1389
Freud, Anna, 2463
Freud, Sigmund, 3610
Frías, José D. , 1390-1394
Friedeberg, Erwin, 1395
Fuente de Peña, Antonio de, 105
Fuentes, Carlos, 2803, 3140
Fuentes Mares, José, 1396, 1397
Fujimori, Seikichi, 1398

G

G. , F. , 1399
Gaddi, Taddeo, 1400, 1401
Gag, Wanda, 1402
Gaitán Durán, Jorge, 2520
Galerna, Francisco, 1403-1407
Galetar, Margarita, 1408
Galíndez, Bartolomé, 1409
Galindo, Marco Aurelio, 1410
Galindo, Sergio, 780, 3302
Gálvez, ?, 1411
Gall, Jacques and Francois, 1859
Gallardo M. , Roberto, 1412
Gallegos, Gerardo, 1999
Gallegos, Rómulo, 687
Gallegos Rocafull, José María, 661, 1413-1415, 1433, 3352

Galliano Cancio, Miguel, 1298
Gallo, Joaquín, 1416
Gamow, George, 3458
Gandhi, Mahatma, 2645
Gangotena, Alfredo, 1417
Ganivet, Angel, 299
Gaos, José, 661, 1418, 2560, 3587, 3968
Garabito Martínez, Jorge, 1419, 1420
Garbedian, H. Gordon, 1924
Garbo, Greta, 1735
García, Genaro, 1421, 1636
García Ascot, José Miguel, 1423-1427, 4024
García Bacca, Juan David, 661, 1141, 1428-1439, 2876, 3510
García Blanco, M. , 1440
García Calderón, Ventura, 1302, 1441, 1442, 1662, 3684
García Godoy, Federico, 1443
García Granados, Jorge, 419
García Icazbalceta, Joaquín, 1326, 1638
García Iglesias, Sara, 2245, 2533, 3243
García Lorca, Federico, 123, 798, 801, 1444, 2711, 2716, 3055, 3332
García Marín, José, 1445-1447
García Maroto, Gabriel, 1448-1455
García Marruz, Fina, 1426, 1456
García Moreno, Gabriel, 3457
García Terrés, Jaime, 1457
Garciasol, Ramón de, 1422
Garcilaso de la Vega, 134, 910
Garcilaso de la Vega, El Inca, 2465
Garfias, Pedro, 1458-1462
Garibay, Angel María, 1109, 1110
Garibay, Ricardo, 1463
Garizurieta, César, 1464, 2841
Garrido, Luis, 1465, 1466, 3655
Garza, Ario, 1467
Garza, Mercedes de la, 1468
Gasch, Sebastián, 1469, 1470
Gastélum, Bernardo J. , 1471-1481

González Rojo, Enrique, 1116,
1645-1663, 2085, 3001, 3925
González Rojo, Enrique Jr.,
1664, 1665
González Ruiz, Nicolás, 3190
González Urízar, Fernando, 2532
González y González, Alicia,
1666
Gooch, G. P., 4002
Gorki, Maxim, 2747
Gorkin, Julián, 2718
Gorlier, Carlos Alberto, 1667
Gorostiza, Celestino, 512, 1668-
1676
Gorostiza, Manuel Eduardo de,
2164
Gorostiza Alcalá, José, 591,
752, 1000, 1677-1697, 2086,
2247, 2435, 3012
Gourmont, Rémy de, 1698
Goya y Lucientes, Francisco
José, 339
Goytortúa Santos, Jesús, 1106
Grabav, Igor, 1699
Graça Aranha, José Pereira da,
1700
Granja Irigoyen, A., 3783
Graves, Robert, 1230
Gracián, Baltasar, 1914
Green, Henry, 3296
Greenwood, Marion, 1701
Grijalba, Fraiz, 1702, 1703
Grote, Barón Heriberto B. de.,
1704
Guardia, Miguel, 1705-1707
Guereña, Jacinto Luis, 1708
Guerrero, Enrique Gabriel,
1709-1711, 2998
Guerrero, Margarita, 3468
Guerrero Galván, Jesús, 20,
1712
Guevara, Fray, 96
Guido y Spano, Carlos, 2417
Guignebert, Charles, 2526
Guillén, Alberto, 1713
Guillén, Fedro, 1714
Guillén, Jorge, 837, 1425, 1715-
1718
Guillén Zelaya, Alfonso, 1719
Güiraldes, Ricardo, 3670, 3825
Gupta, Heramba Lal, 1720, 2001
Gutiérrez, Pedro, 1721, 1722
Gutiérrez, Salvador, 1723

Gutiérrez Cruz, Carlos, 1724
Gutiérrez Gutiérrez, Ernesto,
1725
Gutiérrez Hermosillo, Alfonso,
1072, 1094, 1726-1740, 3078
Gutiérrez Nájera, Manuel,
2239, 2303
Guzmán, Martín Luis, 11,
769, 1173, 1266, 1741-1746,
2795, 3409, 3557
Guzmán, Antonio Leocadio,
2924
Guzmán, Jesús, 47
Guzmán, Raz, 47

H

H., H. W., 1747
Habe, Hans, 1124
Hafiz, 1748, 2125
Halffter, Rodolfo, 1749, 1799,
3062
Hansen, Eva Hemmer, 3453
Hartzenbusch, Juan Eugenio,
1751
Harvey, Guillermo, 291
Harring, María S., 1750
Hayward, J. A., 2538
Heidegger, Martin, 1752
Heiden, Konrad, 3064
Heine, Maurice, 1753
Hemingway, Ernest, 2254
Henestrosa, Andrés, 1754-1762,
2707
Henríquez Ureña, Max, 78,
3450, 3859
Henríquez Ureña, Pedro, 48,
1763-1767, 2229, 2252,
2585, 3769
Heraclitus, 1438
Heredia, José G., 1768, 1769
Heredia, José María, 296, 2214
Hernández, Efrén, 1770-1775,
1975, 2870
Hernández, José, 2241
Hernández, Juan, 1347
Hernández, Luisa Josefina,
2793
Hernández Mateo, 1776
Hernández, Miguel, 144, 2810,
3441
Hernández, Porfirio, 1777-1781
Hernández Bordes, Ernesto, 1782

J

J., R. de, 1905
Jacob, Max, 1906
Jahn, Jan, 1907
Jameson, Egon, 3087
Jammes, Francis, 2174, 3849
Jarnés, Benjamín, 1693, 1908-1932, 2410, 2584
Jaspers, Karl, 1664
Jesualdo, 348
Jiménez, A., 505
Jiménez, Guillermo, 1933-1936
Jiménez, Juan Ramón, 907, 1037, 1166, 1219, 1937-1950, 3912
Jiménez de Asúa, Luis, 416
Jiménez de Quesada, Gonzalo, 2993
Jiménez Mabarak, Carlos, 1951
Jiménez Rueda, Julio, 70, 662, 1110, 1952-1960, 3744, 3931
Jiménez y Núñez, Victoriano, 1961
Jodorowsky, Alejandro, 1962, 3293
Johnson, Eyvind, 1963
Johr, W. A., 3471
Joublanc Rivas, Luciano, 1964-1967, 2087, 2149
Jouhandeau, Marcelo, 1968
Joyce, James, 1180, 1227, 1969, 1970, 3300, 4017
Joyce, T. A., 450
Juárez, Benito, 357
Juárez, Erasmo, 1971
Juárez, Nicolás B., 1972
Juárez Frausto, Manuel, 1973
Juárez Frausto, Pina, 1974-1976
Junco, Alfonso, 1977, 1978, 2081
Jung, C. G., 3378

K

Kafka, Franz, 1606, 1797, 1907, 3011, 3791
Kahlo, Frida, 710, 1979, 1980
Kaiser, Georg, 1990
Kandinsky, Vasili, 1981
Kant, Emanuel, 1397, 3955
Keats, John, 878, 913, 1982
Kegel, Luis Augusto, 1983
Kelatozov, Mijail, 934

Kelemen, Pal, 2756
Kenton, Stan, 2476
Keyserling, Hermann, 1481
Kipling, Rudyard, 1984-1986
Kisch, Egon Erwin, 100
Kitagawa, Tamiji, 1987, 1988
Klemperer, Otto, 616
Kononov, A., 1989
Krauss, Werner, 1990
Kreymborg, Alfred, 1177, 1991
Krimov, Yuri, 1992
Kuniyoshi, Y., 1993

L

L. R., R., 1994
La Danois, Ed, 400
Laborde, Hernán, 1995
Laclos, Choderlos de, 667
Lacomba, Juan, 1996
Lacretelle, Jacques de, 470, 1997, 3653, 3913
Ladrón de Guevara, José, 1998
Lafarga, Gastón, 1999, 2000
Laforgue, Jules, 3234
Lagerkvist, Par, 2774
Lagerlof, Selma, 2916
Lago, Roberto, 1040
Laín Entralgo, Pedro, 291
Lamana, Manuel, 3464
Lamarche, Angel Rafael, 2002
Landaeta Rosales, Manuel, 458
Landsberg, Pablo Luis, 1804, 2003
Lange, Norah, 2054
Lao-Tze, 714
Lara Isaacs, Alfredo de, 2004
Larbaud, Valéry, 2005, 2006
Larra, Mariano José de, 1327
Larrea, Juan, 2007, 2008
Larroyo, Francisco, 2479, 3587
Lasso de la Vega, R., 2009
Lavelle, Louis, 1664
Lavoisier, Antoine Laurent, 576
Lawrence, David Herbert, 596, 890, 1371, 2484, 2872, 3368
Lax, Robert, 782
Lazo, Agustín, 988, 1053, 1194, 1544, 2010-2034, 3829, 3830, 3853, 3854, 3928

Mejía Sánchez, Ernesto, 152, 2301-2303
Mejía Valera, Manuel, 2792, 3303
Mejía Vides, Luis, 2304
Meléndez de Espinosa, Juana, 2305
Melo, Gastón, 2306, 2307
Melo, Juan Vicente, 2308-2316
Melville, Herman, 2317
Hemling, Hans, 382, 2318
Mena, Anselmo, 529, 2319-2322
Mena, Ramón, 2323, 2324
Mende, Tibor, 3447
Méndez, Luis Augusto, 2411
Méndez Dorich, Rafael, 1902
Méndez Plancarte, Alfonso, 887
Méndez Plancarte, Gabriel, 2325, 2326
Méndez Rivas, Joaquín, 2327, 2328, 3907
Mendizábal, Miguel O. de, 1564, 2329, 2330, 2604, 3324
Mendoza, Vicente T., 2536
Mendoza López, Margarita, 221
Menéndez, Miguel Angel, 75
Menéndez Barriola, Emilio, 2705
Menéndez Pidal, Ramón, 62, 65, 1078
Menéndez Samará, Adolfo, 2331, 2332, 3363
Menéndez y Pelayo, Marcelino, 669
Meneses, Padre, 1268
Mérida, Carlos, 794, 969, 1028, 2333-2341
Merino, A., 2342
Mesa, Diego de, 2343
Mesa, Enrique de, 2344
Mesonero Romanos, Ramón, 2345
Meza, Guillermo, 2346
Michel, Alfonso, 2347
Michelena, Margarita, 2348-2352
Mier, Fray Servando Teresa de, 2613
Miguel, Francisco, 2353
Milbreed, Oliver, 2354
Milton, John, 3975
Millán, Marco Antonio, 1120
Millán, María del Carmen, 2355

Millán y M., Ignacio, 2356
Millares Carlo, Agustín, 2137
Miller, Dorothy C., 2341
Mina, Francisco Javier, 2615
Miranda, Carlos Arbulu, 2357
Miró, Joan, 2358, 2359
Misbnun, Virginia, 2360
Mistral, Gabriela (see Godoy Alcayaga, Lucila)
Moctezuma, Isabel, 3243
Mocho, Fray (see Alvarez, José S.)
Modotti, Tina, 2365
Mojarro, Tomás, 2310, 2361, 2362
Molina Enríquez, Renato, 2363-2366
Molinari, Ricardo E., 1650, 3533
Molíns Fábrega, ?, 1514
Moncada Ivar, Luis, 2367
Monsiváis, Carlos, 2368-2375
Montaigne, Miguel de, 511, 2787
Montalbán, Leonardo, 958
Montaña, Antonio, 2376
Monteforte Toledo, Mario, 2352
Montenegro, Carlos, 1506
Montenegro, Roberto, 34, 1019, 1301, 1574, 2377-2388
Monter, Guillermo, 2389
Monterde, Alberto, 1854
Monterde García Icazbalceta, Francisco, 87, 1676, 2084, 2087, 2234, 2243, 2390-2421, 2785, 3534
Montero, José Antonio, 2422
Montes de Oca, Marco Antonio, 2423, 2424, 2437, 2544
Montherlant, Henry de, 1366, 2425
Monvel, María, 2426, 2427, 3743
Moore, George Foot, 2428
Morales, José Ricardo, 1112
Morales C., Arturo, 412
Morales Garcés, Bernardo, 2429
Morales Saviñón, Héctor, 753

Morand, Paul, 1842, 2260, 2430-2432, 2653, 2654
Moréas, Jean, 2132
Moreno, Daniel, 2433
Moreno de Tagle, J. Enrique, 2046, 2434-2438
Moreno Villa, José, 80, 1080, 1114, 1163, 1455, 2166, 2261, 2439-2452
Morgan, Claude, 2453
Morley, Sylvanus G. , 2454
Moro, César, 1053, 2455-2471, 2516, 3902
Mota, Fernando, 2472, 2473
MOTION PICTURES, 192, 193, 481-483, 569, 585, 703, 934, 938, 1385, 2368, 2371, 2595, 2776, 3024, 3145, 3191, 3427, 3804, 3805, 3841
Moussong, Lazlo Javier, 2474-2482
Munguía, Enrique Jr. , 1223, 1371, 2483-2490
Muñoz, Rafael F. , 2491, 2492
Murillo, Gerardo, 2419, 2493-2498
Murray, Gilbert, 64, 2499
MUSIC AND DANCE
  European, 141, 566, 611, 620, 810, 2151, 2487, 2936, 2945, 2947, 3032, 3062, 3428, 3649, 3886
  General, 567, 568, 613, 684, 1476, 1749, 1792, 2937, 2938, 2941, 2944, 2946, 3034, 3416, 3601, 4025
  Mexican, 112, 466, 610, 612, 614, 615, 619, 770, 863, 948, 961, 1042, 1145, 1934, 1951, 1972, 2185, 2186, 2200, 2205, 2289, 2360, 2621, 2862, 2940, 2942, 3499
  North American, 361, 616
  Spanish American, 501, 617, 1552, 1955, 2054, 2079, 2698
Mutis, Alvaro, 2500, 2949

N

Nabokov, Vladimir, 3306
Nadau, Maurice, 1365

Nahui-Olín, 1691
Nalé Roxlo, Conrado, 1107, 2030
Nandino, Elías, 487, 672, 725, 1084, 1133, 1851, 2501-2548, 2791, 3319
Nava, J. Guadalupe, 2549
Navarrete, Fray Manuel, 2253
Navarrete, José Antonio, 2550
Navarrete, Rodolfo, 1590
Navarro, Gustavo A. , 2551
Navarro Luna, Manuel, 730
Navarro Sánchez, José Adalberto, 2552
Navasal y de Mendiri, Joaquín, 3065
Naveda, César A. , 824, 2553
Necker, Anne Louise Germaine, Baroness of Stäel-Holstein, 2098, 2155
Nehru, Jawaharlal, 3447
Nelken, Margarita, 2554, 3155
Nelson, Alma, 2555
Neruda, Pablo (see Reyes, Neftalí Ricardo)
Nerval, Gérard de, 1526, 2556, 2557, 3857
Nervo, Amado, 1291, 2406, 3905
Neuman, Elsa M. , 2558
Neuvillatte, Alfonso de, 2559
Nicol, Eduardo, 661, 2560, 2561
Nielson, B., 2562
Nieto Caballero, Luis E. , 2563
Nietzche, Friedrich Wilhelm, 3410
Noguera, Eduardo, 2564
Nordau, Max, 766
Noriega Hope, Carlos, 1588, 3750
Noulet, Emilie, 2565-2567, 3903
Novo, Salvador, 285, 644, 713, 1775, 1873, 2076, 2248, 2284, 2388, 2575-2600, 3876, 3893
Novaro, Octavio, 2568, 2569
Novás Calvo, Lino, 2570-2574
Núñez y Domínguez, José de J. , 2601-2603, 3988

O

Obligado, Carlos, 2415
Obregón, Alvaro, 1475
Obregón Santacilla, Carlos, 1019, 2605

Ocampo, Isidoro, 2606, 2973
Ocampo, María Luisa, 2607
Ocampo, Victoria, 592
Ocaranza, Fernando, 68
Ochoa, Enriqueta, 2608
O'Gorman, Edmundo, 2609-2616
Ohanian, Armen, 2617
Ohn, Jorge Simon, 2285
Omar-Al-Khayyam, 2125, 2133
O'Neill, Eugene, 1675
Onís, Federico de, 3911
Ontañón, Eduardo de, 754
Ordaz Rocha, Luis, 2618
Orgambide, Pedro G., 2619
Orgaz, Mariano, 1485
Oribe, Emilio, 2620
Orlando, Felipe, 2621
Orozco, Carlos, 708, 2622
Orozco, José Clemente, 337,
    1029, 1041, 1075, 2021, 2623-
    2628, 3802, 3862
Orozco Muñoz, Francisco, 2629-
    2639
Orozco Romero, Carlos, 579,
    2640-2642
Ors, Eugenio d', 431, 2643-2647
Ortega, Gregorio, 2648
Ortega y Gasset, José, 469,
    473, 994, 1010, 1759, 2879,
    3995, 3998
Ortiz, Alfonso, 1985
Ortiz, César, 2649
Ortiz, Fernando, 2650
Ortiz de Montellano, Bernardo,
    752, 994, 1222, 1387, 2006,
    2082, 2651-2714, 3905
Ortiz Monasterio, Manuel, 1041
Ortiz Reyes, José, 2715
Ortiz Saralegui, Juvenal, 92,
    2716, 3405
Ortiz Vidales, Alfredo, 2717
Orrego E., Atenor, 2718
Osorio, Adrián, 2719
Osorio, José Salomón, 2720
Osorio, Miguel Angel, 2744
Ossorio y Gallardo, Angel, 3571
Ostrovsky, Nicolás, 2721, 3244
Otero, Blas de, 2722
Otero Silva, Miguel, 2723, 3570
Othón, Manuel José, 722, 1104,
    2868, 3706, 3987
Ovalle, José de, 2400, 2724

Owen, Gilberto, 744, 1041,
    1134, 2034, 2535, 2725-2746,
    2801, 3657

P

P., D. de, 2747
P., J., 2748
P. S., N., 2749
Paalen, Alice, 2750-2752
Pach, Walter, 2753-2756
Pacheco, León, 2757-2759
Pacheco, Máximo, 2019, 2760,
    2761
Pacheco y Berny, José Emilio,
    623, 937, 967, 2556, 2762-
    2812
Padilla, Hugo, 2813, 2814
Páez de Ribera, Ruy, 2815
Palacios, Alfredo, 423, 825,
    2816-2818
Palacios, Emanuel, 2819-2823
Palacios, Jacinto, 2810
Palafox y Mendoza, Don Juan
    de, 2824
Palencia, Isabel de, 1027
Pallais, A. H., 2825
Pallares, Alfonso, 1019
Papini, Giovanni, 2326
Parada León, Ricardo, 2826,
    2827
Pardo, Wilfredo B., 2828, 2829
Pardo García, Germán, 1858,
    2139, 2830-2834, 3009
Pareja Díez-Canedo, Alfredo,
    686
Pareja Duzcano, Alfredo, 3436
Parés, Nuria, 2525
Paris, Jean, 3300
Parmenides, 2876
Partida, Rafael L., 2835
Parra, Félix, 2836
Parra, Manuel de la, 26, 2837
Pasamanik, Luisa, 2543, 2838
Pascal, Claude, 3067
Paso, Fernando del, 2839
Pasternak, Boris, 933
Pater, Walter, 1
Patte, Richard, 412
Paul, Elliot, 3381
Pavlenko, P., 1510
Pavón Flores, Mario, 2840,
    2841

782, 913, 914, 946, 1013,
1014, 1177, 1218-1223, 1230,
1222, 1225, 1982, 1986,
2134, 2135, 2284, 2600
Chinese
in translation, 136, 2066
Classical
criticism of, 134, 885, 1224
in translation, 2137
French
criticism of, 81, 93, 285,
295, 622, 805, 999, 1004,
1076, 1182, 1203, 1526,
1870, 2129, 2131, 2246,
2397, 2467, 2489, 2565-
2567, 2681, 2696, 2988,
3091, 3107, 3117, 3659,
3849, 3857, 3902, 3910,
4024
in translation, 132, 479,
597, 623, 626, 707, 745,
1012, 1039, 1053, 1175,
1379, 2009, 2045, 2046,
2050, 2132, 2136, 2198,
2430-2432, 2469, 2556,
2713
General, 599, 707, 797, 1456,
1685, 1765, 1997, 2237,
2468, 2470, 2680, 2695,
2714, 2863, 3179, 3180,
3182, 3194, 3279, 3346,
3981
German
criticism of, 1752, 3369
Indian
in translation, 73, 2713,
3566, 3567
Italian
criticism of, 1352, 2918
in translation, 746, 1052,
1053, 2063
Mexican, passim, consult
under author
Persian
criticism of, 2125
in translation, 1748, 2133
Russian
in translation, 3498
Spanish
criticism of
20th century, 44, 79, 90,
147, 153, 209, 415, 462,
537, 539, 590, 642, 661,

662, 665, 801, 837, 907,
1037, 1056, 1085, 1089,
1092, 1096, 1097, 1108,
1114, 1160, 1166, 1383,
1405, 1425, 1447, 1498,
1520, 1607, 1658, 1776,
1802, 1837, 1840, 1941,
2008, 2141, 2210, 2230,
2240, 2281, 2442, 2534,
2711, 1716, 2743, 2842,
2874, 2880, 2983, 3055,
3066, 3092, 3141, 3237,
3332-3334, 3362, 3371,
3412, 3441, 3474, 3480,
3537, 3630, 3658, 3770-
3772, 3912, 3937
19th century, 89, 3052
Golden Age, 12, 468, 659,
910, 1805, 1953, 2745,
3342, 3407, 3989
Medieval, 65, 666, 1799,
2226, 2440, 2582
original works, passim,
consult under author
Spanish American
criticism of
20th century, 71, 82, 92,
93, 122, 152, 237, 348,
362, 366, 372, 538, 588,
641, 726-728, 730, 834,
887, 1038, 1077, 1079,
1088, 1099, 1107, 1166,
1212, 1281, 1286, 1294,
1298, 1375, 1426, 1505,
1538, 1543, 1650, 1661,
1665, 1688, 1755, 1858,
1862, 1927, 1931, 2008,
2117, 2158, 2178, 2187,
2369, 2407, 2411, 2415,
2420, 2505, 2520, 2523,
2532, 2543, 2548, 2563,
2572, 2705, 2708, 2744,
2856, 2877, 2895, 2896,
3009, 3059, 3136, 3267,
3405, 3411, 3434, 3444,
3466, 3475, 3533, 3540,
3731, 3743, 3749, 3793,
3820, 3873, 3879, 3918,
3921, 3923, 3926, 3932,
3933, 3990
19th century, 296, 1311,
1615, 3517, 3261, 3486,
3550, 3702

criticism of, 694, 2326, 2453, 3297
in translation, 900
Mexican, passim, consult under author
Norwegian
criticism of, 2774
Russian
criticism of, 668, 719, 1043, 1044, 1275, 2747, 3244, 3306, 3685
in translation, 777, 1410, 1510, 1989, 1992, 2721, 3018, 3433
Spanish
criticism of, 56, 74, 99, 489, 543, 658, 815, 849, 935, 1172, 1502, 1542, 1690, 1693, 1836, 1838, 1912, 1928, 2257, 2315, 2718, 2784, 3122, 3189, 3348, 3373, 3383, 3436, 3924, 4018
original works, passim, consult under author
Spanish American
criticism of, 498, 553, 592, 670, 685, 687, 718, 1125, 1293, 1506, 1785, 1958, 1999, 2189, 2352, 2429, 2792, 2871, 2949, 3157, 3303, 3367, 3400, 3436, 3462, 3464, 3468, 3489, 3493, 3569, 3570, 3670, 3705, 3746, 3773, 3825, 3893, 3904, 3929
original works, passim, under author
Polacek, Antonín, 777
Poliansky, D., 2934
Proust, Marcel, 549, 1262, 1312, 1322, 1573, 1656, 2686, 3611, 3679
Puente, J. Jesús, 2981
Puértolas, Agustín S., 2982
Puga, Mario, 498, 2983
Puga y Acal, Manuel, 26
Puig Casauranc, José Manuel, 2984-2987
Pujula, Pedro, 2988
Pushkin, Alexander, 1174

Q

Quesada y Miranda, Gonzalo, 1328
Quevedo, Francisco de, 1953, 2989-2991
Quijano, Alejandro, 2992-2994
Quinn, Arthur Holson, 411
Quintana, Jorge, 2995-2997
Quintero Alvarez, Alberto, 585, 1103, 2998-3015
Quiñones, Horacio, 3016
Quiroga, Vasco de, 172
Quiroz Malca, Demetrio, 122

R

R., T., 3017
Radványi, Netty, 1118, 3018
Ramírez, Alfonso Francisco, 445, 3019
Ramírez, Ambrosio, 3986
Ramírez, J. Martín, 3020
Ramírez Cabañas, Joaquín, 3021, 3022, 3492
Ramón y Cajal, Santiago, 425
Ramos, José Manuel, 3023, 3024
Ramos, Leopoldo, 3025-3030
Ramos, Samuel, 1197, 1869, 2332, 2561, 4001
Ramos Gómez, Raymundo J., 2480, 3044-3047
Ramos Martínez, Alfredo, 3048
Réau, Louis, 1852
Rebolledo, Conde de, 3134
Rebolledo, Efrén, 3049, 3890
Rebolledo, J. Enrique, 3050, 3051
Recaséns Siches, Luis, 739, 2829
Rejano, Juan, 539, 590, 1085, 3052-3068
RELIGION, 562, 660, 714, 991, 1204, 1214, 1235, 1414, 1415, 2001, 2319, 2330, 2526, 2912, 3082, 3215, 3352, 3997
Remarque, Enrich María, 3326
Rembrandt van Ryn, Hermensz, 380, 3069
Renan, Ernest, 283
Renard, Jules, 3628

René-Jean, 3072
Reneville, Roland de, 2470
Renn, Ludwig, 552, 3073
Renourad, P., 3074
Requena Legarreta, Pedro,
  2088, 3075
Revueltas, Fermín, 530, 2366,
  3076
Revueltas, José, 3077-3087,
  3359
Revueltas, Silvestre, 466, 610,
  2185, 2186, 2862
Rey, María Ramona, 3088, 3089
Reyes, Alfonso, 3, 49, 95,
  105, 206, 224, 239, 513, 589,
  720, 773, 869, 930, 1195,
  1315, 1334, 1351, 1359, 1529,
  1556, 1680, 1726, 1754, 1770,
  1901, 1933, 2119, 2145, 2173,
  2255, 2297, 2319, 2390, 2579,
  2609, 2629, 2651, 2652, 2908,
  2975, 2992, 3090-3128, 3187,
  3249, 3276, 3314, 3470, 3517,
  3581, 3592, 3671, 3752, 3767,
  3901, 3906, 3909, 3963
Reyes, Fernando, 3129, 3130
Reyes, Neftalí Ricardo, 362,
  366, 2856, 3131-3136
Reyes Nevares, Salvador, 3137-
  3141
Reyes Ruiz, J. Jesús, 3142,
  3143
Ricard, Robert, 2912, 3144
Richards, I. A., 599
Richepin, Jean, 2988
Rigol, Jorge, 3145
Rilke, Cristóbal, 3369
Rilke, Rainer María, 676, 2227
Rimbaud, Jean-Arthur, 805,
  1367, 1368, 2009, 3450
Rinser, Luisa, 3449
Río R., Rafael del, 641, 3146
Rioja, Enrique, 3147-3150
Ríos, Carlos Alfonso, 3151
Ríos, Fernando de los, 3152
Ríos, Juan, 3153
Ríos P., Joaquín, 3154
Ristel-Hueber, René, 2461
Rivas, Antonieta, 2430
Rivas, Antonio, 3155
Rivas, Humberto, 1469, 2151,
  2198, 3156-3166
Rivas Panedas, José, 3167-3175

Rivas Sáinz, Arturo, 3176-3194
Rivera, Diego M., 255, 530,
  970, 1451, 2024, 2504, 2635,
  3041, 3195-3207, 3438, 3801,
  3860
Rivera, Gerardo, 3208
Riverón, Enrique, 3108
Robespierre, Maximilien
  François Isidore, 2804, 3382
Robledo, Antonio, 3209
Robles Gil, Alberto, 1019
Roca, Deodoro, 3210
Rodell, John S., 3211
Rodin, Auguste, 3212
Rodó, José Enrique, 1959
Rodríguez, Claudio, 3213
Rodríguez, Emilia Gaspar, 959
Rodríguez, Eugenio, 3214
Rodríguez, Luis Angel, 3215,
  3216
Rodríguez, Luis Felipe, 2416,
  3217
Rodríguez, Ofelia, 1925
Rodríguez Alcalá, Hugo, 1039,
  3218, 3219
Rodríguez Chicharro, César,
  3220, 3221
Rodríguez Demorizi, Emilio,
  71
Rodríguez Lozano, Manuel,
  149, 972, 2757, 2758, 2969,
  3222-3228, 3336
Rodríguez Luna, Antonio,
  1484, 3229
Rodríguez Mata, Magdalena,
  3230
Rodríguez Orgaz, Mariano,
  3231
Roeber, Cristián, 1294
Roggiano, Alfredo G., 2548
Rojas, Fermín, 3232
Rojas, Fernando de, 109
Rojas, Jorge, 2008
Rojas, Marcial, 2675, 3233-
  3237
Rojas, Mariano, 194
Rojas, Ricardo, 83, 1932
Rojas Garcidueñas, José,
  2412, 2521, 2535, 2775, 3238
Rojas Giménez, Alberto, 3239
Rojas González, Francisco,
  1101, 3240, 3241
Rojas Paz, Pablo, 3242

Rojas Rosillo, Isaac, 3243
Rolland, Romain, 3244
Romains, Jules, 888, 1960, 2978
Romano Muñoz, José, 3245, 3246
Romero, Francisco, 3247, 3248, 3984
Romero, José Rubén, 1117, 2091, 2193, 3249
Romero Brest, Jorge, 3250, 3251
Romero de Terreros, Manuel, 1110, 1982, 3252-3258
Romeu, Octavio de, 3855
Romo, Herbert, 3259, 3260
Rooseroeck, Gust. L. van, 3261
Ros, Antonio, 3262
Rosa, Leopoldo de la, 3263, 3264
Rosa, Pedro de la, 3265
Rosado Vega, Luis, 3266
Rosales, Salatiel, 3267
Rosenzweig, Carmen, 3268, 3269
Rosey, Gui, 3270
Rossi, Attilio, 3271
Rosso de San Secondo, ?, 2034
Rougemont, Denis, 3920
Roura Parella, Juan, 1082
Rousseau, Jean Jacques, 3602, 3812
Roxas, Juan Bartolomé, 3413
Rubalcaba, Gilberto, 1267
Rubio, David, 3189
Rubio, Ricardo, 1949
Rueda, Salvador, 44
Rueda Medina, Gustavo, 104
Ruelas, Julio, 3865
Ruiz, Antonio, 243
Ruiz, Cristóbal, 312
Ruiz, Guillermo, 530, 1341, 3202, 3272
Ruiz, Juan Martínez, 2440, 2582
Ruiz Cabañas, Samuel, 3273, 3274
Ruiz de Alarcón y Mendoza, Juan, 43, 48, 870, 875, 884, 1168, 1582, 1764, 2855, 3128, 3275, 3583
Ruiz Esparza, Juan Manuel, 3276, 3277

Ruiz Harrell, Rafael, 3278
Rulfo, Juan, 967
Russell, Bertrand, 1887
Russell, Dora Isella, 3279

S

S., 3280
Saadí, 2639
Saavedra, Rafael M., 3281-3283
Saavedra Faxardo, Diego, 3284
Sabines, Jaime, 3285-3287, 3393
Sabisch, ?, 3288
Sáenz, Marta, 3289, 3290
Sáenz, Vicente, 3469
Sagües, Isidoro, 3367
Saint-Saens, Charles Camille, 2945
Saint-Exupéry, Antoine de, 2251
Sáinz, Gustavo, 3291-3306
Sáinz de la Maza, ?, 3886
Salado Alvarez, Victoriano, 61, 1093
Salas Viu, Vicente, 3307
Salazar, Adolfo, 568, 1749, 3308-3312, 3357, 4025
Salazar, Juan B., 3313
Salazar, Toño, 3314, 3315
Salazar Bondy, Sebastián, 3316
Salazar Chapelo, Esteban, 3436
Salazar Mallén, Rubén, 121, 2771, 2830, 3317-3326, 3809
Salazar Viniegra, Leopoldo, 3327, 3328
Salazar y Chapela, E., 3329-3332
Salinas, Miguel, 1276
Salinas, Pedro, 3237, 3333-3335
Salmón, André, 3336
Salt, Sidney, 3785
Sánchez, Luis Alberto, 3472
Sánchez, Luis Aníbal, 1293
Sánchez, Pedro C., 3337
Sánchez Barbudo, Antonio, 281, 714, 1214, 1233, 1836, 2064, 2296, 3018, 3338-3383

Sánchez de Ocaña, Rafael,
  3384, 3385
Sánchez Mayans, Fernando,
  2517, 3386-3394, 4026
Sánchez Rivero, Angel, 3395
Sánchez-Sáez, Braulio, 3396
Sánchez Vásquez, Adolfo,
  3397-3413
Sandburg, Carl, 2134, 3414
Sandóiz, Alba, 3415
Sandoval, Adolfo, 89
Sanín Cano, Baldomero, 1169
Sanjuan, Pedro, 2698, 3416
Santa Cruz, Francisco, 3418
Santa Cruz, Mario, 3419
Santacruz, Agustín, 3417
Santaló Sors, Marcelo, 3420,
  3421
Santayana, George, 602, 886,
  891, 3176, 3422, 3476, 3934,
  3935
Santos, Ninfa, 3423
Santos Chocano, José, 3424
Santovenia, Emeterio S., 3446
Santoyo, Matías, 3425
Santullano, Luis, 3426
Sarmiento, Domingo Faustino,
  83, 115, 1755
Sarmiento, Pedro, 2465
Saroyan, William, 600
Sartre, Jean Paul, 1427, 3049
Sayago, Fernando, 3427
Schaeffner, André, 3428
Scheler, Max, 1001, 3379, 3999
Schmitz, Ettore (see Svevo,
  Italo)
Schons, Dorothy, 43, 3429
Schostakovsky, Pablo, 3188
Schwartz-Bart, André, 3305
Schweitzer, Albert, 2798
Schwob, Marcel, 2781
SCIENCE
  Biological, 332, 344, 3147-
    3150, 3313
  General, 1437
  Medical, 356, 416, 628,
    1753, 1897, 2213, 2331,
    2356, 2538, 2650, 3262,
    3328, 3378, 3491, 3610,
    4005
  Physical, 301, 309, 378,
    576, 825-827, 1136, 1247,
    1416, 1924, 2153, 2154,

    2285, 2927, 3023, 3337,
    3385, 3420, 3421, 4004
  Social, 554, 1185, 2824,
    3051, 3591, 3716, 4015
Second, Jean, 2131
Seghers, Anna (see Radványi,
  Netty)
Segovia, Tomás, 936, 3430,
  3431
Ségur, Condesa de, 3432
Seignotos, Charles, 3408
Selke, Angela, 2064, 3018
Selke, Rodolfo, 3433
Selva, Mauricio de la, 2540,
  2834, 3434-3483
Selva, Salomón de la, 3484-
  3493, 3720
Sender, Ramón J., 74, 935
Seneca, 3375
Serge, Victor, 2471, 3494
Serpa, Enrique, 2189, 3495
Serrano, Luis G., 3496
Serrano del Castillo, Manuel,
  2990
Serrano Plaja, Arturo, 1837,
  2842, 3497
Severianin, Igor, 3498
Shakespeare, William, 367,
  3103
Shelley, Percy Bysshe, 3892
Shildt, Runar, 2835
Shoskes, Henry, 3382
Shotwell, James Thomson, 410
Sierra O'Reilly, Justo, 38,
  157, 160, 1446, 1976
Sigüença, Fray Joseph de, 1323
Sigüenza y Góngora, Carlos
  de, 14, 35, 57, 77, 1110,
  2412, 2914
Silva, Jonás de, 3500
Silva, José Asunción, 1038
Silva Valdés, Fernán, 2407,
  2708, 3501
Silva Vandeira, Mariano, 2022,
  3502
Silva y Aceves, Mariano,
  3503-3505, 3558
Sinclair, Upton, 3506
Siqueiros, David Alfaro, 709,
  3507-3509, 3803
Sitwell, Edith, Sachaverrell,
  and Osbert, 625
Sitwell, Sir Osbert, 625, 4028

Smedley, Agnes, 2745a, 3356
Smith, Justin H. , 1304
Smith, Logan Pearsall, 3510
Soby, James Thrall, 2341
Socrates, 3511
Solana, Rafael, 1100, 2168, 2266, 2267, 2773, 2869, 3512-3539, 3792, 3900
Solar, Hernán del, 3540
Solís, José M. , 3541, 3542
Sologuren, Javier, 3543-3545
Sor Adoración del Divino Verbo, 3931
Soriano, Juan, 582, 2847, 3546-3548
Soto, Jesús S. , 2081, 2432, 3549
Soto, Rafael A. , 3550
Sotomayor, Adolfo, 728
Soupault, Philippe, 3551
Spender, Stephen, 1013, 1014
Spinoza, Benedictus de, 4007
Spitteler, Carlos, 290
Spota, Luis, 3445, 3482
Spratling, William, 3071
St. John Perse (see Léger, Aléxis Saint-Léger)
Staël, Madame de (see Necker, Anne Louise Germaine, Baroness of Staël-Holstein)
Steinbeck, John, 585, 2649
Stendhal (see Beyle, Henri Marie)
Stevenson, Robert Louis, 851
Stoyanov, Ludmila, 3552
Strachey, John, 1507
Strawinsky, Igor, 3032, 3428
Suárez, Dolores, 3553
Suay, José E. , 1287
Sucre, José María de, 3554
Supervielle, Jules, 132, 2489, 2696, 3555, 3556
Svevo, Italo, 3297

T

T. , E. B. , 3557
T. , M. , 3558
Tablada, José Juan, 448, 2394, 2430, 2559-2564
Taborda, Saúl, 3565
Tagore, Rabindranath, 73, 1720, 2713, 3566, 3567

Tamayo, Rufino, 586, 981, 1348, 1888, 3573-3575
Tanguy, Ives, 3576
Tapia Bolívar, Daniel, 3568-3572
Tardiff, Guillermo, 1848
Tario, Francisco, 1674
Tarsis y Peralta, Juan de, 3134
Tauro, Alberto, 3577, 3578
Tchaikovsky, Peter, 141
Teasdale, Sara, 2135
Tebo, 3228, 3579
Tejera, Humberto, 2408, 3990
Teixidor, Felipe, 3580
Teja Zabre, Alfonso, 2812, 3581-3583
Téllez Toledo, Juan, 3584
Terán, Juan Manuel, 3585-3589
Teresa de Jesús, Santa, 3661
Téry, Simone, 3590
Thibaudet, Albert, 161, 808
Thomas, Bernhard, 3591
Thomson, David, 2790
Tietze, Hans, 3565
Tíndero, Jorge Celso, 2406
Tirado Guentes, René, 3592-3594
Tizón, Héctor, 3595
Tolsa, Manuel, 3596
Tolischus, Otto D. , 418
Tolstoi, Alexis, 3433
Tolstoi, Leo, 668, 719, 2747
Toral Moreno, Alfonso, 3598
Torner, Florentino M. , 3599-3606
Toro, Alfonso, 3607
Toruño, Juan Felipe, 3608
Torre, Claudio de la, 3609
Torre, Guillermo de, 2431, 2701, 3370
Torre, Miguel de la, 1299
Torres, Edelberto, 3451
Torres, José, 3610
Torres Bodet, Jaime, 101, 478, 752, 818, 1443, 1929, 2081, 2501, 2805, 3322, 3436, 3500, 3519, 3611-3662, 4010
Torres Morales, Rubén, 3663-3665
Torres Ortega, Rebeca, 1111
Torres Quintero, Gregorio, 3747

273

Verhesen, Fernand, 3809
Verlaine, Paul, 2136, 3810
Verzman, I., 3812
Vicens, Josefina, 2539
Vicente, Gil, 1805, 3407
Vico, Gianbatista, 1364
Victoria, Marcos, 3483
Villa, Dr., 3813
Villa, Pancho, 45, 1746
Villamediana, Conde de (see
    Tarsis y Peralta, Juan de)
Villardo, Jorge, 3498
Villaseñor, Eduardo, 474, 2075,
    2892, 3510, 3814-3826
Villaseñor, Jorge A., 3827
Villaurrutia, Xavier, 76, 409,
    457, 585, 560, 679, 693, 752,
    809, 904, 928, 1009, 1011,
    1050, 1135, 1194, 1322,
    1515, 1544, 1659, 1732, 1841,
    1871, 2028, 2032, 2033, 2040,
    2050, 2219, 2235, 2258, 2348,
    2388, 2512, 2514, 2736, 2742,
    3535, 3726, 3828-3938
Villena, Enrique de, 3939
Villiers de L'Isle-Adam, Conde
    de, 905
Vincenzi, Moisés, 1273, 1695
Vinci, Leonardo da, 2031
Virgil, 134, 2328, 3104
Vistel, Agusto P., 1905
Vitier, Medardo, 2612
Vivaldi, Antonio, 2621
Vives, Luis, 300, 353
Volkov, V., 3940
Von Martin, Alfred, 3716
Vossler, Karl, 1704
Voyetejov, Boris, 3380
Vries, Lini M. de, 2806

W

Wagner, Richard, 2947
Walden, Hernwarth, 3941, 3942
Wallace, Elizabeth, 889
Wasilievska, Wanda, 3943
Watteau, Jean Antoine, 393,
    3944
Weber, Alfred, 1899
Weber, Delia, 3945
Weidle Wladimir, 3184
Welsh, Donald, 3946
Wells, H. G., 402, 1803, 3017

Werfel, Franz, 2150
Westheim, Paul, 1388, 1389,
    3947
Weston, Edward, 2395, 2396,
    3948-3951
Westphalen, Emilio Adolfo,
    3952
Whitman, Walt, 2062, 3845
Wilcock, Juan Rodolfo, 3953
Wilde, Oscar, 880
Wilder, Thornton, 603
Williams, Tennessee, 522
Williamson, Rev. P. Claude,
    3604
Windelband, Wilhelm, 3589
Worringer, Wilhelm, 3043
Wright, Richard, 310
Wyld Ospina, Carlos, 3954
Wyzewa, Teodor de, 3955

X

Xavier, Héctor, 3956
Xenophanes, 2876
Ximeno y Planes, Rafael, 3957
Xirau, Joaquín, 3958-3962

Y

Yáñez, Agustín, 1072, 2238,
    2250, 2355, 2789, 2867,
    3354, 3963-3969
Yeats, William Butler, 914
Ygobone, Aquiles D., 3970

Z

Z. V., J., 3971
Zabre, Solón, 3972-3974
Zahar, Alfonso, 3975
Zalamea, Jorge, 2045
Zalce, Alfredo, 3831, 3976,
    3977
Zaldumbide, Gonzalo, 3978
Zambrano, María, 163, 3010,
    3375, 3979-3984
Zamora, A., 1970
Zamora, Lino, 232
Zanuck, Darrell, 585
Zarraga, Angel, 3985
Zavala, Jesús, 2868, 3986-3990
Zavala, Justino, 3186
Zea, Leopoldo, 3325, 3991-4007